MEDIA & JOURNALISM

SECOND EDITION

NEW APPROACHES TO THEORY AND PRACTICE

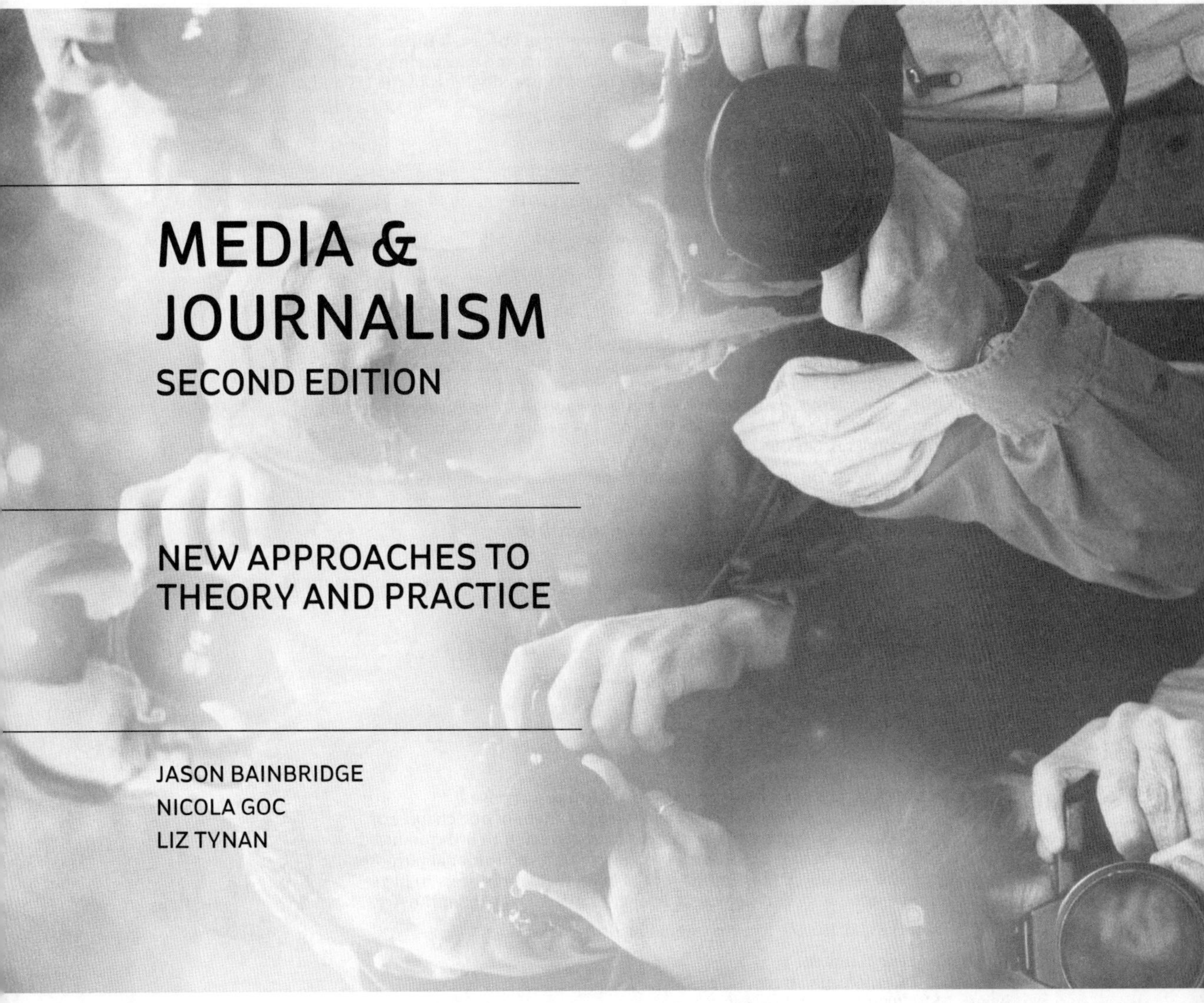

MEDIA & JOURNALISM

SECOND EDITION

NEW APPROACHES TO THEORY AND PRACTICE

JASON BAINBRIDGE
NICOLA GOC
LIZ TYNAN

OXFORD
UNIVERSITY PRESS
AUSTRALIA & NEW ZEALAND

OXFORD
UNIVERSITY PRESS

Oxford University Press is a department of the University of Oxford. It furthers the University's objective of excellence in research, scholarship, and education by publishing worldwide. Oxford is a registered trademark of Oxford University Press in the UK and in certain other countries.

Published in Australia by
Oxford University Press
253 Normanby Road, South Melbourne, Victoria 3205, Australia

The moral rights of the author have been asserted
First edition published 2008

Reprinted 2009, 2010

Second edition published 2011

National Library of Australia Cataloguing-in-Publication data

Author: Bainbridge, Jason.
Title: Media and journalism: new approaches to theory and practice/Jason Bainbridge, Nicola Goc, Liz Tynan.

Edition: 2nd ed.
ISBN: 9780195574104 (pbk.)

Notes: Includes bibliographical references and index.
Subjects: Mass media.
Journalism.
Other Authors/Contributors: Goc, Nicola. Tynan, Elizabeth.
Dewey Number: 070

Edited by Pete Cruttenden
Text design by Sardine
Typeset by diacriTech
Proofread by Sandra Goldbloom Zurbo
Indexed by Jeanne Rudd
Printed by Sheck Wah Tong Printing Press Ltd

DEDICATION

From Jason Bainbridge:

To all the media students, colleagues and friends who have contributed directly and indirectly to this book over the years. To my first mentor, teacher and friend—my Dad, Graham Bainbridge—who read the first draft of this book; I wish you could still be here for this second edition. And to you, the person who is reading this acknowledgments page right now. We wrote this for you, regardless of whether you want to be the next Rupert Murdoch, Julian Assange or Oprah Winfrey.

From Nicola Goc:

To the journalists and media workers—present and in the future—who continue to fight for the public's right to know and who have a steadfast commitment to upholding the ideals of the Fourth Estate, I dedicate this book.

From Liz Tynan:

To the many journalism students who have, over the years, made me think more clearly about my profession, made me value it more highly and inspired in me a conviction that all reports of the demise of a free media are premature. And to my Uncle Don, who died just as this edition was going to press and who was much loved and will be greatly missed.

FOREWORD

Too often, there is seen to be a big divide between the academic study of the media and the professional skills required of job ready journalists. The result is that a book such as this is rare. I was not expecting to find a way of providing my students with an introduction to key concepts and theoretical approaches to media studies as well as engage them with key journalism skills such as news gathering and interviewing in the same text. Yet, in the first edition of *Media and Journalism: New Approaches to Theory and Practice,* that is just what Nicola Goc, Liz Tynan and Jason Bainbridge so impressively brought together. Now with the welcome appearance of the second edition, they have again brought a range of theoretical lenses to bear on the media transformations of recent years and applied those insights to the practices of journalism. The value of this as a way of learning is that the relationship between the academic history of the media, for example, and the current practice of a media interviewer, becomes something we can think about consciously and critically. Surely there has never been a more important time to do so. Our everyday lives are increasingly mediated. We have become more interactive and generative communicators than ever before and there is plenty of debate, considered in this volume, as to how meaningful any more is the difference between the professional and the amateur journalist or media producer. We appear to have so much choice. Without the intellectual tools—including a language—for critical reflection on media practices in which more of us are engaging when once they were available to only a few, we literally have no way of thinking about such crucial questions such as: What do we control and what is controlled for us (by corporate interests and values, for example)? What does privacy mean to us? What information do we really need and want, and who's giving it to us? In giving readers these intellectual tools, through building knowledge of and reflection upon the histories and theories of the media and of journalism, this book encourages critical awareness of the implications of the transformations it documents and analyses, for journalism, for our personal and public lives and for society and culture. This book provides anyone working in the media and journalism or aspiring to do so with understanding and tools to do so. But to get out of it all that it offers, you the reader need to take up its challenges. Do it and you will benefit, no matter where in media and journalism you hope to be.

Anne Dunn
Associate Professor
University of Sydney

FOREWORD TO THE FIRST EDITION

Shock! Horror! Universities are teaching courses in media studies. Students are wasting their time studying *Neighbours* and *Buffy the Vampire Slayer*. It's a regular story in the newspapers. But let's be honest, media studies academics are just as bad. Shock! Horror! Journalists are pandering to their audiences, telling them the stories they want to hear about celebrities rather than challenging the status quo and championing a left-wing revolution.

It's a war out there. But as someone with a foot in both camps, I think it's a shame, because it's clear that the two sides have a lot in common, and that each has a lot to learn from the other. As popular media writers, we could do with understanding the history of our professions, and thinking self-reflexively about our work so we can understand its purpose and how it could be done differently. And as media studies academics, we could do with learning the skills of basic factual research and how to write clearly.

If only somebody would write a book that would show journalists and media studies academics what they have in common. A book that would give journalists an understanding of the context in which they work, and tell media studies academics how to write properly. Oh, wait. They have. This is it. It's good. Jason, Nicola and Liz have produced an audacious book that ranges from the history of the media to the skills of interviewing, from theories of how the public sphere works to basic rules of clear writing, from Habermas to Lindsay Lohan. I haven't seen a book such as this before, and I'm very glad that it exists. Buy it. Read it. Whatever job you aspire to in the knowledge professions, it will be useful to you.

Alan McKee
Professor
Queensland University
of Technology

CONTENTS

GUIDED TOUR

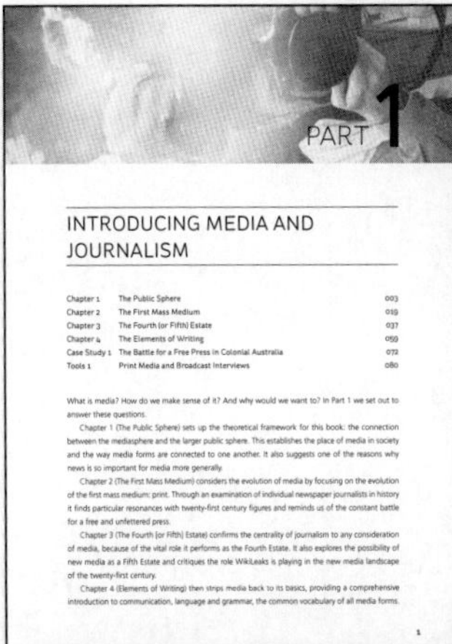

PART 1

INTRODUCING MEDIA AND JOURNALISM

What is media? How do we make sense of it? And why would we want to? In Part 1 we set out to answer these questions.

Chapter 1 (The Public Sphere) sets up the theoretical framework for this book: the connection between the mediasphere and the larger public sphere. This establishes the place of media in society and the way media forms are connected to one another. It also suggests one of the reasons why news is so important for media more generally.

Chapter 2 (The First Mass Medium) considers the evolution of media by focusing on the evolution of the first mass medium: print. Through an examination of individual newspaper journalists in history it finds particular resonances with twenty-first century figures and reminds us of the constant battle for a free and unfettered press.

Chapter 3 (The Fourth [or Fifth] Estate) confirms the centrality of journalism to any consideration of media, because of the vital role it performs as the Fourth Estate. It also explores the possibility of new media as a Fifth Estate and critiques the role WikiLeaks is playing in the new media landscape of the twenty-first century.

Chapter 4 (Elements of Writing) then strips media back to its basics, providing a comprehensive introduction to communication, language and grammar, the common vocabulary of all media forms.

1

Online resources

There are additional resources online to help you get the most from this text at <www.oup.com.au/orc/mediajournalism2e>.

The overall structure

This book is divided into five parts. Each part is built around an overarching theme and contains a number of chapters as well as a relevant Case Study and a 'Tool'. At the start of each part, an overview surveys the themes and content of the section, so you can quickly see what the part includes.

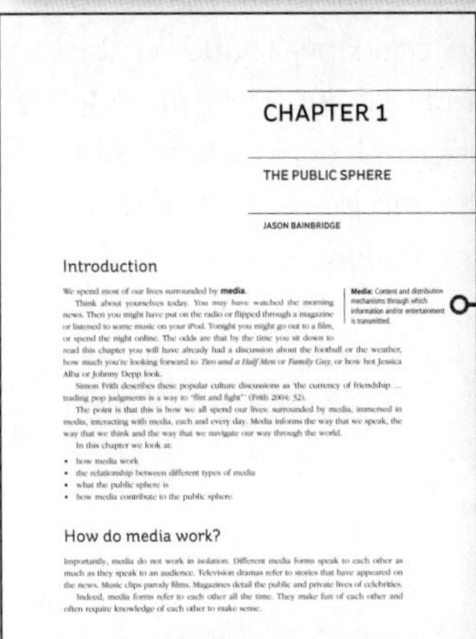

CHAPTER 1

THE PUBLIC SPHERE

JASON BAINBRIDGE

Introduction

We spend most of our lives surrounded by **media**.

Think about yourselves today. You may have watched the morning news. Then you might have put on the radio or flipped through a magazine or listened to some music on your iPod. Tonight you might go out to a film, or spend the night online. The odds are that by the time you sit down to read this chapter you will have already had a discussion about the football or the weather, how much you're looking forward to *Two and a Half Men* or *Family Guy*, or how hot Jessica Alba or Johnny Depp look.

Media: Content and distribution mechanisms through which information and/or entertainment is transmitted.

Simon Frith describes these popular culture discussions as 'the currency of friendship ... trading pop judgments is a way to "flirt and fight"' (Frith 2004: 32).

The point is that this is how we all spend our lives: surrounded by media, immersed in media, interacting with media, each and every day. Media informs the way that we speak, the way that we think and the way that we navigate our way through the world.

In this chapter we look at:

- how media work
- the relationship between different types of media
- what the public sphere is
- how media contribute to the public sphere.

How do media work?

Importantly, media do not work in isolation. Different media forms speak to each other as much as they speak to an audience. Television dramas refer to stories that have appeared on the news. Music clips parody films. Magazines detail the public and private lives of celebrities.

Indeed, media forms refer to each other all the time. They make fun of each other and often require knowledge of each other to make sense.

3

Chapters

At the start of each chapter you will find a brief introduction to the chapter topic and a dot-point list describing what you will learn by reading the chapter. Chapters also feature a 'Key References' list at the end, which provides you with the main sources of information relevant to that chapter.

Glossary margin notes

Essential terminology is defined in the margins for quick and easy reference.

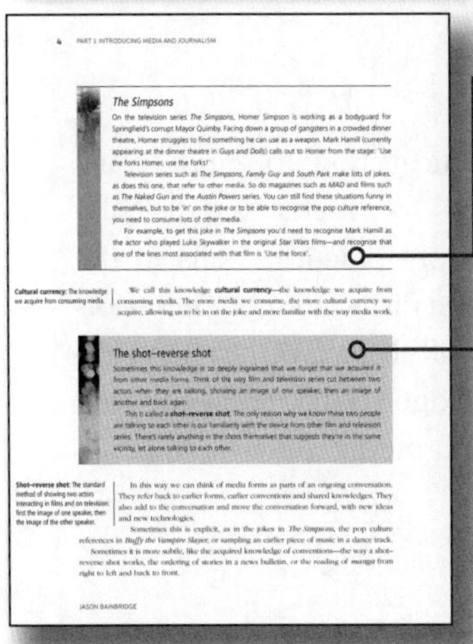

4 PART 1 INTRODUCING MEDIA AND JOURNALISM

The Simpsons

On the television series *The Simpsons*, Homer Simpson is working as a bodyguard for Springfield's corrupt Mayor Quimby. Facing down a group of gangsters in a crowded dinner theatre, Homer struggles to find something he can use as a weapon. Mark Hamill (currently appearing at the dinner theatre in *Guys and Dolls*) calls out to Homer from the stage: 'Use the forks Homer, use the forks!'

Television series such as *The Simpsons*, *Family Guy* and *South Park* make lots of jokes, as does this one, that refer to other media. So do magazines such as *MAD* and films such as *The Naked Gun* and the *Austin Powers* series. You can still find these situations funny in themselves, but to be 'in' on the joke or to be able to recognise the pop culture reference, you need to consume lots of other media.

For example, to get this joke in *The Simpsons* you'd need to recognise Mark Hamill as the actor who played Luke Skywalker in the original *Star Wars* films—and recognise that one of the lines most associated with that film is 'Use the force'.

Cultural currency: The knowledge we acquire from consuming media.

We call this knowledge **cultural currency**—the knowledge we acquire from consuming media. The more media we consume, the more cultural currency we acquire, allowing us to be in on the joke and more familiar with the way media work.

The shot–reverse shot

Sometimes this knowledge is so deeply ingrained that we forget that we acquired it from other media forms. Think of the way film and television series cut between two actors when they are talking, showing an image of one speaker, then an image of another and back again.

This is called a **shot–reverse shot**. The only reason why we know these two people are talking to each other is our familiarity with the device from other film and television series. There's rarely anything in the shots themselves that suggests they're in the same vicinity, let alone talking to each other.

Shot–reverse shot: The standard method of showing two actors interacting in films and on television: first the image of one speaker, then the image of the other speaker.

In this way we can think of media forms as parts of an ongoing conversation. They refer back to earlier forms, earlier conventions and shared knowledges. They also add to the conversation and move the conversation forward, with new ideas and new technologies.

Sometimes this is explicit, as in the jokes in *The Simpsons*, the pop culture references in *Buffy the Vampire Slayer*, or sampling an earlier piece of music in a dance track.

Sometimes it is more subtle, like the acquired knowledge of conventions—the way a shot–reverse shot works, the ordering of stories in a news bulletin, or the reading of *manga* from right to left and back to front.

JASON BAINBRIDGE

Visual Icons

These boxes give you information about something that you can see yourself–for example, in film or television.

Shaded Boxes

Interesting sidelines and illustrative examples are dotted throughout the chapters in shaded boxes. These provide more detailed information to flesh out the ideas being discussed, or simply to provide some fascinating tidbits along the journey.

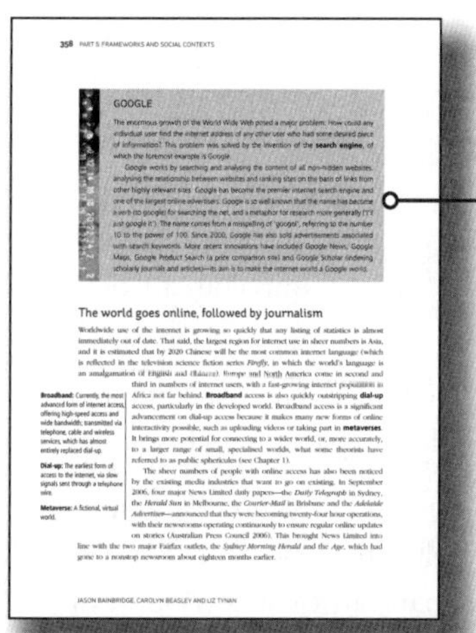

GOOGLE

The world goes online, followed by journalism

Digital Icons

These boxes give you information about the digital media environment.

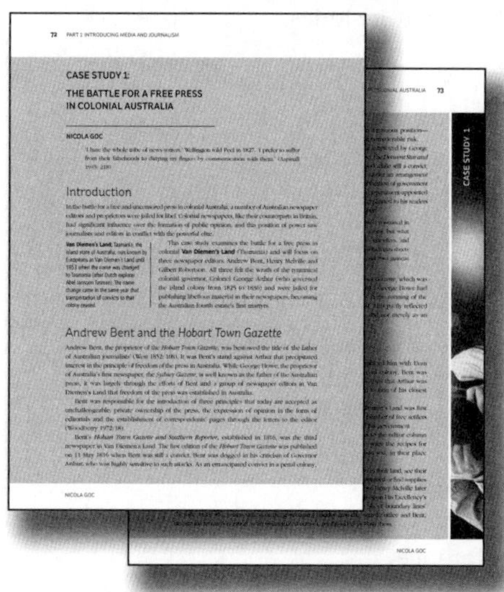

CASE STUDY 1:
THE BATTLE FOR A FREE PRESS IN COLONIAL AUSTRALIA

NICOLA GOC

Introduction

Andrew Bent and the Hobart Town Gazette

Case Studies

These are focused examples designed to illustrate how the concepts found in the chapters play out in real life. They provide specific detail about practical examples of key ideas in media and journalism studies. These will give you insights that will make the theory you encounter clearer.

TOOLS 1:
PRINT MEDIA AND BROADCAST INTERVIEWS

LIZ TYNAN

Introduction

Interviewing for research

Tools

These are practical how-to guides that show you how to master a particular technique or apply practical skills in the media and journalism arena. The tools in this book will help you to develop practical knowledge so that you can work in journalism and media.

CONTRIBUTORS

Jason Bainbridge is Senior Lecturer and Discipline Head of Media Studies at Swinburne University of Technology. He has published widely on media representation, law and popular culture, merchandising and the changing nature of news reporting. Jason has also taught journalism and media studies in Hobart and Brisbane. He has appeared as a media commentator on ABC radio and television and is currently working on a book on movie franchises.

Nicola Goc is a Senior Lecturer and Coordinator of the Journalism, Media and Communications Program at the University of Tasmania. She has previously worked as a news journalist, feature writer, section editor and as a social and cultural historian. She is the author of several social history books and has also published widely on the representation of the 'deviant' woman in the media. Her current project is a study of snapshot photography and the representation of the female sense of self.

Liz Tynan is a lecturer at the JCU Graduate Research School in Townsville, teaching academic writing and critical thinking skills to postgraduate students. She is a former journalism academic with a background in print and electronic media, and a long-standing speciality in science journalism and editing. She has worked for the ABC as a reporter and subeditor, and was later Sydney correspondent for *New Scientist*. She first joined academia in 1997 when she began work in the Journalism program at James Cook University (JCU). She also worked for five years at the University of Tasmania, where she helped set up a community radio station (Edge Radio), before returning for a second stint in the JCU journalism program.

Tim Dwyer is a Senior Lecturer in the Department of Media and Communication at the University of Sydney. He teaches media law and ethics, and his research focuses on the critical evaluation of media and communications industries, regulation and policy. In 2007, Oxford University Press published his co-edited book (with Virginia Nightingale) *New Media Worlds: Challenges for Convergence*. His book *Media Convergence* was published by McGraw-Hill/ Open University Press in 2010. His new book, *Legal and Ethical Issues in the Media*, is to be published by Palgrave-Macmillan in 2012.

Sarah Gillman has worked in the Australian media for more than three decades, including work as a political and legal reporter, news editor, producer, researcher, broadcaster and freelance journalist. Most of her career has been with ABC radio and television, although she has also worked on commercial radio and newspapers. Sarah has taught journalism and media studies in tertiary institutions in Canberra, Darwin and Hobart. Her research interests include the relationship between victims and the media.

Carolyn Beasley is a Lecturer in Writing at Swinburne University of Technology in Victoria, where she teaches Journalism and Electronic Writing in Swinburne's Master of Arts in Writing program. She has worked as a journalist and has won awards for her fiction as well as for her teaching.

ACKNOWLEDGMENTS

Jason Bainbridge A special thanks, first and foremost, to all of my students and colleagues, past and present, at Swinburne University of Technology and the University of Tasmania for their help in shaping, contributing to and workshopping this material, particularly Kerry Tucker. It would be a much shorter and less entertaining book without them. Thanks also to Frances Bonner, Graeme Turner and Alan McKee for initially inspiring me, Alan for his foreword, and Sarah Gillman and Carolyn Beasley for their contributions. Thanks to the team at Oxford University Press who oversaw this project through to completion: Lucy McLoughlin, Karen Hildebrandt, Jessica Hambridge and Natalie Davall for their unflagging support and encouragement, and Pete Cruttenden for his copy editing of the book. A very big thank you to my co-authors, Nicola Goc and Liz Tynan, for their belief that a book on media and journalism would work and was needed, and for all their wonderful work in the chapters that follow. To paraphrase E. B. White, it is not often that someone comes along who is a true friend and a good writer. Nicola and Liz are both, and it has been a pleasure working with them. And finally, to my Mum Pamela and my partner Xandy, who support and sustain me in ways that words have yet to describe.

Liz Tynan I would like to acknowledge my current and former colleagues in Canberra, Hobart and Townsville who have always given me much to think about and many enjoyable interludes discussing ideas and pursuing language pedantry. In particular I would like to mention Sylvia Kelso, Rosemary Dunn and Annie Warburton, magnificent women all. I would also like to acknowledge Helene Marsh, Dean of the Graduate Research School at James Cook University where I work. Her leadership is inspirational to me. I cannot begin to describe the professional and personal fulfilment I have derived from working with Nicola Goc and Jason Bainbridge, first at the University of Tasmania and later in collaboration on this book. They are fine academics and, even more to the point, fine people. To my family and friends, thanks for your support. In particular I would like to mention Mum (Rosemary), Dad (Frank), Inta, Meredith, Sophie, Andrew and Narelle for all the love you have sent my way. And to Brett, thank you for creating our lovely ecohouse in the tropics, a true sanctuary even when the cyclones blow in. I would also like to acknowledge the Oxford University Press team, in particular Karen Hildebrandt and Jessica Hambridge for their publishing nous and friendly efficiency. I would also like to thank Pete Cruttenden for his superb copy editing.

Nicola Goc The genesis for this book was discussions in the corridors and tearooms of the University of Tasmania between myself, Jason Bainbridge, Liz Tynan and Journalism and media colleagues. While Liz and Jason have moved on to different institutions, they have not only remained respected colleagues, but they are also my steadfast friends; I thank them both for their insight, their commitment to the second edition of this book and for their friendship. I also wish to thank the editorial staff at Oxford University Press for their belief in this book and special thanks to our editor, Pete Cruttenden. Finally, I give my heartfelt thanks to my family.

INTRODUCTION

Why a 2.0 edition?

In the short few years between the first edition of this book and the 2.0 edition you are now holding, much has changed and much has stayed the same. We are operating in one of the most dynamic sectors of society and there have been few more dynamic eras than the one we are living through now. In case you missed it, thanks to digital technology, media themselves have been upgraded. This is Media 2.0 and to help you around we have created this 2.0 edition.

Media 2.0 refers to the increasing prevalence of user generated content (UGC), which basically means that for the first time in history anyone reading this book can produce their own media. Indeed, if you have a Facebook page, or tweeted, or blogged, or ever uploaded anything to YouTube, you already have. While it's dangerous to provide a starting point for Media 2.0 (its arguably more of an evolution than a particular point in time) it most arguably crystallised around the terrorist attacks of September 11, where the full potential of internet technologies for surveillance and resistance (protest and alternative forms of journalism) was realised. Now Media 2.0 is commonplace. Popular cultural products, such as BBC's *Doctor Who*, incorporates web content, games, downloads and DVD extras into its distribution and fans of the original series (Russell T. Davis and Steven Moffat) now produce and write it; the consumers have become producers. News programs too, such as ABC's *Q&A*, incorporate Twitter and Skype into their structure, creating a live, interactive audience no longer bound by a studio.

More broadly we are bearing witness to a series of profound changes as a result of this upgrade—to the rise of social media and its increasing importance in times of crisis; to the startling eruption of WikiLeaks; to democracy and demonstrations sweeping across the Middle East, aided by Facebook and Twitter; to rolling coverage of a series of natural disasters, each worse than the one that preceded it; to the all-pervasive nature of digital technology and the (voluntary) erosion of privacy; to the celebrity of Lady Gaga and Justin Bieber; to the proliferation of free-to-air digital television channels; to the success of 3D cinema. All these and many other manifestations of this awesome Media 2.0 paradigm shift are there to be seen, experienced, debated and assimilated. It is the era of Media 2.0 and this 2.0 edition will reflect the seismic changes now underway while emphasising the timeless skills and knowledge bases that set the high quality media and journalism practitioner apart from the dabbler or the hack.

To an extent, this book is based on David Gauntlett's idea of Media Studies 2.0 in the sense that we view you all as empowered users (rather than passive consumers) of media. That's one of the reasons we talk about media *and* journalism. In many respects, the skill sets we refer to as journalistic are active ways of putting media theories into practice. You may also notice that while there are lots of references to other media in this book there are relatively few pictures. This is because we want you to use this book in connection with the media around you. When we talk about television, have a look at what is currently on your television. Listen to music on your iPod. Tweet. Flip through the pages of your magazines. We want this to be a truly immersive experience, as individual for you as possible, and while we do point to certain key texts, we also want to encourage you to make your own links and analyse your own texts with the tools we provide you with. Any of the references we make are available online and you should be able to access most media content via sites such as YouTube. Don't just passively read this text. Be active, follow connections, make links.

To that end we've upgraded all of the information herein, added new material, created new case studies and archived all of our previous case studies online. Furthermore we have additional web content for all of our sections.

Who is this book for?

Since its launch, this book has become many things to many people and in this 2.0 edition we have sought to be just as inclusive, recognising the broad and encompassing nature of so many media and communication professions. So *Media and Journalism 2.0* will be suitable for anyone interested in media and journalism and the relationship between them, particularly:

- undergraduate students
- postgraduate students wanting a refresher course or an accessible introduction to new areas of study
- educators in journalism and/or media wanting to know more about the other area
- early career journalists wondering what to do, and how to do it, now that they have finished their studies
- early career media practitioners who are in a similar position
- those people already working in media who are thinking of changing their career path in some way (from print to electronic media, or journalism to PR, or magazine editor to blogger, for example)
- journalists generally
- people working in PR generally
- media practitioners generally
- people interested in communications
- people in public life who want to understand how media and journalism work.

We have written this with you in mind, making it as accessible and interesting as we can. The ideas in here may be complex, but we have set out to express them as clearly and entertainingly as possible. We hope that you will find this book not only interesting to read, but also fun.

Why should you be interested?

As media forms continue to converge, and the line between entertainment and news becomes harder to define, it is important for people working in media and journalism to have knowledge of the theories and practices that inform media as a whole. This book is designed to be an authoritative and easy-to-follow introductory text that does not abstract journalism or PR from the rest of the media, but rather considers and interrogates their roles in media, through theory and practice. We want you to understand how your profession works in the larger context, and equally, how those skills typically labelled as 'journalistic' are transferable into different jobs within media.

Why is this book different from most of the other media and journalism books?

This book is about media *and* journalism, not media *or* journalism, or media with a hint of journalism, or journalism with a vague reference to the public sphere somewhere towards the end. This is because in the twenty-first century an 'editorial act' can be found among the millions of amateur bloggers as well as the tens of thousands of professional journalists (Deuze 2009). In the era of Media 2.0, the divisions between media and journalism have become virtually non-existent. So this is a book about the relationship between media and journalism, and how a study of one can inform the study of the other. Building on the work of leading theorists and practitioners, this book integrates media theory with journalistic practice, providing you with a complete introduction to media and journalism by drawing on current theories of the media as well as providing practical instruction on how to write journalistic pieces that put these theories into practice.

How is this book organised?

The book is divided into five parts—from an overview of what we mean by media and journalism, to histories and analyses of the media industries that produce them, to the tools we use for analysing media, to the ways in which we produce news, to the ethical and legal frameworks within which media and journalism operate, to the social contexts within which they function, now and into the future—providing a complete handbook of communication. You can therefore follow the flow of information and ideas from news production through to dissemination and negotiation, which will reveal how important media and journalism studies are to each other.

Each part is divided into chapters addressing the major areas of study, which introduce you to the theoretical debates and specialist vocabulary of each area, a case study, which demonstrates some of these theories in practice and a tools section, which offers practical training relevant to each area, through which you can engage with these theories yourselves, and you can put theory into practice. Furthermore, each chapter, case study and tools section is supplemented by web content, including alternative case studies, tutorial exercises, additional examples and assessments.

Built around the notion of the public sphere, the book explores how the history of journalism informs the construction of modern media practice and the democratisation of knowledge. News is the entry point of new information into the public sphere to be negotiated, debated and exchanged. From there we follow how these ideas are disseminated and commodified (by the media industries), analysed and constructed (through media analysis and journalistic writing), framed and discussed (through ethical and legal frameworks) and, finally, contextualised and debated (through new media, convergence and postmodernity).

What this textbook does differently is to bring together media and journalism studies in an interdisciplinary way that sees journalism and news texts as media products that can be considered in relation to other media products, such as television dramas, films and soap operas.

What do we mean by media?

For this book we define media as content and distribution mechanisms through which information and/or entertainment are transmitted. They can be publicly or privately owned, developed with advances in technology and are often economically profitable.

Some things to remember about media:

- Strictly speaking, the term 'media' refers to *anything* through which *something else* can be transmitted.
- We are using the above definition because we will be looking at specific types of media, what are often referred to as *the* media or *mass media*, message transmitters designed to attract the greatest number of audience members, such as newspapers, television, film, radio and the internet.
- This means that the types of media we will be looking at are all involved in *communication*. As Hirst and Harrison (2007: x) note, the crucial difference between communication and media is that 'communication is the process of sending and receiving messages ... media are the means of communication and transmission'. Media are therefore the mechanisms through which we communicate with other people.
- Media are called *media* because they are literally in the middle (*media* means *middle* in Latin). They are the mechanisms that stand between the sender and the receiver of messages, the mechanisms that convey messages between the sender and receiver.
- Journalism is therefore a crucially important media form, as it is involved in the transmission of news (quite literally, 'new information'), whether that is news about the fall of a government, a terrorist bombing or about a celebrity, a new album or a sporting match.
- *Media* is the plural of *medium*: something through which something else can be transmitted. For example, a psychic medium claims to be able to transmit messages between the living and the dead; an electrical cable is a medium of transmitting electricity to appliances in your home. Similarly, a newspaper, a Facebook page or a film transmits information and/or entertainment to an audience. Any one of these would be a medium. In total we call them media.
- In this book, when we refer to a specific type of media we will call it a *media form*, such as television or radio. In Part 3, we will break down these media forms further into *media texts*, *signs* and *signifiers/signifieds*, all of which will be defined in their appropriate chapters (look out for the handy definitions in the book's margins).
- Only rarely we will refer to media as *mass media*, a term you're probably familiar with, for two reasons. First, it carries the connotation of the audience being an undifferentiated lump, whereas, in truth, the various members of 'mass audiences' can behave in very

different ways, based on age, gender, race or a host of social, cultural and economic factors. Second, the era of the mass media is fragmenting, because of the rapid development and implementation of *new media* (a term that we will define later, but which encompasses the internet, social media, games and mobile phones) and the *convergence* (also defined later) of various media forms. Whereas *mass media* was once used, quite correctly, as a term that differentiated media industries from the telecommunications industry (because the telecommunications industry was seen as a one-to-one industry and other media industries as one-to-many), a combination of convergence and new media innovations has meant that media as a whole can no longer be thought of as 'mass'. Instead, person-to-person and many-to-many communication is becoming increasingly common, and the boundaries between audiences and producers are less defined. These changes, which form a running theme of this book, are examined in more detail in Chapters 16 and 17.

- The distinction between old and new media will also be made in Chapter 16, but you should be aware that as the advances in media (technological and otherwise, which are frequently referred to as 'new' media) are so widespread that new media will be considered in most chapters throughout the book.

Who is a media practitioner?

A media practitioner is anyone involved in the production of media. They can include graphic designers, producers, broadcasters, actors, scriptwriters, audio technicians, public relations officers, spin doctors, bloggers, website designers and journalists.

What do we mean by 'journalism'?

Journalism is the gathering and disseminating of new information about current events, trends, issues and people to a wide audience. Journalism academic Barbie Zelizer (2005) argues that it is unsatisfactory to define journalism as a profession, an industry, an institution or a craft. She says that journalism has to be ultimately understood as a culture. Journalism can be defined by the practice of journalists, but for those aspiring to become journalists, a definition that goes beyond 'journalism is what journalists do' is required.

Journalism came out of the creation of a public sphere in which ideas and information could be disseminated, negotiated, debated and exchanged. The Greek *agora*, the Roman Forum, and the European coffee houses all provided the space in which the basic principles of journalism evolved. Through often vigorous (and sometimes fatal) discussions that worked out the principles of checks and balances on truth-telling, point-of-view and accuracy, a consensus was reached on what the citizens would accept as accurate information upon which they could act.

- The fundamental principles of journalism are the respect for truth and the public's right to information.
- It is often said that journalism is the first draft of history, because journalists record important historical events as they are happening.

- Journalism informs a global community of current and future events that have an impact on everyone on the planet: from global warming, war or the threat of a tsunami to global economic downturn and global terrorism.
- Journalism also disseminates information about the day-to-day detail of ordinary life within our immediate community, such as changes to the bus timetables, increases in rates and taxes, the success or failure of a local sporting team and the death of a prominent citizen.

What is a journalist?

While Zelizer's cultural definition of journalism covers a wide field, those aspiring to a career as a journalist most likely want to know just what a journalist does.

A journalist is a person who practices journalism, someone who gathers and disseminates new information to a wider audience about current events, trends, people and issues. The word 'journalist' is taken from the French *journal*, which comes from the Latin term *diurnal* (daily).

Our understanding of the role of a journalist often comes not only from news bulletins and newspapers, but also from films, novels and comics—surely the ultimate heroic journalist is the comic-strip character Clark Kent, the *Daily Planet* reporter who combats evil as Superman. We've all seen in films and television the stereotypical Hollywood journalist hero, the hard-bitten, cynical reporter up against a corrupt world. Harry Shearer's succinct tongue-in-cheek definition captures the stereotypical journalist of old: 'He's a hard-drinking, soft-spoken, burn-up-some-shoe-leather, sort of son-of-a-gun who's seen it all before, and can't wait to see it all again.'

This image is a far cry from reality. For a start, at least half of all working journalists today are female, and most journalists use telecommunications technology rather than shoe leather to gather information. They may start as bloggers, or on Twitter, or just using their Facebook page to tell stories. And occupational health and safety rules have put an end to the whisky bottle in the bottom drawer.

Unlike most other professions and trades, there is no professional body that registers journalists—so anyone can claim to be a journalist, which prompts the question: 'What is a journalist?'

The ideal journalist

Just as the fundamental principles of journalism are respect for truth and the public's right to know, a journalist's first obligation is to the truth and their loyalty is to the public. Journalists must also:

- act independently from those they report on
- operate under a value system, a code of ethics, such as the Media Entertainment and Arts Alliance/Australian Journalists Association (MEAA/AJA) Code of Ethics. The MEAA/AJA Code tells us that:

> Journalists describe society to itself. They convey information, ideas and opinions, a privileged role. They search, disclose, record, question, entertain, suggest and

> remember. They inform citizens and animate democracy. They give a practical form to freedom of expression. Many journalists work in private enterprise, but all have these public responsibilities. They scrutinise power, but also exercise it, and should be accountable. Accountability engenders trust. Without trust, journalists do not fulfil their public responsibilities. (MEAA/AJA Code of Ethics)

All journalists are writers, which is why we devote space in this book to the forms of journalistic expression and the foundations of English grammar.

Ideally, journalists are also concerned with the pursuit of objectivity, and they operate within an environment that should have in place checks and balances ensuring that their journalism is balanced, fair and accurate.

News journalists:

- work differently from the way other journalists work; they are at the frontline of the Fourth Estate (see Chapter 3), and act as watchdogs over government and others who wield power
- report on the news of the day that has greatest impact on the community
- report on all levels of political and public life: police matters, the courts, health and welfare, and on financial, environmental and other social issues deemed to be of public importance
- give us the information that enables us to make decisions about the way we live: timely and accurate information that is in our interest to know.

Part 4 provides you with the essential skills you will need to work as a journalist, while there are parts of other sections of this book that will give you essential information on the role of the journalist in society and the role and impact of journalism in the twenty-first century.

What is the difference between hard news and soft news?

News journalists can find themselves working at two very different ends of the news spectrum, sometimes for the same organisation. A journalist may work on an infotainment-style program for the electronic media, a job that also covers hard news and investigative stories, or they may work on a newspaper that has both hard and soft news sections, or on a magazine where both styles of news are published. Hard and soft news indicate a difference in the standards for news values (for definitions, see Chapter 12).

Hard news

Hard news, closest to the ideal of the Fourth Estate, is associated with the notion of a free press and to the public's right to know. Hard news stories aim to inform the community about events and happenings, and provide citizens with the information they require to be able to participate in the democratic process as fully informed citizens.

Hard news journalists gather and disseminate new information to the public in the interests of animating democracy. Hard news covers topics such as politics, crime, law, environment, conflict, war, disasters, welfare, health, social justice, economics, science and technology.

Hard news needs to be conveyed in a timely manner and cover *current* events. People need to be informed about the most recent developments. The advent of twenty-four-hour-a-day news, digital media and the World Wide Web have made this imperative a lot easier to deliver.

New media (see Case Study 5, Part 4 and 6 and Tool 5) is providing new opportunities—and new challenges—for news journalists: to blog and tweet or not to blog and tweet? Should journalists use social networking services for sourcing? Journalists working in all platforms today, and even more so in the future, will need to be adept at posting stories on multiple platforms. These new demands, at a time when staff numbers are being reduced, place new pressures on journalists. But new media also offer new opportunities for collaboration between journalists and media organisations and the public in the creation of news.

As Australian political journalist, Annabel Crabb, who now writes online for *The Drum*, the ABC's comment and analysis portal, says the loss of control for journalists in the new media environment is about the loss of centrality.

> We are—belatedly, and for reasons entirely unassociated with Government-led deregulation or any of the other usual reasons—contestable. The community of news and commentary is getting stronger and more populous. We are just not necessarily, automatically at the core of it any more. And we are open to criticism—some of it savage, some of it worryingly accurate—like never before. (Crabb 2010)

The death of the business model for journalism in old media and the failure to find a sustainable business model in the online environment threatens the future of professional journalism. Old media, in the rush to engage with their audiences in the new online environment, established online sites in the first decade of the twenty-first century where they posted their breaking news and new content. They let the genie out of the bottle and when, at the end of the first decade of the century, they began trying to charge for this content, audiences rightfully objected. As Crabb rather colourfully puts it:

> Having put the cart before the horse in the first instance, it seems that newspapers often make the same mistake again in trying to get out of the mess. Trying to work out how to charge for the content before working out how you make the content worth charging for. Sounds like we're hitching our horse right back up to the arse end of the cart again. There is such a panic on about how to make money that the larger questions—How will we be relevant? How can we be useful?—often are overlooked.

Crabb argues that the only way forward is to offer something new, something worth paying for.

> Apps for mobile and tablet devices are the obvious vehicle, but it's no good just dumping the copy from the newspaper on some cigarette-packet-sized mega-computer and holding out your hand.

And she says the sheer volume of information on the Web could be the opportunity for journalism:

> There is a market in making sense of things. The problem for the hungry online consumer has become, with vertiginous speed, not 'Where can I find news?' but 'How do I hack my way through all this stuff to find what I want?' (Crabb 2010)

And then along comes a phenomenon such as Wikileaks (see Chapter 3). WikiLeaks is an organisation that solicits, vets and distributes leaked documents via the web. Through its collaboration with several influential newspapers around the world, it is providing a new model for journalism and has arguably become the most significant development in journalism to date in the 21st century. It has reinvigorated the public's interest, on a global scale, in the right to an unfettered press, free from government and industry interference, and the public's right to be informed. And it has provided optimism among those who believe in the importance of a strong and effective Fourth Estate. Indeed, many believe Julian Assange's mission to keep governments and the powerful accountable provides a way forward for journalism and the Fourth Estate in the digital, global environment.

Soft news

Soft news, generally defined as news that does not have a high priority in the news values scale, encompasses such issues as entertainment, sport, lifestyle, human interest, celebrity and the arts (although all of these issues can also be the focus of hard news stories). Soft news is also sometimes called *infotainment* (see also Chapter 2 and Part 4). Governments are rarely brought down by soft news stories, and countries do not go to war over the exposure of a sporting scandal. Soft news does not have the same imperative for timeliness as hard news, and is usually generated by the journalist's or editor's curiosity rather than an event.

The division between soft news and hard news has blurred significantly in recent years with the proliferation of celebrity and entertainment news entering the hard news sections of newspapers and news bulletins.

Today tension frequently exists between traditional hard news journalists and those in media management who have more of an eye on the revenue flows from delivering infotainment and soft news.

By way of example, in America Mika Brzezinski, a news presenter with *Morning Joe* on MSNBC television, refused to lead her bulletin with the latest Paris Hilton story about the celebrity socialite's release from prison before reports on Iraq and developments at the White House. In the first bulletin she screwed up the script and refused to read it; in the second bulletin she took a co-presenter's cigarette lighter and tried to burn the script; and in the third bulletin on air she took it straight to the shredder in the studio and fed it into the machine. Ms Brzezinski told viewers: 'I hate it and I don't think it should be our lead. I just don't believe in covering that story, at least not as the lead story on the newscast, when we have a day like today.' Within a day 250,000 people had viewed Ms Brzezinski's actions on YouTube. Hundreds of viewers posted positive comments, including 'This lady has some serious balls and some serious morals.'

This recent trend, which has seen soft news making its way into hard news spaces in print and in the electronic media, is called the *tabloidisation* of news. (A tabloid is a newspaper that is compact in size. Its content is usually considered to be less serious than broadsheet newspapers. Tabloid news focuses on the sensational and privileges such subjects as crime, sex, scandal and sport, with an informal vernacular delivery.) This does not mean that it is not of value to readers and viewers. While most citizens demand to be informed by a free press about matters that have an impact on their lives within a democratic state, they may also be just as interested in the sporting results or entertainment news. One person may privilege business news over entertainment news, and another may privilege lifestyle news over politics. All of this news comes together to fulfil another aim of journalism—to describe society to itself in all of its complexity.

Dan Okrent, editor of new media for *Time Inc.*, believes that journalists have to be aware of what their audiences want. He says journalists remove themselves from their audiences when they take themselves too seriously. While he believes that, as the public's eyes and ears, journalists are obliged to be honest, accurate and fair, he says that 'sometimes to be a journalist is to report on the new colours for living room sofas' or to 'report on whether the TV star is really happy with his new girlfriend'. He says there are things to do with entertainment and conversation that provide a connection with readers and viewers at a different level.

J-bloggers

Are bloggers journalists? The internet enables any of us to publish our writing, but does that mean that every self-published writer is a journalist? Bloggers who use the medium of the internet, subscribe to the journalistic ideals of an obligation to the truth and the public's right to information, act independently from those they report on, operate under a value system—such as a code of ethics—and scrutinise those in power and who search, disclose, record, question and entertain can be regarded as web journalists, whether they are paid professionals or citizen journalists—are called J-bloggers (see Chapter 3).

Nicola Goc, who coined the term, argues that J-bloggers, working within new media, have reclaimed some of the old traditions of a free and independent press by reporting without fear or favour. They have brought new energy and innovation to journalism, they are breathing new life into the old practices and, along with their colleagues working in the traditional media of newspapers, television and radio, are providing the oxygen of twenty-first century democracy.

What is public relations (PR)?

Public relations is the promotion of a product, idea, event or person with the intention of creating goodwill for it. Public relations can be many different things, some not necessarily closely connected with marketing. In a general sense, you can say that the profession is interested in relationships: reducing conflict and improving cooperation. In the corporate sector, this can certainly serve the marketing objectives of a company to create a receptive environment for the marketing of products. In the government sector, it can help sell policies and ideas and change behaviours in various ways, for example, the various public relations campaigns around health issues or domestic violence. In the community or nongovernment sectors, it can establish useful social connections or spread new knowledge for the benefit of various communities. PR really deals in the flow of information, in many varieties and forms. It is a huge and growing part of the public sphere, a sector that (rightly or wrongly) promulgates much of the information that passes through the media.

According to the Public Relations Institute of Australia (PRIA): 'Public relations is the deliberate, planned and sustained effort to establish and maintain mutual understanding between an organisation and its publics.'

- While its reach and influence may be cause for disquiet among members of the Fourth Estate, it is possible for journalists and other media professionals to engage with public relations practitioners in positive and fruitful ways.

- Mutual mistrust between public relations professionals and the media is unhelpful, and in many ways unnecessary. Finding ways to develop positive relationships is the theme of Chapter 8, while Chapter 15 canvasses some of the pitfalls in the relationship between journalism and public relations, and suggests ways through the ethical minefields.
- Tools 2 gives practical advice on how to run an effective media conference.

Academic approaches to journalism

While journalism has been taught at Australian and New Zealand universities for more than eighty years, traditionally most journalists gained their training on the job through a cadetship. Today, however, the entry-level requirement for a cadet journalist is a university degree.

Academic approaches to journalism have traditionally come from a number of disciplines, and focused on whichever aspect of journalism is most interesting to that particular discipline.

- Sociological studies of journalism tend to focus not only on the journalist's role in society, but also on the practices of journalism, from studies on the selectivity of stories and gatekeeping, through to ethnographies of the newsroom and ideological studies of the institution of journalism. The ideas of *gatekeeping* and *news culture* come from this tradition.
- Historical studies of journalism tend to analyse the impact of journalism at micro, mid and macro levels, through analyses of memoirs and biographies, periods and events, and the development of the nation-state. This approach is reflected in Chapters 2 and 3.
- Language studies of journalism tend to look at journalism in the context of semiology, content analysis, framing and discourse analysis, all forms of textual analysis that are used in media studies as well. These concepts are defined in more detail in Tools 3.
- Political science studies of journalism tend to look at the relationships between journalism, politics and power, particularly around sourcing practices and the role of the journalist. To some extent, the idea of journalism as the Fourth Estate (Chapter 3) has been shaped and developed through a political science perspective.
- Cultural studies approaches to journalism tend to analyse the forms journalism can take, the ways in which journalists are represented and the relationship between journalists and audiences. Again, this clearly intersects with media studies, and directly informs our study of a variety of journalistic forms and our use of the term *representation.*

Why is it important for journalists to know about media?

In Australia, this question has been at the centre of a debate between journalists and media academics for over a decade. The debate is popularly known as the 'media wars'. Several prominent writers have argued that media theory is of no practical use to would-be journalists (Flew and Sternberg 1999; Windschuttle 2000; Flew et al. 2007). These writers point to the number of media courses offered by commercial providers that make no mention of 'theory' (see Flew 2008 for more on this) as evidence that the sector does not require knowledge of theory.

However, once you have graduated from university and are out there seeking a career in journalism or the media you will need to be work ready. You will need to have a very strong portfolio—and preferably one that shows skills across more than one type of media. That's why you may choose to study journalism from many different perspectives: print, radio, television, photojournalism and online. To be able to put these skills into practice, you will also need to gain an understanding of professional practice within a global media sphere, understand the ethical practice of journalism and public relations, and understand the role of journalism in contemporary society within the broader media sphere. In summary, you will need to have a comprehensive knowledge of the twenty-first century media environment.

More specifically, you should know about media because:

- with the ongoing erosion between information and entertainment, news and entertainment, and hard news and soft news, it becomes conceptually important to know about *all* areas of media so you can adapt, resist or at least recognise these erosions as they occur
- you will need to understand how your profession works in the larger context of media
- you will need to understand the theories and concepts behind what you are doing in practice
- you will need to acquire knowledge of a variety of media concepts and practices to make it easy for you if you wish to change media jobs at some point in your working life (such as moving from print to electronic, journalism to PR, or journalism to dramatic scriptwriting) or if you are an academic who wishes to teach in interdisciplinary programs.

Media, journalism, culture and society: the broad relationships

How can we best study the broad relationships between media, journalism, culture and society? We study these relationships by applying theory. For the purposes of this book we define theory as the body of rules, ideas, principles and techniques that apply to a particular subject, as distinct from actual practice.

Theory is not something that is solely the province of academics. Theories range from how to find the best tomatoes, to who will win the football grand final, to how to pick up a date at a club, to Lyotard's theories of postmodernity (see Chapter 18).

Theory in itself is not an evaluative term. A taxi driver's theory that Martians killed President Kennedy can be as theoretical as Cunningham and Turner's theories regarding the operation of the media in Australia.

What makes one theory better than another, or more persuasive than another, or having what we may term more academic rigour than another are two further factors: methodology and evidence. We discuss both of these in the Tools 3.

It is worth noting that not everyone defines theory in this way. Some people would reserve theory for the academy, and would claim that theory does have certain requirements that differentiate it from 'old wives' tales', 'beliefs' or 'conspiracy theories'. But we prefer to separate theory, methodology and evidence. It demystifies theory as a term, and reveals the ways in which we can all contribute theoretically, regardless of whether we are part of the academy or not.

Furthermore, we follow the lead of Gunther Kress (1997) in proposing that theory works best in combination with practice, moving away from theory as abstract critique, towards a model of practice-led theory that is more interested in revealing how meaning is made through representation and design. Therefore you shouldn't be frightened or distrustful of theory, but rather use it as a tool to develop your own work in new and innovative ways.

In this book, we teach theories of media by setting them out, using many examples, and showing how they operate in practice with case studies and tools chapters. In this way we can think of journalism as being, to use Thomas McLaughlin's term, a form of 'vernacular theory', in that it is a set of ideas that has evolved outside academia and, as you can see from the approaches listed above, has only recently been folded back into the academy, usually under the auspices of former practitioners.

In this way we hope to develop the links between media and journalism, and between theory and practice, and provide you with the most comprehensive introduction to media and journalism that we can.

We hope you enjoy the 2.0 edition of *Media and Journalism.* We hope you learn a lot and we hope you have some fun while doing it.

INTRODUCING MEDIA AND JOURNALISM

What is media? How do we make sense of it? And why would we want to? In Part 1 we set out to answer these questions.

Chapter 1 (The Public Sphere) sets up the theoretical framework for this book: the connection between the mediasphere and the larger public sphere. This establishes the place of media in society and the way media forms are connected to one another. It also suggests one of the reasons why news is so important for media more generally.

Chapter 2 (The First Mass Medium) considers the evolution of media by focusing on the evolution of the first mass medium: print. Through an examination of individual newspaper journalists in history it finds particular resonances with twenty-first century figures and reminds us of the constant battle for a free and unfettered press.

Chapter 3 (The Fourth [or Fifth] Estate) confirms the centrality of journalism to any consideration of media, because of the vital role it performs as the Fourth Estate. It also explores the possibility of new media as a Fifth Estate and critiques the role WikiLeaks is playing in the new media landscape of the twenty-first century.

Chapter 4 (Elements of Writing) then strips media back to its basics, providing a comprehensive introduction to communication, language and grammar, the common vocabulary of all media forms.

Case Study 1 (The Battle for a Free Press in Colonial Australia) revisits the beginnings of the news media in Australia and reminds us of the importance of understanding the battle for a free and uncensored press in colonial Australia. At this moment in time, it is particularly significant to revisit these early days and see the resonances with the manufacture of twenty-first century news, and to realise that throughout time journalists and publishers, with influence over the formation of public opinion, have always been a threat to the powerful elite.

Tools 1 (Print Media and Broadcast Interviews) introduces you to one of the most basic research skills, but one that requires a lot of practice to perfect. The interview is the point at which private information becomes public, where much information enters the public sphere. It is the foundation of news reports, features, broadcast journalism, ethnographic research and, frequently, dramatic narratives.

CHAPTER 1

THE PUBLIC SPHERE

JASON BAINBRIDGE

Introduction

We spend most of our lives surrounded by **media**.

Media: Content and distribution mechanisms through which information and/or entertainment is transmitted.

Think about yourselves today. You may have watched the morning news. Then you might have put on the radio or flipped through a magazine or listened to some music on your iPod. Tonight you might go out to a film, or spend the night online. The odds are that by the time you sit down to read this chapter you will have already had a discussion about the football or the weather, how much you're looking forward to *Two and a Half Men* or *Family Guy*, or how hot Jessica Alba or Johnny Depp look.

Simon Frith describes these popular culture discussions as 'the currency of friendship … trading pop judgments is a way to "flirt and fight"' (Frith 2004: 32).

The point is that this is how we all spend our lives: surrounded by media, immersed in media, interacting with media, each and every day. Media informs the way that we speak, the way that we think and the way that we navigate our way through the world.

In this chapter we look at:

- how media work
- the relationship between different types of media
- what the public sphere is
- how media contribute to the public sphere.

How do media work?

Importantly, media do not work in isolation. Different media forms speak to each other as much as they speak to an audience. Television dramas refer to stories that have appeared on the news. Music clips parody films. Magazines detail the public and private lives of celebrities.

Indeed, media forms refer to each other all the time. They make fun of each other and often require knowledge of each other to make sense.

The Simpsons

On the television series *The Simpsons*, Homer Simpson is working as a bodyguard for Springfield's corrupt Mayor Quimby. Facing down a group of gangsters in a crowded dinner theatre, Homer struggles to find something he can use as a weapon. Mark Hamill (currently appearing at the dinner theatre in *Guys and Dolls*) calls out to Homer from the stage: 'Use the forks Homer, use the forks!'

Television series such as *The Simpsons*, *Family Guy* and *South Park* make lots of jokes, as does this one, that refer to other media. So do magazines such as *MAD* and films such as *The Naked Gun* and the *Austin Powers* series. You can still find these situations funny in themselves, but to be 'in' on the joke or to be able to recognise the pop culture reference, you need to consume lots of other media.

For example, to get this joke in *The Simpsons* you'd need to recognise Mark Hamill as the actor who played Luke Skywalker in the original *Star Wars* films—and recognise that one of the lines most associated with that film is 'Use the force'.

Cultural currency: The knowledge we acquire from consuming media.

We call this knowledge **cultural currency**—the knowledge we acquire from consuming media. The more media we consume, the more cultural currency we acquire, allowing us to be in on the joke and more familiar with the way media work.

The shot–reverse shot

Sometimes this knowledge is so deeply ingrained that we forget that we acquired it from other media forms. Think of the way film and television series cut between two actors when they are talking, showing an image of one speaker, then an image of another and back again.

This is called a **shot–reverse shot**. The only reason why we know these two people are talking to each other is our familiarity with the device from other film and television series. There's rarely anything in the shots themselves that suggests they're in the same vicinity, let alone talking to each other.

Shot–reverse shot: The standard method of showing two actors interacting in films and on television: first the image of one speaker, then the image of the other speaker.

In this way we can think of media forms as parts of an ongoing conversation. They refer back to earlier forms, earlier conventions and shared knowledges. They also add to the conversation and move the conversation forward, with new ideas and new technologies.

Sometimes this is explicit, as in the jokes in *The Simpsons*, the pop culture references in *Buffy the Vampire Slayer*, or sampling an earlier piece of music in a dance track.

Sometimes it is more subtle, like the acquired knowledge of conventions—the way a shot–reverse shot works, the ordering of stories in a news bulletin, or the reading of *manga* from right to left and back to front.

In each of these examples, media forms are engaging each other in dialogue through jokes, references, reading conventions or cross-promotional opportunities. We can therefore characterise the relationship *between* different media forms as **dialogic**.

Dialogic: Descriptive of texts that are structured as dialogue.

The relationship between media and their audiences is similarly dialogic. Media forms encourage their audiences to enter into dialogic relationships with them: to contribute, to question, to solve the mystery, to follow the narrative and to seek resolution.

Talkback radio is predicated on this dialogic relationship between a broadcaster and their community of listeners. So are television talk shows, such as *Oprah* and *The Ellen DeGeneres Show*, or letters to the editor in newspapers, comics and magazines.

Crime series such as *CSI*, *Criminal Minds*, *Inspector Morse* and *Miss Marple* feature episodic mysteries that encourage viewers to solve the mystery along with the detectives. *Fringe*, *Lost* and *The X-Files* feature long-running mysteries ('story arcs' over several episodes or seasons) that similarly encourage viewers to seek resolution, to find the answer to what is going on. And some series, such as the short-run *Veronica Mars*, feature both of these types of mysteries. In *Veronica Mars*, episodic mysteries were based around events at Veronica's school, while the ongoing mystery arc of 'Who killed Veronica's friend Lilly Kane?' ran for the first season. By posing a question for the audience, these media forms invite the audiences into a dialogue to answer the question.

Soap operas (such as *The Bold and the Beautiful*), romantic films (such as *Pretty Woman*) and dramatic television series (such as *Grey's Anatomy* and *Sex and the City*, and the earlier *Moonlighting* and *Northern Exposure*), encourage audience engagement by putting impediments in the way of their lead characters coming together. Here the dialogic relationship begins with the question: 'Will X get together with Y?'

Even broadcast news is structured in this way. Newsreaders and reporters address audiences directly. Headlines engage audiences with the stories that will be covered, while sports and weather reports encourage us to stay to the end.

Advances in technology mean that the dialogic relationship between users of media and their audiences is becoming virtually instantaneous. Twitter enables its users to post text-based tweets of up to 140 characters on their profile pages, constantly updating their followers as to what they are doing at any point in time. Other social networking sites, such as Facebook, work in similar way. Voting via mobile phones enables audiences to determine the outcome of talent quests such as *Australian Idol* or *X-Factor*—just as it used to determine who was evicted from the *Big Brother* house. Emails enable audiences to voice what issues are concerning them on morning news programs, actually shaping the content of these series. Some of these ideas are discussed in more detail in Chapters 2, 18 and 19.

The mediasphere

Mediasphere: The subtle and obvious connections between media texts, whether fictional (popular media) or factual (journalism), that form a larger whole.

If we think of the media as being structured like dialogue, then we can move from thinking about discrete media forms (television, film and newspapers) working in isolation, to chains or webs of media all talking back and forth to each other.

This is the **mediasphere**: thousands of media forms connected to each other in subtle and obvious ways.

Of course where there are connections between media, there is also the possibility of someone controlling those connections. As Thwaites, Davis and Mules (2002) note, engaging in dialogue is a fundamental part of social action, but it also means that media can be used to impose cultural *dominance* and offer forms of *resistance*.

This means that the mediasphere is also connected to *power* and *control*.

Figure 1.1 The mediasphere

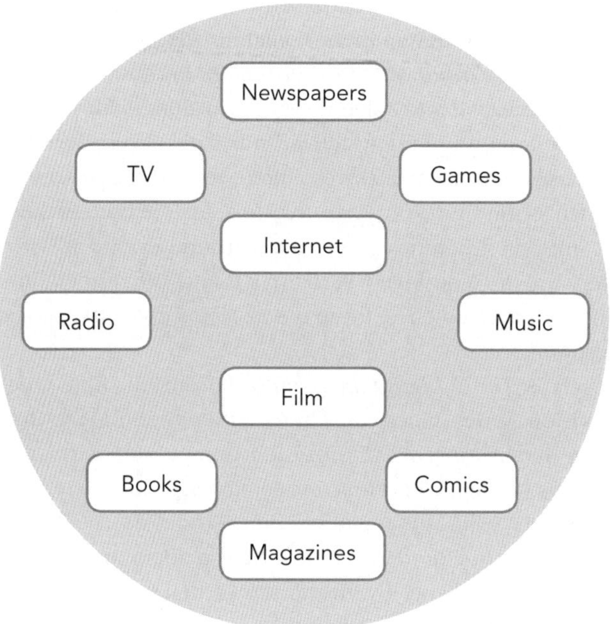

V

The science fiction television series *V*, which first aired in 1983–85 and was reimagined in 2009, deals with ideas of cultural dominance and resistance. In both versions, the series tells the story of Earth being visited by a vast fleet of flying saucers, piloted by apparently benign visitors who look just like us—but are actually cold-blooded reptilians scheming to exploit the Earth in some way (and process us for food). In both series they take control of the media and run a powerful public relations campaign arguing for trust and peace. Similarly, in both series, a human resistance learns the truth and agitates for revolution against them. In 1983, for example, they are led by television journalist Mike Donovan (Marc Singer) and frequently fight for control of the media from the visitors, so they can show the worldwide audience what 'they truly are'. Interestingly, the cultural dominance of the 1980s visitors is made clear through continual allegorical comparisons to the Nazis, through their SS-like black and red uniforms, their swastika-like symbol and their 'visitor youth' program. However, in the 2000s the visitors' cultural dominance is made clear through constant

allegorical comparisons to President Obama's administration, including the reiteration of the buzzwords 'hope' and 'change' and the advocation of 'universal health care'. *V* therefore serves as an example of how ideas of cultural dominance can change over time (from the overt, to the subtle), but constantly depend on who 'controls' (or has access to) media.

Understanding media and power

There are two ways of understanding power relations in the mediasphere. The first is **hegemony** (Gramsci 1971), which is primarily involved in cultural dominance.

Hegemony: The ability of elite groups to acquire and/or remain in power by convincing subordinate groups that it is in their best interests to accept the dominance of this elite.

How is hegemony articulated?

French Marxist Louis Althusser (1971) considered that cultural institutions (such as schools, religious groups and families) helped to construct hegemony by producing 'cultural identities' for people—convincing people that there were particular ways they should act or behave.

The media are clearly other cultural institutions that function in a similar way. Dominant groups use the media to persuade subordinate groups that they should be in power. Here, the media encourages the subordinate groups to accept the leadership and ideas of the dominant power elite. We can refer to this influence as *hegemonic power.*

Importantly, hegemonic power is rarely a product of brute force. It is not like a soldier breaking into your home and convincing you, at gunpoint, that you must do this or that. Gramsci never thought that this concession of power or control by one group to another group was a part of hegemony. Hegemonic power is far more subtle than that. At its most subtle, hegemony is unseen and virtually unconscious.

Hegemony actually encourages subordinate groups to consent to the rule of the dominant power elite. This elite appears naturally superior and the subordinate group comes to believe that the dominant group shares the same ideas and beliefs as themselves. Ultimately, hegemony makes it appear that subordinate interests are best served by this elite group being in power.

Who are these dominant power elites?

> Some groups within a culture—normally those with the greatest economic or cultural capital—have a greater opportunity to promote their ideas to wider audiences, and to convince those audiences to accept their claim to power. (Schirato & Yell 2000: 81)

Dominant power elites might include politicians (such as Kim Jong-il in North Korea), dictators (such as Muammar Gaddafi in Libya) or media barons (such as Rupert Murdoch in general) who can exercise control over the media through political pressure or ownership.

Dominant power elites require great economic or cultural capital because hegemony can rarely work through just one media form. Usually, hegemony requires an accumulation of media, a repetition of the same message over and over again, across different forms. Therefore, dominant power elites have to control vast amounts of media in order to exercise their hegemonic power.

The mediasphere as a political economy

A lot of the terms we are using in this chapter—hegemony, pluralism and even the concept of the public sphere—were first applied to politics, and then imported into media studies. This is partly reflective of a larger shift in society, where dominant value systems (previously the sole province of religion or politics) have come to be embodied, reproduced and contested in the mediasphere. It is also indicative of the way media are increasingly implicated in politics and economics, which leads to a corresponding desire by governments to censor or at the very least regulate the media.

It is therefore possible to think of the mediasphere as a political economy and to study 'the social relations, particularly power relations, that mutually constitute the production, distribution and consumption of resources' (Wasko 2001: 29).

Understanding these power relations is clearly important for concepts such as hegemony and pluralism, as discussed below.

Think again of Rupert Murdoch, who is a recurring figure in this book. Murdoch owns a number of newspapers and television stations in the US, the UK and Australia, among other countries. Following a directive from Murdoch, passed down through his editors and news producers, the editorials in all of his newspapers—and the presenters on his Fox News service—adopted a prowar stance in relation to the US intervention in Iraq in 2003. Murdoch was therefore using his media to support President Bush's policies in relation to the Middle East. Through the media, he was convincing subordinate groups that it was in their best interests that the US invaded Iraq.

Propaganda?

We can link hegemony to ideas of **propaganda**. As is propaganda, hegemony is communication designed to persuade. Hegemony aims to persuade us to think in a certain way, but whereas propaganda is usually overt, emotive and appeals to the nationalism of the audience, hegemony works on a far more covert level.

Propaganda: The deliberate, systematic attempt to shape perceptions, manipulate cognitions and direct behaviour to achieve a response that furthers the desired intent of the propagandist.

Hegemonic power is exercised through the connections *between* media forms. Not only does hegemony convince the consumers of Murdoch's media that the dominant power elite is acting in their best interests, but it also goes a step further to convince them that the elite's interests are the same as theirs and that they actually deserve to rule.

So this dialogic relationship between media forms can work hegemonically to convince audiences that the dominant group is right, the dominant group is good, and the dominant group is actually looking out for them and helping them by being in power.

Diversity and choice

The alternative way of understanding power relations in the mediasphere is the **pluralist** view, which is fundamentally involved in cultural resistance.

Pluralism: Diversity in society, and therefore in the media; pluralist media offer us a wide range of choices.

Pluralism argues that the mediasphere reflects the plurality of the larger society. We always have choice—the choice to ignore certain media, make fun of certain media or seek out alternative media.

> The main function of the media is to please the audience. It therefore seeks to fulfill their needs, and its representations meet with their expectations. Moreover, as media 'texts' are complex and contain multiple meanings, it is difficult to find clear patterns of representation or the distinct exercise of power. Indeed, media representations themselves are pluralistic. (Sardar & Van Loon 2000: 74)

So this dialogic relationship between media forms can also work pluralistically to offer us choices and ways of resisting cultural dominance. They also actively introduce us to different ways of seeing the world by exposing us to different social values and feelings.

Can these views be reconciled?

While these ideas of media and power are clearly in competition with each other—hegemony directs the public to think a certain way, while pluralism offers the public choice—it is possible to reconcile these ideas in the contemporary mediasphere.

Consider the following propositions.

- Most news services (referring here to mainstream news services) work hegemonically, reinforcing ideas about how to understand the world in a certain way.
- The larger mediasphere—the dramas, soaps, comedies, magazines, alternative presses, blogs, etc.—are pluralist, offering us a range of perspectives on the world.

Or to put it another way:

- Rupert Murdoch owns the Fox television network.
- Fox News is generally regarded as being fiercely hegemonic, promoting a right-wing, conservative view of the world.
- The Fox network also screens *The Simpsons*, which is parodic, offering a number of ways of viewing the world, some of which support conservative views (for example, Homer's attitude towards gun control, the liberal media and homosexuals) and some of which openly criticise those views (including portraying Murdoch himself as a 'billionaire tyrant'). *The Simpsons* offers a pluralist view.
- Therefore even though we could argue that the mainstream news industry is largely hegemonic (and we say 'largely' because there are always exceptions), the broader mediasphere is pluralist.

The public sphere

As Gramsci saw it, groups are always struggling for control, for hegemonic power. Power is therefore never secured but always being negotiated, contested and exchanged. So even if we adopt a purely hegemonic approach to media we have to concede that groups are constantly fighting for the consent of the people. Occasionally, we can even see that fight made manifest in ratings wars, the lobbying of governments, regulations, censorship and struggles over ownership and broadcasting rights.

Therefore, regardless of whether the mediasphere is purely pluralist, purely hegemonic, or is ultimately a combination of both, it should be clear that the mediasphere is a space where ideas can be negotiated, exchanged and discussed (as part of that dialogic relationship between media forms and between audiences and media forms.)

Public sphere: The public spaces of work, leisure, politics, religion, academia and the mass media, where issues and ideas are encountered, articulated, negotiated and discussed as part of the ongoing process of reaching consensus or compromise in democratic societies.

This means that the mediasphere is also part of the larger **public sphere**.

> The idea of the public sphere is of something which is open and accessible to all and a key component of modern, participatory, democratic life. (O'Sullivan et al. 1994: 250–1)

Although 'public sphere' and 'mediasphere' are terms that are used fairly interchangeably, especially in the press, it is important to note that the public sphere is larger than the mediasphere. It certainly incorporates the mediasphere—and the mediasphere is centrally important to the functioning of the public sphere (see below)—but it also includes areas well outside the province of the mediasphere.

The public sphere includes conversations at the pub, posting on Facebook, blogging, a debate over dinner, a text message, a noticeboard at the office, a suggestion box at a restaurant or sticky notes on a refrigerator in a share house ('Don't touch my muffin!').

Figure 1.2 The public sphere

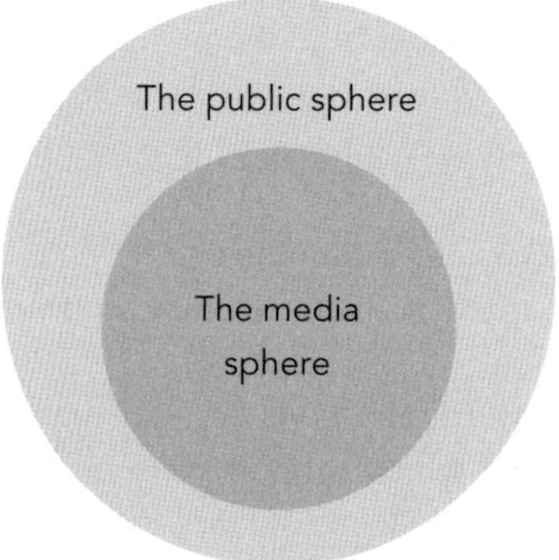

Interestingly, some theorists, such as John Hartley, still prefer to think of the public sphere as being enclosed by the mediasphere—an inverse relationship to the one we have set out above. It really all comes down to how you define 'public'. Is a busker in the street part of the public sphere? Is a presentation in a lecture theatre or an activist on a soapbox? All of these may be unmediated but they certainly all contribute to the public sphere, suggesting to us that the public sphere is the larger of the two.

The public sphere is often defined in opposition to the private sphere (the personal and domestic spaces of the home), but increasingly the media conflate the public and the private. Talk shows (such as *Oprah* and *The Jerry Springer Show*) and reality television (such as

Big Brother) did this throughout the 1990s into the 2000s, and today's social networking sites (particularly Facebook) are similarly predicated on this idea of making the private public (or at least publicly accessible). This means that the public sphere is anywhere 'where information, ideas and debate can circulate in society, and where *political opinion* can be formed' (Dahlgren 1995: ix).

Note the emphasis on 'political opinion'. Again, there is a clear overlap between media and politics, which we return to below.

We can also characterise the public sphere as dialogic, but it is a conversation between ideas and minds rather than between media forms. The mediasphere plays an important role in this meeting of minds and ideas, but, once again, the conversation can clearly extend well beyond the mediasphere.

Increasingly, as communities become larger and larger, the mediasphere plays a greater role in the functioning of the public sphere. Politicians use media to reach potential voters through television appearances and Twitter. Families and friends use media to keep in touch via texting and social networking sites. Audiences learn about the communities of which they are a part through media: print, television and online news informing them about their local community, their state community, their national community and the international community. Indeed, media theorist Alan McKee (2005) suggests that the mediasphere actually functions as the public sphere for modern nations.

Water-cooler show: A film, televison or radio program that generates great interest wherever members of the public gather in discussion, especially around the office water cooler.

The water-cooler effect

A popular way of describing a successful television series in the 1990s was to call the series a **water-cooler show**. The term refers to the way people in offices would gather at the water cooler to discuss the previous night's programs. Such a conversation was indicative of the level of investment by a series' viewers (that they were willing to discuss the series in such detail the following day) and would generate interest in the series among people who had not seen it (encouraging them to tune in or otherwise be excluded from the conversation). *Seinfeld*, *Ally McBeal* and *Sex and the City* have all been examples of water-cooler series. *Underbelly* and *Lost* similarly became water-cooler series for a while.

This water-cooler effect is an example of how the public sphere extends beyond the mediasphere. Ideas generated in the mediasphere are taken up outside the mediasphere (in the office, at the water cooler) and discussed, negotiated and contested.

An even earlier example of the water-cooler effect might be the hairdressing salon where the previous night's television or the contents of a magazine could become the topic of discussion and debate.

The mediasphere has therefore become the place where ideas are articulated and circulated because populations are now too large to gather together in one physical space.

Of course, maintaining this exchange of ideas and information in society is important because it is only through such exchanges—such *participation*—that democracy can function.

Is there anything larger than the public sphere?

Yuri Lotman, using the model of the biosphere, suggested that all communication may be part of something called the semiosphere, which he defined as the 'semiotic space necessary for the existence and functioning of languages' (Lotman 1990: 123). We will be discussing semiotics in more detail in Part 3. As all communication would include communication in both public and private spaces, the semiosphere would be much broader than the public sphere. We can therefore think of communication as mapping across three spheres that are arranged like Russian dolls: the semiosphere, which encloses the public sphere, which, in turn, encloses the mediasphere.

The public sphere as a physical space

Agora: An open space in a town where people gather, especially a marketplace in ancient Greece.

Forum: In ancient Rome, a public square or marketplace where business was conducted and the law courts were situated.

Originally the public sphere was a physical space. From the sixth century BCE, the **forum** was a large, unenclosed area in Roman cities designed for public gatherings. Greece had a similar area called an **agora**.

Hartley (1992a) describes how the forum gave voice to the free man, allowing him to participate in public life 'directly, as a voter, a jurist, a consumer, or as an audience of oratory in the service of public affairs' (Hartley 1992: 35):

> The classic Roman forum [Greek agora] was the place of citizenship, an open space where public affairs and legal disputes were conducted ... In classical Greece or Rome, assuming you were a free man rather than a woman, slave or foreigner, you could walk into the agora or forum and participate in public life directly (Hartley 1992: 33, 35).

In the beginning, each city had only one forum, which performed the dual functions of business (legal, political and mercantile) and entertainment (public games, theatrical performances and gladiatorial combats). In time, separate forums developed, such as the *forum civile* for legal and administrative affairs, and the *mercantile fora venalias* (the marketplace).

Gladiator

For an example of the physical public sphere, see Ridley Scott's film *Gladiator* (2000). Here the gladiator Maximus (Russell Crowe) uses the arena as part of the public sphere to introduce new ideas and issues that challenge the authority of Roman emperor Commodus (Joaquin Phoenix).

The forum is the ancient history equivalent of the town hall where people similarly gather together to discuss and negotiate ideas and issues of common concern. The forum is also the archetype of many of the institutions around us today, including parliament, the courts and even shopping centres. All of these structures developed around the notion of *spectacle*. They conflated the public and the private in the way they brought private matters—such as local interests, and the prosecution of crime and consumption—into the public sphere. And of course this emphasis on spectacle also means that the forum is the archetype of the modern-day stage, as well as mass media forms such as film, television and social networking sites. For more on this see Foucault (1977).

The public sphere as a conceptual tool

Jurgen Habermas was the theorist responsible for introducing the public sphere as a concept in his book *The Structural Transformation of the Public Sphere* (1989). Here the public sphere became a way of theorising about the relationship between media (and communication practices more generally), politics and society.

However, Habermas continues to link the public sphere to a physical space—the coffee house and salon culture of the seventeenth, eighteenth and nineteenth centuries where educated people gathered together to exchange and debate ideas. (In some ways we are seeing a re-emergence of this culture in commercial coffee chains—though the quality of debate would often be less than Habermas would like.)

Habermas saw this (idealised) physical space as providing an opportunity for people to openly and equally discuss their views—particularly in relation to politics. Habermas also linked the public sphere to the new developments in printing at the time, particularly the mediation of issues in newspapers, pamphlets and political journals. So, once again, media are heavily implicated in politics and, most importantly for Habermas, the maintenance of democracy.

In the relationship between the public sphere and democracy, Habermas links the public sphere to a much larger concept—modernity—which is defined in greater detail in Chapter 20. Modernity embodies all of these ideas of democracy, including equality and freedom, and recognises the importance of the individual in contributing to the functioning of society.

In conceptualising the public sphere, Habermas is really moving the public sphere away from a physical space and towards an ideal. This means the public sphere is becoming a **virtual space** and, more particularly, a tool to measure the health of public discussion and democracy in society. The public sphere therefore becomes a way of assessing the mediasphere's role in enabling public dialogue, political participation and, ultimately, sustaining democracy.

Virtual space: An alternative space to generally accepted reality, experienced by people interacting with other people and their environment via media forms like computers and not through face-to-face contact.

Importantly, for Habermas the public sphere is not just a public space and a virtual space—it is also a *political* space. The aim of this Habermasian public sphere is to promote political debate and thus enable democracy. As such, Habermas thought the public sphere should only involve 'rational debate' and engage with 'serious issues', thereby excluding entertainment, emotion and 'soft' news. As such, the Habermasian public sphere is presented as an ideal for how society *should* operate.

Rational media

Media that could potentially fit Habermas's definition of rational media are those promoting political debate, including broadsheet newspapers, political pamphlets, hard news reports, political websites and public television broadcasters—with some concessions. For example, PBS's *Sesame Street* would fail in that it aims to entertain as much as educate and focuses on emotional as much as logical responses, hence the presence of the Muppet characters. This seems a shame. Why should Elmo be excluded from the public sphere?

Ultimately, Habermas wanted to encourage people to work harder to achieve this level of rational discussion. He didn't want the public sphere to be something easily accessible; rather, participation in the sphere was an achievement, a reward for improving yourself. This may seem elitist, but it still carries a certain resonance for lots of people in Western democracies. In some ways it also echoes a lot of the arguments academics make about the value of education.

The public sphere as a virtual space

For Habermas, the public sphere operates as a virtual space because it is an ideal, a concept that can be applied to our present society as easily as eighteenth-century coffee culture or the ancient Roman forum.

In Habermas's recognition of the importance of media in articulating ideas and mediating issues, the public sphere also becomes a virtual space: 'Today, newspapers and periodicals, radio and television are the media of the public sphere' (Habermas 1997: 105).

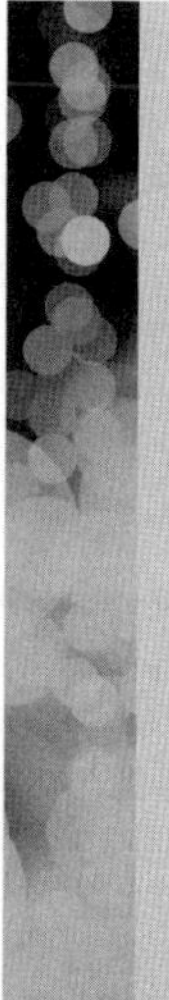

Why is the Habermasian public sphere an ideal?

We can describe Habermas's concept of the public sphere as idealised for a number of reasons.

First, his view of salon culture and media in the seventeenth, eighteenth and nineteenth centuries never actually existed as he described it (see Dahlgren 2002 for more about this). While Habermas believed this public space was universally accessible, in reality it excluded people based on class, ethnicity, geography and gender; only wealthy, white, educated men actually participated in these debates. Habermas has since acknowledged this fault (Habermas 1992).

Furthermore, the media in existence at the time were far more diverse and commercial than Habermas describes.

Finally, Habermas has been criticised for speaking of a singular, unitary public sphere rather than multiple public spheres—a criticism taken up and developed by postmodern theorists (see below). Essentially, it means that Habermas's ideal still excludes a variety of people based on geography, sexuality, race and gender (not just the Muppets).

As the mediasphere is a virtual space, composed of the dialogic relationship between media, the increasing centrality of the mediasphere in the public sphere moves the public sphere further and further away from a physical space towards a purely virtual one.

This is confirmed by the continuing technological developments in media, most notably the internet. Blogging, independent online news sites and personal web pages all confirm the democratising potential of the media (see Chapter 18 for more on these developments). In the US Democratic Party's pre-selection process in 2007, candidates were asked questions directly by voters operating through YouTube.

Increasingly, then, these public spaces are virtual spaces, allowing for the instantaneous dissemination and debate of ideas, and capable of gathering together vast communities of people irrespective of geographical location.

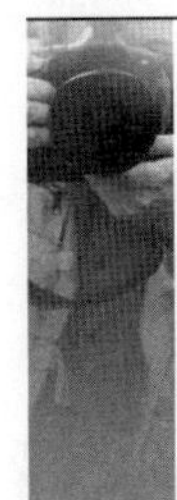

The Social Network

For an example of the virtual public sphere see David Fincher's *The Social Network* (2010). The film uses the story of the founding of the social networking site Facebook (and subsequent lawsuits) as a metaphor for exploring how media have become our primary mechanisms of communication—leaving us virtually unable to communicate without them.

The public sphere as postmodern space

Partly as a response to Habermas—and partly because of the changing nature of the mediasphere—another way of thinking about the public sphere has emerged: the public sphere as a **postmodern** space.

Postmodern: A way of thinking that encourages the consideration of multiple points of view. Postmodern thinking considers that there is no single true representation of any aspect of the world: rather, there are multiple ways of making sense of the world and therefore multiple competing truths.

With advances in technology, population growth and the move towards globalisation, the mediasphere and the public sphere have become almost indistinguishable. More importantly, the contemporary mediasphere is quite clearly not the ideal political space Habermas envisaged.

Of course, this is not to say that the mediasphere does not feature political discussion. As previously noted, politicians, be they members of government or minor parties, or political activists, have long recognised the importance of airing their views through the media. But vast segments of the mediasphere are also governed by commercial imperatives and devoted to entertainment (rather than information). Additionally, an increasing number of media forms (quite apart from news) have brought private issues into the public sphere, including social networking sites (such as Facebook), talk shows (such as *Oprah*), reality shows (such as *Big Brother*), do-it-yourself shows (such as *Changing Rooms*) and talkback or drive-time radio (such as *Hamish and Andy*). In this way the mediasphere has legitimated private issues as being worthy of public discussion.

Popular media

Postmodern theorists tend to be more interested in the value of **popular media** (Hartley 1996: 5–7), such as **tabloid** newspapers, soft news, commercial television, commercial radio, computer games and comic books.

Popular media: Media consumed by the majority of the population; for example, tabloid newspapers, soft news, commercial television and radio, computer games and comic books.

Tabloid: In a literal sense, a type of newspaper that is smaller and easier to read than a broadsheet paper. Generally, it refers to news that focuses on the sensational, and is recognised by an informal vernacular delivery, featuring such subjects as crime, sex, scandal and sport. Today, hard news stories, even in serious news organisations, are often delivered in a tabloid style.

Postmodern scholars argue for recognition of these changes in the public sphere. They claim that popular media actually give voice to the minority groups excluded in both the physical and Habermasian spaces of the public sphere. Essentially, then, postmodern theorists are also arguing for the public sphere as a way of democratising social life. They just think democracy can be achieved in different ways.

First, postmodern theorists see *all* genres of media as being capable of contributing to this exchange of ideas, not just the 'rational discussion' and limited range of factual media Habermas describes. They argue for popular media to be taken seriously—politically, culturally and socially.

Second, postmodern theorists' recognition of many equally valid ways of understanding the world—based on gender, religion or age, for example—means that a postmodern public sphere often celebrates fragmentation. As opposed to Habermas's idea of a homogenous, unified whole, the postmodern public sphere can in fact be a set of multiple, smaller, **public sphericules**, incorporating and overlapping others. We could refer to a queer public sphericule, an Islamic public sphericule, a youth public sphericule and so on, with information and entertainment passing between them and, sometimes, entering into larger mainstream public sphericules. A Facebook page would be a great example of a public sphericule.

Public sphericules: Multiple smaller public spheres—based on particular cultures and subcultures relating to age, sexuality, gender or race—that interconnect with each other.

Digital divide: The gap between those who can access media technology (thanks to wealth, culture and geographical location) and those who cannot.

Fundamentally, then, postmodern theorists view the plurality of the mediasphere as actually assisting democracy. The more diverse media are, the more capable they are of giving voice to all segments of the population. They offer not only information and ideas, but also different perspectives. McKee (2003) maps this approach by reclaiming critiques of the mediasphere to describe how feminine ('trivial'), working class ('commercial'), black ('spectacular'), gay ('fragmented') and youth ('apathetic') issues and ideas are all articulated and debated by popular media.

A question of access?

One of the major differences between these ideas of the public sphere is in relation to access. The pre-modern public sphere excluded women, slaves and foreigners from participating. Furthermore, because it was a physical space, there were physical limitations on how many people could participate. Habermas's ideal public sphere does not have physical limits, but sets other limits to access, excluding anything that does not constitute rational debate, for example. The postmodern public sphere appears completely accessible as it encourages—and celebrates—difference. But with the mediasphere becoming a more important part of the public sphere, even access to the postmodern public sphere can be limited by technology, censorship and ownership.

This is often referred to as the **digital divide**: the gap between those who can access media technology (thanks to wealth, culture and geographical location) and those who cannot. It is the gap between the information rich and the information poor, because without technological access to the mediasphere, these people are effectively being excluded from participating in the larger public sphere.

Why is all of this important for people engaging with media and journalism?

Broadcast: The transmission of knowledge (ideas and information) in the widest possible circles. It can operate as a verb: to broadcast; a noun: a television broadcast; and as an adjective: a broadcast program.

Understanding this relationship between different media forms—and between the mediasphere and the public sphere—is important for three reasons.

First, it reminds us of the centrality of media in contemporary culture. Media provide us with a common knowledge. They show us what is going on in the larger societal groupings to which we belong and, increasingly, they are one of the few ways we can engage with others on a local, national and international scale. They are the primary mechanisms through which issues and ideas are expressed and debated. They are, therefore, vitally important to sustaining our society, our very way of life, because they provide us with the resources for active citizenship.

Broadcasting

This centrality of media in modern societies may still seem surprising to some of you, but, as Jostein Gripsrud (1997) notes, it is a notion embodied in the term 'broadcasting' itself. Originally, **broadcasting** was an agricultural term referring to the practice of sowing seeds by hand in the widest possible circles. Taking this as a metaphor, we can understand broadcasting to mean that 'there are centralized central resources (the bucket of seeds), which, given the widest possible distribution, may yield a rich harvest' (Gripsrud 1999: 37). Broadcasting is really the communication of knowledge (ideas and information) in 'the widest possible circles'. We return to this idea in Chapter 10.

Second, understanding this relationship between different media forms assists us to understand the interplay of ideas between news and the rest of the mediasphere. Indeed, understanding how journalism and media fit together in this dialogic exchange of ideas is one of the rationales for this book.

Why is news particularly important to the public sphere?

As we defined it in the introduction, news is literally new information. Therefore, it is the entry point for the public sphere; the place where new ideas, new information and new issues most often move from the private to the public. From hard news (exposés, investigative journalism, court reporting and political reporting) through to soft news (celebrity news, fashion news, and leisure and lifestyle news) a similar pattern applies: when something becomes news it is moving from the private to the public; it is becoming part of the public sphere.

Of course, news often works with the public relations and celebrity industries to achieve this; they similarly make the private public or generate more public awareness around a certain organisation or individual.

More particularly, journalism also has the potential to act as a watchdog for the public sphere (see Chapter 3).

Third, understanding this relationship provides us with a framework for understanding how issues and ideas are articulated through the mediasphere.

In studying television, John Ellis (1999) refers to the concept of 'working through', which is a psychoanalytic term Ellis defines as 'a process whereby material is not so much processed into a finished product as continually worried over until it is exhausted' (Ellis 1999: 55). In relating this to television, Ellis suggests that television 'can be seen as a vast mechanism for processing the raw data of news reality into more narrativized, explained forms' (Ellis 1999: 55).

> Television works through the material from the news … It uses words, providing forms of explanation and understanding, further information and the kinds of psychological

> perspectives that are impossible within the news format … providing increasing stability to the images of disorder: it reframes and refocuses; it narrativizes and adds production values. (Ellis 1999: 56)

In the context of television, Ellis pursues this articulation of issues and ideas from news through to chat shows (offering psychological frameworks of understanding), to soap operas, documentaries and current affairs (offering narrative frameworks of understanding) and on into drama series, sitcoms and television films.

Agenda setting: The way the media determine what will be communicated as news to influence what audiences think about and discuss.

We can similarly apply this idea of working through to the larger mediasphere. Newspapers, news periodicals, radio, online and television news **set the agenda**, 'breaking' the story. The issues and ideas coming out of the story are then taken up by other media genres, personalised in current affairs series, documentaries and periodicals, and narrativised in television series, films, music and comics. Some narrative forms explicate this: the television franchise *Law & Order* often advertises its stories as being 'ripped from the headlines'. Other narrative media forms, such as hip-hop music, provide a voice to a group underrepresented or negatively represented by the media, often speaking back against mainstream media (and therefore offering a site of resistance). Blogs, text messaging and social networking sites then permit audiences to post, discuss and share their ideas on these stories. The mediasphere, therefore, provides a range of alternative perspectives, adding to the conversation and generating new ideas and new issues, all as part of this process of moving towards consensus or compromise.

In this way we can understand the mediasphere as a more accessible interface between the purely political rational debate demanded by Habermas and the more pluralistic and personal perspectives of the postmodern theorists. It becomes, in effect, a 'forum for interpretations' (Ellis 1999, p. 69) and contributes to the larger public sphere in this way.

The mediasphere provides us with a way of working though ideas and issues. It does not and cannot offer definitive conclusions, but rather is part of this larger process of working towards consensus or compromise.

Conclusion

All media forms are structured like dialogue. They talk back and forth to each other and to their audiences. This creates a mediasphere of media forms in constant conversation with each other. Dominant groups are always seeking to control media, to hegemonically convince audiences to accept their view of the world. But the plurality of media also offers the possibility of resistance. This constant articulation, debate and negotiation of issues and ideas makes the mediasphere an increasingly important part of the larger public sphere. Understanding this relationship enables us to appreciate the role each media form has in this interplay of ideas and the way ideas are continually articulated through the mediasphere.

KEY REFERENCES

Habermas, J. (1989). *The Structural Transformation of the Public Sphere: An Inquiry into a Category of Bourgeois Society*. Trans. T. Burger with F. Lawrence. Cambridge, MA: MIT Press.

Johnson, S. (2005). *Everything Bad Is Good For You: How Popular Culture Is Making Us Smarter*. London: Allen Lane.

JASON BAINBRIDGE

CHAPTER 2

THE FIRST MASS MEDIUM

NICOLA GOC

Introduction

News was first shared around campfires as hunters roasted mammoth flesh and exchanged stories of their latest hunting triumphs and failures. These first oral news stories were surpassed daily when new hunting feats became the next point of discussion. Some of these hunting tales were given permanence through illustrations on the walls of caves, which could be regarded as the world's first news images. We could think of both of these spaces, the campfire and the cave, as being the earliest forms of the public sphere; news was therefore a part of the public sphere from the very beginning. Indeed, as we have seen in the previous chapter, the public sphere could not function without it.

Centuries later, the exchange of news stories took place in the agora of ancient Greece and in the forums of Rome. Later still, in medieval Europe, wandering minstrels roamed from town to town ringing their bells and broadcasting written proclamations. By the sixteenth century, coffee houses were the arenas for the communication of news and for debate on public affairs. Then, a German goldsmith, Johannes Gutenberg, invented a printing press that revolutionised printing, and the process of communication was changed forever.

In this chapter we look at the following:

- the history of the first mass medium
- the impact of Gutenberg's printing press on the creation of news
- the advancement of journalism through the ages
- the challenges the newspaper industry faces in the twenty-first century in the internet age.

Note that the term 'news'—and the associated terms 'hard news' and 'soft news'—are defined at length in the introduction to this book.

The first printed news

Julius Caesar introduced one of the first forms of written news with the *Acta Diurna* (*Daily Events*) in about 59 BC. This laboriously handwritten news sheet told stories of government scandals, military campaigns, trials, executions, battles and conflagrations. The *Acta Diurna* was produced at great expense and sent to the governors of provinces and to private subscribers, while in Rome it was posted in the Forum for all who could read, creating a focus for political and social discourse.

Gutenberg's printing press

From the eighth century in China, newspapers appeared in Beijing as handwritten news sheets, informing merchants and powerful citizens of events. However, the news sheet in this form did not enter Europe until the middle of the fifteenth century, when German goldsmith, Johannes Gutenberg (c. 1398–1468), invented a printing press with replaceable and moveable letters. Gutenberg's invention revolutionised printing in Europe.

Although movable type had been known in East Asia since the eleventh century, it is unlikely that this system was established outside of Asia. A printing trade already existed in Europe before Gutenberg's time, but the woodblock technology was a complex and laborious process. Individual sheets of paper were placed on an inked woodblock and a single impression was taken by rubbing the sheet—a very time-consuming method. Gutenberg's invention was a considerable leap in speed and efficiency, and transformed the printing industry. He had been inspired by the technology used in the screw-type wine presses of the Rhine Valley. His screw press, which he designed to achieve an even transfer of the image to paper or parchment, worked by first rolling ink over the raised surfaces of moveable handset block letters held within a wooden form, and then pressing the form against a sheet of paper. The hand casting instrument—the most significant element of the invention—enabled the printer to quickly cast the required number of a diverse range of characters. The metal used for casting was an alloy of lead, tin and further admixtures, which allowed for rapid cooling and sufficient durability under the high mechanical stresses of the press.

Gutenberg's printing method remained the standard until the twentieth century.

While Gutenberg's press created a revolution in the production of books and pamphlets in the fifteenth century, it did not directly lead to the birth of the newspaper as we know it. Most news sheets were still handwritten in small numbers by official scribes, providing the wealthy merchants and the elite with information about shipping, trade, commerce and politics. Occasionally, when there were important events such as political unrest, war, natural disasters or royal visits, town criers (the first news readers) read out these news sheets in public places. Gutenberg's press did not only fostered rapid development in the sciences, arts and religion, but it also created an environment in which the newly literate populace started to demand information about the noteworthy events happening in their community. However, the high cost of printing, combined with the fact that the majority of people in Europe were still illiterate (with the exception of monks and merchants), delayed the development of cheap, mass-produced newspapers.

Predecessors of the newspaper

In Germany in the late 1400s, news pamphlets or broadsides were printed for the entertainment of the wealthy, educated elite, and contained the first content we would recognise today as news. Each pamphlet or **broadside** published a highly sensationalised story about a natural disaster, a shocking crime, a scandal or a remarkable adventure. Some of the most famous of these pamphlets report the atrocities against Germans in Transylvania perpetuated by a sadistic *veovod*, named Vlad Tepes Dracul, who became the Count Dracula of later folklore.

Broadside: A precursor to the newspaper, cheap single pages of entertaining news, usually crime or sensationalised accounts of disasters. By the 1860s, cheap newspapers had largely taken their place.

Dracula and the evolution of media

Dracula remains a central figure in the development of media. Every generation has reinterpreted the tale of Bram Stoker's vampire, from numerous theatrical productions through to the silent film *Nosferatu* and the youthful *Dracula* of the 2007 BBC television production. There have been American Draculas (Bela Lugosi, Jack Palance), English Draculas (Christopher Lee, Gary Oldman) and even blaxploitation Draculas (the infamous *Blacula* from the 1970s.) The Count has appeared in virtually every media form, from comic books through to Count Chocula's cereal, and shows no signs of diminishing in appeal; he remains the single most represented fictional character in media. A history of Dracula is a history of media, so it seems appropriate that Tsepes's tale, which served as one of the inspirations for Dracula's creator Bram Stoker, should be part of the first mass medium.

Names for early forms of printed news included pamphlet, broadside, broadsheet, newsletter, newsbook, *coranto* and *gazette*.

Corantos

In the English-speaking world, the earliest predecessors of the newspaper were **corantos**, small news pamphlets that were produced only when a newsworthy event occurred. The first English printing press was established in 1477, and London soon became one of the most important centres for printers in Europe. News pamphlets, unlike the newspapers to come, were printed irregularly in London and provided reports of single events. One of these news pamphlets, *The Trew Encountre*, published in England in September 1513 by Richard Fawkes, told the story of the Battle of Flodden Field. By the reign of James I, printers were publishing stories of war, calamity, political intrigue and religious strife in profitable weekly *corantos*.

Coranto: The earliest predecessor of the newspaper, a *coranto* was a small news pamphlet that was only produced when a newsworthy event occurred. From the Spanish *coranto* (runner), that is, fast-delivered news.

News as a commodity

It was in Venice that the commercial value of news as information was first recognised. In the Venetian Republic in the mid-sixteenth century, merchants set a precedent by charging an admission fee of one *gazetta* (a small coin) to public readings of the latest news sheets. Venice was a centre of trade and information, and merchants needed to know the location of vessels and the value of the expensive cargoes they carried. Duplicates of these dispatches were also sold to merchants. In 1556 the Venetian Government ordered the collection of information and the weekly dispatch of news in a **gazette**. The term 'gazette' has since been a popular name for commercial newspapers.

Gazette: One of the earliest forms of a newspaper, including official government information. Named after a *gazetta*, a small coin in the Republic of Venice that was the price of their early news sheets, the name was later applied to many types of newspaper.

Periodical: a magazine or journal published at regular intervals, such as weekly, monthly or quarterly.

In the first half of the seventeenth century, regular newspapers began to emerge to supplement the occasional news sheets and pamphlets. By the early 1600s, the first true news **periodicals** emerged when printers realised that their news pamphlets could be profitable if they were published regularly.

The first newspaper

German Johann Carolus is credited with publishing the first newspaper, the *Relation*, in 1605. The *Relation* was officially titled, *Relation aller Fürnemmen und gedenckwürdigen Historien*, which translates as The *collection of all distinguished and memorable news.* There is argument among scholars, however, as to what constitutes the first newspaper, with some (see Morison 1980) arguing that *Relation* was a newsbook rather than a newspaper because its layout resembled a book: it was printed in quarto size with the text spread across the page in a single column width. Morison argues that the world's first newspaper was the *Dutch Courante uyt Italien, Duytslandt, &c*, which was first published in 1618. Other scholars (see Chappell 1999; Smith 1979) do not make a distinction between the newsbook, the pamphlet or the newspaper.

The *Relation* was soon followed by other newspapers, including the *Nieuwe Tijdingen* in Belgium in 1616, the *Weekly Newes* in England in 1622 and the *Gazette* in France in 1631. By the 1620s printers in Amsterdam were exporting weekly newspapers, published in French and English, to England and other European countries.

Spread of vernacular languages

The advent of Gutenberg's printing system, and the creation of an environment that promoted the spread of knowledge and eventually led to an increase in working class literacy, meant that printing was no longer restricted to the very wealthy. The reduced prices of printed materials made them more accessible to the masses, leading to a freer exchange of knowledge and ideas. Gutenberg's system popularised vernacular languages, such as English, French, Italian and German, saw them replace Latin texts, and saw a larger audience gain access to Luther's German translation of the Bible, accelerating the spread of the Protestant Reformation.

It seems appropriate to think of journalism as a vernacular theory of media (see the Introduction) because its evolution popularised vernacular languages.

Early English newspapers

The first English printer, William Caxton, set up a printing press in England in the early 1470s. In 1474, his translation and printing of *The Recuyell of the Historyes of Troye* was the first book printed in English. Caxton printed nearly 100 publications, about twenty of which he also translated from French and Dutch. The most famous books from his press include *The Canterbury Tales* and *Troilus and Criseyde* by English poet Geoffrey Chaucer. While Caxton did not publish news, he did bring the technology to England that would eventually lead others to establish news publications.

Many scholars regard the *London Gazette*, first published in 1665, as the first English newspaper, because it contained mainly news, and it was produced regularly. The *London Gazette*, which was the only officially sanctioned newspaper (government gazette) of the time, consisted mainly of news items from Europe, and occasionally from America or Asia, but it rarely covered domestic issues. At this time the press was subject to strict censorship as the British government had quickly recognised the power of newspapers to inform the populace, create public discourse and set public agendas. They saw his spread of information as a threat to their power, and sought to limit printing presses to the London district. Laws were passed to license printers and restrict the publication of material critical of governments and royalty. The publisher of the *London Gazette* omitted any domestic news to avoid landing himself in prison, instead reporting on the military blunders and royal scandals of other nations. The first regular daily newspaper, the *Daily Courant*, was not published until 1702.

English Civil War

The outbreak of civil war between the British king and parliament in 1642 transformed the dissemination of news by creating an unprecedented demand for domestic news in Britain: people wanted to be informed of the current state of national affairs. At the same time, those involved in the political struggle realised the power of the press to promote their own political cause, and the press became a powerful propaganda tool. In the breakdown of authority, censorship controls lapsed and partisan newsbooks such as the *Daily Intelligencer* widely reported domestic news for the first time. These political publications, vociferous in support of a particular political perspective, were filled with sensational narratives of heroic battles atrocities committed by the enemy. They had a ready audience in their loyal supporters; circulations rose dramatically, leading to larger and more frequent print runs. One Royalist report in 1645 read in part: 'The Cathedral at Lincolne hath lately been prophaned by Cromwell's barbarous crew … who have filled … that holy place with their own and horses dung' (Patterson n.d.).

At the end of the British Civil War, Oliver Cromwell tried to curtail the unchecked dissemination of political news. On the eve of the execution of Charles I, Cromwell attempted

Broadsheet: Historically, a cheap single page of entertaining news, usually crime or sensationalised accounts of disasters; a precursor to the newspaper. By the 1860s, cheap newspapers had largely taken their place. Today broadsheet refers to a large format newspaper (in Australia, generally 841mm × 594mm). In some countries, including Australia, broadsheet newspapers are commonly perceived to contain more quality or indepth journalistic reporting than their tabloid counterparts.

to suppress all news sheets, but he was unsuccessful and the newspaper headlines announced in dramatic prose the beheading of the king. When the monarchy was eventually restored, press control was reintroduced and government censorship saw a dramatic reduction in the amount of political news being reported. This did not, however, see a decline in newspapers, as the public taste for printed news had been whetted and newspapers were firmly established as a profitable enterprise.

By the 1670s, murders and executions were popular news topics. In late 1677, for example, one English **broadsheet** published a series of murder stories under the title: 'A True Relation of All the Bloody Murders that Have Been Committed in and about the Citie and Suburbs of London, Since the 4th of this Instant June 1677'. Witches were also big news. In 1767, an eight-page news pamphlet was titled 'A Brief Narrative of A Strange and Wonderful Old Woman that Hath a Pair of Horns Growing Upon Her Head'. These sensational broadsides often began 'A True Narrative Of …' ascribing the notion of truthfulness to sensational narratives.

Early terms for journalists: running patterers, hacks, penny-a-liners and muckrakers.

The birth of the journalist

Journalist: A person who practises journalism; someone who gathers and disseminates new information about current events, trends, issues and people to a wide audience; from the French *journal*, which comes from the Latin *diurnal* (daily).

Newspapers now employed reporters as news gatherers to find news and report on events that would attract readers' attention and boost circulation. The word **journalist** came into use as early as 1693 to describe those who wrote of the daily goings-on for the public press. Daniel Defoe, considered the world's first journalist, first published in the *Review* in 1704.

The early broadsheet journalists in Britain were called running patterers, with 'patter' meaning the fast, well-prepared talk of someone such as a comedian or salesperson. These running patterers would run from the courthouse or gallows to the newspaper offices to write up their lurid gallows literature, which often contained true confessions from the hapless criminal about to swing—all conveniently rhyming and written in ballad style. Mayhew described one of these running patterers as a 'seedy, half-starved looking middle-aged man' who came in to the office 'with a bundle of manuscripts in his hand. He had on a shocking bad hat, and a red nose, and smelt of liquor abominably' (Mayhew 1861: 226).

The early broadsheet reporters were also known as hacks (a term that is still used today as a derogatory descriptor for some tabloid journalists) because they often culled their information from reputable daily newspapers, such as the *Times*, and from these reports they created lively stories to entertain their working-class audiences.

Freelance reporters writing for both broadsheets and the respectable press were also known as penny-a-liners, because they received a penny a line for their reports, which gave them the incentive to create florid, verbose stories. These freelancers made up the casual labour force of journalism until the middle of the nineteenth century.

US President Theodore Roosevelt coined the term **muckraker** in 1906 in reference to investigative journalists who challenged his government. While the press of the early twentieth century seized the name as a badge of honour, today it is used more as a derogatory term for tabloid journalists who write sensationalised stories.

Muckracker: A term coined by President Theodore Roosevelt to refer to investigative journalists who challenged his government. The term came from John Bunyan's *The Pilgrim's Progress* (1678), where it was used to describe men who look nowhere but down.

John Wilkes

The courageous actions of one Englishman, the radical journalist, newspaper proprietor, parliamentarian and notorious libertine John Wilkes (1725–98), forever cemented the notion of a free press. It's of interest to us today that another Wilkes-like character, the twenty-first century maverick journalist Julian Assange, has come along to show us that crusading journalism can still enliven the Fourth Estate. Assange, in publishing secret diplomatic cables and government documents, is following in the fine tradition of Wilkes.

In 1771 Wilkes, with the support of several London printers, challenged the law that prohibited the reporting of parliamentary debates and speeches. Until this time, parliamentary proceedings were kept secret because those in power argued that such information was too sensitive to be communicated to its citizens. It was argued that disorder, disturbance and even uprising could result from the publication of parliamentary debates and speeches. Through his actions in challenging the right to publish information, Wilkes (like Assange) brought upon himself the wrath of the powerful elite and (also like Assange) found himself hounded into prison on charges intended to destroy him.

Wilkes established the *North Briton* newspaper in 1762 while a member of parliament, and used his newspaper to criticise the King George III, as well as the prime minister, the Earl of Bute, who was supported by the king and who Wilkes considered to be incompetent. On 3 April 1763, after he published an article critical of the government and the monarch, Wilkes was charged with seditious libel and imprisoned in the Tower of London. However, with the support of influential friends and the defence that as a member of parliament he was immune from prosecution, he was found not guilty and left the court as a champion of liberty.

Wilkes continued to be a thorn in the side of the government and the Crown, publishing articles attacking the king and the government. At one point, a government supporter challenged Wilkes to a duel in a plot to silence the radical newspaper proprietor. There were rumours that the challenger had been practising his shooting skills for months before the challenge. Wilkes was shot in the stomach, but his life was saved by the attentions of a doctor secured by his friends. Soon after the duel, parliament passed a bill to remove a member's privilege from arrest for writing and publishing seditious libels. Still seriously ill from the shooting, Wilkes was spirited away to France by friends before he could be arrested.

During his absence he was expelled from parliament. When he eventually returned to Britain in 1768, he stood as Radical candidate for Middlesex, but immediately after being elected he was arrested and sent to King's Bench Prison. Such was the outrage of his London supporters that large crowds assembled outside the prison to protest his incarceration. By 10 May 1768, the crowd had swelled to more than 15,000. As they chanted slogans demanding Wilkes's liberty, troops opened fire; seven of the protestors were killed. The outcry at what became known as the St George's Field's Massacre saw Wilkes's popularity spread throughout the city and in 1769 he was elected as an alderman of the City of London.

Not long after his election, he was found guilty of libel, expelled from the House of Commons and sentenced to almost two years in jail. Undaunted, Wilkes stood three more times for the seat of Middlesex and was elected on each occasion, only to have the result overturned by parliament. When he was finally released from jail in April 1770, he was still banned from the House of Commons, but continued to be influential in local government affairs and active in the campaign for press freedom.

He now used journalism to challenge the government, reporting parliamentary debates verbatim in the *North Briton*, arguing that parliamentarians were not representatives of the people if the people were ignorant of what went on in parliament. The government was outraged, claiming his actions, and those of several other printers, were a breach of parliamentary privilege. When a messenger was sent by parliament to arrest two of the printers, Wilkes, as a city alderman, had the messenger arrested for violating the privileges of the City of London.

A large crowd surrounded the House of Commons, chanting slogans in support of Wilkes and the printers; the government, aware of the backlash from the St George's Field's Massacre, ordered the release of the two men and abandoned attempts to prevent the publication of reports of its debates. While parliament maintained that the publication of debates was a breach of parliamentary privilege, it made no attempt to enforce its order. Wilkes had won the day and from that moment the freedom of the press was born.

In 1774, Wilkes was elected lord mayor of London and he was also elected to represent Middlesex in the House of Commons. He died on 29 December 1797.

Shorthand

Shorthand: A system of rapid handwriting made possible by using abbreviations of words.

Court and parliamentary reporters were the first newspaper journalists, as we understand the term today. **Shorthand** is a system of rapid handwriting made possible by using abbreviations of words. Scribes in ancient Greece, Egypt, Sumeria and Rome used shorthand systems to record the important proclamations of rulers and religious leaders. Many different systems of shorthand developed during the Renaissance. In 1588, Dr Timothie Bright's *An Arte of Shorte, Swifte, and Secrete Writing by Character* was published in London, and John Willis published the first known alphabet of shorthand in London in 1602. Samuel Pepys used the Shelton system to record his account of the Great Fire of London—perhaps the first journalistic use of shorthand. In 1707, Thomas Gurney developed a system of shorthand that was later taken up by Charles Dickens during his career as a parliamentary and court reporter.

The introduction of shorthand reporters had a dramatic impact on court and parliamentary reportage. The journalist who had the ability to write shorthand became 'the principal broker for the substantial discourse of society' (Smith 1979: 163). The format of parliamentary reports and court reports was transformed from brief summaries to lengthy verbatim testimonials. Shorthand's impact on the manufacture of news was akin to the introduction of live broadcasts almost two centuries later, in that it provided the individual reader with a sense of personal engagement with the court or parliamentary process, while at the same time maintaining their place within the mass audience experience. The fact that these reports were rarely verbatim, or full transcripts, and were in fact still highly mediated texts, was a moot point. The perception was that this expanded version of parliamentary and court proceedings, in conjunction with the perception of neutrality it brought to the journalist's role, conferred a greater authority to these news texts.

The *Times* and the rise of the British press

In 1785, the *Times* (the 'newspaper of record') was first published in London by John Walter I under the title the *Daily Universal Register*. Walter, who in 1788 changed the name to the *Times*, published commercial news and government notices with a smattering of crime and scandal. By the 1830s, the *Times* had developed into a widely respected national journal and daily historical record. In 1852, John Delane told his readers in a stirring leading article that newspapers had a specific and unique responsibility for the shaping of ideas and the forming of public policies. Late in the nineteenth century, the *Times*'s reputation and circulation declined; however, under the ownership of Alfred Harmsworth, Viscount Northcliffe, who purchased the newspaper in 1908, the *Times* was restored to a position of influence and financial security (see below for more about Northcliffe).

The imposition of a stamp duty

Between 1801 and 1851, the population of England and Wales grew from nine million to eighteen million, due mainly to a decline in infant mortality. At the same time, the number of literate citizens began to increase significantly. Aware of the political power of the newly literate masses, and of the dangers of allowing the working class to create a public discourse through newspapers, in 1819 the government imposed a stamp duty on newspapers. The *Newspaper Stamp Duties Act* created a tax on 'small publications which issue from the press in great numbers at a low price'. This tax kept the price of newspapers out of the reach of most of the literate working class, who resorted to reading their news in libraries at a cost of a penny an hour. The tax remained in place for almost forty years, until it was finally abolished in 1855, enabling cheap newspapers to flourish.

Rise of the penny press

By the 1850s, working-class literacy was between 65 per cent and 75 per cent, providing a ready audience for the popular press. There were three significant technical developments in the printing industry in the early 1800s that, when combined with the abolition of the stamp duty in 1855 and the rise in working-class literacy, advanced the rise of the newspaper industry. These developments were the introduction of:

- continuous rolls of paper
- the steam-powered press
- iron to replace the wooden press.

Penny press: Cheap nineteenth-century newspapers that cost a penny and were marketed to the newly literate working class, leading to a dramatic increase in newspaper circulation.

Tabloid in size, the **penny press** presented news on crime, calamity, scandal and sport for the literate working class. The growth of railway networks also had a dramatic impact on the distribution of newspapers across the world. In London, newspapers could now reach regional areas on the day of printing, leading to the development of London-based national tabloids. By 1855, two London newspapers, *Lloyd's Weekly News* and *News of the World*, each had achieved circulation figures of more than 100,000 copies a week. Their success, according to Francis Williams, rested on a formula 'as old as that of the first broadsheets and as up to date as that of next Sunday's *People* or *Sunday Pictorial*: crime (especially when violent), sex (suitably shrouded) and sport' (Williams 1957: 103).

Nineteenth-century advances in the newspaper industry

- American Richard Hoe's invention of the rotary printing press in 1843 made printing much faster than it was with the old flat-bed printing press.
- The invention of the telegraph in 1844 transformed the content of newspapers, because information could be transferred within a matter of minutes, allowing for more timely, relevant reporting. The telegraph also saw the birth of the inverted pyramid news format.
- The growth of railway networks led to the development of national tabloids based in capital cities.
- The invention of the system of offering newspapers to newsagents on sale or return in the middle of the nineteenth century led to an enormous uptake of newspapers by local shops and newsagents.

The telegraph and the advent of the inverted pyramid

Inverted pyramid: The style of writing news that places the most important information at the beginning of the story, followed by less important information, and so on to the end of the story; this enables the story to be cut from the bottom in order to fit the available space.

It was the technology of the telegraph that produced the wire services and the distinctive who, what, where, when, why and how format of printed news. This style of news writing, known as the **inverted pyramid**, placed important facts at the top of the story to ensure that as much information as possible was transmitted in case a wire broke and the connection was lost. The inverted pyramid style of writing remained the dominant news writing style for more than 100 years. However, in recent times, with the advent of the internet, new media and the proliferation of soft news, the inverted pyramid has been challenged as the dominant news writing style (see Chapter 14).

The tabloid

Alfred Harmsworth, Lord Northcliffe, is credited with inventing the tabloid newspaper in the early 1900s. Scandal, crime and sport were already popular topics in newspapers in the first half of the nineteenth century, and long before Northcliffe entered the scene

Lloyd's Weekly News had exploited the crime formula so successfully that it became the first newspaper in the world to reach sales of a million. Fox Bourne (1887: 370–1) lamented the fact that many newspapers gave people what they wanted: sport and 'loathsome court cases'.

Northcliffe made reading newspapers appealing to a mass readership by redesigning the layout of the newspapers, introducing illustrations, and presenting the news in an attention-grabbing narrative style. When Northcliffe purchased the *Evening News* in 1894, the paper was nearly bankrupt. But by dramatically changing its content and appearance, the paper's circulation rose to almost 400,000 within a short time, and by 1896 its circulation approached 800,000. Northcliffe reduced advertisements to a single column on the left, leaving six columns of news broken up by attention-grabbing headlines and illustrations. He also made the content of these news reports more accessible to the working class by introducing a vernacular style. Headlines such as: 'Was it Suicide or Apoplexy?', 'Another Battersea Scandal', 'Bones in Bishopgate', 'Hypnotism and Lunacy' and 'Killed by a Grindston' were guaranteed to attract readers.

Buoyed by this success, Northcliffe launched a new paper, the *Daily Mail*, on 4 May 1896. This eight-page newspaper, with its innovative banner headlines that went right across the page, ran with the slogan 'The Busy Man's Daily Newspaper', and aimed to provide a simpler, shorter style of news stories based on scandal, sex, crime, human interest and sport. It was also the first newspaper to include a women's section. The *Daily Mail* was an immediate success and circulation quickly reached 500,000. The national interest in the Boer War in 1899 saw sales go over one million. Northcliffe also founded the *Daily Mirror* in 1903 and in 1908 he purchased the *Times*, transforming it into a modern newspaper.

Northcliffe's greatest influence was in shifting the press away from its traditional informative role to that of the commercial exploiter and entertainer of the masses, a tradition taken up by media magnate and head of News Corporation, Rupert Murdoch, in the late twentieth century. While Northcliffe is still considered by some to be the most successful publisher in the history of the British press, Murdoch is challenging this mantle.

The first media barons

Between 1890 and 1920, the period known as the golden age of newspapers in Britain, the press was dominated by the **media barons**: Viscounts Northcliffe and Rothermere, and Barons Ridell, Beaverbrook and Dalziel, who exerted enormous influence. These powerful newspaper lords shaped the attitude of governments and influenced major decisions in the First and Second World Wars. Along with their counterparts across the Atlantic—William Randolph Hearst and Joseph Pulitzer—they built huge publishing empires and were notorious for the ways in which they wielded their power. Lord Beaverbrook, the owner of the highly successful British newspapers the *Evening Standard* and the *Daily Express*, was also a member of the British parliament. As the first minister for information during the First World War, he created a propaganda model for publishing news stories that showed the government in a favourable light.

Media baron: The term that replaces *press baron*; refers to the early British newspaper proprietors, such as Lords Beaverbrook, Rothermere and Northcliffe, and contemporary media owners such as Rupert Murdoch.

Early Australian newspapers

In the early years of settlement in the Australian penal colonies, the first printed news was official government gazettes, which provided information on convict musters and the arrival of ships, as well as announcements on rules and regulations for the military, convict and free populations. Australia's earliest newspaper, the *Sydney Gazette and New South Wales Advertiser*, was first printed by a former convict, George Howe, in 1803. This weekly newspaper was 'moral to the point of priggishness, patriotic to the point of servility, pompous in a stiff, eighteenth century fashion' (Ferguson, Foster & Green 1936: 98). Howe encouraged colonists to submit articles for his newspaper, and to accommodate them he hung a slip box in front of the store where the paper was issued. Poems, literature and religious advice were published alongside official reports, shipping news, auction results, crime reports and agricultural notices.

The second newspaper to be published in New South Wales was the *Australian*, established by the explorer William Wentworth in 1824. (This should not be confused with Australia's current national newspaper, the *Australian*, which was launched in 1964 by Rupert Murdoch.) By the 1830s there were seven newspapers in the colony. Australia's longest-running newspaper, the *Sydney Morning Herald*, was first published as the *Sydney Herald* in 1831.

The first commercial newspaper in Van Diemen's Land (Tasmania) was the *Derwent Star and Van Diemen's Land Intelligencer*, first published in 1810. (For more on early Tasmanian newspapers see Case study 1.) By the mid 1850s, Australia's smallest colony boasted a vibrant newspaper industry with eleven titles, including two newspapers still in publication today: the Hobart *Mercury* (1854) and the Launceston *Examiner* (1842). Reverend John West, the first editor of the *Examiner*, wrote a stirring leading article in the first edition on 12 March 1842 in which he spoke about the important role of the press in Australia, sentiments that, despite their antique phraseology, are just as relevant today:

> The legitimate province of the press has long been settled and defined, and notwithstanding its occasional perversion, its immense public utility is fully perceived and admitted. Stronger than charters and laws for protection of the people, it has raised a tribunal, before which the best of rulers bow, and the worst of depots tremble. With telegraphic rapidity it announces the approach of political danger, and preserves the social edifice form injuries, which could not be averted by arms.
>
> Keen to discover and prompt to tell obnoxious truth, its collective voice cannot be restrained by terror, or stifled by corruption.
>
> Representatives may be intimidated or bribed, and the forms of freedom may survive its principles, but so long as the press exists the spirit of liberty can never perish: its summons will arouse the people to defend their rights when they are invaded—to recover them when they are lost.
>
> The press has other important functions to perform.
>
> All the complicated concerns of man, his wide-spreading relationships, his intellectual achievements, his commercial enterprise, his duties, his wants, his sorrows—all these combine to form the field from whence the diligent journalist may gather instruction, and give importance, variety, and interest to his labours. But a newspaper may be a curse; it may disturb and disfigure the operations of that mighty agency to which it

> belongs, and tarnish the triumphs of the press. A newspaper may be the organ of vice and the instrument of prejudice, a mere channel to ignorant vituperation, a dagger pointed, ready for every assassin of private reputation, who is malignant enough to employ it, and has cash enough to pay for it.
>
> Yet it is not enough that a newspaper should be innocuous—it ought to be useful. A false delicacy that does not disturb the quiet of peculators or impostors, or shrinks from correcting the errors of well meaning but blundering functionaries, may secure a journalist from opposition, but he must speedily drivel into contempt and drop into oblivion. (West 1842)

Today the *Examiner* is Australia's second-oldest newspaper after the *Sydney Morning Herald*, having been published continuously since 1842.

The first Victorian newspaper, the *Melbourne Advertiser*, was published in 1838, with the *Port Philip Herald* following in 1840 and the *Argus* in 1846. The *Argus*, a conservative newspaper for most of its history, was a Melbourne institution until its closure in 1957. When it was acquired by the London-based *Daily Mirror* newspaper group in 1949, the newspaper adopted a left-leaning approach. Its main competitor was the *Age*, which was launched in 1854 at the height of the gold rush. In its first decade the *Age* established itself as a newspaper with a radical viewpoint, publishing strident editorials in support of the miners at Ballarat, and later supporting the eight-hour working day and reforms to land laws. Competition between the *Argus* and the *Age* was fierce. Legend has it that the reporters at the *Argus* once handed telegraph operators a copy of the Bible to transmit in an attempt to take over the wires and prevent other newspapers from sending their stories. The gold-mining boom led to the birth of several newspapers in Victoria, including the *Herald*, which in 1853 was first produced on a steam press, and the *Melbourne Australasian*, which was first published in 1854.

Early Western Australian newspapers included the *Fremantle Journal and General Advertiser* (1830), *West Australian Gazette* (1830), *Fremantle Observer* (1831), *Perth Gazette* (1831), *Western Australian Journal* (1831) and *Western Australian Colonial News* (1833). The *Perth Gazette* (1833) was the forerunner of today's *West Australian*, which is one of Australia's oldest continually published newspapers.

Brisbane's *Courier Mail* is descended from one of Queensland's earliest newspapers, the *Moreton Bay Courier*, which was first published in 1846. Other early Queensland newspapers include the *Moreton Bay Free Press* (1850), the *Queensland Guardian* (1860), the *Ipswich Observer* (1870) and the *Daily Observer* (1880).

In South Australia, there were five weekly newspapers in the 1830s and rivalry was fierce. Competitors frequently published attacks on other newspapers, as illustrated by the following editorial, published in the *South Australian Register* attacking the *Southern Australian* in 1838:

> Though we think it scarcely necessary to pollute our columns with examples of the trash doled out by the persons who club their wits to rake together a weekly sixpence worth of scum, still, as a friend, blessed with a stomach not easily turned, has ventured to gather a few specimens out of the nauseous and disgusting puddle, we print these lies with a running commentary. (Pitt 1946: 31)

In 1848, the first issue of *Deutsche Post fur die Australische Colonien*, a bilingual English–German newspaper, was published in South Australia. The proprietor later moved the newspaper to the Barossa Valley, where a large number of German immigrants had settled. In 1862, the first edition of the *Telegraph* newspaper was published in Adelaide to mark the connection of the telegraph from Melbourne to Adelaide. This newspaper is said to be Australia's first penny evening daily. The *Telegraph* soon had competition from the *Adelaide Express*, another penny evening newspaper that was published by *South Australian Advertiser* (1858) and was launched in 1862. South Australia is the birthplace of the most powerful media mogul in the world today, Rupert Murdoch, whose father's company News Limited owned the *Adelaide News*.

The *Koori Mail*

Australia did not have a national Aboriginal and Torres Strait Islander newspaper until the *Koori Mail* was launched in 1991. Regarded as 'The Voice of Indigenous Australia', the newspaper is owned jointly by five small Aboriginal organisations in Bundjalung country, on the far north coast of New South Wales. Significantly, profit from the newspaper goes back to Indigenous Australians in the form of dividends, sponsorships and scholarships. The *Koori Mail* is published fortnightly, and has an Australia-wide circulation of 90,000.

Early newspapers in the Pacific and Asia

The first newspaper to be published in New Zealand was the *New Zealand Gazette*, which was launched by journalist Samuel Revans in April 1840. The *Wanganui Chronicle* was first published as a daily newspaper in 1856 and the *Otago Daily Times*, New Zealand's longest-running daily newspaper, was first published in 1861. By 1866, thirteen newspapers were being published across the country.

One of the longest-running newspapers in Asia is Singapore's *Straits Times*, which was first published in 1845. Japan's first daily newspaper, the *Yokohama Mainichi Shimbun*, began publication in 1870, although printing from movable type had been introduced into Japan in the late sixteenth century. Japan's longest-running newspaper is the *Mainichi Shimbun*, which was first published in 1872.

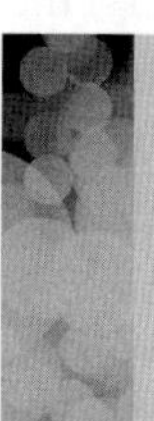

The world's first newspaper weather chart

The world's first weather chart to be published in a newspaper—a map of the east coast of mainland Australia—was published in the *Sydney Morning Herald* on 5 February 1877.

The news image

Photographic technological advances in the 1880s led to the first photographs, in the form of lithographic illustrations, appearing in newspapers and periodicals. But it was the development of the half-tone process, which enabled the publication of photographic images directly rather than through engravings, that transformed the format of newspapers and eventually led to the pictorial layouts that we are familiar with today.

The digital camera

The greatest advance in press photography was the arrival of the digital camera at the end of the twentieth century. While this new technology, to date, has not changed the look or format of newspapers, it has created new ethical dilemmas about photographic manipulation. Additionally, combined with computer programs such as PhotoShop, it has enabled citizens with few photographic skills, who witness a news event, the opportunity to contribute to newsmaking. For more on the impact of digitalisation generally, see Chapters 18 and 19.

A rival—the advent of the broadcast media

When broadcast radio entered the media scene in the 1920s, newspapers were forced to re-evaluate their role as society's primary information provider. As with the advent of the internet and new media technologies of today, the development of the radio—a low-cost alternative news source—sparked fears that it would overtake the newspaper industry. To respond to this new competition, editors revamped the format and content of newspapers to broaden their appeal. Stories were expanded to provide more indepth coverage, with longer feature stories and pictorial supplements introduced.

No sooner had newspapers adapted to radio than they were forced to re-evaluate themselves once more following the introduction of television following the Second World War. In the USA between 1940 and 1990, newspaper circulation dropped from one newspaper per every two adults to one per every three adults. Despite this sharp decline, television's omnipresence did not render the newspaper obsolete.

Technological advances in printing technology in the late twentieth century enabled newspapers to introduce colour printing and high-resolution images, which saw a proliferation of lifestyle supplements and a reduction in the hard news content. **Infotainment** news—in the form of lifestyle, travel, finance, education, showbiz and book sections—dramatically changed the style and content of newspapers.

Infotainment: Originally, a term that referred just to television programming that dealt with serious issues or current affairs in an entertaining way; today the term applies across all media, and refers to the way in which soft news style, in both form and content, is delivered in news and current affairs stories.

Computers

Perhaps the biggest revolution in the printing industry since the steam-powered press in the nineteenth century was the advent of computer technology in the 1970s. The introduction of the first daisy-wheel printer signalled the end of the mechanical printing press that had developed out of Gutenberg's screw press 500 years earlier. The daisy-wheel printer was soon superseded by the dot-matrix impact printer, which was faster and could print graphics and use different fonts. By the end of the 1980s, the ink-jet printer had overtaken the dot-matrix printer, followed by the laser, and then the thermal-transfer printer. The immediate impact of these changes was in the loss of employment for printers, linotype operators and compositors. The electronic computer-based typesetting system gave direct access to typesetting by journalists and the telesales staff who typed out classified advertisements, thus bypassing the linotype operators in the composing room and reducing the workforce by 75 per cent. Most linotype operators and compositors were forced to take redundancy or retire, although some were retrained.

The World Wide Web: the beginning of the end?

> Cybermedia will make every man his own editor, which in turn makes every writer a fool. The internet will transmit misinformation very efficiently. We will miss the gatekeepers. (Freeman 1995)

Today, newspapers across the world are facing declining circulation and profits. The technological revolution in the mass media is creating new challenges and opportunities for newspapers. Never before has so much information been so accessible to so many. The World Association of Newspapers (WAN) claimed in 1997 that 'by whatever criteria one may choose to measure it—advertising levels, circulation, time spent reading—newspapers are in decline and have been for decades' (WAN 2000: 8).

While the advent of television, the development of new media and the threat from online news sources have been blamed for the acceleration in the global decline of newspaper circulation, there are a number of other factors that have also contributed to this downward trend, which has been occurring since the 1960s. These factors include:

- fewer young readers (Ewart 2005)
- the demise of afternoon newspapers and consequent loss of blue-collar readers (Ewart 2005)
- the global financial crisis (from 2007) along with spiralling costs and reader dissatisfaction with content (WAN 2000: 8).

Changing formats: the twenty-first century

In the early years of the twenty-first century, newspapers have been forced to implement radical changes to their layout and news content to compete in the internet age. Newspapers have begun offering digital innovations such as weekly politics **podcasts**, links to their online news editions and news updates on mobile phones. Opinion and analysis has substantially increased and hard news content has decreased in a bid to stem falling circulation.

Podcast (iPOD broadCAST): An audio broadcast that has been converted to an MP3 file or other audio file format for playback in a digital player. Although today many podcasts are played on a computer, the original idea was to listen on a portable device; hence, the 'pod' name from 'iPod'. Although podcasts are mostly verbal, they may contain music, images and video.

Many serious newspapers have also reduced their physical dimensions from the larger broadsheet format to the **Berliner** (or compact size), and in a bid to attract reader attention, celebrity and soft news stories now sit side by side with hard news. The once clear line between entertainment and news is blurring. Today, stories about the war in Iraq sit on the front page beside stories of Madonna's bid to adopt an African child and Paris Hilton's release from jail.

Berliner: A compact newspaper measuring 470mm × 315mm, which has become a popular newspaper format in recent years.

Citizen journalist: A member of the public who acts in the role of a journalist by gathering news and new information (including images) that are communicated to an audience.

Citizen journalists have been given editorial space, with guest contributors providing copy on pages previously reserved for journalists. In a bid to keep circulation figures from falling, the British broadsheet, the *Independent*, has embraced 'editorial stunts' usually found only in the realm of the tabloids. In 2006, the newspaper handed over of the reins for the day to Irish rock star Bono, sharing its revenue for that day with charitable causes such as Bono's RED campaign (Sellers 2006).

In an even more controversial editorial policy the *Independent* has displaced front-page news with opinion and analysis, transforming the newspaper into what its editor, Simon Kelner, has called a 'viewspaper'. Unlike other newspapers that have embraced online content, Simon Kelner is not interested in trying to keep readers by developing the *Independent*'s online presence. He says online news is 'not central to his strategy', which is to sell newspapers. The *Independent* hopes to survive by refusing to compete with the internet, and instead to shift the emphasis 'away from scoops to magazine-style roundups, opinion and analysis' (Sellers 2006).

In contrast, one of the *Independent*'s competitors, the *Guardian*, has embraced new technology to 'create a flexible media company that can provide news in many formats, one of which remains (for the time being, at least) newsprint' (Sellers 2006). Journalist Frances Stead Sellers says the internet is 'the bull's-eye of Alan Rusbridger's strategy for the *Guardian*'. She continues:

> These days, he is in the business of selling news rather than newspapers, and he is experimenting with doing so not only in print, but online, on podcasts, on mobile phones—indeed, on whatever technology looks as if it may ultimately make commercial sense. The paper has a circulation of some 380 000, but its website, Guardian Unlimited … has more than 13 million unique visitors each month and has begun making a modest but real seven-figure profit. (Sellers 2006)

Conclusion

Journalism was born out of Johannes Gutenberg's printing press and the development of the newspaper industry. Today, we live in a multimedia world where the first mass medium has to fight for its share of the news market. WAN remains naturally upbeat about the future of newspapers, arguing that newspapers continue to have a significant role in the dissemination of news, estimating that one billion people in the world today read a newspaper daily. WAN claims that although today the amount and immediacy of information on the internet is unparalleled, it has not signalled the end of the newspaper's relevance. Newspapers in print, WAN (2000) argues, 'remain a popular and powerful medium for the reporting and analysis of events that shape our lives'. There is no doubt that newspapers, in the age of the World Wide Web and new media, have challenges ahead if they are to maintain a presence as news providers. The challenge is for a new generation of newspaper proprietors, editors and journalists to find ways to capture the public in the twenty-first century and to continue the centuries-old tradition of providing printed news.

KEY REFERENCES

Bishop, J. & Woods, O. (1983). *The Story of the Times*. London: Michael Joseph.

Boyce, G., Curran, J. & Wingate, P. (eds) (1978). *Newspaper History: From the Seventeenth Century to the Present Day*. London: Constable.

Chappell, W. (1999). *A Short History of the Printed Word*. Vancouver: Hartley & Marks.

Curthoys, A. & Schultz, J. (eds) (1999). *Journalism: Print, Politics and Popular Culture*. St Lucia: University of Queensland Press.

Kirkpatrick, R. (2000). 'Covering Every Dogfight: A Century and a Half of Local News in the Provincial Press'. *Australian Journalism Monograph*, 5–6, May–November.

Lindoo, E.C. (1998). *The Future of Newspapers: A Study of the World Wide Web and its Relationship to the Electronic Publishing of Newspapers*. <www.wan-press.org/article.php3?id_article+2821>. Accessed 12 April 2007.

World Association of Newspapers (2004). *Newspapers: A Brief History*. <www.wan-press.org/article2821.html>. Accessed 20 April 2007.

WEBSITES

Australian Media History Database: <www.amhd.org.au/associations.html>

Australian Newspaper History Group: <www.uq.edu.au/journ-comm/?page+8634>

The Gutenberg Press: <www.mainz.de/gutenberg/english/erfindun.htm>

CHAPTER 3

THE FOURTH (OR FIFTH) ESTATE

NICOLA GOC

> The most obvious lesson is that [WikiLeaks] represents the first really sustained confrontation between the established order and the culture of the internet. There have been skirmishes before, but this is the real thing. (Naughton 2010)

Introduction

Almost a decade ago, citizen journalist website New Directions for News reported that 'journalism finds itself at a rare moment in history where … its hegemony as gatekeeper of the news is threatened by not just new technology and competitors, but, potentially, by the audience it serves' (cited in Rosen 2005: 30). American journalism academic Jay Rosen (2005: 30) said professional journalism is 'no longer sovereign over territory it once easily controlled', but he also acknowledges that:

> This does not have to mean declining influence or reputation. It does not mean that prospects for the public service press are suddenly dim. It does, however, mean that the old political contract between news providers and news consumers will give way to something different, founded on what Curley correctly called a new 'balance of power'.

Tom Curley, the CEO of Associated Press, says there has been a huge shift in the balance of power from content providers to the content consumers in the first decade of the twenty-first century.

This chapter examines the notion of the **Fourth Estate** in the twenty-first century by posing the following questions.

The Fourth Estate: Journalists as a group

- Are we witnessing the demise of the Fourth Estate?
- Has infotainment taken over the role of the Fourth Estate?
- Has the advent of the internet threatened the Fourth Estate?
- Are bloggers journalists?
- Are new media the Fifth Estate?
- Does WikiLeaks provide a new model for the Fourth Estate?

By the end of this chapter you should have an understanding of what is meant by the term 'the Fourth Estate', and you should be able to form an argument about the relevance and importance of the news media in the twenty-first century.

The death of the Fourth Estate?

Twitter: An instant messaging system launched in 2006 that enables users to send brief text messages of up to 140 characters to a list of friends and approved followers.

Facebook: An online social networking site.

Blog: An online journal comprising links and postings; a noun and a verb with various inflections, such as 'blogger' and 'blogging'. It's origin is from 'we*blog*'.

As we enter the second decade of the twenty-first century, the new online news providers of the first decade, such as *Huffington Post* and *Crikey*, have cemented their place in the mainstream news process, while citizen news sites, such as *OhMyNews* and *DigitalJournal.com*, continue to evolve and gain credibility as they adopt the work practices of traditional journalism. The predicted death of old media has not eventuated. While new technology has changed news practice forever, and audiences (through social media such as **Twitter** and **Facebook**, and through **blogs**) are actively participating at a far greater rate in the manufacture of news, our reliance on traditional news sources for news and information is still dominant, particularly for news on significant events, as was clearly illustrated in Australia during the devastating 2010–11 Queensland floods.

The Fourth Estate and disaster coverage

During the floods crisis, traditional media outlets—particularly television and radio, and their online sites—provided the most accessible and comprehensive real-time coverage of the unfolding disaster. While individuals communicated their personal experiences through Twitter and Facebook, and uploaded their photos and videos to online news sites, it was the traditional news organisations that comprehensively and authoritatively communicated up-to-the-minute news and information to the public.

Audiences tuned into television, radio and online news sites to hear Queensland Premier Anna Bligh and emergency services personnel regularly updating Australians on the situation. Through regional and national networks, television stations Channel Nine and the ABC (on its news channel ABC24 and on ABC1) set aside regular programming to broadcast comprehensive reports to the people of Australia.

Channel Nine Queensland Managing Director Kylie Blucher said during the crisis: 'Information is paramount and it has nothing to do with ratings. Our focus is to get the information out there, get hotlines out there.' A national appeal was launched on Channel Nine, drawing the nation together with a sense of common purpose as celebrities and politicians were filmed taking part in a telethon and reporters brought regular updates to the screen. The local knowledge of rural reporters and on-air talents proved invaluable in providing accurate and credible information.

The death of the old media business model

While this disaster news coverage potently illustrates how traditional broadcast media continue to serve the public well in times of crisis, the reality remains that the business model for old media, particularly newspapers, is broken but a sustainable business model for new media has yet to be found. Until a sustainable way of bringing in revenue for both old and new media eventuates, newsrooms will continue to contract, and journalism as the public watchdog will continue to weaken.

Content changes

While significant changes to journalism practice have been brought about by new technologies and delivery systems in the past twenty years, perhaps the biggest contemporary threat to the Fourth Estate is the dramatic change in the content carried by the media. Since the last decades of the twentieth century, there has been a readjustment in the core business of news journalism from primarily scrutinising government and those in positions of power to providing a greater proportion of celebrity news, infotainment, opinion and lifestyle articles. Today, entertainment values often override traditional news values (see Chapter 12), and although some of us bemoan the displacing of hard news with soft news, the consuming patterns of the majority reinforce society's desire to be entertained.

While citizens of democracies still expect their news media to be the watchdogs of government, and to expose the wrongdoings of those in positions of power, they now also demand to be informed about the latest celebrity scandals and lifestyle trends. However, a 2007 Pew Research Center survey showed that the public are not as hooked on celebrity gossip as news editors might have us believe. Almost 90 per cent of those surveyed believed celebrity scandals receive too much news coverage; only 2 per cent believed there was too little celebrity scandal coverage (Pew Center for Research 2007). More than 50 per cent of those who said celebrity news was over-covered also believed news organisations were to blame for giving these stories so much coverage. So it would appear that audiences (at least in the US where this study was conducted) are not to blame for the rise in celebrity news in the hard news sections of newspapers and broadcast bulletins. In fact, part of the public's disengagement with the news media could be due to the disengagement from hard news by journalists and editors.

And then along comes a phenomenon such as the WikiLeaks organisation (discussed at length later in this chapter), which has ignited a global interest in hard news. Founder of WikiLeaks Julian Assange is on a mission to keep governments and the powerful accountable; perhaps this courageous journalist, editor and publisher and his organisation have provided the Fourth Estate with a way forward in the contemporary global environment.

The Fourth Estate in history

More than 250 years ago, English playwright and journalist Henry Fielding (1707–54) introduced the idea of the Fourth Estate. Fielding was a notable playwright, whose sharp burlesques satirising the government of the day gained him the wrath of the then prime minister, Sir Robert Walpole. In a bid to stifle Fielding's voice, the British government introduced the *Theatrical Licensing Act*; undeterred, Fielding became the editor of a journal that continued to scrutinise Walpole's government. It was in 1752 that Fielding famously wrote in his *Covent Garden Journal*:

> None of our political writers … take notice of any more than three estates, namely, Kings, Lords and Commons … passing by in silence that very large and powerful body which form the Fourth Estate in this community … The Mob.

We will return to Fielding's notion of the Fourth Estate as 'the mob' later in this chapter, when we look at the advent of the internet and web blogs, and what some have called the 'Fifth Estate'.

It was the actions of another Englishman, the radical journalist, newspaper proprietor, parliamentarian and notorious libertine John Wilkes (1725–98), that forever cemented the notion of a free press (for more on Wilkes, see Chapter 2). Wilkes is of particular interest to us today because, more than 240 years after his death, we have seen another maverick journalist, editor and publisher in Julian Assange. By publishing secret diplomatic cables and government documents, Assange has shown the world how a new style of journalism—a collaboration between old-world journalism and the new-world journalism of the internet—can enliven the Fourth Estate.

James Mill

In the late eighteenth century, another Briton played a significant role in the development of the Fourth Estate and a free press. Scottish philosopher James Mill (1773–1836) advocated for press freedom because, he said, it could make known 'the conduct of the individuals who have chosen to wield the powers of government' (cited in Jarlov n.d.). At about the same time, Thomas Jefferson (1743–1826), America's third president and author of the US Declaration of Independence, reiterated Mill's position, arguing that citizens needed access to reliable information about matters of state. Jefferson famously said: 'Were it left to me to decide whether we should have a government without newspapers or newspapers without a government, I should not hesitate for a moment to prefer the latter' (Jefferson 1787: 48–9). Although Jefferson understood the importance of having a free press, he did not always speak kindly of the Fourth Estate, once stating that 'the advertisements are the most truthful part of a newspaper'.

Carlyle's Fourth Estate

The most quoted reference to the Fourth Estate is by Edmund Burke, an Anglo-Irish statesman, author and political philosopher who served in the House of Commons, and was one of the finest parliamentary orators of his day. His pronouncement was quoted by noted Victorian historian and author Thomas Carlyle in 1841:

> Does not … the parliamentary debate go on … in so far more comprehensive way, out of Parliament altogether? Edmund Burke said that there were three Estates in Parliament, but in the Reporter's Gallery yonder, there sat a Fourth Estate more important than they all. (Carlyle 1841: 349–50)

Thomas Carlyle also argued that printing was equivalent to democracy. Invent writing, he said, and democracy is inevitable:

> Whoever can speak, speaking now to the whole nation, becomes a power, a branch of government, with inalienable weight in law-making, in all acts of authority. It matters not what rank he has, what revenues or garnitures: the requisite thing is that he have a tongue which others will listen to; this and nothing more is requisite. (Carlyle 1841: 349–50)

Here Carlyle was describing the newly found power of the man of letters, who would evolve into the news reporter of today. When Carlyle was writing about the Fourth Estate in the nineteenth century, it was accepted that the other three powers were the priesthood, the aristocracy (the House of Lords) and the House of Commons. Later, these powers were seen as the church, parliament and the judiciary, while today, in our more secular society, the three powers are generally regarded as the government, the public service and the judiciary.

The nineteenth-century press soon developed into the watchdog not just of the first three estates, but also of all those in positions of power. As we have seen in the previous chapter on the rise of newspapers, the rise of a radical press in the early nineteenth century saw unprecedented numbers of newly literate citizens gaining access to printing presses and establishing newspapers that addressed the social issues of the day. The radical press gained a large audience, establishing unprecedented political discourse among the working class.

Independent of political pressures and financially self-sufficient, the Fourth Estate was difficult for governments to control, so in 1819 the British government introduced a newspaper stamp duty. When the tax was eventually repealed in 1855, the subsequent free-market environment saw a transformation of the newspaper industry. Improving technologies meant that the cost of production dropped as the rate of production rose, providing the masses with access to the cheap penny press. With industrialisation came commercialisation and a reliance on advertising revenue, which transformed news into a very profitable commodity.

The Fourth Estate today

For more than 200 years, journalists have seen their role as informing the public and ensuring accountability. However, there are those who would argue that rather than scrutinising government, business and the powerful elite, the Fourth Estate works to reinforce and sustain these institutions. Certainly, in totalitarian regimes, government-controlled media are instruments of the state, but it is also claimed that in Western democracies some media outlets uncritically promote, rather than scrutinise, government ideologies. Radical left-wing thinker Noam Chomsky, for instance, argues through his **propaganda model** (Herman

Propaganda model: Noam Chomsky's argument that the mass media are tools used by their owners and by governments to deliver a capitalist ideology, rather than to scrutinise governments and other powerful groups in society.

& Chomsky 1994) that the mass media are tools used by their owners and by governments to deliver a capitalist ideology rather than scrutinise government and the powerful. He argues that the media work hand in glove with governments and big business. From the political economy perspective, the mass media are seen as representing the interests of those who own them. Chomsky argues that these owners influence public discourse for their own commercial and ideological motives (Herman & Chomsky 1994).

What Chomsky is really talking about here is a form of hegemony, which we define at length in Chapter 1. We look in greater detail at the term 'ideology' in Chapter 9.

An example of Chomsky's argument is one we have already considered in Chapter 1: media mogul Rupert Murdoch's influence over his newspapers during the lead-up to the 2003 US invasion of Iraq. As you may recall, Murdoch publicly declared his support for the proposed invasion, and also outlined his viewpoint in a letter to each of the 175 editors of his newspapers across three continents. All of his newspapers took a pro-invasion editorial stance. At the time, media commentator Roy Greenslade (2003), a former editor and journalist, wrote:

> What a guy! You have got to admit that Rupert Murdoch is one canny press tycoon because he has an unerring ability to choose editors across the world who think just like him. How else can we explain the extraordinary unity of thought in his newspaper empire about the need to make war on Iraq? After an exhaustive survey of the highest-selling and most influential papers across the world owned by Murdoch's News Corporation, it is clear that all are singing from the same hymn sheet.

This is nothing new. During the first half of the twentieth century, the English newspaper lords (Viscounts Northcliffe and Rothermere, and Barons Riddell, Dalziel and Beaverbrook) played highly influential roles not only in promoting but also in influencing government policies on major decisions in the First and Second World Wars.

News audiences as consumers

Consumerist model: Under the consumerist model the manufacture of news is profit driven; news is seen primarily as a business enterprise, with news as a commodity.

There has also been a significant shift in recent decades in the way media proprietors view their audiences. Media owners now see readers, listeners and viewers as the **consumers** of their commodities, in much the same way as the owners of retail chains see their customers as the consumers of the products they sell. As Hirst and Patching (2005: 104) claim, media industries today 'treat their audiences as "consumers" of news, entertainment, information, sport, and associated product packaging'. Again, this shift might not be as recent as we think. Fifty years ago, at the height of Senator Joseph McCarthy's anticommunist campaign in the USA, television and radio journalist Ed Murrow criticised the media for entertaining the masses at a time when they should have been informing the public of the threat to free speech and personal freedom.

Fifty years later, Ed Murrow's prescient words resonate in a world unsettled by threats to global peace, and where hard news and investigative reporting are being increasingly replaced by infotainment. In the early twenty-first century, celebrity news often dictates the news agenda. While often quoted, Murrow's criticism of the lack of endeavour by journalists and news corporations at a time when the USA was swept up in a wave of anticommunist sentiment, had little influence on stemming the tide of the commercialisation of news. With an increasingly affluent consumerist public that demands to be entertained as well as informed, the role and relevance of the crusading investigative journalist—the muckraker—increasingly is being challenged.

Good Night, and Good Luck

The film *Good Night, and Good Luck* tells the story of Ed Murrow's career. In his famous address to the Radio–Television News Directors Association and Foundation, Murrow (1958) told the American people:

> Our history will be what we make it. And if there are any historians about fifty or a hundred years from now, and there should be preserved the kinescopes for one week of all three networks, they will there find recorded in black and white, or color, evidence of decadence, escapism and insulation from the realities of the world in which we live … during the daily peak viewing periods, television in the main insulates us from the realities of the world in which we live. If this state of affairs continues, we may alter an advertising slogan to read: LOOK NOW, PAY LATER.

'The infotainment monster that ate the news industry'

Infotainment, it has been argued, is not only now fulfilling the role of the Fourth Estate, but it is also engaging, informing and entertaining the public far more effectively than the traditional news outlets. Australian media academic Stephen Stockwell (2004) says that television infotainment (here he includes subgenres such as lifestyle shows, reality television, docusoaps, **docugames**, tabloid news, talk shows, **mockumentary** and news sitcoms), when considered as a totality, actually offer greater diversity of viewpoints, acuity of representation and depth of critique than traditional news and current affairs programs in Australia presently provide (Stockwell 2004: 14).

Stockwell (2004: 14) argues that reality television 'provides a more intense account of experience than either news or entertainment can supply and a deeper reading of what it is to be a human'. He points to amateur footage of natural disasters, which places the viewer with the citizen at the dramatic moment of challenge; for example, the amateur footage of the devastating 2004 Boxing Day tsunami, which provided an immediate and shocking understanding of the horror and devastation of that disaster in a way that no journalist reporting in the aftermath could hope to accomplish.

Docugames: Interactive reality games in which players are involved in role-play scenarios that are based on real events. They blend reality with interactive entertainment by allowing the player to control and alter historical figures and events. Throughout the game there are links to articles and interviews from or about the real event.

Mockumentary: A melding of the words 'mock' and 'documentary'; a film or television program presented as a documentary recording real life but which is in fact fictional—a commonly used medium for parody and satire.

By 2011 traditional news outlets had learnt their lesson, and had the resources in place—along with a well-established online presence—to reverse this deficiency in disaster coverage. As mentioned earlier, the news coverage of the 2010–11 Queensland floods saw mainstream news journalists filing reports and footage from the epicentre of the unfolding floods. It was this ability of journalists across the vast flood regions to file timely stories and footage of the unfolding disaster—both on traditional formats (particularly television and radio) and online—that brought audiences back to mainstream news coverage.

Nonetheless, audiences today still often engage with news and current affairs through outlets other than news bulletins. In general, it is evident from the ratings that the public are turning to infotainment shows, tabloid current affairs, YouTube and Facebook for their information. Stockwell says infotainment shows on Australian television (such as *Big Brother*, *Survivor*, *Good News Week*, *Better Homes and Gardens*, *Getaway*, *Frontline*, *The Games* and *Spin City*) and tabloid current affairs programs (such as *Today Tonight* and *A Current Affair*) offer 'opportunities for new forms of democracy to develop based in an expansion of social reflexivity' (Stockwell 2004: 17).

Current affairs: The news media's delivery, usually on television or radio, of political and social events or issues of the present time.

There is no doubt that the tabloid entertainment style of journalism captures our attention. In her work on media effects, Grabe (2000, cited in Stockwell 2004: 7–8) found that the flamboyant tabloid—or infotainment style of packaging news and **current affairs**—increased arousal and attention.

Academic John Hartley, who calls journalism the 'sense-making practice of modernity', and sees it as the very foundation of democratic politics and the primary wiring of popular culture, argues that the 'tabloidisation of journalism is not a diminution of its ambition, but an extension of its reach; another unfolding layer in the story of journalism's role as the oxygen of democracy' (cited in Hargreaves 2003: 23).

While audiences voraciously consume stories about Madonna adopting babies from Africa and Paris Hilton's time in jail, they still expect their news media to provide reliable information from trustworthy sources in a timely manner, and to expose corruption and wrongdoing.

The former president of NBC News in the USA, Reuven Frank, said the following about the news media's capitulation to audience demands for infotainment and entertainment:

> This business of giving people what they want is a dope-pusher's argument. News is something people don't know they're interested in until they hear about it. The job of a journalist is to take what's important and make it interesting. (Hickey 1998)

Epistemology: The use of logic, psychology, philosophy and linguistics to study knowledge and how it is processed by humans.

Fifth Estate: The new media technologies, such as the internet, as modes of news delivery; originally applied to radio and television.

eZine: A magazine that is published in an electronic form.

Carl Bernstein, veteran journalist of Watergate fame (cited in Stockwell 2004) maintains that the problem with news and news journalism today is **epistemological**: journalism has become 'illusionary and delusionary—disfigured, unreal and disconnected from the real context of our lives … distorted by celebrity and the worship of celebrity; by the reduction of news to gossip; by sensationalism'. By giving way to the audience's base desires, one commentator claimed that it was 'the infotainment monster that ate the news industry' (Rapping, cited in Stockwell 2004).

While audiences continue to enjoy lifestyle and infotainment programs, in recent times it has become clear that they are also extremely interested in seeing governments and the powerful elite held accountable. The public reaction to WikiLeaks not only shows how interested the global community is in significant news, but also that, by using the WikiLeaks model, journalism has an opportunity to re-engage with its audience.

The Fifth Estate

With the introduction of radio news in the early twentieth century, a new term was coined for this new news medium—the **Fifth Estate**—which was later extended to include television. However, the term did not become established as a distinction between the old and new media of news because it was generally agreed that radio and television news continued to fulfil the same Fourth Estate role as the press.

Today, the Fifth Estate is sometimes used in reference to new media, but only if the new media manufacture news in a way markedly different from that of traditional news media.

The term has also been taken up by Canada's premier television news magazine program, *The Fifth Estate*. *Fifth Estate* is also the name of an **eZine** produced by the journalism program at RMIT University in Melbourne, Australia, that focuses on media analysis, news and comment.

Does the internet threaten the Fourth Estate?

YouTube and Facebook

The digital and electronic revolution of the past twenty years has had a significant impact on the way we access news and information. While the most dramatic impact of the internet on the traditional news media has been on the decline of newspaper circulation figures, the more recent phenomenon of sites such as **YouTube** and **Facebook** have started to have a significant impact on television viewing. According to Sorensen (2007), 'Every day millions of people choose to watch dubious quality amateur videos on the screens of their personal computers'. She said that no one anticipated the trend, and 'no one foresaw that, within a couple of years, media watchers would be talking about an end to the TV era'.

YouTube: A user-created online video bank.

Facebook: An online social networking site.

However, not only has the death of the television era not yet occurred, but a 2011 Deloitte study has also found that television will retain its global leadership of all media forms in terms of total revenues, including advertising revenues, subscriptions, pay per view and licence fees. In 2011, television will account for about 41 per cent of all advertising revenues and grow its share to 42 per cent by 2012. According to the report, television advertising revenue grew almost 10 per cent between 2007 and 2010, from 37 per cent to more than 40 per cent (Deloitte 2011). Deloitte predicts television will solidify its status as the 'current super media', defying some commentators' prophecies of imminent obsolescence. According to the report, television audiences around the world will watch 140 billion more hours of television. Further:

> Revenues from pay TV in the BRIC countries [Brazil, Russia, India and China] will rise by 20 per cent, worldwide TV advertising will increase by $10 billion, and 40 million new

> viewers will be added; TV chefs will sell tens of millions more cookbooks than their non-televised peers; TV shows will be the most common conversation topic around the world and the subject of more than a billion tweets. In short, television will likely continue to command a growing share of the world's attention and pocketbooks. (Deloitte 2011)

New media are transforming traditional television: the old inflexible program schedules are disappearing and individual consumers can now access programs whenever they want. The convergence of free-to-air and pay television with the internet and radio is transforming the way we are entertained and informed. The televisions in our homes (whether laptops, giant LCD screens or 3D screens) are being transformed into multimedia platforms and these new technologies are providing new formats for news and current affairs to be brought to the world.

Wikipedia: An online encyclopedia that is continually edited and added to by its users.

Australian academic Axel Bruns (cited in Sorensen 2007) claims that what we are seeing with YouTube and **Wikipedia** is the 'user-led future of communications'. He says that YouTube and Wikipedia are changing the power relations between producers and users, and that we are seeing a 'fundamental shift in the model of consumption that grew out of the industrial revolution'. Bruns (2007) says that Industrial Age approaches to the production and distribution of goods rely on a one-way value chain from production through distribution to consumption, but this traditional way of accessing the media is under threat in this user-led revolution. Not only are citizens producing the editorial content of such video-sharing sites, but companies are also starting to leverage the user-led approach. For example, companies have started to invite people to create advertisements about why they like a certain product, with the 'winner' having their advertisement chosen as the company's new video advertisement. According to Sorensen (2007), many of the entries are posted on YouTube, so the site provides a quick, free, widespread ad campaign and the advertiser doesn't even have to pay to create the advertisement.

One company using this adaptation of the 'produsage model' to advertise its fast food argues that people become not just customers but also fans who feel a personal connection with what they choose to eat or what they view on screen. Citizens making commercials about their favourite fast food or perfume is one thing, but what happens when citizens start creating their own political advertisements?

In March 2006, a posting on YouTube highlighted how the internet is becoming increasingly influential in political campaigns. A 2008 US presidential election campaign advertisement was created by taking Ridley Scott's classic '1984' Macintosh television advertisement for Apple Inc. and reincarnating it as a satirical attack against presidential candidate Hillary Clinton. Within two weeks, the 74-second clip had been viewed more than 2.6 million times on YouTube, and had created a political storm. The creator of this 'sizzling guerrilla advertisement' (Hecht 2007) anonymously signed themselves as 'ParkRidge47' (Hillary Clinton was born in Park Ridge in 1947). They had replaced the demonic Big Brother figure in the advertisement with the figure of Hillary Clinton.

Mashup: A website or application that combines content from more than one source into an integrated experience.

This video **mashup**, in support of Clinton's opponent Senator Barack Obama, ends with an Apple-like logo that has been converted into an 'O' for Obama. Senator Obama's campaign denied any knowledge of the making of the video. The story about the advertisement became national news across the traditional news media. According to *Seattle Post* columnist D. Parvaz,

'It … kicked off quite a storm … with both the mainstream media and the bloggerati. It was featured on the evening news as well as on entertainment shows and industry gossip sites' (Parvaz 2007). When Micah Silfry, a blogger from Techpresident.com, emailed ParkRidge47 in a bid to identify the creator soon after the video clip was posted, she received the following reply:

> Thank you for your interest in the video. It has been amazing to watch it explode on the viral scene. At one point it was the #3 most watched video on YouTube and is at 108,000 views and growing.
>
> Considering Hillary Clinton's biggest video has only received 12,000 views on YouTube, I'd say the grassroots has won the first round.
>
> The idea was simple and so was the execution. Make a bold statement about the Democratic primary race by culture jacking a famous commercial and replacing as few images as possible. For some people it doesn't register, but for people familiar with the ad and the race it has obviously struck a chord.
>
> A friend suggested the idea after reading a *New York Times* article about the Clintons' campaign of bullying donors and political operatives after the Geffen dustup. (Silfry 2007)

The identity of the creator became an issue of national importance, with more than 2.6 million viewers—and potential voters in the 2008 general election—logging onto the site within two weeks. The news media, as well as citizens on the World Wide Web, started a quest to identify the creator. Parvaz claimed that 'everyone but Deep Throat himself was suspected of loading up the mysterious anti-Hillary Rodham Clinton viral video on YouTube' (Parvaz 2007). In an example of the message trumping the medium, it was not a traditional news medium that exposed the creator of the video mashup but an online blog. Acting in the traditional role of the Fourth Estate, Arianna Huffington's blog *Huffington Post* exposed the creator of the video as Phil de Vellis:

> For the last two weeks, the internet has been buzzing about the hottest online mystery since lonelygirl15: who was behind the 'Hillary 1984' video mashup?
>
> Some suspected right wing SwiftBoaters. Some speculated it was the work of disaffected Democratic consultants. One blogger even pointed the finger at me.
>
> As the intrigue deepened, the mainstream media joined the fray, with Hillary Clinton and Barack Obama both being asked about the viral smash—and much talk about the impact user-generated political videos will have on the 2008 race.
>
> Well, today I can end the guessing. Last night, we sent out a challenge to the HuffPost team asking them to hit the phones and contact all their sources. As a result, we have learned the video was the work of Philip de Vellis, who was the internet communications director for Sherrod Brown's 2006 Senate campaign, and who now works at Blue State Digital, a company created by members of Howard Dean's Internet Team. (Huffington 2007)

And it was another online news blog, *Rawstory*, that exposed the link between Obama's campaign team and Phil De Vellis, proving that Senator Obama's claims that his campaign staff had no way of knowing who Phil De Vellis was were false. *Rawstory* posted a photograph of De Vellis in 2006 with his housemate, who just happened to be Senator Obama's Washington press secretary, Ben LaBolt. This is a fine example of J-bloggers in action (for more on the role of J-bloggers, see below).

Edward Helmore of the *London Observer*, in a story titled 'YouTube: The Hustings of the 21st Century?, claimed that the 1984 advertisement points to the future of campaigning. Helmore wrote that the video posting 'raised questions about the power of the internet in the political process—and the opportunities for subterfuge this presents'. He argues that the video:

> was one of the most talked-about items in the political press. And while initial excitement that this was an inspired and spontaneous piece of citizen action was undermined by the unmasking of de Vellis's Obama connection, it remains proof of the political power that YouTube and social networking sites such as MySpace now offer. (Helmore 2007)

According to Helmore (2007), the media giants were not slow to notice the shift in political campaigning from traditional media to the internet, and that media corporations were 'rushing to establish political sites'.

Because of the Clinton video, Rupert Murdoch's MySpace launched MySpace Impact, a political site that enabled candidates to use the network's first viral fund-raising tool. It was also announced that MySpace would host a series of online political events through the 2008 elections, with MySpace CEO Chris DeWolfe claiming that the site would play a 'powerful role' in the election campaign. *Washington Post* media columnist Howard Kurtz and colleague Jose Vargas wrote an opinion piece, 'A Brave New World of Political Skulduggery? Anti-Clinton Video Shows Ease of Attack in the Computer Age', in which they said that the 'ad's reach blows up any notion that candidates and mainstream media outlets can control the campaign dialogue. Especially online' (Kurtz & Vargas 2007).

Reporting war in cyberspace

In a world of **network-centric warfare**, a propaganda war is played out in cyberspace. In the case of the second Gulf War, combat film footage from Iraq was posted on YouTube from the perspectives of the insurgent forces and the Americans. Clean, crisp images from unmanned US aerial vehicles were brought to the public through internet forums such as YouTube by 'warrior intellectuals' (Correy 2007). The Americans fought the insurgents in **cyberspace**, on blogs, in **chatrooms** and on YouTube, where they delivered the message that tribal leaders were fighting against Al-Qaeda and that the US troops were doing better than the mainstream media was portraying. The same practice is still occurring in Afghanistan where combat film footage is regularly posted on YouTube. In February 2011, a search of YouTube showed that there were more than 500 individual postings under the 'Afghanistan war' title and similar numbers under 'Afghanistan war footage'.

According to David Morris, academic, former US marine and the author of *Storm on the Horizon* (2004), guerrilla film directors used film as a weapon in the Iraq war. But Morris says the Americans did not anticipate how quickly and effectively insurgent groups would take up the new medium and use it for their own propaganda purposes. Insurgent groups were able to use cyberspace within Arab cultural and language groups to get their message across, with footage of captured Americans posted within minutes of offensives. According to Morris (2004), the Iraq war was a storytelling war that was fought from the perspective of who could get the first footage out on the World Wide Web.

Network-centric warfare (NCW): A new military doctrine or theory of war, pioneered by the US Department of Defense, which seeks to translate an information advantage into a competitive war fighting advantage through the robust networking of well-informed, geographically dispersed forces that enables new forms of organisational behaviour.

Cyberspace: The notional realm in which electronic information exists or is exchanged; the imagined world of virtual reality.

Chatroom: A site on a computer network where online conversations are held in real time by a number of users.

J-bloggers and the Fourth Estate

As has been argued in the Introduction, bloggers who act in the role of journalists and use the medium of the internet—subscribing to the journalistic ideals of an obligation to the truth and to the public's right to information, acting independently from those they report on, operating under a value system (such as a **code of ethics**) and scrutinising those in power—can be regarded as web journalists. These new-age, new-media journalists are **J-bloggers**.

J-bloggers: Internet bloggers who act in the role of journalists disseminating newsworthy information, and who subscribe to the journalistic ideals of an obligation to the truth and the public's right to know.

code of ethics: A set of rules prescribing the ethical practices that all members of a profession should follow.

new media: The mechanisms for digitally transmitting information and entertainment.

Op ed: Contraction of 'opinion editorial'.

J-bloggers working within the **new media** have reclaimed some of the old traditions of a free and independent press, reporting without fear or favour. The new technologies of the internet and new media have brought the opportunity for J-bloggers to storm the ramparts of traditional journalism. Rosen (2005: 33) refers to the blog system as a 'new press online'. He says that there are certain things about blogs and the sphere of blogging that are dramatically different from what came before in publishing and the media (see the box below).

However, in a world saturated with news blogs, the public will likely gravitate to particular sites that will come to be regarded as the most credible and trustworthy—whether these are run by amateur or professional J-bloggers—thus in time creating a new hierarchy of influence.

Many journalists who have gained credibility and respect through working in traditional media have already established an influential blog presence. The blogs of Australian journalists Annabel Crabb and George Megalogenis, for example, operate in much the same way as the commentary and **op ed** columns in traditional media, but, significantly, they offer audience participation not possible in the traditional media formats.

Ten things radical about the blog in journalism

1 The blog comes out of a gift economy, whereas traditional journalism comes out of the market economy.
2 Traditional journalism is the domain of professionals, and amateurs are sometimes welcomed into it, whereas the blog is the domain of amateurs, and professionals are welcomed to it.
3 In traditional journalism, barriers to entry have been high. With the blog, barriers to entry are low: a computer, a new connection and a simple software program is all that's needed.
4 In the blog world every reader is actually a writer, who writes not so much for the reader but for other writers.
5 In traditional journalism, we imagine the public record accumulating, that is, becoming longer. In blogs, we imagine the public record tightening, becoming stronger, as links produce more links.

6 A blog can work journalistically if it reaches fifty or 100 souls who like it, use it and communicate through it. In traditional journalism, such a small response would be seen as a failure, but with blogs the intensity of a small response can spell success.

7 A blog is like a column in a newspaper, but whereas a column written by twelve people makes little sense and wouldn't work, a blog written by twelve people makes perfect sense, and does work.

8 In traditional journalism, the story went to an editor and the editor represented the reader. With a blog, the story goes directly to readers, and the readers represent an editor.

9 In traditional journalism, information flows from the press to the public. In the blog world, information flows from the public to the press.

10 Traditional journalism assumes that democracy is what we have and information is what we seek. In the weblog world, information is what we have and democracy is what we seek.

Source: adapted from Rosen (2005: 21–36).

Arianna Huffington

Arianna Huffington is an independent blogger who can rightfully claim the mantle of J-blogger. Born in Greece in 1950 and educated at Cambridge University, Arianna Huffington is the co-founder and editor-in-chief of the *Huffington Post*, an online news and blog site launched in 2005. She is also a nationally syndicated columnist in the USA, an acclaimed author and the co-host of *Left, Right and Center*, an American public radio political round-table program. Following its launch in May 2005, the *Huffington Post* quickly became one of the most widely read, linked to and frequently cited news sites on the internet. In 2006, Huffington was named in the *Time* 100, *Time* magazine's list of the world's 100 most influential people.

In addressing the issue of new media and the Fourth Estate, Huffington argues that the question as to whether blogs and other online media will eventually displace the traditional Fourth Estate (newspapers, television and radio) is the wrong question to ask. She claims that newspapers and television are not 'going away any time soon'. She says that, on the contrary, 'they complement each other; each one's weakness becomes the other's strength' (cited in Davis 2000). The mainstream media, she says:

> Sometimes suffers from attention deficit disorder—flooding the zone on stories like the death of Anna Nicole Smith, only to drop them after several weeks. On the other hand … the blogosphere tends toward obsessive-compulsive behaviour, picking over the tiniest details until a larger story emerges, as happened recently when Joshua Michael Marshall of *Talking Points Memo* recently began piecing together the details surrounding the firings of US attorneys.
>
> *Huffington Post* itself, while in some ways a symbol of the digital media revolution, also relies on older tools. Consider, not all of the company's 800 unpaid bloggers

transmit their columns via computer. The late Arthur Schlesinger, for instance, used to fax over printed versions of his copy, while Larry David phones his blog posts in from the set of *Curb Your Enthusiasm*. (Davis 2007)

News blogs and news websites offer an immediacy that newspapers can never match, and because of this they are attracting a new breed of journalists (the J-bloggers) who embrace the flexible delivery and nonstop nature of the new media. While these news blogs and news websites generally are the medium of the younger generation—most of whom rarely buy a newspaper but regularly log onto the World Wide Web for information and news—they are increasingly attracting a larger slice of the traditional audience market.

Stephen Mayne: J-Blogger

In 2000, former business journalist Stephen Mayne created *Crikey* (<www.crikey.com.au>), an independent Australian online news service that carries email commentary, analysis and gossip. His combination of gossip and anti-establishment reporting got Mayne into legal trouble several times, but he was still able to sell his site in 2005 for $1 million to publishers Eric Beecher and Diana Gribble, and it remains a popular and influential independent site today. In October 2007, Mayne launched a new site, *The Mayne Report*, a daily videoblog and subscription newsletter that focus on shareholder activism and corporate governance issues.

Are blogs the new mob?

If J-bloggers are the new journalists, then are blogs the new mob? Remember Henry Fielding's claim: 'None of our political writers ... takes notice of any more than three estates, namely, Kings, Lords and Commons ... passing by in silence that very large and powerful body which form the Fourth Estate in this community ... The Mob'? Media commentator Shelly Palmer (2006) refers to web blogs as **moblogs**, arguing that they form like 'regular mobs'. She says that they can 'be constructive or destructive, patriots or rebels—but unlike their flesh-and-blood counterparts, their ideas can have immense, virtually instantaneous impact on a worldwide platform' (Palmer 2006). She likens moblogs to a living thing:

Moblogs: Blogs where participants appear to behave like regular mobs, but unlike their flesh-and-blood counterparts, their ideas can have an instantaneous impact on a worldwide platform.

> Information now displays many of the characteristics we attribute to living things. It is born, it evolves, it eats, it excretes, it mutates—but, interestingly, it can no longer die. This was true on a small scale even before the 'great unwashed' learned to blog. However, this is the first time in history that an idea (good or bad, true or false) can travel worldwide instantaneously and live on with a permanent, un-erasable, record of itself. Burn all the books you like, the knowledge lives on in the ether. (Palmer 2006)

Palmer says that the most interesting attribute of moblogs is the way they self-assemble, evolve into points of view, then metamorphose and mutate into the next phase of their existence—gaining or losing the power to influence their audience. She argues that it is a 'fascinating twist' on our ability to communicate, which, for organisations that rely on central control, such as governments and corporations, it is not necessarily a good thing:

> No gatekeepers, no pundits, no leadership, just passionate points of view. Perhaps the legacy of RSS (Really Simple Syndication—the specification which enables blogging) will be the empowerment of a true Fifth Estate with a collective mind all of its own and the ability to amplify the voice of the people above all others. (Palmer 2006)

Blogs, or moblogs, are spontaneous, unedited first takes on the issues of the day; they are creating a global public discourse on unlimited issues, providing everyone with a platform upon which to express his or her view, much like the soapbox at Speaker's Corner in Sydney's Hyde Park. But are these sites, and the bloggers who post their opinions on them, all representative of Henry Fielding's mob (the group of individuals sitting in the reporter's gallery in parliament) or are these mobloggers the other mob: the masses protesting outside of the parliament? Is the new medium of the World Wide Web merely providing the soapbox—or the protest meeting place—for the masses in the twenty-first century? Does the speaker on the soapbox or the blogger act under the journalistic rubric of the Fourth (or Fifth) Estate, or is she merely expressing a right as an individual to free speech?

One important point of difference sets the blogger apart from the public orator of times past: accountability. While the hecklers in the crowd would have publicly challenged the soapbox speaker—wanting to know where the speaker got his or her information, who was the source, and what was the agenda—today's web orators can sidestep accountability by posting opinions anonymously. Without accountability and without gatekeepers to question their utterances, anonymous bloggers face the criticism that they are no more than poison-pen letter writers of the twenty-first century. These anonymous bloggers, who sidestep accountability, surely cannot claim the mantle of J-bloggers.

Julian Assange and WikiLeaks

> WikiLeaks is a non-profit media organisation dedicated to bringing important news and information to the public. We provide an innovative, secure and anonymous way for independent sources around the world to leak information to our journalists. We publish material of ethical, political and historical significance while keeping the identity of our sources anonymous, thus providing a universal way for the revealing of suppressed and censored injustices. (WikiLeaks n.d.)

WikiLeaks is arguably the most significant development in journalism in the twenty-first century to date. The collaboration of traditional news organisations with the WikiLeaks organisation opens up new possibilities for the development of the Fourth (or Fifth) Estate. Australian Julian Assange founded the not-for-profit organisation WikiLeaks in 2006 as a user-editable **wiki** where people could anonymously post secret and classified documents. Within a year of its launch the site claimed to have a database of more than 1.2 million documents. It soon changed from the wiki format by disallowing comments or edits, and today works in a traditional publication role with an editorial team that vets material from anonymous sources.

WikiLeaks: A non-profit online media organisation that publishes otherwise unavailable documents from anonymous sources.

Wiki: A server program that enables users to collaborate in forming the content of a website. Users edit the content of other users.

The site gained worldwide attention in April 2010 when it posted a video on a website called *Collateral Murder*, which showed US forces killing Iraqi civilians and journalists. Three months later WikiLeaks released 76,900 secret documents about the war in Afghanistan, called *Afghan War Diary*, and then in October 2010, in collaboration with leading world newspapers, the organisation released 'The Iraq War Logs', 391,832 reports that document the war and occupation in Iraq, from 1 January 2004 to 31 December 2009 (except for the months of May 2004 and March 2009), as told by soldiers in the US Army. Each is a SIGACT or significant action in the war. They detail events as seen and heard by US troops on the ground in Iraq and are the first real glimpse into the secret history of the war that the US government has been privy to throughout (Schechter 2010). In November 2010, WikiLeaks began publishing 251,287 leaked US embassy cables, the largest set of confidential documents ever to be released into the public domain. According to the WikiLeaks: 'The documents will give people around the world an unprecedented insight into the US Government's foreign activities' (WikiLeaks 2011a).

WikiLeaks's founder, Julian Assange, an internet activist and journalist, is an elusive character, who until his arrest in late 2010 was reluctant to expose his private life. Concerns that he may be killed saw Assange sign a publishing deal for his autobiography, which was released in April 2011 by Canongate Books. 'I hope this book will become one of the unifying documents of our generation. In this highly personal work, I explain our global struggle to force a new relationship between the people and their governments,' Assange said of the memoir.

Assange was born in Townsville in northeastern Australia where he was predominantly home schooled by his mother. He became interested in computers from a young age and by sixteen was hacking computers, 'reportedly assuming the name Mendax—from the Latin *splendide mendax*, or "nobly untruthful"' (Harrell 2010). Four years later, Assange and some fellow hackers broke into the master terminal of Nortel, the Canadian telecom company. According to *Time* magazine, 'He was caught and pleaded guilty to 25 charges; six other charges were dropped. Citing Assange's "intelligent inquisitiveness", the judge sentenced him only to pay the Australian state a small sum in damages' (Harrell 2010).

Assange studied physics and mathematics at The University of Melbourne, but dropped out 'convinced that work by others in the department was being applied by defense contractors and militaries' (Harrell 2010). He founded WikiLeaks in 2006 under the Sunshine Press organisation. In December of that year the website published its first document:

> a decision by the Somali Islamic Courts Union that called for the execution of government officials. WikiLeaks published a disclaimer that the document may not be authentic but 'a clever smear by US intelligence'. The website went on to get several prominent scoops, including the release in April 2010 of a secret video taken in 2007 of a US helicopter attack in Iraq that killed a dozen civilians, including two unarmed Reuters journalists. Assange helped post the video from a safe house in Iceland that he and the other WikiLeaks administrators called 'the bunker'. (Harrell 2010)

Assange is not a trained journalist, and has not worked in traditional news media; his expertise is in information technology. But in establishing WikiLeaks and disseminating secret documents, he is acting in the role of a journalist. Remember, our definition for a journalist is 'someone who gathers and disseminates new information about current events, trends,

Source: In journalistic terms, someone who communicates information to a journalist.

issues and people to a wide audience'. Assange and his fellow workers at WikiLeaks gather and disseminate previously secret information on important political, social and economic issues. They are the gatekeepers between the whistleblower (the **source** in journalistic terms) and the public. Assange and his fellow workers employ journalistic routines in vetting and fact-checking material that is leaked to them. It is WikiLeaks's organisational review structure (the traditional gatekeeping of journalism) that sets WikiLeaks apart from other online sites that upload secret documents. As journalism academic Christian Christensen argues:

> There are literally hundreds of videos on YouTube from Iraq and Afghanistan showing coalition forces engaged in questionable, and in some cases obviously illegal, acts of aggression. Yet none of these clips have had anything like the impact of the single video posted to WikiLeaks showing scores of civilians (and two Reuters journalists) gunned down by high-powered aircraft artillery in a Baghdad suburb. (Christensen 2010)

Following the release of the *Afghan War Diary* and the leaked US embassy cables, it was WikiLeaks's partnership with old media, and its adherence to traditional journalistic practices, that gave these documents immediate credibility and increased their impact. This partnership with the influential mainstream newspapers, such as the *Guardian*, the *Times*, the *New York Times*, *Der Spiegel* and the *Sydney Morning Herald*, is an acknowledgment of the role WikiLeaks is playing as a part of the Fourth Estate.

The global public support for WikiLeaks grew throughout 2010 as those with much to fear from the organisation pressured businesses and institutions to cut WikiLeaks adrift. First, WikiLeaks was removed from the servers of Amazon, its US host, then it was removed from a smaller back-up host. In response, it moved to a Swiss domain, and then to a simple numeric web address. The attempts to shut down WikiLeaks saw Assange's supporters strike out online by setting up mirror sites to help WikiLeaks stay live. According to *Time* magazine's Massimo Calabresi:

> By December 8 WikiLeaks had listed more than 1,200 Web addresses that it said were hosting the site worldwide. WikiLeaks continued to publish about 100 cables a day from its vast trove of classified material. And before he surrendered in London, Assange distributed a heavily encrypted 1.4-gigabyte file to supporters that he said contained unedited secrets from WikiLeak's stash; a handful of trusted advisers hold the key to decode the file, said Assange, and will release it if he dies or WikiLeaks is destroyed. (Calabresi 2010: 12)

It was the development of this new dynamic between the public and the journalist that set WikiLeaks apart from other citizen journalism sites and potently demonstrated the influence the organisation has. Crucially, for the Fourth Estate, it also opened up new possibilities for collaborations between citizens and traditional journalism. The spark was the decision of several financial institutions—including PayPal, MasterCard and Visa—to block donations to WikiLeaks. However, the organisation and its worldwide supporters were prepared: the financial institutions found their own online sites temporarily brought down by hackers supporting Assange. According to Michael Elliott, 'In the supposedly virtual world of cyberspace, an army of real people were anointing their new hero' (Elliott 2010).

As the organisation came under siege from financial institutions and web hosts, WikiLeaks forwarded the following post from John Perry Barlow, former Grateful Dead lyricist and founder of the Electronic Frontier Foundation (a First Amendment advocacy group in the USA) to 300,000 of its own followers: 'The field of battle is WikiLeaks. You are the troops.'

And when Assange was imprisoned in London in December 2010 to await possible extradition to Sweden to face charges of sexual abuse (with resonances of John Wilkes; see Chapter 2), leading law experts, including Australian Geoffrey Robertson, offered their services free of charge, and funds came into the organisation to assist Assange.

US Republicans announced that they wanted Assange extradited to the USA to be tried and they were willing to pass new legislation specifically tailored to enable this to happen. The US Department of Justice began looking at the *Espionage Act* of 1917 to see if any charges could be laid. Even traditional journalism organisations in the US were initially critical of WikiLeaks and denied it was journalism. The Society of Professional Journalists and the Newspaper Association of America, which had been working for years with members of Congress to pass a federal reporter's shield law, felt their efforts were 'imperiled by WikiLeaks' (Peters 2010). The groups said the website did not do journalism and thus the shield would not protect it (Lee 2010). The executive director of the Reporters' Committee, Lucy Dalglish, criticised WikiLeaks as 'not journalism', claiming it was 'data dissemination' (cited in Lee 2010).

Journalism academic and member of the Ohio bar, Douglas Peters, argues that WikiLeaks and Assange would fail the US First Amendment–based journalistic privilege because 'WikiLeaks is not involved in investigative reporting and that the content disseminated is not news … it is not engaged in investigative reporting, a process that involves more than the mere dumping of documents and requires the minimization of harm' (Peters 2010: 11). Journalist Douglas Lee saw this announcement as 'journalists marking their territory':

> Whatever awkwardness previously existed as journalists desiring a federal shield law wooed the legislators they're supposed to be watching, it's now worse. In recent weeks, the two groups have publicly joined forces to exclude WikiLeaks from possible protection under the bill. In doing so, journalists have managed both to look territorial and to endanger the independence they're striving to create. (Lee 2010)

Then New York Democrat and Senate sponsor of the *Free Flow of Information Act*, Charles Schumer, and California Senator Dianne Feinstein announced that they were 'working with representatives of the newspaper industry in crafting the new language that will explicitly exclude organisations like WikiLeaks—whose sole or primary purpose is to publish unauthorized disclosures of documents—from possible protection'. In response, Lee commented, 'It doesn't seem all that long ago that representatives of the newspaper industry would have recoiled from working with Congress to deny legal protection to anyone who leaked confidential or classified documents. Today, however, they seem happy to be doing so' (Lee 2010).

According to Lee, the president of the Society of Professional Journalists Kevin Smith acknowledged that 'he was concerned that WikiLeaks's posting of the classified documents might derail the shield law. This is the closest we've come to getting something moved and it's unfortunate that this WikiLeaks situation's come up' (cited in Lee 2010). Lee argued that it would be 'more unfortunate, however, if journalism organizations, in their zeal to see a federal shield law finally pass, encouraged Congress to restrict the Act's protection to those who practiced journalism only in a particular way' (Lee 2010).

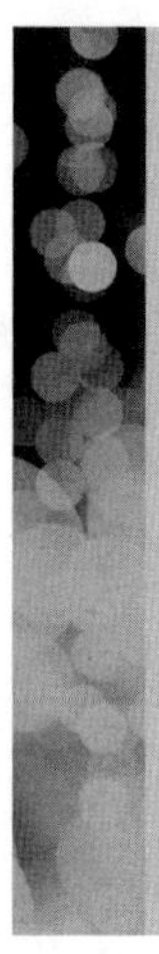

'The big game has been changed forever'

Australian broadcaster Phillip Adams, who is a member of the WikiLeaks advisory board, said the following at a WikiLeaks support rally in Sydney, Australia, on 15 January 2011:

> The big game has been changed forever—the mighty will always be looking over their shoulders and find it harder to lie. Or at least find new ways to do it. Democracy is being democratised, tyrannies exposed and millions who've been fed bullshit for generations are now able to confirm their suspicions. Any attempt to hand over Assange to the US—or any other country seeking to silence WikiLeaks—must be resisted. Australian governmental attacks on WikiLeaks? A disgrace.

What of the claims that WikiLeaks is not practising journalism and Julian Assange is not a journalist? WikiLeaks's explanation of its practice—'We publish material of ethical, political and historical significance while keeping the identity of our sources anonymous, thus providing a universal way for the revealing of suppressed and censored injustices'—mirrors traditional journalistic practice. Assange and his workers receive secret documents from the public, just as traditional journalists receive secret documents from whistleblowers, and Assange and his workers use traditional journalistic gatekeeping practices of verification and fact checking (in collaboration with traditional news outlets) to publish material that questions the actions of governments and powerful elites.

Whether WikiLeaks is stand-alone journalism or a part of a new journalistic process is still under discussion, but the important point is that the WikiLeaks model has changed the way traditional news organisations access leaked documents, and it has changed the way citizens and sources interact with the news media.

WikiLeaks, importantly, does not see its role within the business model of journalism; it describes itself as a 'not-for-profit media organisation' that has adopted 'journalism and ethical principles' to guide its operations, characterised on the site as journalistic in nature:

> When information comes in, our journalists analyse the material, verify it and write a news piece about it describing its significance to society. We then publish both the news story and the original material in order to enable readers to analyse the story in the context of the original source material themselves. (WikiLeaks 2011b)

Assange and WikiLeaks have increasingly been singled out for new media awards. In 2008, WikiLeaks won the *Economist*'s New Media Award; in 2009, Assange won the Amnesty New Media Award for work exposing hundreds of recent extrajudicial assassinations in Kenya; in 2010, the New York City *Daily News* listed WikiLeaks as the preeminent website 'that could totally change the news'; in 2010, Assange was named *Time* magazine's people's choice person of the year; and in early 2011, WikiLeaks was nominated for a Nobel Peace Prize. Norwegian parliamentarian Snorre Valen entered WikiLeaks as a candidate for the prestigious prize because, while WikiLeaks's work in exposing government secrets had earned it the enmity of countries around the world (and especially the USA), the organisation deserved the prize for contributing to world peace. 'One instance is the exposure of the corruption in Tunisia, where [ousted president Zine El Abidine] Ben Ali, the dictator, was exposed. That contributed, in a small part, to the fall of a more than 24-year-long regime,' Valen said.

Assange and his team claim they have been careful not to recklessly endanger the lives of vulnerable individuals, for example, by withholding more than 15,000 documents about the war in Afghanistan in 2010 until the names of Afghan civilians, who might be endangered if their identities became known, were redacted. However, there have been instances where it has been argued that WikiLeaks has unwittingly placed sources at risk, and the organisation has changed some of its practices to ensure greater protection of its sources.

Like the crusading eighteenth-century journalist John Wilkes, Assange is on a mission to make the powerful accountable. By challenging powerful institutions, WikiLeaks is augmenting democratic discourse. By publishing leaked documents that expose the actions of governments and the powerful, and making them more accountable for their actions, WikiLeaks is an organisation that upholds the ideals of the Fourth Estate as laid down by Henry Fielding. Indeed, *Time* believes that WikiLeaks 'could become as important a journalistic tool as the Freedom of Information Act'. Further, efforts, particularly in the USA, to use 'a high-minded debate about freedom of speech' to try to shut down WikiLeaks will 'surely succeed in energizing all sorts of new Web publishers based on the WikiLeaks model' (Calabresi 2010).

Conclusion

The news media do not always serve us well. Across all platforms—newspapers, television, radio, mobile phones and the World Wide Web—news is often fragmented and inconsistently delivered. Misinformation and untruths often spread like wildfire, and this information, once out in the global community, is almost impossible to rectify or to correct. The multiple platform delivery of news in the twenty-first century provides consumers with many choices, but it can also cause information overload, resulting in consumers looking for news sources they can trust.

There is reason to be concerned that the tabloid style of news is becoming the dominant format for delivering news, leading to a reduction in hard news content and a rise in infotainment, and resulting in far less public scrutiny through investigative reporting of those in positions of power. As consumers of the news media, as media practitioners and as media academics, we all must be vigilant in our scrutiny of the role of the Fourth Estate in the twenty-first century, and we must be outspoken in our concerns.

Despite these challenges, the Fourth Estate is alive, and it will continue to exist in the traditional form of the Fourth Estate and in the world of new media, of J-bloggers, WikiLeaks, Indymedia, text news messages and video blogs, where it may well wear the mantle of the 'Fifth Estate'. The WikiLeaks case speaks to the power of technology to make us rethink what we mean by 'journalism' and the Fourth Estate in the early twenty-first century. Fielding's Fourth Estate will survive wherever individuals, acting as journalists, are committed to respecting the truth and the public's right to information, are dedicated to informing citizens and to exposing abuses of power, and are committed to accurately describing society to itself.

To draw from that famous journalist and novelist Mark Twain, reports of the death of the Fourth Estate have been greatly exaggerated. In the 1770s it took a radical journalist and newspaper publisher, John Wilkes, to bring about a free press; in the twenty-first century it has taken another radical journalist and publisher in Julian Assange to remind us of what is possible in the digital age, and to potently demonstrate that journalism, far from being dead, has new technologies at its disposal to reinvigorate both journalistic practice and the Fourth Estate, and to remind all of us of the crucial role journalism plays in informing global citizens and in keeping those in positions of power accountable.

KEY REFERENCES

Ester, H. (2007). 'The Media'. In C. Hamilton & S. Maddison (eds) *Silencing Dissent.* Sydney: Allen & Unwin.

Flew, T. (2002). *New Media: An Introduction.* South Melbourne: Oxford University Press.

Lee, D. (2010). Trying to exclude WikiLeaks from shield law stinks. First Amendment Centre, 25 August. <www.firstamendmentcenter.org/commentary.aspx?id=23303>. Accessed 18 January 2011.

Rosen, J. (2005). 'Each Nation Its Own Press'. *Barons to Bloggers: Confronting Media Power.* Melbourne: Miegunyah Press.

Zelizer, B. (2004). *Taking Journalism Seriously: News and the Academy.* California: Sage.

WEBSITES

WikiLeaks: <http://wikileaks.ch>

Huffington Post: <www.huffingtonpost.com/>

CHAPTER 4

THE ELEMENTS OF WRITING

LIZ TYNAN

Introduction

As an aspiring writer, you should understand the foundations of our language, whether you plan to be a journalist, scriptwriter, public relations practitioner or a producer. As your career progresses you may well subvert everything you learn here, but only people who understand the rules can break them and not compromise their ability to convey meaning. The theme throughout this chapter is the need to analyse and hone your own writing to make it grammatically correct and to conform to professional style and convention. This chapter should be read in conjunction with Chapter 14 ('Subediting, News Language and Convention'). English grammar is a very large subject, and it is not all covered here. This chapter simply provides an overview, with special reference to what professional writers of all kinds will find helpful to know.

In this chapter we will look at:

- why journalists and other media professionals need to understand grammar and writing conventions
- the nature of grammar and why we need it
- recognising important parts of speech
- writing correct grammatical sentences.

An interesting observation

It is telling that most people who rail in various public forums against the imposition of grammatical rules usually do so in impeccably correct English—to ensure that the rest of us clearly understand their meaning. Even people who claim not to like grammar will still use it to make a point against grammar.

What does grammar have to do with journalism and the media?

Language is a clever, intricate machine that can run smoothly and get you where you want to go without breaking down. Or it can splutter and cough and sound wonky and get you nowhere. In this chapter we are going to pare the language back, take it apart and see how it operates. We need to understand it at its most basic level before we put it back together. It is certainly possible for people to make themselves understood without ever understanding the inner workings of the engine of language. But for the elite professional writer, it is necessary to go a bit further: to introduce not just correctness but also grace and economy, power and control.

Expanding on the car analogy may help. Most people who use cars have no idea what goes on under the bonnet. This ignorance is not helpful, though, if you want to run your car at its best and develop it into a performance vehicle. To do that, you have to understand its mechanics. It's the same with writing. To be a reader you don't necessarily need to understand the technicalities of **grammar** and usage. To be a writer—to be a good writer anyway—you have a responsibility to know your way around the intricacies of the language so that you can use it as a precision instrument. You must learn correct grammar, punctuation and word usage to have complete control over your writing. You may find that when you work in a communication profession there will be some flexibility in the application of grammatical rules, but it is essential that you know those rules first before you attempt to vary them. Grammar is an important tool (though not the only one) for ensuring that your message can always be understood without delay or difficulty.

Grammar: The rules of the relationship that words have to one another in a sentence.

George Orwell

One of the greatest writers in English, George Orwell, famously said, 'Good prose is like a window pane'. He meant by this that clarity is the prime requirement of prose writing. Good writing helps people to see concepts, ideas and actions clearly. One of the most important tools for achieving clarity is grammar. Always keep in mind that grammar is not an end in itself but a means by which you can make yourselves better understood. In any communication activity, aim for clarity. All prospective journalists should read Orwell's essay on writing, 'Politics and the English Language' (Orwell 1946), which expands upon the reasons clarity is so important. Orwell was a journalist as well as a fiction writer. Here are his timeless hints for great writing:

1. Never use a metaphor, simile or other figure of speech that you are used to seeing in print.
2. Never use a long word when a short word will do.
3. If it is possible to cut out a word, always cut it out.
4. Never use the passive when you can use the active.
5. Never use a foreign phrase, scientific word or jargon word if you can think of an everyday English equivalent.
6. Break any of these rules sooner than say anything outright barbarous.

What is grammar, and why do we need it?

Grammar has come to mean the description of the relationship words have with one another in a sentence. Although for centuries the word 'grammar' specifically related to ancient Greek and Latin, grammatical analysis is possible for all the languages of the world. English owes much to Greek and Latin, and many of the grammatical forms of ancient times apply today. More modern concepts of grammar have evolved too, and these have challenged some of the tenets of traditional grammar. But it remains true that traditional grammar is helpful to know, particularly for the student of writing. Good grammar is not pedantry; it is a courtesy to your reader and a sign of true professionalism.

Language is our dominant form of communication, and humans need to be able to speak and write using a set of rules common to everyone, so that we can all understand each other. Grammar provides the rules that enable us to express our inner thoughts to the external world in a cogent and consistent manner. It is the structure into which we can pour our ideas, with the hope that the listener or reader can make sense of what is being said or written; if you do it properly, your reader will be able to process the information without having to spend much time trying to decipher what you mean. Ungrammatical, unstructured writing invariably is hard to read, and it puts an unnecessary burden on the reader. In a profession devoted to efficient, rapid communication, this is not an option.

The elements of English: nouns, verbs, adjectives and adverbs

In English, nouns, verbs, adjectives and adverbs make up the largest part of the vocabulary. They are often called the **content words** of a language, and in English new ones are added frequently (words such as 'cyberspace', 'phishing', 'googled' and 'downsize', for example). The other main kinds of words are **function words**. These are conjunctions, prepositions and articles, which, in various ways, join together related parts of sentences. It may be helpful to think of these words as the glue that holds the sentence together. These tend not to be added to in English—we just stick to the same ones that have been used for years. Among these words you will find conjunctions such as 'and' or 'but', prepositions such as 'on', 'by', 'with' or 'from', the definite article 'the' and indefinite articles 'a' or 'an'. In this chapter we are concerned mostly with the content words rather than function words.

Content words: Nouns, verbs, adjectives and adverbs; the largest part of the English vocabulary and the words that supply substance.

Function words: Conjunctions, prepositions and articles; words that help to show the relationship between content words, thus giving meaning to the content words.

Taking the content words one at a time, let's start with nouns. The simplest possible way of defining them is to say that they are used to name objects (such as 'tree') and abstract concepts and feelings (such as 'discussion' or 'affection'). Nouns fall into two main groups. People who play Scrabble will know that they can't get away with using proper nouns, which are specific in naming individual people or entities, and are written with an upper case first letter, such as Canberra or Murray River. Scrabble players are, however, allowed to use common nouns, which are generic, that is, they refer to any member of a class of things. You will also come across another class related to common nouns, called collective nouns.

These refer to collections of items, for example, a company, organisation, team, crowd or community. Collective nouns operate grammatically in the same way as singular nouns.

Collective nouns are an important concept in news writing and a source of common errors among people new to professional media work. We will come back to them later, as it is important to link nouns to the correct form of verbs in order to make sense.

Nouns have an important associate, known as the pronoun. Pronouns are words such as 'it', 'him', 'her', 'their' and many others, which stand in for a noun. Pronouns are useful for making the language flow more smoothly. For instance, it is quite natural to say 'Chris is going overseas and she can hardly wait'; the pronoun here is 'she'. It would sound odd to say 'Chris is going overseas and Chris can hardly wait'. When you use a pronoun, the noun to which it refers is known as its antecedent. The antecedent of 'she' in our example is 'Chris'.

Pronouns may also be in first, second or third person: 'I bring the picnic basket' uses a first person pronoun; 'You make the salad' uses second person; 'He opens the bottle' uses third person. Pronouns are interesting because they inflect. This simply means that they change their form depending upon their role in the sentence. Consider the following:

> *I* am going with Mark to the movies.
> Mark is going with *me* to the movies.

Here we are talking about the same person, but we use two quite different words: I and me. Why is this? Pronoun inflection is a remnant from ancient times, reflecting that fact that in the early languages to which English can be traced back, all nouns and pronouns were inflected. You can see this clearly if you look at, for example, ancient Latin. In this language you might see a name such as Marcus at the beginning of the sentence, but it could appear as Marcum or perhaps Marco when the word is needed to fulfil a different grammatical role. This was also the case for pronouns. In English we do not inflect nouns, but we do inflect pronouns. This means that the form of the word will depend on whether it is being used as a subject or an object. In the sentences 'I am going with Mark to the movies' and 'Mark is going with me to the movies', my grammatical position changes, in this case, from subject to indirect object, and therefore the form of the pronoun must change. Usually, people instinctively inflect pronouns without knowing anything about their special nature, but errors can easily creep in. Consider these two sentences:

> My husband and I will open this fete.
> This fete is to be opened by my husband and I.

One of these is incorrect, even if you may have heard something like it said by royalty. In the second sentence, note what happens when you remove 'my husband and': the sentence becomes 'This fete is to be opened by I'. It is clearly incorrect when you look at it like this. Always check your pronouns to ensure that you have inflected them properly. Here's another example:

> Him and me went out to dinner.

By testing each pronoun in turn here, you can better see what the problem is: 'Him went out to dinner' and 'Me went out to dinner'. These sentences need to have their pronouns inflected correctly, to become 'He and I went out to dinner'.

Verb: The word in a sentence that conveys action.

Next we turn to **verbs**. Verbs may well be the most important words in news media because journalism is always about things happening, and concepts of action can only be conveyed by verbs. We know that nouns name the items being referred to. Verbs describe what the items do. They are commonly known as the doing or action words, and they drive the action of the sentence. Some simple examples are 'horses gallop' and 'journalists write'. The verbs 'gallop' and 'write' are simple verbs, that is, they are only one word. But verbs can also be more complicated than that. For instance, compound verbs are made up of two or even more words. An example might be

She turned off the television.

or indeed

She turned the television off.

or even

She was turning the television off.

Verbs may be in the past, present or future tense. For example, consider:

wrote (past tense)
writes (present tense)
will write (future tense)

Note that the future tense in English cannot be rendered with just one word. You always need another word to convey the sense of something that hasn't yet happened.

Also, less familiar verbal tenses, such as the past imperfect, past perfect and past continuous, are available in English to help us convey meaning. Think of some other forms of these verbs:

He has written
He is writing
He will be writing

So verbs take different forms, depending on their function in the sentence and the subtleties of meaning they are reporting. Their exact form changes depending upon the meaning you wish to convey. Understanding how to use verbs properly helps journalists to convey the complexities of stories. You should also understand the need for strong verbs, the verbs that carry meaning most clearly. For example, 'impacted on' or 'facilitated' do not carry as much meaning as 'damaged' or 'made possible'.

Remember: verbs are the powerhouses of sentences. They are the grammatical tools needed to indicate action, the main point of the many forms of media writing.

The foundation of journalistic sentences: S–V–O

Using nouns and verbs, we are now in a position to make the simplest of all sentences in English. This is called the subject–verb sentence, which consists of a noun and a verb. For example, we can say 'Annette writes'. This is grammatically correct, and contains

Subject: The topic of a sentence; what or who is performing an action in a sentence.

a **subject** (in this case, Annette) and a verb (writes), which stands on its own as descriptive of the action taking place. Note that, in grammatical terms, the subject is sometimes referred to as the topic, although it doesn't always mean that the sentence is only about the subject.

Intransitive and transitive verbs

In our example here, 'Annette writes', the present tense verb 'writes' does not need an object (that is, something being acted upon). Therefore, this particular verb, used in this particular sentence, is known as intransitive, which is the only kind of verb you can use in simple S–V sentences. You couldn't use a transitive verb in this sentence, for example, 'Annette sends', and still make sense. Some verbs have to have something to act upon and some don't. In the case of 'writes', this verb can be either transitive or intransitive, depending on the context of the sentence. In our S–V–O example, 'Annette writes a story', it is transitive.

Object: The thing being acted upon in a sentence; the subject of the sentence acts on its object.

S–V–O (subject–verb–object) sentence: A standard sentence structure in English containing a subject (what is acting), the verb (the action being taken) and object (what is being acted upon).

Most sentences do not have a structure as simple as containing just a subject and verb. The classical sentence construction in English has that other element referred to earlier: the **object**. This is the **subject–verb–object sentence**, often shortened to the **S–V–O** sentence. In this form, the verb connects the topic of sentence, Annette, to the thing being acted upon: the object, also known as the predicate, the comment or (in classical terms) the accusative case. So we might have another sentence such as 'Annette writes a story'. In this sentence, the object is 'a story'.

To recap, the subject (or topic) of this sentence is Annette. The direct object is 'a story', because this is the thing being acted upon by way of the verb. You may also have an indirect object, for instance, another sentence might be 'Annette writes the editor a story'. Here the indirect object is 'the editor'. The sentence will still have meaning without the indirect object. The purpose of the indirect object is to add more information about the direct object, to make the sentence more complete.

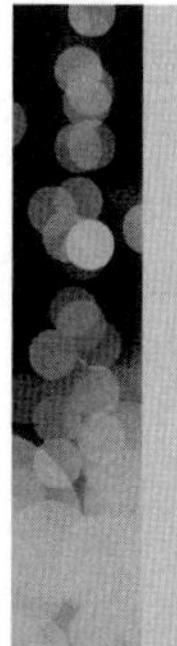

Spotting the grammatical subject

Keep in mind that subjects can have more than one element. For example, in the sentence

> The old man and his dog walked through the park.

the subject is 'The old man and his dog'.

Also note that the subject is not necessarily the first thing you read in a sentence. For example, in the sentence

> After visiting his patients, the doctor returned to the surgery.

the subject is 'the doctor'.

The S–V–O construction provides a simple sentence that fulfils the requirements of sentences in English, to convey meaning via a linear progression. In reality, most sentences are more complex than this (see later in this chapter for complex and compound sentences), but they still have this underlying structure, which, with practice, you will be able to discern. Being able to identify the parts of speech is the first step to really controlling your writing. Too often words are strung together to look like sentences: they start with a capital letter and end with a full stop, but what appears in between is not complete and is therefore ungrammatical.

Table 4.1 Identifying parts of the sentence: a guide to recognising the subject, verb, direct object and indirect object in a selection of sentences

	Subject	Verb	Object	Indirect object
He and I set up the projector.	He and I	set up	the projector.	
After eating at the restaurant, we saw a movie.	We	saw	a movie.	
Fire destroyed the building.	Fire	destroyed	the building.	
Police shot a man dead last night.	Police	shot	a man.	
Bernard is telling you the truth.	Bernard	is telling	the truth.	you
The editor bought the cadets a round of drinks.	The editor	bought	a round of drinks.	the cadets
I asked her a question.	I	asked	a question.	her

To be correct, sentences must be powered by the right verb. In the S–V–O formulation, only what is known as a finite verb is correct. In our S–V–O example, the finite verb is 'writes'. It is recognisable by the fact that it can be changed to indicate past, present or future tense: wrote, writes, will write. Verbs appear in many different forms, but what you have to look for are those verbs that indicate the driving action of the sentence. A common error is attempting to use the word 'being' for this purpose. This construction is wrong:

> This being the way the company has always operated.

Because the verb is wrong, this is not a complete sentence. The verb that has been used here is 'being', which cannot be used to create an S–V–O sentence. This string of words does not have a finite verb to power it, and it can only be grammatical if it is part of a bigger sentence:

> The driver delivers the products by truck, this being the way the company has always operated.

The operating verb in this construction is now the word 'delivers', which is a suitable finite verb. In this case, you could quite comfortably say 'delivered' for past tense, or 'will deliver' for future tense, and the sentence will still hold. You cannot do this with the verb 'being'.

Another way to fix this sentence would be to change the verb to something suitable. This may lead to a new sentence, such as:

> This is the way the company has always operated.

Your sentences are rarely as straightforward as 'Annette writes a story', but they will still display this logic even when they are more complicated. A journalistic sentence, such as 'Police charged a man yesterday with murder after the discovery of a body at the university', is an active and newsy sentence that has a subject–verb–object structure, with the addition of extra descriptive information. The part of the sentence that reads 'after the discovery of a body' is an adjunct phrase, but the subject–verb–object part is 'police charged a man', which you can see clearly conveys something that has happened and therefore informs the reader. Try to analyse your own sentences in terms of subject–verb–object to see if you can stick to this form as much as possible.

Remember: you can tell if a verb is the correct one to operate the sentence if you can change its tense to past, present and future. Other forms of verbs cannot do this.

More complicated sentences

Most journalistic writing will be simple, clear and straightforward. This can be achieved not only through the simple S–V–O construction, but also through a grammatically more complicated structure that has more than one clause. A clause is a group of words, containing a subject and verb, that forms part of a sentence; it is joined with another clause or clauses to form the complete sentence. Without getting too technical, these kinds of sentences are known either as complex sentences (a main clause and attached subordinate clause/s) or compound sentences (containing clauses of equal grammatical status). More than two clauses can make sentences convoluted, which is best avoided in media writing.

Here is an example of a complex sentence containing a main clause and a subordinate clause. Note that subordinate clauses are joined to the main clause either by a conjunction or, in certain cases, by a semicolon:

> The prime minister yesterday announced a sweeping review of the 1992 *Broadcasting Act*, though it was unlikely to reform the sector.

Here the conjunction is the word 'though'.

There are many other kinds of conjunctions. The most common (coordinating clauses)—which often joins clauses of equal status—is 'and', followed by 'but' and 'or'. Consider this sentence:

> The prime minister yesterday announced a sweeping review of the 1992 *Broadcasting Act* and she established an inquiry into the commercial radio sector.

In this case, both clauses can stand alone grammatically, once you remove the 'and'. This can't happen with the subordinate clause, earlier, where the second clause was dependent on the first.

There is disagreement on whether a comma should be used between clauses, particularly before 'and'. You will find some pedantry around this one—some editors swear blind that it is never acceptable to put a comma before a conjunctive 'and'. Yet many grammar books insist upon a comma before the 'and' in complex or compound sentences. This is often called the Oxford comma, in honour of the publisher of this book you are reading. What to do? Since

Australian media style is tending towards reducing the use of commas as much as possible, but correct grammar requires that commas be used to aid clarity, may we suggest the following rule? If, as we have seen in the compound sentence above, the clauses are coordinating and joined by 'and', then you don't use a comma. If, however, you are using a subordinate clause, then use a comma. Think of the following sentence:

> The prime minister yesterday announced a sweeping review of the 1992 *Broadcasting Act*, and about time too.

You will note that in our earlier complex sentence there was a comma before 'though'. To eliminate the comma between clauses entirely could cause confusion, but leaving it out between the clauses of compound sentences seems to work without upsetting the pedants too much.

Other punctuation elements can cause confusion. For example, the semicolon (;) is used to substitute for a conjunction—this is almost its only function, apart from separating elements of a list. Here is an example of it being used to stand in for a conjunction:

> Mary Shelley's works are entertaining; they are full of engaging ideas.

In this sentence the semicolon is taking the place of a conjunction such as 'because'. Semicolons and colons (:) are not interchangeable. They have different functions. To quote from Strunk and White (2000: 7):

> Use a colon after an independent clause to introduce a list of particulars ... an amplification or an illustrative quotation. A colon tells the reader that what follows is closely related to the preceding clause. The colon has more effect than the comma, less power to separate than the semicolon and more formality than the dash.

Here is an example of correct colon use:

> The squalor of the streets reminded her of a line from Oscar Wilde: 'We are all in the gutter, but some of us are looking at the stars.'

Subject–verb (S–V) agreement

As is often the case in English, the rule is simple but the execution more difficult. The subject of a sentence must agree with the finite verb of the sentence; if the subject is singular then the verb must be singular too. If it is plural, then the verb must be plural. This means that we write:

> The lawyer discusses her strategy.

and not

> The lawyer discuss her strategy.

Most people with a reasonable grasp of English will have no problem understanding S–V agreement here. But what happens when the sentence is a little less clear-cut? Consider these sentences:

> The adventure of professional writing—its trials, its joys, its challenges—are not soon forgotten.

and

> The adventure of professional writing—its trials, its joys, its challenges—is not soon forgotten.

The correct sentence here has to be the second example, even if it doesn't immediately seem right. Words that intervene between subject and verb do not affect the number (singular or plural) of the verb. But you can probably see how this could be a trap.

There are other traps as well. Consider the following:

> He is one of those people who is never ready on time.

or

> He is one of those people who are never ready on time.

Here the second sentence is correct. It is a common mistake to use a singular verb in a subject construction such as this, but you have to remember that the word 'people' here is the key part of the subject, rather than the singular 'one'.

Note that words such as 'no one', 'each', 'everyone' and 'everybody' generally take a singular verb. For example, 'Everyone is happy; no one is sad'. There can be a problem with the word 'none', which may operate as either singular or plural. In the following case, it is singular: 'None of us is perfect', in the sense of no one, or not one. However, it may be used in another sense as well, when 'none' is intended to mean more than one thing or person: 'None are so cherished as those who are no longer here.'

Collective nouns

Perhaps the biggest issue concerning subject–verb agreement, certainly in media newsrooms, is the form of the verb used in the case of collective nouns. This rule may appear to be counterintuitive, which may be why it is such a common error. It simply means that words such as government, council, university and many others take a singular verb (and a singular pronoun). The difficulties often arise in the case of collective nouns that sometimes have a plural sense. For example, in most cases 'family' is a collective noun that is treated singularly. But when there is a sense of the constituent parts acting plurally, it is slightly less clear-cut. For example, in the sentence 'The family put down their dishes', you would need to accept that this is a plural sense of a collective noun: to write 'The family put down its dishes' wouldn't sound right. Also, in sports journalism the rule often is quite flexible, to account for the fact that while a team is a singular entity, it is made up of constituent parts that act plurally.

ABC: The Australian Broadcasting Corporation (the Australian Broadcasting Commission from 1932 to 1983), Australia's public broadcaster, which is funded by the federal government rather than advertising.

The most important time to remember this rule is when writing about an organisation or company. Say you are talking about the **ABC**. This organisation is treated grammatically as a collective noun, and collective nouns always take singular verbs (and pronouns):

> The ABC broadcasts from its studios in the city.

Note that the finite verb in this sentence is the word 'broadcasts', and it is singular. You do not write:

> The ABC broadcast from their studios in the city.

As much as the tendency exists to think of an organisation or company as a plural entity, you must see it as a collective noun and always choose a singular verb to go with it. This applies to companies such as Microsoft or Nike, federal and state governments, and organisations such as the Red Cross and the army.

Active and passive voice

In English, unlike in various other languages, word order is crucial. It is not okay to reorder the words in our original sentence 'Annette writes the story' to become 'Annette the story writes'. But there is another way to convey the same message in a different word order. The concept of active voice and passive voice is important in journalism. 'Annette writes the story' is in active voice, because it follows the S–V–O construction. By its nature, it makes the topic of the sentence the most prominent. But you can also say 'The story is written by Annette', and what was the object now starts the sentence instead of appearing at the end, thus making this part of the sentence more prominent. It has swapped positions, and the subject (Annette) is now called the agent—'by Annette'. Note also that the verb has undergone a change. You must add in a new word (in this case 'is') to preserve the original meaning. The original verb also changes, from 'writes' to 'written'.

Passive voice is not recommended as a writing style because it tends to sound stilted and wordy. This sentence style always guarantees a compound verb, because passive verbs are always at least two words. But you can't always avoid passive voice. It may be necessary, for example, if the active subject is unknown or not easily stated. This might lead to a sentence such as 'Walter's father was killed in the Second World War', which is in the passive form. Because we don't know who or what actually killed Walter's father, it cannot be rendered in active voice. In this case, there can be no agent because we don't have enough information to be able to say who carried out the action of the sentence.

Sometimes, even when the agent is known, it is not stated. This is because it is common for passive voice to be used to distance the writer from the reader, and from responsibility for the action in the sentence, to lend the appearance of objectivity. You may have noticed that government papers and other official documents are filled with sentences in the passive voice. Consider, for example, this passive voice sentence:

> The hospital beds have been shut down.

There is no agent in this sentence, which has the effect of holding no one responsible for the action. It may well be that the sentence could correctly be rendered as:

> The hospital beds have been shut down by the Health Department.

In this case a journalist would rewrite it as:

> The Health Department shut down the hospital beds.

As professional writers, you must be sparing with the passive voice, because it can remove responsibility for actions as well as being difficult or confusing to read. You can't always eliminate it, but you can minimise it. The only way you can do this, though, is if you can recognise it when you see it. Also note that the concept of active and passive voice does not refer to tense. It is a common misconception that active voice is simply a sentence in the present tense. Either voice can be in any of the tenses. Table 4.2 lists some examples:

Table 4.2 Voice and tense

	Active	**Passive**
Past	I wrote the story.	The story was written by me.
Present	I write the story.	The story is written by me.
Future	I will write the story.	The story will be written by me

Passive voice tip

You can usually tell if you have written a sentence in the passive voice if, first, it has a compound verb such as 'was written', and also if the word 'by' is used to indicate the passive agent. Note, however, that in those sentences where the subject is not known (such as 'Walter's father was killed in the Second World War') or where the agent is being concealed ('The hospital beds have been shut down'), there is no agent indicated, and therefore no use of the word 'by'.

Adjectives

Adjectives describe a noun, adding further information of various kinds, for example, desirable, fatal, beautiful, allergic, happy, active, monstrous, nosy and angry. In English, adjectives may be recognisable because they have characteristic endings, such as -able, -al, -ate, -ful, -ic, -ive, -ous, -y and others. Adjectives also can be formed from verbs; for example, riding competition, sliced bread, deserted beach. And nouns may be used as adjectives: consider, for example, the Gillard government or tennis lessons. Adjectives usually do not have plural forms, but they may have degrees; for example, happy, happier and happiest.

Adverbs

Adverbs give more information about the action of the verb. An adverb can indicate time, manner, place, reason or purpose. It offers the answers to questions about the verb, such as where? why? when? how? what for? how long? how often? how much? Many adverbs of manner are formed from adjectives by the addition of -ly; for example, rapidly, smoothly, cleverly, stupidly, wildly and boldly. Other kinds of adverbs that indicate time, place and degree have no particular distinguishing form, so we must look at them in context to identify them as adverbs. In the sentence 'Let's go now', for example, the word 'now' is an adverb. You can recognise it by the fact that it adds more information to the verb 'go': it answers the question 'when?'

Adjectives and adverbs can be useful when used sparingly by media writers, but be ruthless in cutting out those that don't add sufficient information to justify their inclusion. Always weigh up the usefulness of every word in your sentences. This especially goes for adjectives and adverbs. Note also that adverbs and adjectives can lend bias to a piece of writing and may be a subtle form of editorialising. Note, for example, the differences in tone in the following sentences:

> At least five states have sensibly decided to give terminally ill patients the right to refuse medical treatment.

Or

> At least five states have decided to give terminally ill patients the right to refuse medical treatment.

The addition of the adverb 'sensibly' changes the tone of the sentence completely and adds editorial comment.

Conclusion

Language has a great deal of power in our culture, and perhaps nowhere more so than in the media. Powerful images are certainly important, but sometimes there is no substitute for crafting a strong news story, a vivid word picture, a telling line of dialogue or a masterful statement. The ability to write powerful, meaningful prose is a great responsibility as well as an enduring source of satisfaction for everyone who works in the media. Eloquence, grace and crispness are also highly regarded virtues. The foundations of the language will hold firm while you take your own writing to lofty heights. Without strong foundations, the heights may be harder to achieve.

KEY REFERENCES

Kaplan, B. (2003). *Editing Made Easy.* Melbourne: Penguin.

Orwell, G. (1946). 'Politics and the English language'. First published in *Horizon*, April 1946. Accessed: <www.orwell.ru/library/essays/politics/english/e_polit>.

Strunk, W. & White, E. B. (2000). *The Elements of Style* (4th edn). Boston: Allyn & Bacon.

Truss, L. (2003). *Eats, Shoots and Leaves.* London: Profile Books.

Watson, D. (2003). *Death Sentence: The Decay of Public Language.* Sydney: Random House.

CASE STUDY 1:

THE BATTLE FOR A FREE PRESS IN COLONIAL AUSTRALIA

NICOLA GOC

> 'I hate the whole tribe of news-writers,' Wellington told Peel in 1827. 'I prefer to suffer from their falsehoods to dirtying my fingers by communication with them.' (Aspinall 1945: 218)

Introduction

In the battle for a free and uncensored press in colonial Australia, a number of Australian newspaper editors and proprietors were jailed for libel. Colonial newspapers, like their counterparts in Britain, had significant influence over the formation of public opinion, and this position of power saw journalists and editors in conflict with the powerful elite.

Van Diemen's Land: Tasmania, the island state of Australia, was known by Europeans as Van Diemen's Land until 1853 when the name was changed to Tasmania (after Dutch explorer Abel Jansoon Tasman). The name change came in the same year that transportation of convicts to that colony ceased.

This case study examines the battle for a free press in colonial **Van Diemen's Land** (Tasmania) and will focus on three newspaper editors: Andrew Bent, Henry Melville and Gilbert Robertson. All three felt the wrath of the tyrannical colonial governor, Colonel George Arthur (who governed the island colony from 1825 to 1836) and were jailed for publishing libellous material in their newspapers, becoming the Australian fourth estate's first martyrs.

Andrew Bent and the *Hobart Town Gazette*

Andrew Bent, the proprietor of the *Hobart Town Gazette*, was bestowed the title of 'the father of Australian journalists' (West 1852: 108). It was Bent's stand against Arthur that precipitated interest in the principle of freedom of the press in Australia. While George Howe, the proprietor of Australia's first newspaper, the *Sydney Gazette*, is well known as the father of the Australian press, it was largely through the efforts of Bent and a group of newspaper editors in Van Diemen's Land that freedom of the press was established in Australia.

Bent was responsible for the introduction of three principles that today are accepted as unchallengeable: private ownership of the press, the expression of opinion in the form of editorials and the establishment of correspondents' pages through the letters to the editor (Woodberry 1972: 18).

Bent's *Hobart Town Gazette and Southern Reporter*, established in 1816, was the third newspaper in Van Diemen's Land. The first edition of the *Hobart Town Gazette* was published on 11 May 1816 when Bent was still a convict. Bent was dogged in his criticism of Governor Arthur, who was highly sensitive to such attacks. As an emancipated convict in a penal colony, where the power of the authorities was all encompassing, Bent was in a tenuous position—publishing his criticisms of the government put his personal freedom at considerable risk.

Bent arrived in Hobart Town in 1812 aged 22. Soon afterwards he was employed by George Clark, who in 1810 had established the first, short-lived Tasmanian newspaper, the *Derwent Star and Van Diemen's Land Intelligencer* (Pretyman 1966: 86). Within four years, and while still a convict, Bent had established the *Hobart Town Gazette*, receiving a small subsidy under an arrangement with Governor Davey by which his *Gazette* was the official organ for the publication of government notices. The newspaper remained entirely Bent's own property, but with a government-appointed editor to oversee the publication of the government notices. In 1825, Bent explained to his readers the significant production issues he experienced in producing his newspaper:

> Our type was so limited that we could not compose at once more than is contained in one of our present-sized columns. There was no printing ink in the colony, but what we were necessitated to manufacture in the best possible manner for ourselves, and common Chinese paper, no more than half the size of foolscap, and of which two sheets were consequently obliged to be pasted together for each gazette, cost two guineas sterling per ream! (*Hobart Town Gazette*, 6 January 1825)

In 1824 there were still only two newspapers in Australia—the *Sydney Gazette*, which was still closer in control to the government, and Bent's *Hobart Town Gazette*. George Howe had a far more cordial relationship with the New South Wales government in the running of the *Sydney Gazette* than did Bent with the Van Diemen's Land government. This partly reflected the fact that Bent's newspaper was the first to function as journalism and not merely as an adjunct to official news and reports (Miller 1952: 248).

Governor Arthur's arrival

In May 1824 Bent dismissed the government-appointed editor and replaced him with Evan Henry Thomas. A week later Colonel George Arthur arrived in the penal colony. Bent was blissfully unaware of Arthur's antipathy to the press and did not know then that Arthur was so opposed to a free press that he had previously refused permission to one of his closest supporters to create a newspaper in Honduras (Giblin 1939: 629).

However, within days of his arrival Arthur made it clear that Van Diemen's Land was first and foremost a penal colony. Arthur had little regard for the increasing number of free settlers and made it clear that he would not tolerate a press that was critical of his government.

Despite the risks of speaking out against Arthur's regime, the letters to the editor column in the *Hobart Town Gazette* began to take on a political tone. Gone were the recipes for snakebites, typhoid cures and tips on growing wheat in the antipodean soil; in their place were letters critical of the new regime.

A settler who wrote an indiscreet letter to the editor could lose the title to their land, see their allocation of convict servants withdrawn, discover important mail had disappeared or find supplies to the government store rejected—in effect he or she could be ruined. As Henry Melville later wrote: 'Scarcely is there a single settler in the Island, who is not dependent upon His Excellency's will and pleasure, either for his grant, or his decision in some dispute about boundary lines' (Melville 1835: 46). Letters critical of the government flooded into the *Gazette* office and Bent, despite his tenuous position as an emancipated convict, continued to publish them.

Arthur, incensed at the thinly veiled criticisms of his regime, was determined to gag the press and in June 1824 he publicly proclaimed the *Hobart Town Gazette* as government property. Bent immediately sent his editor Evan Henry Thomas to Sydney to seek redress. Months later Thomas returned 'big with glory' (Miller 1952: 227)—Arthur had no legal right to pirate the *Gazette*. The tone of Bent's editorial on 8 October was one of triumphant rectitude: 'Even yet the sling of an outraged "weak one" when brandished against the Gideonite of tyranny, must be, Laus deo, irresistible' (*Hobart Town Gazette*, 8 October 1824).

The newspaper remained in Bent's hands and the editorials and letters continued their anti-Arthur sentiment. Behind the scenes Arthur was planning to gag the press. In April 1825 he was negotiating for the purchase of the newspaper plant of the newly established Launceston newspaper, the *Tasmanian and Port Dalrymple Advertiser*. The irony was that the owner, George Terry Howe, son of George Howe of the *Sydney Gazette*, was supported in the establishment of the *Tasmanian* by none other than Bent, who acted as his Hobart Town agent. Bent knew that Howe was planning on relocating his press and newspaper to Hobart Town and supported the move 'in the hope that a cause of the freedom of the press might be strengthened' (Miller 1952: 71). But he didn't know of Arthur's involvement. Meanwhile, Bent's newspaper continued its attacks on Arthur's administration:

> It is much better that a few supine, ignorant and extravagantly-hired Public Officers should be galled for their misconduct than that a whole community should be crushed, enslaved and subjugated. (*Hobart Town Gazette*, 20 May 1825)

Separate editions of the *Hobart Town Gazette*

On 25 June 1825 Arthur played his trump card. Two separate editions of the *Hobart Town Gazette* appeared before the public: Bent's *Gazette* and another with identical masthead and volume number, which was filled with pro-Arthur sentiment and declared to be the 'official organ' of the colonial government.

An anti-Arthur letter, which had earlier been published by Bent under the pen name 'A Colonist', was boldly reprinted in Arthur's *Gazette* with every 'no' turned into a 'yes' and every 'unsatisfactory' into 'satisfactory' (Miller 1952: 248). Bent, incensed that he had been betrayed by a man he had supported, branded Howe a 'pirate' who had conspired to ruin him. He published a scathing attack regarding Arthur's alleged misdeeds while governor of Honduras, which led to the following correspondence between Governor Arthur and his attorney-general:

> Seeing that he [Bent] has continued week after week to insert in the *Gazette*, both in the leading article and under various signatures, the grossest falsehoods, and is systematically endeavouring to degrade the public functionaries of this Island, and to scandalise the government, I can no longer hesitate in desiring you to prosecute forthwith the various libels which have appeared in the *Hobart Town Gazette*—reflecting either upon the Government or the Governments officers. (*Historical Records of Australia* 111, vol. 6: 238)

Bent was sued for libel for the 'Gideonite of tyranny' editorial and the Honduras editorials. A public meeting was called by Friends of the Liberty of the Press, which raised £250 for Bent.

The public saw the suit as a persecution of the champion of the free press by a tyrannical governor. The first trial was abandoned and another held in April 1826 before a military jury of seven officers, all in the pay of the government. Not surprisingly, it found Bent guilty and he was sentenced to six months imprisonment and fined £518 (*Colonial Times*, 23 April 1826).

Word of the imprisonment of a newspaper proprietor in the Australian colonies for libel brought against him by a governor reached the London newspapers. The concept of the freedom of the press was by no means an accepted principle in England and was being fought out there in a series of clashes between newspapers and authorities. The *London New Monthly* reported on the colonial newspaper war:

> The printer of the *Hobart Town Gazette*, which the government seems anxious to suppress, has been found guilty of libel. The list of special jury is amusing in a colony where there are men to be found in a civil life equal to any that sat on that occasion … The matter charged as libellous would not have been thought so in the Mother Country. (*London New Monthly*, April 1826)

Arthur's Newspaper Act

A year later Arthur found other ways of gagging the press. On 29 September 1827 the *Hobart Town Gazette* published an announcement of the introduction of 'an Act to Regulate the Printing and Publishing of Newspapers, and for the prevention of blasphemous and seditious Libels' (*Hobart Town Gazette*, September 1827). The Act required proprietors to hold a licence to print or publish a newspaper. If the licensee published any matter tending to bring into contempt or hatred the royal family, the government or the Constitution of the United Kingdom or of Van Diemen's Land, the licence could be cancelled at once. Each licensee was also required to enter into a recognisance with surety of £400 and three guarantors, each with surety of £400, that no libel would be printed. The icing on the suppression of the free press cake was another Act imposing a stamp duty of three pence per copy. Naturally, Bent was refused a licence to print. A protest signed by fifty leading citizens claimed that the restrictions on the press were 'needless, unconstitutional and debasing—an insult to the colony, and contrary to the implied engagements of the Crown when emigration was invited'.

In the meantime, Bent was struggling financially to keep control of his newspaper, which he had renamed the *Colonial Times*. To add insult to injury, Arthur decreed that convicts could not be employed in printing houses, forcing Bent to dismiss his editor, the convict novelist Henry Savery. What really galled Bent was that convicts were employed in the government press. Arthur's actions were nothing short of persecution. Bent lost his battle to keep the *Colonial Times*, but kept his printing press and established a monthly news magazine, the *Colonial Advocate and Tasmanian Monthly Review*, in March 1828, thus avoiding the newspaper licence.

After being rejected by Arthur, the settlers' petition supporting Bent and freedom of the press was sent to the home government and in December 1828 news was received supporting the colonists and annulling both Acts (Melville 1835: 70). But it was too late for Bent's *Colonial Times*. With Bent effectively sidelined, Arthur turned a blind eye to the weekly attacks from other publications, but his patience reached its limit when the wild and headstrong journalist, editor and proprietor of the *True Colonist*, Gilbert Robertson, hit a raw nerve.

Gilbert Robertson and the *True Colonist*

By the 1830s, the public was under no illusions about Arthur's regime—cronyism was rife and most settlers knew of it. His nephews, Chief Police Magistrate Captain Matthew Forster and Colonial Secretary John 'Warming Pan' Montagu, were hated, feared and much resented for their blatant misuse of convict labour and public materials. Montagu was derisively called 'Warming Pan' because he was always ready to turn his hand to profitable enterprises using government labour and supplies (Goodrick 1978: 142). Arthur's cronyism and the relationship between Arthur's nephews and the editor of the *Tasmanian*, Robert Lathrop Murray, became the subject of much copy in Robertson's *True Colonist* (1834–44).

Murray, regarded as a turncoat, was known to his enemies as 'Old Scapenoosc' (Woodberry 1972: 143). It had been his anonymous letters opposing Arthur, published ten years earlier in Bent's correspondents' pages that had, in part, landed Bent in goal. Murray had then been unswerving in his criticism of Arthur's piracy of Bent's *Gazette* and of his attempt to control the press, but in the latter part of Arthur's governorship Murray had come full circle and now indulged in adulation of Arthur and sycophantic support of his nephews (Miller 1952: 24).

Robertson, a Creole brought up on his Scottish father's plantations in British Guyana, arrived in Van Diemen's Land in the mid 1820s to take up the position of superintendent of the government farm at New Town. He soon became interested in the press and at various times edited newspapers in opposition to Arthur. In 1834 he established the *True Colonist* and *Van Diemen's Land Political Dispatch and Agricultural and Commercial Advertiser*. The *True Colonist* became a political voice in vigorous opposition to Arthur and, it must be said, moderation was not high on Robertson's agenda.

In February 1834 Robertson was charged with three counts of libel: first, that he had made the assertion that Arthur had made a correction of a clerical error after the enrolment of a grant of land (the imputation being that if he corrected clerical mistakes he could make other alterations); second, that Robertson had claimed that hay from the government farm (which Robertson once supervised) was for Arthur's own use (a suggestion of larceny); and third, that Robertson made libellous comments regarding T. W. Rowlands, an Arthur supporter.

Robertson was swiftly found guilty and sentenced to thirteen months in jail. While he was incarcerated he was tried and found guilty on another count of libel against Warming Pan Montagu (*True Colonist*, 23 January 1835). Robertson conducted his own defence through the pages of his newspaper. When sentencing Robertson to a further year in the fetid Hobart Town jail, Attorney-General Gellibrand made the heated claim that a press such as Robertson's 'was like a firebrand in the hand of a madman' and that his articles were 'a pest even to Botany Bay' (*Colonial Times*, 14 July 1835).

Bent had remained steadfast to his principles of a free press, and when no one would print Robertson's newspaper after his imprisonment, Bent agreed to print the *True Colonist*, despite being on the brink of financial ruin. Bent, with costs and fines of £1500, and having served three terms of imprisonment, was still determined to fight for the principles of a free press. Robertson wrote of his gratitude to Bent:

> When we experienced some difficulty in getting our Journal printed at any office, our 'Tasmanian Franklin' immediately threw open gratuitously the use of his office, type and press to us, merely upon paying our workmen the amount of their wages. (*True Colonist*, 27 March 1835)

Henry Melville and the *Colonial Times*

Robertson soon found himself keeping company in jail with the highly regarded author, journalist, newspaper proprietor and editor Henry Melville. Trumped-up charges against innocent men and women who were perceived as enemies of the government were not uncommon during Arthur's regime. On a daily basis, spurious cases were brought before the courts against innocent and respectable citizens by corrupt convict constables who pocketed half of the fines imposed. Within this environment of corruption, the Robert Bryan case is particularly distasteful. Robertson avowed in the *True Colonist*: 'They may hang Robert Bryan, and imprison all the Editors in the Colony, but they may rest assured that justice will overtake them' (*True Colonist*, 13 November 1835).

The trial of Robert Bryan was no ordinary trial of a settler who had run afoul of the authorities. Bryan was the nephew of the influential and wealthy Irishman William Bryan, who arrived in the colony in 1824 and was appointed to the magistracy. After a falling out with the police magistrate, William Bryan resigned his position, and not long afterwards Arthur refused William Bryan's application for a land grant. When he was publicly critical of Arthur's administration, his convict labour was withdrawn at harvest time (Robson 1983: 298–302).

William Bryan formally charged Arthur and his nephew, Chief Police Constable Forster, with misuse of government property and labour, and made it known that he had sent his complaints back to the home government.

William Bryan also fell out with the local constabulary, known colloquially as 'Arthur's felon police' (*Colonial Times*, 15 September 1835). The stage was set for retribution, and William Bryan was charged with cattle duffing, a popular trumped-up charge of the day. After being found guilty and fined, he left the colony to return to Britain to personally make complaints to his influential contacts in the home government. It was while he was on this mission that Arthur extracted his revenge, seeing to it that Bryan's young nephew, Robert, was charged with the capital offence of cattle stealing.

The Crown case was based on the evidence of three convict constables who had been planted among the convict work party assigned to Bryan's property and who claimed to have witnessed Robert Bryan driving cattle onto his property. Such was the lieutenant-governor's interest in a case of cattle stealing that he travelled to Launceston in his personal carriage with, as his travelling companion, none other than Chief Justice Pedder, who was presiding over the case (*Colonial Times*, 3 November 1835). Arthur made sure that his three influential nephews daily attended the trial. Lengthy reports of the trial were published in the *Colonial Times*, the *Cornwall Chronicle*, the *Hobart Town Courier* and the *True Colonist*.

Arthur was still using military juries, despite the direction from the Secretary of State for the Colonies that civil juries should be instituted. Melville reported in the *Colonial Times* that the jury was 'packed by Colonel Arthur' (30 October 1835) and accused the constables of being 'perjurers' and the foreman of the jury of being 'a miserable quibbler when on oath'.

Robert Bryan was found guilty. Under British law, although a sentence of death was recorded, convicted cattle stealers were no longer hanged, but in Bryan's case Pedder ordered that the death sentence be carried out.

A concerned citizen, who knew the statements of the convict constables to be false, took out a complaint of wilful and corrupt perjury against them, but Chief Justice Pedder refused to act on the information. Several people of influence, who were in court throughout the trial, signed a document stating that from the evidence they had heard they 'verily believed the prisoner innocent' (Melville 1862: 51). Several other prominent citizens, upon reading the newspaper reports of the trial, signed another petition that was sent to the home government. Melville gave a scathing appraisal of the whole proceedings in the *Colonial Times* (3 November 1835):

> This prosecution was in every sense of the word a 'prosecution of the Government', how got up none but those concerned can tell. We ask why was it that the Governor left Launceston as soon as Mr Bryan was found guilty—was it that the authorities might communicate through the Secretary of State, to Mr W. Bryan that his nephew was found guilty of felony in Botany Bay? Such has been the fate of Mr Robert Bryan; reader, you may tomorrow be charged with an unnatural crime, felony or murder—and are there not hundreds ready to swear you guilty for half a crown—nay, for a glass of rum? (*Colonial Times*, 3 November 1835)

The judges of the Supreme Court immediately ordered a warrant be served on Melville. He was brought before the court and found guilty of contempt of court and sentenced to twelve months in jail, fined £200 and ordered to find sureties of £500. The unprecedented severe sentence for contempt of court was aimed at financially destroying Melville, who found himself incarcerated in the jail in Hobart Town while a condemned Robert Bryan waited in a cell at the Launceston jail for his death sentence to be carried out.

Two colonial editors in jail

With two newspaper proprietors incarcerated in the Hobart jail, a visiting US sea captain observed: 'In all America, there was only [ever] one Editor of a newspaper incarcerated in jail, and he was there for telling a 'parcel of lies' (Goodrick 1978: 191).

The *Colonial Times* countered that in Van Diemen's Land 'there were two editors, two publishers and two printers in gaol for telling the truth!' (*Colonial Times*, 3 November 1835, cited in Goodrick 1978: 191). Melville told his readers that 'In these times of terror the safest place is the gaol!' (Goodrick 1978: 191).

Melville spent his time in prison writing a commentary on prison discipline, as well as completing a critical and descriptive account of Arthur's administration, *A History of the Island of Van Diemen's Land from 1824 to 1835*, which was published to great interest in 1835 without outside interference or censorship or fear of imprisonment.

Conclusion

Journalism and freedom of the press finally triumphed. In December 1835, Arthur released Robertson, and in January 1836, after spending a miserable Christmas in the 'unwholesome dungeon', Melville also was released—possibly due to pressure from the home government.

With Arthur's recall in 1836, the anti-Arthur press could not contain themselves. Robertson's *True Colonist* 'called upon every resource of type to announce the happy fact' (23 May 1836). Arthur's recall signalled an end to an oppressive period in the history of the press in Australia. His attempt to gag the press was deliberate, calculated and relentless.

While Governor Sir John Franklin and subsequent Van Diemen's Land governors were often harshly criticised in the Tasmanian press, never again did a governor endeavour to destroy the free press and deny the citizens the only public forum for comment available to them.

KEY REFERENCES

Cryle, D. (1997). *Disreputable Profession: Journalists and Journalism in Colonial Australia*, Brisbane: Central Queensland University Press.

Ferguson, J. A. (1965). *Bibliography of Australia, Vol. 1 1851–1900*. Sydney: Angus & Robertson.

Goodrick, J. (1978). *Tales of Old Van Diemen's Land*, Adelaide: Rigby.

Historical Records of Australia III, vol. 6.

Melville, H. (1835). *A History of Van Diemen's Land*. G. Mackaness (ed.). Sydney: Sydney Review Publications.

WEBSITES

Colonial Times: <http://trove.nla.gov.au/>

Hobart Town Gazette: <http://trove.nla.gov.au/>

TOOLS 1:

PRINT MEDIA AND BROADCAST INTERVIEWS

LIZ TYNAN

Introduction

A journalistic interview is often said to be a conversation with intent. While it may have some of the characteristics of a social conversation, it has a specific information-gathering goal that should never be forgotten. It is always structured, and should be strictly controlled by the reporter, whether in print or electronic media (allowing for key differences between the various media). Interviews are often exercises in psychology, intellectual jousting, nuance and subtle manipulation as much as straightforward information gathering. They can be stressful, and require the reporter to be fearless and well prepared. Reporters use interviews as a major method of gathering material from primary sources. They can be as simple as a quick phone conversation to confirm minor details, to a full-blown studio production with all the trimmings. Sometimes you may even find it is better not to use the word 'interview' when arranging to speak to a source, but rely instead on words such as 'chat', 'checking', 'confirming' or some other reassuring word to take the heat off. Here in Tools 1, we look at print and broadcast interviewing, beginning with principles common to both.

Interviewing for research

The interview is, among other things, a research device. The information gathered during this stage must be treated with the same scepticism as all other material that will be used to prepare a story. The fact that someone has made assertions during an interview does not guarantee that a single word they have said is true. Reporters must always substantiate the statements they include in their news and feature stories, even if those statements come from primary sources.

The interview is a staple of the journalistic process, whether for hard or soft news, features or profiles in print, or news, current affairs or documentaries in the electronic media. As do all other research techniques, the interview has varying degrees of reliability; however, direct interaction with the characters who contribute to a story has many benefits:

- It provides a means of verifying the information through attributing it to a source.
- It is a means of assigning responsibility for the information (or possibly misinformation) to someone other than the reporter and/or the media outlet.
- It gives your story authority and credibility.
- It provides quotes and anecdotes.
- It enables the writer to find out more about a subject.
- It sometimes reveals more than words can convey about the person, such as gestures, personality traits and habits that might add to the writer's understanding of the subject.

The words of the interviewee are not the only basis for the understanding that a writer gains from a face-to-face interview. The rest comes from impressions, countenance (facial expressions and body language) and sometimes the surroundings in which the interview takes place. These can give the reporter hints about the interviewee's state of mind, and also help them find their way into the story itself, adding descriptive detail to the story.

Mark Colvin, the ABC's radio current affairs show *PM*: 'I've come to believe that the great secret of interviewing is really just one word: listening.'

Interviewing for print

The print interview brings the reporter into direct dialogue with primary sources. Some reporters new to the profession feel uncomfortable with the interview process as it involves close engagement and potentially a high level of vulnerability. New reporters may try to wriggle out of interviews and depend on arm's-length written sources, such as media releases or material on the internet. But in many cases journalistic stories cannot be complete without interview material, and young reporters have to face up to the challenge.

Strategies for contacting people for an interview depend on the type of story and the reason for the interview. A late-breaking major news story will obviously dictate when and how you contact your sources. For more routine stories, use your common sense. If the interview concerns the person's work, call the workplace during business hours if possible. If it is for a profile or a feature story, it may be acceptable to call the person at home, so long as you are mindful of a few guidelines:

- Call at a convenient time. Bad times include weekdays at 7'o clock in the morning when people are getting ready for work, at dinner time, and after 9'o clock at night.
- Declare fully your reason for calling. You must state your name and your news organisation, and that you are seeking an on-the-record interview.
- If the response is negative, accept this and thank the person for their time. Do not be pushy. The person may reconsider your invitation to an interview, so leave your contact details.
- Arrange a mutually suitable location.
- The optimum time to set aside for a print news interview is 30 to 40 minutes, but you might need considerably more time for a feature. Predict a time and try to stick to it.
- Strict laws govern any publicity involving children. Before attempting to interview anyone under the age of 18, consult with a senior editorial person.

Interviews, as much as possible, should be held in places where interruptions are likely to be minimal. Mobile phones belonging to both parties should be switched off. It is very insulting (and counterproductive) for the reporter to take a call while interviewing someone. Don't do it. While some reporters prefer not to eat while interviewing, others happily conduct interviews over lunch; this is a matter of personal preference, but decide ahead of time whether you really want the ordering and consuming of food to punctuate the interview. For a straightforward news story interview, it is often enough just to catch up with the person in his or her office and carry out the interviewed quickly and efficiently. A news interview is not a social visit; it should always take the shortest amount of time to get the job done.

The first key to mastering the interview is preparation. Being prepared provides you with an armoury. It helps to minimise the risk of being conned by the interviewee or being unable to recognise a stunning admission or a whole new line of enquiry. While you must always be alert to any new information in an interview, your mind will be more receptive to that new information if you have a firm grasp on the existing information available through research.

You may have already decided on your angle and who the other interviewees should be. Sometimes the interview itself will change the plan you have drawn up; in journalism, flexibility is a virtue. You should have read widely and deeply beforehand, and formulated a range of questions.

Closed questions: Questions whose answers are limited to yes, no, or similar precise information.

Open questions: Questions whose answers can elicit a wide range of responses; usually these questions begin with the words Who?, What?, When?, Where?, How? or Why?

News interviews tend to have two basic kinds of questions:

- **closed questions**, which usually have yes or no answers
- **open questions**, which may elicit a range of possible responses within the constraints of the question; these are questions that begin with the words Who?, What?, When?, Where?, How? or Why?

Both types of question have their purpose. A closed question may quickly get you the answer you need without further elaboration, so it has its place in an interview, particularly when establishing baseline information. A skilled interviewer knows how to balance closed and open questions so that the interview yields the kind of responses needed for the story.

One of the real skills of the journalist is to formulate questions that will fully reveal the story. Questions should be structured logically and thought through, even when following an unanticipated line of enquiry: 'The reporter should resist preconceived ideas, recognising that an open mind can achieve unexpected results' (Conley 2002: 193). Allowing the interviewee to see how much research you have done and what conclusions might be drawn from that research—while still allowing them opportunities to confirm or deny information or previous statements—is more effective than going in with a judgmental mindset that has the story set beforehand.

The rhythm of an interview may benefit from you beginning with simple closed questions to avoid initial confrontation that may cause your interviewee to clam up. Closed questions are usually specific and fact based, for example, 'Will you be attending the conference?' or 'Are you planning to vote for the amendment?' These questions are a good opportunity to get standard but essential and uncontested information. This part of the interview is often also a good time to check spellings and titles, and other factual information. You then move on to the open questions, which are more opinion based and invite open-ended responses.

By all means, during this part of the interview, be confrontational if that is needed. Part of being a journalist involves pursuing important lines of enquiry, especially if someone is trying to stop you. Never raise your voice or be aggressive. Be persistent and don't let the source off the hook. Not all interviews become confrontational, but sometimes they must be. Don't be confrontational just to maintain a gung-ho reporter image. The story is always the thing, not the image.

If the interviewee fails to answer your questions, that will tend to be a warning signal. If you let the talent get away with not answering the questions, then you may lose control of the

Being the people's witness

Journalism, or at least the more elevated and noble forms of journalism, is often referred to as 'the people's witness', which may be a useful way of seeing your role in an interview. Ask the questions that you think average people want and deserve to have answered, so that their view of an event is as complete as possible. This generally means that you run through the closed, factual questions to establish the essential features of the issue or event, then go on to ask open questions that begin with Who?, What?, When?, Where?, How? or Why? Most standard news stories will answer these questions.

interview and hand the advantage to the interviewee. Use evasion as a cue, formulate follow-up questions and dig accordingly later.

One of the biggest problems that reporters, particularly inexperienced reporters, face is being too wedded to pre-prepared questions. While it is crucial to formulate questions based upon a range of research ahead of time, do not let your questions blindly dictate the course of the interview. Listen as well as ask.

Matt Brown, ABC news and current affairs political journalist: 'Governments have power, and I have an obligation to scrutinise it ... You are here, professionally, to negotiate your way through telling the story of what they are doing. You can't do that as an unequivocally hostile person. You can't do it as a compliant, obsequious reteller of their words.'

Take special care to ensure that your questions are not long and convoluted, requiring multifaceted answers. Always focus on one question at a time, and don't make a difficult interview even harder and almost certainly less effective by stringing two or more questions together. Keep your questions blunt, almost to the point of rudeness, while not actually being rude. Ask this sort of question: 'What is the city council planning to minimise the risk to residents of rising sea level?', rather than 'Do you think that climate change is likely to cause rising sea levels in coastal development areas, what are you planning to do to help home owners in those areas deal with the problems of rising water, and should there be global mandatory targets to cut down on greenhouse gases?' The latter questions will either have the interviewee floundering or will give the person an opportunity to evade answering in the ensuing confusion.

Students often ask whether audio recording of print interviews is necessary. This is a judgment call for you, and possibly a policy issue in the newsroom you join. Many reporters always record, and just as many others never do. It is a hotly disputed topic. To help you make up your own mind, here are some points to ponder. A recording is a strong piece of evidence should your story be disputed by the source/s. It will also help if your written notes turn out to be inadequate. However, you must always take notes, even if you are recording. Recording equipment can easily break down, and if you have no recording and no notes, you are in big trouble. Memory is notoriously unreliable, particularly if the interview has been at all stressful. Trying to recreate direct quotes from memory almost never works—human memory is not that efficient.

The downside to making recordings is the process of transcribing. It may not be essential to transcribe the whole thing, and you should note down exactly where in a recording you can find the quote you need, so that you can return to it easily to check what was actually said. Some reporters (often specialists, such as science journalists) do prefer to work from a full transcript, but there is a price to be paid in terms of time and repetitive strain injury. Few daily journalists have the luxury of obtaining a full transcript, which is why you need to find your place in the interview quickly to avoid wading through masses of recordings. In the print media, a small and inexpensive note-taking recorder with a built-in microphone is usually sufficient.

Shorthand

Most mainstream media organisations require their cadets to learn shorthand. It is a useful skill, and may obviate the need for a tape recorder. But you have to be really proficient to rely on it. Even those journalists who do take notes in shorthand will sometimes record as well.

For legal reasons, journalists usually keep their notebooks for at least seven years. It may take a while for someone to dispute your version of the story. Don't rush to throw out your raw materials. Store them away for future reference, if needed.

Off the record

A request for a part of an interview to be off the record may come up, possibly unexpectedly. It generally means that the interviewee wants the information to be public, but doesn't want to be associated with it for some reason. Off-the-record statements must be respected, and preferably an agreement about this form of information would be negotiated before the start of the interview. If a source wishes to go off the record during the interview without prior warning, most journalists will be interested to hear what they have to say. Problems may arise if sources retrospectively wish to change some information from on the record to off the record. This is why it is important to be clear on the exact nature of the information you are receiving during an interview and why some journalists prefer to first discuss and reach agreement with sources on the prospect of off-the-record information.

Technology has enabled writers to gather interview material without meeting the source. Two methods in particular have become widespread: email and telephone. While some older journalists may doubt whether an email interview is a proper interview at all, it is increasingly common. News and information gathering by email has benefits and drawbacks. The benefits may be summarised as:

- certainty of content (with written responses to questions)
- time efficiency

- absence of inhibitive environmental factors
- absence of phone call costs and time zone issues for overseas interviewees.

Email correspondence can produce certainty on the part of the respondent, because there is more time to think about the answers to questions. Written responses also eliminate any possibility of the writer misinterpreting her or his own notes. Emails can be really useful when checking facts with, for example, a scientist or other expert overseas.

The drawbacks are that email responses may be spun and carefully planned rather than being spontaneous and perhaps more truthful. It is easier, too, for interviewees to simply not answer questions that have been sent by email, or be selective in their answers. Also, the reporter can't quickly follow up a new angle that presents itself. Be aware that the interviewee may have more control over this kind of interview.

Telephone interviewing is common and convenient. Sometimes journalists use telephone recording devices (not phone taps, which are illegal, but just simple telephone pick-ups of various kinds) to ensure accuracy. You must never record an interview without first getting permission from the interviewee. Do not make secret recordings. Be up front about everything you are doing; you are not a spy.

The telephone interview is the quickest way for a newspaper journalist to gather primary source information, and its speed and the absence of inhibitive factors can produce a degree of honesty that may not be achievable in either face-to-face or written interviews. But there is a trade-off. The main disadvantage is that you can't pick up on most of the nonverbal signals, mentioned earlier, that are available in a face-to-face interview.

Broadcast interviewing

Interviewing in the broadcast media has a twofold purpose: it is intended to gather the information that forms the basis of news stories or other forms of journalistic content, and it has to provide a range of sound to give radio or television broadcasts a multiplicity of voices (and vision in the latter case). This section focuses on broadcast-quality audio interviews, but does not deal with the specialised area of capturing images.

Broadcast news thrives on variety, so reporters are always looking to make their packages as lively and as authoritative as possible. Liveliness and authority come from having lots of people contributing their voices to your broadcast. The diversity of voices makes it lively; the qualifications of the interviewee lend authority.

Standard radio news interviews intended to provide grabs for regular bulletins—the bread and butter of radio news—tend to be shorter, simpler, more formal and more structured than a print interview. For news, you are aiming to obtain your grab and the main facts or opinions, then get out as quickly as possible to package your story for the next bulletin. News happens very quickly in radio in particular, so you don't have the luxury of time.

As a general rule, it is wise to limit the number of questions for a broadcast news story to no more than four. Even this might be too many. Sometimes you will get all you need with two or three well-directed, well-worded questions. This is particularly the case with news. Current affairs and documentaries are more probing and will require more questioning. Even so, you must be careful not to get an hour's worth of recording, and then suffer agonies trying to edit all your sound down to the two-to-five minute package often required for current affairs.

Despite the fact that you don't have much time, you still need to do your preparation. Without this preparation you won't know what angle to pursue, and angle is everything in broadcast news. A single strong news angle is the basis of all broadcast news stories.

Talent: In electronic media, the person interviewed for a story.

You will do your own research first; then, when you are with the **talent** (interviewee), you will first talk informally to provide an outline of what is to be discussed. In all kinds of broadcast interviews you should give your subject a chance to prepare for the interview before you start recording. There are some obvious exceptions to this—a prime ministerial doorstop for one, or a hurriedly arranged interview with someone at the scene of a disaster—but for your standard news story you would let the talent know which angle you are going to be taking so that he or she can be prepared for what is to come. Spend a few minutes chatting to your source before you begin the formal part of the interview. This is also an opportunity to do a sound check on your talent's voice.

You will also need to decide on the location for the interview. Will it be done in the field, in the studio or on the telephone? Increasingly these days, radio journalists undertake phone interviews in the production studio, where a broadcast-quality recording can be made. However, sometimes a story benefits from the associated atmosphere being incorporated as soundscape. An example might be at a demonstration, where you can capture the sound of the crowd chanting or other relevant background noise. These environments are less controlled, and you do have to take care to ensure that ambient noise does not render voice recording unusable. You will need to get your talent away a bit from the other noise and get the microphone close enough to them.

Another option is a studio interview, where sound conditions are optimal for good recording as you are in a soundproof environment. This is a good option for a longer interview, perhaps for documentaries or current affairs. It is also a setting where the journalist tends to have more of the upper hand than elsewhere, as the talent may feel that he or she is outside of their comfort zone.

If you have to interview someone in their own space, such as an office, ensure that the person takes the phone off the hook and switches off their mobile phone. It would help also if they could hang a 'Do not disturb' sign on the door. If you have a choice, select a carpeted room, without much furniture, to provide the best audio recording environment.

In any setting, you always need to control the interview. You must have a clear idea of the outcome you are seeking, and not let the talent take you off on different tangents or dominate. You should retain your objectivity at all times, and ensure that you stay professional, even if you are being confrontational.

Avoid verbal reassurance

In a print interview, you will often give your interviewee clues about how you are responding to what he or she is saying. Often this will be saying things like 'Yes' or 'Right' or some other cue word. You might also make noises like 'Hmmm' or 'Ohh'. For broadcast interviews, you must resist the temptation to offer any sort of verbal reassurance. It will render your recording confusing or irritating for the listener, and in fact may make it unusable. Instead, get into the habit of nodding or making some other noiseless gesture if you feel you need to encourage your interviewee.

Always keep your eyes focused on the talent. If you are drifting away and not apparently listening to what the person is saying, they will start to lose the thread, and again, your recording quality will be compromised. Always be involved in the interview. Try as much as possible to use the open question technique (Who?, What?, When?, Where?, How?, Why?). You want the interviewee to supply a usable and informative grab, not just a yes/no response to your supply of information. Yes/no answers are almost always useless in the electronic media.

Getting broadcast-quality quotes from interviewees requires you to control the way the interview unfolds. Take care in live and recorded interviews not to ask double-barrelled questions. These are likely to result in the interviewee being confused, or answering only one of the questions. Even more so than in print interviews, you must keep your questions really short and simple, to the point of bluntness (again, without being rude). You want the interviewee to understand the question immediately, and not flounder around trying to figure out what you are getting at. The only way to do it this way is to think through your questioning ahead of time. It is recklessly optimistic to believe that you will always be able to think cogently and comprehensively on your feet. You must always prepare.

TIPS ON WHAT TO DO AND WHAT TO AVOID

Make sure you always:

- select quotes carefully
- honour all confidences
- remain calm and professional
- for print, record the interview carefully, take notes and possibly make an audio recording as well
- for broadcast, choose a good sound environment and limit your questions to the essentials.

Make sure you never:

- attempt an interview without solid preparation
- push your personal opinion
- misrepresent the purpose of the interview
- secretly record the interview
- take a phone call during an interview
- ask convoluted, multipart questions
- get sidetracked or railroaded by the interviewee.

To really shine:

- be as well prepared as possible to make the most of your time with the primary source and listen attentively to everything that is said.

Conclusion

Interviews are the front line in the interaction between the media and sources, and they are where the people's witness does much of the actual witnessing. You will find interviews easier once you become more comfortable with the idea of being a representative of the people for whom you are reporting. Part of being an effective representative involves being well prepared, which will help you stay in control. A well-controlled interview is a good interview, and a good interview usually means a good story.

KEY REFERENCES

ABC Radio (2002). 'The Art of the Interview', *National Cultures of Journalism.* 13 November.

Conley, D. & Lamble, S. (2006). *The Daily Miracle: An Introduction to Journalism* (3rd edn). Melbourne: Oxford University Press.

Johnson, C. (2005). *21st Century Feature Writing.* Melbourne: Pearson Education.

PART 2

MEDIA INSTITUTIONS

Media industries are the engine rooms of our culture. They produce the images, words and stories that inform and entertain us. They tell us what is going on in the world and they offer us different ways of seeing and being in that world.

This means that media industries are also creative industries: they combine creative skill with media production, distribution and technology to manufacture products that can be industrial yet innovative. It is the media industries that produce the dialogic webs that make up the mediasphere.

In Part 2, we look at each of the major media industries, including radio, film, television and public relations.

Case Study 2 ('Spinning the War: How PR Made the First Gulf War') shows one of the most profound and significant shapers of the modern world—public relations—in action. This case study takes a look at the way public relations has shaped the way media cover and interpret warfare.

Tools 2 ('How to Conduct a Media Conference') introduces media practitioners and journalists to some of the basic elements of promotional culture: how to plan it, how to create it, how to work with it and how to use it effectively and ethically.

CHAPTER 5

RADIO: THE TRIBAL DRUM

LIZ TYNAN

Introduction

Listen to the radio—really listen to it. What do you hear? Voices talking, voices singing, instruments playing music, maybe machinery, maybe animals: the sounds of life in various forms. Your ears are picking up soundwaves that have been created and sent by some surprisingly simple electronic equipment into your brain, into your mind. You then construct the meaning according to your own unique brain wiring, according to the sounds that have significance for you. This is the medium that Marshall McLuhan (1967) called a 'tribal drum' that turns society into a 'single echo chamber' and thus, he claimed, was more buried in our psyche than any other medium. Even the advent of digital recording and editing equipment in most Australian radio newsrooms some years ago hardly changed the medium, and radio remains a simple technology that works best when people understand its essential simplicity and therefore can tap into its strength.

Notice that you imagine things when you listen to sound from the radio. You might picture the lead singer of the band whose music is playing, or you might imagine a forest or a beach, a cityscape or a farmyard, depending on the sound that is being sent to you. You might picture the DJ or the guest who is speaking, even if you have never seen either of these people before. You might only be half aware that you are doing this, but in some way your brain is filling in the gaps of an enticing little world that is being created for you. All you have to do is provide the imagination.

In this chapter we look at:

- how early radio quickly established its special power
- the Marshall McLuhan interpretation
- how radio has developed many different uses, including propaganda
- why radio has a unique place in mass communication.

Beginnings

Radio: The wireless transmission through space of electromagnetic waves, and the device designed to collect these signals and turn them into sound that you can listen to.

Antenna: The device used to send or receive electromagnetic signals, a crucial part of radio broadcasting.

Radio began in the first half of the twentieth century, and quickly spread around the globe. The technology had flowed from physics research, from basic investigations into electricity and electromagnetism. This evolved into the capture and transmission of sound waves in the latter years of the nineteenth century and early years of the twentieth century. It was called 'wireless' technology because electromagnetic waves were sent and received via the medium of air, without wires to carry the signal, unlike the earlier telegraph technology. This was almost like magic at the time. Italian physicist Guglielmo Marconi took up earlier work by the pioneering theorist James Clerk Maxwell and the experimental scientist Heinrich Hertz to send a telegraphic (dot–dot–dash–dash) wireless signal in 1901. A few years later, the first radio signal of a human voice was sent and received. Transmitters and **antennas** of increasing strength were built in a short space of time. Radio became a reality.

Radio stations started springing up in the northern hemisphere in the early 1920s. Australia was not far behind; this country is known as an early adopter of new technology. The very first person heard on Australia's airwaves was a young soprano named Miss Deering. At 8 o'clock on the night of 23 November 1923, her voice went to air on Australia's first radio station, 2SB, in Sydney, singing the now-forgotten song 'Farewell in the Desert'. This station changed its name soon after to 2BL to avoid confusion with the second Australian radio station, 2FC. Over the next few years, radio stations began in most Australian capital cities and in some country towns.

After initial confusion about how Australian stations would be licensed, Australia established two systems of broadcasting: commercial and national. Commercial stations raised their income from advertising. In July 1932, the Australian government took a significant step when it set up a national broadcaster. Originally called the Australian Broadcasting Commission, and now the Australian Broadcasting Corporation (the ABC), it was based on the British Broadcasting Commission, which started broadcasting in 1923. At the time income for ABC stations was raised from radio licences that had to be bought by every household that owned a radio. The ABC has since then played an important social and cultural role and is embedded in Australian society, even though it is often a source of controversy.

The three decades from the early 1930s are often referred to as the golden years of radio, when it was a familiar and much-loved fixture in most family homes and the source of information and entertainment in most Western countries, Australia predominant among them. During those years, radio featured many types of entertainment that can now be found on television, such as drama, documentary and concerts. The years of the Second World War, 1939 to 1945, reinforced the importance of radio. In September 1939, most Australians heard that Australia was at war with Germany via the famous broadcast by Robert Menzies, then prime minister, a broadcast that still has the power to evoke memories of a long-departed era. The words on the page don't do justice to the unadorned eloquence of the recorded voice. Find a recording on the internet and hear the tribal drum resonate through this famous piece of radio.

Media students should also listen to the milestone in early radio, *The War of the Worlds*, a radio drama that was broadcast throughout the USA from New York on Halloween Eve, 30 October 1938. Recordings are readily available to download from the internet. Listen in

Transcript of the first minute of Menzies' declaration of war

Fellow Australians, it is my melancholy duty to inform you officially that in consequence of a persistence by Germany in her invasion of Poland, Great Britain has declared war upon her and that, as a result, Australia is also at war. No harder task can fall to the lot of a democratic leader than to make such an announcement. Great Britain and France with the cooperation of the British Dominions have struggled to avoid this tragedy. They have, as I firmly believe, been patient. They have kept the door of negotiation open. They have given no cause for aggression. But in the result their efforts have failed and we are therefore, as a great family of nations, involved in a struggle which we must at all costs win and which we believe in our hearts we will win.

Robert Menzies, 3 September 1939

as this most famous—and infamous—of radio shows weaves its magic, even now. It was a memorable use of a still relatively new medium.

The brilliant young actor, Orson Welles, aged only twenty-three but already with a sonorous voice and a hefty reputation as a stage and radio actor and entrepreneur, introduced a daring new style of broadcast that had consequences not even Welles could have predicted. *The War of the Worlds* radio show, which lasted just one hour, has gone down in history as the moment that the power of radio was first felt to its full extent. It created mass panic: tens of thousands of people tried to flee New York to get away from the alien invaders from Mars, and many people reported seeing the destruction wrought by the Martians. It seems incredible now that so obviously a fictional piece, based upon a well-known piece of literature by H. G. Wells, could have this effect.

But remember that this broadcast was made less than a year before the Second World War broke out in Europe, and this program tapped into the prevailing sense of unease. People tuning in late to the program heard what sounded like a plausible real-time unfolding of events, with news flashes breaking into the usual radio fare of band music, followed by what seemed to be a live cross to a reporter at the scene of a spacecraft landed in a farmer's field. The subsequent apparent death of the reporter and the bystanders sounded realistic to the listeners, many of whom hurriedly packed their bags.

Paul Heyer (2003) looks afresh at this amazing milestone in the development of radio, showing how Welles summoned all the powers of 'the theatre of the imagination', as Welles called radio. Heyer describes how Welles deliberately exploited radio's characteristics of immediacy and spontaneity to convince large numbers of people that the Earth was being invaded by aliens from Mars. He was so successful, and frightened such a large number of people, that he was taken in for questioning by the police.

Although at the end of the broadcast Welles told the audience that *The War of the Worlds* had been a big Halloween trick, by then a number of New Yorkers had fled their homes. The broadcast had far-reaching consequences, leading academics to study radio as a unique communication phenomenon for the first time.

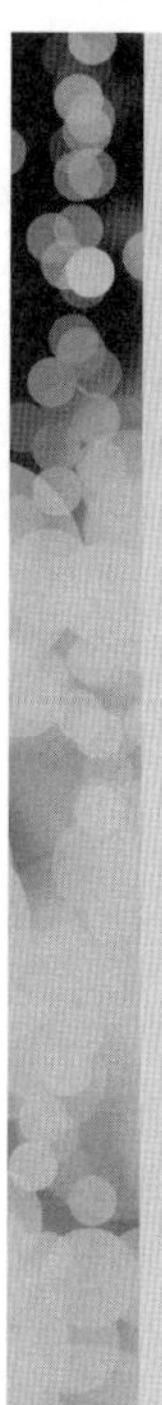

Orson Welles' opening narration from *The War of the Worlds*

We know now that in the early years of the twentieth century this world was being watched closely by intelligences greater than man's and yet as mortal as his own. We know now that as human beings busied themselves about their various concerns, they were scrutinised and studied, perhaps almost as narrowly as a man with a microscope might scrutinise the transient creatures that swarm and multiply in a drop of water. With infinite complacence people went to and fro over the Earth above their little affairs serene in assurance of their dominion over this small, spinning fragment of solar driftwood, which by chance or design man has inherited out of the dark mystery of time and space. Yet across an immense, ethereal gulf, minds that are to our minds as ours are to the beasts in the jungle, intellects vast, cool and unsympathetic, regarded this Earth with envious eyes and slowly and surely drew their plans against us.

In the thirty-ninth year of the twentieth century came the great disillusionment. It was near the end of October. Business was better. The war scare was over. More men were back at work. Sales were picking up. On this particular evening, October 30th, the Crosby Service estimated that 32 million people were listening in on radios. (Welles 1938).

The McLuhan interpretation

In 1964, pioneering Canadian media theorist Marshall McLuhan published *Understanding Media: The Extension of Man*, which used the Welles broadcast to help elucidate how radio operated—how it gets into our heads. McLuhan wrote, in his typically colourful prose, that radio was a tribal drum and that it had a power to 'involve people in depth'. 'Radio affects most people intimately, person-to-person, offering a world of unspoken communication between writer–speaker and the listener' (McLuhan 1967). He was concerned to distinguish between the effects of different media, and famously called radio a 'hot' medium. The term 'hot' is intended to refer to the level of participation in a medium. At the time that this analytical approach was formulated (that is, the early 1960s), participation phenomena—such as talkback radio, listener polling or competitions that required listeners to phone in—were not prevalent in the USA, and rare in Australia.

The McLuhan interpretation is frequently misunderstood, mainly because it employs terminology ('hot' and 'cool') that seems unrelated to meaning. It can perhaps be most simply interpreted as meaning that radio required little direct participation and could be absorbed while a person was doing other things. This was in contrast to television (and various other media), which tended to engage more than one sensory perception, and so required more direct attention. Radio is an altogether more intimate, inward experience. This made listening to the radio an essentially different experience from watching television or using a telephone.

Further, McLuhan maintained that Welles used 'the auditory involving power of radio to tap primal fears and emotions—anticipating what Hitler was about to do in reality' (Heyer 2003). McLuhan used *The War of the Worlds* broadcast to illustrate his point that 'the subliminal depths of radio are charged with the resonating echoes of tribal horns and antique drums'; in other words, that radio has a deeply evocative capacity. A population already primed by fear caused by the rise of Hitler could very easily be prompted to believe in an alien attack. Any medium that can do this must have tremendous power.

A unique place

Radio occupies a unique place in modern mass communication. In many ways, it is mass communication at its most simple and basic. This, perhaps paradoxically, gives it its special power. It engages one sensory perception only, which happens to be the most fleeting of human perceptions: hearing. It's always in the now. Newspapers are more lasting, even if they only last a day. Television imprints visual images on our memories that may stay there for years. Not so radio. More than any other form of mass communication, radio engages human imagination. For this, and many other reasons, it did not disappear when television rose to its gargantuan proportions. At the time there were plenty of people who said that radio had had its brief and shining moment and that it would die out, but that has not happened yet. Recent research shows that radio as a medium is actually on the rise again—it has experienced a resurgence in audience numbers in the past few years in Australia, particularly among youth.

Before radio, access to information was largely confined to the literate. This meant that the educated minority controlled the flow of information to the uneducated masses. Information, as many commentators have noted, is power, and literacy itself has always been a method of exerting social control. So it is not surprising that in the twentieth century, during a period of great social upheaval, sources of information were wrenched from the hands of existing elite groups and put into different hands, whether into those of another kind of elite or even into the hands of less powerful groups in the population. Where power had once been held by, for example, the monarchy, the aristocracy and the clergy, now new power groups were emerging. These included those who had access to the airwaves, such as media owners or public relations practitioners—those who were able to use emerging media power to speak directly to the people. And if people could be reached, they could be swayed. The advent of radio marked a change in how power groups operate, with calculations about mass appeal suddenly becoming possible. That's not to say that information was necessarily democratised, but it did become possible to reach and mobilise more people than ever before, including those who could not read.

This has had a wide range of implications. In totalitarian and authoritarian states, for example, radio is always a state-controlled entity with enormous propaganda power. Propaganda on a mass scale began as a twentieth-century phenomenon. While radio in itself is ethically neutral, the way it has been used by power groups has given it moral content. In a military coup or a revolution the leaders will quickly take control of the radio stations. This is not because military leaders want to become broadcast stars, but because they want their message to reach the vast majority of people. In many countries, the only way to do this is via the radio.

George Orwell, who fought on the anti-Franco side during the Spanish Civil War in the 1930s, wrote eloquently in his book *Homage to Catalonia* (1938) about what happened in Barcelona during the factional infighting on his own side—the capture of the radio station symbolised the supremacy of a particular winning faction. In more recent times, a successful coup (in Thailand, for example) is always heralded by a sudden change in radio programming as a particular military commander and his troops take control of the radio stations.

The intimacy of radio

Another key characteristic of radio is its intimacy. When you listen to an interview on radio, it is intrinsically different from watching the same interview on television. This has to do not only with sensory perception but also the mirage of apparent closeness to the two or more people engaged in the discourse. When you watch television, on some level you are well aware of the unnaturalness of the medium and your mind automatically compensates. For one thing, the people are a fraction of normal size in most cases, unless the camera has zoomed in to extreme close-up.

When you listen to a radio interview, it almost feels as if you are the third person in the conversation. This illusion is heightened by the fact that you can take the radio with you to your place of work, to the beach or to sporting events. When it was introduced, the portable miniature television was supposed to fulfil the same function, but it has never really become popular. Perhaps this is because television tends to create a sense of being part of a wider, less personal community, while radio reinforces a sense of community intimacy. The rise in Australia of community radio since the 1970s is testament to the medium's community-building capacity, and is one positive exploitation of this special characteristic.

Talkback radio: Radio programming that includes telephone conversations with members of the audience.

Opinion making has become an important feature of much radio in Australia. Some radio **talkback** stars have demonstrable influence on political and social policy, again through this ability of radio to create a sense of a community. Whether these communities exist mainly to satisfy the station's ratings and the talkback person's ego, rather than contribute to informed debate, is an ongoing subject for discussion in this country, but there is no denying the power wielded by the most popular talkback broadcasters. Alan Jones, one of the highest-rating talkback broadcasters in Australia, attempted to impose the talkback model on television during the 1990s. He even placed an old-fashioned radio microphone on his desk. It simply did not work: the medium was wrong for this kind of community creation. When the program failed, many commentators also repeated the oft-quoted maxim that Jones had a 'very good face for radio'.

Other powerful uses of radio

During the Great Depression of the 1930s, and later during the US involvement in the Second World War, President Franklin Roosevelt used radio to broadcast fireside chats, during which his audiences felt that he directly spoke to each of them. He broadcast thirty-one of these radio addresses, ranging from fifteen to forty-five minutes, during some of the most tumultuous times his country had experienced. They became compulsive listening for large numbers of Americans—a significant factor in the domestic propaganda effort. Here was the president actually speaking to individuals in their own homes, at a time when radio was still relatively new as a form of mass communication.

Other uses of radio as a propaganda mechanism include Radio Free Europe, Radio Liberty (in Cuba), Radio Free Asia and the more recent Radio Free Afghanistan and Radio Free Iraq, all of which have been used to support US policies in strategically important areas. The propaganda possibilities of radio first became important during the Second World War, when the Nazis broadcast to Britain the messages of 'Lord Haw Haw', whose real name was William Joyce. During the same war, the Japanese sent out broadcasts by Tokyo Rose, and in the Vietnam War, Hanoi Hannah broadcast from North Vietnam.

Veteran Australian broadcaster Phillip Adams often refers to 'the listener' (in the singular) during his nightly show *Late Night Live* on ABC Radio National. He is highlighting the fact that the radio announcer effectively is talking to just one person—each person receiving the message is the only one being spoken to at any given moment. As we have seen, this ability to speak directly to people has been harnessed for both noble and dubious reasons throughout the history of the medium.

Radio, propoganda and war

Lord Haw Haw, aka William Joyce

William Joyce was born in the USA to British parents and travelled on a British passport. Before the Second World War, he was a member of the notorious British Union of Fascists, led by Oswald Mosley. Using his pronounced British accent, Joyce broadcast Nazi propaganda in British to Allied troops throughout the conflict. When the war was over, he was hanged for treason by the British, which was controversial since Joyce was still an American (despite holding a British passport) and no US court had condemned Second World War propagandists.

Tokyo Rose

Tokyo Rose was not one single person but a range of young women. The person most associated with this identity, however, was a Japanese-American woman called Iva Ikuko Toguri, who claimed to have been stranded in Japan just before the Pearl Harbor bombing that brought the USA into the war. Toguri died in 2006, aged about ninety-eight. It is reported that she was much less enthusiastic about her propaganda role than was Lord Haw Haw about his. She was forced into broadcasting, and is said to have subverted her broadcasts by incorporating scripts actually written by Allied prisoners of war. She used the on-air name of 'Orphan Ann', but was known to the Allies as Tokyo Rose. She was convicted of treason after the war, but was pardoned in 1977 by US President Gerald Ford.

Not 'television without pictures'

Radio is not television without pictures. As McLuhan (1967) identified, all the media operate in distinctly different ways, providing specific sensory input. Therefore, information from the radio is processed in the human mind differently from information presented via television or newspapers.

While we are listening to radio, the visual cues we are used to in everyday life and in other media are not in play. Body language is not an issue on radio, so listeners have to use other clues to decide how to assess the information they are receiving. The sort of accusatory, aggressive or coquettish body language that you might find displayed by television interviewers cannot be discerned on radio. Interviewers can't stab the air with their pen or lean forward menacingly to make a point about where they stand on an issue. A radio interview may still be tough and demanding, and the interviewer can interrupt the flow of a person's answers, but the medium cannot convey the visual cues that give the interviewer the status of equal participant in a drama. Therefore, the radio experience is seen by many—rightly or wrongly—to be more detached than the television experience.

All considerations about a person's appearance—the sorts of things that can make a huge impact in nearly all other media—are not an issue in radio. This can have something of a democratising effect, in that it removes discrimination on the basis of appearance. Conversely, the fact that listeners cannot see a person's eyes might detract from the ability to determine whether the person speaking is telling the truth.

Interviewees on the whole tend to be less nervous and more voluble on radio than they are on television. Someone being interviewed on television is very aware of a camera being pointed at them. On radio, the apparatus is less intrusive. Once they get over their initial reserve, most radio interviewees are able to forget about the recording equipment. It is less easy to ignore a television camera.

The imaginative dimension of radio brought with it the possibility of artifice. An early and famous example of this is the 'broadcast' of 1930s test cricket matches being played in England to audiences in Australia. The technology of the 1930s did not enable broadcast of the actual voices of the commentators from the British cricket grounds. The match description was sent in code by telegraph. The illusion of real time was achieved by the commentator improvising live commentary using the telegraphed match description. A technician or the commentator himself added sound effects; for example, knocking a pencil onto wood to sound like a bat hitting a cricket ball and using recordings of cheering crowds. Cricket enthusiasts in Australia were glued to their wirelesses, and imagined every ball of the match. It is easy to understand why these broadcasts were popular, and why such an illusion could work only on radio.

During the 1950s, the celebrated British program *The Goon Show* used a bizarre and diverse range of sound effects; in fact, the show was a pioneer in this technical field of expertise. The special effects staff perfected the sound of a custard hitting someone in the face or just about anything exploding. To the generation of people who listened to the Goons, their surreal antics had their own reality. Members of the radio audience *saw* the characters Neddy Seagoon, Bloodnok or Eccles in their imagination. During the 1960s and 1970s, Spike Milligan, one of the Goons, attempted to bring some of this same madness to television with a series called *Q*, but it only started to succeed when he abandoned radio techniques and adapted his ideas to television by inventing original visual effects. Also during the early 1970s, the Monty Python team, the natural successors to the Goons, were visual from the start. While still retaining the surreal mood of the Goons, they were able to carve a place for themselves on television.

Situation comedy and drama were staple programs on radio for quite a while, but they almost disappeared from radio after the introduction of television to Australia in 1956. However, radio continues to meet demands from youth for music, and from older listeners for information: news, current affairs and documentaries. The rise and rise of the iPod has changed the way many people consume music, and this will affect how radio stations present their programs. At present, most people remain habituated to radio, although they increasingly complement their radio listening with self-compiled iPod playlists. Radio has always had to adapt to keep up with changes in tastes and demands, and the present situation is no different.

Nonetheless, some traditional uses of radio have maintained their popularity. For example, many people choose to listen to football and cricket commentary on radio rather than watching the television coverage because it gives their minds material for imagination or simply because it is a more convenient way to enjoy coverage of sport while out and about. Additionally, radio stations often inspire great loyalty, with listeners staying tuned exclusively to particular outlets throughout lengthy periods of their lives.

Since the 1950s, radio has also been a major force in the rise of the youth culture. During the 1950s and early 1960s, rock'n'roll music became a form of mass entertainment largely because radio took up this music enthusiastically, often playing music that was seen by the prevailing conservative culture as subversive. Bob Dylan, considered by many to be the most influential songwriter of the second half of the twentieth century, has often been quoted as saying that he spent his youth during the 1950s listening to the great rock'n'roll and blues musicians on the radio, and this helped to form his musical idiom. A case could be made that radio has actually become more conservative and less daring in musical matters in recent times, and this is one area where the visual senses have become dominant in what was once firmly an aural domain. Now popular, youth-orientated music doesn't get very far without a striking video clip on one of the many television-based music programs or channels, and radio programmers (with some notable exceptions) feel obliged to follow rather than lead in these matters. It could well be that in some cases the visual imperative has become more important than the music itself. But once that popular song has won acceptance, it will be played on the radio stations, sometimes ad nauseam.

The future is here

Radio has reached several crossroads since its inception. One of these was presaged by the arrival of digital technology. Radio newsrooms started switching from analogue to digital in the 1990s, initially reflecting the evolution in recording technology. Digital recording technology was followed by a revolution in transmission technology, making possible digital broadcasting. This new era has been embraced by a number of Australian radio outlets, particularly the ABC. To listen to ABC digital channels such as Dig Music or ABC Jazz, consumers may purchase a digital radio receiver that they can use in much the same way as old-style receivers—that is, they are small, portable units—but they do not tune in to the old AM or FM frequencies.

Instead, listeners locate their station by name on the receiver. In fact, digital broadcast uses quite different technology that also enables pause, rewind and storage functions on the receivers, which are known as DAB+ receivers. DAB stands for digital audio broadcasting and DAB+ is the digital radio technology standard for Australia. Jolly (2008), in a parliamentary report on the advent of digital radio in Australia, says: 'Some have labelled the improvements over AM and FM radio broadcasting that digital radio can deliver as "electrifying". While this assessment is overly enthusiastic … there appears to be general agreement that digital radio has the potential generally to provide an improved listening experience for audiences.'

Radio greatly increased its accessibility when some stations began using the power and reach of the internet, just over a decade ago. Now, the new digital channels can be accessed there, too. When radio stations stream on the internet, they are using a different delivery system again, specially developed for the internet rather than for broadcasting on the airwaves. Wherever a personal computer is connected to the internet, web radio is readily accessible. It is now possible to listen to radio from around the world via the internet.

Conclusion

Radio does have a distinct and continuing role in mass communication. Certainly, it has adapted in many ways, but these adaptations appear to have strengthened it—at least for now. New technology is gathering pace, and soon we may get all our information from a multimedia system of some kind. For the moment, though, the popularity of radio is not seriously threatened. Its unique capacity to involve people emotionally—even as they are doing other things and going about their lives—gives it an enduring quality. Radio is an important part of most people's soundscape, and one that will continue for the foreseeable future. It is the grandfather of entertainment, news and information, and creates a community that an iPod cannot yet replace. To study radio, you have to approach it quite differently from both print and television. It is unique. People who choose a career in radio soon face the reality of dealing with sound alone—with no other sensory perception—and that dictates everything they do, whether they write news for the hourly bulletins or craft a story through documentaries or drama.

KEY REFERENCES

Heyer, P. (2003). 'America Under Attack 1: A Reassessment of Orson Welles' 1938 War of the Worlds Broadcast'. *Canadian Journal of Communication*, 28, 149–65.

Kent, J. (1990). *Out of the Bakelite Box: The Heyday of Australian Radio*. Sydney: ABC Books.

McLuhan, M. (1967). *Understanding Media: The Extensions of Man*. London: Sphere.

Phillips, G. & Lindgren, M. (2006). *Australian Broadcast Journalism* (2nd edn). Melbourne: Oxford University Press.

CHAPTER 6

FILM: THE SEVENTH ART

JASON BAINBRIDGE

Introduction

Film is perhaps the only popular media form to be referred to as art. Structurally, the comparison seems appropriate: what is film, after all, but an image framed on a wall? And who has not been moved by a film in the same way that one can be moved by a painting? From a baby's pram rolling out of control down the Odessa steps, to a door quietly closing between a Mafia don and his wife, to a Dark Lord reaching out to his enemy and telling him that 'I am your father', film images haunt us long after the films they belong to have run their course.

Film is also an industrial product: the product of writers, directors, producers, studios and art departments, among many others. Just look at the list of credits at the end of any major film and it becomes quite clear that, unlike a painting, which is usually the product of a single artist, films are massive industrial productions manufactured by vast numbers of people. How then can we reconcile these ideas? And where does film sit in the larger mediasphere?

While it seems logical that film would be part of a book on media studies, at the same time it is always slightly removed from the other media industries, in terms of its study (as an art form it is regularly subsumed into literary studies courses) and its reception (viewed in a cinema, as opposed to the domestic spaces of the radio, television or newspaper). But films can also be viewed on televisions, iPads and online. Film has been implicated in convergence (the coming together of what were once separate media texts and industries; see Chapter 19) almost from its inception. It is film that provides us with a vocabulary for analysing moving and still images.

In this chapter we look at:

- a history of the film industry
- the domination of Hollywood
- approaches to studying film
- the impact of technology on film.

What is film?

When people talk about film they often refer to 'motion pictures' or 'flicks'. Both terms are important because they point to what makes film such a unique media form: motion (or, to be more precise, the appearance of motion—hence the word 'movie'). Indeed, this is how we would now define film—a series of still images providing the illusion of motion—because films are increasingly not even captured on film (photographic) stock but as digital images, in films such as *Slumdog Millionaire or Avatar.* Structurally, a film is a series of photographs (still images) called *frames.* When members of an audience watch a film, their eyes are tricked into seeing a series of static images as a single unbroken and continuous movement.

Films are shot and projected at twenty-four still frames per second, with the light being broken twice—once when a new image appears and again while it is held in place—which has the effect of projecting each frame onto the screen twice. This creates the illusion of continuous motion, thanks to our neural and cognitive processes misperceiving what we are actually being shown.

Why does this happen? A number of overlapping theories have been put forward, including:

- *persistence of vision* (known to the ancient Egyptians and scientifically described in 1824 by Peter Mark Roget), which maintains that the brain retains images on the retina for one-twentieth to one-fifth of a second longer than when they are first shown
- *the phi phenomenon* (or the *stroboscopic effect,* discovered in 1912 by psychologist Max Wertheimer), whereby a spinning colour wheel or the blades of a fan are perceived as being one circular form and/or colour
- *apparent motion,* by which rapid changes to a visual display can fool our eyes into seeing movement, for example, a girl jumping rope in a flashing neon sign
- *critical flicker fusion,* whereby flashes of light (at around fifty frames per second) are perceived as a continuous beam of light.

The crucial thing to remember is that film offers us the illusion of movement. As you will read in Chapters 9 and 10, all media forms are mediations of reality, that is, they all represent reality, whether in sound or words or images. An added part of film's representation, then, is this illusion of movement. It is an illusion that depends very much on technological development and it is this often antagonistic relationship between film and technology that will become a feature of our discussion below.

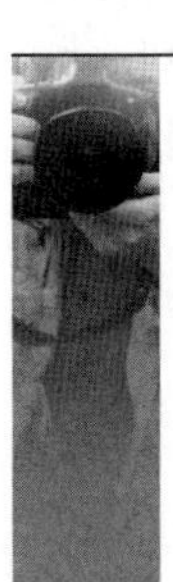

Inception

For more on the relationship between film and illusion, look at Christopher Nolan's 2010 film *Inception*, which tells the story of a corporate espionage thief, Dom Cobb (Leonardo DiCaprio), who extracts information from the unconscious minds of others while they are sleeping. In many respects the film is a meditation on the nature of filmmaking itself: the levels of dreaming Cobb and his team work through echo various film genres (see below) and a central question throughout is whether something is reality or fantasy—has the dream ended? Does it even matter? This, more than anything else, seems to be the secret of a film's success—whether it does or does not provide an illusion you are completely immersed in.

Why flicks?

The term 'motion pictures' is pretty straightforward (films are a series of pictures that provide the illusion of motion), but 'flicks' is a little more obscure. It relates to this idea of critical flicker fusion. Early silent films were shot at sixteen to twenty frames per second and the light was broken only once per image, leaving the films with a pronounced flicker, which led to the slang term 'flickers' or 'flicks'.

A brief evolution of film

As we have seen, the development of mass media is marked by a series of technological developments, and film is no exception. Like radio, it began as a scientific exploration—of why we perceive continuous movement from a series of still images—by inventors such as Joseph Plateau and William George Horner. It may have remained that way had not technology and a series of shrewd businessmen stepped in to turn it into an entertainment.

The early nineteenth century ancestors of film were optical toys such as the thaumatrope, a child's toy paper disc with strings that could be spun to simulate movement between the two images printed on either side of the disc. Later, patrons of arcades and fairgrounds paid money to look at more sophisticated toys, such as the phenakistoscope in 1832, the zoetrope in 1834 (both machines spun their images on strips of paper in rotating drums) and the mutoscope, which created movement by flipping cards in front of a peephole. But all of these devices could only simulate movement—they couldn't actually record movement as it occurred.

This fell to Anglo-American photographer Eadweard Muybridge, who recorded the movement of a horse with twelve separate cameras to create a type of series photography. Other pioneers, such as the American W. D. L. Dickson, refined and developed the equipment, which led to the production of the Edison Laboratories motion-picture camera of 1892: the kinetograph.

Such devices were exhibited in the same arcades and fairgrounds that had been home to the phenakistoscope and zoetrope, but the mass commercial appeal of film remained unappreciated. Thomas Edison had first run 50 feet of film in 1888, but he mistakenly believed moving pictures should be individually exhibited via a coin-operated kinetoscope (in 1894). After much trial and error, French inventor and businessman Louis Lumière, and his brother Auguste, were the first to capitalise on the mass commercial appeal of film. They perfected the cinematographe—a machine that served as camera, film printer and projector—so the moving images could be projected onto a screen, to be enjoyed by an audience rather than an individual person, all from a machine that weighed only 6 kilograms and remained small and portable. From this cinematographe machine comes the term **cinematography**, which refers to the whole industrial process of shooting, manipulating and developing film.

Cinematography: The industrial process of shooting, manipulating and developing film.

On 22 March 1895, the Lumière brothers projected a moving film titled *La Sortie des ouvriers de l'usine Lumière* (*Workers Leaving the Lumière Factory*) to a private Parisian audience. The commercial possibilities of film were finally realised on 28 December, when the

Lumières projected a program of about ten films to a paying audience at the Grand Café on the Boulevard Capucines in Paris; film had become a mass medium and a potentially lucrative commercial venture. This prompted Edison to respond with his own film projection system, the vitascope, often showing films that were illegally copied from the Lumières' catalogue. Many imitators followed.

The next major development—the addition of narrative structure rather than the mere recording of scenes—came from a magician, George Méliès.

Méliès began producing films in 1896, inventing a range of special effects (optical tricks involving framing and sets; see below) and technical conventions (such as the fade-in, dissolve and fade-out; also see below), following a happy accident in which his camera jammed and the bus he was filming was replaced by a hearse. Importantly, Méliès was the first filmmaker to realise the possibilities that film editing contained for manipulating real time and space: that crucial distinction between screen time (where events can be compressed and not everything has to be recorded) and real time (what you are currently experiencing as you read this chapter). This culminated in his (and perhaps the genre's first) science fiction film: *Le Voyage dans la lune* (*A Trip to the Moon*) (1902), with its famous image of a rocket in the eye of the moon.

The film enjoyed wide international circulation, and within ten years the narrative film was well on its way to dominating film output (with the first western, Edwin S. Porter's *The Great Train Robbery*, following shortly thereafter in 1903). The more complex and story-driven these films became, the more they began to attain respectability among the middle and upper classes. Filmgoing was no longer just a working-class pursuit; it was truly becoming an entertainment attractive to a mass audience, regardless of class and (increasingly) regardless of nation.

While the date of the first narrative film remains an ongoing source of debate (though in a burst of nationalistic pride we would suggest Australia has the strongest case with *The Story of the Kelly Gang* in 1902), filmmaking continued to be dominated by the French. The Lumières sold their commercial interests to Charles Pathé in 1900, and his company, Pathé Frères, became the world's largest film producer, while France's Gaumont became the world's largest film studio.

The onset of the First World War curtailed production throughout Europe, affecting France, Italy (another major player in the nascent film industry), Germany and Britain. As Turner (2006) notes, this left the way clear for the US film industry to move into the European, Latin American and Japanese markets: 'American film exports rose from 36 million in 1915 to 159 million in 1916; by the end of the war the US was said to produce 85 per cent of the world's movies and 98 per cent of those shown in America' (Turner 2006: 14).

The USA's domination of film was maintained by three factors: aggressive **vertical integration** (of production, distribution and exhibition) at home and abroad (finally outlawed in the USA by the US Supreme Court in 1948), the Second World War's destabilisation of European cinema's growth (following the introduction of sound in countries where English was not the national language) and the rise in costs for film production and promotion.

Vertical integration: The ownership by one company of all levels of production in an industry; in the film industry, it was the combined production, distribution and exhibition of films in the USA before the 1950s.

As the single biggest film market in the world, the USA remains one of the few countries where local productions can recoup their costs without having to rely on foreign sales. By way of contrast, foreign-made films rarely achieve mainstream distribution in America, as they require the support of a major distributor whose films are already in competition with this foreign product. This means that for most people, in most countries of the world, when they think of film they still think of US film and, more specifically, Hollywood film.

What is Hollywood?

First, Hollywood is a place: a section of Los Angeles, California, that was, for many years, the centre of US film and television production (it replaced New York as the centre of film production). Second, it is a form of factory-style film production, almost a genre in its own right; by 1920 Hollywood was turning out almost 800 films a year, with contract actors and actresses swapped between studios like players on sporting teams. Third, and perhaps most importantly, it is a state of mind, a synonym for magic and glamour and an aspiration for actors and actresses all over the world. For more on Hollywood the place see Billy Wilder's *Sunset Boulevard* and Robert Altman's *The Player*. For more on Hollywood the dream see Garry Marshall's *Pretty Woman*. Where else but in Hollywood (diegetically and extradiegetically) could the tale of a wealthy businessman who breaks up companies and a prostitute hired to be his escort be turned into a romantic comedy with a happy ending?

Why is Hollywood important?

Not only are Hollywood films still the bulk of films in circulation and consumption, particularly in English-speaking countries, but they also form the **mainstream** of film, against which independents and **film movements** often position themselves. An understanding of this mainstream is vital to understanding the innovation of these other forms and to understanding how ideas of genre, auteurs and film style (the various theoretical approaches to film) emerge in practice as well as theory.

Mainstream: The most familiar, popular or otherwise generally available of any art form, especially films.

Film movement: Groups of films loosely directed towards similar formal or social ends.

Furthermore, given the dominance of US film internationally, the imprint of Hollywood can also be seen on a variety of international films, for example, Australia's deliberately derivative **10BA cycle of films**, Italian 'spaghetti' westerns, the French New Wave's hardboiled detective films (such as *Alphaville*) and Japanese *anime* (such as *Akira*), all of which were influenced by Hollywood.

Similarly, Hollywood has absorbed international filmmaking practices and filmmakers into its own structure—think of the Hong Kong-style action films and Jackie Chan, the Chinese *wuxia* martial arts movies such as *Crouching Tiger, Hidden Dragon*, the J-cycle of Japanese horror film adaptations, or the more recent adaptations of India's Bollywood style of films.

The studio system and the creation of film genres

10BA Cycle of Films: A group of Australian films produced in the 1980s, assisted by the 10BA tax scheme, introduced in 1981, that provided generous tax relief for film investors. The films spanned a number of genres (horror, exploitation and action) and were particularly commercial, stylistically imitative of Hollywood and more focused on the US film market than providing any quintessential depictions of Australianness.

Studio system: The set of practices that dominated the US movie industry from the 1920s to 1950s, chiefly based around vertical integration and the conception, scripting and production of films with a factory-style efficiency.

Show business: The business of entertainment, especially in the USA, that seeks to strike a balance between the show (entertainment spectacle) and the business (making a profit).

From 1915 to 1930, experimentation with film was steadily standardised and economised into what became known as the **studio system**, so that by the 1920s (following the example of Thomas Harper Ince and his trendsetting Inceville studios with its five self-contained shooting stages) the film industry was made up of great factories devoted to the large-scale production of film for a mass audience as a commercial undertaking.

What film studios set out to do was create events. As French critic and filmmaker Francois Truffaut noted, 'When a film achieves a certain success, it becomes a sociological event, and the question of its quality becomes secondary' (Truffaut 1977). This was partly because the industry was trying to reach a mass audience, and partly because people had to be attracted to see a film (increasingly in picture palaces, the forerunners of cinemas and multiplexes designed for the exhibition of film)—and what better attraction could there be than an event? These events were managed through the successful interplay of the movie production itself (the film text), the distribution (and attendant opening night and star endorsements) and exhibition and promotion (marketing).

In the creation of film we find the perfect example of **show business**. On the one hand, the artist (or artists: the filmmakers, designers and stars) try to develop film as the 'seventh art' (see below), relying on the narrative tropes and traditions of drama and literature (the show). On the other hand, the studios, producers and exhibitors promote the film as they would any form of mass entertainment, such as vaudeville or a fairground attraction, while always watching the bottom line (the profit result). Hollywood in particular was all about trying to negotiate this tension between the show and the business.

However, it was this mass audience for film that also helped build the studio system. Their attendance ensured that filmmaking could be a commercial enterprise, which encouraged the investment of bigger budgets and more complex filmmaking techniques, as well as determining which conventions and trends would be successful. The popularity of one story or particular form of cinematic expression would inspire repetition, so originality involved making something inventive to satisfy the audience's demand for novelty without alienating the audience by giving them something incomprehensibly new.

The end of the studio system and the recognition of the auteur

A movie: In a double bill at a movie theatre, the feature attraction, made with higher budgets and well-known stars.

By the end of the 1930s, the studio feature film was itself a genre. A night at the cinema (or movie theatre) was usually made up of a newsreel (giving you headlines and international news), a cartoon, a serial, a **B movie**, and then the featured attraction, the **A movie**.

Until the 1970s, studio films were part of a much larger program of entertainment, much as a particular television series may be part of a night's viewing. (In the days of silent film, until 1928, this was heightened by the fact that larger cinemas still supported film screenings with the vestiges of vaudeville: an orchestra might play or some other live musical entertainment such as an organ player.)

B movie: In a double bill at a movie theatre, the supporting or second feature, made with lower budgets and lesser-known stars.

While today we think of films being part of huge merchandising and composite commodity programs involving spin-offs, tie-ins and memorabilia, usually associated with the blockbuster film, we can see that film has been an event-based form of entertainment for almost a century.

Indeed, film had only become the feature attraction thanks to another advance in technology: the introduction of a soundtrack, which was pioneered in Warner Brothers's *The Jazz Singer* (1927), starring Al Jolson. This advance seems slightly ironic, given the fact that Edison had only experimented with film initially as an accompaniment to his sound machines. Jolson's line, famously recorded in *The Jazz Singer*, was: 'You ain't seen nothing yet.'

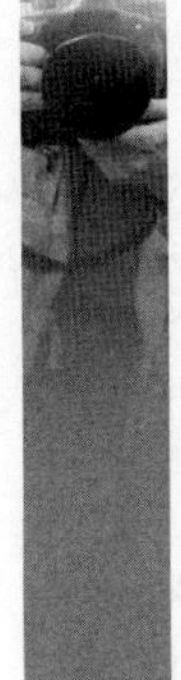

Singin' In the Rain

Improvements in film technology led to the development of a wholly original American genre of filmmaking: the musical. *Singin' in the Rain* was made several times before the most famous version starring Gene Kelly, Donald O'Connor and Debbie Reynolds was released in 1952. The musical as genre is exemplified in Gene Kelly's title song-and-dance performance of 'Singin' in the Rain' or Donald O'Connor's song-and-comedy act in 'Make 'em Laugh'. Musicals such as *Singin' in the Rain* combined a rigorous exploitation of new technological breakthroughs in sound with the old pre-movie conventions of vaudeville—the perfect balance between novelty and convention that studios and audiences demanded at the time.

By the 1930s, the big five major studios (or the majors)—MGM, Paramount, Twentieth Century Fox, Warner Brothers and RKO—and several significant minors (such as Columbia, Universal, and the semi-independent Republic, Monogram and United Artists) had consolidated their control over budgets, exhibition and distribution in the USA and throughout much of the rest of the world, as well as over the contracting of directors and stars and other filmmaking personnel. But less than a decade later the studio system started to fall apart.

The break-up of the studio system began with the US Supreme Court's 1948 Paramount decision, which forced the majors to sell their theatre chains, ending their vertical monopolies over exhibition. Then the developing power of celebrity (see Chapter 11) led to many stars and directors setting up their own productions, resulting in a loosening of the studio's control over the filmmaking personnel and a diminishing number of contract players. The arrival of television (see Chapter 7) also reduced audience numbers. By the end of the 1950s the studio system had come to an end.

The United States Production Code of 1930 was a set of censorship guidelines governing the production of motion pictures in the USA. It spelt out what was and was not morally acceptable content for films produced for a public audience. Among its many provisions were the prohibition of nudity, 'sex perversion' (homosexuality) and the avoidance of 'excessive and lustful kissing'. Often referred to as the Hays Code, after the original head of the Motion

Picture Association of America (MPAA), Will H. Hays, it was adopted by the MPAA in 1930, enforced in 1934 and abandoned in 1967 in favour of the more permissive MPAA ratings system, which ushered in a wave of pornographic films and other more confrontational films collectively referred to as the American New Wave.

So what became of the majors?

With the exception of RKO, the major companies of the 1920s and 1930s survived, changing hands as they became part of larger and larger conglomerates. In the 1960s, they became little more than distributors for the new television and drive-in markets, and, later, distributors and financiers for independent production companies. Today's seven major studios—Disney, Paramount, Sony, Twentieth Century Fox, United Artists–MGM, Universal and Warner Brothers—have independent production arms and are closely linked to television (Disney, for example, owns the US ABC television network).

Exploitation films and youth films flourished, and arthouse and adult cinemas opened in more locations. By the end of the 1970s an alternative infrastructure of festivals had sprung up (for example, the Sundance Festival began as the US Film Festival in 1978) to support alternative productions. Outlets for showing films increased rapidly after the 1970s, from multiplex cinemas (buildings with a large number of small cinemas) to cable television stations such as HBO.

Blockbuster film: A very costly film that the studio hopes will make a profit as a result of the enormous amounts of money spent on publicity and wide distribution.

Hollywood increasingly derived its main income from **blockbuster films**, beginning with *Jaws* (1975) and *Star Wars* (1977). Such films incur enormous production costs, but can make far more money in a short time than films could during the 1940s. By contrast, the independent companies attempted to spend relatively small amounts on experimental productions that were still capable of large earnings. The first successful low-budget film was *Easy Rider* (1969). Others included Steven Soderbergh's *sex, lies, and videotape* (1989), which cost $1.2 million to make, but made $24.7 million in its initial domestic release and had made over $100 million by 2001.

Star Wars

An important film in terms of convergence (see Chapter 19) and the science fiction genre, *Star Wars: A New Hope*, is also very much structured as a love letter to film itself. It uses elements of other film genres (and even other films) to create a new mythology that is surprisingly fresh but also strangely comforting. A supreme example of world building on a grand scale, the Star Wars franchise continues to wear its love for film proudly on its cybernetic arm (I'm looking at you Anakin) with episodes of its more recent animated iteration, *Star Wars: Clone Wars*, paying tribute to westerns, samurai movies and Godzilla films.

The studio system had promoted the use of house styles, under which few but the most popular directors, such as Alfred Hitchcock and Billy Wilder, could retain their independence. The end of the studio system and the rise of the independents refocused attention not only on the individual styles of these indie (independent) directors, but also on the directors and films made under the studio system. Who really were the authors of films: directors or studios? This tension underlies **auteur theory**.

Hitchcock's *Rear Window*

Arguably still the most famous director of all time and an auteur in every sense of the word (he even indicated where he thought the editor should cut the film), Alfred Hitchcock understood that one of the real pleasures of film was its sense of voyeurism, of sitting in the dark and seeing something you were not meant to see. This was never better expressed than in his film *Rear Window*. In telling the tale of a wheelchair-bound photographer who suspects his neighbour may have murdered his wife, Hitchcock cannily predicts media interest in reality television (the windows of the apartments across the way are like a series of little television screens) and the increased desire for interactivity (Grace Kelly's character ultimately feels compelled to go across to the apartment under suspicion, with almost disastrous results).

Why the 'seventh art'?

The heading of this chapter, 'Film: the seventh art', is not just a cliché—many filmmakers, writers and critics place film alongside the six arts identified by the philosopher Hegel in the early nineteenth century (architecture, sculpture, painting, music, poetry and philosophy). Why then did film come to be regarded as the **seventh art**? As far back as 1915, the US Supreme Court ruled, among other things, that 'the exhibition of motion pictures is a business pure and simple, originated and conducted for profi'. Similarly, producers generally have been less interested in thinking of cinema as art, and more interested in selling, franchising, replicating and copying films to make money.

The idea that film could be art began with the filmmakers themselves, starting with Griffith and Méliès, who argued that filmmaking could be considered as an art form; it was the critics and the academics, especially during the 1960s, who seriously suggested that it could be. Within fifteen years of its initial development, film was on its way to becoming the twentieth century's first original art form: the seventh art, a new aesthetic form as important as painting or sculpture or literature.

In 1915, D. W. Griffith's epic *Birth of a Nation*, the longest feature made until then, received great public and critical acclaim. In the same year, US poet Vachel Lindsay's *The Art of the Moving Picture* was released, equating film with high art. As such, film was the first media form to be taken up by academics as an artistic medium worthy of study.

Auteur theory: From the French *auteur*, meaning author; at its most basic, it is the theory that a film has an author, just as a book does, and the author of a film is its director. In its more complex variations, it is a theoretical tool that concedes that while it is impossible for there to be a unitary author of a film, given the number of people who contribute to its making, it is still possible to analyse individuals' ability to leave some form of distinctive style or signature on what is essentially an industrial product.

Seventh art: As an art new to the twentieth century, cinema was added to the traditional arts: painting, sculpture, architecture, poetry, theatre and philosophy.

Since then approaches to film have tended to follow two streams:

- *aesthetic studies*, which apply literary studies paradigms to film
- *industrial studies*, which focus on the social practice and reception of film.

Let's look at each of these in more detail.

Aesthetic studies

Film style

- *What it is*—Film style is a particular form of textual analysis specific to film, which attempts to understand how meaning is made.
- *Where it came from*—It arose from a combination of film movements in Europe from the 1900s to the 1940s. In the days of the silent films, in state-funded film industries such as those of Germany and Russia, film was being developed as an **expressive** or **formalist medium**. This gave rise to movements such as **German expressionism** and **Russian montage**, which stated that, rather than simply reproducing the world, film actually created its own heavily stylised worlds, though which filmmakers could make statements on important issues. Following the introduction of sound, there was a return to a more **realist filmmaking** mode, particularly after John Grierson's documentary movement in the UK (see below) and the neorealist film movement in Italy. Together, these movements contributed to a vocabulary of film, a way of describing how films are composed and how they make meaning.
- *Key theorists and filmmakers*—A central figure in film style was Sergei Eisenstein, a Russian filmmaker and critic who is perhaps best remembered for *Battleship Potemkin.* Like Méliès, Eisenstein believed that film made meaning through editing a combination of shots—as exemplified by his famous Odessa steps sequence from *Potemkin.* Eisenstein was particularly interested in the juxtaposition of separate shots, which created a montage. Another key theorist was André Bazin, French critic and founder of the enormously influential French journal *Cahiers du Cinema*, who believed that film made meaning through **mise en scène**: the composition of elements within a shot (Bazin 1997).

Expressive medium: The notion that film works best by expressing the feelings of the artist, through metaphor, allegory and performance.

Formalist medium: The notion that film works best by presenting the best possible examples of film styles and techniques (the form).

German expressionism: A form of filmmaking, developed in Germany, particularly Berlin, during the 1920s, that featured highly stylised sets and symbolic acting to reveal the internal emotional struggles of its protagonists (and society).

Russian montage: A form of filmmaking developed in the USSR in the 1920s, based on Sergei Eisenstein's notion of using separate, contrasting images to construct combined new images for the viewer.

Realist filmmaking: A style of filmmaking seeking to show great fidelity to real life, often through unscripted dialogue and the use of handheld camera and long takes, necessarily limiting the intrusion of the filmmaker; best seen in the British documentary movement and the neorealist movement in Italy.

Mise en scène: Literally 'placing on stage' it refers to all the physical elements of a shot, that is, everything that is placed before the camera—props, sets, actors, costumes, make-up and lighting—and how these are arranged to tell the story (for example, revealing narrative information, emotion or even a character's mental state).

Why film style is important

First, it refocused attention on European films after a long period of ascendancy of the US film industry. Second, Eisenstein's notion of montage and Bazin's notion of *mise en scène* together became the basis of a new vocabulary for analysing moving images. For a complete listing of this vocabulary, see Tools 3: Textual Analysis and Media Research.

Citizen Kane and *Psycho*: textbooks in film style

While you can read about the elements of film style, as film is a medium that blends sight and sound, film style is much better experienced on the screen. There can be no better examples than Orson Welles's *Citizen Kane* and Alfred Hitchcock's *Psycho*. Both are films about complicated men—one a public figure (Charles Foster Kane, played by Orson Welles), the other a very private one (Norman Bates played by Anthony Perkins)—and both films will provide you with all you need to know about shot construction, lighting, editing, music and sound.

Documentary films

Documentary films are fact-based films that depict actual events and people.

- In the early 1900s the French used the term *docummentaire* to refer to any nonfiction film, including travelogues.
- John Grierson, the famous Scottish documentary film pioneer, first used the term 'documentary' in a review of Robert Flaherty's 1926 film *Moana* (Cunningham 2005). This landmark film told the story of Samoan Pacific islanders.
- It was another Flaherty film, *Nanook of the North* (1922), that is regarded as the first official documentary or nonfiction narrative film. It was an ethnographic depiction of the austere life of Canadian Inuit living in the Arctic, although some of the film's scenes of obsolete customs were staged.
- Flaherty's first sound documentary feature film was the *Man of Aran* (1934). It depicted the rugged Aran islanders and fishermen off the west coast of Ireland's Galway Bay.
- Documentaries can be a form of journalism (Australian journalist John Pilger is one of the best-known journalist filmmakers).
- Documentaries can also be a form of social commentary.
- Documentaries can also be a conduit for propaganda or personal expression. During the decade before the Second World War, Leni Riefenstahl, who is known to have sympathised with the Nazi government in Germany, made a powerful propaganda film, *Triumph of the Will*. In the following decade, Frank Capra's *Why We Fight* series (1942–45) and the British film *London Can Take It* (1940) were persuasive nationalistic documentaries.
- The important distinction separating documentaries from other films is that their purpose is to show us reality rather than invented stories.
- Because they are factual works, they are sometimes known as *cinema verité*, a term that became popular in the 1960s when documentary films began to emphasise a more informal and intimate relationship between camera and subject.

Continued

- Because they usually do not reach the large audiences that attend showings of major fiction films, documentaries are generally considered a subgenre of nonfiction, alongside concert films, large format (IMAX) films, compilations and reality films.

John Grierson: the pioneer of documentary filmmaking

Scotsman John Grierson (1898–1972) was the most influential pioneer of documentary film. In the 1920s, he recognised the potential of films to shape people's lives, and promoted the use of film for educational purposes. He wrote an important essay, 'First Principles of Documentary' (Fowler 2002), on documentary filmmaking, taking the French term *docummentaire* and transforming it from a word for the classification of travel films into the title of a new film genre. Grierson first used the term in a review of Flaherty's *Moana* in the New York *Sun*, writing that Flaherty's *Moana* 'has documentary value' (8 February 1926). This remark saw the creation of a movement that still influences documentary filmmakers today.

Grierson was the founder of the British documentary film movement and its leader for nearly four decades. In the 1920s, after graduating from Glasgow University, he won a Rockefeller Fellowship to study in the USA, where he developed an interest in mass communications and the theories of Walter Lippmann. On his return to Britain, Grierson was commissioned to make *Drifters* (1929), a documentary about the North Sea herring fleet. *Drifters* includes many of the attributes that would later characterise documentary filmmaking, particularly an emphasis on the social interaction and daily routine of the fishermen, and the economic value of their work. This film, and Grierson's involvement in the making of *Night Mail* (1936), a film about loneliness and companionship, as well as about the collection and delivery of letters, were pivotal to the creation of a British film culture.

Frank Hurley: Australian pioneer documentary filmmaker

Frank Hurley—adventurer, photographer and polar explorer—was one of Australia's first documentary filmmakers. In December 1911, Hurley travelled to Antarctica on the expedition led by Douglas Mawson. His feature-length documentary, *Home of the Blizzard*, was released to great acclaim in 1913. In 1917, Hurley released his second documentary film on polar exploration, recording the expedition to the Antarctic led by Ernest Shackleton in 1915–16. The success of *In the Grip of Polar Ice* saw Hurley hailed as Australia's greatest documentary filmmaker. During the First World War, Hurley produced films for the Australian War Records Office. In the 1920s, he shot several Cinesound features, including *The Silence of Dean Maitland* (1934) (Pike & Cooper 1998: 131–2).

Rules of the documentary film genre

- Documentary filmmakers, like journalists, are committed to truth telling in documentary films, and this ideal is reinforced by guidelines and codes of conduct that are issued to producers by broadcasters and commissioning authorities.
- While there are no official rules for documentaries, most documentary filmmakers subscribe to certain ideals, which include filming events as they happen rather than recreating events, representing people as themselves, recording events in a manner that is consistent with available historical evidence and not overtly presenting the filmmaker's point of view.
- Having noted these ideals, it has to be acknowledged that some of the most influential documentaries have broken these rules. The highest-grossing documentary films of recent times have certainly not adhered to these guidelines (such as Morgan Spurlock's *Supersize Me,* for example).
- Nonfiction films have a long history of being used as persuasive tools—overtly, as in Michael Moore's *Fahrenheit 9/11*, and as nationalist propaganda, as in Frank Capra's *Why We Fight* series and Leni Riefenstahl's *Triumph of the Will*.
- Michael Moore, the advocacy filmmaker, is the most successful documentary filmmaker of all time. He uses a potent mixture of facts, attention-grabbing journalism and opinion, placing himself on the screen in what has been called **performative documentary**, a style in which the documentary film is constructed around a performance by the filmmaker (Bruzzi 2000: 154).
- The highest-grossing documentary film of all time, Michael Moore's 2004 *Fahrenheit 9/11*, took $US119.2 million in ticket sales, and was the first documentary to attain the status of a mainstream blockbuster. It was the third Michael Moore film to top the list of highest-grossing documentary films. The others were *Bowling for Columbine* (2002) and *Roger and Me* (1989).
- Al Gore's 2006 success, *An Inconvenient Truth*, billed as 'the most terrifying film you will ever see', is another example of documentary filmmaking where the filmmaker operates in a performative role. This film has been credited with putting climate change on the political agenda of many countries.

The introduction of animation and special effects

Animation and special effects have become a part of documentary filmmaking in recent times. While the purists may lament the use of fictional techniques in nonfiction films, this technique has been used to great effect, and can engage audiences in a way that straight delivery cannot. The Australian documentary *After Maeve* (2006) used animation in an emotionally affecting documentary about the sudden death of young Maeve Coughlan. The National Geographic documentary, *March of the Penguins*, which made $US77.4 million in 2005 and was one of the highest-selling documentaries of all time, it used actors' to provide the voices of the penguins in some parts of the world and the actor Morgan Freeman to provide a third-person narrative for its English language release.

Genre theory

Documentary film: A fact-based film that depicts actual events and people.

Performative documentary: A style of documentary film that is constructed around a performance by the filmmaker.

Iconography: From icon; the most recognisable aspects of a text's form and content, which represent that text, for example, white hats (the good guys) and black hats (the bad guys) in western movies.

Narrative tropes: Words, phrases or expressions that recur in particular narratives, for example, the *femme fatale* (the sexually attractive but dangerous woman) in crime movies of the 1940s.

Genre: Categories of texts according to shared narrative and iconographic features and codes, as well as categories of commercial products provided by producers and marketers and expected by audiences of texts.

- *What it is*—'Genre theory' is a term used to describe how **iconographic** elements (such as setting—temporal and physical—lighting, music and format) and **narrative tropes**, the accepted clichés of the medium, such as the possibility of a positive resolution, the presence of monsters or otherworldly things, a strong romantic plot and people breaking into song to express their feelings, can be organised into and classified according to recognisable types of narrative entertainment, such as science fiction, horror, the western or the musical.
- *Where the term came from*—Genre is an aesthetic term coming out of literary studies, treating the film as another bounded text such as a book. But genres are also industrial products. As Schatz (1981: 4) writes:

> In their continual efforts to reach as massive an audience as possible, early filmmakers investigated areas of potential audience appeal and, at the same time, standardized those areas whose appeal had already been verified by audience response. In the gradual development of the business of movie production, experimentation steadily gave way to standardization as a matter of fundamental economics.

Through a combination of audience expectation and consumption, filmmakers' repetition and variation on common themes, and studios' economic imperatives, a set of stylistic and narrative conventions emerged that we can think of as **genre**.

Film genres are shaped by production, distribution and reception. For while a genre is defined by the film industry, it must be capable of being recognised by the audience.

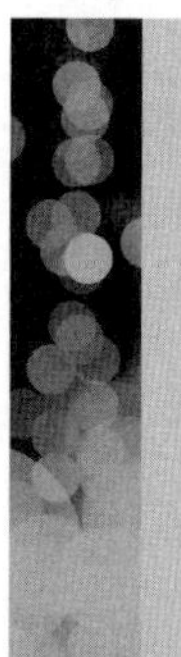

Great genre films

To sample some of the genres that are out there, here are a few films that not only function as good genre films but also reflect on the nature of their genres:

Action: *Die Hard*
Animation: *Who Framed Roger Rabbit?*
Film noir: *Double Indemnity*
Horror: *The Mist*
Melodrama: *Imitation of Life*
Musicals: *Cabaret*
Romantic comedy (rom com): *There's Something About Mary*
Science fiction: *Serenity*
Westerns: *Unforgiven.*

Steve Neale (2000: 7), quoting Tom Ryall describes it this way:

> The master image for genre criticism is the triangle composed of artist/film/audience. Genres may be defined patterns/forms/styles/structures which transcend individual films, and which supervise both their construction by the filmmaker, and their reading by an audience.

In this way, genre theory is more than just a literary model applied to film. When talking about literature, we tend to think only about the writer and reader, and the relationship between them. When talking about film genres, we need to consider the entire process of production, distribution and consumption. Therefore, it may be better to think of genre as a negotiation between the filmmakers, the producers, the distributors and the audience.

- *Key theorists and filmmakers*—Genre theory tends to be applied to popular US directors (because it is, essentially, looking at the most popular and formulaic films). However, canons of genre have also been established to focus on certain auteurs (see below), as well as innovators who have been able to stretch and adapt genres in new and interesting ways, such as Steven Spielberg, Martin Scorsese and Quentin Tarantino.
- *Why genre theory is important*—Genre theory is important for a number of reasons. First, while genre theory tries to classify and archive films, it also directly deals with power. When we try to decide whether a film succeeds or fails as a genre film, we need to decide what can and cannot be considered as part of a **canon**. We might therefore ask how does this film fit into, or develop or otherwise challenge the canon? Second, genre theory provides us with a way of considering the most basic and formulaic of films and understanding how they negotiate the balance between repetition and innovation that is so vital to being considered a good genre film. Third, a study of genre (and more particularly which genres are popular at certain points of time or in certain parts of the world) is also a way of studying changing patterns of taste and consumption. So, genre is not only a way of understanding the relationship between filmmakers, the industry and the audience, but also between filmmaking, filmgoing and the larger culture.
- *Why the idea of the canon is important*—The term, derived from religion, refers to the essential books of scripture, such as the accepted books of the Bible. Within popular fiction, there is, for example, a canon of Sherlock Holmes books, that is, all those written by Sir Arthur Conan Doyle. Anything not written by Doyle is noncanonical. Only televised episodes of *Doctor Who*, for example, may be considered canon by the fans of the series and its producers (the BBC), rather than the various books, recordings or stage shows based on the series. In the context of film studies, genre theory makes us think about filmic canons and whether a certain film can be considered to be part of a particular generic canon (or not) based upon its generic attributes (plot, setting, etc.).

Film genres: Film categories, such as westerns, mysteries and melodramas, produced in order to keep costs low while building presold audiences.

Canon: The set of texts regarded as forming the essence of a particular body of work.

Toy Story 3

For a broad overview of genre, look at this 2010 Disney Pixar release. In this story of toys learning to find a new place for themselves in the world now that their owner is preparing to leave for college, the narrative moves through a number of different genres, including romantic comedy, prison film, disaster film and even film noir. See how many you can identify according to their tropes and iconography.

Auteur theory

- *What it is*—Auteur theory is the form of textual analysis that emphasises the importance of the auteur of a film. The director is usually regarded as the film's auteur. Auteur theorists concentrate on those textual elements (signature touches) that recur in a number of the same director's films and as such can be considered as evidence of that director's particular style or preoccupations.
- *Where it came from*—It emerged in France during the mid 1950s and early 1960s, particularly through critics writing for the journal *Cahiers du Cinema*. Whose ideas were picked up by American, British and Australian critics and filmmakers during the 1960s.
- *Key theorists and filmmakers*—They include André Bazin, founder of *Cahiers du Cinema*, whose ideas were taken up by such people as French critic and filmmaker François Truffaut, who wrote about the notion of the *la politique des auteurs* (the policy of auteurs) in 1954. Auteur theory was subsequently taken up by US critic Andrew Sarris and many others, and has been applied to a range of American directors, including Alfred Hitchcock (director of thrillers), John Ford (director of westerns) and Douglas Sirk (director of melodramas).
- *Why auteur theory is important*—It is a literary and aesthetic framework that places an emphasis on the role of the author in media studies, and so it contradicts most of the other approaches in this book. This theory also focuses our attention on the craft of filmmaking and, more specifically, how an artist can function and leave a distinctive signature touch while working within an industrial framework.

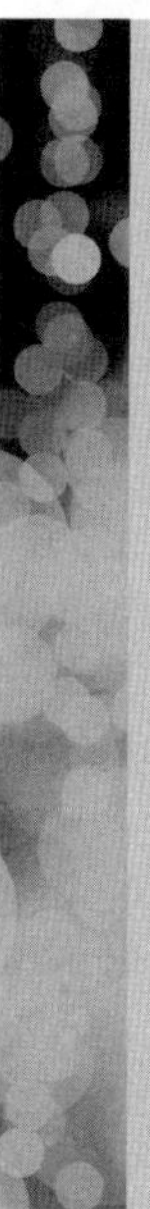

Art in the age of the blockbuster?

Can film still be regarded as the seventh art in the age of the blockbuster, when special effects flood the screen and film franchises based on recognisable brands dominate the box office? There is an argument for it, depending on your perspective. Those seeking more diversity in filmmaking can look to the rich collection of films from national cinemas and independent features. Ironically, though, the increased availability and advancement in special effects has provided auteurs such as George Lucas or Steven Spielberg with more power than ever before. The use of digital filmmaking enables directors to maintain control over every aspect of what appears in the frame. In this way we could argue that films such as *Avatar* and *Lord of the Rings* are in fact closer to art than many low-tech arthouse films, because the ability to manipulate film digitally makes it a more painterly medium. As a result, the notion of film as art may require some redefinition in the future, lest it simply become a matter of comparing the number of pixels in a sequence on Pandora with the beauty of Ray Harryhausen's stop-motion skeletons in *Jason and the Argonauts*.

Industrial studies

- *What it is*—This is a form of analysis focusing on the construction and place of the filmmaking industries themselves, rather than their individual films. Industrial analyses tend to analyse filmmaking practices, costs and the way individual countries' industries fit into the pattern of global production and circulation of film.

- *Where it came from*—Industrial studies of film emerge from media studies, as well as from a desire to understand how industries local to the concerns of theorists (such as those in Australia, New Zealand, the UK and Hong Kong) fit into the larger global (US) film culture.
- *Key theorists and filmmakers*—Notable theorists on the Australian film industry include Tom O'Regan and, as part of her larger work in Australian cultural studies and the Asia–Pacific region, Meaghan Morris, both of whom have mapped the changes in an industry that has long sought to balance telling Australian stories with being commercially viable. O'Regan has, for example, written extensively on the way Warner Brothers' Gold Coast studios have been used for international productions.
- *Why this approach is important*—Industrial studies of film refocus attention on the behind-the-scenes costs and practices of filmmaking. The idea of film as art is therefore subordinated, so that analysts can focus on such matters as the difficulty of making films within these systems. Industrial studies also focuses attention on international filmmaking, highlighting the difficulties for many local industries in making their stories and having them distributed. Often they highlight the need for greater government funding in national industries, the ways in which local filmmaking can compete and how local industries can survive through a combination of international infrastructures (as happened in New Zealand with *Lord of the Rings* and in Australia with *The Matrix*) and a small export industry.

Wolf Creek and *Australia*: working at the edges of the Australian film industry

Unlike the US industry, the Australian film industry has always carried the added burden of having to provide a representation of Australian national identity, tales that reflect the quintessential essence of what it means to be Australian and to live in Australia. This has produced some unique and moving films, such as *Picnic at Hanging Rock, The Adventures of Priscilla, Queen of the Desert* and even *Mad Max* (if you like cars, guns and a young Mel Gibson). But it has also presented challenges to filmmakers who want to make good genre films, such as the horror film *Wolf Creek*. This is despite the fact that our genre films—and *Mad Max* could be included on that list—are among the best-known Australian films internationally. *Wolf Creek* also travelled well, but there was some concern it wouldn't do anything for the tourist industry. (Ironically it did, with Wolf Creek becoming quite a tourist site.) Sitting somewhere in between is Baz Luhrmann's *Australia*, a genre film, in that it is both a melodrama and a blockbuster, the latter being a genre that Australian films typically don't do, owing to budgetary constraints, that also seeks to represent the quintessence of what it is to be Australian (a battler) and what it means to be living in Australia (the vast outback, the sumptuous natural beauty). Unlike *Wolf Creek*, this became part of a Tourism Australia campaign—a campaign that was ultimately deemed unsuccessful given the (relative) failure of *Australia* at the US box office. The future of the industry may lie with more of an embrace of genre films (the horror genre, particularly, has smaller budgets and reaps good box office returns) or more international production using Australia (and its actors) as a setting.

JASON BAINBRIDGE

The video and DVD revolution

Given the queues at the cinema and the enormous grosses of film franchises such as *Iron Man* and *Batman*, you might not realise that audience attendances for film peaked in the mid 1940s, and that film audiences have been steadily declining since 1946. Because the introduction of sound had been so successful in the early 1930s, the film industry believed that any technological innovation could arrest this slide in audience numbers. Therefore, over the years the industry has tried the following innovations (with varying degrees of success):

- *colour*—Technicolor, introduced in the mid 1930s, was seen as a luxury for filmmakers until the 1960s, but now very few films are made in black and white (monochrome)
- *widescreen formats*—such as Cinemascope and Cinerama (early 1950s)
- *innovative experiences*—such as 3D films, in which the image seems to jump out of the screen at the audience and each audience member had to wear red and blue glasses, Aromarama, and Smell-O-Vision, with cards that had scratch-and-sniff smells, which date from the 1950s and 1960s.

Recently, digital filmmaking has allowed an increased blurring of the distinction between live-action and animated filmmaking, for example, where live-action actors perform digitally animated stunts against digitally animated creatures in digitally animated landscapes. Following the success of *Avatar*, 3D made a return in a big way. But this time it added depth to the image; rather than things jumping out at audiences, it was more like looking through a window on images that seemed to spread beyond the screen, an experience akin to Dorothy opening her black-and-white Kansas home door onto the Technicolour of Oz in *The Wizard of Oz.*

Ironically, advances in technology have also done the most damage to the film industry. In the 1950s, the introduction of television almost ruined the film industry for about ten years. Later, the introduction of home-theatre technologies, such as videotape, provided new threats to films. Digital video discs (DVDs) and their variations (such as Blu-ray) are the most recent challenge.

The advent of home videotape players in the late 1970s challenged the historic logic of filmgoing—films that had once been inaccessible after their theatrical run (save for a limited re-release or broadcast on television) could now be accessed at any time from a consumer's home and watched as many times as a consumer wanted. Furthermore, the film could be stopped, started and paused, enabling audiences to edit the film's presentation as they saw fit.

This was an enormous change in the way films were consumed, as it enabled audiences to develop relationships with particular films and filmmakers based around re-viewing the film rather than relying on some memory of seeing the film in a cinema.

Despite the film industry's fears, video did not destroy box-office takings. A night out at the cinema remained the most popular way of consuming films. Videos became an important, but ultimately subsidiary, extension of that experience.

DVDs alter that experience in two main ways. First, the DVD can provide a viewing experience of a higher quality than that experienced in the theatre. Digital sound technologies in home-theatre systems have helped to make the viewing of a digital film on a digital television a more desirable—or purer—experience than viewing that same digital film at a cinema that often lacks in digital technology. DVD viewing is not a subsidiary extension of film, but may actually be a preferable alternative.

Second, and perhaps more significantly for the future, DVDs feature a variety of extras (something the home video market never really took advantage of), including outtakes, director's commentaries, alternative endings and background information, some running hours longer than the film itself. DVDs, then, provide a more complete viewing experience than the film did during its initial release. Increasingly, the film is becoming a teaser for the DVD release rather than the DVD being a subsidiary extension of the film.

The use of DVD illustrates the ideas of show business—the negotiation between art and commerce—discussed above. In their commentaries, directors will often discuss the tensions involved in bringing their vision to the screen and the concessions that had to be made to the industry.

It is important to think of film as art, because like art it can be communicated through a variety of media. Art exists in sculpture, on canvas, on city walls and, yes, in images, too. Film can similarly exist without cinemas, through DVDs, iPads, home theatres and downloads—basically, anywhere an image can be shown on a screen.

Conclusion

Film is both an artistic endeavour and an industrial product, a negotiation between the demands of art and commerce. It is has provided us with some of the most recognisable representations and ways of understanding the world, as well as a vocabulary for understanding how still and moving images make meaning. While the future of film distribution may be in doubt, there is no doubt that filmmaking and filmgoing will continue to exist, in many forms, for many years to come.

KEY REFERENCES

Bordwell, D. & Thompson, K. (2008). *Film Art: An Introduction* (8th edn). Boston: McGraw Hill.

Cook, D. A. (1996). *A History of Narrative Film* (3rd edn). New York: W. W. Norton.

Neale, S. (2000). *Genre and Hollywood.* London: Routledge.

Turner, G. (2006). *Film as Social Practice* (4th edn). London: Routledge.

CHAPTER 7

TELEVISION: THE ZOO

JASON BAINBRIDGE

Introduction

Since 1956, when it was first introduced in Australia, television has been our pre-eminent media industry. As a domestic form of media, it is part of almost everyone's home. A magpie medium, it has appropriated earlier forms from vaudeville to radio shows, updating and adapting them to suit its own requirements. As a mass media form, shared by billions of people across the globe, it has remained the most successful medium for bringing vast groups of people together around commons issues, passions and ways of thinking while seeming as intimate as a voice in the room or a window in the wall.

But television's position is under siege. It is being displaced by YouTube, downloads and DVDs, and its mass audience is fragmenting across a multiplicity of cable stations and other media platforms. At the same time, television sales are the strongest they have ever been. Australia has never had a greater choice of channels, and a large proportion of television output is available on demand, either through DVDs or downloads. Television itself is in a state of change, reinventing itself and moving forward in an attempt to re-assert its dominance as the preeminent media form.

In this chapter we look at:

- a history of television
- the principles of television
- new approaches to television in the age of the download and the DVD.

The importance of television

Television maintains a privileged position in the public sphere for three main reasons:

- *It remains the communal site for large groups of people*—For fifty years no other medium has brought together large groups of people more effectively than television, whether to find out who shot J. R. Ewing on *Dallas* in the 1980s, to commemorate the life of Diana, Princess of Wales in the 1990s to see Prime Minister Kevin Rudd say sorry to Indigenous

Australians, to take part in the opening ceremony of the Sydney Olympic Games in 2000 or to share the grief of seeing floodwaters rise across the Brisbane CBD in 2011. Television has replaced, or at the very least displaced, the town or church hall as the meeting place for large groups of people. Even now, in the post-broadcast era (see Chapter 10), it still remains the central medium in the public sphere; while online audiences may be getting larger, they tend to be more fragmented.

- *It is a domestic form of media*—Television is a part of people's homes. People don't have to go to television; they simply have to switch it on.
- *It is a common ground for large groups of people*—Television is a source of shared knowledge between people, often regardless of geographical location.

Table 7.1 Television milestones in Australia

1956	Television introduced to Australia to coincide with the Melbourne Olympic Games. Internationally, television is often introduced to capitalise on a spectacle.
	In the early years of Australian television, the major form of local content was low-cost variety and quiz shows, such as *In Melbourne Tonight* and *Pick-a-Box*. Successful radio formats were imported to television, starting with Australia's first local drama, the courtroom-based *Consider Your Verdict*.
1964	80 per cent of households owned a television set.
1974	90 per cent of households owned a television set.
	Broadcasting in the 1970s became a highly profitable enterprise, with profit margins of between 15 and 20 per cent.
1975	Introduction of colour television.
	Local dramas, based around Australian locales and concerns, continued to be important in Australia throughout the 1970s and into the 1980s.
1980s	Start of a localising trend, largely prompted by regulatory requirements for Australian content. This saw the introduction of a number of new long-running dramas, such as *Prisoner* and *Number 96*, and lavish miniseries such as *Bodyline, All the Rivers Run* and *Return to Eden*.
1990s	Inexperienced operators, high interest rates and the 1987 stock market crash reduced profits in the Australian television industry—Channels Seven and Ten went into receivership. Throughout the 1990s, the stations all reduced production of expensive local dramas, making significant cuts in local programming and seeking low-cost formats in an effort to reverse their fortunes. This led to an increase in lifestyle and reality series, as well as the increasing reliance of channels on imported programming.
1995	Cable television station Foxtel began broadcasting in Australia. Formed via a joint venture between Telstra and News Corporation, this was not the first cable television provider in Australia, but it soon proved to be the strongest: it acquired Galaxy TV subscribers, formed a partnership with Austar and entered into a content sharing agreement with Optus TV.
2001	Digital television began broadcasting in Australian metropolitan areas, with regional areas following.

Continued

Table 7.1 Television milestones in Australia (*continued*)

2008	The launch of Freeview, a consistent marketing platform for Australia's digital terrestrial, that is, free-to-air (FTA) channels. Each FTA was allocated three digital channels, offering viewers a total of fifteen channels from the Freeview brand in direct competition to cable channels such as Foxtel, in part to encourage viewers to embrace digital technology.
2009	The first of the new Freeview channels was launched: Channel Ten's formally sport-only channel, One.
2013	Predicted date for the switchover to digital, when the rollout of digital television will be complete and the last of the analogue signals will be switched off.

What television is really doing is providing audiences with knowledge of nations. Media theorists such as John Hartley, John Fiske and Alan McKee note the ways in which television enables audiences to place themselves in relation to the rest of the world. This occurs not only through news, which provides audiences with knowledge of local, national and international issues, but also through sport, which enables us to compete as nations and as parts of nations, and dramas, which give us some insight into how we and the peoples of other nations present ourselves.

This knowledge of nations is acquired in two ways:

- *through national events*, which bring audiences together as nations, such as during sport and large dramatic moments, such as the final episode of *Seinfeld*, a televised funeral or a wedding
- *through internationalisation*, through foreign infrastructure investment, which promotes production, for example, US production houses in New Zealand, and through the sale and exchange of formats and series overseas. Endemol, for example, a Netherlands production company, is one of the major providers of reality television in the world.

A double-faced culture

Media theorist Tom O'Regan refers to Australian television as being 'double-faced': a blend of local and imported product that produces 'an amalgam of different cultures ... and multiple identities' (O'Regan 1993: 96). Australian television drama relies on 'innovation through producers adjusting—and audiences adjusting to—local program and cultural traditions with common international formats evident from contemporaneous US and British imports' (O'Regan 1993: 87). This leads to innovative Australian formats with, say, our own type of soap opera, such as *Neighbours* or *Home and Away*, which blends American melodrama with British social realism.

O'Regan's (1993) notion of double-faced cultures was developed around Australian television, but it can apply to a range of television industries outside the USA, that is, any television industry composed of one or more imported cultures, such as US or British, and a very small local export industry.

Principles of television

Television has, historically, been based upon three apparently contradictory principles: show business, flow and delay.

Show business

Television shares film the notion of maintaining the balance between *creativity* and *cost*—between the *show* and the *business*. This is especially important for commercial television and is as true of news production as any other genre. Commercial television is a medium designed to sell goods and services; it also sells audiences to advertisers. This is what drives production—to create something desirable for audiences to watch, and thereby attract audiences to advertisers—and drives television's search for global export and growth.

Flow

In television, **flow** is the way in which one moment of drama or information leads to the next, encouraging us to watch television in a certain way—through narrative ('Will X end up with Y?' or 'Will Y survive the train accident? Join us again next week', or scheduling—*Beautiful Sunday* on Seven or Friday Night Football.

Flow: In television, the way one moment of drama or information leads to the next.

Delay: The way in which consumption of television is indefinitely postponed through advertising, narrative or scheduling.

Delay

Delay is the way in which consumption of television is always indefinitely postponed: through advertising ('We'll return after this commercial break'), narrative (the cliffhanger, the 22-minute episode) and scheduling (sports being presented towards the end of a news bulletin, a daily serial or a weekly series). Media industries such as television produce goods that are never completely consumed. Complete consumption of the programs audiences watch is always delayed, as a result of which, audiences are continually being returned to advertisers so that they can consume a little more of the programs they enjoy.

The significance of television

But is television really still such an important medium in the face of increasing audience demand for social media (see Chapter 18)? The answer is yes—at least for now.

Social media remain, for the most part, extensions of traditional media outlets, and television remains at the centre of this shift. For example, iPod, Disney and ABC have a deal whereby a missed episode of *Desperate Housewives* can be downloaded to an iPod for $1.99; CBS has entered into a partnership with Google to sell programs online; Fox and the BBC have offered downloadable mobisodes (television segments for mobile phones) of their programs *24* and *Doctor Who*; and the US network NBC and the Australian network Nine are both allied with Microsoft (forming MSNBC and ninemsn respectively), while Seven has a partnership with Yahoo (forming Yahoo7). All television news is regularly updated online and all bulletins point viewers to the web for additional, usually audience-generated, content, such as your footage of the fires, ways in which you can help out, etc.

Television, then, remains at the centre of this convergence, and because it remains the major source of content for new media forms, television will remain the content provider for new media distribution platforms. In addition, audiences will always watch television shows—but maybe not always on a television set. Futurist Mike Walsh, for example, suggests that we are fast approaching a time where the main purpose of television will be to drive us to the accompanying website, where television will exist only to support web content. Television may come to refer to content (the programs you watch) rather than a specific medium (that increasingly large and crystal-clear screen you have at home).

Home theatre

Is television, as a medium, really going to die any time soon? In recent years, enthusiastic acceptance by Australian audiences has led to the rapid adoption of **home-theatre** technology. Despite the variety of distribution platforms on offer, audiences continue to spend large amounts of money updating their televisual technology, and because of the adoption of large screens and complex sound systems, television has again become a design feature of the home. With added features—such as more free-to-air digital channels and advancements in 3D technology—it seems that television is more likely to displace cinema than be displaced itself.

Home theatre: Electronic facilities in the home, such as large screens and five-speaker sound systems, that emulate facilities once found only in cinemas and theatres.

Spoiler: Details about a narrative that are revealed before the wider audience has gained access to them.

Bingeing: The watching of a succession of television episodes in one sitting.

These changes in distribution affect the principles of television outlined above. Accessing television through distribution means such as downloads, DVDs or even TiVo, a system that tapes television programs and removes the advertisements, clearly challenges the notions of flow and delay because television becomes accessible on demand and show business because, while producers and networks still need to cover their costs, advertisers are taken out of the supply of entertainment.

Two of the most important phenomena that challenge these principles are spoilers and bingeing.

- **Spoilers** are important details about television narrative that are revealed before the wider audience has gained access to them. To some extent these have always been part of television culture—daytime soap operas encouraged viewer interest by revealing information about upcoming storylines to viewers; viewer pleasure was then derived from seeing how these events played themselves out. The practice of downloading television series and accessing online reviews has increased access to spoilers which means that they have to be built into the program to generate a desire to keep watching.
- **Bingeing** is the watching of a succession of television episodes in one sitting. Bingeing can occur via downloading episodes from the internet or, more commonly, watching a large group of episodes in a DVD package. Some consumers will watch all of a boxed set of

DVDs, a season, up to twenty-two episodes, of a television series in a short period of time. This has led to a change in the production of television drama, with episodic series giving way to longer, arc-driven programs that can be enjoyed sequentially in DVD bingeing: series such as *24, Prison Break, Heroes* and *Lost.*

New perspectives on television

As television adapts to the new media environment, a new set of principles for television is needed to describe what it is that television is doing—and continues to do—throughout these changes in distribution.

Television scholar Robert C. Allen (2004) says that because television is ubiquitous and so much a part of our lives, it has become almost invisible to us. To focus on television as an object of study, we need to make it strange. As academic interest in television has increased, a number of possible models for thinking about television have been advanced.

Drawing on Baratay and Hardouin-Fuger's cultural study of zoos, *Zoo: A History of Zoological Gardens in the West* (2004), I suggest another model for television: the zoo—or more particularly 'the enclosed space containing a collection of animals' (Baratay & Hardouin-Fuger 2004: 10) that came into existence in the sixteenth and seventeenth centuries, when the idea of establishing 'a single place for their exhibition' developed, and 'the first theatres of the wild were created in the grounds of grand princely residences; these establishments which turned the act of keeping animals into a spectacle' (Baratay & Hardouin-Fuger 2004: 13).

Zoo TV

On 29 February 1992, the Irish rock group U2 began an elaborate worldwide arena tour entitled Zoo TV, which was to last almost two years. The tour marked a change in U2's music. With its incorporation of techno pop and a change in performance style, the earnestness of their earlier hit album *The Joshua Tree* was replaced by a technological marvel of a stage designed by Peter 'Willie' Williams that incorporated numerous television cameras, 176 speakers and thirty-six video monitors that featured everything from random slogans and multimedia performance artists Emergency Broadcast Network, to videotaped 'confessions' of audience members.

The tour was a satirical response to CNN's coverage of the first Gulf War in 1991, emblematic of what Bono and the other band members saw as the media overload that was dominating the 1990s. But during the European leg of the tour (Zooropa) something else happened: the band began initiating live link-ups to people in wartorn Sarajevo. Inspired by Bill Carter's documentary *Miss Sarajevo*, the band intended to highlight the suffering of a people they considered were being ignored by the bulk of the world's media. Over the course of the tour, U2 members came to realise how television could function as a cultural resource—and all through this metaphor of the zoo.

Why is television like a zoo?

Similarity of aims

Baratay and Hardouin-Fuger (2004) write about the zoo's development from the time in the sixteenth, seventeenth and eighteenth centuries when cabinets of curiosities were favoured by the aristocracy, scholars, doctors and affluent bourgeoisie. In these cabinets a clear parallel with television is made:

> They were envisaged as microcosms, as condensations of the perceivable, understandable world. They contained disparate collections of all the rare and curious things that would best express the diversity and power of human, divine and natural invention. (Baratay & Hardouin-Fuger 2004: 30)

Zoos carry on this idea by exhibiting a diversity of animals from different areas; television carries on this idea by exhibiting a diversity of programs.

Similarity of structure

- *Both zoos and television programs present themselves as a series of scenes separated from us* by a screen, a railing or bars. Television, like the zoo, is a microcosm, an observational space, a way of containing the world, of presenting 'the wild' in a domestic setting (your home). This is particularly apparent in news reports that can take us around the world ('the wild') in a matter of minutes, but is also true of documentaries and other programming that exposes us to other parts of life and living we may not otherwise experience.
- *Both zoos and television programs use natural resources,* the zoo in its exploitation of wild animals, the television in its use of naturally occurring waves. As Allen explains:

> The [television licensing] system rests upon a policy established by the US government more than half a century ago—and subsequently 'exported' to countries around the world—regarding how the nation's airwaves would be utilized, by whom, and for what purposes. Television signals travel through the air as electromagnetic signals riding on naturally occurring waves. They share the electromagnetic spectrum with other forms of electronic communication [radios, microwave transmissions, etc.] ... By the 1920s, it had become clear in the United States that, as a public utility belonging to a nation as a whole, the finite spectrum space had to be regulated if this natural resource was to be utilized beneficially and if broadcasting chaos was not to ensue. The [Federal Communications Commission] was formed to allocate spectrum space to various services, assign stations in each service by issuing operating licenses, and regulate existing stations by establishing guidelines and acting on requests for license renewals (Allen 1992: 17).

- *Both zoos and television environments are laid out for us,* but there is freedom for us to stray from the directed pathways. In both, there is a sense of moving in certain way: zoos are mapped and arranged for us (aquariums, aviaries, petting zoos, baby animals, reptile house, wild cats' area, etc.), while schedulers and network executives map out television for us (news, current affairs, drama, the late movie, etc.). In both there is the opportunity for viewers to make their her own way, either by moving between exhibits at the zoo at will, for example, lions first, then reptiles, and then the aviary, or by viewing television through other distribution systems, such as DVDs or downloads, or simply by channel hopping via a remote control.

The news hour

The centrepiece of most television stations' scheduling is their news block, the idea being that if viewers watch the news they will stay with the network for the rest of that night's schedule. It also attracts a great deal of advertising revenue, particularly from high-end products such as cars. For many years Channel Nine dominated with its news hour of *National Nine News* and *A Current Affair* (from 6pm to 7pm). But recently, capitalising on the success of their morning news–entertainment show *Sunrise* and its evening lead-in *Deal or No Deal*, Channel Seven has been winning the news hour with *Seven News* and *Today Tonight*. Even more recently, Channel Ten entered the news war with (originally) not one but two-and-a-half hours of news (from 5pm to 7.30pm), a 5pm–6pm news bulletin targeting an older audience, *6pm with George Negus,* promoted as offering depth and experience, and an alternative to the other channels' 6pm bulletins, a 6.30pm local news bulletin, again offering an alternative to the 6.30pm current affairs programs, and *The 7pm Project*, targeting a younger audience, with a mix of news and humour. The limited success of this schedule demonstrates how difficult it can be for networks to reman connected with their audiences.

- *Both zoos and television environments exist as perfect laboratories* (Baratay & Hardouin-Fuger 2004: 10). Just as the zoo trades in ideas of nature, control and curiosity, television trades in ways of representing the world and in ways of thinking about the world. Television becomes a way of testing out different ways of thinking about the world (see Chapter 10) by wedding theory (ideas) with practice (narratives). This is especially apparent if we think about the variety of genres of television, Soap operas, for example, provide ideas of ethics ('How should I behave in this situation?'), science fiction series provide ideas of philosophy ('Who am I?' and 'What is my place in the universe?') and police series provide ideas of sociology ('How should society be organised?' and 'What is justice?').

What about smell?

One of the things that strikes us whenever we visit a zoo is the smell: all those different smells from all those different animals. Television cannot replicate that … or can it? This is not a reference to Smell-O-Vision, but the idea that media products have distinctive odours. This idea, put forward by media theorist Koichi Iwabuchi, suggests that media products have traces or elements that reveal their place of origin. They could be accents, particular locations or particular expressions. By contrast, an odourless media product would be one where it is hard to know where it came from, because it is hard to identify any traces of its country of origin. Just as we can use smells at a zoo to differentiate between animals, we can use odour on television to differentiate between, for example, US, British and Australian television programs.

Similar patterns of study

The study of zoos also parallels the study of television in other ways. Baratay and Hardouin-Fuger (2004: 80) note the early distinction between the word 'zoo', which focuses attention on 'the contents of the space (zoology)', and the phrase 'zoological gardens', which focuses attention on 'the space itself'.

Students of television studies have continued to divide themselves between institutional and industrial analyses (the 'zoological garden') and textual analyses of particular programs (the 'zoology'), though we'd argue that the best analyses contain elements of both. With the rise in alternative distribution platforms for television content, the message is beginning to exist independently of the medium. Future analyses of television may focus more on the interplay between, for example, the DVD industry and television series, than on the television industry and television series.

Similarity of functions

The four functions of the zoo can also be understood as the four functions of television. Again, as Baratay and Hardouin-Fuger (2004) write, these are:

- recreation
- education
- research
- conservation.

We now look at each of these functions in more detail.

Television and recreation

Zoos and television both appear to have been designed for recreation. Pleasure parks and zoological gardens 'responded to a growing desire among worthy citizens to escape, just for a moment, from urban noise, dirt and crowds … to distinguish private and working life' (Baratay & Hardouin-Fuger 2004: 100). Sitting down and watching television, regardless of the delivery system, has also typically marked the demarcation between work time and leisure time.

Both similarly depend on spectacle to attract audiences, particularly the spectacle of the exotic. Exotic animals (the odd, the ferocious and the wild) always draw record numbers to zoos. Similarly, television viewers gravitate towards the exotic on television. They enjoy seeing familiar places (note the popularity in Australia of local accents and locations in programs such as *Homicide*), but exotic stories—police procedurals, medical dramas and science fiction series—are always popular. Although audiences enjoy seeing domestic dramas (domestic in the sense of being local, and featuring stories and people they can relate to), on television the emphasis has always been on drama, hence the weddings, births and deaths that draw big audience numbers for soap operas, or the volume of police and hospital shows dealing with serial killers or freakish death. Both are providing an entertainment service.

In both cases this function of recreation disguises the true industrial nature of these organisations: they are designed to attract a profit. This applies to commercial television networks, not government-owned or community broadcasters. It can also apply to news services that blend humour or feature a mix of soft news stories, such as does *The 7pm Project*. In the context of the zoo, its patrons 'still [see] nature less as a community to be conserved than as a commodity to be consumed (environmentalist Aldo Leopold, cited in Baratay & Hardouin-Fuger 2004: 280). Similarly, for commercial networks 'the principal aim of broadcasting is not to entertain, enlighten, or provide a public service; it is to make a profit' (Allen 1992: 17).

The economy of television

Networks sell air time, with the price of thirty seconds of air time being determined by the statistical probability that a certain number of people fitting certain demographic descriptions will be tuned into the station at the moment the ad is being broadcast. Importantly, television sells audiences to advertisers, not advertisements to audiences. It does this by placing advertisements during programs that are popular with audiences or certain segments of the audiences.

John Fiske (in Burns & Thompson 1989) suggests that a dual economy works in commercial television: *a political economy* that produces an audience that can be sold to advertisers as a commodity, and *a cultural economy* that reflects the way audiences' consumption produces meanings and pleasures.

As we have seen above, the cultural economy is structured around delay—audiences are continually being returned to advertisers so they can consume a little more of the programs they enjoy.

How do the producers of the program make money?

Apart from being paid by the network for their show, program makers have traditionally made most of their money through syndication, whereby the program is sold overseas or 'stripped' (syndicated) for repeat screenings. Money can also be made through merchandising and DVD sales. DVD sales made *Buffy the Vampire Slayer*, for example, highly profitable for Warner Brothers, and kept it on air for five seasons.

Merchandising is something television shares with the zoo. Baratay and Hardouin-Fuger (2004) write that in the early 1800s, 'London's hippopotamus was welcomed by an immense crowd, becoming the hero of *Punch* cartoons and a multitude of engravings ... Small silver reproductions of him were sold at the Strand, while the "Hippopotamus Polka" was a hit in London's salons' (Baratay & Hardouin-Fuger 2004: 170). We discuss merchandising in more detail in Chapter 19.

The dual economy of television—the content of television and the cultural values it represents and responds to—are inseparable. They fit together to create the recreational aspect of television that audiences enjoy.

Even when transferred to DVD, television is still presented as entertainment and remains a commodity that must make a profit. Delay still functions in terms of narrative, which is structured into the episodes themselves irrespective of whether the format is the original program, a DVD release or a downloadable file.

Television and education

Zoos and television are both democratised spaces, designed to be accessible to the public and to draw massive audiences all over the world.

Zoos justified this democratisation when they were 'proposed as venues for the entertainment and moral improvement of the working classes' (Baratay & Hardouin-Fuger 2004: 105), a process of liberalising admissions in the 1950s that was concurrent with the general rise in living standards in the West (Baratay & Hardouin-Fuger 2004: 201). Television has similarly tried to justify its democratisation by appealing to education.

This is because democratic spaces often create anxieties and tensions. A writer of a stroller's guide in Brussels (1856) wrote: 'The zoological gardens have today passed so completely into public habit that one must ask oneself what, three years ago, the inhabitants of Brussels did between coffee time and tea' (in Baratay & Hardouin-Fuger 2004: 100, n. 34). John Hartley (1992b) similarly suggests that television's populism and immediacy make it an unreflective and 'scandalous' medium, while Graeme Turner (Turner & Cunningham 2000) notes the ambivalence with which television is regarded—blamed for violence, depression, sexism and racism, but also regarded as so trivial as to not be deserving of study.

As we noted earlier, television is a domestic medium. To watch television, you don't need to leave your house, as you do when you want to visit a zoo. Television is always there and anyone can access it. Such unmediated access has prompted governments to set up regulatory authorities to restrict **cross-media ownership**, prohibit some types of advertising (such as tobacco products), provide a ratings system and, most importantly, decide what can and cannot be broadcast. In countries such as Australia and New Zealand, with small domestic television markets, government regulation extends to ensuring that certain programs are shown: there are minimum national content quotas that television stations are obliged to fill, to ensure that audiences are seeing their own stories in their own accents and their own locations.

Cross-media ownership: The ownership of one major source of news and information (such as a television station) in the same territory as another other major source (such as a daily newspaper or radio station).

Anxiety arises in part because zoos and television traditionally have been seen as family entertainments, led by children. During the twentieth century, children enjoyed an increasingly privileged place in the family, and both zoos and other media forms contributed to the dominant position of animals within children's imaginations. In this respect, television particularly perpetuates the work of books and films.

As Baratay and Hardouin-Fuger note (2004: 207), television and zoos exist in an inverse relationship to each other, with television 'transforming real creatures into imaginary ones, [inverting] the process that had taken place in the early modern era of enhancing the reality of animals that had seemed fantastical'.

One of the ways of combating anxieties around democratised spaces was to push for these spaces to be educational. Scholars were responsible for the creation of many zoos, though their stewardship was later replaced by businessmen and politicians. Popularising natural history has always been a popular function of zoos and television, though in practice the entertainment value of both triumphed (Baratay & Hardouin-Fuger 2004: 209).

Similarly, television has apportioned some of its air time to educational programming—such as documentaries, historical pieces, art shows, plays and other forms of children's education—though increasingly these have become the province of national broadcasters and cable channels. While television is often criticised for not lifting the standard of public education, it does contribute in its own way to the public sphere by advancing pluralist discourses and encouraging research. Perhaps television's great educational ability is in telling us what is regarded as important by different members of society.

Television and research

Bizarre as it initially may seem, television also shares the zoo's practical objectives for natural history, including:

- observation and theory
- ideas of nationhood
- acclimatisation
- classification and genre
- reality.

Observation and theory

Television presents us with events from across the globe, and a range of different ideas about the world and the institutions therein.

As with a zoo, television reveals 'unknown worlds and diverse life forms; they pose the eternal questions of identity, challenging or reinforcing life's certainties' (Baratay & Hardouin-Fuger 2004: 9). This is true not only of genre television, with its insistence on otherworldliness, as in *True Blood, Star Trek* and *Doctor Who*, but also of television that depicts certain areas of society, such as the *Law & Order* franchise, with its depiction of the legal and police processes, *ER*, with its representation of hospitals, and *The West Wing*, with its depiction of US politics, and subcultures (youth culture on *The Hills* and queer culture in *Queer as Folk*).

Baratay and Hardouin-Fuger (2004: 181) write: 'The public's relationship with the animals in a zoological garden was therefore based on attraction and repulsion, curiosity and fear.' This ambivalence is made visible in the use of railings, and later wooden joists, bars and cages, to contain the animals in zoos. A similar relationship occurs between television series and the television viewer: think of your own reaction to the violence of *The Sopranos*, the misogyny of *Mad Men* or the carnage of *World's Worst* [Whatever] *Disasters*.

Sometimes this even carries over to interactivity. In zoos, this took the form of feeding the animals—'the desire for exchange' (Baratay & Hardouin-Fuger 2004: 185)—while in television, texts provide their viewers, through cliffhangers and interactivity, as in the voting practices in *Australian Idol*, with delay tactics. DVDs allow us to control the flow of television: we can pause, replay or fast-forward the narrative as we wish, or simply skip ahead to our favourite scenes.

Generally, the rise in interactive television seems to correspond with the rise in new media: the ultimate interactive media form (see Chapter 18).

Ideas of nationhood

In relation to zoos, Baratay and Hardouin-Fuger (2004: 9) argue that 'the exhibition of wild-life in the midst of civilised societies has been a constant of human history because it has helped people to place themselves in relation to the rest of the world. Human beings need the wild and endlessly seek it out'. Television similarly allows us to place ourselves in relation to the rest of the world. It gives us a sense of nationhood, and presents us as a nation with local, national and international issues. Think of the appeal to the nation to assist during times of natural disasters, for example.

Acclimatisation

Just as zoos were involved in the 'the domestication of exotic species with the aim of introducing new resources to society at large' (Baratay & Hardouin-Fuger 2004: 141), television provides popular knowledge about professions that are exotic species we may not otherwise know about, introducing their practices (sometimes challenging them, sometimes supporting them) to society at large. Television programs have featured such professions as ad men (*Mad Men*), funeral directors (*Six Feet Under*), politicians (*The West Wing*), private eyes (*The Rockford Files*), lawyers (*Boston Legal*), writers (*Castle*) and members from all strata of society (*Dynasty, Gossip Girl* and *Shameless*).

Just as 'zoos often participated in the long process of understanding wild animals, despite the fact that the specimens they offered for observation were more virtual than natural' (Baratay & Hardouin-Fuger 2004: 281), our knowledge of law, for example, comes almost entirely from television, through series such as *Perry Mason, LA Law, Law & Order* and *Boston Legal*. These are constructed representations, which are often highly stylised and exaggerated—'more virtual than natural' (Baratay & Hardouin-Fuger 2004: 281)—and we don't think that they're real, but they do provide us with a working knowledge of legal processes.

Classification and genre

Zoos and television, then, also exist as forms of classification. The creation of the menagerie at the Jardin des Plantes in Paris was in part a result of a desire among scholars of the time (1792) to create a place where animal behaviour could be studied and classified.

Television similarly offers us a way of classifying media texts by genre. As we have seen in the context of film (Chapter 6) and will see in media more generally (Chapter 9), genre is a way of categorising the output of media industries based on particular codes embedded in the media form itself—be they temporal, structural or textual—and this is a method that can be equally applied to television.

In television, this idea of genre doesn't work as well as it does in film or popular literature because programs are becoming increasingly hybridised. Even in the early days of television, series combined genres: the variety shows, *Dark Shadows* (horror and soap opera), *The Wild Wild West* (western and spy series), *Robotech* (soap opera and anime) and *V* (soap opera and science fiction). Other series give viewers narrative pleasure by moving through different generic forms—for example, *Picket Fences* or *Doctor Who*—and some series themselves became labelled as genre (for example, *Max Headroom* or *The Prisoner*) or postmodern (*Twin Peaks, Wild Palms* and *Moonlighting*) because they defied conventional generic classification.

This has led to genres being invented for series that exist as hybrid genres (such as 'dramedy' for *Ally McBeal*) and providing contexts for television series as they continue to diversify (from funeral homes in *Six Feet Under* and plastic surgeons in *Nip/Tuck* to prisons in *Oz* and the White House in *The West Wing*). Often, all that connects these forms is the term 'drama'. Even drama can hardly function as a category, as it ranges from highly structured dramas such as *The Edwardian House* to game shows such as *The Amazing Race* and *Survivor*, and further, to combinations of the two, such as *Big Brother*. Even the news genre covers types of program as diverse as news services, current affairs shows and chat shows. However, television continues to present the appearance of a classification system, which is replicated in television guides around the world, and in the blurbs and marketing used to sell DVDs.

Interestingly, television programmers speak of formats—the time a program runs and the number of weeks it runs for—rather than genres, so 'genre' is not an industry term.

Reality

From 1792, zoos sought to recreate the original environments of their animals, and these modifications (for example, soil or turf on the floors of aviaries) continued into the second half of the nineteenth century. This slow process of naturalisation, culminating in zoos without bars, started to emerge after 1907, representing what actually occurred in the wild. Stellingen Zoo in Germany was one of the first of these 'replacing the image of a confined animal with that of one at liberty' (Baratay & Hardouin-Fuger 2004: 237), becoming what Baratay and Hardouin-Fuger term the 'imitation of nature' (2004: 265).

Over the course of its evolution, television has similarly moved away from the wholly artificial towards realism. This move towards reality not only includes the increase in the popularity of documentaries (see the box, 'Documentary films on television'), reality series, such as *MasterChef* and *The Block*, and do-it-yourself programs, such as *Better Homes and Gardens*, but also series such as *Dexter*, *Breaking Bad* and *The Sopranos*, which, it can be asserted, provide drama that is more real (the characters swear, have sex on screen and engage in graphic violence) than that which is shown in the usual run of television programs. As Bauman notes, the reality conferred by television itself remains compelling to audiences:

> Being 'shown on TV' [has become] the certificate of reality … it is the condition of being real and that is why, when there are family events, to make sure they are real you put them on video. Being seen on a screen is the contemporary definition of being 'really real'. What used to be a reflection of reality has become the standard of reality. (Bauman 2000)

Zoos and television are therefore 'interested in a new form of exhibition—an imaginary realm that simulates and stimulates the illusion of escape' (Baratay & Hardouin-Fuger 2004: 237). Increasingly, this has also lead to more complex forms of television programming, from the genre-defying *Twin Peaks*, which made television more cinematic, to the intricately plotted *The Wire*, which was more like a Russian novel than a television program.

Television and conservation

The one scientific area that zoos could claim as their own was the preservation of species; today they implement breeding programs for pandas, snow leopards and Tasmanian devils, among many other endangered species.

Documentary films on television

Documentary television programs have the power to expand on issues covered by news journalists. Since the 1960s, television has became an important medium for documentaries, enabling journalists to present long, filmed investigations of a single issue or event, in the style of CBS's *Harvest of Shame* (1960).

In Australia, the ABC's *Four Corners* (started 1961) set the benchmark for standards of investigative documentary television, producing influential films such as *The Moonlight State* (1987), which reported on alleged corruption within the Queensland police force and led to the establishment of a commission of inquiry into police corruption.

Australian journalist John Pilger has also played an influential role in the promotion of documentary television programs, covering a host of geopolitical and social-justice issues, from the Vietnam war and the independence struggles in East Timor to refugee rights and the plight of Indigenous Australians.

Nicola Goc

Television is similarly engaged in the preservation of genres (think of the western being preserved by *Deadwood*, melodrama in soap opera and the musical in *Glee*), formats (talk shows and radio game shows) and stars (Keifer Sutherland in *24* and Patricia Arquette in *Medium*, film stars who revived their careers by starring in popular television programs). Appearances on television also preserve the performances of people long gone, for example, the classic clips of Elvis Presley from *The Ed Sullivan Show* or *The Beatles at the BBC*.

Perhaps, most importantly, it is the conservation of television series on DVD that points the way forward for television as a media form. DVD sales have saved many low-rating shows from cancellation (see Chapter 19), and DVD increasingly becomes a way of accessing older series or providing new audiences with access to rarely seen series. This creates an archive, overcoming the transitory nature of television broadcasts, and as an archive, television can potentially exist as a cultural resource. Indeed, this seems to be the reason for the popularity of some of the newer free-to-air channels; 7mate, for example, featured a run of action series from the 1980s (*Airwolf*, *The A-Team* and *Knight Rider*) that have connected with a younger audience that would never have seen them previously, while also proving nostalgic for viewers who did. Channel Nine's Go! channel works in a similar way.

Television as a cultural resource

So what does all of this mean for the future of television? As Alan McKee (2001) notes, television can potentially serve a number of useful social and cultural functions:

- *as a public and popular archive,* where analyses of television enables us to track the changing tastes and values of the culture
- *as a source of political critique,* not only through news and current affairs, but also through humour and satire

- *as the basis for a common language between people, regardless of geography, class or culture,* we can share a common language that we have learnt from *The Simpsons* or share the latest popular televisual catch phrase with people with whom we otherwise may have nothing in common.

Therefore, and regardless of the delivery system, television will continue to provide a window on the world and a way of thinking about the world.

Conclusion

Media scholar John Hartley famously suggested that television 'stood in place of "the bard": as the culture's storyteller, oral historian and entertainer' (Hartley, in Turner 2006: 7). Certainly this has been the case for many years. But even if television's position at the focal point of the mediasphere does change with the change in delivery systems, from television units to online delivery options and DVDs, there is no reason to think that these basic storytelling functions of television content will change. The function of television will remain recreational although the business models behind it may change, educational as a useful research tool for classifying and acclimatising us to the world around us and an important way of conserving media traditions and ways of being. Indeed, as television becomes a more on demand service, it will become even easier to achieve these aims—though, perhaps, at the cost of the common language and diversity afforded to us during the last fifty years. Television will remain a storyteller, finding new ways of sharing its stories. The message, it seems, will survive without the medium.

KEY REFERENCES

Allen, R. C. & Hill, A. (eds) (2004). *The Television Studies Reader.* London, New York: Routledge.

Baratay, E. & Hardouin-Fugier, E. (2004). *Zoo: A History of Zoological Gardens in the West.* (trans. Oliver Welsh). London: Reaktion.

Ellis, J. (2000). *Seeing Things: Television in the Age of Uncertainty.* London: Tauris.

Fiske, J. & Hartley, J. (2003). *Reading Television* (2nd edn). London: Routledge.

Holland, P. (2000). *The Television Handbook* (2nd edn). London: Routledge.

McKee, A. (2001). *Australian Television: A Genealogy of Great Moments.* Melbourne: Oxford University Press.

CHAPTER 8

PUBLIC RELATIONS: SPIN CYCLE

LIZ TYNAN

Introduction

There are two main ways to approach public relations (PR): from the point of view of a media practitioner, and from the point of view of a PR practitioner. While these are often held to be diametrically opposed positions, this is not necessarily the case, because they share a great deal of common ground. The reality is that many people who have trained in journalism—including some who have been successful journalists—do become PR people. People with journalism training have long been considered suitable for PR because of the very skills that made them good journalists, although it is important to note that PR involves far more than just media liaison. Journalists often face a steep learning curve when they shift to PR, as they must acquire a number of new skills. No matter where in the media you end up working, understanding this huge and growing phenomenon is going to help you. It is not overstating the case to say that PR has implications for how our society functions, driving change and fundamentally altering the way human beings organise themselves. This chapter provides an overview of how PR operates, and advice to those on both sides of the line between the two professions.

In this chapter we look at:

- how public relations has developed as a societal force in the past 100 years
- why media practitioners, and particularly journalists, should exercise caution when using the PR products
- the role of media releases and media conferences
- how PR practitioners and media professionals can fruitfully work together.

The big picture

The twentieth century saw unprecedented change in Western society, largely because of the rapid and seemingly inescapable and unstoppable increase in mass communication and global corporate culture from a time when notions such as celebrity-style fame, economic globalisation and spin doctoring did not exist.

Public relations as a discipline did not exist then, as least not in the way we think of it now. Some say that public relations has been a recognised profession for only about 100 years; certainly, it had its beginnings as a conscious form of activity not long before then, but why is that?

Public relations (PR): The controlled release or exchange of information in various ways and through various outlets, most visibly through the news media.

Public relations occupies a part of the mass communication continuum. Consequently, as mass communication has become increasingly important, so too has PR. Mass media demands information in many forms, and relentless pressures have been exerted on governments, organisations and businesses to provide information for an enormous variety of purposes.

How do you convince large numbers of people to give up smoking? How do you create a buzz around a particular product and make lots of people want to buy it? How do you engender an image for an organisation to target a particular demographic? How does a government persuade the governed that it has their best interests at heart? These questions, and many others like them, face public relations companies and practitioners. Their task is to manage information—but this simple statement has endless complexities. Why should anyone manage the information people receive? Isn't it enough for them to be told the plain truth? Truth can be a tricky concept, as anyone in the information business can confirm.

Philosopher and media commentator Noam Chomsky (Herman & Chomsky 1994), challenging current ideas about reality and truth, is famously associated with the concept of 'manufacturing consent', which echoes the related idea of 'engineering consent'. These are both rather disturbing terms that relate to the way information can be mass manipulated within a democratic system. Interestingly, Chomsky's term '**manufacturing consent**' is intended to be derogatory, while 'engineering consent', made famous by Edward Bernays (the so-called father of PR), was merely intended to be informative.

Manufacturing consent: The way in which Western mass media act to subdue popular dissent and to assist in the realisation of political and corporate objectives while giving the illusion of freedom; coined in 1922 by US writer Walter Lippmann and popularised later by Noam Chomsky and Edward Herman.

The Chomsky–Herman model

Noam Chomsky and Edward Herman deal with the manipulation by Western media in their much-quoted text *Manufacturing Consent: The Political Economy of the Mass Media* (1994). One of the filters that influence what becomes news is the sourcing of information, and it is here that information management becomes a force in moulding the news agenda. As Chomsky and Herman (1994) write: 'The magnitude of the public-information operations of large government and corporate bureaucracies that constitute the primary news sources is vast and ensure special access to the media. The Pentagon, for example, has a public-information service that involves many thousands of employees, spending hundreds of millions of dollars every year and dwarfing not only the public-information resources of any dissenting individual or group but also the aggregate of such groups.'

PR's beginnings

Humans have a long history of showing off and publicising themselves in various ways, but it was only in the twentieth century that people started making formal careers out of it. Presumably, in the unsentimental world of corporate enterprise and government, sectors that employ armies of PR people, this is seen as money well spent. Why is it so important now to use PR? What is it about the modern world that makes PR an essential activity?

There are some high-minded answers about the need for PR, and these certainly have some legitimacy. For example, it is said that the modern democratic process survives only by public consent based upon freely available information. The more people know, the better equipped they will be to make sensible decisions. This is undoubtedly true. Public relations, by its nature, is a broadly-based activity, and is not necessarily preoccupied with selling products.

Public relations is not advertising, although advertising can form part of a PR person's kitbag. Advertising, in most (though not all) cases, is clearly recognisable paid image making. It is Ronald McDonald singing a song to encourage children to take their parents to a McDonald's outlet. It is the annoying jingles used to flog cars, and skateboarders selling Fanta.

PR is different. It is the controlled release or exchange of information in various ways and through various outlets, though most visibly through the news media. It may take the form of a conference, a public meeting or series of meetings with decision makers. An organisation, whether a corporation, government department or interest group, has a public voice through its PR activities, contributing to the flux and flow of information. This is over and above merely trading goods and services in the marketplace, although marketing activities are certainly linked.

Like so many features of modern Western culture, PR started in a professional sense in the USA. The person widely credited as being the first true PR practitioner was Edward L. Bernays, the nephew of Sigmund Freud, who was the father of his own field, psychoanalysis. Bernays was impressed by his Uncle Sigmund's world-changing theories and applied psychological techniques in his attempts to influence people on a mass scale (Tye 2002).

Bernays and Goebbels

In a cruel twist, Edward Bernays's well-known book, *Crystallising Public Opinion* (1923), became the inspiration and handbook for Nazi propaganda minister Joseph Goebbels. Edward Bernays was Jewish and the Nazi regime was dedicated to destroying European Jews—and came close to succeeding. Goebbels is widely held to be an evil genius who refined propaganda into an indispensable tool of despotism. As Bernays (1965) said himself: 'Goebbels ... was using my book *Crystallising Public Opinion* as a basis for his destructive campaign against the Jews ... Obviously the attack on the Jews of Germany was no emotional outburst of the Nazis, but a deliberate planned campaign.'

Bernays was the first person to really pitch cigarette smoking to women, representing the practice as healthy and an aid to beauty and femininity, and also linking the practice to notions of freedom and equality. Bernays organised a march in New York by women allegedly asserting their right to smoke, the famous Torches of Liberty Contingent. Bernays had been paid a lot of money by the American Tobacco Company, makers of Lucky Strike cigarettes, to promote cigarettes. He staged the march because he identified an enormous market—women—for whom it was at the time socially unacceptable to smoke. By dressing up the sales pitch in ideas of equality, he secured a whole new market for the product. This approach was hugely successful and guaranteed Bernays a long and lucrative career.

Ivy Lee: another father of PR?

The title father of PR is sometimes also bestowed on a slightly earlier identity, the former journalist Ivy Lee (Bates 2006). Lee is said to have started the field of crisis management, although it wasn't called that then, putting the best spin on less-than-favourable circumstances. Some of this work led to him being nicknamed 'Poison Ivy'. Lee, with a colleague, founded a PR company as early as 1905. The company, Parker and Lee, was set up to publicise the activities of the big US industrialists, who were extremely unpopular and facing government regulation for the first time. He also worked for the coal industry and the railroads. He was noticed by the biggest industrialist of them all, oil magnate John D. Rockefeller, and created a new and more altruistic public image for this ruthless American tycoon. Later, Lee carried out PR, and other management functions, for the American Red Cross during the First World War, and later still campaigned for diplomatic recognition of the fledgling Soviet Union.

Like Edward Bernays, Lee had his reputation tainted by the Nazis. He worked in the early 1930s with an organisation seeking to improve US–German relations, which led to charges that he was a Nazi propagandist. Lee also wrote books on public relations, as did Bernays, and was a relentless self-promoter, providing quite a bit of prepared favourable material on himself for any interested journalist, as any good PR person is well placed to do. He died much younger than Bernays, aged only fifty-seven. Maybe this accounts for the fact that he is given less prominence than Bernays: he had less time to work on the spin.

A profession founded on engineering consent

While Noam Chomsky and Edward Herman were alarmed by the manipulation of the democratic process that they called manufacturing consent, Bernays saw engineering consent as an informative term pointing to a useful phenomenon. He had what many would consider a rather undemocratic mindset, and saw nothing wrong with outright manipulation, as he outlined in his book, *Propaganda*.

Bernays and *Propaganda*

Here is the opening passage from Bernays' other famous book, *Propaganda* (1928):

> The conscious and intelligent manipulation of the organised habits and opinions of the masses is an important element in democratic society. Those who manipulate this unseen mechanism of society constitute an invisible government which is the true ruling power of our country. We are governed, our minds are moulded, our tastes are formed, our ideas suggested, largely by men we have never heard of. This is the logical result of the way democratic society is organised. Vast numbers of human beings must cooperate in this manner if they are to live together as a smoothly functioning society. (Bernays 1972)

The idea of engineering consent is to make whatever it is you are trying to sell 'the thing'—the current must-have—and this trick must be worked by subtle, public relations-based methods rather than straight advertising. This principle was completely new when Bernays propounded it, but it is so woven into the fabric of contemporary Western society that we can't always see what is happening. Yet all of us are subjected to it every day.

Both Bernays and Lee began their activities at a time of rapid modernisation and the rise of capitalism on a global scale, the start of what later became known as 'The American Century', in which capitalism was triumphant. Their era encompassed the first of the world wars, which was itself a tragic reminder of how society was changing towards a more global entity, with positive and negative consequences. Communications were becoming more sophisticated, the media more widespread and important (particularly when radio began in the 1920s), and means of transportation faster and more readily available. All the things we associate with the modern era—electricity, cars, air transportation, the telephone and electronic media—had their beginnings at this time, and it is no coincidence that PR also was born then.

PR in Australia

The first Australian described as a public persuasion practitioner was George FitzPatrick of Sydney. His career began just before the Second World War (Tymson, Lazar & Lazar 2000: 35). He listed himself in the Sydney phone book as a 'registered practitioner in public persuasion, propaganda and publicity', and organised public charities and various publicity activities for companies. The word 'propaganda' was freely used in connection with this activity back then, but the Second World War put an end to that usage. Two years after that war ended, there were just two PR-related telephone directory listings, but the industry started to grow as more businesses started to see the benefits of having their stories told in the media. This growth created the need for a forum to allow the exchange of information between practitioners. The **Public Relations Institute of Australia** (PRIA), held its first meeting (Tymson, Lazar & Lazar 2000: 36)

Public Relations Institute of Australia (PRIA): The peak professional body for PR practitioners in Australia.

in 1949, and this is regarded as the official start of public relations as a profession in Australia. The postwar era in Australia was a time of rising prosperity and consumerism, combined with political and economic stability. The new profession had found its ideal time to be born, and it thrived and grew.

PR evolves

Inevitably, PR has evolved from its media-focused beginnings. While getting stories into media outlets remains an important activity, the contemporary industry sees itself as more subtle than that. The aim is not just scoring media hits (a measure of uptake of stories by the media), but a more interactive process has also developed, involving studying the demands of a variety of **publics**. This is a concept in PR circles that refers to different audience sectors, such as employees, investors, media, community sectors and government, all of which require separate communication skills, with an emphasis on two-way rather than unidirectional communication. PR practitioners study the way these sectors operate and communicate, and use what they know about them to enter into their conversations.

Publics: In PR, a buzzword that refers to the different audience sectors, such as employees, investors, media, community sectors and government, that often require separate communication skills, with emphasis on dialogue rather than one-way communication.

The profession has gradually become more knowledgeable about what does or does not work in communication, developing and refining factors such as the psychological aspects of the audience's interest, theories on how to persuade people and other evolving ideas about the way people think and make decisions. Given the foundations of the profession in the ideas of Sigmund Freud, the rise of psychology as a professional discipline is important in this process. Freud was famous for drawing attention to the role of the unconscious in human behaviour, proposing that an unconscious element in the mind influenced consciousness in ways that are not readily apparent (Beystehner 1998). The growing field of psychology pointed to new prospects for understanding human behaviour, and thereby directing it or even controlling it. The behaviourist theories of B. F. Skinner, for example, also contributed ideas of stimulus and reward: people could be effectively influenced to behave like rats in mazes. Behaviourism suggested that they could be persuaded to spend their money on the shiny new car because the car gave them the reward of status. Unfortunately for the eager new public relations practitioners, they found that human behaviour does not necessarily fit all the formulae put forward. But enough data were being gathered on how people actually responded to public information to make it possible to direct and segment public opinion.

In the modern era, PR is at least as important as advertising; maybe even more so. As long as mass media has existed, advertising has been around. It is an inescapable feature of most successful businesses. But the continuing growth of advertising also brought a growth in cynicism in the market. The general public, and the segments therein, do not regard advertising to be part of public information as such. It is just seen as selling products by whatever means possible. PR takes a different approach, even if its goal is to sell products. **Proactive PR** (often called agenda setting) creates a story, usually a positive story, where none existed before, such as

Proactive PR: Often called agenda setting; the creation of a story, usually a positive story, where none existed; examples include calling a media conference to announce the establishment of a new award, or sending out a media release about the findings of a specially commissioned study.

sending out a media release about the findings of a specially commissioned study or staging a glitzy launch of some kind.

The pace of change in public relations has been accelerating recently. Some commentators predict that PR will drive the policy of many large organisations in the future, rather than remaining as just one of several important factors. The need to communicate will be the main focus of any sort of strategic management.

Is this a good thing? What do you think? Is this a case of companies and other organisations going for appearance over substance, or is it just a reflection of the desire to give consumers exactly what they want? Given that we are now in the midst of the information age, it does seem a natural evolutionary process for the forces of communication to rise to the top. Information implies communication, and that is essentially what PR is.

Example of presenting a consistent image

Not all public relations is concerned with selling products; some is related to securing informed public consent for certain activities. The public relations activities of the Australian Institute of Marine Science (AIMS), for example, seek to present a consistent set of views that accord with its organisational goals, and its public image is based around what people know about its public stance on tropical marine science and Australia's marine resources, including the Great Barrier Reef. Journalists may well seek out AIMS's input when writing stories about anything to do with Australia's tropical marine environment, because the organisation has ensured, through its PR effort, that journalists know that it is available to comment. This powerful process establishes AIMS as an authority in this field.

Journalists: take care

Media release: A document, written by a PR practitioner in journalistic style, that provides a story intended for use by the media.

For the media practitioner, there are advantages and pitfalls in using public relations material. One of the main contacts media people have with PR people is through the **media release**. A media release is prepared by a public or private agency, group or person to inform the media about the specific activities, opinions or reactions of an organisation. It is a way of managing the release of information, which has advantages and disadvantages for the journalist who wants to get to the truth of a story. Large numbers of media releases arrive in newsrooms every day, usually by email or fax.

Of course, media releases emphasise news (or something that looks like news but really is not) that reflects favourably on the institution or individual for whom it was prepared. They are not always written with deliberate bias or distortion, but a journalist should always be careful when using them. The advantage is that they may distil lots of complex information into a readily understood form. The journalist is rarely an expert in any field, and may need guidance through the intricacies of, for example, medical research, engineering or public policy.

Information provided by expert organisations such as the CSIRO, the Institution of Engineers or a university's public affairs office can helpfully bring out the pertinent information to save the reporter valuable time and to clarify facts of a story, when they might otherwise be very unclear indeed. This time-saving aspect is very important. Such PR can also save the reporters the embarrassment of forming the wrong conclusions about complex information that they might have gone through quickly and not really understood.

The rise of the PR professional has meant that, to a certain extent, the news agenda is set by organisations and individuals outside the traditional news arena, and in most cases their first priority is not the public good. Too often, media releases from big companies, government departments, agencies and organisations are taken at face value and run as news: the term often used is that they are **cut and pasted** from media releases. This means that the journalist has not used initiative and a news sense to find the news, and this has an effect on the quality of the media product over time.

Cut and paste: The transfer of information, by a journalist, from a PR release to a news item, without the application of journalistic editing skills or judgment.

Types of PR professional

There are two main types of PR practitioner. One kind is hired by an organisation as a staff member to work on behalf of that organisation and no other. Such people may be called PR officers, PR managers, communication managers, public affairs officers or a variety of similar titles. They are generally part of an organisation's management team, and they can be found in many sectors, such as corporate, government, non-government and community. The other kind of PR practitioner belongs to a **consultancy** or agency. These are companies expressly set up to be available for hire to undertake public relations activities. A PR consultancy might have a large number of clients from diverse sectors, and will spread the work among its consultants.

The rise of PR has changed news media. There are now more PR practitioners in the USA than there are reporters (Stauber & Rampton 1995), and that is probably the case in Australia as well, though exact figures are unclear. Nonetheless, public relations is a huge and growing industry. News reporting has diminished somewhat in recent years, and newsroom resources are often stretched to the limit. Therefore, there is an unfortunate tendency in newsrooms to rely on PR material to provide content for news items. This has the effect of letting PR practitioners, rather than members of the news media, decide what is going to be news. Skilled PR practitioners are able to predigest information and put it into a media-friendly format so it is easy for a reporter to use as presented and not research further. This is not true journalism, and should be resisted.

PR consultancy: A company set up specifically to carry out contract public relations work, in contrast to a PR person who is on the staff of a company or organisation.

However, journalists can certainly make use of public relations material, including media releases and backgrounders, and attend PR-convened media conferences, and still maintain their all-important independence. It is a matter of not being beguiled by the easy option that PR presents.

Media releases

PR practitioners are trained to write media releases exactly like a news story. These documents usually display the journalistic convention of one sentence per paragraph, use direct quotations in the same way reporters do and are written in the inverted pyramid form. This is specifically intended to make it easy for the journalist to place the contents of the media release into the news outlet; that is, to cut and paste.

Many PR professionals worked as journalists before switching professions. At the very least, they would have received training in journalistic practice, and the most successful ones adopt the same writing forms to gain access to the media. For straightforward informational media releases, this may not be too much of a problem, although it remains undesirable for media outlets to accept this material at face value and without input from other sources.

Spin doctors: People who are paid to bend information to the needs of their bosses or clients, often beyond what a PR person might normally do.

Spin: The process whereby an organisation or individual ensures that information placed into the public sphere, usually through a PR channel, puts them in the best possible light. This word has a negative connotation, as it implies information manipulation.

The main problem arises, when information is being spun, often by a **spin doctor**. This is where an organisation or individual presents information designed to show them in the best possible light. The spin doctor's professional expertise is the selective use of information and subtle manipulation of emphases. **Spin** may not involve outright lying (it rarely does), but is more likely to be found in the information that has been omitted, the tone that has been adopted and the way some elements have been played down and others emphasised. Information is prepared to look like an objective, dispassionate news story, but in fact is seriously skewed in favour of a vested interest.

It is generally acceptable to use media releases as a starting point for a story. Journalists should always speak to a human being and not just rely upon direct quotations in the PR release. Releases will always contain contact details to reach the people named. Use those details to get direct comment from the source. Not to do so means that you are allowing yourself to be manipulated by the PR person who wrote the release. You also must find balancing points of view, perhaps contrary to the information in the media release. Never take media releases as the whole truth, because they probably are not. A good journalist is sceptical, and checks everything.

Media conferences

Another form of interaction between the media and PR is the media conference, also known as the news conference, which is a long-established method for releasing news to a lot of journalists in one go (see Tools 2 for more on conducting a media conference). It is one of the media's big set-piece events, where a source is questioned by a room full of reporters.

Sir Joh's chooks

The late Sir Joh Bjelke-Petersen, the legendary former premier of Queensland, memorably described media conferences as 'feeding the chooks', a term that conveys something of the atmosphere of a feeding frenzy that can be found at such events.

Media conferences remain an important means for relaying information from entertainers, sportspeople and leaders of industry, science and business; however, they are becoming less common in the political sphere. Nowadays, many politicians stage 'door stops' at the entrance to parliament—an informal, impromptu media gathering—or they make policy announcements on talkback radio or via Twitter or Facebook. At political media conferences, the questioning is more likely to be adversarial, which can be risky for politicians, who will have more difficulty controlling the spin of their particular message.

Still, media conferences are an integral part of a journalist's work. You need to overcome any fears you have about speaking up in front of a room full of people, because you need to pose your questions to the subject of the media conference. If you don't, the more assertive journalists will monopolise proceedings. It is best for a journalist to steer the course of the conference by preparing strong, effectively worded questions that are confidently stated. By all means write questions down in your notebook, but also listen carefully to what is being said at the conference, and ensure that you don't miss an unexpected angle should it arise. Do try to keep your questions short and to the point: rambling, multifaceted questions tend to be ineffective, and possibly ambiguous or even laughable.

Advice for the PR practitioner

The media and PR can and do work harmoniously, though not in all cases. It is now entrenched behaviour for media practitioners to deride PR people, often using the derogatory term '**flack**' or saying that journalists have gone over to the dark side. A typical comment about PR people, specifically those who specialise in science, was broadcast by Robyn Williams, the ABC radio *Science Show* presenter, on 24 October 2004. He said: 'Do you know about the dark side? It's what journalists have to do if they can't report and need to promote instead. A job's a job. For every science journalist in Australia there are between ten and twenty working in PR, members of the dark side.' This dismissive view is widespread among journalists. But survey after survey shows that much of the content of newspapers and electronic media news would not exist without PR material. Today, reporters phone PR practitioners as often as PR practitioners phone reporters. Instead of sniping, a more fruitful approach is for media practitioners to accept that PR is a fact of life, and for PR people to ensure that their behaviour displays high ethical standards.

Flack: A term often used to describe PR practitioners; thought to have been formed by melding 'flak'—for flak catcher, someone paid to catch the flak directed at their employer—with 'hack', a mediocre writer.

On the day-to-day level, the ethical management of information is a useful job. It helps those outside the organisation make sense of incoming information. This is especially the case for dealings between a public relations practitioner and a hard-pressed journalist, who does not have time to process all relevant information and still produce a coherent story. An ethical PR person is expected to anticipate the needs of the journalist and prepare adequate and succinct material.

The ethical PR person is a middle person, an interpreter, a service provider, an information coordinator and an adviser. The PR person's employer expects him or her to provide a window to the world, perhaps tidied up and prettified, but essentially useful and clear. They are also expected to advise senior management on presenting themselves and their key messages, and possibly on improving interdepartmental communication. Increasingly, the PR practitioner is part of senior management, reflecting PR's growing societal role.

Media journalists tend to pride themselves upon their independence and commitment to digging up the truth, especially when it has been obfuscated by PR professionals. This often produces a cat-and-mouse game as journalists try to either dodge official messages or hold them up to ridicule. Even so, the PR person is often the journalist's first source for readily accessible information, resulting in a somewhat disingenuous attitude on the part of journalists who are perfectly prepared to use PR's helpful services while simultaneously deriding them and their profession.

Conclusion

While media practitioners may sometimes sneer at PR people, they are demonstrably happy to use PR materials. The widespread use of information generated by PR people is, of course, partly needed because of the declining number of journalists as newsroom budgets are cut. Some PR material is also newsy, useful and fits the media agenda, as it is designed to do. It is up to journalists to ensure that the information is balanced with contrary opinion or fact. No one can really blame the PR practitioner if the journalist doesn't complete the extra information checking and gathering steps while preparing a story.

These are the two main sides of the argument, and both are partly right. Some PR is concerned with image manipulation, spinning messages, blatant stonewalling (offering 'No comment' to all enquiries) or even with lying. However, public relations practitioners contribute greatly to the availability of easily accessible information. Companies and other organisations have to engage with the information demands of modern society, and the best way to do this is via trained, skilful people who can manage the information exchange between experts and the general public, usually via the media. Part of the PR person's job is simply that of translator. PR practitioners who recognise this important task and do it well are the ones cherished by journalists, even if the journalists don't often admit it.

KEY REFERENCES

Bernays, E. L. (1947). 'The Engineering of Consent'. *Annals of the American Academy of Political and Social Science.* New York: Sage.

Herman, E. S. & Chomsky, N. (1994). *Manufacturing Consent: The Political Economy of the Mass Media.* London: Vintage.

Johnston, J. & Zawawi, C. (2000). *Public Relations Theory and Practice.* Sydney: Allen & Unwin.

Tymson, C., Lazar, P. & Lazar, R. (2000). *The New Australian and New Zealand Public Relations Manual.* Sydney: Tymson Communications.

CASE STUDY 2:

SPINNING THE WAR: HOW PR MADE THE FIRST GULF WAR

LIZ TYNAN

Introduction

The first Gulf War, which took place in 1991, was a triumph of information management and media access control led by the US government with the cooperation of allied governments, including Australia. The US military heeded the hard lessons it had learnt about media coverage from the Vietnam War of the 1960s and 1970s, in which a far less regulated media were able to report on and show conflict like never before. Following a period of reflection after Vietnam, a plan evolved for a different way to manage media. This plan was tested first in several small conflicts before being put into full-scale operation in the Gulf War. It worked brilliantly. This case study first examines the influence of media coverage on the outcome of the Vietnam War, and how this led to measures such as press pools being used to ensure information control and restrictions on the flow of media information in subsequent conflicts. It then outlines the role of public relations in obtaining public consent for the Gulf War.

The media and modern conflict

To understand how PR was able to influence the conduct of modern warfare, we need to look briefly at where it all began—Vietnam. The Vietnam War is often referred to as 'The Living Room War', or the first television war. For the first time in history, people witnessed the detail of a military conflict while they were sitting in their safe suburban houses. The Vietnam War occurred at an important time in the development of television. The few people who had television in the early 1950s in the US (it was not yet available in Australia) had witnessed some of the Korean War, but it was really Vietnam where war entered the mass communication age. The military wasn't used to television at all, so a significant proportion of the imagery that went into people's homes wasn't censored, despite some attempts at restriction. These images ended up having a profound effect on the outcome of the war, although in its early stages the media actually supported the war effort.

This war, conducted by four US presidential administrations, began in 1962 and ended (from the point of view of the USA, at least) in 1975. Out of the Vietnam War came some of the most chilling and compelling news images ever displayed in the public arena. Some of those images still resonate today: Nick Ut's photo of the young girl running down the road, naked, her flesh burning from the napalm that had engulfed her; Eddie Adams's shot of the Commander Nguyen Ngoc Loan of the South Vietnamese National Police summarily executing a suspected Vietcong soldier in the street; and the self-immolation of Buddhist monks in protest against the conflict.

These images, all of which are celebrated as great news photography and some of which won Pulitzer Prizes, influenced how the Western audience perceived the Vietnam War. The images made the consequences of war inescapable for the average person. The exact role the visual media played in deciding the outcome of the Vietnam War is a matter of scholarly dispute to a certain extent. What we do know is that no war before Vietnam had been so graphically reported.

Despite clear evidence that the war effort was less than successful in objective terms, popular opinion and much expert military opinion regard the Vietnam War as one that could have been won on the battlefield, but instead was lost in the living rooms of the US public. This conflict proved to be a great lesson for the US military and the perceived mistakes were not allowed to happen again. By the time of the first Gulf War, these lessons had been completely assimilated.

Testing a new approach

Before the Gulf War, a new military approach to the media was tried in some small-scale conflicts. The October 1983 invasion by US military of the Caribbean island nation of Grenada, for example, was an experiment in barring media access altogether. No media were allowed to report for 72 hours after the invasion, which resulted in a media outcry. This complete lack of access was unprecedented, certainly in a US conflict. To quote from *NBC Nightly News* commentator John Chancellor, the invasion of Grenada was 'a bureaucrat's dream. Do anything. No one is watching.'

Press pools

Furious protests by media about denial of access to the conflict on Grenada led to the next stage of the evolution of military media management. The press pool was born, a system in which a small number of reporters are given access to gather information, which is then shared with other members of the pool and the wider press outside the pool. The press pool concept was tested a few years later during the US invasion of Panama. That invasion was undertaken to arrest the country's president, General Noriega, and put him on trial for drug trafficking. Although press pools were formed for the Panama conflict, there was still no media access for the first 24 hours of operations. Once the pool journalists did get in, they just saw the sanitised aftermath of what had gone on.

By the time the Gulf War erupted in 1991, the pool system was fully in place. The Gulf conflict arose in response to Saddam Hussein of Iraq occupying neighbouring Kuwait in August 1990. Unlike the later Iraq conflict that began in 2003, this was a United Nations-sanctioned war with military forces from a number of countries involved, such as France and Germany. Australia also was there, committed to the war by then Prime Minister Bob Hawke. In Operation Desert Storm, also known as the Gulf War, it is said that the military didn't need to use overt censorship techniques—just implementing a press pool was sufficient control. In the Gulf War, pools were made up of small numbers of physically fit reporters who were given limited access to combat zones under strictly controlled conditions. All despatches by journalists had to be viewed in advance by a military censor, a process known as a 'security review'. In the Gulf, about fifty representative journalists and their crews were included in the press pool at the start (although this number rose as the conflict continued), and their reports were made available to the rest of the media. The non-pool journalists were forced to hang around their hotels in Riyadh or Dhahran in Saudi Arabia waiting for the pool reports to arrive or taking in the heavily spun daily media briefings presented by military personnel. Most pool slots went to US journalists. In fact, there was only one position available for the entire international media contingent (Benjamin 1995). Many journalists were dissatisfied with this system since it not only greatly restricted most reporters' access to events, but the military also limited what even the pool reporters could cover.

Pools are seen by the military as a way of maintaining military security and preventing a massive influx of reporters into the war zone. Certainly a great deal of thought was given to how the pool concept might be used to optimum effect in the Gulf. According to David Benjamin, in his 1995 article 'Censorship in the Gulf:

> The military won extremely positive coverage during the war at the price of a dissatisfied press corps and lingering doubts about whether the press saw the whole story. The same factors that produced the military victory over the Iraqis aided the military victory over the media. Empty deserts and vast distances provided both an ideal theatre for mobile armoured warfare and for keeping the press at the mercy of the military.

Pulitzer Prize-winning journalist Sydney Schanberg of the *New York Times*, writing five days before the bombing of Baghdad started, claimed that the hard news had been taken out of war reporting, to be replaced with soft stories, with 'human interest pieces about how our soldiers are faring in the heat, features about planes being refuelled in mid-air, stories about [then Vice-President] Dan Quayle's visit, stories about the lousy military food, etc., etc. And this soft journalism is the direct result of the press controls.' Robert Goldberg in the *Wall Street Journal* said: 'Mostly, this is news by press release.'

Retired US General Sidle had headed a special internal Pentagon commission into media coverage during the Grenada invasion, and went on to work as a consultant to the United States Department of Defense. The Sidle Commission formalised the pooling idea as official Pentagon policy in 1984. Sidle argued that in dealing with the press, security and troop safety must be the military's first concern and that if news organisations would not limit the numbers of reporters they sent to a battle area, then the military would have to. Certainly it is the case that news organisations do seek to send more reporters to conflicts these days than they did at the time of the Vietnam War. In Vietnam the maximum number of reporters in the field at any one time was fourty-seven, a peak that occurred during the Tet offensive in 1968. In all, only about 400 journalists were present in Vietnam during the war. This relatively low number could be explained by the fact that the ones who were there did a very thorough—indeed, extraordinary—job in conditions that the majority of journalists would not be able to stomach.

By contrast, in the Gulf War, according to Benjamin (1995), there were 1600 journalists and support crew in Saudi Arabia, all of them tightly controlled. Some 400 were assigned to the units doing the fighting during the ground war. For the 1200 journalists who were not at the fighting, the press pools were an endless source of frustration, hampering their efforts to cover the action. One reporter claimed that 'each pool member is an unpaid employee of the Department of Defense, on whose behalf he or she prepares the news of the war for the outer world'.

Restrictions on reporting

The allied coalition that conducted the war imposed a number of conditions on reporters operating in Saudi Arabia. Failure to follow the guidelines would lead to expulsion from the country. Here are some of those conditions:

- No mention could be made of the specific numbers of troops, planes, supplies, etc. Only general terms could be used to describe the forces available.
- No mention could be made of future plans.
- No mention could be made of specific locations of units.
- The rules of engagement—that is, the rules specifying under what conditions coalition forces would use force—were off limits.
- No mention could be made of intelligence-gathering operations, the points of origin for air missions, information on the effectiveness or otherwise of enemy military measures, or operating methods and tactics in general (Benjamin 1995).

These are only some of the many restrictions. The most controversial of all was the obligation for reporters to stay with a PR escort on Saudi bases—at the discretion of the commander on US bases. This severely restricted access by reporters to the combat area and to troops. The actions of the PR escorts varied enormously, with some clearly helping the reporters to get what they wanted and others taking it upon themselves to censor reporters' work. All pool reports had to be submitted to the Joint Information Bureau in Dhahran, the official censoring site, for security review.

Unilaterals

Some journalists decided to break away from the pool system and set up as so-called unilaterals. They did manage to get stories that were at odds with the official line, for instance, about coalition troops not being equipped with adequate maps. But the unilaterals were a small minority. Most journalists in the region were only too mindful of the experience of a CBS television crew who went missing across the Kuwaiti–Saudi border days after the war began and who spent the next forty days in an Iraqi prison cell. Only a year earlier, the Iraqis had executed a journalist—Farzad Bazoft from the *Observer*, a London-based newspaper—who had gone investigating inside Iraq for himself.

The celebrated New Zealand-born reporter Peter Arnett, who had been one of the leading journalists covering the Vietnam War, was famously in Baghdad when the bombs first started falling in 1991. At that stage he was with the new Cable News Network, CNN. The Gulf War established CNN as a major source of news. Arnett was not part of a pool, because he was on the ground in Baghdad, which at the start of the war was of course outside the command of the allied military. He was not strictly a unilateral either, as he was covering not allied operations but conditions inside Iraq at the time of the attack. His view, therefore, was necessarily different. Here's what Arnett had to say about the conflict:

> The media with the coalition forces felt censored because they were not given easy access to the troops on the ground and were not able to go with the jet bombers bombing Baghdad. In Baghdad itself, the main form of censorship by the Iraqis was

> denying us visits to military areas and interviews with military personnel. So there was much frustration on the part of the American journalists. On the other hand, we had open access to report freely on what we saw of the bombing destruction. And we could travel around the countryside; they did not allow us to talk about military equipment we saw, but we were able to discuss civilian problems and comment on the general atmosphere. Overall, I felt that the reporting experience on the Iraqi side was satisfying and informative. (Arnett 1994)

Missing the story

In an interview on ABC Radio National's *The Media Report*, the Australian polemical journalist John Pilger talked about the effect of press pools in the flow (or otherwise) of information during the Gulf War. He said:

> This was the most covered war in history. And pretty well everyone missed the story. That's how organised it was. It was organised to the point that journalists ceased to be journalists. They became functionaries. And the few journalists who were able to escape this pooling system and to escape this organisation did so at their peril... They missed the story, because the story was that 200,000 Iraqis were killed. And many of them were killed at night. And many of them were buried alive in their trenches. There was the most awful carnage. But at the end of the war we came away with the idea ... that casualties were light, that it was something of a kind of high tech surgical strike type war, and that it was a great victory. (*Media Report* 2003)

The Gulf War was short compared with the Vietnam War, and that in itself changed the dynamics and made information control more feasible and easier to refine. Also, because the military had found ways to control exactly how reporters went about their work, through the use of pools and censorship requirements, they had completely changed the conduct of war reporting—changes that persist and still influence coverage of military conflicts today.

The Kuwaiti babies

Public consent for the Gulf War was established in part by use of a fabrication. A so-called Kuwaiti nurse named Nayirah told the US Congress that she had witnessed Iraqi soldiers removing premature babies from humidicribs. This was reported by journalists and provoked a degree of outrage among Western audiences. It was revealed after the war that the whole story was a stunt invented by the huge PR company Hill & Knowlton for a fee of $US11 million to create what journalist Rick MacArthur described as 'one of the most brilliantly orchestrated public relations campaigns in history'. Nayirah turned out to be the daughter of the Kuwaiti ambassador to the USA.

The role of PR is crucial to understanding what happened in the Gulf, and a reflection of the sophistication of the Pentagon in understanding the audiences they needed to influence. Hill & Knowlton was not directly hired by any member of the US government; it was hired by a front organisation known as Citizens for a Free Kuwait (CFK). To quote from MacArthur, who uncovered the PR stunt:

> I went to visit Citizens for a Free Kuwait, or what was left of it, a few months after the Gulf War ended when I was doing research on my book. I went to see a Mr Ibrahim, who was the titular head of CFK. The first time I realized something fishy was going on when he pulled out a stack of atrocity photographs. I went through them and thought this looks pretty awful—people with odd pieces of metal jammed into their bodies in various places. It looked quite horrible, but the photographs were a little out of focus. I went through them a second time and I realized that they were mannequins. They had literally dressed up mannequins as torture victims! This is not to say that Saddam did not kill Kuwaitis and did not torture Kuwaitis but these fraudulent photographs became the stock in trade of the Hill & Knowlton campaign.
>
> Nobody at the [Congressional] hearing, no reporter said, 'Nayirah, that is a terrible story; I am on the verge of tears. But what did you do after you put the babies on the floor to die? Did you call for help, did you try to pick one up, what happened then?' The most fundamental and most elementary questions that a reporter is supposed to ask were not asked. Nayirah was a fantastic propaganda success. Hill & Knowlton made a brilliant little video news release out of it, which they beamed all over the world. It was on *NBC Nightly News* and millions and millions of people saw this ... The campaign had begun to 'get legs' as we say in the public relations and news business. (MacArthur 1992)

Almost certainly there are people who still believe that Iraqi soldiers took babies out of incubators in Kuwait and left them to die. While the allegations about Iraqi soldiers were widely reported at the time, there was little later mass media coverage of the uncovering of the Hill & Knowlton public relations campaign.

Conclusion

Overall, the media probably did not change the course of the Gulf war, certainly not in the way that they did the Vietnam War. The restrictions on their reporting were too stringent. The media, of course, preferred the way they were able to operate in Vietnam and would have liked, in the Gulf, to find the information that could change the public's perception of the war. The military preferred to manage the media in such a way that there was no possibility of Vietnam-style imagery and reporting that could jeopardise the possibility of victory. The military prevailed and the role of PR is now well entrenched in the conduct of modern warfare.

KEY REFERENCES

Arnett, P. (1994). *Live from the Battlefield: from Vietnam to Baghdad: 35 years in the world's war zones.* New York: Simon & Schuster.

Benjamin, D. (1995). *Censorship in the Gulf.* <http://web1.duc.auburn.edu/~benjadp/gulf/gulf.html>. Accessed 11 November 2010.

MacArthur, R. (1992). *Second Front: Censorship and Propaganda in the First Gulf War.* New York: Hill and Wang.

The Media Report (2003). 'Propaganda Wars', ABC Radio National, interview with John Pilger, 30 January. <www.abc.net.au/rn/talks/8.30/mediarpt/stories/s771659.htm>. Accessed 10 November 2010.

TOOLS 2:

HOW TO CONDUCT A MEDIA CONFERENCE

LIZ TYNAN

Introduction

Media conference: A public relations event in which a major news announcement is made to assembled journalists. The announcement is usually followed by journalists questioning the news source.

One of the great set pieces in public relations practice is the **media conference**. Media conferences are a bit like a stage play in that they involve setting up a suitable venue, scripting, rehearsals, planning, obtaining an audience and putting on a performance. They should not be done half-heartedly; you must plan every stage to optimise the process. Being slapdash is anathema to this work. Bad things can happen if the event is not carefully worked out—never forget that you are dealing with demanding and impatient media practitioners who don't like to be mucked about. However, getting all the ducks to line up and presenting an effective media conference is the source of much job satisfaction for PR professionals. A media conference should also be useful and efficient for reporters. It is intended to provide an information service and the opportunity for streamlined delivery of a strong news story.

Assessing whether to hold a media conference

The most important factor in this decision can be simply expressed—is your announcement newsworthy? Only through a thorough understanding of news values (see Chapter 12) will you be able to make the call. Journalists will not come to an event that does not carry the promise of a true media story. You must have something of substance to report and you must provide the information in a media-friendly way. You must also be clear that a media conference, which involves briefing a number of journalists in one go, is the best way to make your story known. You may at this point give some thought to whether your story might be best announced through electronic distribution of a media release alone or by simply briefing a key journalist. If you decide that you need to have a room full of journalists potentially asking difficult questions of the spokespeople you put in front of them, then proceed.

The basic elements

Assuming that you have a newsworthy story to announce, there are a number of elements that you need to consider (and to manage) to ensure that everything comes together at the appointed time. These are outlined below.

- *Setting a date:* The exact date of your media conference will be determined by the news value of timeliness. If you have a government report, a major research finding or an important book coming out on a particular day, that is the day the media conference must be held—not the day after, or the day after that. Some senior managers have been known to try to put off a media conference until a day that *they* prefer, in the mistaken belief that holding out will intensify interest in the story. As a PR professional, you will have to do your best to convince them otherwise. Timeliness of provision of information is of utmost important and journalists may well ignore your otherwise impeccably organised event if the story actually happened the day before.

- *Setting a time:* Generally you will schedule your media conference for mid-morning to help ensure that there is ample time for all kinds of journalists—electronic and print—to prepare the story for their deadlines later in the day. You don't want it to be too early, though, as newsrooms tend to have their news meetings to assign the day's tasks around 8am to 8.30am. Most proactive public relations media conferences—the kind where you are introducing a story to the news agenda, not responding to outside events or a crisis—tend to be held within the timeframe of 9.30am to 11am. You are asking for trouble (and indifference) if you schedule your event for 4pm. Any announcement made at that time would have to be of broad national importance to be picked up. Note that most media conferences are quick: generally, you will not need more than one hour for the whole event, and sometimes less than that. The formal part of the event, in which your spokespeople make the actual announcement and give brief statements about issues, should be no more than 15 minutes. The longer part of the event involves media questions and one-on-one interviews.
- *Identifying and booking a suitable venue:* The venue should be a room that is large enough to cope with all potential participants but not too large that it looks sparsely populated to the attendees, or on the television news. You may want to consider a venue that offers good visuals of various kinds so that television can get overlay and/or decent backgrounds—examples of these settings include art galleries, museums, aquariums, sports stadiums, etc. It is a good idea to provide chairs for media representatives as most of them will wish to take notes, which is hard to do standing up. It is standard practice to provide simple refreshments of some kind, usually coffee, tea, orange juice and biscuits, but don't bother offering full meals. Someone in the PR department or agency—usually the PR person responsible for the event—will need to obtain costings for the refreshments and ensure that people are on hand to set up, serve and remove them. Also, you may need to investigate a suitable sound system and recording facilities so that the speakers can be heard and so that you can keep your own electronic record of the event. Be wary of holding media conferences outdoors without some sort of shelter. If you are determined to hold an outdoor event, it may be safest to set up a waterproof marquee and, if the worst happens and there is a thunderstorm, have an alternative indoor venue available that can be pressed into action at short notice.
- *Sending out a* ***media alert:*** This brief (two- to three-paragraph) document, which is described in more detail later, is a mini media release that functions as an invitation. It should not give away too much about the actual announcement, but be informative enough to ensure media interest. Send it up to a week before the actual media conference, and no later than the day before. It should state very clearly and boldly exactly when and where the conference is to be held. Always keep it simple and provide a map if necessary.

Media alert: Also known as a diary note; a document used by PR practitioners to alert journalists and editors to a forthcoming event, often a media conference or a speech by a prominent person. It is a form of invitation tailored to the needs of the media, and is generally distributed by email or facsimile between one week and one day before the event.

- *Preparing the main media release:* This should follow normal media release format, and either be distributed electronically under embargo earlier in the day or handed to journalists as soon as they arrive at the media conference so that they are prepared for the talking heads and are able to start formulating questions. You may also wish to prepare other items of background information, such as reports or tables, for inclusion in a media kit. More detail on media releases and media kits appears later.
- *Identifying and briefing the spokespeople:* Most likely you will have at least one senior person from your organisation or company in attendance to speak and to answer questions. In some cases, you will have a high-profile person such as a government minister as well. Having more than one authoritative person sitting at the front making the announcement is a good idea. You should not be making any announcements yourself; as a PR person you are the facilitator rather than the source. Ensure that everyone involved at your end understands the key points that must be relayed through the media conference—you do not want a situation in which people are contradicting each other (or the media release) publicly. You may need to hold several meetings with key spokespeople before the media conference to make sure all participants understand their exact roles and the order of service. During these meetings, establish no more than three essential take-home messages to impart at the media conference. Coach your spokespeople not to use technical language or jargon. Always make sure their messages are fully accessible to non-specialists.
- *Contacting media representatives by phone:* It is good practice to ring the people to whom you have sent the media alert to ensure that they have received the information and so you can obtain a good idea of exactly who will be there. When making these phone calls never be pushy—never insist that journalists attend the media conference—just call to gather information. Keep a list of who is likely to attend and brief your spokespeople on what to expect in terms of numbers of journalists and the outlets they will represent. It may be necessary to wait a few moments before starting the conference if someone you are definitely expecting hasn't arrived yet.
- *Placing corporate or organisation imagery around the room:* You will probably need to at least place a logo on the lectern or the main table, and it is a good idea to place other large images on the walls as suitable background for newspaper photographs or television footage. You will probably confer with a graphic designer or production manager, either a staff member at your organisation or a contractor, to ensure that the imagery fits the occasion. It should always be big, striking and simple. Don't put up posters showing lots of words and complicated tables—whatever you put up should be instantly understandable.
- *Introducing the speakers:* At the start of the media conference, the PR practitioner may need to call the room to order and make clear and brief introductions of the spokespeople. You do not need to reel off a whole CV, just offer some quick information about who is speaking and ensure that there is no ambiguity about exactly who is who. It is a good idea to practise public speaking yourself, because you need to sound fluent and confident. Dithering or confusing announcements by the PR person will get the event off to a bad start.
- *Lining up one-on-one interviews:* After the main part of the media conference, you may need to race around assisting reporters to set up one-on-one interviews. One of the reasons it is useful to have more than one spokesperson (though not too many) is so you can have several interviews going at once, and so the television and radio reporters have access to a diversity of talent to make their reports more interesting. Calmly and politely keep

your spokespeople moving around to the various reporters and ensure that no one is left wondering what to do next.

- *After the media conference:* Depending upon the nature of your announcement, media interest may continue through the day. Indeed, you may still be answering calls and providing photographs and other requested information well into the evening. A media conference is a special event day and you should be prepared for anything. You may find it sensible not to make any plans for that evening.

When it is over

At the end of a media conference, and after all follow-up issues have been dealt with, you normally feel exhausted but high. You have done your hard work; now it is time to relax a little and enjoy the aftermath—assuming that no media liaison disaster becomes apparent. This is where the job satisfaction comes in. PR can be an enormously satisfying job, even if its rewards are rather different from those of a reporter. It can be fascinating to observe how the media deal with your announcement after the media conference, particularly if the conference has been properly stage managed and the chance of the information being misconstrued has been avoided. With any luck, your organisation's senior management will be able to bask in a little glory, and hopefully, they will indicate satisfaction with the job you have done to make it all happen. You will, of course, be carefully monitoring the outcome of your media announcement. Using the services of a **media monitoring organisation** is the most reliable way to ensure comprehensive monitoring. Management may require a report summarising the cost and benefit of the event.

Media monitoring organisation: A company that may be contracted to track media activity and provide print media clippings and audio and video recordings of media coverage. These companies generally also offer analysis of news trends. Media monitoring organisations are used extensively by PR professionals to measure the impact of publicity activities.

Essential documents 1: the media alert

The media alert, often known as a diary note, serves a specific purpose that is related to but separate from the media release. It is used to let journalists and editors know about a media conference and to ensure that they have all the information necessary to get them to come along. It is a special media form of invitation.

There are two keys to preparing a successful media alert or diary note:

1. Your note must be absolutely clear, with easy-to-follow directions and all relevant information prominently displayed.
2. It should not reveal too much because you don't want the story to be released before the media conference and hence compromise its news value.

If you wish, you may place **embargoed** information about the substance of the media conference into the media alert, as metro journalists in particular will not commit to an event unless they know exactly what is being announced. However, as a PR person you must ensure that your announcement is not pre-empted in the media, thus

Embargo: A notice forbidding release of information about an event before a certain time or date.

rendering the media conference redundant and probably ensuring that no one turns up. Always remember the purpose of media alert: to get media representatives to come to your event and report on it. They won't do this if the story has already been released, if you make it too difficult for them to get there or if they are confused about dates.

For examples of good and bad media alerts, go to this textbook's online resources at <www.oup.com.au/orc/mediajournalism2e>.

Essential documents 2: the media release

Once your media alert has done its job and enticed reporters to come along to the media conference, you will pass around copies of the full **media release**, containing all the information you want journalists to have. As mentioned earlier, you may also have distributed the release electronically, either before the media conference (under embargo) or at the time it is scheduled to begin.

Media release: A document, written by a PR practitioner in journalistic style, that provides a story intended for use by the media.

Media releases take many formats and styles that are all perfectly acceptable. The exact look of a media release is often a matter of the style and taste preferences of the organisation issuing it. However, there are still some rules that apply in all cases and that are known to assist in the uptake of material from releases.

Media releases v press releases

While many people still refer to press releases, this term is held by many industry practitioners to be outdated as it implicitly excludes the electronic media. While not everyone sees this as an important issue, it is wise for PR people to be as inclusive as possible. This also holds for media conference being preferred to press conference.

The media release is a long-standing method for reaching journalists quickly, mostly because no better way has been found. An effective media release is much like a well-written news story—it should have a clear opening sentence, and then an inverted-pyramid structure that takes the reader though a hierarchy of information from most importance to least. It is best to deal with one fact at a time in each sentence and, like news stories, make each sentence its own paragraph.

Your media release may be either one or two pages long. A two-page release is fine if the information warrants it, but never go beyond two pages. If you have other information that you must supply, put it into a backgrounder and attach it as an extra document. (Backgrounders are discussed in more detail below.) The release should feature a simple, eye-catching headline in journalistic style. Try not to use clichés or be too clever. A simple, straightforward statement is all that is required; newspaper subs prefer to be clever on their own behalf.

Address the Who?, What?, When?, Where?, Why? and How? formula that also applies to news stories. When you look at what you have written, make sure that all these questions are answered. Your prose should be brief, well expressed and couched in the active voice as much as possible. It should never sound like an advertisement—this is media death. In most cases, journalists are repelled by the advertising writing style and will only respond to material that is not only written like news but also contains actual news. In a media release that will be issued in association with a media conference, you must include direct quotes from those spokespeople present at the conference. What they are quoted as saying in the media release should exactly reflect what they are going to say in person at the conference. Your media release must also follow journalistic style in its use of language (see Chapter 4 and Chapter 14 for detailed discussions of grammar and news language, respectively).

Your releases should always look good. Never use hard-to-read typefaces; stick to clear, clean typefaces such as Times New Roman. Similarly, avoid blocks of impenetrable text; there should be plenty of white space and a pleasing, uncrowded appearance. Don't try to fit too much on the page. If it looks too busy, do what you can to simplify it. Use your organisation's logo every time. A consistent look for each alert and release you send out is helpful. If you are doing your job properly, a quick glance by an editor or journalist will assure them that the document they have received is going to be useful.

Clearly list all the means by which journalists can contact you, the PR person, for further information. In the case of a big story announced at a media conference, it is often the case that the senior people quoted are attending to media queries while other journalists are trying to get through, so you have to help take that overflow. Your role is not the same as the spokespeople's who provide quotes for the journalists' stories. It is more likely that you will take journalists' names and phone numbers and get your talent back in touch with them as soon as possible.

Media kits

Media kit: A folder that contains a range of material relevant to a media event such as a media conference. As well as a media release, it may include background information, photographs and pens.

A **media kit** should contain a useful collection of information that will assist the journalists attending your media conference. It will include the main media release as well as a backgrounder and any other relevant material, all contained in a special folder. The kit folders are often A4 cardboard, folded to make a pocket inside to hold material. If your organisation doesn't already have such a folder, you will need to allow plenty of time for one to be designed, approved and printed well ahead of the media conference. Apart from a media release, the kit will often contain background information of various kinds, including fact sheets giving technical information, graphs, photos, pens, coasters or whatever your organisation deems useful for a journalist to have.

Backgrounders

Often, media releases are accompanied by supplementary media material known as a **backgrounder**, which may take several different forms:

Backgrounder: Material provided in addition to a media release, consisting of more detailed information than the release and providing journalists with a range of new angles.

- a page or two of brief dot-point notes, perhaps providing key dates and history in the form of a timeline
- essentially, a feature story, written journalistically and provided to flesh out the news story contained in the media release proper.

Your background feature may be up to about 2000 words long and will probably contain subheadings to break it up.

You may include relevant images, such as photos, drawings and graphs, as well as a list of further reading and additional contacts. The idea is to give the story more depth and provide the journalist with more options for angles.

TIPS ON WHAT TO DO AND WHAT TO AVOID

Make sure you always:

- ensure that your media conference announces a story that is genuinely newsworthy
- schedule your media conference on a date of optimum news timeliness and at a time of day that accords with media deadlines
- book a suitable venue that will provide a pleasing and relevant backdrop and be just the right size for the event
- brief your spokespeople carefully ahead of time and agree on simple take-home messages and jargon-free delivery
- play a facilitating role and ensure that your spokespeople are efficiently matched with journalists for one-on-one interviews
- ensure that your associated media materials are professional, informative, accurate and newsworthy.

Make sure you never:

- ignore media news values
- set dates and times that accord with priorities other than those of media needs and deadlines
- arrange a huge venue that makes the event look sparse when viewed on the television news that night
- allow your spokespeople to obfuscate or waffle
- give away too much about the story in your media alert or reveal the story ahead of time without applying an embargo to the information
- fail to follow through with further media enquiries after the event.

And to really shine, your media conference should:

- offer a timely, important story in an efficient manner allowing all media representatives access to well-briefed spokespeople who are able to explain the story clearly and simply. If you get a reputation for being able to do this, journalists will find your media conferences useful and reliable, and they will be more likely to attend them in future.

Conclusion

If you think about what you are trying to achieve as a PR person, the requirements of the media conference become just common sense. You want to supply information to the media sphere in a way that benefits your organisation and accords with media priorities and conventions. If you keep these overall goals in mind, your media conference will be a success.

KEY REFERENCES

Tymson, C., Lazar, P. & Lazar, R. (2000). *The New Australian and New Zealand Public Relations Manual.* Sydney: Tymson Communications.

PART 3

MEDIA ANALYSIS

Media are products—industrially produced and usually made in great numbers—but they are also unique in the sense that media, regardless of their form, carry meanings. In Part 3 we explore the ways in which we can analyse media.

In Chapter 9 (Media Texts) and Chapter 10 (Audiences and Representations) we look at the elements of media, the commonalities they share, and what it is they ultimately do. We explore the role of the audience and the way media forms are connected to economics and power. In this way, we can start to think of media in terms of textual systems, composed of industries, products and audiences, and recognise that journalism is an important textual system in modern society.

In Chapter 11 (Celebrity) we consider one of the most commonplace yet complex media products—the celebrity—and the ways in which the current proliferation of celebrities is altering the mediasphere.

Case Study 3 (The Politician, the Journalist, Privacy and the Public Right to Know) analyses the case of a commercial television station outing a state politician, former New South Wales Minister for Transport David Campbell, as leading a double life as a bisexual man. The broadcast of the story by Channel Seven's Adam Walters sparked a debate across Australia about media ethics, the issue of privacy and the public right to know.

Tools 3 (Textual Analysis and Media Research) provides an introduction to the basics of media research, and a variety of tools for and practical approaches to analysing and producing image and written media texts.

CHAPTER 9

MEDIA TEXTS

JASON BAINBRIDGE

Introduction

In media studies and journalism our objects of study are very diverse.

The mediasphere is filled with many different forms of media, from films to comics, video clips to television miniseries, podcasts to talkback radio programs, and cooking shows to current affairs exposés. How can we possibly analyse them all? What could a game show about twelve strangers locked together in a house have in common with the nightly news? How can we compare an adaptation of Shakespeare's *Richard III* with *SpongeBob SquarePants*? Is there even a word for all these media forms or some underlying commonality that they might all share—from a German drama such as *Inspector Rex*, to a Japanese cooking show such as *Iron Chef*, to a Broadway extravaganza such as *Wicked*?

The answer is yes. Simply by being part of the mediasphere, all media forms provide a representation of the world. Furthermore, we can refer to all of these diverse forms—and many more besides—as *texts*.

In this chapter we look at:

- what a text is
- the basics of textual analysis
- where we find texts.

What is a text?

Traditionally, when people refer to a **text**, they are referring to something they have sent or received on their phone, or a book. Indeed, the very book you're reading now has probably been described as an academic text, a reference text, the set text or the best text ever written on the relationship between media studies and journalism (we can hope, can't we?).

In media studies, texts can refer to a lot more than just a book. **Media texts** can include not just books but also magazines, newspapers, advertisements, films, television and radio programs, comics, web pages,

Text: Anything we can make meaning from.

Media text: Anything produced and/or distributed by a media industry from which we can make meaning.

tweets and phone messages. Texts can also include graffiti, articles of clothing, works of art, animation cels, pieces of furniture, architecture, sculpture, action figures, plush toys and even people ... basically, anything from which we can make meaning.

Why use the term 'text'?

This broad definition would seem to be unworkable. After all, what can't we make meaning from? But that's precisely why the word is important—it's a very democratic term. There's no value judgment attached. If, for example, you were told that you would be studying Tolstoy's *War and Peace* (a book), an episode of MTV's *Jersey Shore* (a television show) and a Barbie doll (a toy), you might be tempted to value the book more than the other two items. However, by referring to them all as texts we can remove any evaluative judgment. Suddenly a Barbie doll is as worthy an object of study as a Tolstoy novel; similarly, a piece of graffiti written on the back of a toilet door is as important as one of Shakespeare's folios, and a Britney Spears song is as valuable as a Robert Frost poem. This is not to say that some texts don't have more impact or influence than other texts, but it does mean that we can analyse all of them without preconceptions.

However, this type of approach can also lead to all sorts of criticisms.

The trouble with Harry

A. S. Byatt (2003), writing on the incredible interest in the Harry Potter novels, films and merchandise, claimed that:

> It is the substitution of celebrity for heroism that has fed this phenomenon. And it is the levelling effect of cultural studies, which are as interested in hype and popularity as they are in literary merit.

This levelling effect is another way of describing the democratic effect of using the term 'text'. It is a levelling effect because it creates a level playing field, erasing distinctions between high culture and popular culture, mainstream and alternative, local and international.

Literary merit: Intrinsic value or worth of a literary work based on the quality of writing, inventiveness of story or ability to capture a certain period of time or emotion; often used to demarcate literature from other formulaic or genre fiction and from the wider body of popular culture.

Remember that media studies, like cultural studies, as a discipline is not saying that **literary merit** is not important. It is not suggesting that Shakespeare, Dickens and Orwell are not worthy of study—indeed, all of these authors are mentioned in this very book. It is certainly not saying that media studies should replace literary studies, any more than it should replace political science or law. The real point is that media studies, like cultural studies, is not just interested in literary merit. Media studies is also interested in concepts such as celebrity, **hype** and popularity, and in why some things become a phenomenon (to use some of the words that Byatt uses in her criticism of the academic approaches to the Harry Potter novels and films). We do this because what are often regarded as the most trivial aspects of our culture (the popular) are also sites of profound importance in terms of power, economics and understanding—as we shall see.

That's why we study media, and why we use the term 'text' to describe what we study.

Hype: Extravagant and overstated publicity; a contraction of the word 'hyperbole', which means an exaggerated statement not meant to be taken literally.

Texting

The idea of the text is crucially important to mobile phone communication. Thousands of these brief, simultaneously written and visual texts, composed of letters, words and numbers, are produced and distributed every day. Similar to Telex speak, mobile phone texting is a modern form of shorthand that evolved from the limitations of the phone keyboard and the limitations of early SMS (short messaging service) facilities, which only permitted the use of 160 characters. But even with developments in phone technology, and the increased use of predictive text, texting (also known as SMS language, txt or txt talk) continues to be used. Indeed, texting conventions are so commonplace that they are often referred to in other media, as in the title of Fall Out Boy's 2007 song 'Thnks fr th Mmrs' ('Thanks for the Memories').

How do we make meaning?

Having defined what a text is and why we use the term, let's now consider how we make meaning from a text.

In Tools 3, we outline a number of ways of analysing specific texts in greater detail. Following McKee, we call all of these methods of analysis 'sense-making practices'. Here, however, we just want to think about what happens when we first encounter a text; generally, we start off by **reading a text**.

Reading a text: The first act in interpreting the text; the point at which we start to make meaning.

Reading occurs when people first interact with a text. Therefore, in media studies we can say that we read film and television. This may sound strange to you, but it's something that you do all the time, every day, when you consume media. A few examples appear in the following boxes.

Reading media

When you sit down at the end of the day, turn on the television and start to channel surf, you're reading texts very quickly. If you pause on a program with a laugh track, you will probably read that text as a comedy program. If horses and big hats are involved, you will probably read the program as a western. If it is in black and white, then you might read it is a relatively old text. Something similar occurs when you are searching for information on the internet. You will Google a search term or phrase and then scroll quickly through the results that come up, reading through the information to see if it is relevant to your search.

Continued

In both cases you are reading the text, that is, you are interpreting and making meaning from the text. It may not always be the most likely reading, but you are engaging and interacting with the text in some way.

Reading something new

When you go to a new city or country, or are exposed to a foreign culture, you will be acutely aware of reading texts as you try to make meaning from things that are otherwise strange. If you are looking for a toilet, you will be reading texts for male or female signs. If you are looking for an airport, you will be reading texts for symbols that could represent an airport—like the symbol for a plane, or the letter 'A'.

You don't really need to go somewhere new to do this. You could simply try reading a foreign film without subtitles. How much meaning can you make through the images—the clothing, the looks people give one another and the locations? Can you tell where the film is set? What it is about? In each case, interpreting the film will be informed by the ways you read the text.

Reading advertising

Some texts are so simple that reading a text is all you have to do to understand it. Advertisements are often remarkably simple texts because they want to sell a product. The classic advertising axiom 'Sex sells' is a great example of this: an attractive girl standing beside a sportscar or a great-looking guy with a girl are both examples of texts we can read so easily that they have become clichés: 'If I buy this product, then I will be as sexy as this, or can attract someone as sexy as that.'

Some advertisements do work via obscurity, encouraging you to stay with them or return to them to work them out like a puzzle. However, ads are most often designed to be read as quickly and simply as possible, to encourage you to buy a product.

Analysing a text

Reading a text is such an automatic response that we are often unaware that we're even doing it. It takes something foreign or strange (as mentioned above) to make us recognise that we are involved in the process. Additionally, when we're confronted with a very difficult text, we may struggle to make meaning from it. Again, simply reading a text is not always a very accurate way of making meaning.

What we need to do is educate our guess. The first thing we should do is slow down the process of reading, to make us aware of each step that we are taking in interpreting the text. Then we need to inform our reading by looking at things outside the text, such as other texts or the place where the text is located. In this way we're moving from simply reading a text towards **analysing** a text. Each step we take educates our guess. Some textbooks also use the term 'close reading' to describe this process.

Analysis: Examination in detail of the elements of something in order to determine how the whole functions.

A complete textual analysis is usually a combination of three approaches:

- breaking down a text into its various components
- **framing** a text (becoming aware of how the text is presented to us and where we find the text)
- looking at the relationship between texts.

Framing: A process of selecting and rejecting information in the construction of a news story by placing emphasis on a particular aspect or angle.

You might think that this seems an exhaustively long process. Furthermore, you might notice that to describe these approaches we use a number of terms that will be new to you, but in the immortal words of *The Hitchhiker's Guide to the Galaxy*: DON'T PANIC!

While the terms may be unfamiliar to you, the practices they describe will not be. This is because you are already reading texts, so you're already analysing texts, too. The process seems exhaustive only because all we are trying to do is slow down the process of making meaning, and one of the best ways to do this is to name each part of the process, one by one. Just remember:

- You do all of these things so quickly they are practically unconscious processes.
- By breaking them down and naming each step we make them conscious processes, so you become aware of the decisions you make and, ultimately, how meaning is made.
- Best of all, once you have learnt the concepts in the chapter, you will find that you can apply them to any and every text you encounter—from a simple radio jingle through to an exotic foreign film.

A forensic examination

John Hartley (1999) describes this kind of analysis as being akin to a 'forensic examination'. As with the television series *CSI*, *Bones* or *Silent Witness*, or the Kay Scarpetta novels of Patricia Cornwell, we are confronted with a mystery: how do we make meaning? In place of a body on the slab, we have a text, and like those forensic examiners we need to consider each piece of the text, the text's relationship with other texts and where the text was found in order to solve the mystery.

What is textual analysis?

Because there are many different types of texts, there are also lots of different ways of analysing texts. We look at a number of these in Tools 3. But for our purposes now, we will use Alan McKee's definition (2003: 1):

> When we perform textual analysis on a text, we make an educated guess at some of the most likely interpretations that might be made of that text.

Note that this is an educated guess. Also, 'educated' here means informed by theory and research, reading around the text and finding plenty of evidence to support your guess. By educating your guess, you can move from simply reading the text towards making the most likely interpretation of the text.

Origin of textual analysis

Textual analysis: An educated guess at some of the most likely interpretations that might be made of the text.

This idea of **textual analysis** emerges from work done by theorists known as the French structuralists in the 1960s, and more particularly from the work of Roland Barthes (1915–80). Barthes believed that any kind of popular cultural product could be 'decoded' by reading the 'signs' within the text (Barthes 1957). The version of textual analysis in this book is a blend of the approaches put forward by Barthes, Hartley, McKee, Thwaites, Davis and Mules.

Why is it important to understand how we make meaning?

You may be wondering why it is important to understand how we make meaning. After all, if it is something we all naturally do, then why are we trying to understand it in such detail?

The main reason is that certain media industries claim to be able to affect people's thoughts and behaviours. They claim to know how people will make meaning from certain texts and, in some cases, how they can direct people to make a certain meaning. These industries include:

- *advertising, marketing and public relations*—who want audiences to accept their messages as being right and correct
- *filmmakers and other popular media practitioners*—who similarly construct texts in such a way that they will produce certain meanings or elicit certain emotional responses; think of how Steven Spielberg creates sympathy and sadness for the plight of the lost *E.T.* in the film of the same name
- *activists and speechwriters*—who also aim to incite or inflame the emotions of the audiences to win their support or allay their fears
- *news organisations, documentary filmmakers and journalists*—because the selection of items during a report or broadcast can alter people's perceptions (see Chapter 12). The story may be edited or put together in such a way as to elicit a certain emotional response. Look, for example, at the way in which documentary filmmaker Michael Moore uses music and editing in his documentaries (such as *Fahrenheit 9/11* or *Bowling for Columbine*) to mobilise an audience around an issue.

Ultimately, what all of these industries and individuals have in common is the claim that they can predict, with some certainty, how their texts will affect people. But the best they really can do is perform their own textual analysis, that is, make their own educated guess about likely interpretations of, and responses to, the texts they produce.

If you want to become one of these individuals or work in one of these industries, it is important that you can make an educated guess as well. Similarly, understanding how we make meaning will empower you as a consumer of media, enabling you to negotiate, resist and enjoy media texts in more detail. It will actually enable you to appreciate how media function in relation to communication, economics and power, which will enable you to be a more successful media producer as well.

Figure 9.1 Signs are the structural elements of the text

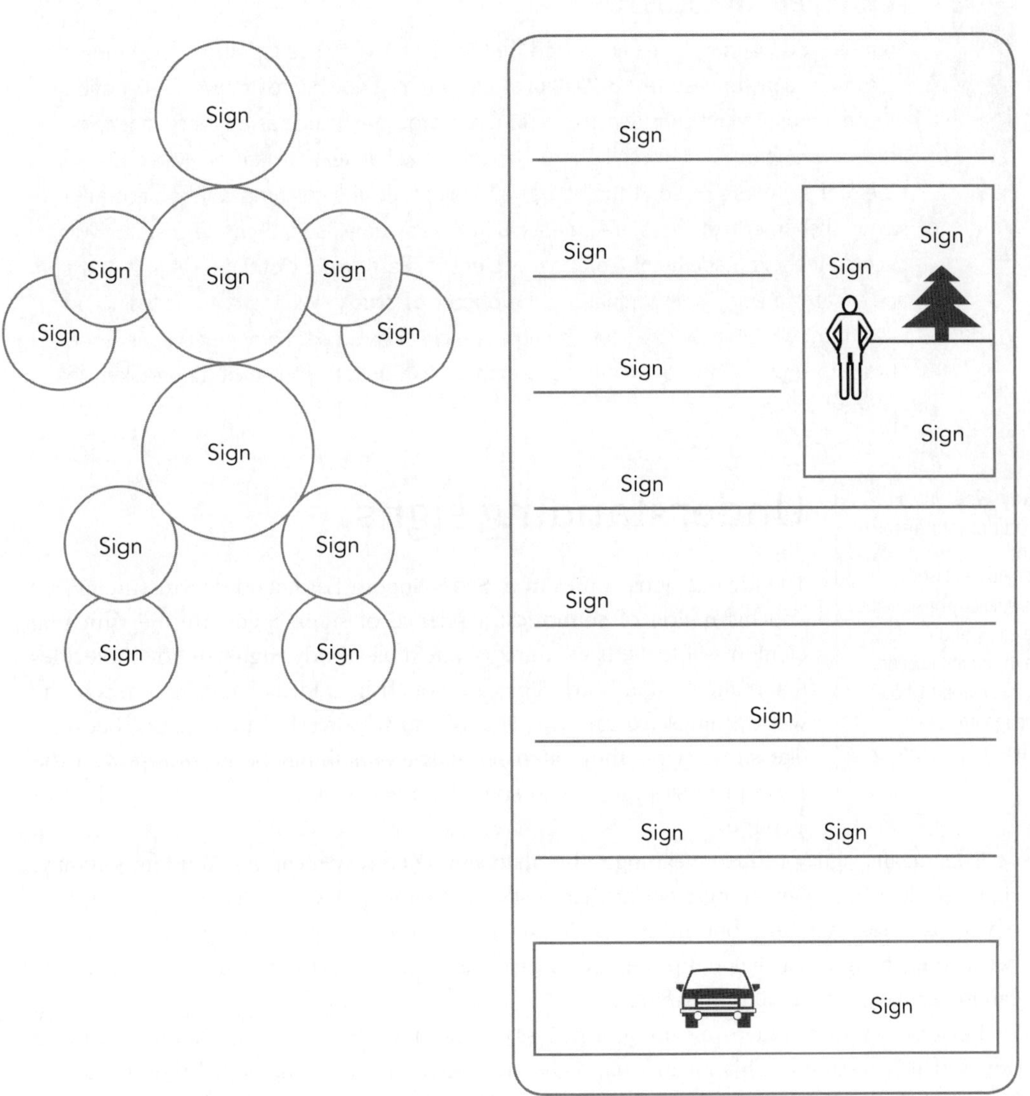

Breaking down the text

Every text is a combination of signs.

Signs are those elements of a text that enable us to read a text in a certain way. If we are analysing a film, we could look at the location, costumes and colours as signs. If we are analysing a magazine article, we could look at the typeface, the words and the accompanying pictures as signs.

Sign: A unit of meaning; a structural element of a text that produces meaning(s).

A problem of focus

Some of you will have already noticed that texts and signs overlap. We could study a costume or a picture as a text in itself (and then break it down into its own combination of signs) or we could consider it as a sign in a larger text, such as a film or magazine article (see Figure 9.1). It really does depend on what text we are analysing at the time. If we are interested in the film as a whole, then the costume will be become a sign in the larger text. If we are interested in the costume itself, then the costume will become the text made up of a number of signs (the articles of clothing). What is a text and what is a sign is determined by the **object of study**. What we are focusing on will inform whether we treat something as a sign or as a text. Remember: your aim is always to understand how meaning is made. Your analysis should be undertaken to achieve this aim.

Object of study: What you are studying; the focus of your research.

Semiotics: Sometimes also referred to as semiology or semiotic studies, it's the study of the role of signification in communication, including, but not limited to, how meaning is made (both how it is produced and how it is understood by an audience member).

Understanding signs

The idea of signs comes from Swiss linguist Ferdinand de Saussure (1986) and his notion of **semiotics:** a science of signs. Signs are the structural elements of texts. If we think of a text as a body, signs are the molecules that make up that body. Signs are not abstract ideas: they are things in the world, things we can see. This is also why we call them signs, because, like street signs, they often represent something (be it an airport or the concept of stopping) with something else (a physical object, a colour or a shape).

This means signs produce meaning rather than simply convey meaning. More importantly, signs produce many meanings, rather than just one meaning per sign. This is why we can never say a text has only one meaning—it can have a more likely meaning, but ultimately, because each sign that makes up the text is capable of many meanings, the text as a whole can never have one, unitary meaning.

Because a sign produces meaning, it necessarily requires an audience, someone to make sense of that meaning. This means that signs are social, and in being social they make the texts social, too. They resemble a needy person who just wants to be the centre of attention all the time, waving his or her hands about saying, 'Look at me, look at me'. How signs—and texts—attract attention is dealt with in greater detail in Chapter 10.

Reading socially

Whenever you are out socially, you will analyse people as texts.

If, for example, you are out at a club and see someone you 'like', you will break the text (the person) down into a number of signs. You might look at the articles of clothing that the person is wearing, whether they have any jewellery or tattoos and what they are drinking. You will certainly be looking at their physical attributes (we'll let you think

of an example for this) and how they interact with surrounding people (whether they are alone or part of a group, their closeness to or distance from other people, whether they seem to be enjoying themselves and whether they appear to be single or attached).

You are trying to make meaning from what you see, that is, you are reading socially to decide: Am I attracted to this person? What attracts me to them? Am I going to ask this person out? Is this person already with someone?

Once again, you are interpreting this text. This time, however, you are not simply reading the text, but also engaging in a textual analysis—breaking the text down into its component signs because you want to make the most likely interpretation to save yourself from the embarrassment of rejection.

Signification

Having broken the text down into signs we can now break down each sign into two parts—the signified and the signifier:

Signification: The *signifier* is the physical part of the sign. The *signified* is the mental part of the sign, the abstract concept represented by the sign. *Signification* is the relationship between the signifier and the signified.

Figure 9.2 A sign

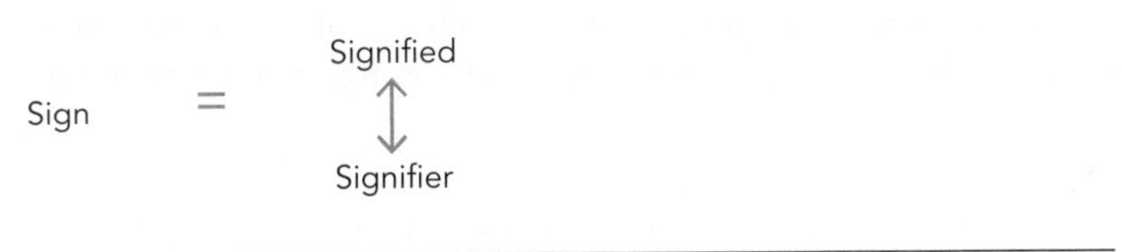

The signifier is the physical part of the sign. The signified is the mental part of the sign, the abstract concept represented by the signifier. We call the relationship between the signifier and the signified the process of signification. These two elements are part of every sign. You can never have a signifier without a signified, or a signified without a signifier. You can move each part around (see below), but both parts must always be present to produce meaning.

Once again, this is why we call these elements of a text signs, because they work just like street signs.

- Think of a STOP sign.
- The signifier is the physical aspect of the sign itself: the symbol, the shape, the colour, the pole sticking into the ground and the word 'STOP'.
- The signified is stopping: slowing down to a complete stop.
- In this way, the stop sign signifies the concept of stopping.

Note that the link between the signifier and the signified is arbitrary, that is, there is no natural link between the signifier and the signified.

There is nothing about a stop sign that has any natural link to the concept of stopping. It has simply been agreed, by custom and usage, that this colour, shape and word signifies the concept of stopping. Similarly, the link is arbitrary between most words (especially in English) and the concepts they represent. The classic example here is 'cat'. There is nothing in the word 'cat' (the signifier) to suggest a furry, four-legged animal who occasionally allows humans to pat it. Indeed, Thwaites, Davis and Mules (2002) note that this signifier can also refer to a piece of earthmoving equipment (bearing the Cat brand), a medical procedure (a cat scan) or, in education, can be the abbreviation of a Common Assessment Task (CAT), a written assignment.

In other written languages, such as Chinese ideograms, Egyptian hieroglyphics or Japanese kanji, there is more of a link between the words (the signifiers) and the concepts (the signifieds), because the words themselves evolved out of symbolic visual representations of certain things in the real world (see Figure 9.3).

Figure 9.3 Japanese kanji for tree (*ki*)

But even visual signifiers share an arbitrary relationship with the signified. For example, both of the images in Figure 9.4 are signifiers of 'dog', even though they are widely disparate.

Figure 9.4 Dog

This means a number of signs can become signifiers for signifieds that seem completely unrelated; for example:

- *celebrities:* these are people who are often referred to as being emblematic of their times (celebrity is discussed in detail in Chapter 11). Marilyn Monroe, for example, is frequently referred to as being representative of the 1950s, that is, Marilyn Monroe functions as a sign—the person (the signifier) signifies the 1950s (the signified)

- *iconic news images:* these also function as signs: the image (the signifier) signifies the issue, story or event (the signified).

The X-Files and *Fringe*

Depending on your object of study, entire media texts can function as signs. The television series *The X-Files*, for example, which revolves around the efforts of two FBI agents to uncover a vast government conspiracy, was seen as being representative of the paranoia of the 1990s. As such, in a study of the 1990s, *The X-Files* could function as a sign, that is, the television series (the signifier) signifies the paranoia of the 1990s (the signified). In contrast, the television series *Fringe*, which revolves around the efforts of a special FBI Fringe Division team to stop an invasion from a parallel universe, can be read as being representative of the paranoia of the 2000s. Whereas *The X-Files*'s shadowy government conspiracy signifies that particular paranoia of the 1990s, the doppelgangers of *Fringe*'s parallel universe signify the particular paranoia based on terrorism and the fear of sleeper cells: people who look like us but are actually plotting against us. This paranoia has had particular cultural resonance since the 11 September 2001 terrorist attacks on the USA. In this way *Fringe* also functions as a sign: a television series (the signifier) signifies the paranoia of the thousands (the signified).

We see these ideas come together in the figure of the newsreader or news presenter. Media organisations invest great sums of money in their on-air news presenters in the hopes of branding certain news stories and media events as their property. If audiences begin associating exclusive stories and breaking news with a certain presenter on a certain network, then the network itself becomes a signifier of breaking news and exclusivity (the signified). This can translate to greater audience share, greater advertising revenue and the perception that this is the network to watch for news.

Signification, therefore, is the process by which meaning is produced. Breaking texts down into their component signs—and then understanding the relationship between the signifier and signified(s) that make up each of these signs—brings us one step closer to understanding how meanings are produced and, ultimately, how we make meaning.

Connotation and denotation

But there is still a problem here. Think of our Marilyn Monroe example. Monroe doesn't just represent the 1950s. She can also represent femininity, or glamour, or stardom or tragedy. Similarly the word 'cat' can represent an animal, a piece of earthmoving equipment, an assessment task or a medical procedure. In each instance, the signifier remains the same, but attaches to a variety of different signifieds. Each of these signifieds appears equally valid—so how do we determine which meaning is produced?

It may be more appropriate to think of a sign in graphic way, as illustrated in Figure 9.5.

As the relationship between the signifier and signified is an arbitrary or unclear one, there is nothing in the nature of the sign itself to tie a signifier to just one signified.

Why you will never look at a bouquet the same way again

Think of a man giving a girl a bunch of flowers.

- These flowers are the signifiers, that is, they are the physical part of the sign.
- The most obvious signified is love: the man is giving the girl these flowers because he loves her.
- But the signified could also be guilt—because the man just cheated on the girl with someone he met in a bar.
- Or the signified could be grief—because the girl's mother just passed away.

The signifier (the flowers) remains the same. But the signified changes, and each signified is equally valid.

Connotations: The possible signifieds that attach to a signifier.

Denotation: The most likely connotation of a signifier, often determined as a matter of common sense or by looking at the relationship of the text to other texts or the context in which the text is found.

Rather than the pattern shown in Figure 9.3, we can think of the one signifier having a spread of possible signifieds, as in Figure 9.5. We call this spread of possible signifieds **connotations**.

And the most stable or verifiable or likely connotation we call the **denotation**.

To understand which one is the most likely connotation (the denotation) for a sign in any given text, we need to consider two further things:

- the context in which the text is found
- the relationship between the text we are studying and other texts.

Figure 9.5 Signifier and signified

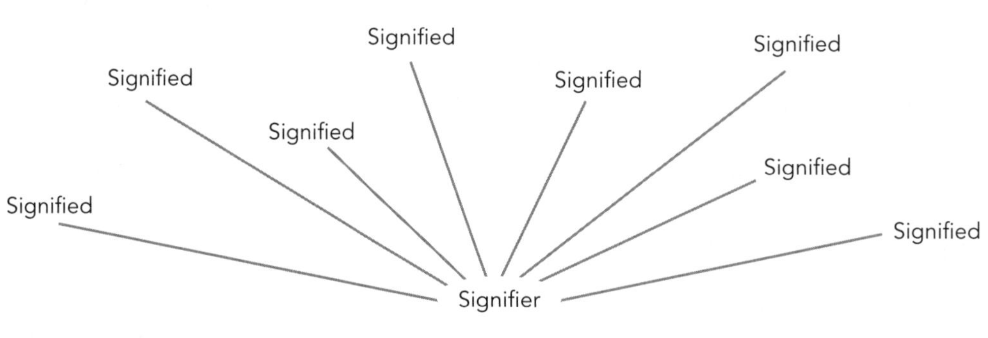

Polysemy: The openness of texts to many different interpretations; a splintering of interpretations.

Think about how this might affect the larger text. As the link between the signifier and the signified is arbitrary, this means that media texts are naturally **polysemic**, that is, 'open to many interpretations'. This is why we can only ever say there is a more likely interpretation; there can never be a definitive right or wrong answer—that a text means this or that—because texts lend themselves to being read in lots of different ways.

In and Out

Frank Oz's 1997 film *In and Out* provides an example of how connotations work. In the film, an actor publicly thanks his drama teacher when he wins an Academy Award—and publicly outs him as gay at the same time. The teacher denies this, but is surprised to discover that most of his students—and the town—think he is gay because of certain things he does: waving his hands around as he speaks, being neat, being well spoken and liking to read.

'Gay' is the signified. Usually, the signifier of gay would be a same-sex relationship, but in this film, all of these other activities become signifiers of being gay, that is, each of these signifiers carries the connotation of being gay. This is only one of the signifieds that using your hands when you speak could carry—but in the film it becomes the denotation, or the most likely connotation. Indeed, the connotations become so convincing that by the end of the film the teacher himself is even questioning his own sexuality, despite being engaged and never having been previously attracted to a man.

'Dog'

For a more general example, think of the word 'dog'. One of the signifieds of dog is a furry, four-legged animal that barks and likes to be patted by humans. But dog can also be used as a derogatory term for a woman, or a way of praising the sexual activity of a man ('You dirty dog'). As unfortunate as it is to admit it, if a woman carrying a dog walked through that door behind you right now, and someone said 'Look at that dog', it might be unclear which signified was being referred to, as these are both currently used connotations of the word dog.

This can make it very difficult for those industries and individuals we described earlier—such as directors, public relations firms and journalists—to produce the meanings that they want to. What they have to do is reduce the polysemy of the text, or to limit the range of connotations. We call this process encoding a text, and it is described in detail in Tools 3.

Framing the text

In determining the denotation (the most likely signified) we make one other, very fast decision—we consider how the text has been framed, that is, how the text is presented to us. This involves two elements: the frame (the limits of the text itself) and the **context** (where the text is located).

Context: The location of the text; the point in time and space where an audience will locate it.

Frames

All texts have frames. Sometimes we are very aware of them, such as the individual frames of a film, the screen on which a television show is displayed, the edges of a photograph or the panels of a comic book. But every text has a frame, even when we may be unaware of it. This is because all texts are bounded in some way: think of the limitations of a telephone text message (limited by the dexterity of the user and the amount of space on a phone), a newspaper report (limited by column inches) or a radio program (limited to a certain bandwidth at a certain time). Even website displays are somewhat limited by the size of the screen on which they are displayed (though hyperlinks can overcome these limitations to some extent).

Frames are important because an awareness of what is inside the frame also makes us aware of what has been left out. This directly relates to ideas of power, access and control, all of which we will be looking at in more detail in Chapters 10 and 12. As Entman (1993: 52) points out: 'To frame is to select some aspects of a perceived reality and make them more salient.' Framing, therefore, is the selection of elements that make up the text.

Framing is a particularly crucial term in understanding how journalists work, for at each stage in the production of a news story we can see frames being used:

- the event or issue is first framed as news by editors, producers and journalists, that is, it is considered worthy of being reported
- these gatekeepers set the frames of reference by which audiences interpret the news
- the story is then framed as a media text for publishing or broadcast
- the story itself then serves as a frame, to set the agenda (or frame the agenda) for further discussion of the issue or event.

As Gitlin (1980: 7) puts it, framing becomes a way to 'organise the world both for journalists who report it and, in some important degree, for us who rely on their reports'. We look at the processes involved in framing news texts in Chapter 12.

Contexts

All texts have a location, that is, a point in time and space where we encounter them. Remember, no text exists in isolation. In reading texts we are always aware of the texts' dialogic relationship with other texts (which we call intertextuality, something we return to in Chapter 10), and we are always aware of the context, the point at which we encounter them.

There are nine basic contexts—structural, physical, temporal, political, textual, narrative, generic, industrial and sociocultural—which all overlap to some degree, and a de facto tenth context, the mediasphere (see Figure 1.1). Simply by virtue of being media texts, all media texts are contextualised into the larger mediasphere, that is, they are all part of that web of dialogic relationships outlined in Chapter 1.

Codes: Usually, parts of the signs that make up texts, including such elements as colour, dress, lighting, angles, words used and format on the page or screen.

Assisting us in finding a context for a text is a series of codes embedded in the text. **Codes** are usually parts of the signs that make up texts. These codes could include such elements as colour, dress, lighting, angles, words used and format on the page or screen.

Codes will differ between media texts. Indeed, on the most basic level, they will often indicate what form of media we will be dealing with:

- An aural text with a lack of visuals, for example, would suggest a radio text.
- A visual text broken up by advertising would suggest a televisual, rather than filmic, text.

Codes may also help us to determine in which of the nine contexts a text can be found. Some of these contexts will already be familiar to you from previous chapters; others we will return to later in the book. Each in its own way can assist us to understand how meaning is made, because each gives us an idea of where the text comes from and what its place is in the wider world. It is another important step in educating our guess as to the most likely meaning of this text.

The structural context: the form or shape of the text

- Is it written, oral, aural or visual—or a combination of them?
- What is the shape of the text? A certain type of arrangement of words on a page, for example, can suggest a letter; the use of the inverted pyramid style of writing can suggest a news article. By contrast, an interplay of words and visuals might suggest a comic.
- How does the shape of the text alter the way you make meaning? Do you, for example, privilege a text more if it is written than visual?

The physical context: the physical location where we encounter and/or engage with the text

- Think of the difference between seeing a film in a cinema and seeing it on television. There are the obvious differences in being out of your house (as opposed to watching something in your home) and the size of the screen—but the differences also have an impact on the way the film might be cut (if it's being aired by a free-to-air television network it could be cut for censorship or advertising requirements) or how you consume the film. Are you doing something else while it is on? Are the lights on or off?
- What difference do censorship or classification make?
- What difference does it make to read a newspaper at a cafe rather than at a library?
- What expectation might you have of a magazine labelled as, say, a men's magazine?
- How does where you encounter the text alter how you make meaning from it?

The temporal context: the time when the text was produced or first encountered

- Think of when the text was created. This may account for certain ideas on racial, political or sexual equality that may seem strange to you, or the use of technologies or fashions that may seem outdated.
- It may also account for technical deficiencies, such as the quality of the film stock, or the absence of colour or sound.
- Was the text particularly revolutionary for its time? Did it challenge the prevailing ideas of its time? Or is it a relatively conservative text? Does it look back to a particular idea of the past? Or is it the forerunner for current texts?
- The temporal context can also refer to when audiences encounter the text—either the time it appears on a schedule (as in a morning radio show, a daytime soap or the late news) or the age of the audience member when they encounter it (the popularity of *Starsky and Hutch* in the 1970s, and *Pokemon* in the 1990s).
- Think about how the time of the text's production and whether the time of its reception could have an impact on the way meaning is made. Does it make you reconsider how ambitious or how tame the text actually was?

The political context: the political regime under which the text was created or to which it responds

- How has the text been informed by the politics of its time? Arthur Miller's play *The Crucible*, for example, uses the Salem witch trials as a metaphor for the ideas of McCarthyism that were prevalent in the USA when the play was published (in the late 1940s). Similarly, Alan Moore and Guy Davis's *V for Vendetta* comic book uses a story about a futuristic British government to provide a critique of the political climate of the 1980s United Kingdom.
- How does the text relate to the politics of the present? Has it taken on a new meaning, a new resonance or a new relevance? Or does it come across as conservative now, whereas once it might have been seen as radical?
- How does this relationship to politics alter how meaning is made? Does it depend on how explicit or implicit the relationship is?

The textual context: where the text sits in relation to other texts

- Think about how this text's relationship to other texts may affect how meaning is made, for example, does it require a greater level of cultural competency from the audience than some other texts?

The narrative context: where the text fits into a larger story or narrative

- How does a text advance a story or narrative? Is it part of a larger narrative? Is it initiating a narrative or does it come at the end of a narrative?
- How does recognising how a text fits into a larger narrative alter how meaning is made?

The generic context: what genre the text might belong to

- How might we classify the text in terms of genre?
- What elements of a text assist us in determining the genre it belongs to?
- How does belonging to one genre rather than another affect how meaning is made? For example, do you privilege something in the news genre more than something in the science fiction genre? How closely is the notion of genre related to notions of exclusion and inclusion, and power and control?

The industrial context: the media industry that has produced this text

- How can we work out which media industry has produced this text? This will involve questions of structural context, the shape of the text and the physical context.
- How have the work practices of the industry shaped the text, especially in film and television? How might this affect how meaning is made?

The sociocultural context: the position of the text in the wider culture and society

This encompasses all of the above contexts, as well as considerations of the ethical and legal frameworks within which the text was constructed, and the overall impact and influence of the text in the wider culture and society.

- How can we understand the ethical and legal frameworks in which media texts are produced?
- How can we measure the impact or influence of a text? How might both of these considerations alter how meaning is made?

These questions are all addressed in other chapters. The relationship between texts is discussed in Chapter 10, as are the ideas of exclusion and inclusion, power and control, and impact and influence. Genre was discussed in Chapters 6 and 7. For more detail on ethical–legal frameworks, see Part 5. For more detail on the wider social context, see Part 6.

The relationship between texts

Thinking about the relationship between texts is a crucial element of textual analysis and media texts in general; it is developed in more detail in Chapter 10.

As we have already seen in Chapter 1, media texts rarely work in isolation. Texts are interdependent, that is, they often make meaning through their relationship with other texts. They establish conventions (ways of reading texts, such as the shot–reverse shot mentioned in Chapter 1) and, sometimes, they explicitly reference another text for purposes of parody, pastiche or homage. The presence of just one actor can signify a whole body of work; it is easier to accept Harrison Ford in the role of a hero, for example, because you have already seen him as a hero in most of his other films. Other conventions are so commonplace that they become generic, that is, indicative of the film belonging to a certain genre. So, for example, suspenseful music on the soundtrack might indicate that a character is facing great danger.

This idea of texts not existing in isolation, but rather depending on each other to make meaning, is called **intertextuality**. This really flows back to that earlier idea (again in Chapter 1) of **cultural competency**. You can still enjoy *The Simpsons, Austin Powers* or *Mad Magazine* without knowing all of the intertexts they are referring to and/or quoting from. But you will find it easier to make meaning, whether it is understanding a reference or getting a joke, if you are aware of the intertexts.

Intertexts inform us, enlighten us and help us make sense of texts. They include everything from previous episodes of a television series (imagine trying to make sense of *24* or *Breaking Bad* without having seen any of the early episodes) and guidebooks, to other films by the same director.

Intertextuality: The idea that texts do not exist in isolation, but rather are interdependent. Texts frequently make meaning through their relationship with other texts. These other texts (secondary texts) are called *intertexts*.

Cultural competency: Knowledge and ideas that are gained from experience; cultural knowledge is insider knowledge that is known only by people within a particular culture or by people who have learnt about the culture through interaction with it.

Intertextuality also assists us in two ways to understand how meaning is made:

- it provides a textual context for the text, a way of placing the text in relation to other texts
- it provides a way of understanding how the text works in relation to these other texts. Intertextuality, therefore, becomes not only a way of connecting texts, but also a way of determining the significance of an individual text. (This is covered in more detail in the next chapter.)

Once again, intertextuality can also act as a way of including or excluding the audience. Those who are aware of the intertexts are included, and those who are not are excluded. Think about how a knowledge of intertexts assists you in understanding how meaning is made. What conventions is this text drawing on? What references to other texts does it make? What are the differences in making meaning when the text is read with intertextual knowledge compared with it being read without intertextual knowledge?

Conclusion

Media texts offer a number of ways of representing the world. We can break down texts into units of meaning (signs), and can further break down signs into a physical element (the signifier) and a range of mental concepts (the spread of signifieds). These spreads of signifieds are called connotations. The most stable, verifiable and likely connotation is the denotation, usually determined by reference to the situation (the context) in which the text is found. Audiences are so media savvy, and make meaning from media texts so quickly, that it is almost an unconscious process. We refer to this process as reading a text. It is only through the process of analysing a text that we can slow down this process, which is what makes us aware of how meaning is made.

Textual analysis is a three-stage process of breaking down the text, framing the text (considering how the text is presented and the context in which the text is located) and looking at the relationship between texts.

In the next chapter we look at texts from the perspective of the audiences to explore the ways in which audiences engage with texts and conclude with a consideration of what it is that texts actually do.

KEY REFERENCES

Hartley, J. (1999). *Uses of Television.* London: Routledge.

McKee, A. (2003). *Textual Analysis: A Beginner's Guide.* London: Sage.

Thwaites, T., Davis, L. & Mules, W. (2002). *Introducing Cultural and Media Studies: A Semiotic Approach.* Basingstoke: Palgrave.

CHAPTER 10

AUDIENCES AND REPRESENTATIONS

JASON BAINBRIDGE

Introduction

You have probably heard that famous philosophical question: 'If a tree falls in a forest and nobody hears it, did it really fall at all?' In a similar vein, we could ask if a text can truly function as a text without an audience to read it.

In Chapter 9 we explained what a text was, broke it down into its component signs and considered some of the contexts in which texts are situated and the relationship between texts. But this is really only half of the story. A text presupposes an audience: texts cannot produce meaning without having someone to make meaning from them. To appreciate how a text can actually function as a representation of the world, we need to think about the people who are making meaning: the audience and how their relationships with texts are constantly changing, thanks to advancements in technology.

In this chapter we look at:

- the relationship between audiences and texts
- ways of thinking about audiences
- what it is that texts actually do.

The social function of signs

In the previous chapter we saw that texts are made up of units of meaning called signs, and that each sign is composed of a signifier and a possible spread of signifieds called connotations. The most likely signified is referred to as the denotation.

This idea of denotation is important, because it is at this point that industries and individuals work to make meaning; the producers of media texts do this by encoding a text in a certain way (see Tools 3) and the receivers of media texts do this by analysing a text following those steps we went through in the previous chapter.

Both processes are social processes, because signs require someone to create them and someone to make sense of them. As we noted in Chapter 9, this means that signs themselves are social and, in being social, they make texts social, too.

Sender: The text's point of origin.

Receiver: The text's destination.

As signs are social, we can say that they have a point of origin and a destination. We call the point of origin the **sender**. A sender might be any or all of those individuals or industries who encode a text in anticipation that the audience will read the text in a certain way.

We call the destination the **receiver**: the audience that analyses signs. Members of the audience analyse texts every time they break texts down into signs and then break signs down into signifiers and spreads of signifieds. As already noted, this is often done so quickly that we are rarely conscious that we are even doing it.

Signs need an audience—they cannot function without one. Therefore, signs need to attract audiences, and they attract audiences through the process of address. Address is the first stage in the dialogic relationship between texts and audiences we mentioned in Chapter 1. In effect, it is the text's attempt to enter into a dialogue with someone.

What is the process of address?

Address: The way the text hails us, calls us over or otherwise demands our attention.

Addresser: The position that is actively attracting us to the text.

Addressee: The audience implied by being addressed.

The process of **address** is the way the text hails us, calls us over or otherwise demands our attention.

The position that is actively attracting us to the text we call the **addresser**. For anyone familiar with the Australian television series *Kath & Kim*, the addresser is the textual equivalent of 'Look at me; look at me'.

The audience implied by this position is called the **addressee**.

Note: The addresser and addressee are both textual constructs, that is, they only exist inside the text as opposed to the sender and receiver, who are real people in the real world and as such exist outside the text.

When we say that the addresser and addressee are textual constructs, we mean that we can identify the addresser and addressee (as they are actually parts of the text we are analysing), whereas we can never really identify the sender and receiver with any degree of certainty.

What is a lot easier to determine is the addresser and addressee because they are textual constructs. We simply need to look at the text to understand who they are.

Why is it difficult to work out who is the sender of a media text?

Unlike literary texts, which we can usually attribute to a single author and even that can be problematic; look at, for example, the debates over who really wrote Shakespeare's plays. Media texts are usually the products of vast teams of people, making the apportionment of responsibility very difficult and identification of the sender even more so. Look at the

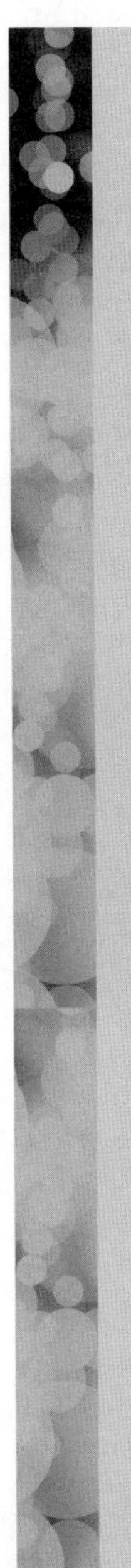

credits for a film or a television series—it would be almost impossible to say who was the sender of these texts. Who was responsible for each element? Who was responsible for the original idea? Similarly, who is the sender of a song: the writer, the singer or the producer? Who is responsible for a news report: the reporter, the camera operator or the editor? What about comic books? Do we say that the writer or the artist is the sender, or maybe both, or maybe the editor?

The death of the author

Roland Barthes and Michel Foucault, the most prominent French cultural studies theorists of the last forty years, addressed this issue when they referred to the concept of the death of the author. Here, they are not referring to the literal homicide or suicide of authors, but are arguing for less attention to be paid to the intention of the author, in favour of focusing on the text itself. In part, this is because the intentions of the author (the sender) don't matter as much as the text itself and the meanings that the text carries. When we are no longer looking at literary texts, this argument gets around the difficult question of apportioning responsibility where the sender (or senders) are hard to identify. Most importantly, it means that texts can transcend their creation to evolve and change with the times.

Why is it almost impossible to work out who is the receiver of a media text?

Determining who is the receiver can be just as difficult. A finance report may be designed for a business audience, but some viewers may tune in because the host is well known. *Cleo* magazine is designed for a female audience, but is sometimes read by men trying to understand the female mind. *Fantasia* was an animated Disney film designed to introduce audiences to classical music, but it enjoyed renewed popularity in the 1960s because of drug users who found watching the film while high provided a great trip. Even the media texts we refer to in this book were intended primarily for entertainment, not academic study. It's therefore next to impossible to determine who the receiver will ultimately be.

For an alternative view of the relationship between authors and media texts, and one of the ways authors can still have an impact on media texts despite the death of the author, see the discussion of auteur theory in Chapter 6.

The addresser

Addressers can be identified as characters within a text who address us in some way. They may be looking at us, as models do in advertisements, or as people do from the covers of magazines or from their photos on social networking sites. Or they may speak to us, as talk show hosts do, or journalists, comedians, entertainers and bloggers. The addresser is the 'I' of the text.

- There are often multiple addressers in any one text, especially where there is a combination of written and visual elements, so a photo and a headline may each act as an addresser.
- Addressers are signs that encourage us to engage with the text, and then go on to read the text.
- Addresser is most often a dual role, in which two aspects of the text simultaneously address the audience. On the one hand the text itself addresses us via a headline on a newspaper, a strong visual in a television series or the opening chords of a song. On the other hand, a character inside the text, such as a newspaper columnist, a narrator or a singer can address us.
- We can think of the addresser as a dual role, because the addresser is simultaneously the newspaper and the columnist, the television series and the narrator, and the song and the singer.

Name badges

Think of one of the simplest texts, the name badge worn by staff in retail stores such as Myer or Coles. Typically, these badges include the name of the store and the (first) name of the staff member. Even this simple text has a dual-addresser position: the addressee is simultaneously addressed by the store and the staff member as an agent for that store.

The implied addressee would be someone in that store, implied by the addresser store name, seeking service, implied by the staff member's name.

The addressee

You might be confused when we say the addressee is implied by the text. What we mean is that addressees are implied by the text because the addresser(s) necessarily imply a corresponding addressee, that is, someone it is hailing. Let's look at an example:

- An attractive, semi-clad woman on the cover of *Playboy* implies a male addressee.
- We can find out more about the addressee by reading the titles of the articles, looking at the age of the woman, the price of the magazine and any age restrictions on purchase.
- By looking at a combination of signs, we can build up quite a detailed picture of who the intended addressee might be.
- This does not prevent the magazine being bought by a lesbian or stolen by a twelve-year-old boy—but we can gain an idea of the audience the magazine is constructing for itself.
- The addressee is, therefore, as much of a textual construct as the addresser.

By looking at how texts address us, we could construct similar addressee profiles for the addressees of *Cleo* and *Fantasia* (referred to above) as well as certain songs, television programs and newspapers. By looking at the evidence in the text itself, we could determine an addressee's gender, age, financial resources and location—and sometimes even their political leanings.

Be aware of the advertisements

One of the best ways of determining the constructed addressee is to read, watch or listen to the advertisements that appear during, after or before the text that you're analysing. They give a clear indication of the audience that the text wishes to reach, because the advertisers are targeting audience members with items they want them to purchase.

Why is identifying the addresser important?

Identifying the addresser is a way of determining the implied addressee, and this is important because it provides us with information about whom the text views as being part of its intended audience. As will be made clearer below, this can (sometimes) help us understand what the text is trying to do. Furthermore, it can better enable us to understand the possible relationships between a text, power and money, because audiences are the basis on which decisions are made about what is going to be produced, broadcast and printed. Audiences provide much of the commerce for the functioning of commercial media organisations.

The ways in which signs hail audiences

There are two ways in which signs seek or hail audiences:

- the passive form, called address
- the more active form, called interpellation.

These two ways of hailing audiences are not exclusive. Often they are layered, so a text can address us, and then interpellate us into the text.

Address

The first way signs seek out an audience is through this process of address. Signs construct an addresser that implies a corresponding addressee. The really interesting thing about address is that it creates ideas of **inclusivity** and **exclusivity**: some parts of the audience are addressed by the text (that is, they are included), while others are not (they are excluded). As we have seen in the examples above, this does not mean other members of the audience cannot access the text (unintended receivers, for example), but it is interesting that it is already establishing a power relationship between the text and its audience.

Inclusivity: The inclusion of an audience member, as if he or she belongs to a certain community.

Exclusivity: The exclusion of an audience member, as if he or she has been excluded from a certain community.

Address is an essentially passive way of seeking out audiences because it amounts to little more than the text looking at us or talking to us until we notice and engage with it.

Interpellation

Interpellation: Actively seeking out an audience; encouraging the audience to contribute to the text in some way.

The process of address is not the only way texts seek out audiences. A more active way is through the process of **interpellation**. Often, address and interpellation can work together, with address encouraging us to engage with the text, and then interpellation actually making us a part of the text. Signs invite, direct or encourage the audience to become a part of the text.

Interpellation, a term first used by Althusser (1971), is an essentially active way of seeking out an audience, because it encourages the audience to actually contribute to the text in some way. Interpellation seeks out an audience, involving it in a variety of strategies to get the audience into the text—and each strategy involves a different level of audience investment.

These interpellation strategies take three forms, encouraging audiences to engage through:

- identification
- interaction
- narrative.

Understanding each of these strategies is important for media practitioners who want to build an audience for their texts, and for media consumers who want to be aware of how the media works.

Identification

She looks great in that, so I'll look great in that …

In a number of narrative (and increasingly non-narrative) texts, audiences are encouraged to identify with a particular character, that is, an addressee position is not only implied by the text but actually created as a space within the text itself.

Audience identification: Encouraging audiences to adopt the viewpoint and share in the emotions (especially hopes and fears) of a character in the text.

Subjective viewing position: The taking on of the viewpoint of a character in a text by an audience member; the addressee position actually created as a space within the text itself.

This space is cultivated through **audience identification** with a particular character in the text, which creates what we can term a **subjective viewing position** for the addressee to occupy.

Often, this identification might be with the hero (we empathise with Peter Parker's plight and take pleasure in him becoming Spider-Man), but other positions may be created, too, for example, the audience often shares the point of view of the jury in legal dramas.

This idea of identification is also becoming more common in non-narrative forms:

- Talkback radio hosts often portray themselves as one of the people, encouraging identification.
- Notoriously, the idea of embedded journalists in Iraq (journalists who were part of military deployments) also constructed subjective viewing positions, leading to claims that this undercut their journalistic objectivity.

Identifying with advertising

Advertisements are still the primary media texts that construct an addressee position within their texts, encouraging you to identify with the person in the advertisement by suggesting that if you use their product you can become like them.

In this way the addresser becomes an aspirational figure for the addressee.

Interaction

Phone in now!

Interaction interpellates the audience into texts by making the texts dependent on their involvement, for example:

- talkback radio requires callers to phone in to generate discussion around particular issues
- reality television series are structured around the decisions audiences make to vote people in or out.

In each case, the audience is interpellated into the text, moving the text forward or deciding how the text will develop by deciding what gets discussed, who goes and who stays.

Narrative

And that means the killer must be …

Narrative is not just a way of structuring meanings into the form of a story (as defined in Schirato and Yell 2000), but also a desire among members of the audience to make a structured story out of the texts they engage with.

We can call narrative an active way of seeking out an audience because it actually involves the audience in the text. The audience can, for example, be encouraged to discuss who the murderer might be in a murder mystery, how people are related in a soap opera or whether characters will end up together in just about anything. The audience's implication in the text is an important way of generating extratextual discussion (think back to our discussion in Chapter 1 of the water-cooler television series). Narrative also encourages and rewards ongoing investment in a series of media texts, thereby interpellating more audience members into the text.

What are audiences?

Having said that signs can hail audiences in these different ways, we really need to pause for a moment and think about what it is we actually mean when we say 'media audiences'. Thanks to technological advancements in media, today's audience for a television series such as *Mad Men* is very different from the audiences that would have existed in the era in which that show is set (the 1960s). Indeed, technology means that the nature of being an audience member is in a constant state of flux and change.

By way of example, think of the 2009 Britney Spears's song 'Circus'. It opens with the line: 'There's only two types of people in the world, the ones that entertain and the ones that observe.' This is certainly how it has been for many years: the classic idea of the media network where one group (the ones who entertain, or the producers) broadcasts and/or performs to many (the ones who observe, or the consumers). But this is increasingly no longer the case. The lines between those that entertain and those that observe are being blurred all the time. Today, for the first time in history, anyone reading this textbook has the ability to make their own media—through websites, mashups, blogs, Twitter, posting on YouTube, etc. This means the mediasphere has moved away from being composed of one-to-many media networks

Audience networks: Where audience members themselves access media texts through links with other audience members, replacing the broadcast one-to-many media networks.

towards **audience networks** where audience members themselves access media texts through links with other audience members, whether it is via a blog, a Twitter or Facebook account or through statistically similar watchers of YouTube or buyers on eBay or Amazon. It is sometimes referred to as the *post-broadcast era*. This is once again a confirmation of the mediasphere's functioning as (arguably) the most important part of the public sphere and an indication of how the producer–consumer distinction is rapidly becoming a thing of the past, something we will return to in Chapters 18 and 19.

Ways of understanding audiences

Something that has not changed is that audiences consume media for different reasons and in different ways. You may watch reruns of *Star Trek* for pleasure or you may feel compelled to watch them as part of a media studies course. Similarly, you might pay far more attention to a film that you have paid money to see than you might to the Top Forty on the radio while you're completing an assignment.

With audiences having so much power and choice, media companies and producers need to know their audiences. They need to understand why audiences are consuming their media and how this particular audience is consuming them. Audiences are where media industries make their money; therefore, audiences actively determine what media texts industries will create—and distribute—throughout the mediasphere.

The audience equation

Audiences + advertisers = money = further media production.

Commercial media produce content that delivers audiences to advertisers. Advertising revenue enables further media production.

Media effects model: The injection (like a hypodermic syringe) of ideas by media into an essentially passive and vulnerable mass audience. Sometimes also referred to as the direct effects or hypodermic syringe model.

For many years, the dominant way of thinking about the relationship between media and their audiences has been the **media effects model**.

This was the dominant way of thinking about the relationship between media and audiences, particularly in the 1970s and 1980s, when it formed the basis of a number of media effects studies that attempted to measure scientifically psychological and/or behavioural reactions to media content.

The media effects model is still occasionally rehearsed by psychologists or policy makers today, as a popular commonsense or monkey see, monkey do approach to how media influence the people who consume them. Think of, say, the debates over violence and sexual content in video games or music or film; they are said to promote violence and moral degradation. These are all debates generated by a media effects model of media.

But it is important to remember that the media effects model has been criticised as being theoretically unsophisticated, especially in its treatment of audiences as unthinking, completely passive and willing to accept whatever is put in front of them.

Anyone who has ever had to share a television or babysit a young child knows how hard it is to get someone to sit down and watch a television program that they are not interested in. The idea of a purely passive audience falls apart when compared to one's own experience.

Furthermore, the media effects that are measured under this model are relatively short-term changes in attitudes and behaviours, without considering the broader social, historical and cultural contexts of the media, and how they may have an impact on individual audience behaviours.

Ways of measuring audiences

Unsurprisingly, media organisations spend vast amounts of money in market research to try to measure audiences. These ways of measuring audiences take the following forms:

- pure statistical information
- demographic information
- focus group surveys
- reception studies.

Pure statistical information

Pure statistical information tells us about the number of people consuming media. This information includes:

- ratings (for television and radio)
- box office or gross ticket sales and income (for films)
- hits (for online media)
- sales and orders (for merchandise, games, books and comics)
- circulation and readership (for newspapers and magazines).

We refer to this way of measuring audiences as pure statistical information because it is solely interested in measuring the number of audience members consuming the text at any point in time. Such information does not tell us anything about the audience, or how members of the audience consume the text. Television **ratings**, for example, are simply 'the mechanism by which people watching television are made into a commodity to be sold in lots of one thousand' (Allen 1992: 19). They determine the percentage of homes using television at the time, but do not actually tell us anything about how individual audience members engage with the text.

Ratings: Nightly and weekly surveys conducted to determine how many viewers are watching particular programs on particular channels. The results are used to attract advertisers and determine programming schedules. The practice of ratings surveys is often referred to as the 'ratings war' between commercial television or radio stations.

Demographics

Demographic studies tell us about the types of people watching. This is usually statistical information broken down according to the age, gender, socioeconomic bracket and/or geographical location of the audience consuming the text, for example, women 18–39 or children 5–12 in the eastern suburbs. However, unlike pure statistical information, demographics do tell us something about the audience—for example, age and/or gender—though they still don't tell us anything about how audiences consume a text.

Tied into demographics is the notion of niche audiences (see below): the creation of media products that appeal to a certain demographic that is likely to consume it, likely to invest heavily in it or likely to buy ancillary products connected to it (through advertising), rather than simply appealing to the greatest number of people at any one point in time.

Focus group surveys

Focus group surveys tell us how and perhaps why audiences consume texts. Some studies can tell us more about the audience and how and why members of that audience consume texts. Sample questions could include:

- Do you consume the text every day?
- Do you sit down to watch television or do you move around the room while it is on?
- Do you listen to a radio or an iPod?

Reception studies

Reception studies: Studies of the ways in which audiences consume (receive) media.

All of the ways of measuring audiences are **reception studies**, in that they are studying the receivers of media. But reception studies also exist as a discrete catch-all category to cover those audience measures that combine a variety of measures or, alternatively, targeted or focused studies that tell us about a particular audience, how it consumes texts, and where it consumes texts.

Reception studies, for example, could look at the difference between consuming films in a cinema compared with watching them on television at home.

Types of audiences

Measuring audiences in different ways means we can also talk about different *types of audiences*, of which there are four main groups:

- mass audiences
- niche audiences
- fan audiences
- culture jammers.

Mass audiences

Mass media: Media designed to attract the greatest number of audience members.

Traditionally, we describe media audiences as mass audiences. This refers to the fact that these are **mass media**, that is, media designed to attract the greatest number of audience members. Successful media texts can draw audiences in the millions, so mass audiences seems a good way of describing media audiences.

However, mass audiences can make it sound as if audiences are a passive, undifferentiated mass that all respond exactly the same way to the same media texts. When we look at the media effects model, we see why this cannot be the case: audiences are engaged by media in different ways, and they consume media in different ways and for different reasons.

The idea of a mass audience in which everyone thinks the same way does not really make sense. If media producers knew exactly how audiences would respond to any given media product at any given time, they would simply produce the same successful media products over and over again.

The media effects model depends on the idea of the mass audience. The ratings system for measuring audiences also depends on the idea of the mass audience, as it breaks audiences down into numbers: it is a purely quantitative analysis.

More significantly, mass audiences have been the product of traditional broadcast media, such as film and television—media that attempted to reach the broadest audiences possible. With the advent and increasing importance of new media (as we have seen throughout this book and return to in Chapter 18), media are moving away from traditional notions of mass audiences and broadcasting towards niche audiences and **narrowcasting**.

Niche audiences

Niche audiences are measured through **demographic analyses**: the percentage of consumers in a particular category—such as age, gender, race, sexuality and income band—who are consuming this particular media product. Media texts can now be directed towards certain audience types and remain profitable without having to appeal to every member of a mass audience. The value of a niche audience has been recognised in traditional media for some time (in television, for example, since at least the debut of *Hill Street Blues* in the 1980s), but is increasingly the province of new media.

Just as mass audiences are associated with broadcasting, niche audiences have become associated with narrowcasting (Hirst & Harrison 2007: 378).

Demographic analysis: Statistical analysis of audiences based upon selected population characteristics such as age, gender, race, sexuality, income, disability, mobility, education, employment status and location; showing distributions of values within a demographic variable and changes in trends over time.

Narrowcasting: The distribution of media content to increasingly segmented audiences, to the point where the advertising or media message can be tailored to fit the special needs or consumer profile of members of the targeted audience.

The digital revolution

For an example of a media industry targeting niche audiences, look at a couple of the new free-to-air channels that have been launched by Australia's television networks as part of the changeover to digital television. Channel 7, traditionally a mass audience, family network, has launched 7mate (targeted to a largely male demographic). In contrast Channel Nine, traditionally a mass audience network that skews male, has launched Gem (targeted to a largely female demographic). Look at their programming to see how this targeting occurs in practice. Unlike their parent networks, these new free-to-air networks are driven by demographics rather than ratings.

Fan audiences

Fan (short for 'fanatic') audiences refer to audience members most likely to invest emotionally in a particular media text and its ancillary products, including merchandise. Fan audiences are not independently measured by media industries, but the importance of the fan audience is certainly changing, and is dealt with in greater detail in Chapter 19.

Culture jammers

Culture jamming: Resistance to cultural hegemony by means of guerrilla communication strategies such as graffiti, satire or some other reappropriation of the original medium's iconography to comment upon itself. It differs from other forms of artistic expression or vandalism in that its intent is to subvert mainstream culture for independent communication or otherwise disrupt mainstream communication.

Détournment: The reuse of a well-known text to create a new text that often carries a message contrary to the original.

Paradigm: The greatest spread of possible connotations that any signifier can have.

Syntagm: The selection that an audience member makes from the paradigms of possible connotations.

These are audiences who actually speak back to media or otherwise interact with media in ways that are almost certainly unintended by the media producers. They could be graffiti artists, producers of publications such as *Adbusters*, slash fiction writers who publish fiction exploring pornographic or homosexual relationships between characters in television series, or satirists who use media properties in a variety of ways, usually to comment on or make fun of the media. The process of **culture jamming** is sometimes also referred to as **détournment**.

Ways of reading media texts

Quite clearly, each of these audiences reads texts in different ways, and within each of these audiences, individual audience members also read texts in different ways.

Remember, texts are made up of signs. Signs are naturally polysemic; that is, each has many meanings (many signifieds arranged in spreads of connotations). We can call this spread of signifieds or connotations a **paradigm**.

When we read a text we make a choice or selection from this paradigm. We call this choice the **syntagm**.

So when we read signs, we make a syntagmatic selection from the paradigm of possible signifieds or connotations. The most obvious selection is the denotation (see Chapter 9).

But, as we know, advertisers, spin doctors, directors and a number of other media producers are trying to encode signs to be read in certain ways. They are trying to make one set of connotations seem like the denotation. Media practitioners do this through metaphor, metonymy and anchorage, each of which is described in more detail in Tools 3.

This means individual audience members can undertake a variety of readings. They can make:

- a *preferred* reading, where they believe all of what they're told
- a *negotiated* reading, where they believe some of what they're told
- an *alternative* or *oppositional* reading, where they don't believe in what they are told, or they completely reject it.

In this book we're trying to provide you with another way of reading a media text—an **empowered reading**—by which you accept only some of what is being presented to you, because you are now aware of how media work, how you can be manipulated and what choices are being offered to you by the larger mediasphere.

Empowered reading: A reading of media informed by an understanding of how media work, how audiences can be manipulated and the choices being offered to audiences in the larger mediasphere.

The way you can make an empowered reading is by performing textual analysis (see Chapter 9), understanding the concepts presented in this chapter and the one before it, and applying the tools presented in Tools 3. We want to make you aware of how you can break down a text, how texts work together and how texts are framed.

But at this stage you may still be wondering why this is all so important. To understand this, we need to think about what it is that a media text actually does.

What does a media text actually do?

So far we have seen that texts are made up of signs, and that each sign is composed of a signifier and a possible spread of signifieds called connotations. The most likely one is the denotation.

Every media text, regardless of whether it is a video clip or a breaking news bulletin, shares these same structural features. This is because all media texts are involved in **mediating** something, that is, they are all involved in communication: communicating a message, whether information, entertainment or a mixture of both. This also means that every media text is fundamentally doing the same thing: providing a **representation** of the world.

Mediation: The function of media; the communication of messages, whether information, entertainment or a mixture of both, by media.

Representation: The selection of elements that media communicate to audiences; those aspects of the world that media re-present to audiences.

Why are media texts representations?

In mediating information, every text has to make a selection of what to include, what to focus on and what to discard when presenting its message to you. Because of this, no media text can be reality—rather, it is a mediation of reality, a selection of elements from reality that is then communicated to you.

This selection of elements—the representation within each and every media text—represents the world in a different way, whether within a film, a television series or the nightly news.

This becomes easier to understand if you look at media texts from other cultures. If you have ever watched a film or read a book in translation, you will know that there are some words that have no corollary in English. This is how the English language has developed: by appropriating words from other languages to fill the gaps in its own.

Cultural representations

As McKee (2001) notes, every culture and every part of these cultures (what we might call subcultures, based on gender, age, race and sexuality) represents the world differently, from extremely dissimilar cultures, such as Indigenous cultures, which are primarily oral, and Anglo-Celtic ones, which are primarily written to subtly different ones of the same nationality, such as men and women, senior citizens and youth, and queer and straight people.

What does this mean for realism and authenticity?

When we talk about the world, we are really talking about reality: the world as it exists for us in our day-to-day lives. As we cannot experience all that the world has to offer—and sometimes we might not wish to—we rely on media to present us with entertainment and/or information on events and situations to which we would not otherwise have access. This could be a news report on unrest in Tibet or a film about a voyage under the sea.

But as we have seen, all media, whether a fictional television program or a news radio report, represent the world to us. No media text can ever fully reproduce reality; it can only communicate parts of it. Even the most graphic photograph of a war zone, for example, cannot provide the sound of battle. Even the most immersive virtual reality game cannot provide the smell of a flower. Every media text is the product of a vast number of decisions about what to include and what not to include in its representation, as well as being limited by time, finances and other resources, and the particular nature of the medium.

Think of the different ways of seeming real that appear in a variety of media texts, from documentaries, photojournalists' images and embedded journalists' reports to programs such as *Judge Judy, Survivor, Mad Men, Boston Legal* and *Grey's Anatomy.* Each media text is negotiating a different relationship with reality, making you forget (or reminding you) that this information and/or entertainment is just a representation.

This is important for two reasons. First, it raises a number of questions about human beings' peculiar relationship with reality, ideas we will return to in Chapter 20 (on postmodernity).

The uncanny valley theory

Japanese roboticist Masahiro Moti developed the uncanny valley theory in the 1970s. This principle states that as something is made more humanlike in its appearance and motion, the emotional response from a human being to the creature or object will become increasingly positive and empathetic, until a point is reached at which the response suddenly becomes strongly repulsive. 'This chasm—the 'uncanny valley'—represents the point at which a person observing the creature or object in question sees something that is nearly human, but just enough off-kilter to seem eerie or disquieting' (Bryant 2006).

We increasingly empathise with something that looks more human (think of C-3PO from *Star Wars*), but if that creature or object appears too humanlike our compassion peaks, then plummets into a chasm of emotional detachment and disgust—because we become hypercritical of the creature or object's lack of humanity, such as shadows on a face, eyes not moving quickly enough or a failure to subtly change facial expressions.

Originally, this idea was applied to robotics, but now it is increasingly used to account for the relative success and development of *anime*, special effects, digital game characters and even audience receptions of animated features such as *The Incredibles* and *The Polar Express*. That is, animated characters can look real, but not too real to be 'eerie or disquieting', something *The Adventures of Tintin: The Secret of the Unicorn* had to negotiate when it presented the Belgian comic characters in motion capture 3D.

Second, it raises questions about how reality can be simulated. You can, for instance, think about these ideas of **realism** across a spectrum of filmmaking practices:

Realism: The way in which media try to represent ideas or situations in ways that members of the audience believe are real.

- From the 1940s to the 1960s, black-and-white film stock was considered more authentic, more real, than colour film stock—perhaps best demonstrated by the black-and-white scenes shot in Kansas (the real world) compared with the colour scenes shot in Oz (the fantasy world) in the film *The Wizard of Oz*. This assumption continued until the advent of colour television.
- Today, gritty film stock and handheld video cameras seem more real, more authentic, than glossy colours and steadicam photography. This was originally a style used for documentary filmmaking, but is now also used in police series (starting with *NYPD Blue*) and music videos.
- You could also think about ideas of the filmic real, for instance, the way a flare or drops of water are left on a camera lens or reproduced in an animated film to demonstrate how a particular image was captured; or the way live television represents liveness through the use of an audience, apparently ad-libbed remarks or presenters breaking up on camera or otherwise fluffing their lines.

Any and all of these techniques were, at one stage or another, perfectly legitimate ways of seeming real and each of these ideas of realism can be compared and contrasted with ideas of **authenticity**. Whereas realism attempts to merely simulate reality, authenticity intends to hone as closely as possible to reality—to reproduce what actually happened.

News reporting and documentaries attempt to provide, as far as possible, an unmediated, truly **objective** view of what is occurring in the world. They aim to be as authentic as possible and avoid **subjectivity**.

Authenticity: The way in which media try to represent ideas or situations as near as possible to how they occur in reality—the principal aim of journalism.

Objectivity: The application of observation and experimentation to reality in order to avoid bias or prejudice; the principle that requires journalists to be fair, nonpartisan, disinterested and factual.

Subjectivity: The addressing of reality through individual experience, perception and interpretation; the expression of an individual's point of view.

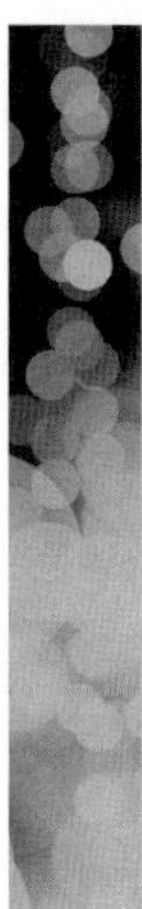

Reality and journalism

If we claim that reality is just a representation, it can seem as if we're sitting at odds with the requirement that journalists report the truth. Sometimes journalists have a problem with this idea of news being just another representation, but this should in no way stop journalists from undertaking truthful reporting. Rather, the idea of reality as a representation must be something journalists should be aware of, because good journalists should always try to ensure that their report is as real, truthful and authentic a record of what is happening as possible. Being aware that reality can be just another representation should make journalists aware of the many instances of bias that can creep into news production and make them try to compensate for that.

What is representation?

Representation is both the process and the product of media texts—the practice and the result. Media texts do not present the world to us. That can only happen if we were there at the time. Instead, media texts represent the world to us. They frame the world in a certain way, conveying a message to us through the signs used. This is the process.

Media texts are also a representation of the world. Newspapers, television series, comic books, radio, films and news reports all offer us a product that represents the world in a certain way. So mediation is the act of re-presenting information to an audience (that's the process) and providing us with a representation of information (that's the end result).

All texts do this, from your great uncle's home movies to the latest Spielberg blockbuster. What is clearly different is that some texts—and therefore some representations—will be more significant than others. This significance depends on the text's place in the mediasphere and the larger public sphere.

Figure 10.1 Representation: a mediation of the world

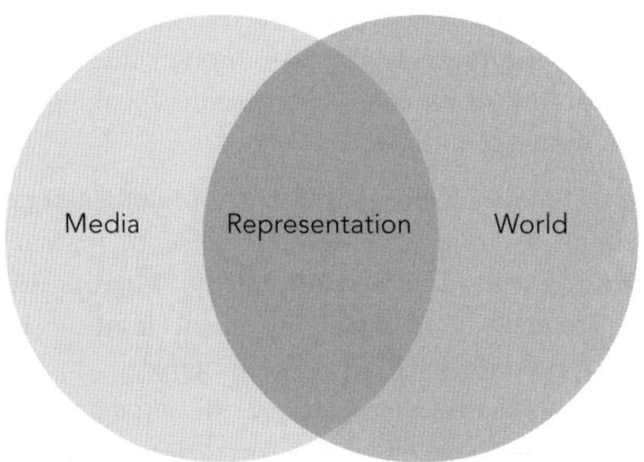

How do media texts become significant?

Significance, whether social significance or political significance, cannot be achieved via a single text. Therefore, the logic of representation in popular culture is intertextual. Remember from Chapter 9 that intertextuality is the relationship between texts, which do not exist in isolation but are interdependent. Texts frequently make meaning through their relationship with other texts.

Significance: The impact of a particular media text's representation of the world. It refers to social and political significance, and is derived from the number of times a media text is referenced in other texts; the more it is referenced, the more significant a media text will become, and the more impact that text's representation of the world will have.

The more a text is referenced in other texts, the more significant the text becomes and the more impact that text's representation of the world has.

How do media texts work together?

If we think of media texts as intertextual, then we return to thinking about texts as chains or webs, rather than rather than operating in isolation. This is the mediasphere (see Chapter 1), which is composed of thousands of texts that provide thousands of representations of the world, connected to each other in subtle and obvious ways.

In this way, texts speak to each other as much as they speak to an audience. We can characterise this relationship between texts and between texts and audiences as dialogic (see Chapter 1), which means that:

- texts engage each other in *intertextual* dialogues
- texts engage audiences (through the process of address or interpellation) in *textual* dialogues
- as we have already noted in Chapter 1, engaging in a dialogue is a fundamental part of social action, which means that texts and readings can be used to impose cultural dominance as well as offering sites of *resistance*
- in this interaction, we can begin to understand the connections between *textuality* and *power*
- representation therefore also gives us information about the process of power and politics.

If you're unclear how these ideas of representation, significance and power interrelate, think of this in relation to **stereotypes**: those neat little labels that categorise people in easily recognisable social or cultural groups, usually in negative terms (Sardar & Van Loon 2000: 75).

Stereotype: An oversimplified, standardised image or idea held by one person or social group about another.

Stereotypes

Think about your reaction to these words:

- Aboriginal
- Muslim
- blonde
- American
- academic

Write down a list of your immediate reactions to each word.

Look at each list again. Do you actually know any person who fits all or any of your negative stereotypes? Think about how people in each group are represented in the media. This is often their denotation: a particular stereotype that is reinforced through multiple media representations.

Stereotypes are not always false. Sometimes a generalised representation of a group in society may contain an element of truth that is universally applied or blown out of proportion.

While the media certainly contribute towards inventing or reinforcing stereotypes, they can also subvert them, as illustrated by the *Queer as Folk* television show.

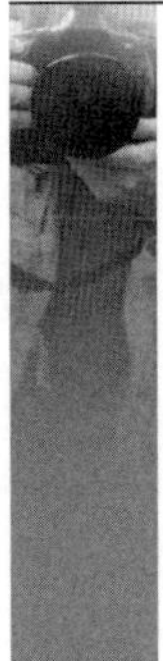

Queer as Folk

The English (and later US) series *Queer as Folk* presented a full and frank discussion of homosexuality in the 1990s. Without being overly sentimental, it revealed the lives of homosexual people in a funny and often touching way to a mixed straight and gay audience. Along with series such as *Queer Eye for the Straight Guy* and *Will & Grace*, it was one of a number of positive representations of homosexuality in the media that subverted a lot of the then current stereotypes of homosexuals, something maintained by later series such as *Glee, Beautiful People* and *Torchwood*.

How do representations function within the process of power and politics?

When we look at texts intertextually, we can start to consider their representations in aggregate. You may already be familiar with some of the words that academics use to describe representations, but you should also be aware that they have a number of meanings, depending on who you ask, and in which subject and which context you are using them.

Three of these terms are:

- discourse
- ideology
- myth.

These words all describe how media representations function in relation to power and politics, so let's look at each one in more detail.

Discourse

Discourse: A way of representing the world.

For our purposes, **discourse** is a way of representing the world. You could think here of medical, legal, religious, academic or political discourses, as well as the discourses of slang, comic books or romance fiction. We can think of each of these as a discourse because each offers a different viewpoint of the world, founded on, for example:

- rights or duties (political or legal discourse)
- morals and ethics (philosophical discourse)
- a belief in God or gods (religious discourse)
- a belief in transcendent power (comic book discourse)
- a belief in fair representation and due process (legal discourse)
- a belief that all men have powerful, muscular chests and all women have heaving bosoms (romance fiction discourse)
- a belief that all redheaded men can be called Bluey (slang discourse).

Further, each of these discourses is made up of a number of representations across a range of (inter)texts. So, for example, legal discourses are constructed out of case law, statute law, court rituals and popular representations of law, to name just a few.

How do discourses and texts fit together?

Central to our understanding of texts and representations is the work of Michel Foucault, which provides a theoretical framework for focusing on representation and understanding under discursive regimes (hierarchies of discourses). Our approach is to read texts for their meanings, bearing in mind the discourses they work within, and that part of their function is to act as a representation of the world. This is why, when we look at texts, we break down the text (look at its meaning), consider its context (as an indicator of the discourse(s) they work within) and explore their intertexts (as an indicator of how they may be representing the world).

Ideology

An **ideology** is a set of assumptions or ideas about the world, which is often more overtly political or religious than a discourse. Communism and humanitarianism are major ideologies, believed in by millions of people, that in part derive from such documents as *The Communist Manifesto* and the *International Declaration of Human Rights*.

Ideology: An all-encompassing set of ideas for thinking about the world.

The word 'ideology' has a lot of baggage around it. Some scholars see the concept as virtually the same as discourse, others see it as quite different from discourse, and still others see it as capable of being reconciled with discourse (ideologies being the ideas that underpin a discourse).

Myth

In media studies, **myth** is not just a collection of tales from ancient Greece or Rome—it is an ideology that has become so accepted, so commonplace, that we no longer recognise it as an ideology. To most people in a particular society, it seems real and right; there seems to be no other way of viewing the world.

Myth: An ideology that has become so accepted, so commonplace, that it is no longer recognised as an ideology.

But myths change over time. They have included, during different periods of history, the idea that the world was flat, the idea that some races are superior to others, the idea that women are inferior to men and the idea that some wars are justified.

Myth is denotation on the broadest possible scale. Several stereotypes have become myths, for example, the Nazi myth, by which the government in Germany before the Second World War took some old-fashioned stereotypes about Jewish people, then expanded those ideas into an ideology in order to justify their attempt to destroy the whole Jewish people. More often, a myth that can seem perfectly acceptable (indeed, commonsense) in one cultural or historical context can be completely unacceptable in another; for example, the myth of imperialism, which is the assumption by European countries before the nineteenth century that they had the right to take control of any non-European country that seemed uncivilised.

Importantly, myths are not always negative or pejorative. Examples of myths that have long been a part of Australian society include that of the Aussie battler, the concept of mateship, the idea of a fair go and the importance of sport in our national identity. We are not saying that these myths are right or wrong; we are just identifying them as ideologies that have become so widely accepted, so commonplace, that they seem to be essential parts of being Australian and therefore go largely unquestioned.

As consumers of media you should be aware of how myth functions, and the myths that may be currently circulating through the mediasphere. Similarly, when approaching texts from other cultures and other times, be aware of the myths that inform these texts and factor those into your reading.

Back to the mediasphere

The acceptance of discourse and ideologies—and the way in which some ultimately become myths—occurs through two terms you will already be familiar with: hegemony and pluralism. As you may recall from Chapter 1, hegemony is the ability of the ruling classes in any society to rule by consent, because the media persuade us that it is in our best interests to accept the dominance of this elite. **Pluralism** is the term we use for diversity in society, including in the media. Pluralist media offer us a wide range of choices. Again, some scholars prefer to link this term to discourse, proposing that a range of discourses offers us a truly pluralistic view of society.

Pluralism: Diversity in society, and therefore in the media; pluralist media offer us a wide range of choices.

Conclusion

In Chapters 9 and 10 we have broken the idea of the mediasphere down into the concept of separate media texts, which can be further broken down into signs, signifiers and signifieds. We have analysed how these signs engage with audiences. We have then put texts together again, to explore how they work as representations, discourses, ideologies and myths in the larger mediasphere. In doing so, we have come full circle in our consideration of media texts.

For practical examples of the analysis of texts and discourses, see Tools 3.

KEY REFERENCES

Hartley, J. (1999). *Uses of Television.* London: Routledge.

McKee, A. (2003). *Textual Analysis: A Beginner's Guide.* London: Sage.

Thwaites, T., Davis, L. & Mules, W. (2002). *Introducing Cultural and Media Studies: A Semiotic Approach.* Basingstoke: Palgrave.

CHAPTER 11

CELEBRITY

JASON BAINBRIDGE

Introduction

A film star from the 1950s. A fortysomething politician in an openly gay relationship. The teenage star of a television sitcom. The thirty-year-old single mother who has just won a reality television series. An overweight British director. The winner of the 2007 Nobel Peace Prize. A boy caught enthusiastically swinging a lightsabre on YouTube. The chief executive officer of New York's most famous hotel chain. Two miners who spent an agonising fortnight trapped beneath the earth. The author whose books sell a million copies a day. Lindsay Lohan.

All of these people are celebrities. Some will remain celebrities longer than others. Some will have vast amounts of column space devoted to their private lives, their relationships and their affairs. Some will start their own clothing brands. Some will fade back into obscurity. But for a while, each and every one of them will be famous.

Celebrity: The familiar stranger; a celebrity is simultaneously a text and an industry.

What is it that fascinates us about celebrities? Why is so much of our journalism devoted to reporting what they do? And why do so many of us want to be one?

In this chapter we look at:

- what a **celebrity** is
- types of celebrity
- why celebrities are important.

What is a celebrity?

In Part 2 we looked at media industries ranging from print to radio to film to television.

As well as calling each of these a media industry, we can also call these industries cultural industries because of 'their crucial role in producing and disseminating the most popular forms of cultural expression in modern societies' (Turner & Cunningham 2002: 14).

This means that the texts these industries produce—for example, the magazines that are produced by the print industry, the television series that are produced by the television industry, and the radio programs that are produced by the radio industry—can also be thought of as **cultural products**.

Cultural product: A product that contains meanings, values and ideas, that is, a product that functions as a form of communication.

Examples of these cultural products include the film *Psycho*, the television series *Gossip Girl*, the magazine *Vanity Fair*, the *Times* newspaper, *The War of the Worlds* radio broadcast, a Justin Bieber video or Marvel's *Avengers* comic books.

Each of these media texts functions as a cultural product because it communicates a series of meanings, values and ideas. Some, the *Times* newspaper or a documentary on Iraq, seem to be more involved in communicating information. Others, such as television series such as *Gossip Girl*, or *Cleo* magazine seem to be more involved in constructing or negotiating different forms of identity based on gender, age or more nebulous ideas of taste and style. Some, such as the nightly news, seem to be doing both.

Celebrities are also cultural products, communicating a variety of ways of being. Celebrities construct or negotiate forms of identity, and can be both inspirational ('I want to be like that person') and aspirational ('I want to be that person').

What makes celebrities significant texts is the increasing attention they receive in the news and mediasphere as a whole. As more and more attention is devoted to celebrity—reporting who they are, what they do and how to become one—we might well ask: Is the mediasphere itself becoming more about providing ideas of identity than information? If so, this is a significant shift, which may have some serious implications for the perceived functioning of journalism as the Fourth Estate.

One way of describing this shift in attention is to refer to **celebrity culture**, which is a culture based on the individual and individual identity, for example, newspapers that consist mainly of gossip, scandal and PR material issued by celebrities' agents. In celebrity culture, social issues are ignored, or told only in terms of the activities of celebrities.

Celebrity culture: A culture based on the individual and individual identity, for example, news that consists mainly of gossip, scandal or snippets from celebrities' PR handouts, or where social issues are constantly reframed as personal issues.

Since the notion of celebrity is today part of the notion of news, it becomes important to understand how the celebrity functions: what celebrities are, the elements of celebrity and what celebrities do.

Where does celebrity come from?

Academic interest in celebrity originally sprang from an interest in film stars (a star being a particular type of celebrity). For simplicity's sake, we'll use the term 'celebrity' in this chapter because, as you will see in the table further on, celebrity has become a catch-all term for a type of individual whose image circulates in the media, of which the film star is just one example.

Todd Gitlin (2001) defines the celebrity as 'the familiar stranger'. The definition is a good one because it refers to the way celebrities can simultaneously be known by the audience and yet must necessarily remain, forever, at a distance.

Members of the audience feels as though they know the celebrity through media appearances, the gossip they read in magazines and the photos they see, that is, they become familiar. At the same time, the audience can never really know the celebrity, because all the information they consume is mediated through various media texts, that is, the celebrity remains a stranger. All the audience really knows about the celebrity is the image that they see in the media.

The parasocial relationship

Chris Rojek (2001) describes the way audiences can develop parasocial relationships with people they know only through the media, in ways that are similar to real friends and colleagues. This is especially applicable to celebrities who we might see over and over again as, for example, hosts on morning television or film stars we continually watch in the cinema. In this way we start to feel as though we know the celebrity as well as the other people we encounter in our day-to-day lives.

The celebrity is not a new phenomenon. As Gitlin (2001: 22) notes, the celebrity is not 'unprecedented in history':

> People have long imagined a world populated by figures who were not physically at hand and yet seemed somehow present … What has changed is the magnitude of the flow, the range of characters that enter our world, their omnipresence, the sheer number of stories.

According to Miller (1998: 599), 'by the Depression, Hollywood stars were the third biggest source of news in the United States', but today's growth in media forms is creating a greater proliferation of a wider variety of celebrities than we have seen before. As Catharine Lumby (2004: 112) sees it, the 'evolution of celebrity in the twentieth century is intimately related to the evolution of technologies for making individuals public'. Celebrity is a creation of this ongoing blurring of the private and public spheres, first discussed in Chapter 1.

The history of celebrity

Like so much of modern society, the origins of celebrity can be found in ancient Rome, where rulers would use statues and coins to promote themselves, so they would become known to all the members of their society. Today, that practice continues: Australian coins bear the face of the head of state (the Queen), while US currency bears the face of former heads of state (presidents). When Iraq fell to US forces, among the first things US troops did was tear down the statue of Iraq's ruler, Saddam Hussein, and take all the currency bearing his image out of circulation.

Famed documentarian David Attenborough, who has become a celebrity himself, explains that as tribes became bigger, those with power sought ways to reach all members of their tribe, to make themselves as visible as possible (*The Human Face* 2001: pt 2). Clearly, those with power could no longer meet with all the members of their tribe in person, so they had to create something that would stand in their place, something that could function as a signifier of themselves. They used a **celebrity image**, an image specifically designed to convey ideas of the celebrity and their values. They placed their image on artwork—pottery, statues and pictures—as well as currency, to make themselves visible, to make themselves known and to circulate their image among the tribe.

Celebrity image: The image of the celebrity as it appears in the media; a construction designed to connote the ideas and values of the celebrity.

Until the twentieth century, artwork and currency functioned in a way similar to the modern media, standing between the tribe and the person with power, mediating that person to the tribe through products bearing their image.

With the advent of the printing press, celebrity was developed through advertising, monographs and volumes. Chapbooks sensationalising the stories of highwaymen and rogues such as Dick Turpin and Jonathan Wild made these people celebrities in much the same way as outlaw Jesse James became a celebrity in the American West and the bushranger Ned Kelly became a celebrity in the Australian bush. As early as the 1820s, theatres were advertising certain actors' names to promote their productions; the Shakespearean actor Edmund Keane became famous as a result. In Victorian England, entire compendiums of celebrity were produced. These celebrities were high-profile people of the time, including scientists, authors and other great thinkers.

As media continued to develop, so too did the ability to capture the image, through photography and film, rather than engravings and woodcuts, and circulate that image to wider and wider audiences.

The close-up

As the BBC documentary series *The Human Face* (BBC 2001) notes, one of the key advancements in the development of celebrity came with the advent of the close-up. Before this, stage actors always remained in the distance, as slightly obscure figures. The close-up meant that, for the first time, people could see the faces of those acting on the screen. For film actors, this had the effect of making their head seem twice as big as everyone else and therefore seem twice as important. The close-up provided an intimacy and a point of identification between the audience and the actor—it made the stranger familiar. The close-up is still a common device in film, often replicated in different ways in other media, such as the standard two-shot in television, the head shot that adorns magazines and the way news readers (and often reporters) are framed as they speak to camera. If you ever want a reminder of how important the face is for celebrity, just look at a PEZ candy dispenser; the only recognisable sense of character is the plastic head that tops the dispenser tube and yet it is enough to signify celebrities from NASCAR drivers and Elvis to the crew of the USS *Enterprise*.

The changing notion of celebrity

We can now start to map the ways in which celebrity is considered in culture. Allied to the developments discussed above were two important changes in the way celebrities were presented, and in what they could do.

First, a number of separate industries developed around the celebrity. These became devoted to promoting and publicising them, and to exploring the parallel narratives of their personal lives, their backgrounds and their scandals. This started with early gossip magazines such as *Broadway Brevities* (1916), and continued through publications such as *Confidential* (1950s) and the sexually explicit *Hollywood Star* (1970s) to the supermarket tabloids such as the *National Enquirer*, magazines such as *People* and *OK*, and television programs such as

Entertainment Tonight. A great number of these stories were created and circulated by the film studios themselves as part of their promotion and publicity campaigns, products of the overlap between cinema and public relations. For more on this see Chapter 8, as well as the film *LA Confidential* for more about the early gossip magazines and the television series *Entourage* for more on the role of the agent in promotion and publicity.

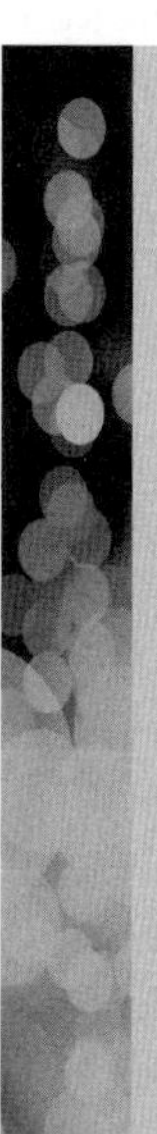

The celebrity timeline

Antiquity

Images circulated on coins and through statues:

- The people represented had real political and social power.
- Example: Julius Caesar, emperor of Rome.

1800

Images circulated through engravings, illustrations, photographs and the popular press:

- The people represented were either leading social figures, scientists and writers or scandalous, murderous lowly criminals.
- Examples: Mark Twain (writer), Madame Curie (scientist) and Dick Turpin (criminal).

1900–today

Images circulated through film with the development of the close-up, magazines and tabloid newspapers, producing the notion of celebrity culture:

- The people represented come from many walks of life, but are predominantly actors, musicians or famous simply for being famous.
- Examples: Charlie Chaplin (film star), Madonna (singer–actor), Paris Hilton (not quite sure really ...)

This growth in celebrity culture is fuelled by three overlapping phenomena:

- the development and proliferation of media
- globalisation, leading to greater international circulation
- convergence, the coming together of media forms.

The second major change was in the power held by the celebrity. Celebrity originated in the desire of people who had real social and political power to be known by all of their tribe. As time went on, the wheel was to turn full circle, because celebrities (Hollywood stars this time), who otherwise would have held little political power, began to claim social power for themselves.

The birth of the Hollywood star

The Hollywood star was generated by the development of the close-up, which led to recognition and identification, along with an interest among the audience in the off-screen lifestyles of their favourite stars. US silent film comedian Charlie Chaplin could be recognised throughout the world. Wherever he went with his fellow silent film stars Mary Pickford and Douglas Fairbanks, he would be mobbed and questioned about every detail of his marriages.

The star system

Originally, Hollywood was dismissive of stars, reluctant to lavish the costs in promotion required to make them famous for fear that they would become too powerful. Slowly, Hollywood started to realise the wealth of stars as **commodities**. They could brand certain films (a Gary Cooper western, for example), celebrities could be traded between studios and celebrity endorsements became a valuable form of advertising. Then actor Ronald Reagan, for example, advertised cigarettes during the 1940s.

So the star system was born. Studios kept stables of stars in much the same way as sporting organisations keep teams of athletes. Hollywood studio MGM, for example, used to promote itself as having 'more stars than there are in Heaven'. The star system continued until the break-up of the studio system in the 1940s and 1950s (see Chapter 6).

The first forms of power celebrities enjoyed were recognition, leading to further work in advertising, and remuneration, through the large salaries they received. Increasingly, they sought out more power, especially in terms of controlling their careers, which, under the star system, were still at the whim of film studio heads such as Louis B. Mayer of MGM and Jack Warner at Warner Brothers. This led Mary Pickford, Douglas Fairbanks, Charlie Chaplin and film pioneer D. W. Griffith to form their own studio, United Artists, on 5 February 1919, thus demonstrating the increasing power of celebrities and their desire to control their own careers.

The Society of Independent Motion Picture Producers was founded in 1941, with the aim of preserving the rights of independent producers in an industry controlled by the five major film studios. This contributed greatly to the demise of the studio system and the rise of the independents (again, see Chapter 6).

The stars thrived in the new Hollywood. No longer locked into seven-year contracts with studios, they could exercise more control over their careers and command higher and higher salaries from independent studios eager to attach them to their projects. They became **bankable** stars, that is,

Commodity: An economic good; in relation to celebrities, it refers to someone who is subject to ready exchange or exploitation within a market.

Bankability: The ability of a celebrity to make a guaranteed profit for their employer; a bankable Hollywood star can make a film succeed on the strength of his or her name alone.

their films were almost guaranteed to succeed simply because they appeared in them. We can see this power manifested in a number of ways, from Nicole Kidman's fee per film (reported as $20 million or more) through to Angelina Jolie's social power as an ambassador for the United Nations.

Fears in Hollywood over celebrities' power may also be destroying the system. On 22 August 2006, Paramount Pictures ended its fourteen-year contract with arguably the most powerful star then working in Hollywood, Tom Cruise. The company cited economic damage to his value as an actor because of his controversial public behaviour, particularly on the *Oprah* television show as the reason for the termination. Ironically, the fact that Paramount dropped Cruise because of damage to his image really illustrates how important his Cruise actually was to them; his value had dropped, so they dropped him. Even more ironically, in November 2006 Cruise and his production partner Paula Wagner took over United Artists, the company that was originally formed because of the star system.

Elements of a celebrity

In his book *Understanding Celebrity*, Graeme Turner (2004: 1) lists four elements that are part of every celebrity:

- Someone who emerges from a certain industry or otherwise attracts public attention—his or her fame does not always have to depend on the position or achievements leading to prominence in the first place. Madonna, for example, began as a respected figure in the music industry, but has attracted more media attention for her private life. Paris Hilton's main ability seems to be attracting public attention. Indeed, she is paid to attend parties because she is so good at it.
- Someone who is made highly visible through the media—this includes politicians, such as the US President, criminals, businesspeople … and Paris Hilton.
- Someone whose private life often attracts greater public interest than their professional life. While Angelina Jolie's recent films still attract attention (*Salt*, *The Tourist*), she remains a celebrity more because of her work for UNICEF, her relationship with Brad Pitt and her adoption of children from a wide variety of backgrounds. Paris Hilton's private life has filled far more magazines, papers and websites than has her professional life as an actress, author and fashion designer.
- Most importantly, a celebrity is a construction—what is referred to as a celebrity's persona, aura or image. Lady Gaga gains constant media attention because of her ever-changing media image, usually as a result of her fashion choices, be it her outfit made out of Kermit the Frogs (in 2009) or her meat dress at the MTV Video Music Awards (in 2010). Paris Hilton exists purely as an image, a fun-loving socialite, though she has attempted to deepen this image by presenting herself as a savvy businesswoman, with mixed results.

Turner (2004: 8) believes that 'we can map the precise moment a public figure becomes a celebrity … it occurs at the point at which media interest in their activities is transferred from reporting on their public role … to investigating the details of their private lives'.

Can journalists be celebrities?

As the above discussion shows, journalists also can be celebrities. The term 'celebrity journalist' was coined by James Fallows in 1986 when he stated that '[their] names appear in gossip columns and society pages ... We know when they wed ... when they become parents ... and when they get divorced' (in Shepard 1997: 26). Shepard links the appearance of the celebrity journalist to the work of journalists Bob Woodward and Carl Bernstein, whose relentless investigative work led to the resignation of President Richard Nixon in 1974. Shepard (1997: 26) writes: 'The Watergate affair changed journalism in many ways, not the least of which was by launching the era of the journalist as celebrity.' In contrast, S. Robert Lichter (in Levy & Bonilla 1999: 84) believes that the era of celebrity journalism may have officially begun in 1976, when Barbara Walters became the first million-dollar anchor on ABC. As Boorstin (in Shepard 1997: 27) writes: 'A celebrity is a person who is known for his well-knownness ... journalists are the creators of well-knownness. In the process of creating well-knownness for others, it's not surprising that some of them become celebrities too. It's inevitable.'

What is the celebrity image?

The celebrity's image is, like other representations, not a real thing but a construction that appears in the media. It is, therefore, similar to the divide between sender and addresser (see Chapter 10): we can never really know Brad Pitt, just as we can never really know the sender, but we can study and analyse 'Brad Pitt' as he appears in the media, just as we can study the addressee. Like the addressee, 'Brad Pitt' is a textual construct, a mediation of the real Brad Pitt and an image generated across a number of different texts. Indeed, some people like to spend a lot of time analysing Brad Pitt.

Sometimes the construction of an image is so complete that it supplants the individual. Entire lives, off screen and on screen, can be devoted to the maintenance of the image. Archie Leach, for example, was an actor who arrived in Hollywood in the late 1920s, then took the name of Cary Grant and constructed the image of Cary Grant, off screen and on screen. He had a particular look, a particular set of mannerisms and a particular way of being in the world. Similarly, Norma Jean Baker constructed the image of Marilyn Monroe. No doubt both did so with the support of their publicists and the rest of the Hollywood industry, but the fact that Marilyn Monroe and Cary Grant are remembered today, long after the deaths of Norma Jean Baker and Archie Leach, is a testament to the power of their images.

The celebrity image is an on-screen and off-screen construction. This is quite different from a celebrity assuming a role. We recognise, for example, that the Terminator, Dutch, Quaid and Jack Clayton are all roles assumed by Arnold Schwarzenegger in a variety of films. These roles work together, with the off-screen texts (his marriage to Maria Shriver and his early career as a body builder) to create the image of 'Arnold Schwarzenegger', of which the latest manifestation was the 'Governator', while he was governor of California. But in 2011 this on-screen heroic paternal image was disrupted by off-screen revelations of his infidelities and his fathering of (at least one) illegitimate child. Schwarzenegger's celebrity image became less stable as a result leading some commentators to wonder what the name Schwarzenegger would now signify for future audiences.

The celebrity image, therefore, is an intertextual construction (see Chapter 10). Like any representation, the celebrity image is constructed across a variety of intertexts.

Previous scholars, such as Richard Dyer (1998), writing on Hollywood stars, and Andrew Goodwin (1992), writing on music stars, drew attention to the fact that stars' images are constructed through a series of intertexts. Dyer stated that:

> A star's image is also what people say or write about him or her, the way the image is used in other contexts such as advertisements, novels, pop songs, and finally the way the star can become part of the coinage of everyday speech. (Dyer 1998: 2–3)

So a film star's image is not only established by the films in which he or she appears, but also by the interviews the star gives, and the scandals and gossip that surround their name.

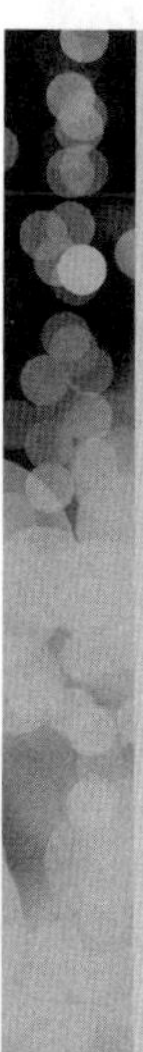

The music celebrity

In popular music, the images of celebrities such as Lady Gaga, Rhianna, Justin Timberlake, Michael Jackson, Justin Bieber or Madonna are created by intertexts of gossip, film and video clips, together with their public appearances, music and lyrics. This may help to explain why the music celebrity, rather than the film star, is currently at the top of the celebrity hierarchy. Whereas for many years everyone aspired to be a film star, since the 1960s the music celebrity has become the more aspirational figure, thanks to Frank Sinatra, the Beatles and Elvis Presley. It may be because, especially with the advent of MTV in the 1980s, it is music celebrities who are best poised to take advantage of all that media has to offer. They operate at the intersection of a wide variety of industries (print, music, online, film, television and merchandising) and have a product, their song, that can, and often does, travel globally without the need for complex translations. You can hear Katy Perry songs in Italy and Lady Gaga is loved in Japan.

Metanarrative: A supernarrative constructed from multiple narratives. An example would be a metanarrative of celebrity, built from all of the narratives in all of the intertexts that represent that celebrity.

The cumulative result of these intertexts is referred to as a **metanarrative** of the celebrity. It is built from all the narratives in all of the intertexts that represent the celebrity. Think of it as a kind of supernarrative; the narratives of Brad Pitt, Tom Cruise or Madonna, for example, are their images assembled through all of these intertexts.

Table 11.1 The celebrity of Michael Jackson

Let's look at how these intertexts work together in relation to Michael Jackson, the late, self-proclaimed king of pop. You may need to Google some of these names and references to find out more about them.	
Born	29 August 1958, Gary, Indiana, the seventh child of the Jackson family.
1964	At age five, he joins his brothers in the Jackson 5.

Table 11.1 The celebrity of Michael Jackson (*continued*)

1970	He becomes eleven-year-old frontman of the Jackson 5; they spend thirteen weeks at Number 1 on the pop music chart: four releases sell more than 15 million copies. Their first album is called *Diana Ross Presents the Jackson 5*. The Jackson 5's first performance on the Motown label was appearing as special guests of Diana Ross and the Supremes, beginning Michael's lifelong friendship (or obsession) with Diana Ross.
1971	Jackson is now twelve, and the Jackson 5 cartoon from Hanna Barbera appears on Saturday morning television. Some commentators have claimed that seeing an animated version of himself at such a young age contributed to some of Michael's image issues.
1972	The single 'Ben' is No. 1 on the US pop singles chart. It is a song about a young man's affection for a rat. Again, some commentators claim this is an early example of Jackson's freakish tendencies.
1973	Jackson turns fourteen—and is already a millionaire.
1978	Jackson acts as the Scarecrow in the film *The Wiz*. (Diana Ross acts as Dorothy in the same film, the first filmic intertext between the two stars.)
1979	Jackson is regarded as a mature singer for the first time when he releases the single 'Don't Stop Till You get Enough', which becomes No. 1 in the US. His album *Off the Wall* sells more than 10 million copies.
1980	At the American Music Awards, Jackson wins awards for Favorite R&B album, Favorite Single and Favorite R&B Male Artist.
1982	Jackson's album *Thriller* sells over 40 million copies and becomes No. 1 in every major record-buying country in the world, providing Jackson's seventh US Top 10 single. He wins eight Grammy Awards. Singles taken from the album that become independently successful include 'The Girl is Mine', 'Thriller', 'Billie Jean' (dealing with issues of gender) and 'Beat It' (dealing with issues of race). Jackson becomes the first African-American performer to gain major airplay on the MTV channel, with the video clip for 'Billie Jean'.
1984	Jackson wins a record seven awards in the American Music Awards. Jackson's hair catches fire while shooting a commercial for Pepsi Cola. Because he receives second-degree burns, he requires plastic surgery.
1985	Jackson appears as a superhero on the compilation album *We Are the World*, which was recorded to raise money for a worldwide charity.
August 1985	Jackson outbids Paul McCartney and Yoko Ono to buy the ATV music publishing catalogue for $US47.5 million, which gives him the rights to more than 250 Beatles songs. Jackson is now seen as a major businessman. He secures a $5 million sponsorship deal with Pepsi Cola, although, because of his religion, he cannot drink it.
1986	Jackson makes *Captain Eo*, a fifteen-minute Disneyland film (continuing the discourse of 'Jackson as hero'). This month also marks the first appearance of the infamous *National Enquirer* picture of Jackson; he apparently sleeps every night in the oxygen tank.

1987	Jackson's *Bad* album goes directly to No. 1 on the US albums chart. Newspapers feature reports that Jackson has offered $50,000 to $100,000 to buy the remains of the Elephant Man from London Hospital; this episode is later parodied in his 'Leave Me Alone' video clip.
1988	Jackson acquires a ranch in Santa Ynez Valley, California, which is converted into the Neverland ranch. Newspapers make claims that Jackson has undergone large amounts of plastic surgery in order to look white. By the end of the 1980s Jackson has sold more records than any performer alive.
1994	Although newspapers constantly insist that Jackson's sexual orientation may be homosexual, he marries Lisa-Marie Presley. This heterosexual image of marriage is undercut by a very awkward forty-five-second kiss at the MTV Music Awards.
1995–2005	Allegations of child sexual abuse, marriages, rumours of surgeries, the mysteries of Neverland ranch, the birth of his children and subsequent commercial failures and antics (most significantly, holding his youngest child over a balcony) are repeatedly reported by the press as bizarre, and destabilise his celebrity image.
June 2009	While preparing for his comeback concert series, Jackson dies from cardiac arrest. As did Princess Diana before him, Jackson's death led to a very public and widespread outpouring of grief, with reportedly as many as one billion people tuning in to watch his funeral on television.
March 2010	Sony Music Entertainment signs a reported $US250 million deal with Jackson's estate to retain until 2017 distribution rights to his recordings and release seven posthumous albums.

Up to 1994 we can see that Jackson's intertexts often worked against each other, creating a tension in his celebrity image. These tensions became more pronounced in the decade following 1994. Ironically, in death Michael Jackson became very much the king of pop and the king of popular culture, in that his life embodied all the aspects of celebrity culture discussed in this chapter. His death confirmed that it is the image that is most important for the celebrity to function, because Jackson's death removed the problematic man beset by rumours and scandal, and left his audience with the image of a driven, talented and tragic artist, dancer and performer. Brand Asset Consulting's quarterly survey of more than 16,000 Americans found that after his death, Jackson's relevance had increased by 125 per cent and his esteem by 32 per cent. Like Princess Diana and Marilyn Monroe before him, Jackson's death rewrote some aspects of his life, which points most powerfully to the difference between a star and a celebrity, something we return to further on.

The example of Michael Jackson also illustrates how important it is to maintain control over an image; otherwise, the metanarrative starts to fall apart. This might suggest that a celebrity image can only function when public and private lives are in relative harmony. Small tensions (a drug habit, bad marriage or wild lifestyle) can be tolerated, and may actually deepen and develop a celebrity image, but where the intertexts work against each other, as in the case of Arnold Schwarzenegger's infidelities and Charlie Sheen's increasingly bizarre behaviour, the overall representation of the celebrity—the metanarrative and the image as a whole—starts to fall apart. We can no longer feel as though we know the celebrity—the familiar part of the familiar stranger becomes lost. The person might maintain a celebrity status, but it will function at a different level on the hierarchy of celebrity (discussed below).

Celebrities, then, exist at the intersection of different media industries. In so doing, they come to function as industries in themselves. They are simultaneously a commodity, in that they can be analysed as another cultural good, another media text and another representation, and an industry that produces that commodity. Celebrity can, in effect, become self-fulfilling. This, ultimately, seems to be the goal of a celebrity.

Madonna

While initially regarded as a chameleon because of the rapid changes in style in video clips such as *Material Girl*, *Like a Virgin*, *Cherish* and *Vogue*, Madonna has taken control of her celebrity image to reconstruct herself as Madonna-as-musician, embodying that feminist ideal of a woman able to make it in a man's world on her own terms. When the video clip for 'Justify My Love' was released, despite it being little more than a form of sexual exploitation, it was widely hailed as a blow in favour of cultural freedom and feminism.

Of all her intertexts, the 1991 documentary film *Truth or Dare (In Bed with Madonna)*, showing backstage footage of Madonna preparing for a rigorous concert tour, perhaps did the most to exploit and develop her image as sexually alluring and honest. But even Madonna's bad films serve as intertexts, in the sense that they suggest she is authentic ('If Madonna can't act, this must be *her*') or that she cannot be restrained ('She is mutable and therefore cannot be limited to just one role').

A hierarchy of celebrities

It is possible to map a hierarchy of celebrity based on fame. Increasingly, celebrities seem to be interested in deepening their celebrity or otherwise extending and developing it. Actors choose meatier roles, athletes become commentators, YouTube sensations make the jump to concert tours and reality television stars write tell-all books and magazine columns.

In mapping this hierarchy of celebrity, the three important factors are prominence, power and longevity. A celebrity seeks to be prominent in the public sphere. Similarly, a celebrity seeks to gain control over his or her own image, that is, to gain power to develop and deepen and enrich that image. This enables them to become, in effect, the industry responsible for the creation of their image, and to be in control of their own mode of production. Allied to this is the drive to maintain celebrity, or to increase the longevity of their image. Of course, celebrities aim to make a considerable amount of money, but in terms of celebrity, it is long-lasting fame, born and developed as a result of control, that ultimately seems most important.

If we imagine celebrity as a graph, we can plot a hierarchy of celebrity across two axes, as depicted in Figure 11.1.

Figure 11.1 Hierarchy of celebrity

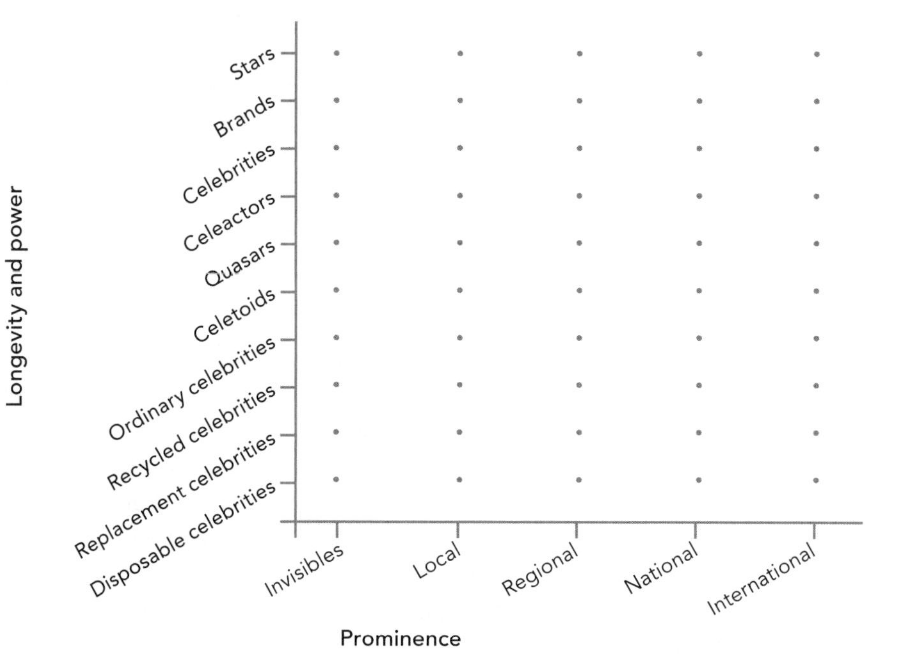

The first axis maps the prominence of the celebrity in the public sphere, which is similar to the way a media text achieves significance, as outlined in Chapter 10. Rein and colleagues (2006: 94) suggest a hierarchy of prominence rising from invisibles to local celebrities, regional celebrities, national celebrities and finally, international celebrities. Local celebrities, for example, are 'somewhat well known in their own geographical areas … In the past, most local celebrities did not seek visibility, they acquired it as a by-product of their occupations or lifestyles' (Rein et al. 2006: 94–5). Local newsreaders or politicians or people working in local radio or on community access television could all be examples of local celebrities.

In order for a person to move along this axis, a celebrity will need to develop an increasing number of intertexts, thereby increasing their significance and prominence in the public sphere.

The second axis maps the longevity and power of the celebrity, using the subsets discussed in more detail below.

The counterfeit people

Daniel Boorstin (1961: 57) famously referred to celebrities as 'the counterfeit people' who are 'famous for being famous'. The term seems apt as a way of describing the way celebrities, particularly celebrity images, can accommodate a wide variety of behaviours. Counterfeit people can move between multiple roles, for example, from actor or

musician to politician (Ronald Reagan, Arnold Schwarzenegger and Peter Garrett), actor to activist (Sean Penn and Audrey Hepburn), company executive to media personality (Donald Trump, Richard Branson and, briefly, the reverse in Eddie McGuire's case) or journalist to friend (the *Sunrise* team and US newsreader Katie Couric). Part of the skill of being a celebrity appears to be being able to deepen, widen or otherwise develop the celebrity image so a person can move successfully between these roles and thus prolong that celebrity.

Stars

Richard Dyer's *Stars* (1979) was one of the first texts to consider celebrities in the context of film stars. Stars exist at the very top of the celebrity hierarchy, and increasingly, as noted above, these are *music* stars because of their earning power through music sales, concert appearances, record box office receipts and/or fees per film. More importantly, they're at the top due to the longevity of their careers their ability to have a great deal of agency (control) over their careers and their tendency to be supported by a wide range of intertexts, such as gossip magazines and entertainment shows. They are the apex of the aspirational celebrity hierarchy because they are self-fulfilling, and able to produce and reproduce their own star images (think, for example, of Oprah Winfrey or Madonna).

A **star** refers to any of a range of celebrities exhibiting these features, whether they are based in film, television, radio or music. A star tends to be linked to a particular industry (a film star, a pop star or a television star), whereas celebrities can be more transient and thereby can exist without a clear institutional affiliation.

Star: A celebrity who commands prominence, longevity and power in his or her particular field.

But the most significant part of being a star, as Michael Jackson demonstrates, is that like the celestial bodies to which the term refers, their images often persist after the actual person has died. Marilyn Monroe, Elvis Presley, James Dean, Humphrey Bogart and scores of others have maintained celebrity power and continue to make money though they are long gone and all we are left with is their image. This, then, seems to be the true test of star power—the ability to exist as a celebrity after the person has passed away. We would suggest that in the future, as celebrities continue to proliferate, this may be what the term 'star' is reserved for.

When does a celebrity become a star?

If it isn't death that makes a celebrity a star, then when does it occur? Media writers frequently refer to a star-making moment: a particular film or album or television series that enables the transition from being just another celebrity to becoming a star capable of exercising control over a career and attaining some sort of longevity (and greater sums of money). Judging this moment can be a subjective determination, but star-making moments could include Samuel L. Jackson's performance in *Pulp Fiction* and Daniel Craig's starring role in *Layer Cake*, which gained him the role of the new James Bond in *Casino Royale*.

Brands

One of the ways celebrities can become self-perpetuating and thus make the transition to star is by becoming a **brand**: someone whose name and/or likeness can be used to sell and/or represent certain goods. Brands seem to exist in this nebulous zone between celebrities and stars. Celebrities such as Martha Stewart (through the Martha Stewart Living Omnipedia), Jamie Oliver and Elle Macpherson experience longevity through merchandising, but often seem to fall short of real stardom. An example is former heavyweight boxer George Foreman, who has maintained a kind of celebrity through his George Foreman Grill. Once again, a brand raises the possibility of the celebrity image persisting after death; the director Alfred Hitchcock, himself a former advertising man, reconstructed himself as a brand for his films, television and even books so successfully that 'Hitchcockian' now exists as a an adjective to describe film styles and themes similar to his own body of work.

Brand: A name, person, sign, character, colour, font, slogan, catch-phrase or any combination of these that operates as the signifier of a particular product, service or business. A legally protected brand is called a trademark. A brand is a perfect example of metonymy and an aspiration for many celebrities.

Athletes and models, whose celebrity is tied to a necessary expiry date—how long they can keep performing at a peak physical level—often seek to make the transition to being a brand; Air Jordan (or Jordan) shoes continue to be produced by Nike, even though their namesake, former professional NBA basketball player Michael Jordan, retired from the NBA in 2003. Indeed, they are now sold by the Jordan Brand, a subsidiary of Nike.

Oprah's Australian adventure

Perhaps the best example of the power of the celebrity brand is Oprah Winfrey. A six-month campaign by Tourism Australia (costing an estimated $150 million, including associated advertising), wooed the talk-show host to Australia in December 2010 for four episodes, in which she extolled her love of Australia to audiences in over 150 countries. While its net effect may take up to five years to quantify, everyone concerned agreed that it was money well spent.

Celebrities

As we have seen above, celebrities are 'familiar strangers' (Gitlin 1980). To be a familiar stranger implies that the celebrity has both a public (familiar) and a private (strange) life: the audience desires to know more about the celebrity's private life—the 'real' or 'authentic' person. Of course, the irony is that this can never be achieved, for as soon as the private becomes public it becomes mediated, and thus part of the celebrity image. There are many types of celebrity, and sitting just under brands are those celebrities who have maintained some level of prominence, longevity and power.

Celebrity activism

One of the most common forms of celebrity branding is that of events and causes: celebrity activism. Angelina Jolie and Nicole Kidman are both ambassadors for the United Nations. Bono talks to politicians about the environment. Even celebrity magazine *Vanity Fair* ran concurrent issues on two celebrity causes: the environment and Africa. This can be a very productive use of celebrity, using a profile to draw attention to causes that may not otherwise be on the agenda. But celebrity activism can also be cynically motivated, so that a celebrity increases their exposure by becoming attached to a hot issue.

Politicians, academics, writers, editors, agents, broadcasters, sportspeople, supermodels

Celebrities can and do appear in every field, not just in the film, television and music industries. J. K. Rowling (writer), Stephen King (writer), Howard Stern (broadcaster), Barack Obama (politician), Simon Schama (academic), Tiger Woods (sportsperson) and Naomi Campbell (supermodel) are all celebrities in their respective fields; they have become familiar strangers, with their audiences becoming interested in public and private lives. Other examples include public figures (the royal family), commentators (Richie Benaud), photographers (Annie Leibowitz), newsreaders (Brian Henderson), current affairs presenters (George Negus), editors (Anna Wintour), media creators (J. J. Abrams and Joss Whedon) and newspaper columnists (Phillip Adams and Andrew Bolt), to name just a few. Of course, as also noted earlier, these celebrities also move between media industries, as demonstrated by Hamish and Andy moving between television and radio, or Will Smith moving between music and film.

Are heroes celebrities?

Daniel Boorstin (1961) clearly differentiates heroes from celebrities in terms of achievement: heroes are famous for doing something (heroic); celebrities are famous just for being famous. This is not always true, but it does demonstrate how celebrities and heroes can be differently thought of. Heroes can be celebrities as well (as they become familiar strangers), but it is relatively rare for a celebrity to become a hero. Exceptions could include victims of great tragedy or record-breaking sporting figures (who are also referred to as 'legends'). Steve Irwin, the late crocodile hunter, for example, was clearly a celebrity in life, but has been referred to as a hero since his death, because of his work for the environment.

Familiar strangers, whose private and public lives are equally interesting, can include criminals, victims of crime and people involved in the criminal justice system, such as lawyers and police. As demonstrated by both Jesse James and Ned Kelly, criminals have long been considered celebrities. In Australia, 'Chopper' Read, who had spent much of his life in jail, made himself into a celebrity through his books and the film based on his life. People whose lives were featured in the *Underbelly* series, such as Mick Gatto, similarly attracted a degree of celebrity following the success of that television series, slipping between infamous celebrities and quasars (discussed below). Italian-American gangster Al Capone is another example of an infamous celebrity with some longevity and prominence in the mediasphere.

Celeactors

Celeactor: A fictional character who has a private and public life, and exists independently of his or her creator; for example, Dame Edna Everage.

Some fictional characters have a private and public life, which often exist quite independently of their creators. Examples of **celeactors** include Dame Edna Everage, Ali G, Borat, Norman Gunston and Alan Partridge. Frequently, they interact with real people who may be unaware that they are in fact fictional constructs, and they may move between different texts. Dame Edna Everage, for example, played a character on the television series *Ally McBeal.* It also means that the creators of such characters (Barry Humphries, Sascha Baron Cohen, Garry McDonald and Steve Coogan, respectively) can have separate careers and celebrity images quite apart from their creations.

Can fictional characters be celebrities?

With the exception of celeactors, the answer would seem to be no. Characters such as Homer Simpson, Kermit the Frog and Mickey Mouse simply don't have the private life that the familiar stranger requires—they can only exist within purely fictional constructs. But this might change in the future with the advent of new technologies.

Quasars

Quasar: A shooting star; a celebrity whose popularity remains only for the duration of a major event. The term is scientifically inaccurate, as a quasar is not a shooting star (transitory), but a quasi-astronomical object, a mysterious far-off object that might be a star, or perhaps a mini-galaxy in violent turmoil.

Celetoid: A celebrity created to fill a gap in an industry, or for some specified purpose (such as reality show winners).

A **quasar** is a celebrity whose fame usually lasts only for the duration of an event. Quasars can include reality television stars, lawyers on a case that gains media coverage, victims of crime, or criminals (see also 'Disposable celebrities' below).

Celetoids

Celetoid is Rojek's (2001) term for a type of celebrity specifically designed to be a celebrity. Often we are made aware of the celetoid's construction, for example, the Spice Girls, bands featured on *Popstars* or the winners of *Pop, American Idol* or *Australian Idol.*

Ordinary celebrities

Ordinary celebrities arise from lifestyle and reality television series that appeal to audiences because of their authenticity, chefs such as Curtis Stone, for example, or gardeners such as Jamie Durie. Such people appear to be so authentic that members of the audience feel as though they know them. However, as Frances Bonner (2003) points out, this 'ordinariness' is itself another performance—that of being ordinary. A more recent example of ordinary celebrities would be the spate of celebrities coming out of YouTube: ordinary people caught doing silly or amazing things. As Justin Bieber, who first came to fame as a YouTube sensation, demonstrates, it is always possible for ordinary celebrities to move up the hierarchy and become celebrities in their own right.

Recycled celebrities

Some people maintain their celebrity through cameo or guest appearances in other media or in game and reality television series. Originally, it used to be on shows such as *The Love Boat* (who remembers Charo?) but now it is in series such as *Dancing with the Stars*, *I'm A Celebrity, Get Me Out Of Here!* and *Hollywood Squares*.

Replacement celebrities

Replacement celebrities are types of celetoids groomed to replace one currently in existence, often referred to as the next so-and-so or the next big thing. Replacement celebrities occur in a variety of industries, often on talent series or reality television series. The annual winners of *X Factor*, *MasterChef* or *Australian Idol* could fall into this category.

Disposable celebrities

Chalke's (2005) notion of the **disposable celebrity** describes the virtual production line of celebrities produced by reality television series, that is, the commodity that is created to be used for a brief period of time and then disposed of. Often, these are not the winners (these are replacement celebrities) but the other contestants, who emerge from reality television series such as *Big Brother*, *Survivor* or *Australian Idol*, which run season after season. They are manufactured with a built-in expiry date—to release X number of singles or make X number of appearances—before they are disposed of and replaced by the next wave of disposable celebrities from the new season of the program. In this way they have no power over their image; to maintain their celebrity they must develop their celebrity—assert control over their image in some way—otherwise their celebrity will end with the commencement of the next season of the show. Often the best they can hope for is to become a recycled celebrity on another reality television program, but as Ryan 'Fitzy' Fitzgerald and Chrissie Swann (former *Big Brother* evictees rather than winners) prove, it is still possible to move up the celebrity hierarchy to become media commentators.

Disposable celebrity: A celebrity manufactured on a production line in order to be replaced in the near future by the next disposable celebrity.

How can we analyse celebrities?

As we have seen above, the celebrity is a textual construct, a commodity and an industry. Celebrity can therefore be analysed as:

- another media text (through textual analysis; see Chapter 9 and Tools 3)
- an industry in its own right (through notions of public relations; see Chapter 8)

- a particular type of commodity designed to sell products and ideas, market films and other media texts, brand events and protests, and provide endorsements.

Why are celebrities important?

While celebrities may seem incredibly superficial and undeserving of much attention, they are culturally significant for several reasons:

- *They offer their audiences a wide variety of identities and different ways of being.* The celebrity can be understood as a condensation of values, either at a particular time (Marilyn Monroe and Americans during the 1950s) or in order to challenge existing identities (which is one of the arguments for Paris Hilton or Lady Gaga's appeal). This means celebrities can be both inspirational ('I want to be like that person') and aspirational ('I want to be that person').
- *The celebrity shows an ability to function as a counterfeit person.* This enables them to move between different roles, which reflects a perceived need of people to transform, remould and recreate themselves. This is perhaps best embodied by the actor Hugh Laurie who was best known as a British comedian (on *Blackadder*) then became a dramatic American actor (as the titular character on *House*) and most recently became a musician. This desire is mirrored in other aspects of today's society, such as therapy groups, plastic surgery, and job-changing. It is an element of postmodernity that we return to in Chapter 20.
- *The celebrity indicates a shift in the mediasphere as a whole, from the dissemination of information towards the dissemination of identities.* This can be viewed as a negative—a move 'towards a culture that privileges the momentary, the visual and the sensational over the enduring, the written, the rational' (Turner 2004: 4). It also can be viewed as a positive—a move towards a more democratised culture in which different identities are constantly on display, offering potential choices to everybody in society.

Is celebrity a negative aspect of society?

If you described a journalist or newsreader as a celebrity, it could be interpreted in one of two ways. Either the person has done very well and become very well known (positively), or the person lacks credibility and is more concerned with image than with information (negatively). But are the traits of celebrity really negative? If we take Rojek's (2001) idea of parasocial relationships, outlined earlier in this chapter, we can see that these are potentially advantageous to the journalist or newsreader, because celebrity enables the person to form a link with their audience. Such skills helped to make Katie Couric a success in the USA and the *Sunrise* team so successful in Australia. Is celebrity really such a bad thing?

Conclusion

The celebrity is best described as the familiar stranger, a definition that acknowledges both the parasocial relationship created by the celebrity (familiarity) and the fact that a celebrity is a highly constructed image (therefore the real person always remains a stranger). Part of the appeal of the celebrity for audiences is in trying to close this gap, to know the unknowable; in many cases it is analogous to a religious experience. Fans of particular celebrities will gather information, opinions, views and images of the celebrity to get to know them better.

As a result the celebrity is an intertextual construction: a balance of the public and the private. If these are out of alignment, the celebrity may slip down the hierarchy of fame, though an increase in the private element of the celebrity's fame does not appear to be a problem (think, for example, of Paris Hilton). For the people who promote their celebrity, such as Tom Cruise or Lindsay Lohan, the private element may become embarrassingly out of balance with the public element.

Celebrities' increasing dominance of the mediasphere, and their increasing proliferation, particularly through YouTube, Twitter and reality television series, means that they are important objects of study for the ways in which they are transforming the mediasphere, for good or ill, and as an indication of how the mediasphere might function in the future.

KEY REFERENCES

Gitlin, T. (2001). *Media Unlimited: How the Torrent of Images and Sounds Overwhelms Our Lives.* New York: Metropolitan Books.

Turner, G. (2004). *Understanding Celebrity.* London: Sage.

Turner, G., Bonner, F. & Marshall, P. D. (2000). *Fame Games: The Production of Celebrity in Australia.* Cambridge: Cambridge University Press.

CASE STUDY 3:

THE POLITICIAN, THE JOURNALIST, PRIVACY AND THE PUBLIC RIGHT TO KNOW

NICOLA GOC

Introduction

In Australia in 2010, a commercial television station outed a state politician as leading a double life as a bisexual man. The broadcast of the story by Channel Seven's Adam Walters sparked a debate across Australia about media ethics, and the issue of privacy and the public right to know. This case study examines the actions of Channel Seven and the subsequent public and media discourse on the state of the media and the right to privacy, and examines the ethical issues related to personal privacy and the actions of journalists going about their daily work.

Channel Seven's exposé

In May 2010, Channel Seven's New South Wales chief political reporter, Adam Walters, produced a story on the then New South Wales Labor Minister for Transport David Campbell, exposing Mr Campbell, a married man, as leading a double life. Channel Seven filmed Campbell leaving a gay sauna in Sydney and within 24 hours of the broadcast a humiliated Campbell resigned from his ministerial portfolio, telling the public that he was sorry for his actions. Campbell said that while his decision to frequent Ken's Bar had hurt his family, there had been no impact on his professional life in parliament.

Adam Walters said a Seven crew had started following the minister for transport some months earlier, after the minister refused to disclose his whereabouts during a notorious traffic jam on the F3 freeway in northern Sydney on 12 April. Walters had received a tip-off about Campbell's steam-bath trips at the same time as the Seven crew began their surveillance of the minister.

Walters argued that it was a matter of hypocrisy that a married minister of parliament should be leading a double life, and said his actions compromised his ministerial position and made him vulnerable to blackmail.

Campbell's record on gay-related legislation was clear. As the *Sydney Morning Herald*'s Brian Robins reported, Campbell was not hypocritical in his voting record, having supported—sometimes vocally—every major piece of gay reform legislation that had come before the New South Wales parliament during his tenure:

> Debating superannuation entitlements for same-sex partners in 2000, not long after he had joined Parliament, Mr Campbell made it clear he thought society was changing, moving away from the era of the 'white picket fence with a nuclear family of a husband, a wife and two kids'.
>
> 'We are a changing community,' he said. 'We need to … understand that people who want to share a same-sex relationship will do so openly.'

> In a similar vein, last month he voted in a conscience vote in favour of setting up a relationship register, which is aimed at strengthening the legal standing of same-sex and de facto couples, although he did not take part in the debate. (Robins 2010)

The journalist under scrutiny

As the media debate over the ethics of Walter's reporting spread, the journalist himself came under scrutiny with claims that he may not have been working from a dispassionate position. Andrew Crook, writing for Crikey.com.au, argued that Walters had 'scores to settle' with Campbell and that 'bad blood' circulated between Walters and the mother of his child, the former Labor Minister for Health Reba Meagher. In 2008, when Walters had been working as the communication minister to former Premier Morris Iemma, his relationship with Ms Meagher began. Crook wrote that 'Some sources are claiming the hatchet job on Campbell was payback for Walters' emotional distress after the power couple's relationship turned sour last year' (Crook 2010). According to Crook, Walters later said Iemma's office was 'a circus full of clowns' and that he was planning his departure from his first day in the job (Crook 2010).

Channel Seven justified the station's actions under the right to know defence, initially arguing that the minister had wrongfully used his ministerial car to attend the gay venue; however, the station retreated from this defence when New South Wales Premier Kristina Keneally said ministers routinely use their ministerial vehicles for private tasks, including picking up their kids from school.

The public interest defence

News organisations argue that it is the role of journalism to report the details of a person's private life when it is in the public interest to do so. The public interest defence is often hotly debated when the issue of unethical media behaviour is discussed.

The Australian Press Council (APC), in its Statement of Principles, defines 'public interest' as 'involving a matter capable of affecting the people at large so they might be legitimately interested in, or concerned about, what is going on, or what may happen to them or to others' (APC 2009). According to the APC, public figures necessarily sacrifice their right to privacy, where public scrutiny is in the public interest, but that 'public figures do not forfeit their right to privacy altogether. Intrusion into their right to privacy must be related to their public duties or activities' (APC 2009).

If journalists have the right to breach an individual's privacy when it is in the public interest to do so, then it would be fair to assume that it would be desirable to have a categorisation of which matters are private and which are not. Yet the public right to know is a term with different definitions in different temporal and geographic locations. What may be considered an adequate public right to know defence in one jurisdiction might differ elsewhere, depending on the court of law, the decade and the jurisdiction.

Privacy

What is meant by privacy? Privacy has to do with keeping personal information non-public or undisclosed. Personal information is that set of facts about oneself that a person does not wish to see disclosed or made public (Archard 1998). Personal information can be inferred from a photograph, film or sound recording. However, the issue is more nuanced because what one person strives to keep private, another might be happy to see as common knowledge.

In the digital age people are often naively uninhibited when posting comments and pictures on social networking sites such as Facebook and Twitter. People have been known to post intimate images and personal comments on these sites, believing only friends would access the material—only to later find the material in the public domain. In 2010, a University of California and University of Pennsylvania survey found that more than 50 per cent of the 1000 adults surveyed were more anxious about their online privacy in relation to their public image than they were five years earlier.

Celebrities, politicians and privacy

It is well known that some in the entertainment industry see the exposure of personal scandal as a useful strategy to place them into the public spotlight. 'Bad news is good news', as some public relations strategists argue.

The groups most likely to have their private lives exposed through the media are politicians and others in positions of power, celebrities and personalities, and people unexpectedly thrust into the public eye.

Most of us, though, would probably think of our sexual and financial affairs as our private affairs. Richard Archard argues that the publication of the details of someone's personal circumstances constitutes an invasion of privacy, for example, that someone is gay, is HIV positive, is having an extramarital affair, engages in a certain kind of sexual activity or has an illegitimate child (Archard 1998).

There are two issues involved here:

- the right of the individual to protection against intrusion into her or his private concerns
- the duty of the media to report information that the public has a right to know.

Karen Saunders (2006) looks to the approach of Besley (1992) and Kieran (1998) to argue that 'privacy attaches to people according to their position'.

Sir Zelman Cowen, former governor-general of Australia once argued: 'A man's privacy is his safety valve; he has in it his permissible area of deviation, his opportunity to give vent to what he would not express or do publicly; within these private limits he may share confidences and intimacies with those he trusts and he may set boundaries to those confidences' (Cowen 1969).

Privacy and journalism

The notion of privacy and journalism can be understood in juxtaposition to the concepts of public interest and larger social purpose, which, as Nalini Rajan argues, are 'broad expressions and do not lead themselves to precise definition' (Rajan 2005: 76). Saying the public has a right to know—that it is in the public interest to publish or broadcast certain material—is not the same as the public being interested in knowing something.

Brandeis and Warren, and the right to privacy

The issue of privacy and journalism became a topic of legal discussions in the USA in the late nineteenth century when Judge Cooley described the protection of the person—and the protection of the individual's right to privacy—as the right 'to be let alone' (Cooley, cited Brandeis & Warren 1890).

In their seminal 1890 paper, 'The Right to Privacy', Louis Brandeis and Samuel Warren argued that 'recent inventions and business methods' had called attention to the issue of privacy and the media:

> Instantaneous photographs and newspaper enterprise have invaded the sacred precincts of private and domestic life; and numerous mechanical devices threaten to make good the prediction that 'what is whispered in the closet shall be proclaimed from the house-tops.' For years there has been a feeling that the law must afford some remedy for the unauthorized circulation of portraits of private persons; and the evil of invasion of privacy by the newspapers, long keenly felt, has been but recently discussed by an able writer. (Brandeis & Warren 1890)

Brandeis and Warren were the first to articulate the issue of privacy and journalism more than a century ago, and they provided guidelines that are still relevant today:

> In general, then, the matters of which the publication should be repressed may be described as those which concern the private life, habits, acts, and relations of an individual, and have no legitimate connection with his fitness for a public office which he seeks or for which he is suggested, or for any public or quasi public position which he seeks or for which he is suggested, and have no legitimate relation to or bearing upon any act done by him in a public or quasi public capacity. (Brandeis & Warren 1890, cited in Padmanabhan 2005: 76–7)

Privacy v the right to free speech

There are those who believe that truth is valuable for its own sake. Nineteenth-century utilitarian John Stuart Mill, in his famous treatise 'On Liberty', extolled the virtues of the 'free market place of ideas', arguing that anyone who wanted to contribute to public discourse should be permitted to do so for four reasons:

- Silencing an opinion risks silencing the truth.
- A wrong opinion may contain an element of truth, which helps to find the whole truth.
- Even an opinion that is the whole truth has to be tested and defended.
- A commonly held opinion must be challenged in order to retain its vitality and effect.

In the Campbell case, sections of the Australian media, particularly the commercial broadcast stations and the tabloid press, supported Channel Seven's actions. David Penberthy, writing for *The Punch*, a News Limited online journal, argued that David Campbell had a lesser right to privacy than an ordinary citizen because 'as a politician his entire existence is underwritten by the taxpaying public—his salary, his car, his living arrangements, his ability to travel, all of it is fully or partially funded by the public, and to an extent which massively eclipses the average wage earner'. He went on: 'As a politician he wields enormous and direct power over the way we live our lives, even own financial status' (Penberthy 2010).

In contrast, Eric Beecher, publisher of Crikey.com.au, was scathing in his criticism not only of the station's actions but also of the rallying cry in support of Channel Seven that came from the tabloid media. Beecher wrote that the 'debate' about the media and privacy was a 'sham conducted by people who are paid extremely well to legitimise something nasty and indefensible' (Beecher 2010). He went on:

> The editorial culture of the organisations that routinely invade personal privacy—tabloid TV, certain newspapers and weekly 'women's' magazines—is aggressively, deliberately and explicitly led from the top. (Beecher 2010)

He argued that the newsroom culture in certain media organisations is one that is 'constructed, in part, to invade privacy. It is a practice that sits at the heart of their editorial DNA. It is one of the core tenets of the way they do their journalism, and the way their journalism is internally judged and rewarded' (Beecher 2010).

Privacy laws in Australia

The need to balance respect for privacy with standards that recognise freedom of speech and of the press is recognised by the *Privacy Act 1988*. This Act provides an exemption for acts done or practices engaged in by a media organisation in the course of journalism, if the media organisation is publicly committed to observing standards that deal with privacy in the context of the organisation's activities, and those standards have been published in writing either by the organisation or a body representing a class of media organisations. The *Privacy (Private Sector) Amendment Act*, which came into effect in December 2001, has a similar exemption.

In response to these Acts, the Australian Press Council (APC) developed such a set of standards, known as the Statement of Principles. Principle 4 states that:

> News and comment should be presented honestly and fairly, and with respect for the privacy and sensibilities of individuals. However, the right to privacy is not to be interpreted as preventing publication of matters of public record or obvious or significant public interest. Rumour and unconfirmed reports should be identified as such. (Australian Press Council 2009)

In determining whether Channel Seven was unethical in broadcasting video footage of David Campbell coming out of a gay sauna, the case has to be subjected to the public interest defence. If a person's private actions have actual or potential consequences for the public, the public is entitled to know, through the media, what is happening, whether or not that person is embarrassed or harmed by the disclosure of private activities. The public could, for example, be disadvantaged if certain private actions remained hidden, such as a junior sporting coach or a pre-school teacher who has committed a paedophile offence.

Because the circumstances differ from case to case, journalists are opposed to arbitrary rules defining where they should or should not go, and what they should or should not do. They believe they should be bound by ethical guidelines based on generally accepted standards of taste and decency, and respect for individual rights.

Privacy and codes of ethics

How do journalists process sensitive information they come across as they go about gathering news? All professional journalists work within the constraints of a code of practice, or a code of ethics, which sets out certain principles that are guidelines to ethical journalistic practice (see Chapter 16). It is universal that journalism codes contain a clause relating to individual privacy. The US Society of Professional Journalists (SPJ), for example, under the 'Minimize Harm' section of its code of practice, states that journalists should:

> Recognize that private people have a greater right to control information about themselves than do public officials and others who seek power, influence or attention. Only an overriding public need can justify intrusion into anyone's privacy. (SPJ n.d.)

Journalists in Australia who are members of the Media Entertainment and Arts Alliance (MEAA) are bound by the MEAA/Australian Journalists Association Code of Ethics. Clause 11 relates specifically to privacy: 'Respect private grief and personal privacy. Journalists have the right to resist compulsion to intrude.' This clause is, however, a general statement that does not guide specific advice (beyond 'private grief') to journalists. Clause 2 also relates to the disclosure of private material: 'Do not place unnecessary emphasis on personal characteristics, including race, ethnicity, nationality, gender, age, sexual orientation, family relationships, religious belief, or physical or intellectual disability' (MEAA n.d.).

Code 8 of the Australian Press Council's Statement of Principles states: 'Publications should not place any gratuitous emphasis on the race, religion, nationality, colour, country of origin, gender, sexual orientation, marital status, disability, illness or age of an individual or group. Where it is relevant and in the public interest, publications may report and express opinions in these areas' (APC 2009).

Broadcast media and the internet in Australia come under the Australian Communications and Media Authority (ACMA), an Australian government agency whose main roles are to regulate broadcasting, radio communications and telecommunications, and to regulate internet content standards.

Commercial television stations also have a self-regulatory code of practice. It covers matters relating to program content that are of concern to the community, such as accuracy, fairness and respect for privacy in news and current affairs, as well as the matters prescribed in section 123 of the *Broadcasting Services Act*. Section 123 of the *Broadcasting Services Act* lays out the federal government's policy on the development of codes of practice for commercial and community radio and television industry groups. Under the Act, radio and television industry groups are required, in consultation with ACMA to develop codes of practice. Codes of practice developed for the broadcasting industry should, according to the Act, relate to, for example, methods of classifying programs that reflect community standards; and promote accuracy and fairness in news and current affairs programs (*Broadcasting Services Act 1992*).

The Australian Broadcasting Corporation (ABC) has a Code of Practice that includes the provision that every reasonable effort must be made to ensure that the content of news and current affairs programs is accurate, impartial and balanced (ABC 1994).

The Special Broadcasting Service (SBS), under the *Special Broadcasting Service Act 1991*, requires SBS to ensure that the gathering and presentation of news and information is accurate, and balanced over time and across the schedule of programs broadcast (SBS 2010).

Conclusion

Channel Seven's public interest defence fails if one applies the standard that journalists have no right to hold a public figure to account for their personal moral choices unless that person's private life impacts on their public life. But the public right to know standard is far less straightforward. Channel Seven's claim that Campbell's private actions reflected on his public life and that voters had a right to know about this received considerable support from sections of the public and the media. The question for the public is simple: if voters knew that Campbell was bisexual or gay, should this information be considered relevant to their voting decision?

In this moment of media navel gazing, it was perhaps surprising that in the Campbell case: two high-profile journalists from very different perspectives—David Marr, journalist, author, and political and social commentator noted for his liberal stance on social and politician issues; and Miranda Devine, columnist and writer, who is equally well known for her conservative stance on a range of social and political issues—both came to the same conclusion: it is not up to us (neither the public nor the media) to judge the status of relationships in the Campbell family. They both determined that there was clearly no public interest in this case, except a prurient one.

KEY REFERENCES

Archard, D. (1998). 'Privacy, the Public Interest and a Prurient Public'. In M. Kieran (ed.) *Media Ethics*. London: Routledge, 82–96.

Beecher, E. (2010). 'Tabloid Media Laughing All the Way to the Pub on Campbell'. *Crikey*. 24 May. <www.crikey.com.au/2010/05/24/beecher-tabloid-media-laughing-all-the-way-to-the-pub-on-campbell/>. Accessed 3 June 2010.

Brandeis, L. D. & Warren, S. D. (1890). 'The Right to Privacy'. *Harvard Law Review*. IV (5), 193–220.

Crook, A. (2010). 'The Minister, the Gay Sauna, and a Reporter with Scores to Settle'. *Crikey*. 21 May. <www.crikey.com.au/2010/05/21/the-minister-the-gay-sauna-and-a-reporter-with-scores-to-settle/>. Accessed 3 June 2010.

Penberthy, D. (2010). 'Why David Campbell has a Lesser Right to Privacy'. *The Punch*. 21 May. <www.thepunch.com.au/articles/why-david-campbell-has-a-lesser-right-to-privacy>. Accessed 12 November 2010.

WEBSITES

Australian Press Council: <www.presscouncil.org.au/pcsite/complaints/sop.html>.

Australian Government Information Sheet (Private Sector) 12–2001 Coverage of and Exemptions from the Private Sector Provisions: <www.privacy.gov.au/materials/types/infosheets/view/6544>.

Society of Professional Journalists: <www.spj.org/ethicscode.asp>.

Media Entertainment and Arts Alliance, Code of Ethics: <www.alliance.org.au/documents/codeofethics.pdf>.

TOOLS 3:

TEXTUAL ANALYSIS AND MEDIA RESEARCH

JASON BAINBRIDGE

Introduction

In the preceding chapters we have explained what textual analysis is and why you might undertake it. In this Tools section we want to show you how textual analysis is done, some different forms of textual analysis and some additional tools to help you conduct your own textual analyses.

Where does textual analysis come from?

As you saw in Chapters 9 to 11, textual analysis comes out of the work of theorists known as the French structuralists in the 1960s, particularly the work of Roland Barthes (1915–80). Barthes believed that any kind of popular cultural product could be decoded by reading the signs within the text. Today, this approach is one of the primary tools media researchers use to understand how meaning is made from media texts. As media theorist McKee (2003: 1) puts it:

> Textual analysis is a way for researchers to gather information about how other human beings make sense of the world. It is a methodology—a data-gathering process—for those researchers who want to understand the ways in which members of various cultures and subcultures make sense of who they are, and of how they fit into the world in which they live.

Textual analysis is also the perfect starting point for somebody writing a news story, analysing a public relations campaign or developing a television series, and an effective way of assessing, comparing and understanding media texts. It is something we all do instinctively, to some extent, but if you follow these steps, textual analysis can become a skill that, as a person involved in media, journalism, business or public life more generally, you can use to understand why certain media texts are successful, subversive or popular.

Ultimately, textual analysis is a toolkit for examining the media, which is applicable to very simple media forms, such as advertisements, as well as more complex forms, such as news narratives, television series and films. It is also a toolkit for media practitioners who want to convey a certain message or try to convince audiences to think in a certain way. There should be something here of use to you, regardless of your future career in media.

As noted by McKee (2003: 1), 'When we perform textual analysis on a text, we make an educated guess at some of the most likely interpretations that might be made of that text'. The important thing to note is that this is an educated guess. Your educated guess will be informed by research and completed by utilising the tools outlined below.

What is structuralism?

Structuralism is a French intellectual movement that began with the linguistics work of Ferdinand de Saussure, and was subsequently used as a model in anthropology, psychoanalysis and literary theory. Structuralists include Roland Barthes, Michel Foucault, Jacques Lacan and Claude Lévi-Strauss.

Structuralism seeks to analyse social structures such as language and narrative to determine the structures that underlie them. Such structures often take the form of binary oppositions (hot–cold, being–nothing, culture–nature), which can then be broken down into units, such as signs, codes and rules. Structuralism is the basis of semiotics and our form of textual analysis, which includes understanding how the text is encoded, breaking down the text and framing the text.

Is there only one form of textual analysis?

There are many different ways of defining textual analysis. When, for example, US Supreme Court Judge Antonin Scalia refers to the textual analysis of the US Constitution, he is referring to having regard to the original intentions of the drafters of the Constitution, something completely at odds with the ideas of polysemy and the death of the author that we've presented in previous chapters.

Our form of media studies follows the form developed by fellow media and cultural studies theorists such as Hartley (1999) and McKee (2003).

There are three important things to remember about this form of textual analysis:

- As discussed in Chapters 9 and 10, it involves a new and unique vocabulary. Don't panic! While the terms may be unfamiliar to you, the practices they describe won't be, because you engaging with them every day.
- As with other media tools, you will find different uses for different tools in different situations. Not every tool is applicable to every text. They are here to help you make meaning. Use only the ones you need to make a persuasive and compelling argument.
- Practise using these tools on the media you encounter in your daily lives. The more often you use them, the sooner you will feel comfortable applying them.

Why textual analysis differs from the other tools in this book

Theory: The body of rules, ideas, principles and techniques that applies to a particular subject, as distinct from actual practice.

Generally, the tools in this book are practical applications of some of the concepts presented in the preceding chapters. They are skills we most often label as 'journalistic', but are, in fact, transferable to a number of occupations. Textual analysis differs from these other tools in that it is a mixture of **theory** and practice.

The way we study the relationship between media, culture and society is by applying theory, and for the purposes of this book we define theory as being a critical reflection on the actual world. Furthermore, theory in itself is not an evaluative term. What makes one theory better than another, more persuasive than another or have what we may term more academic rigour than another are two further factors: methodology and evidence.

Media research basics: theory, research, methodology and evidence

Theory

You start with a theory, a critical reflection on the world that takes the form of a rule, idea or principle that applies to a particular subject that you want to test.

Research questions

The theory you choose becomes the basis of your research question(s), which might include, for example, How can this text be understood?, Why is it popular, and How does it relate to other media texts?

Methodology

A **methodology** is a technique designed to answer such questions, a systematic way of producing knowledge that involves the production and analysis of data. A methodology is a way of testing, accepting, developing or rejecting theories.

Textual analysis (see Chapter 9) is one such methodology for testing and developing the theories raised about texts in the preceding chapters. But textual analysis is not the only methodology media researchers use. Other methodologies include taking ratings, conducting interviews (see Tools 1) and compiling audience surveys. To answer some research questions you can even develop new methodologies, and frequently researchers use different methodologies together to do just that. This is because different methodologies produce different kinds of information.

Methodology: A systematic way of producing knowledge, involving both the production and analysis of data; a way of testing, accepting, developing or rejecting a theory.

Evidence: Signs or proofs of the existence or truth of some proposition; information that helps somebody to reach a particular conclusion, through empirical materials (physical items) and observable phenomena (such as heat or cold).

Textual analysis is a useful methodology because it focuses on the media texts themselves. Whenever you're involved in audience research through interviews or surveys you are, in effect, creating more texts to analyse, such as statistics, articles, books and surveys. In textual analysis we always remain focused on the primary media text itself (we define what that means below).

Evidence

The **evidence** that we will be looking at will be media texts, such as films, television programs and magazines.

Evidence can be broken down into two forms: primary evidence and secondary evidence. As all of our evidence can be found in two types of texts, we can refer to these texts as being either primary texts or secondary texts.

Types of texts

Primary texts

Primary text: The original information that forms the basis of the rest of textual analysis.

Primary texts comprise the original information that you begin with: the primary object of study. If you were analysing an episode of a sitcom, a magazine or a particular film, you would call this text the primary text.

Depending upon your research question, you could look at more than one primary text, for example, you could be writing a historical overview of the Walt Disney Corporation, so your primary texts would include the Disney films, Disney television series and Disney-linked products.

For a constitutional lawyer, the Constitution will be the primary text. For an investigative journalist writing an exposé of potentially criminal business dealings, the primary texts could include business documents and interviews with the people involved. For a surgeon, the body itself becomes the primary text.

Secondary texts

Secondary texts: Analytical or descriptive studies that interact, inform or otherwise elucidate the original information you are studying.

Secondary texts are the texts that make an analytical or descriptive study of the primary text or texts. They help us to understand the primary text, or otherwise clarify our analysis of the primary texts.

For academics and students, secondary texts are usually reference works taken from the body of academic literature around a subject. They could include textbooks or academic articles, lectures and seminars. For journalists, these could include other articles on the subject or interviews. For people working in public relations, they could include analyses of audience surveys or statistics.

Tools for all types of texts

Some tools are applicable to all types of texts, regardless of whether they are image or written.

Encountering the text

- Take notes about where and how you encounter the text for the first time.
- Make notes about why a text produces certain responses or encourages audiences to react in certain ways.
- Make a guess at how meaning is made; this will remain a guess (or hypothesis), but through analysis you will unpack how this meaning is made, educating your guess by continuing examination of the primary material.

- As you build up primary and secondary evidence, you may be quite surprised by how correct your gut instincts or first impressions were. They should be, because you've been unconsciously training yourself to analyse texts every day, as you live in a multimediated world.

Analysing the text

This is the way in which we educate our guess.

Break down the text

- Break down the text into its component signs, or units of meanings.
- Focus on the relationship between the physical part of the sign (the signifier) and what the sign signifies (the signified), that is, how each part of the sign makes meaning.

TIPS FOR BREAKING DOWN THE TEXT

As we have seen in Chapters 9 and 10, a sign is anything that produces meaning. In analysing signs, remember the following:

- Signs do not merely comment on things in the world; they are things in the world, for example, street signs, clothing or parts of a magazine.
- Signs are also units of meaning: they produce meanings.
- Signs can produce many meanings, not just one per sign. We call this spread of possible signifieds connotations. The most stable and verifiable of these we call the denotation.
- Signs are social: they require an audience to function, and often hail this audience by addressing them in some way.

Encoding texts

As the link between the signifier and the signified is arbitrary, media texts are naturally polysemic, that is, open to many interpretations. In their attempt to ensure that a particular meaning is made, the industries and individuals responsible for these texts attempt to manipulate the relationship between signifier and signified in order to direct receivers to adopt an intended message.

Therefore, the sender is encoding the text in a certain way, which means that we can classify texts as being either open or closed:

- **Open texts** have many meanings, depending on time, gender, race, politics, place, class, age and experience.
- **Closed texts** encourage a specific meaning and permit little space for the reader to generate different interpretations.

As a (very) general rule, the more complex the text, the more open it will be, allowing many different readings. Equally, the simpler the text, the more closed it will be, allowing relatively fewer readings. A great deal of textual

Open texts: Texts that have many possible meanings.

Closed texts: Texts that focus on a specific meaning and permit little space for the reader to generate a variety of interpretations.

analysis will be spent understanding how the text is encoded, for as a creator of media texts you need to understand how and why you can encode a text. Similarly, as a consumer you should be able to identify the ways in which the text is being encoded.

TIPS FOR DETERMINING WHETHER A TEXT IS OPEN OR CLOSED

There are three principal ways senders attempt to produce closed texts in order to limit the range of connotations available or specifically encode a spread of signifieds around a certain signifier:

Anchorage: The tying of an image text (through a caption) or a written text (through a headline) to a certain meaning.

Metaphor: An implicit or explicit comparison between signs, where the qualities of one are transferred to another.

- **Anchorage** is the use of captions or commentary designed to select and/or control the connotations that can be made by a reader. This anchors an image text (through a caption) or a written text (through a headline) to a certain meaning.
- A **metaphor** is an implicit or explicit comparison between signs by which the qualities of one are transferred to another. Imagine a big equals sign between two aspects of the text, whether words or pictures or a combination of the two. An advertisement showing an attractive woman using a brand of lipstick, for example, metaphorically means that if you use this lipstick, you can also become glamorous, sexually attractive and slim: the lipstick, becomes the metaphor for personal success.

Metonymy: The standing in of a part or element of a text for the whole.

- **Metonymy** is a part or element of something used to stand for the whole. At its simplest, a pair of muscular legs in an advertisement represents an entire person. We assume that the rest of the person continues outside the frame; we are not looking at just a pair of dismembered legs. In complex metonyms, a person can stand for all people, a colour can represent an entire product (such as Coca-Cola's use of red and white), a symbol can represent a company (the Nike swoosh or the McDonald's arches) or a particular writing style can represent a particular way of being (class, taste or passion).

These methods of encoding, anchorage, metaphor and metonymy can also work together. A strong arm wearing a watch with the slogan 'Testosterone Watches—for real men', for example, would be a combined example of anchorage, metaphor and metonymy. The caption anchors the image: we know it refers to a particular brand of watch, as it is a watch advertisement. The arm works metonymically, in that it stands in not just for the rest of the model (who we assume continues outside the frame of the ad) but also for all men. The arm also works metaphorically, that is, it transfers the strength of the arm to the strength of the watch. The implication is that if you wear a Testosterone watch you, too, will be a strong man—a real man. This could appeal to women, too; if they buy their boyfriend, husband or colleague a Testosterone watch, it will make him a strong man, a real man, and by inference a man who appeals to a woman.

Advertising

Still having trouble breaking down texts? Try these tools on some of the advertisements you might encounter on public transport, on television, in newspapers or in magazines. Advertisements are often the simplest texts, because they are so clearly encoded to make you think a certain way, that you need to buy this product or service. It is estimated that the average Australian sees 1500 marketing messages every day and 240 thirty-second television commercials per week.

Cultural studies theorist Raymond Williams (2000) once called advertising the 'official art of modern capitalist society', for the following reasons:

- Advertising is one of the oldest forms of media.
- Advertising informs much of the media we consume, as it provides the main source of income for media owners.
- Advertising orients the range of entertainment and information produced by the media towards those audiences advertisers want to reach. In developing a program or publication, the question of who it may appeal to is an artistic and commercial matter, though public broadcasters such as the ABC and the BBC are seen to be exceptions to this. This is the idea of show business we discussed in Chapters 7 and 10.
- Advertising is all about image (signifier) and association (signified), rather than product (see below).

Framing the text

Framing the text involves two considerations:

- the frame of the text is the way the text is presented to us
- the context is where the text is located, and how it is encountered by use.

In looking at the frame of the text, ask yourself not only why certain elements have been included, but also what has been left out. Ask yourself why these elements have been left out. How does this affect the possible meanings the text might have?

In thinking about what is not included in the frame, look at **structuring absences**: what is missing from a text, and what meaning these omissions might connote. Since all media texts are mediations of the world, affected by a series of choices and selections, and framed in a certain way, we must always be aware of what is not included in the text. For example:

Structuring absences: Elements in the text that have meaning despite (or because of) the fact they have been left out.

- What is missing?
- What choices have been made in leaving out this or that element?
- What meaning might be elicited from this absence(s)?
- What selection of images and information has occurred?

In thinking about analysing what is included in the frame, use the exnomination and commutation tools to help you determine how meaning is made:

Exnomination: The process by which dominant ideas become so obvious they don't draw attention to themselves; instead they just seem like common sense.

- **Exnomination** is the process by which dominant ideas become so obvious they don't draw attention to themselves; instead they just seem like common sense, and subsequently are rarely challenged. When you nominate something, for example, a skin-coloured bandaid in a text, you draw attention to it. The bandaid is pink and therefore the implication is that anything other than pink cannot be considered skin coloured. The phrase 'skin-coloured bandaid', therefore, works hegemonically to reinforce certain ideas of race, which is a form of racism that doesn't draw attention to itself. Therefore, you need to be aware of exnomination so that you can draw out the subtleties of power relations in texts, particularly where they work with other intertexts to support a certain ideology of the world.

Commutation: The replacement of one element of a text with another to see how this affects how meaning is made.

- **Commutation** is the replacement one element of a text with another one to see how this affects how meaning is made; for example, substitute man for woman, black for white, arm for leg or young for old to find out how these substitutions alter the meaning of the text.

Context

When looking at the context of a text, consider the following:

- What is the time in which the text was created?
- In what type of media product is the text located?
- Where is the media text placed in that product? For example, is it located towards the front of a newspaper or magazine, or does it go to air during prime time or late at night?
- What is the country of origin (and reception) for the text?
- Which industry is responsible for the text's creation?

Recognise that the context may be somewhat artificial. You could be encountering the text as a result of an assignment from your boss or an academic exercise set at university. Try to keep in mind the regular context for such a text, otherwise it will remain abstracted from the wider culture and society.

Intertexts

While the primary text should remain the focus of textual analysis, intertexts can help us understand how meaning is produced by a text. As we saw in Chapter 9, intertexts are interrelated, interdependent texts that relate to either primary or secondary texts, and can inform us about how meaning is made from the primary text. They can include production records, academic articles or other media programs in a similar genre.

Texts frequently make meaning through their relationship with other texts. Indeed, as we have seen time and again, the logic of representation in the mediasphere is intertextual, because social and political significance cannot be achieved by reading a single text.

Specific tools for specific types of texts

Because of the variety of texts, we also need specialised tools designed for particular texts. Some texts, such as newspapers, novels or letters, are primarily written, others, such as films, television programs or computer games, are primarily image based. Still others, such as comic books or websites, are combinations of the two. Just as you would select a screwdriver for some household jobs and a hammer for others, you would use these specific tools for some specific textual jobs and not others. The following sections examine the process of analysing image texts and written texts.

Analysing image texts

As we saw in Chapter 6, films can provide us with a vocabulary that we can use to analyse still and moving image texts, that is, photographs and films. This involves breaking down these image texts into their individual components, naming each component and seeing how each works as a unit of meaning. These parts of an image's composition are similar to the signs we discussed earlier, in that they are all comprised of a signifier (a physical or aural element) and a signified (the mental element we associate with that physical part).

This means we can read image texts just as we would a written text. This shouldn't be that surprising—after all, the literal definition of photography is 'writing with light'.

When we read a still image text such as a photograph or a piece of art we look at two aspects of the text:

- *the form of the text:* the shape of the text and the way it appears before us
- *the content of the text:* what is actually there, what is the subject of the text and how that subject is presented to us.

When we read a moving image text such as film or television, we not only look at the form and the content, but also the way the film is put together—the camera movement, the sound and the editing.

Tools for still image texts

The **form** is the shape of the text and the way it appears before us.

Form: The shape of the text and the way it appears before us.

Components of the form

- *Frame:* what is the size of the image and how has the image been presented?
  - Has the image been cropped or cut?
  - Why have particular elements been cut out?
  - Where is the centre of the image?
  - Does the important part of the image fill the frame, or is it alone in the centre of the frame?
  - Does this make the image dominant or isolated?
- *Lens type:* which lens has been used to shoot the image?
  - A telephoto lens can signify voyeurism, giving the impression that you are seeing something you shouldn't see.
  - A standard lens can signify normality, placing the audience at ease.
  - A wide angle lens can signify drama, placing the audience in a state of anticipation.
- *Film stock:* is it a digital shot or a shot created on film stock?
  - Think about why the producer of the image has made the choice they have.
  - Has the image been shot digitally so it can be manipulated in some way?
  - 'Fast film' and 'slow film' are terms that refer to the speed at which the film stock responds to the light. A fast film stock produces a grainy, documentary look that can

appear unguarded and real. A slow film stock produces a high resolution image that can appear more normal.

- *Camera angle:* how has the image been shot?
  - Are you looking up at the figure (implying a low camera angle) or are you looking down at the figure (implying a high camera angle)? Low angles often reinforce the power of the figure on the screen; high angles may signify subservience.
  - For drawings or pieces of art, you can substitute the words point of view for camera angle.
- *Height:* at what height was the shot taken?
  - Is the shot taken higher or lower than how you would normally view this image?
  - Does it encourage you to look at the image in a certain way? Does it, for example, offer a child's-eye view of the world or a bird's-eye view of the world? (The most common height is eye level, which is just under 2 metres.)
- *Level:* what level was the camera when the shot was taken?
  - Usually, this will be straight on (0°), but altering the level of the camera can create a feeling of disorder, unease or chaos.
- *Distance:* what distance is the object from the camera?
  - *Extreme long shots* are for landscapes or aerial photography.
  - *Long shots* (for groups of people) are for setting a scene; that is, placing subjects into a context.
  - *Medium shots* (one or two people) place members of the audience at a safe distance to observe without feeling as though they are intruding.
  - *Medium close-ups* (part of body) focus the audience's attention on something important.
  - *Close-ups* (face) place the audience in an intimate relationship with the subject, usually signifying an emotional moment.
  - *Extreme close-ups* (part of face) can, conversely, create distance by making something familiar appear strange.
- *Depth of field:* what was the focus range of the shot?
  - *Deep focus* (where the whole scene is in focus) is an expressive technique by which the entire content of the shot becomes unnatural and strange. All parts of the content (or *mise-en-scène*; see below) add to this.
  - *Selective focus* (where some parts of the shot remain indistinct) signifies what is important in a shot.
  - *Soft focus* (where the shot appears fuzzy or somewhat indistinct) can signify nostalgia in the form of a flashback, a dream state, romance or glamour.

Components of the content

Content: The subject of the text, and how that subject is presented to us.

The **content** is what is actually inside the frame: the subject of the text and how that subject is presented to us. In film, this is often referred to as the *mise-en-scène* (French for 'put on stage').

- *The subject(s):* What was the focus of the shot?
- *The setting:* What was the background (an indication of the physical and temporal location for the shot)?

- *The lighting:* How was the shot lit? Lighting often signifies mood. High-key lighting can indicate optimism, low-key lighting can indicate a sombre mood, back lighting can create a halo effect around an actor, making him or her appear glamorous, fill lighting can appear natural and a lack of fill lighting can highlight the contrast between light and dark, something particularly common in the film noir genre.
  - Be aware of where the lighting is coming from (above, behind or in front).
  - Be aware of whether the lighting is of equal intensity (which is unlikely), and think about why certain elements are better lit than others.
  - Be aware of where the light is supposed to be coming from: is this because natural light is being used, or is the lighting being used to convey a certain mood?

Tools for moving-image texts

For moving-image texts, in addition to looking at form and content, also look at the following:

- *Camera movement:* How was the camera moving? Why was this decision made? How did it position the audience in relation to the subject?
  - *Pan* is where the camera moves horizontally from a fixed position, to enable the audience to survey an area or follow a subject at a distance.
  - *Tracking (or dolly) shot* is where the camera moves on tracks (a very smooth movement), positioning members of the audience so they can follow a movement from a close proximity.
  - *Tilt* is where the camera moves to the left or right, enabling an audience to follow a movement up and down.
  - *Crane shot* is where the camera moves up or down, ultimately, a helicopter shot, signifying drama through the rapidity of the movement towards or away from the subject.
  - *Handheld* is the shaky documentary style that can appear natural or create a point-of-view shot.
  - *Zoom* involves altering the focal length of a shot to bring us closer to an object. A zoom in enables the audience to see detail from a distance, akin to a telephoto lens. A zoom out places the subject into context.
- *Sound:* Where was the sound coming from, and why might was it used in this way?
  - *Diegetic sound* comes from within the film shot, such as somebody talking or somebody singing, a gunshot from a gun, a tyre bursting or a laser firing.
  - *Extradiegetic sound* comes from outside the film shot. It is only on the soundtrack; it has no obvious source in the diegesis of the film (the world of the film). Music is often extradiegetic, and signifies an emotional state; in a horror film, for example, it can signify tension, imminent peril or a madman with a very big knife standing just behind you.
- *Editing:* How was the film cut and put together (creating the illusion of continuous motion)?
  - *Montage* is the compression of time and space through the juxtaposition of a series of images. Why are the scenes being cut in this way? What does the juxtaposition of these images signify?
  - *The 180-degree rule* establishes an axis of action that shows us where the characters are (for example, the two shot, shot–reverse shot and establishing shot).

- *The cut:* How does a particular cut (or edit) highlight a particular scene or signify a change in mood between scenes?
  - *Fade-out* is a fade to black as the scene ends.
  - *Fade-in* is the reverse of a fade-out.
  - *Dissolve* is where a second shot fades in, superimposed over the first shot.
  - *Wipe* is where it appears as if a curtain has come across the screen.

Tools for analysing written texts

Written texts include books, magazines, newspapers, phone messages and captions for images. The following tools enable written texts to be analysed in terms of their individual components (content analysis) and for their contributions to wider social and cultural ideas (discourse analysis) (also see Chapter 10).

While content analysis and discourse analysis are usually applied to written texts, there is no reason why they could not also be applied to image texts. You could do a content analysis based on the frequency of John Wayne's appearances in film westerns of the 1950s, the frequency of underweight models in the pages of a fashion magazine or interviews on current affairs television programs about Indigenous communities.

Content analysis

Content analysis: Analysis that focuses on the frequency of the presence or absence of words or categories within texts.

Content analysis is a type of textual analysis that focuses on the frequency of presence or absence of certain words or categories within texts, often involving the estimation of how often a word, phrase or name recurs in the media.

Content analysis can inform a study of representation. If, for example, you were studying the impact of Al Gore's documentary *An Inconvenient Truth* on people's perceptions of climate change, you could count and list how many times *An Inconvenient Truth* appeared in news reports. Furthermore, you could list how many times the words 'climate change' appeared in print before and after the release of the film.

Content analysis is a unique form of textual analysis, in that it can be used by itself as a quantitative measure, or as part of a larger textual analysis once you have completed your content analysis, you can then look at how meaning is made by breaking down the texts where the relevant terms appear. It has the advantage of requiring precise research objectives and sample sizes, but at the same time can be a subjective measure as the researcher develops his or her own categories for research. This is, though, frequently limited by time and budget, so content analysis is best used in a pilot study, in conjunction with detailed textual analysis or audience research that can demonstrate how frequency relates to how meaning is made.

Discourse analysis

Discourse analysis: Analyses how texts support or subvert overall views of the world, such as patriarchy or media power.

Discourse analysis is a specific form of textual analysis that focuses on the ways in which media texts support or subvert such aspects of the world as the unequal distribution of power in society, or the legitimisation or subversion of one presentation of the world (white or patriarchal, for example) while excluding others (African, queer or feminist, for example). In the context of journalism studies, discourse analysis has been rigorously applied to journalistic texts such as British newspapers to explore how the routine practices of journalism, and the interdependence of news reports and interviews on government reports and press releases, help legitimate certain positions at the expense of others. Elements that scholars have looked at include the choice of words, the tense and the expert voice used in stories on riots, youth issues and Indigenous issues.

Discourse analysis, therefore, focuses on the way texts work together to provide certain ways of representing the world. It works best on a sample of texts, rather than individual texts, looking at the intertextual relationship between these texts and the larger ideas of representing the world that are produced as a result. But as it requires a sample, it is also subject to the same accusations as content analysis; that is, it can be used in a subjective way. Discourse analysis is best applied in tandem with some more detailed individual textual analysis to demonstrate how the production of discourse affects how meaning is made.

Conclusion

Using textual analysis as a toolkit to analyse media should enable you to make educated guesses about how media texts function and the meanings that can be derived, a skill that is as necessary for the work of journalists, writers and public relations campaigners as it is for media producers and students of media. Use it frequently and have fun with it, and it will soon enable you to move from being a consumer of media to an educated consumer of media, and then to a skilled media practitioner in your own right.

KEY REFERENCES

Hartley, J. (1999). *Uses of Television.* London: Routledge.

McKee, A. (2003). *Textual Analysis: A Beginner's Guide.* London: Sage.

Thwaites, T., Davis, L. & Mules, W. (2002). *Introducing Cultural and Media Studies: A Semiotic Approach.* Basingstoke: Palgrave.

PART 4

MAKING NEWS

News is new information. It is the start of the dialogue, the introduction of new information into the mediasphere. In Part 4 we consider how news is made. We look at news values and news culture, how news is selected and the culture of the newsroom, before turning to the specifics of broadcast news, subediting, news language and convention and specialist reporting.

Case Study 4: Uncovering Maralinga shows the specialised skills and Fourth Estate ethos that led to the breaking of one of Australia's most significant hidden stories, the long-lasting plutonium contamination at the Maralinga nuclear test range in South Australia.

Tools 4: Writing Features provides the knowhow needed to bring together the strands of journalistic endeavour we have looked at to date, to produce high-quality journalistic writing in the longer and more creative formats of features.

CHAPTER 12

NEWS VALUES AND NEWS CULTURE IN A CHANGING WORLD

SARAH GILLMAN

Introduction

There is an old French proverb, *Plus ca change, plus c'est la meme chose*, which translated into English means 'The more things change, the more they stay the same'.

In recent years, the production of news in Australia has been undergoing significant change due to technological developments and changes in news culture. And yet, despite these changes, journalists and other professionals working in the media, such as photographers, camera operators, editors, producers and researchers, are still using core criteria to determine what information is newsworthy and how it will be covered. Even those news producers such as bloggers, tweeters and online writers operating outside the mainstream media use the same basic criteria known as **news values**.

News values: Criteria that the media apply to determine if and what information will be produced as news, including impact, proximity, prominence, human interest, novelty, conflict and currency.

In this chapter we look at:

- defining news
- news values
- news culture and newsroom socialisation
- news discourse, narratives and framing
- gatekeeping and agenda setting
- how news values remain a consistent guide in a changing media landscape.

Defining news

Think about the term 'news'. How do you define news? Perhaps you think of it as being a piece of information that you didn't know about before. But then you might say to yourself: 'Well, so what? Just because I didn't know something before or just because something is new doesn't make it newsworthy to me.' In other words, just because information is previously unknown, it is not necessarily enough to make you sit back and take notice of it. So think about a piece of information that does do that. How is it different? What factors contribute to making it interesting and noteworthy and perhaps something you'd pass on in conversation with your friends? Is it a piece of information about someone you know, for example? Or is it about where you live? Does it have a direct impact on your life? Are there consequences for you as a result of receiving this information? Does it involve conflict? Or is it just a bit weird and unusual? Now think about a piece of information that stops you in your tracks. What elements does it contain? Does it combine several or all of these elements?

Just like you, journalists and media professionals ask similar questions about information they receive. They apply news values.

News values

The most cited journal article on news values was produced by Norwegian academics Galtung and Ruge (1981). Interestingly, they did not set out to produce a form guide to news values, but uncovered a set of criteria they argued helped to explain why and how information became news stories. Since then, there have been a number of studies undertaken of news, newsrooms and media professionals to assess what criteria are used to judge whether something becomes a news story. The results reveal a general consensus on key characteristics. Despite some minor variations that go to the actual terms used, they show that professionals working in news apply the following characteristics to pieces of information to decide whether they are newsworthy:

- impact
- proximity
- prominence
- human interest
- novelty
- conflict
- currency.

Impact

One of the first values that journalists and media professionals apply to a potential news story is **impact**. What are the consequences of this piece of information? The greater the impact or the wider and deeper the consequences, the bigger the story will be. A big story is one that captures attention and comes to dominate the top of bulletins and front pages of newspapers. As we'll see, the concept of a big news story is undergoing some transformation due to changes in news production, culture and consumption, but to understand what journalists mean when they use the term 'big', think about an event you are probably familiar with: the 2009 Victorian bushfires. This event had significant impact or consequence for the people directly and immediately affected by the fires: 173 people died, 414 people were injured and many others lost their homes. Buildings were destroyed, along with stock, other animals and forest. The fires also had significant impact for people living throughout the state of Victoria, as everything from the air quality to resources were affected. Afterwards, the

Impact: The size of the consequences of a news story: the greater or wider the consequences for society of a news story; the greater will be its impact.

Victorian government established a royal commission to investigate the causes and responses to the bushfires. The commission's findings and recommendations have also had an impact, not just in Victoria but also on fire services and government agencies across Australia via changes to regulations on warning systems and the coordination of emergency services. The impact of a news story can be defined as the strength of its effect on a society. As with all the values that are applied in determining news, measuring the impact of a piece of information can change when combined with the other values, such as proximity.

Proximity

Proximity relates to the place where an event is happening. Information often becomes newsworthy if it is about something happening in the immediate vicinity or close to where the media are producing news and to where audiences are consuming it. Proximity relates to the idea that we notice or care about things that relate to our own environment. For example, a story about a bushfire will be extremely newsworthy to people living in the vicinity, but may have less newsworthiness to people who live thousands of kilometres away. However, as the Victorian bushfires show, when the event escalates and people die, hundreds of houses are destroyed and everyday living is disrupted, there is greater impact and so its reach or conceptual sense of being nearby extends. New media technology such as the internet and satellite communication means that news events happening at a distance appear to be closer to us than ever before, because we are provided with up-to-the-minute information. Proximity originally reflects the concept that if information is happening in our environment, then it is likely to impact on us or involve people we know. This touches on another value, prominence.

Proximity: The distance of the news event from the audience: the closer the proximity of news to the environment of the person absorbing a news story, the greater the impact of the news item.

Prominence

When journalists and media professionals are assessing information to determine its newsworthiness, they check to see whether it involves people who are well known. **Prominence** may be measured on a variety of levels, from the very local to the international. Traditionally, information regarding significant people within a society, such as political leaders, has become news because their actions can impact on many others. When the prime minister makes announcements, for example, they are reported because they will have some level of impact on us. But prominence also demonstrates that names make news. Prominence as a news value has been significantly influenced in recent years by the rise of celebrity in our society (see Chapter 11). While the antics of an individual celebrity may not impact on us at all, the information becomes newsworthy because it is about someone who is prominent. Interestingly, when the media confers celebrity status on someone, he or she is subsequently deemed to be prominent and potentially newsworthy. Following the 2006 Beaconsfield Mine Rescue in Tasmania, the two rescued miners, Todd Russell and Brant Webb, were elevated to celebrity status in the media. News reports provided us with information about their personal lives that wasn't specifically connected to their work as miners or the plight they had endured. Subsequently, as their media profile expanded, they became prominent and other things they did were judged newsworthy. The two miners as news names continue to be contacted for

Prominence: The likely impact of a news item, according to whether the person in the news is already well known.

comment about stories such as the successful 2010 rescue of thirty-three trapped Chilean miners. We can better understand the change in the way prominence is being applied as a news value by looking at another value, human interest.

Human interest

Human interest news: News stories that revolve around stories of ordinary people, or issues judged to be socially interesting or important.

Human interest stories revolve around stories of ordinary people, or issues that journalists and media professionals decide are socially interesting or important. Often they can be called colour stories, soft news or features, and will be used to provide a human face to a harder, more complex story. Every year after the federal treasurer brings down the Budget, the media carry reports about how the Budget will impact on 'ordinary people'. This provides a human interest element to the drier financial and political news of this story. Human interest news stories also tend to give us glimpses into the experiences of other people, to publicise their achievements or their difficulties, enabling us to compare and measure our own status and well-being. Just as celebrity has impacted on the value of prominence, it has tended to elevate human interest as a news value in some cases. When, for example, the 2005 London bombings happened, the media provided stories about the Australians who were injured and killed. These stories included information that personalised the tragedy. In many ways, journalists and media professionals working in the fast-paced global world of news find it easier to produce human interest stories because they don't usually require long periods of investigative reporting or many resources. They can be produced by turning interviews into stories that carry to audiences around the world. Often, human interest as a news value is coupled with another value, novelty.

Novelty

Novelty news: News that reveals rare, unusual or bizarre information.

Information that reveals something that is rare, unusual or even bizarre is potentially newsworthy. **Novelty** as a news value reflects information that is noteworthy, which attracts attention and provides a talking point (of the 'Man Lifts Forklift Truck' variety).

Conflict

Conflict: A state of opposition or hostilities. In the context of judgments about what makes news, this might be a significant violent conflict such as a war, or a non-violent conflict such as a disagreement.

Journalists and media professionals consider information potentially newsworthy if it involves **conflict**. This can be a significant violent conflict such as a war, or a non-violent conflict such as a disagreement. Often, conflicts simmer for a time, but when they erupt they have impact and consequence, and so attract attention. Conflict as a news value is connected to our basic need for security and well-being. Some of the earliest forms of what we can define as journalism are about wars and battles. These early forms also relay stories about disasters such as earthquakes and floods that involve people battling natural phenomena, or otherwise being in conflict with nature. Conflict, then, involves information that creates uncertainty or has an uncertain outcome. If you study the words, pictures and sounds of news, you will notice that conflict also underpins a lot of the language used in news. You may also find examples of how a sense of conflict is created by journalist and media professionals. A 'War in the Boardroom' headline, for example, usually doesn't mean that company directors launched missiles and grenades at each other, but it probably points to a major disagreement they had. Similarly, when one cricket team 'destroys' another's attack, it's unlikely to be a literal report of the match but a metaphorical one, using words and images to create drama and conflict.

Currency

Finally, in terms of news values, journalists and media professionals assess whether information given to them is current. **Currency** as a news value relates to information that is currently being discussed as news. If, for example, information about internet crime comes to light, it can generate more news stories because both the media and the public's awareness of, and interest in, the issue/s are heightened. Think of a time when you've learnt the meaning of a new word. Often, straight afterwards, you seem to see it everywhere. A similar thing can happen in the media. When a topic is the focus of a story, the currency of it can generate subsequent stories. Currency also often arises from news stories that provoke controversial and emotional reactions. When a crime has been committed, for example, it can often be the subject of public discourse, in some cases prompting calls for changes to the law. Stories will be produced that background the development of the law, and give voice to the various sides of the debate while it remains a current focus of attention.

Currency of news: The impact of recent and breaking news arising from controversial and emotionally charged events.

At this point you are probably starting to assess these values for yourself and you might notice that they can be qualified and there is no specific order to their application. News values are not fixed. Instead, news values are relative and fluid, that is, they are applied and assessed against each other and often in various combinations. For example, a conflict may be far away but involve prominent people, or an event may be about ordinary people doing something unusual. Every day in newsrooms, journalists and other media professionals debate whether information is newsworthy, both informally among themselves and in formal editorial conferences. However, when something happens that journalists and media professionals assess as encompassing many or all of the news values, then it is judged to be a big story and can develop into a **media event**.

Media event: A news story that becomes a historically important communication event, interrupting the flow of all other news.

Using Dayan and Katz's (1994) definition, a media event is a news story that can be described as a historical mass communication event. Coverage interrupts the normal flow of news as media outlets dedicate staff, resources and space to generating material about the event. Many media events are pre-planned, such as royal weddings and federal elections, but increasingly, with the aid of new technology, media events can arise from unexpected events such as the 9/11 attacks on New York and Washington in 2001, the London bombings in 2005 or the Japanese earthquake and tsunami in 2011. Bromley (2005: 313) describes this splurge journalism as 'the instant, sweeping coverage of major events'. **Splurge journalism** has been aided and abetted by technical developments, but even when deciding how to cover these events, and indeed whether to actually cover them at all, journalists and other media professionals still rely on the application of news values.

Splurge journalism: The up-to-the-minute, immediate saturation coverage of major events.

News values, then, not only determine whether a piece of information becomes a news story, but also how it will be covered, who constructs the news story and where, and how it will appear in a newspaper, news bulletin or web page. In assessing news values, journalists and media professionals apply the basic criteria of who, what, where, when, why and how.

News values are a model for processing information to assess newsworthiness. If you think about how you process information given to you, you will notice you make subjective judgments about it, that is, you make decisions about how to process the information based on your individual experiences and understanding of the world. The way you process information will be different from someone else. And you will change the way you process information as you experience more of life and develop connections with other individuals.

When we look at news values, then, we can begin to see that news is a product resulting from a series of processes and these processes involve the application of commonly and broadly shared values. To quote one newspaper editor:

> We make choices about which facts and quotes to use, and we make choices about the order in which we use them. We make choices of emphasis. We make choices in the layout about which stories get prominence and which stories get length. Those choices are based on our training and our experience and our individual views of the world. (Kirkman 1999)

As a model, news values provide a framework by which those producing news can select newsworthy information and process it into stories. It also ensures that news can be produced. It's highly unlikely that any contemporary newsroom would announce, as the BBC did in 1930, that 'there is no news tonight' (Bell 1991: 1).

News culture and newsroom socialisation

How are news values learnt and developed? Traditionally, they have been fostered in newsrooms through the socialisation of journalists and other media professionals. The process of socialisation occurs when members of a group learn and adopt commonly shared customs, attitudes and values. We all undergo periods of **socialisation** throughout our lives. Think about how you learnt to fit in at high school or worked out how to behave in a job. Similarly, think about how your behaviour and beliefs change in different circumstances. If you play sport, for example, you might find your actions and language are slightly different from when you are attending a family get-together. Through this process of socialisation we are acculturated, that is, we learn and take on the characteristics of a specific culture.

Socialisation: The process by which individuals are embedded into a culture, therefore learning, absorbing and practising particular characteristics of that culture.

News culture: The predominating attitudes and behaviours that characterise the operations of newsrooms and media organisations.

The socialisation of journalists and other media professionals embeds them into **news culture**, which we can define as the predominating attitudes and behaviours that characterise the operations of newsrooms and media organisations. Journalists and other media professionals adopt the patterns and beliefs of their respective industries and institutions. For example, a journalist or camera operator with Channel Seven's *Sunrise* program might have slightly different views on what a news story is, and how it should be pursued and presented, from someone working at the *Financial Review*. This reflects their embedding into a particular news culture. Traditionally, in Australia, news has been produced on the basis of a hierarchical and bureaucratic system, with newsrooms generally having a chain of command to process information into news stories. This has been a powerful force in socialising new recruits into news culture. In fact, it has meant the production of news culture starts before new recruits join the newsroom. The selection criteria used to determine who gets a cadetship or a job in itself reflects previous socialisation and shows the ongoing influence of news culture. Tapsall and Varley (2001) undertook a survey of experienced Australian journalists to find out what skill and attributes were needed to work as a journalist:

> Based on 'Definition: Journalist' survey responses, the top skills and attributes identified as necessary for a contemporary Australian journalist (in rank order) are:
>
> - communication skills
> - a questioning, curious, and inquisitive mind
> - writing abilities
> - news sense
> - knowledge of computers, technology literate
> - listening skills
> - general knowledge
> - empathy, patience and understanding
> - a sense of working for more than self (the notion of a public responsibility)
> - language skills
> - interviewing skills.
>
> Other abilities mentioned—far less frequently than those above—include the ability to meet deadlines, thinking/knowledge analysis skills, resourcefulness and persistence, truthfulness, accuracy and integrity. (Tapsall & Varley 2001: 11)

Since the survey was done in 1998, there have been significant developments in media technology. News is produced around the clock across multiple outlets or platforms, and yet editors and others responsible for recruiting cadet journalists and media trainees still look for recruits who display similar characteristics listed by Tapsall and Varley. If you think about some of the attributes and skills identified, then you will notice that many of them require a degree of subjectivity in judging whether a potential recruit has them. This judgment again reflects socialisation into news culture.

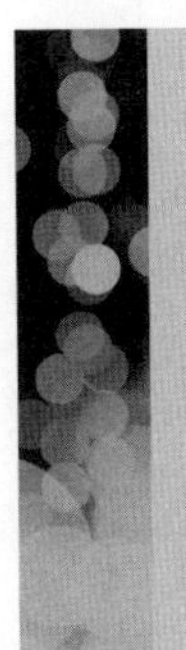

Socialisation and news culture

Socialisation produces news culture that is learnt and refined via:

- education (such as the study of journalism and media at university)
- training
- cadetships
- contacts
- immersion into particular rounds
- social relationships with colleagues
- assignment of roles within newsrooms
- promotion of positions within news organisations.

News culture produces news values, which are expressed in the selection of information as stories, which are produced in a narrative form using news language or discourse. You might want to think about how new technology and news platforms such as social media and online journalism are impacting on this, and on what you consume as news.

Discourse and narratives

News discourse: The way in which news professionals express ideas in written and spoken language, including their evaluation of such elements as newsworthiness.

Hard news: News that aims to inform the community about events and happenings and to provide citizens with the information they require to be able to participate as fully informed citizens in the democratic process.

Soft news: News (sometimes called infotainment) that does not have a high priority in the news values scale, and encompasses such fields as entertainment, sport, lifestyle, human interest, celebrity and the arts.

News story: Information packaged in order to afford maximum readability, either in the pattern of beginning–middle–end, or in the inverted pyramid pattern of most important–slightly less important–least important.

News culture produces a **news discourse**. Discourse is the way we express ideas in written and spoken language. Journalists and other media professionals regard information as newsworthy when they can talk of it using news terms such as *story*, *lead* and *angle*. News discourse reflects news values that are applied to also determine whether a story is **hard news** or **soft news**.

In newsrooms, information using news discourse is framed within narratives, so we get the term **news story**. Information is packaged into a format with a beginning, a middle and an end, even if the beginning and end are not conclusive. This narrative style of news reflects the way we generally tend to process information. Think about the way you pass on information to friends. It probably follows a pattern—a hook to grab their attention, some background to make sure they know who or what you are talking about, and then some detail, with a conclusion of sorts. This is narrative style. When information is not conveyed in a general narrative style, it can be frustrating and difficult to understand. There's nothing worse than being subjected to a conversation that seems to start mid-sentence and assumes you know all the previous information required to make sense of it. News stories tend to follow a narrative pattern that news consumers can understand and expect. In media and cultural studies, this is described as encoding and decoding texts (see Chapter 9). Journalists and media professionals encode information into news stories and news consumers decode them. At the encoding stage, journalists and other media professionals apply news values to turn information into news (although, as we'll discuss, changes to the way producers of news and news consumers interact are changing this flow of information).

Framing

Framing: The process of selecting and rejecting information in the process of constructing a news story and placing emphasis on a particular aspect or angle.

The way journalists and other media professionals create a news story is regarded as **framing**. One way to understand this is to think about the way in which photographers frame pictures. Obviously, when they look at a scene, there are many angles and ingredients present, but by focusing on, and capturing, a particular aspect of the scene, they apply framing and consequently represent a version of reality. In a similar way, journalists and other media professionals processing information into news stories select a particular approach, or frame, that can be reflected in a headline or lead (introduction). Essentially, framing provides a context for news consumers to comprehend information in a particular way. Framing also enables news consumers to control or manage the information provided to us, because it is set out within limits, just like a frame contains a photo or picture. Journalists and other media professionals again use news values to frame stories as they decide what information to include and exclude, and what aspects should be emphasised over others.

Structuring and framing information into news stories mean that journalists and other media professionals are able to determine the news agenda.

News agenda

The **news agenda** operates on four main levels:

News agenda: The influence of news providers on the way members of the public and people in power absorb and react to public events.

- It influences what we talk about in general conversation as a result of consuming news.
- It influences how we react to events and information.
- It influences how stakeholders (people with an interest in a particular development) will react.
- It influences how other journalists and other media professionals produce information as news.

Gatekeeping and agenda setting

If you've lived on or visited a farm, you'll know the significance of closing gates (or perhaps forgetting to close them and letting animals escape). By selectively opening and closing information gates, journalists and other media professionals decide what information becomes news. Every day, newsrooms and individual journalists and media professionals receive huge amounts of information that is potentially newsworthy. Not all of it becomes news. News values are applied to determine what information is selected, what is rejected and what importance it will be given in the overall output. As a result, journalists and media professionals have been described as **gatekeepers**.

Gatekeeper: Media professional, such as a subeditor, who decides which news stories or other types of information will be selected or rejected for public consumption.

Tiffin (1986) argues that news values result from three influences: audiences, formats and competition. As audiences change the way they consume news, as new formats develop and others become redundant, and as competition for news and audiences increases, news values reflect these changes that impact on their application in the production of news. As Tiffin notes:

> The content of news values is not subject to explicit codification. At any one time, ideas about newsworthiness are a response to presumptions about current audience interest, to the mutual monitoring and shoptalk that accompany the industry's competitive ethos, and to the agendas of major sources. Reporting is shaped by understood formats

> of presentation and organisational priorities and by a shared sense, no matter how vague and shifting in its foundations and how commonly breached, of the rules of fair reporting, and the proper role of news. (Tiffen 1986: 68.)

New influences and challenges

Over the past decade, news production, culture and consumption in Australia have undergone major changes. News is now produced and available twenty-four hours a day, compiled and sent by professionals and non-professionals with the assistance of, for example, the internet, digital cameras and mobile phones (see Chapter 19). Professional journalists are increasingly required to be multiskilled—to know how to capture images, write text, edit stories, to file for their own organisations as well as overseas outlets and still try to find an exclusive angle.

Technological and social changes mean news organisations are relying more on content produced by non-professionals. Most media organisations now solicit content from non-media people that can directly influence the news agenda, or what we see, read and hear about in our media. Examples of this content include amateur images of the Queensland floods and the Victorian bushfires, as well as the demonstrations in Egypt, by mobile phones. New collaborative online sites such as TAO of Journalism allow web users to submit story ideas and, in some cases, to act as co-editors. Others canvass the 'your story' style of information that is bought and turned into traditional tabloid news. Individual bloggers and tweeters can also generate news, which is picked up by mainstream outlets.

New technology also facilitates the very fast collection and dissemination of pictures, often close-up photos of high quality. For many media outlets, this graphic revolution means that images have become more important in news than words and ideas. The tabloidisation of news enforces this. When Australian beauty therapist Schapelle Corby was sentenced to prison for drug smuggling in Bali in 2005, many newspapers and web pages simply carried the news with a large close-up photo of her face and two words: 'Twenty Years'. The challenge is to ensure that what is being reproduced and published (or broadcast) at such a fast pace is in fact authentic.

One of the defining images of the 2009 Victorian bushfires was the video of Sam the Koala being given a drink by fireman David Tree. It went around the world, but turned out to actually have been taken the week before the worst of the Black Saturday bushfires. Similarly, in 2009, Sydney resident Clare Werbeloff duped Channel Nine and its viewers about a shooting in Kings Cross. Footage of Werbeloff portrays her as an eyewitness, retelling audiences what happened. Her colourful language subsequently saw the grab uploaded onto YouTube, where she quickly became known as the 'chk chk boom girl'. She attracted greater attention when she revealed she'd made the whole thing up.

Commodification of news: The view that news is a commodity that can be valued, and bought and sold like any other good in the marketplace, reflecting the globalisation and deregulation of news.

Many former and current media professionals, as well as academics, argue that journalism is in a state of crisis, that external factors have led to increasing **commodification of news**: news can be treated like any other good for sale and can be given an economic weight that reflects how much money it generates and how much it costs to produce. Investigative journalism, for example, can be time consuming and expensive, and while it can produce important and new information, many media outlets have cut back on funding it. Instead, they're opting for news that is cheaper to obtain and attracts immediate attention, or relying on mass-produced wire copy and media releases—or **churnalism**. Allan (2005) says the commodification of news has seen a subtle osmosis of corporate interests influencing news content and values. Information that aims to promote these interests is dressed up as news and blurs the line between cross-promotion, advertising and news. One example of this was when the Seven Television Network's news programs reported the death of the fictional Mel Rafter from the popular *Packed to the Rafters* program, which also screens on Seven. Mel 'died' in a car accident when she went through a stop sign while looking at her mobile phone. In some news items, this was the news hook—a warning to not use mobile phones while driving. This suggests that, even in these cases, media professionals are applying traditional news values to translate this infotainment into a news item.

Churnalism: A term coined by British journalist Nick Davies to describe the way media rely on media releases, public relations and wire copy for most content.

Fairclough (1995) argues these developments are further refined via the **conversationalisation** of news language—in other words, while most news is by nature public, much of it is consumed in private places, especially broadcast and online news. Conversational news language helps blur the line between news and entertainment, between checked and sourced news, and between fact and gossip.

Conversationalisation of news: The way the language of news is structured to mirror ordinary conversation, blurring the boundary between the public and private and reflecting the fact that while most news is public in nature, much of it, especially broadcast and online news, is consumed in private domains such as lounge rooms.

Conclusion

As new technology influences how news is generated, how it is made public and how it is consumed, the debate about what news values are will continue. There will be ongoing discussion about what really influences the production of a news story—which brings us back to the old French saying. However the wording might change, or the context of actually utilising them in practice, the key news values outlined in this chapter will continue to be the pivotal influence on how news is selected and shaped. Think again about how you decide whether information given to you can be defined as news. Even if you receive this information via new technology such as a text message on a mobile phone, or from an interactive blog, you will decide on its newsworthiness by applying criteria that resemble the news values that media professionals use to decide what and how information becomes news.

KEY REFERENCES

Bell, A. (1999). *The Language of News Media.* Oxford: Blackwell.

Bromley, M. (2005). 'Subterfuge as Public Service: Investigative Journalism as Idealised Journalism'. In S. Allen (ed.) *Journalism: Critical Issues.* Maidenhead: Open University Press.

Dayan, D. & Katz, E. (1994). *Media Events: The Live Broadcasting of History.* Cambridge MA: Harvard University Press.

Tiffin, R. (1989). *News and Power.* Sydney: Allen & Unwin.

SARAH GILLMAN

WEBSITES

Australian Press Council: <www.presscouncil.org.au>

Cyberjournalist.net: <www.cyberjournalist.net>

Journalism Education Association of Australia: <www.jeaa.org.au>

Media, Entertainment and Arts Alliance:<www.alliance.org.au>

TAO of Journalism: <www.taoofjournalism.org>

CHAPTER 13

BROADCAST NEWS: KEEP IT SIMPLE

LIZ TYNAN

Introduction

One of the defining characteristics of the broadcast media is its immediacy: its drive to be on the spot and first with the sound and pictures from wherever news is breaking. This places pressure on broadcast journalists to work quickly, because stories can move quickly, and journalists don't want their work to look dated. The two dominant broadcast media, radio and television, are mass media capable of bringing the news almost instantly to a mass audience, supplemented increasingly by the internet. The broadcast media also provide a crucial source of news for millions of people. While radio and television have some obvious differences, they have more in common with each other than they do with print. This chapter is most concerned with writing broadcast news, rather than the specific technicalities of, for example, television visuals or radio audio editing. The first thing, and often the hardest thing, that must be mastered in broadcast media is the writing style. This chapter will help you through that process.

In this chapter we look at:

- what broadcast news is
- the transformation of print style to broadcast style
- the notion of signposting
- good broadcast journalism practice, including pacing, scripting and style.

What is broadcast news?

On radio, brief broadcast news items are usually packaged into regular hourly news bulletins. While important breaking stories may go to air at any time, the vast majority of radio news is scheduled into these regular bulletins. Television has its equivalents, usually in the form of the major early evening news shows—generally of a half-hour's duration—and shorter news updates at various times during the day and evening. An army of reporters works around the clock in broadcast media newsrooms creating carefully packaged news vignettes that can be slotted into bulletins and news updates. The range of news covered tends to be more restricted than you will find in a newspaper, mostly because of time restrictions, but also because of the nature of the media involved: undertaking this work successfully involves a broad range of reporting, writing and technical skills, but most critically, an appreciation of the need for speed.

One of the addictive aspects about both radio and television for the journalist is the magic inherent in seeing and hearing one's story on the air, often quite soon after the outline of the story has first formed in your mind. Radio is often somewhat faster than television in getting material to air, but both media are considerably faster than print. Of course, the fastest of all is live broadcast work, which has its own pressures and rewards. This chapter is most concerned with the work of the broadcast reporter who writes scripts and prepares recorded packages for news bulletins.

Broadcast reporters must have robust writing skills and a poised manner. They must be able to produce lots of super-brief and correct prose in ridiculously tight timeframes. It is not unusual for a professional radio journalist to produce eight to ten stories in one eight-hour shift; the television journalist produces fewer due to the greater technical requirements, such as filming and video editing, which are more time-consuming than audio recording and editing. Another advantage for radio journalists is that they can obtain their raw materials from broadcast-quality telephone interviews. A journalist may certainly get out into the field to interview someone—for example, at a protest rally or a bushfire—but a lot of interviewing for radio is carried out by telephone. By contrast, a television reporter will usually be required to go out with a crew to get footage of various kinds before heading back to the studio to create a script and edit the story.

Helpful qualities in a broadcast journalist

All news journalists, no matter which medium they work in, must show impartiality, a nose for news, insatiable curiosity and a sense of ethics. In the broadcast media it also helps to have the following characteristics:

- grace under pressure
- the ability to think on your feet
- a sense of urgency
- large reserves of energy
- an ability to switch quickly between different topics
- an affinity with technology
- the talent to conceptualise a broadcast story as an audio and/or video package
- a capacity for heightened and critical use of one's ears (for radio) and eyes (for television) to ensure that the audio and visuals work.

One of the things that sets broadcast news apart from print is its writing style. You have to get used to extreme brevity, which is a hard thing to do. It means having a news sense so finely honed that you can pick the obvious broadcast news angle immediately, and write about it in a brief but still engaging and conversational way. You can't elaborate much in broadcast. You have to find the essential feature of the story and go with that, leaving out anything extraneous.

Broadcast journalists should always be good writers, within the specific broadcast idiom. There are several features that broadcast news shares with other forms of news writing. The most important three are:

- accuracy
- clarity
- completeness.

Accuracy requires solid information, carefully checked and attributed; clarity requires clear, grammatically and stylistically correct English, containing nothing that has listeners scratching their heads, particularly unexplained technical terms; and for completeness the writer should be able to answer the standard Who?, What?, When?, Where?, Why? and How? questions (see Chapter 14). These must be in place in your stories, as they must be in other forms of journalism.

Print versus broadcast writing

Often a journalist starts in print journalism, and then moves over to the electronic media. Similarly, most journalism courses at university begin by teaching print before moving to broadcast. When you make this transition, one of the most difficult things you have to do is change your writing style.

You have to pare things down so much that it sometimes seems that there is not much left at all. You must be able to say what the story is about, with a minimum of words conveying a maximum of information. Your vocabulary and sentence structure have to become not merely simple but also (to some people, at least) simplistic. Keep in mind that most radio news stories are generally between thirty and sixty seconds long, and television news stories only a little longer, maybe as much as 120 seconds.

At three words a second (see 'Pacing' below), your radio story may contain only ninety or 180 words, and your television story no more than 360 words (probably fewer, because you let the pictures do some of the talking). What you write must still be informative and go to the heart of the matter. It must also capture and keep the attention of the listener. Perhaps your biggest challenge will be to ensure that you encapsulate the news comprehensively in as few words as possible.

Your language should be simple and the sentences should (as much as possible) be short. Avoid overly complex sentences with more than two clauses; likewise, avoid unusual vocabulary. Listeners will find it difficult to follow convoluted sentences with lots of long words. Even sentences that would be perfectly acceptable in the print media may be too much for a broadcast audience to take in. This is the consequence of the two quite different forms of sensory perception involved in reading and listening. Consider the following print media lead:

> Studies on the impact and usefulness of a method to extract coconut oil for use as a fuel alternative in South Pacific villages will get underway this year in Fiji, under a grant allocated by the Australian Research Council (ARC).

This is acceptable as a print story lead, and this example comes from a real print news story. But it will not do as a broadcast story lead, which you will notice if you read it out loud.

To begin with, the words 'Studies on the impact' do not set the context sufficiently for the radio listener, so this is not a good signpost (discussed below). Also, it comes to a total of forty words, which is a feasible lead paragraph for a broadsheet newspaper, but too much for radio, where fewer than twenty-five words per sentence is more the norm. It is difficult to say a long sentence with one breath, which is why broadcast sentences are kept short: the person speaking the script has to sound natural and not strained.

This is how we might rewrite the above lead for broadcast:

> Villages in the South Pacific may be able to use coconut oil as fuel, following a study this year in Fiji.

This lead is now twenty-one words. You would add in the detail about the Australian Research Council in the next sentence, or in the voiceover. Note that, in this radio version, you set the context by beginning with 'Villages in the South Pacific', so the listener can get ready for a story on that subject. Listeners don't need to think back to the crucial bit of information that was relayed to them before they were mentally prepared for it. In a sense, you begin your lead with information that is not the most crucial part of the opening paragraph. The scene-setting information leads the listener to the crucial information.

The same story packaged for television not only would have a brief introduction, but also relevant visual images that serve as a powerful signpost to complement the words.

A variety of news outlets

There are significant stylistic differences between the mainstream electronic media outlets in Australia. The ABC has a different news agenda and house style from most of the commercial radio and television stations. The advent of community radio and television has introduced new voices to electronic media news; again, each station has its own way of doing news. Make a point of listening critically to the different electronic news outlets and note the differences and the similarities. As an exercise, listen intently for how different electronic media outlets use verbs, the words that power sentences. See if you can detect any significant differences between the ABC and commercial outlets. (See Chapter 4 for a discussion of the role of verbs.)

Radio demands that its reporters harness the fleeting nature of the medium without being defeated by it. If you don't capture the listener the first time around in your radio script, you have probably lost that person forever. This is a powerful difference from the way print media works if a newspaper reader does not understand something in print, they can read the story again until the meaning is clear. Radio news is ephemeral, so this is not the case. On television, there are pictures to assist the viewer get the meaning, and pictures are very powerful for creating meaning in people's minds—on radio, you are on your own.

When people listen to the radio they are usually doing something else at the same time. Newspapers tend to engage their readers' attention fully, and this is also the case, perhaps to a lesser degree, with television. Radio has to compete for listener attention with many other distractions, such as traffic, children, the work on your computer or the dinner you are cooking.

Those writing for radio must always remember that if a story is not written well enough to be understood the first time, then it's all over. At best, the listener may catch it again in the next bulletin, but only if it is repeated, and this is not always the case.

It requires greater skill to write briefly than to write at length. Precision of language is supremely important in a broadcast news bulletin. Well thought out, clear language is the first requisite, so aim to use language in such a way that the listener does not have to labour to understand; it must sound natural and conversational. The words must be easy to say, so that you don't stumble when recording your voiceovers, and the newsreader doesn't stumble when reading live. While ruthlessly paring back vocabulary can seem authoritarian and even rather Orwellian, there is good reason to select from a small range of short and easy-to-say words, rather than trying to demonstrate a fancy vocabulary and tripping up yourself and the newsreader in the process.

Before recording your voiceovers, read your scripts out loud to yourself (nearly all broadcast journalists do this). It is a good way of picking up problems of delivery that are not apparent on the page. The words on the page may look OK, but only by saying a sentence out loud will you find, for example, a jarring run of alliteration that sounds silly when spoken. In fact, the last phrase of that last sentence probably would sound silly because of a string of words beginning with 's'.

Broadcast journalists conveying the news of the hour should write as if speaking directly to their audience. You are telling a story, not writing text. Avoid being too formal and artificial, but don't jar your listeners by being too casual and sloppy.

Be brief, but be careful

When stories are truncated for electronic media, it's important that they retain their meaning. Brevity serves no purpose if clarity is lost. If the story takes too many words to tell, that's poor broadcast writing, but if it takes so few that it fails to convey meaning, then you might as well not bother.

To break down the differences to an essence: radio is confined within the limits of sound alone. Sound and silence are the only things you have to work with. As long as you keep in mind that your work is going to be heard, and not read, then you will be able to conceptualise, and then implement this approach. On television you are also writing words that are to be spoken, but in addition they must match and complement (not duplicate or clash with) the visual images.

Signposts: Words and sentence structures that show listeners, readers or viewers the context of a story and/or the way in which they should react to it, for example, broadcast news journalists structure their lead stories in such a way as to provide context for the story first before revealing the new thing that has happened.

Signposting

In the world of radio, the ear can only take in so much at a time—and on the radio, sounds just keep coming at you. Radio journalist must learn to give their listeners clues by using what are known as **signposts**, which are simply ways of letting your listeners know the context of the story they are about to hear. They can take various forms, and while they are also useful in television, they are most useful in radio.

Signposts in your scripts

Signposts simply give context in radio. They prepare your listeners for what you are about to say, remind listeners of what has already been said, or provide a **segue** between different contexts.

For instance, a journalist might begin her story with, 'Astrophysicists studying the beginnings of the universe …' Beginning sentences such as this immediately creates a context for what is to come, so the listener can get ready for the content of the story. In this case, listeners will know that the story is going to concern astrophysics so they can mentally prepare for the new information. The second half of the sentence will contain the news, 'have confirmed a key aspect of the Big Bang theory'. Turning it around into a non-signposted story ('A key aspect of the Big Bang theory …') does not provide enough information to prepare a listener for a story on astrophysics.

You should always signpost your radio stories. This often means that you say who is involved in the action before you say what the action is. Again, in the above example, you have broadly identified the 'who'—astrophysicists—before providing the news. The action will be the main point of the story, but the 'who' will often set the scene. If the 'who' of the story is not sufficiently clear in context, then the 'where', such as 'in Canberra' or 'in Iraq', may be able to do the job.

The kind of signposts you might use at the end of a story or between stories might involve restating who has just been speaking (in **actuality** or **voiceover**), for example, 'Meanwhile, in Washington, President Barack Obama says …'.

The essential point to observe in writing for radio is that listeners cannot go back to check what they have missed or forgotten. You have to keep reminding them where you are up to, but do it in a way that is not needlessly and annoyingly repetitive.

Segue: Pronounced *seg*-way; the transition between elements of a broadcast story or show, including the throw that the news reader uses to introduce a pre-recorded package.

Actuality: Location sound, which may sometimes be an interview with talent, and in some newsrooms is used interchangeably with *grab*.

Voiceover, voicer or VO: The recorded voice of the reporter explaining an aspect of the story.

In broadcast, because you are telling a story rather than writing for the constraints of newspaper layout, you are not confined to the strict inverted pyramid construction (discussed in Chapter 2). Telling is more like a conversation, and the inverted pyramid construction in this context could be rather unnatural. Your aim is to tell a story with such clarity that the listener does not have any questions still to ask at the end. Set the scene of every story you write before you say what the news thing is. All stories have a context. Here is a real example from the ABC:

> A United Nations agency warns that two-thirds of the world's population will not have enough water within twenty years.

Note that the 'who', in this case 'a United Nations agency', is established first, before the main point of the story. In this way the listener is prepared for the news itself, and has a better chance of being able to absorb it efficiently. A 'who' signpost, as this example shows, does not have to be a person: it can be an organisation of some kind. It can also be a description of a person. For example, a real radio story about a potential hijacker started like this: 'A Melbourne man who tried to hijack and crash a Qantas plane last year has been found not guilty due to mental impairment.' This is a 'who' description that most listeners will recognise even if they don't know the man's name.

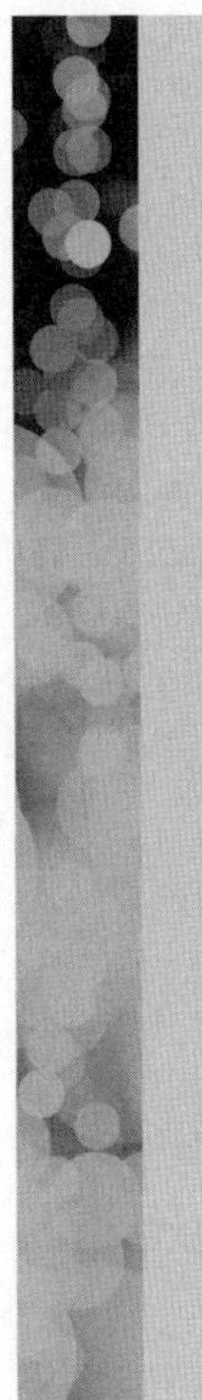

Some possible elements of a broadcast script

While scripting styles can vary enormously, and even the terminology is sometimes used differently in different settings, some things are common to broadcast scripts. These include the following terms:

- **intro or announcer read**: the introductory part of the story, usually read live by the newsreader, and scripted by the reporter
- **throw**: a brief line introducing the person who is about to speak, often the reporter whose voiceover is about to be played
- **grab**: an excerpt of your interview with the talent (or source)
- actuality: sound gathered by a reporter on location or by telephone; it usually refers to an interview with talent and in some newsrooms is used interchangeably with grab
- **outro or back announce**: the announcement made by the live announcer or newsreader after the packaged part of the script is finished
- **timing**: the times allowed in the script for various sound elements: an overall timing for the whole package, and a timing for the pre-recorded part of the package; estimates of how long it will take for the live announcer to say the intro and outro are worked out using the three-words-per-second standard
- **natsound**: natural sound, recorded on location.

So signposts signal to listeners what the story will be about and get them mentally prepared for what is to come. Once you have written your lead, you then take the listener through the rest of the story in the most logical and natural manner possible, repeating key words if necessary to maintain the context.

Intro or announcer read: The introductory part of an electronic media story, usually read live by the newsreader, and scripted by the reporter.

Throw: A brief line introducing the person who is about to speak, often the reporter whose voiceover is about to be played.

Grab: An excerpt of a journalist's interview with the talent (or source).

Outro or back announce: The announcement made by the live announcer or newsreader after the packaged part of an electronic media script has finished.

Good broadcast journalism practice

In broadcast stories, you attribute facts and opinions at all times, as you would in print, but put the attribution first, as in 'Carol Smith says …' It is not natural speech for 'she said' to be tacked on to the end of a sentence, even though that is the print convention. Always put the name of the speaker first.

Timings: The times allowed in the script for various sound elements: an overall timing for the whole package, and a timing for the pre-recorded part of the package.

Natsound: Natural sound, recorded on location.

Note that you will generally use present tense rather than past, so long as it sounds natural. You are not obliged to put your news story into the past tense as (often) you are with print news, though sometimes past tense is the only way to make a story sound natural. If you have to use past tense, you still must take care that your story doesn't sound out of date. Instead of writing, for example, 'Federal parliament last night voted to end refugee detention …', a more signposted version might be, 'Detention of refugees will end following a vote in Federal parliament.' Here the verb is 'will end', which is in the future tense.

Pacing

Pacing: The speed at which a reporter, newsreader or presenter speaks.

Pacing your stories correctly can help make your broadcast writing easy for the listener to comprehend. For most people, information is more efficiently absorbed by the eye than the ear. The eye can take in 250 words a minute or more. But if you speak that quickly, no one will understand you, because the ear doesn't work that quickly.

News presenters and experienced reporters speak at about three words a second, or about 180 words a minute. If you go much slower than that it sounds rather dull and maybe even rather patronising. If you go much faster it becomes difficult to understand.

Practise your pacing: practise reading as close to the professional rate as possible by preparing a story of exactly 180 words and recording it in exactly one minute.

When you time your story, it will be done on the assumption that both you and the newsreader will hit the mark fairly closely. Broadcast news bulletins often operate within very tight time constraints, and you simply can't run over by thirty seconds. If a radio or television bulletin were to do that on any station, it would probably be cut off as the next program kicked in. You should get into the habit of providing timings for all your stories.

Broadcast scripts

Script: The written part of a radio or television story.

Your written story is known in radio and television as a **script**. The technical differences between radio and television mean that the two types of script are set out differently. Different stations employ different styles as well, so a truly standard format does not exist. There are, however, elements you will find in all broadcast scripts, even if they are set out differently.

Your script will begin with words to be spoken by the announcer, presenter or newsreader. Note that reporters are responsible for scripting all parts of the story, including those that they are not themselves going to record or say live.

The intro (or announcer-read) part of the script may contain one short lead paragraph, and possibly more, before throwing to voiceover and/or actuality or grab. These introductory statements are intended to be read by the newsreader or presenter. Each paragraph normally will be no more than about twenty-five words.

Every news script you write for either radio or television must have a reader intro: there is no other way for your script to have context within the news bulletin unless you provide something for the live announcer to say before playing the rest of the story.

Every script will also contain other sound elements, pre-recorded and ready to be played in the bulletin. It is important to ensure that the newsreader or the news producer knows exactly how long the recording will run, so that she is ready to begin speaking live again at the end. Therefore, all of your written scripts will contain timings. Exactly what gets timed (all parts of the package separately or just the recorded part/s) and how it is expressed (in seconds, or in minutes and seconds) varies depending upon the style of the station for which you are working.

Voiceovers are vital on radio, because they add life and interest to a story; having a different voice from that of the newsreader offers the variation that a bulletin needs to keep the attention of the listeners. They are also essential, on both radio and television, for explaining the details of the story, a task that generally can't be done just by using grabs from talent.

Every word of a voiceover, whether recorded at the scene or in the studio, should be thought out carefully for maximum impact, accuracy and brevity, and then spoken with equal care. Write VOs to suit your own way of speaking, so that they sound natural. Everyone has words that he cannot say with ease, and you need to know what your own bogey words are. For some, they might be words such as 'meteorology' or 'nuclear', and others seemingly simple ones like 'familiar' or 'sentiment'. If you have difficulty getting your tongue around particular words or sentence constructions, then rewrite that part of the voiceover to make it right for you. Your delivery should be effortless.

Pronunciation

One of the most difficult aspects of perfecting a broadcast technique is dealing with the issue of pronunciation. The English language is large, complicated, various and (sometimes) illogical, so it is difficult always to know exactly how to say certain words. To deal with this ongoing challenge, the Australian Broadcasting Corporation has a body known as the Standing Committee on Spoken English (SCOSE), which assesses and adjudicates upon issues of pronunciation and advises broadcasters on an agreed correct version.

While we can usually agree on how to spell words, we can't always agree on how to say things. The word 'manufacturing', for example, is commonly rendered as 'manner-facturing', but is this correct and acceptable? Many people would say it is not: to sound correct and pleasing to the ear, it should be spoken as 'man-YOU-facturing'. There are many other examples. Also, as reporter it is your responsibility to find out the correct pronunciation of unfamiliar names. Not correctly pronouncing the name of a person or a place betrays ignorance, which leads to doubts over credibility. Also, getting people's names wrong is not only a great insult but just plain sloppy. Most people don't give this issue a thought, but in the broadcast media it is necessary to find a pronunciation for many different words and names that will be understandable and will not cause offence or irritation.

Phonetic spelling

Broadcast journalists often insert into their written scripts the phonetic spelling of difficult or unfamiliar words. A linguist would not recognise it as phonetic at all, but rather a sounding out of the syllables of a word so that it can be easily said without stumbling. If, for example, you are referring to the French writer Camus you would provide, inside square brackets, the correct pronunciation. This is how it might appear: 'Author of the famous novel, *The Plague*, Albert Camus [CA-MOO] ....'

As you will discover, the process of packaging radio news stories is an activity that makes radio news rather different from television. Sometimes, with quite minimal training, radio journalists are expected to audio edit sound (either on a computer or on a recording device) and create material that will be broadcast. On television, various other people, such as the camera crew and video editor, are involved in the creation of a news story, but in radio often it is just up to you.

Writing in simple broadcast style

One way of achieving clarity is to minimise the number of facts you try to cram into one sentence. There is no rigid rule here, but generally it is accepted that each sentence should contain one fact only, or, at a pinch, two. Do not try to fit too much into each sentence or it will sound too complicated and the listener will give up.

Go easy on adverbs and adjectives; they add to the clutter and often are superfluous. Get rid of any words that are likely to annoy or confuse your listeners, whether because they are obscure or just long and pretentious. It is wise to stick to everyday, straightforward English—although keep in mind that it is jarring to use slang or folksy expressions.

When you place numbers and initials in your story, write them as you would want them spoken by the newsreader. Don't write '1,200,000', because it may be difficult for the newsreader to think quickly enough to convert this to normal speech. Write 'one-million-two-hundred-thousand' in the body of your story. Use precise figures only when they are important to the story; otherwise round the numbers out. For instance, 'four-million-nine hundred-and-ninety-eight-thousand' in most cases could be rounded off to 'about five million'. Because you need to tally up the words in each story to work out your timings, it is important to write out the numbers as words so that they can form part of the overall word count.

Try not to use too many initials in your story, because they may trip up the newsreader. For instance, the US may come out on air as 'us', so it might be better to spell out the United States, or else use America.

If you are talking about dollars, write 'three-thousand-dollars'; don't use a dollar sign. Join the elements together with a hyphen. Don't use the percentage symbol ('%'); write out the words ('per cent').

Use punctuation properly in your stories, because punctuation is the written expression of natural pauses in speech, and as such will help the newsreader to pace the reading of the story correctly. Also, if you are doing a voiceover of your own story, correct punctuation will help you to get it right in the heat of the moment. Therefore, use a comma where there should be a very brief pause in a sentence. A dash may indicate the sort of abrupt pause that comes with a change of intonation, as when inserting a clause or a phrase that need not be there for the rest of the sentence to make sense. For instance, you could say, 'The science minister said the CSIRO—a statutory authority—was funded on a three yearly basis'.

You should avoid direct quotes in your broadcast scripts, because it is hard to convey them by reading. You or the newsreader can make elaborate attempts to show by intonation that what you are saying is a direct quote, but really you may as well just run some actuality of the person concerned speaking rather than try to quote them directly in your script. On television, you may be able to put direct quotes onto graphics and show the viewer what has been said, but obviously that is not an option on radio.

Intros can be as short as one sentence, but should rarely more than three sentences. The throw is just a few word: 'Jane Brown reports …' or 'John Peters reports from Bowen …', or, for variation, 'As Karen Jones reports, the bushfire appears to be out of control …'

The voice report that follows should not repeat what has just been said in the intro, but should expand on the theme and introduce new information, adding as well the authentic information and the atmosphere that can only be obtained at the scene of an event. Remember: the voiceover must follow logically from the throw, otherwise you will actually disorient your listeners and therefore lose their attention. Signpost between sections of script and at the end by writing an outro or back announce, which reminds listeners of who was just speaking.

In both radio and television scripts, you should be able to produce efficient, brief and stylistically correct sentences that clearly identify the key point of the story up front and use signposting to lead the listener/viewer through the facts needed for understanding the story. It all has to be written quickly, often in the station car returning from the recording location.

Key messages for broadcast writing

- Aim for short, sharp, informative sentences that don't exceed twenty-five words.
- Telegraph your intentions at the start of your story, and at other key points, by using signposting.
- Write out all elements of your script, including the voiceover and transcript of the grab.
- Time both the recorded part and the entire script, keeping in mind the standard three words per second.
- Don't write anything that is hard to say.
- Practise saying your words aloud.
- Be mindful of the fact that you will have between ninety and 360 words (depending on whether you are writing for radio or television) to tell the entire story, from start to finish.
- Pare back adverbs and adjectives.
- Don't use complex, convoluted sentences.
- Make every word count.

Conclusion

The best broadcast journalists are those who don't have to strain to write a script. A broadcast newsroom is a fast-paced environment, where robust generic skills are expected. Have a journalistic vocabulary at your disposal, made up of short, sharp and strong words, and a news sense that can quickly pick out the main point of the story. You won't have the capacity in broadcast news to go into depth, but what you do choose to include must provide the audience with the essential facts in a style that facilitates rapid understanding. To cope with the pace, and indeed to even get a job in the first place, you have to have impeccable generic skills. Often the process of getting a job in the industry is demanding, and you will have to demonstrate that you are a confident, well-spoken and poised individual who can discern a news angle and come up with a perfectly balanced and nicely written script. It must display a sophisticated knowledge base as well as easy-to-follow, simple English and correct broadcast style. Do these things, and you are on the way to the top of one of the world's great professions.

KEY REFERENCES

Phillips, G. & Lindgren, M. (2006). *Australian Broadcast Journalism* (2nd edn). Melbourne: Oxford University Press.

WEBSITES

Australian Broadcasting Corporation: <www.abc.net.au>

CHAPTER 14

SUBEDITING, NEWS LANGUAGE AND CONVENTION

LIZ TYNAN

Introduction

People new to media writing often bristle at the notion that they have to follow someone else's writing rules. A common argument is that rules stifle people's creativity through prescriptive and arbitrary pedantry imposed by people who have no life; and grammar rules keep changing so why should we have to learn them? We don't speak the same way as William Shakespeare did. English evolves ... Yes, it does evolve, and it is a wonderful process, and one that continually enriches our primary communication tool. But a language without rules, even transitory ones, is not a language at all, because it cannot be fully understood by all who use it. Rules are there to create meaning, and meaning is vital in all media professions. Also, high-quality media value consistency, which boosts the overall quality of the product. Consistency helps to put the reader or the listener at ease, as it removes irritation or confusion over trifles and leaves them free to consider the main point of what you have written. Many media settings require employees to adhere to a style, which helps to ensure consistency. The subeditor is often the custodian of a publication's language and style, but all subs appreciate the reporters taking pains in this area as well, so they don't have to spend too much time making small, annoying corrections. Consistent writing styles can vary quite a bit; it is not a science, so you will find different media jobs require different approaches. On the following pages are some common principles that should serve as a guide only. The magnificent variety of work in the media throws up a matching multiplicity of writing requirements. In this section the more familiar and common ones are on display, but be prepared to be flexible once you find a job in the industry.

In this chapter we look at:

- subeditors and subediting
- news language
- journalistic convention
- a sample style guide
- diagnosing common language problems.

Subeditors and subediting

Subeditor (sub): A member of a media organisation who edits and corrects material submitted by other people, such as reporters and columnists.

In a media organisation, **subeditors** (subs) edit and correct material submitted by other people, such as reporters and columnists. They are called upon to do many different tasks very quickly. They have saved the jobs and reputations of many reporters, because they act as the guard, the gatekeeper, preventing unwarranted, stupid, illogical, tasteless or actionable words being published or broadcast. They are sometimes not held in particularly high regard by those in the industry who are not subs. The show ponies are the reporters and the workhorses are the subs—or so the usual stereotype goes. Often, their work is simply resented by the reporters, who don't appreciate having their writing questioned and altered. In truth, the sub is indispensable and, if pushed, a reporter may even admit it. Journalism has never been a solitary occupation; it always requires teamwork.

One of the hallmarks of a quality publication is decent subediting, even though it is manifestly deficient in some popular publications. Good subediting brings ordinary text to life, it eliminates irritating or confusing language, and it helps break down those inevitable communication barriers between the producer and the consumer of information. This list of overall subediting principles, in no particular order of importance, shows characteristics that are applicable in Australian media:

- correct English usage
- consistent written style
- accuracy of content
- adherence to journalistic convention
- adherence to deadlines.

In Chapter 3, we considered the importance of good grammar for creating meaning. In this chapter we link these overarching principles more closely to media industry work. Communicating with a mass audience carries significant responsibilities, not just to write nicely but also to ensure that what you write can take its place in public information. It is often said that journalism is the first draft of history. The word 'journalism' obviously is linked to **journal**, which means, strictly speaking, a daily record of events. The emphasis here is on 'record'. Journalists participate in the keeping of records, and it is to be hoped that their record-keeping shows some concern for the gravity of their task. Journalism is a record of the times, demonstrating passing trends and the shifting consensus among practitioners of the language codes, with the symbols of language simply being things that we agree upon as reflecting meanings we hold in our minds: a seemingly mild clause that has masses of philosophical implication.

Journal: From the French *journal*: a daily record of events; therefore, a daily newspaper or magazine.

Language is ever evolving, of course, and there is no custodian or arbiter of correct English. We need to decide what we are going to call correct. One test for correctness involves considering the standards educated people adopt when they are paying due attention to their language. What sort of language use is prevalent among people who are obviously taking care of language and using it optimally for communication? This is not intended to sound elitist. There are reasons why language needs some form of protection among its practitioners, the most important being the need to keep it firmly attached to semantic content (meaning) and hence to the world of ideas. Lose the ability to convey nuance, complexity and abstract ideas, and you lose some of your culture.

Lofty as this may sound, there is a strong sense of guardianship of the language among the best of journalists. Some of the world's most ferocious language pedants are also the most prized subeditors on the best publications. Subeditors often teach new journalists, through not very gentle means, that language use is to be taken seriously. You may or may not share this sense, but the chances are that you will encounter this notion during the twists and turns of your careers in the media. If you don't understand and appreciate these principles straight away, it is likely that some rather insensitive editor or subeditor will let you know in less than flattering terms later on, and that process may involve a certain amount of humiliation.

You should aim not only for the lofty goals of eloquence and correctness of language use, but you should also aim for consistency. Your goal here is ensure that your readers are not irritated or confused. Like static on your television, inconsistent style in any publication can have readers throwing things at the walls and writing furious letters. This inconsistency might, for example, be as simple as offering different ways of spelling 'colour', 'travelling' or 'organise' in the same story or the same publication, differing styles for percentages or page numbering or differing depth of indent, body font height, caption style and style of titles for individuals: a wide variety of elements that fall within a strictly correct usage range but vary enough to cause anguish among readers. The best subeditors will always aim for consistency, and see it as a matter of professional pride. Consistent style imposes a discipline that should run through all the activities of a journalist and a subeditor. It implies that those in these roles are precise not only with writing but also with facts and thought.

Accuracy of content is a central issue: there is no substitute in journalism for accuracy. It is a matter of concern for the reporter as well as the subeditor. However, the subeditor, and ultimately the managing editor, take the responsibility. You will not be able to check everything yourself if you are subeditor, but you must check key points that could, if wrong, become extremely embarrassing or even actionable.

If you are required, say, to subedit text from a reporter whose story asserts that a major tourist attraction is about to close down because it has failed a safety inspection, don't just assume that the reporter has got the facts correct. Confer first with the reporter to find out how the story was obtained, then obtain your own verification of the facts if you are in any doubt. Don't put through any information that seems questionable. Other more common difficulties can include a misspelt name, or a person's name spelt several different ways in a story. Misspelt names have the potential to cause enormous anger and resentment among the wronged parties, and in some cases may lead to legal complications if you identify someone wrongly. It also makes your work look shoddy. Double-check all name spellings, and that includes place names as well as the names of people.

News language

What is news language? There is no simple answer to that question. Journalistic writing has a distinct but hard-to-define form. This form is also echoed in much public relations writing. Australian journalism has writing conventions different from those in other countries, but in no country are the conventions rigid and unchanging. Journalistic writing always evolves. However, some usages persist long enough to be seen as firm rules. Hard news writing (see Chapter 12) is perhaps the most robust form of journalistic writing, and tends to be quite prescriptive, that is, the rules of what not to do tend to outweigh what is allowed.

This leads to a variety of consequences for the reporter, who must try to eliminate long, Latinate words and opt for short Anglo-Saxon words as much as possible. Instead of 'commence', choose 'start'. Instead of 'prior to', use 'before'. We are fortunate in some ways to have a multifaceted language that has drawn on so many other languages. Because English is rich in synonyms, often there is a short version of a word that will convey the same meaning as the longer word. Short words tend to be more instantly understandable. Also, in print media space is limited, and short words use up less space. There is a common misconception that sophisticated writing requires lots of long words and convoluted sentence structures. This is not so: the best writing conveys complex ideas in simple language.

Short words

Journalists usually will choose a short word if possible. This drive for short words is particularly evident in tabloid headlines. Words such as 'probe', 'fury', 'shame', 'agony', 'bid' and 'joy'—short, emotive words that are easy to fit into a newspaper layout—are in popular use, and are often derided and satirised as well. 'Star's Shame over Baby Agony' is the kind of headline that has a familiar ring. The general rule is to always keep your journalistic writing simple and straightforward. Some of the world's best writers are to be found in journalism, or at least in the more exalted forms of it. George Orwell's writing is well known not just for its profundity but also for its brevity and crispness. This is what the best of news language displays.

Redundancies

One quick way to simplify your writing is by eliminating redundancies. For example, there is no need to write 'completely destroyed'. It is enough to say something has been 'destroyed'. The same goes for common redundancies such as 'this point in time' (write 'now'), 'join together' ('join'), 'serious fatality' ('fatality'), 'killed dead' ('killed') and many others. Read your work with the aim of getting rid of unnecessary words. There is always something that can be cut. A first draft is rarely, in journalism, good enough. Even good writing has to be edited.

Strong words

As mentioned in Chapter 3, good journalistic writing is driven by verbs: strong, meaningful, well-chosen finite verbs that power your sentences and give you the ability to tell precisely what is happening. Also important in news writing are powerful, straightforward nouns, such as 'death', 'lie', 'war', 'prison' and 'murder'. News is often about harsh realities. Journalists tend not to write that people 'passed away', so eliminate **euphemisms** as much as possible too.

Euphemism: A mild or vague word or phrase that is used instead of a blunt, harsh word.

Tone

The tone of media writing can be important. Words often have both denotations and connotations, and understanding both forms of certain words may be an issue. Take the example of 'green'. This word means the colour green, but it has political and social connotations as well. In some contexts, it could be taken as derogatory or dismissive, but it could be taken the opposite way in other contexts. A word such as 'claimed' might be problematic for news journalists. In some contexts it is quite straightforward, but in others it will connote the idea that someone has something to hide. Often, bias is betrayed in your use of adjectives and adverbs—these are the words that add colour to nouns and verbs, so do be sparing with them. For example, the sentence 'The government has introduced legislation decriminalising the use of some drugs' is neutral, but see what happens when modifiers are added: 'The government has irresponsibly introduced legislation decriminalising the use of some socially devastating drugs.' Choose your words carefully, being mindful of all their possible interpretations and potential for bias. A neutral tone is usually needed for news writing.

Somewhere between conversational and formal

News writing is not strictly conversational, even though it needs to be simple. Conversational writing is often too vague to work in journalism. Spoken language lacks the formal grammar of properly written prose, and may be filled with slang or other kinds of vernacular. Just listen to random conversations in your everyday life and you will hear sentence constructions that would not survive a subedit. Journalism requires efficiency and precision, qualities often lacking in general conversation. Informal, conversational chat between people who know each other can be filled with verbal short cuts and repetition, because much in conversation is either understood or redundant. This doesn't work in good journalism. Overly informal writing is just as bad as stuffy formal writing.

Convention

Inverted pyramid

The best known of all journalistic conventions is the inverted pyramid form for news stories (see Chapters 2 and 4), which enables stories to be cut from the bottom to accommodate the constraints of page layout. This practical consideration has helped shape the well-written news story into a finely honed method of efficient communication, by placing information in a hierarchy. The inverted pyramid is not generally chronological, because the emphasis is on the most important fact or event, not the first. It begins with the intro or lead, which will always answer one or two of the classic journalistic questions; 'Who?', 'What?', 'When?', 'Where?', 'How?' and 'Why?' The body of the story follows, revealing more details of the story and answering all the rest of the questions. While some news organisations have proclaimed the death of the inverted pyramid, news of its demise may be premature. The inverted pyramid remains a remarkably efficient way to convey information, and it seems unlikely that it will disappear altogether, even as more narrative formats arise.

Leads and other sentences

Journalistic convention on most major Australian newspapers dictates that each sentence in a news story will be its own paragraph. This is not the case in other countries, but is well established here. Journalistic convention used to be that lead paragraphs in newspapers were no more than twenty-five to thirty words. This standard has become more liberal, as a skim through the daily press will show. It is still advisable to keep your sentences short, particularly your lead sentence. However, the whole story will read better if it displays a combination of short and longer sentences.

Attribution

Using the word 'said' is considered to be neutral and without value judgment, and therefore journalistically sound. Mainstream journalistic convention in Australia bars most synonyms of the word 'said', and it is considered acceptable to repeat this word, in a journalistically conventional pattern, throughout a story. This differs from some elements of the non-mainstream press, where you will find people quoted who 'offered' or 'grumbled'—as in '"I didn't think it was a particularly good game," he offered'; or '"That wasn't such a great movie," she grumbled'—usages that are patronising and value laden. Media releases should follow this convention, as they should be written in journalistic language. Public relations practitioners should not attempt to strengthen an assertion with a value-laden attribution word (such as 'insisted' or 'hailed'). It tends to put journalists off.

Direct quotes

All newspaper stories that are not just one-paragraph brief items contain direct quotes of some kind. They are often worked into the piece at around about paragraph four or five, and are usually introduced by some indirect speech that sets the scene. The same applies to media releases. You place the quote first, then the name and position of the speaker. Make sure that you get the punctuation around direct quotes right. Here is a correct pattern:

> 'The research so far is showing promising results,' project leader Professor Carol Smith said.
>
> 'We plan to begin a new trial next year,' she said.
>
> 'We hope to have a new treatment on the market by 2015.'

Third person

Journalistic writing is usually third-person writing, certainly in the case of news journalism. This is the journalistic way of removing the writer from the action. The news reporter must keep some distance from the matters being reported, even if the ideal of strict objectivity cannot be attained. The use of first person 'I', 'me', 'we' and 'us' can be annoyingly cosy, but paradoxically alienating for the reader. Also, using the second person 'you' may be patronising: 'How would you feel if you had been in that car crash?' or 'These measures mean the family grocery bill can be reduced to something you can afford.' Consumers of news don't want to know what the reporter does or thinks, or to be told in the second person how to feel or think. News is about things happening in the world—to people other than the reporter.

There are exceptions. For example, the rules change in the case of certain kinds of feature writing. First-person features are increasingly common, though ideally they should still be about the activities of people other than the reporter. They can show the reporter's response to events, but should not put the reporter at the centre. The kind of journalism that has the reporter as the main character in the story is problematic, though it can be worthwhile if done by a skilled writer who has a good reason for being at the centre. It is not, however, generally a form recommended for those beginning in journalism.

Style

Most media newsrooms, public relations offices and other professional writing settings in the media use a style guide of some kind to guide staff writing. **Style** is a combination of grammatical rules, journalistic convention and the individual preferences of news editors, chiefs-of-staff or managers. It is a good idea to get used to adapting your writing according to a set style. Professional communicators need to ensure that their work does not contain elements that may confuse or irritate the reader. Clear, correct style is essential in this process. While some rules of journalistic writing are common across most Australian media organisations, there are often individual differences between outlets that mean you have to change your writing depending upon where you work. For example, **house style** will differ between broadsheets and tabloids. There are also substantial differences between newspapers and magazines, and between print and broadcast media. Some style guides are extremely detailed and helpful, while others are just sketches. The point of a style guide is to get all journalists on a publication—or public relations people writing media materials or publications—heading in the same direction, employing correctness and consistency. The main style gatekeeper in news is the subeditor, but all journalists are expected to help out by producing what is known as clean copy, copy on which the sub doesn't have to waste precious time correcting small grammar or style errors. The same goes in a public relations office, where a senior manager is likely to fulfil the gatekeeping role, and would be much obliged if the public relations officers took care with their original copy to minimise the possibility of errors passing through unnoticed.

Style: The overall use of a language, whether written (journalism, broadcasting, television or literature), aural (film and television sound) or oral (radio and television presentation); in journalism, it combines grammatical rules, journalistic conventions and the individual preferences of writers, editors and managers.

House style: The particular set of grammatical rules, conventions and organisation preferences chosen by individual publishers and media organisations; usually prescribed in a style guide.

Some common elements in media style guides

As mentioned above, elements of style can vary quite a bit, within and between various media outlets or public relations offices. The style elements below tend to be fairly common in many settings and are useful to know (keeping in mind the need to adapt to a particular house style).

NUMBERS

- Standard newspaper number style is one to nine in words, then 10, 11, 12 … in numerals.
- Sentences should not begin with a numeral.
- When writing journalistic copy, use a comma between numbers greater than 999—1,000, 10,000, 100,000, etc.—but for book publication, use a comma between numbers greater than 9999—10,000; 100,000, etc.
- For millions of dollars, use $10 million.
- Avoid using numerals in headlines.
- Dates should be either day–month–year, such as 2 August 2012, or month–day–year August 2, 2012. Never use the 2nd of August.

WORDS

- Most Australian media environments use standard Australian spelling, not American spelling; for example, colour, harbour (not color, harbor); travelling, not traveling; and catalogue, not catalog. Use centre and theatre, not center and theater. Never use gotten instead of got.
- Use -ise, not -ize; for example, in recognise and organise.
- Dr, Ms, Mr, etc. should not have a full stop.
- NSW, QC and other acronyms should not have full stops between letters, and should not have apostrophes for plurals (QCs).
- Minimise use of capital letters, and use them only to start proper nouns or the first word of sentences.
- Avoid synonyms of said, such as added.
- It is no longer journalistic style in Australia to use whilst, amidst, amongst or similar archaic forms. Use while, amid and among instead.
- Do not use alright; use the correct term, all right.
- Last does not mean the same as past. For example, do not write, 'That is the way we have done it for the last century.' This means the last, then no more. You should write, That is the way we have done it for the past century.
- Some pairs of words are habitually confused; make sure you are not one of the offenders. These pairs include disinterested/uninterested, imply/infer, alternate/alternative, bought/brought, refute/dispute, compliment/complement and affect/effect. If unsure, always look them up.

SYMBOLS

- Use 'per cent', not 'percent' or '%'.
- If you need to distinguish between Australian dollars and the currencies of other countries, use $A100 for Australian, $US100 for American or $NZ100 for New Zealand dollars.
- Use km for singular and plural forms of kilometre; for example, 'The house was one km from the shop' and 'The house was 10 km from the shop'.
- The same applies for the abbreviations of measurements such as millimetre, kilogram and metre.

PUNCTUATION

- Exclamation marks are generally not used in either journalistic or public relations writing.
- Use double quotation marks (“) around direct quotes and single marks (‘) for quotes within quotes. Note: this usage in newspapers and magazines is the opposite of the usage in books published in Australia, where single quotation marks surround double quotation marks.
- Do not use a comma between the subject and verb of a sentence unless it is to insert a non-essential phrase or clause, and therefore ends with a comma: ‘The woman, who was increasingly impatient, waited in line.’ In this case, the phrase ‘who was increasingly impatient’ must be opened and closed with a comma to mark the fact that it is an addition to the sentence that could be removed without damaging the S–V–O sentence structure.
- Always use apostrophes correctly. Not to do so can serious impair one’s credibility, as well as create confusion. Correct apostrophe use dictates that apostrophes are used when indicating a contraction (‘It’s a nice day’) or for noun possession (‘The woman’s book’). Note that possessive pronouns do not take apostrophes (‘The cat chased its tail.’)

CLICHÉS

A simple rule: don’t use clichés. Therefore, you will avoid the following:

- size is not important
- strutting her/his/their stuff
- mum’s the word
- shaken not stirred
- in the nick of time
- at the end of the day
- […] is the new black
- anything being dubbed [something]-gate, such as Camillagate or Walletgate
- the humble [potato, bedspread, kitchen cupboard, or whatever]
- if you think [something], then think again.

There are many other examples, all regularly featured in lazy journalism and mediocre writing. It is important to care about your writing enough to employ originality.

Diagnosing common language problems

There are many things that can go wrong with language, and various contentious issues that don’t necessarily have clear-cut solutions. Even if you don’t agree with some hard-line points of view on these usage issues, it is helpful to be aware of them before going against them. Here are a few of the more common issues.

Split infinitives

‘Don’t split infinitives’ is a rule you will often hear. This is a controversial issue, and you will find vehement opinion on both sides of the argument. Some people maintain that it is an arbitrary, meaningless rule imposed by horrible, prescriptive grammarians wedded to Latin and unable to cope with the twenty-first century. They also generally have no friends and wear only hand-knitted grey cardigans. Others think that splitting an infinitive is always poor writing, and indicates a lack of sensitivity to the language and a general lack of education. Most writers concede, though, that sometimes, for grace and clarity, you may need to split an infinitive.

What is an infinitive? It is a kind of verb, distinct from the finite verb (see Chapter 4). Among its distinguishing characteristics, it does not indicate tense or singular/plural. It is often (though not always) made up of the word 'to' and the so-called dictionary form of a verb, such as 'be'. The most famous infinitive of all is found in Shakespeare's *Hamlet*: 'To be or not to be.' In English, words change their shape for various reasons, and we call this inflection. The dictionary form is the uninflected form. So, for example, we could have the word 'run', which can inflect to 'ran', 'runs' and 'running'. Its dictionary form will always be 'run'. Its common infinitive form is 'to run'. In this case, the second word in this construction never inflects—you can't have 'to ran', for example. It is one of those little tests we have in grammar to see if you have got the definition right. In the case of infinitives, see if you can inflect it. If you can't, then it may be an infinitive. Note that infinitive verbs cannot drive a proper English sentence; only finite verbs can do that.

The world's most famous split infinitive comes from the classic television series *Star Trek*, in which the denizens of the USS *Enterprise* vowed 'to boldly go where no man has gone before'. Here the adverb 'boldly' has found its way between the two elements of the infinitive. Grammarians around the globe clicked their tongues at that one, and the more fervent almost certainly boycotted the show forever more. According to Bruce Kaplan (2003):

> In the publishing world, a split infinitive usually shows that the writer does not understand a basic rule of grammar. Veteran editors on the receiving end of split infinitives can sometimes be seen waving their arms, shouting or sobbing at their desks. These guardians of language purity are the true believers in the crime of the split infinitive. So in your own interests, when writing or editing your own or someone else's work, do not split the infinitive.

But that timeless classic of English, first published in 1926, H. W. Fowler's *A Dictionary of Modern English Usage* (latest edition 2006), defends splitting the infinitive in certain cases. In making his case, Fowler divides the English-speaking world into five classes: those who neither know nor care what a split infinitive is, those who do not know, but care very much, those who know and condemn, those who know and approve and those who know and distinguish—a useful and accurate division. He reserves his scathing wit most for those who rant about not splitting the infinitive while not really knowing what an infinitive is or why splitting it is a problem. Moreover, he says that sometimes, to match the natural rhythms of English, it is far better to split an infinitive than to slavishly keep it intact. Note that the use of the term 'to slavishly keep' is a split infinitive. Not splitting it would result in wording like this: 'It is far better to split an infinitive than slavishly to keep it intact.' Which sounds better? You decide.

Whatever you decide to do, do it knowingly. That way, when a grumpy old sub questions your defiant split infinitive, you won't be taken by surprise and say something lethal like: 'What's a split infinitive?'

Ending with a preposition

'Don't end a sentence with a preposition.' This is just as controversial an edict as the one about the split infinitive. It is also common for subeditors to have conniptions over this one, but there are many dissenters. Winston Churchill famously mocked someone who criticised him for ending with a preposition with the line: 'That is something up with which I cannot put.' Less ridiculous examples of sentences ending with prepositions might be:

> That is the house I live in.
> Who did you give the flowers to?

The rule about ending with a preposition arises because a preposition is supposed to be placed before a noun, a role implied in the literal meaning of the word preposition (pre-position). A preposition is a class of word that governs relationships between the content words (see Chapter 4). The nouns behave in certain ways, depending on what the preposition makes them do; for example, not 'above ice' or 'in ice', but 'on ice'. If the preposition is the last word of a sentence, obviously it does not appear before a noun.

There are arguments for saying that this doesn't matter. Here is Fowler (2002) again:

> It was once a cherished superstition that prepositions must be kept true to their name and placed before the word they govern in spite of the incurable English instinct for putting them late ... The fact is that ... even now immense pains are sometimes expended in changing spontaneous into artificial English ... Those who lay down the universal principle that final prepositions are 'inelegant' are unconsciously trying to deprive the English language of a valuable idiomatic resource, which has been used freely by all our greatest writers except those whose instinct for English idiom has been overpowered by notions of correctness derived from Latin standards. The legitimacy of the prepositional ending in literary English must be uncompromisingly maintained ... In avoiding the forbidden order, unskilful handlers of words often fall into real blunders.

Strunk and White, in *The Elements of Style* (2000), write:

> Years ago, students were warned not to end a sentence with a preposition; time, of course, has softened that rigid decree. Not only is the preposition acceptable at the end, sometimes it is more effective in that spot than anywhere else. 'A claw hammer, not an axe, was the tool he murdered her with.' This is preferable to 'A claw hammer, not an axe, was the tool with which he murdered her.' Why? Because it sounds more violent, more like murder.

Like the split infinitive, ending with a preposition is something to be aware of (or something of which to be aware) but not necessarily cowed by (or by which not necessarily cowed). Use you writer's ear to find what sounds more graceful and vivid.

Mixed metaphors

Don't mix your metaphors. Metaphors can be a wonderful explanatory tool. They work really well for many kinds of writers, whether working in fiction or in, for example, science journalism. In a metaphor, one thing is likened to another: 'my love' to a 'red, red rose'

(Robert Burns), or a cat in a box becomes a metaphor for an unseen physical principle called uncertainty (Schroedinger's Cat). But you must beware the unintentionally hilarious misuse of metaphors, which tend to render your words risible rather than rousing.

Apart from the tendency of metaphors to descend into cliché when you are not looking, they can also cast doubt upon your abilities to write vivid and coherent prose. Consider the following example, from Fowler (2000: 350), who is quoting a political speech:

> No society, no community, can place its house in such a condition that it is always on a rock, oscillating between solvency and insolvency. What I have to do is to see that our house is built upon a solid foundation, never allowing the possibility of the Society's lifeblood being sapped.

Oscillating rocks and lifeblood: the metaphors are ridiculous together. Sadly, this sort of writing is remarkably common, even in prestigious outlets. Consider the following from Revkin, in the *New York Times* (11 June 2001):

> Over all, many experts conclude, advanced climate research in the United States is fragmented among an alphabet soup of agencies, strained by inadequate computing power and starved for the basic measurements of real-world conditions that are needed to improve simulations.

Make sure you know when you are using a metaphor (people don't always realise this) and that you haven't mixed it with something that doesn't make any sense. It is part of the quality control process.

Misuse of apostrophes

The misuse of apostrophes is a subeditor killer. Subeditors find it difficult to understand why people who want to be paid to write sometimes find the apostrophe impossible to master. It couldn't be simpler—the rules are really straightforward. It is important to get this right, if only to save the sanity of the poor old senior sub, who has probably seen a few too many misplaced apostrophes than is safe for the ageing mind.

Here are the rules, which will require some elaboration, but not much. Apostrophes are used:

- to indicate contraction: 'It's [It is] a pity that people don't [do not] care about apostrophes.'
- to show possession (in nouns, not pronouns): 'The subeditor's lament' for singular; 'The subeditors' lament' for the plural.

Possessive pronouns (his, hers, ours, theirs, yours) never take an apostrophe. They exist as words only to show possession, and no further symbol is needed for this function. Consider, for example, 'The cat chased its tail', in which the possessive pronoun 'its' does not require an apostrophe.

The apostrophe is needed in, for example, 'two years' jail' or 'one week's notice': take note of the difference in plural and singular here.

An apostrophe is not needed in, for example, the 1970s, or to show the plural of acronyms such as QCs or MPs. Just a lower case 's' is sufficient. Note that if you are writing, for example, 'the '70s', you do need the apostrophe to show the omission of the first part of the year, but you don't use it between the number and the 's'.

Note that, in the noun possession function, it is important not to get mixed up with adjectives. For example, 'Melbourne citizens' is different from 'Melbourne's citizens', and it is the adjectival form (the first example here) that is more usual in journalism. This can lead to some confusion. It is linked to the word order convention in English, where it is usual to place both an adjective and a possessive before a noun. Because they sometimes look similar, they can be confused.

Persistent usage has meant that some place names don't have apostrophes even when, strictly speaking, they should; for example, Wilsons Promontory, St Andrews, Badgers Creek and so on have lost their original apostrophes, much as it pains the pedantic writer.

Dangling or hanging modifiers

Some sentences have additional information placed at the start, in the form of a participle phrase or some other kind of modifier. This kind of phrase must attach correctly to the sentence proper. If it doesn't attach properly, the problem is known as a dangling or hanging modifier (or dangling or hanging participle). Here are some examples:

- Having written the essay, the lecturer complimented the student on her strong argument.
- After being convicted of robbing a bank, the judge sentenced Joe Bloggs to five years in jail.
- Climbing to the top of the building, the city stretched out before us.

These sentences contain nonsense, because the modifier that begins them is incorrectly attached. The first sentence here is really saying that the lecturer wrote the student's essay, which was surely not the writer's intention. The second sentence says that the judge was convicted of robbing a bank, while the third sentence says that the city climbed to the top of the building. Remember that the participle always relates to the first available noun or pronoun. For these sentences to be made correct, they will have to be restructured. There are different ways to rewrite all these sentences. Here are some possible options:

- The lecturer complimented the student on the strong argument in her essay.
- The judge sentenced Joe Bloggs to five years in jail after Bloggs was convicted of robbing the bank.
- When we climbed to the top of the building we saw the city stretched out before us.

Commas

There is perhaps more reason for confusion over commas than there is over apostrophes. The rules for apostrophes are clear-cut, but the rules for commas are not. These little marks are used to separate ideas in a sentence and otherwise make meaning clear. The trend these days in the Australian media is to cut down on the use of commas where possible. That's fine to a certain extent, but you must always keep in mind that commas can change the meaning of a sentence:

> The politicians, who liked to talk, were appointed to the committee.
> The politicians who liked to talk were appointed to the committee.

The following guidelines may help comma use.

- To avoid ambiguity:
  When the father finished washing, the children went to the beach.

Without a comma here, ambiguity may arise over joining 'washing' and 'the children'.

He was bitten by a mosquito, which annoyed him.

Without a comma, this sentence would indicate annoyance with the mosquito before it bit the man.

- Between adjectives before a noun:

  A large, black van.

- In a list to separate the elements:

  The basic stages of writing a story are: researching, interviewing, drafting, checking and confirming facts, and editing.

- To distinguish parenthetical words and phrases:

  My view, therefore, is that editors should always be consistent.

Parenthetical commas

Pay special attention to parenthetical words and phrases. Commas must always be used in pairs in this case. You cannot open such a phrase with a comma and not close it with one. In the sentence 'My view, therefore, is that editors should always be consistent', to not place the second comma after the word 'therefore' would be grammatically incorrect. An easy way to determine if you need a pair of commas is to see if the word or phrase could be taken out without damaging the grammatical integrity of the sentence. If it can be taken out, then you must use commas around it.

TIPS

Make sure you always:

- turn your words into galley slaves: they must do your bidding; to have this level of control over your words, you must know the purpose of each one
- observe the work of great writers and think about how you can incorporate their techniques into your own writing
- recognise the power inherent in using language in the public sphere, and take it for the serious task that it is
- understand any rules you are breaking before you break them. If you don't, it will just look like you didn't know what you were doing.

Make sure you never:

- sit down to write without access to a dictionary
- just place apostrophes randomly, hoping they are more or less okay
- fall into the lazy habit of writing a cliché when a fresh expression will enliven your work
- submit a first draft—writing can always be polished, even in a high pressure environment.

And to really shine, you should:

- find joy and satisfaction in your writing, beyond just completing a functional task. When you do this, hopefully your readers will feel the same way.

Conclusion

Media writing always has a public role, whether it is for a newspaper, a magazine, a film script or a media release. Communication barriers are common as we share information around many different contexts and individuals in society. Professional writers strive to minimise those barriers inherent in our multifaceted language. Due attention to good grammar, combined with an understanding of relevant language and style conventions, and an appreciation of eloquence and grace, will assist in turning you from a dabbler to a professional who people are willing to pay.

KEY REFERENCES

Fowler, H. W. (2002). *A Dictionary of Modern English Usage.* Oxford: Oxford University Press.

Kaplan, B. (2003). *Editing Made Easy.* Camberwell: Penguin.

Revkin, A. C. (2001). 'US losing status as world leader in climate change'. *New York Times.* 11 June. <www.nytimes.com/2001/06/11/us/us-losing-status-as-a-world-leader-in-climate-science.html>. Accessed 12 March 2004.

Strunk, W. & White, E. B. (2000). *The Elements of Style* (4th edn). Boston: Allyn & Bacon.

Truss, L. (2003). *Eats, Shoots and Leaves.* London: Profile Books.

CHAPTER 15

SPECIALIST REPORTING: DOING THE ROUNDS

LIZ TYNAN

Introduction

Young journalists entering the profession are wise to keep their options open and gain an overview, generally through a cadetship, of what reporting can offer. However, there usually comes a time when you will be ready to work at a deeper level than is possible through general reporting. The general reporter quickly and efficiently has to cover a wide range of breaking stories, from a cat up a tree to a local government resolution to a robot landing on Mars. By contrast, a specialist reporter narrows the focus to a particular field and adds depth. Reporters do not always have a say in exactly which speciality comes their way; indeed, they may arrive at work one day to find they are the new court reporter and are due at a rape trial in twenty minutes. (Part of the fun of a career in journalism is its unpredictability.) Also, in many cases reporters, as part of their training, are assigned to a succession of rounds to gain specialist knowledge in each. Eventually, many reporters settle in one particular area, building their expertise and becoming increasingly adept at spotting stories on the horizon in their field. Many media outlets capitalise on the knowledge bases of their roundspeople and cultivate an image of authority and expertise in areas of greatest interest to their audiences. Media outlets value roundspeople who have made a name for themselves in their specialities and have developed great insight and competence. Roundspeople tend to be more autonomous than general reporters and have greater capacity to drive the news agenda, rather than simply responding to daily events. The most useful roundspeople will be alert to breaking news, will recognise new developments and will appreciate the complexity of these developments when they arrive.

In this chapter we look at:

- how you may progress through your journalism career by taking on a specialised round
- why you do not need to be an expert in the subject to become an effective roundsperson
- how the best roundspeople become part of the milieu of their round

- how you can guarantee effectiveness through actively seeking to increase your knowledge
- some of the particular issues and dilemmas often faced by police roundspeople
- why you may wish to consider becoming a specialist journalist in the trade media.

Moving onwards and upwards

If you join a metropolitan media outlet as a cadet, you will probably be called upon to do many types of reporting tasks. These might include weather reports and stories about accidents, local politics, birthdays of people turning 100 and the local agricultural show—sometimes even cooking up the astrology column. In other words, a whole range of things that will give you broad experience and allow you to become comfortable covering topics of which you do not have direct experience and knowledge. This is part of what being a journalist is about: being able to ask the right questions and write about things that you didn't know about before—and without delay. A cadetship ideally provides a solid foundation and a capacity to develop quick-wittedness, self-reliance and assertive confidence, qualities that are valuable for all reporters.

You will want to give some thought to a long-term career path, and as you develop your professional experience you will seek to cultivate your expertise. Journalistic expertise is often best developed and cultivated in a **round**. Once you progress through the ranks of journalism and begin making your mark, it is likely that you will be given a round to cover. In the USA, this same role is known as a 'beat'. This work does tend to allow for long-term job satisfaction because you will be able to delve more deeply into an area than you can as a general reporter. To do it well, you must become immersed in your round.

Round: A form of reporting where the journalist specialises in a particular subject area and covers that area in depth. Examples include court or police rounds. This same role is known as a 'beat' in the US.

Contemporary media outlets in Australia have become increasingly diversified, embracing more rounds than ever before. At one time, it was not unusual for a reporter to remain a generalist throughout a long media career, and some still do. But there is an increasing demand for specialists who can provide indepth coverage of a particular area. Both kinds of journalist are necessary, according to Osmond:

> You've got to have the generalist philosophy, which says basic journalistic training can be applied to any field, regardless of the content. But then you've got to get a bit more realistic and concede that the world is very complicated and there are highly specialised and highly technical fields all around us ... That's the point at which generalists' skills may break down because ... it requires knowing a specialised field on its own terms and within its own discourse, being able to work within the discourse, but also to translate it into a more general kind of intelligibility. (Osmond 1998, quoted in Tapsall & Varley 2001)

The most common rounds in Australian newsrooms are:

- courts
- local government
- police
- sport.

While these are found in most mainstream media outlets, the big newspapers and broadcasting newsrooms now have many other rounds as well. These may include:

- business
- defence
- economics
- education
- environment
- health
- law
- lifestyle
- religion
- science and technology
- transport.

Major newspapers may have twenty or more rounds. Have a look at a metro paper, such as the *Australian* or the *Sydney Morning Herald*, and identify the rounds those papers maintain. As Conley (2002) points out, among the most sought-after rounds are those involving foreign postings, and the big media organisations often have specialist reporters stationed in, for example, Washington or London. Often, when you are a roundsperson, your byline will describe you as a correspondent, as in 'Science correspondent Freda Nurk'. This should not imply that being a roundsperson is same as being a columnist. Columnists provide analysis and comment and are often senior editorial staff or, indeed, people from outside the newsroom, such as academics, politicians or well-known pundits. As a roundsperson you will generally be expected to write news and associated features, although on occasions, and if you are extremely experienced, you may be allowed to include a comment piece in a sidebar next to your main story. Smaller regional newspapers or broadcast outlets may well give you more responsibility, more quickly, than a metropolitan outlet would. Do not get the wrong idea that reporters are often called upon to put forth their opinion. Opinion column writing remains a minority activity in mainstream media journalism, even if it has grown to dominate much online media.

Not an expert

Becoming a roundsperson in the first place does not mean that you are an expert in that topic—or even have much of an interest in it. You might just happen to be there when the editor wanted to assign a new roundsperson. Former science editor of the *New York Times*, Cory Dean, had been a Washington-based political writer, but then the managing editor of the newspaper saw her in the cafeteria with a copy of the magazine *Scientific American* under her arm. Suddenly she was in charge of a highly respected, 24-page, weekly science supplement in one of the world's leading newspapers. She had to learn very quickly, on the job. Such is the fate of all journalists—you are constantly having to learn new tricks. In Ms Dean's case, she did it so well that she developed an interest in a scientific subject herself and went on to publish books on coastline management. While you may certainly express an interest in a particular round, and the editor may be receptive, on the whole the forces that dictate the allocation of rounds in the mainstream media may well be outside your control. Go with it and enjoy the fact that you get to learn a whole new range of knowledge that you never knew existed. It could end up being an unforeseen and ultimately fortuitous fork in your particular road.

Become part of the furniture

Being assigned to a round means that you have to become, in many ways, a part of the milieu of that round. In other words, if you are an industrial roundsperson, then you will be a familiar figure at Trades and Labour Council meetings, at individual union and employer group meetings, at strikes, rallies, media conferences and announcements and in the corridors and offices of the people from whom you obtain your news. A local government roundsperson attends all relevant meetings, announcements and events, and will have a contact list filled with relevant local players and a head filled with detailed knowledge of local issues. A science correspondent will hang out in laboratories, talking to scientists and reading their published papers. She will attend important scientific conferences and become familiar with the current controversies, conundrums and important personalities. A court reporter will be at court most days of the week and will also cultivate a range of sources among the practitioners and academics relevant to the field. He also will know how to read a court transcript. A court reporter will pay careful attention to detail and, of course, will understand the implications of not being able to record events in court using a tape recorder. Excellent listening and note-taking abilities go with this patch, as does a solid understanding of the law and its conventions. The court reporter may also be called upon to report more broadly on issues in the justice system.

You can see that as a roundsperson you will need to know the lie of the land, and to understand the issues of the round, so that you will know about stories before they break, and will be able to write about them in a well-informed manner.

Do your homework

You may have to do a great deal of your own background reading and other research to get yourself familiar with the territory you will be expected to cover. A courts roundsperson, for example, would be well advised to revise the laws of *sub judice*, defamation and other matters relating to the coverage of legal matters (see Chapter 17 for an overview of need-to-know legal information). Journalists who breach the laws of *sub judice* while covering a trial may be responsible for the whole trial being aborted—this has happened many times in Australia. In extreme cases, journalists can be found to be in contempt of court and be sentenced to jail when convicted of this charge. There is a good reason that media law is a compulsory part of most journalism degrees or majors in Australia. These issues are not trivial in journalism generally, and knowledge of them is an everyday necessity for courts roundspeople. You also need to be aware that as a court reporter you will have no more rights to interact with the courts than any other member of the public, and you will not necessarily be granted any special access. However, in practice, courts often do provide areas in courtrooms that are set aside for reporters. Most court reporters adhere to the conventions and courtesies of courtroom life, including bowing their heads slightly towards the magistrate or judge upon entering the court.

As a roundsperson you have a serious responsibility to understand what you are dealing with in your round. The courts round is the most obvious example of this, owing to the potentially severe penalties for getting it wrong, but the same goes for the other rounds as well. You need to understand the basic issues and the major players, and you must be able to recognise a big story when you see one developing. You should be able to avoid having too many surprises sprung upon you if you are an effective roundsperson.

One of the most important tools for the roundsperson is the telephone. You will have to develop a network of contacts in your round, and ring them frequently—sometimes every day, in the case of police roundspeople—to keep abreast of developments. According to experienced Australian television police reporter Mike Smithson, quoted in a profile by Williams (2009), 'Unless you've got good contacts, all you'll be doing are the bleeding obvious stories, the stories that everybody else does. If you've got good contacts, you'll be doing the extraordinary stories.'

Further, it helps to cultivate the support staff of your contacts. Executive assistants, administrative officers, research assistants, information officers—these people usually are repositories of information and generally are able to facilitate access to your main contact. Sometimes the support staff will have all the information you need anyway, so you won't need to go any further. They may, for instance, be able to provide you with a report you are looking for, or the name of a person who has been involved in a project, or the date of a forthcoming international conference.

According to Conley (2002: 170) the rounds system establishes a 'knowledge bank' for a media organisation, and information is channelled accordingly. The chief of staff, or whoever is running the newsroom, will automatically direct incoming material on a particular topic to the relevant roundsperson. A round, says Conley, tends to give reporters a sense of autonomy and responsibility. Often, it means they are left alone to pursue their own priorities. When assigned a round, a reporter should chase up every clipping file (whether physical or electronic) related to the round for background on issues and develop a good understanding of how their media outlet has dealt with these stories in the past. The new rounds reporter should contact key news sources to organise meetings to familiarise each with the other. Gaining the confidence of sources and being able to talk to them freely are crucial to successful rounds work. Reporters must quickly grasp how the system of their round works—the relevant processes, politics and personalities, and their interrelationships. Additionally, they must be sure to read all important documents related to the round, such as Royal Commission reports or Senate inquiries.

Special issues for police roundspeople

One of the most common of all rounds—and one you are likely to encounter if are employed in daily journalism—is the police round. For many media outlets, this is where the action is. Crime has been a daily staple for media since media began. This is the very archetype of the hard news round and it calls for fast reflexes, quick thinking, ingrained ethics and a good nose for news. According to Conley (2002), police reporters are close to a community's most dramatic events: murders, robberies, fires, sieges, traffic accidents and natural disasters. These are all tried and true topics that the audience consistently wants to consume. Indeed, through monitoring emergency services radio communications (something of a legal grey area, but nevertheless common practice throughout Australian newsrooms), quite often the police reporter finds out about the latest crimes and crises at the same time as emergency services personnel. Needless to say, this requires a strong ethical sense among police roundspeople to ensure that this information is used responsibly.

Reporting on police investigations of crime provides essential media stories, but it can also throw up some challenges for the reporter who seeks to behave as a true representative of the Fourth Estate. Striking the right balance in reporter–police relations can be genuinely difficult. Reporters new to the speciality will be watched closely by the police to see if they are trustworthy, and are likely to be kept at arm's length, at least initially. If there is no trust, there is no relationship. On the other hand, the reporter still has a watchdog role, even if she must work closely with the people being watched over. A reporter should never be a PR person for the police; a professional distance must be maintained. In some cases, reporters become too close to police sources who turn out to be corrupt. The infamous history of police corruption in this country is testament to the fact that many reporters have faced this very issue. If reporters have evidence of corruption, they may find themselves in a difficult situation of potentially losing the trust they had nurtured by revealing the information they have. It is important to note that to conceal such information isn't an option, because this would make the reporter as culpable as the corrupt police.

There are many other potentially tricky issues to contemplate. For example, part of being a police roundsperson involves interviewing eyewitnesses to distressing events. You must be mindful of your ethical responsibilities that include considering the public interest issues around reporting grief (see Chapter 16). While you may certainly be persistent in obtaining all relevant eyewitness accounts to, say, a highway pile-up, a plane crash or a major flood, you must never hound people or pursue a sensationalist angle. Likewise, children who are eyewitnesses should be approached with extreme care, and there is an argument for not interviewing them at all in these circumstances. Your ethical decision not to interview children will generally be accepted by senior editorial management, so don't be afraid to make that decision. In the end, you have to exercise your own conscience and not step outside your own ethical boundaries.

The role of public relations in police reporting

Another increasing issue is the rise of public relations in managing the flow of information. This is an issue in all rounds, but it can be a particularly vexing roadblock when dealing with police stories. Getting quick and decisive information on breaking crime stories is essential for the specialist reporter. While in many cases the staff of the police public relations (PR) unit will be allies for the reporter in getting exactly what is needed without delay, sometimes public relations practitioners, often acting under orders from senior management, can act to block access and slow down the information-gathering process. As a specialist police reporter, you will need to deal with this issue and find ways to overcome this obstacle. There is no substitute for doing your job professionally and maintaining integrity and honesty—these are timeless qualities that will mark you as someone worthy of trust. Public relations in sensitive areas, including crime, has more scope than other areas for over-protection and (occasionally) paranoia, so a reputation for being straight will assist you throughout your career. This does not mean that you will obey police public relations directives not to approach your own police sources for inside information. It simply means that you will follow the story using all the ethical means you have at your disposal, and will write it with honesty and without an external agenda. If the police PR unit helps you do to do that, then great, but if it doesn't, then you must go your own way. As always, you have to represent the interests of the general public.

Professional detachment

The most important feature of rounds is that you need to immerse yourself in your round, while still, of course, maintaining professional detachment from your contacts. The roundsperson role is an important one, because in a sense you become a part of the scene and, therefore, you are best placed to report on major developments in a depth that would not otherwise be possible. Therein lies something of a trap—a too-cosy relationship can sometimes develop between contacts and roundspeople, to the point where reporters may become reluctant to be frank about a developing story because of a sense of allegiance to sources within the sector. One criticism often levelled at political reporters who work out of the federal press gallery is that they live in press gallery world, where they work and socialise with the people they are attempting to scrutinise. This is not a trivial issue—objectivity can disappear when you become drinking mates with key players. While no one would suggest that you become a social outcast in your round, it is your responsibility to ensure that you do not lose your ability to report impartially and comprehensively.

Specialising in the trade media

There is a whole world of employment opportunities for specialist journalists in the trade media. The publications to be found in this sector are generally known only to professionals in particular areas. They are often available only by subscription and deal with sometimes highly specific topic areas, such as air-conditioner engineering, boat building, surfboard fabrication, cardboard box manufacture or organic farming—with correspondingly low circulation rates to a tight-knit audience. Some are rather broader, including various business and commerce journals, travel industry newspapers, science and technology magazines, and the fashion industry press. These publications have launched many a glittering media career and should be weighed up as potential workplaces by aspiring journalists. An excellent listing of all publications in Australia, including some extremely specific and obscure publications, may be found in the Margaret Gee's *Media Guide*. Working as a journalist on a trade publication can be similar to being a roundsperson on a metropolitan publication, and just as satisfying. Because they often have a small editorial staff, it is possible to be given quite a bit of responsibility quickly, as long as you do a good job and establish clear competence in the field. You may well find that more senior responsibilities come your way more quickly than might have been the case on a larger publication. You will also develop extremely good contacts and, if you want to move to the mainstream media at some stage, you will take with you an extensive **contact book**.

Perhaps one of the biggest ethical dilemmas facing specialist reporters on trade publications is the absolute requirement not to be swayed by advertisers. Often within the rather narrow specialities of the trade press, advertisers have quite a bit of clout and may attempt to influence what appears in the editorial pages of the publication. This is a perennial problem in the trade press, but an ethical reporter will never be swayed by demands from advertisers either to report favourably on their new product or event, or to decline to report anything contentious or critical. The only possible exception to this is the so-called advertising feature (or advertorial), which is clearly identified as advertising and is combined with associated editorial that has been paid for as a piece of advertising. In the end, all publications, no matter how specialised, need to maintain high standards of objective journalism—and this means not being beholden to advertisers when it comes to accurate and comprehensive specialised reporting.

Contact book: An electronic or hard copy listing of journalistic sources of information, often with notations to update the information. Journalists refer to their contact book regularly when seeking comment for stories.

Conclusion

Reporting is a multifaceted occupation that has to span a range of topics few other professions require. While a reporter cannot be fully knowledgeable about all the many topics on the daily news agenda, she can find a niche in which the development of a knowledge base is encouraged and rewarded. Having a round is a great opportunity for a reporter and represents, in many cases, a step up the reporting ladder. It can also be the most satisfying kind of reporting, involving as it does a closer intellectual affinity with a topic area and a greater capacity to develop a depth of understanding and a more extensive contact base than a general reporter can hope to do. Doing it well will probably get you noticed within your media outlet and in the milieu of your round. This recognition brings with it a strong obligation not to be seduced by the entreaties from sources to neglect your professional ethics. You may also become uncomfortable with the idea of being typecast by your round and may seek to move around and try other fields; this is fine as long as the opportunities present themselves. In the end, though, most reporters enjoy the challenge and satisfaction of deepening their knowledge and expertise in a specialised field. Part of the excitement of this may even come from discovering that you are fascinated by a topic area you never thought about at all when you were at university. So keep an open mind and reap the rewards that are there to be experienced.

KEY REFERENCES

Conley, D. (2002). *The Daily Miracle* (2nd edn). Melbourne: Oxford University Press.

Tapsall, S. & Varley, C. (2001). *Journalism: Theory in Practice*. Melbourne: Oxford University Press.

Williams, B. (2009). 'Good contacts, extraordinary stories'. *Police Journal*, February.

CASE STUDY 4:

DIRTY DEEDS: UNCOVERING MARALINGA

LIZ TYNAN

Introduction

Maralinga: The nuclear weapons test site established in the South Australian desert where the United Kingdom tested seven major atomic bombs and conducted hundreds of smaller nuclear experiments between 1956 and 1963.

As we have shown in this textbook (see Chapter 4), in a democratic society the media ideally act as a watchdog over the holders of power in government, the legislature and the judiciary, in a role traditionally known as the Fourth Estate. The **Maralinga** case study shows what can happen if the Fourth Estate is not in operation. It also shows how a deficit in reporting can also be at least partially remedied once journalists become motivated and able to cover a story of national importance. Media coverage of the British nuclear tests at Maralinga, both during and long after they took place, reveals a tale of two eras. The strong contrasts that emerge in Australian media output at the time of the tests (from 1952 to 1963), compared with the later era (1978 to 1993), suggest entirely different approaches by the media. This is particularly evident in relation to the most dangerous scientific experiments ever undertaken in this country, the Vixen B minor trials at the Maralinga atomic weapons test range in South Australia between 1960 and 1963. Of all the tests carried out by the British atomic weapons authorities (with the cooperation of the Australian government), these left the biggest legacy of long-lasting radioactive pollution at the site. This pollution was allowed to remain in place for many years, potentially exposing any visitors to the site to grave danger.

In the earlier era—in which the Cold War was under way and several nations had begun building nuclear arsenals—journalists and their editors complied with official directions on what was allowed to be covered and based their stories almost entirely on official sources. The Fourth Estate's watchdog role was not applied to Vixen B and there was no contemporary journalistic coverage of these tests. The later era was characterised by more independent journalism that did not rely upon officially sanctioned information and that uncovered facts that government authorities from both eras had attempted to keep secret. In the later era, the truth about Vixen B was revealed by journalists who actively sought to place these dangerous experiments, and their long-term effects, on the public agenda. This case study is a clear example of why the Fourth Estate is needed in a democracy.

Only when the Australian media ceased their reliance on official sources did it become possible for the whole Maralinga story be uncovered and placed into its correct context. In a sequence of revelatory mainstream journalistic stories beginning in 1978, Maralinga secrets started being revealed to the Australian public. The sources for these stories were often leaked secret documents and the testimony of participants, all of which were actively pursued by journalists. Arguably, the capstone story in the saga was written by the pioneering Australian science journalist, Ian Anderson, and published in *New Scientist* in June 1993, based upon expert analysis of highly technical information.

The two eras

During the first era in this saga, the Australian government committed this nation to another country's nuclear test program, which contaminated a large part of this country's land. Intertwined with this is the later era, when the secrecy unravelled and some important names in Australian investigative journalism, such as Brian Toohey and Ian Anderson, used their formidable, independent journalistic skills to fight through the outright lies, official roadblocks and technical impenetrability of that earlier time to find out what really happened—and then tell the nation about it.

Maralinga

Maralinga, or 'Fields of Thunder', was the name given by anthropologists to part of the traditional home of the Pitjantjatjara and Yankunytjatjara (also known as the Tjarutja) peoples, 1000 km northwest of Adelaide, on the edge of the Nullarbor and just north of the Indian–Pacific train line. It is not their own name for the area, but was borrowed from a Northern Territory language group to give a more colourful appellation to an area known to surveyors simply as X300. The site's new name was made official in November 1953, as secret plans for a permanent British atomic test site in Australia gathered pace. The British atomic tests in Australia had been under way since the year before, when Britain exploded its first nuclear bomb, codenamed Hurricane, from a navy vessel docked at the Monte Bello Islands off the northwest coast of Western Australia on 3 October 1952. In October 1953, more ambitious bomb tests had been held not far from Maralinga, at a place called Emu Field. It was to be at Maralinga, however, where the British chose to establish the full infrastructure for extensive atomic weapons testing in Australia. The 3200 square kilometre desert site was to be a permanent base for these tests, although in the event it was shut down in 1963 as new international bans on atomic weapons testing came into force.

As well as living up to its moniker of Fields of Thunder, the place certainly fits the clichés of Australian outback landscape: it is dusty, flat, absurdly hot, barren, (seemingly) lifeless and waterless, and it's a long way from anywhere. In those days, just two generations ago, it was convenient vacant land, and sufficiently far away from the British voting public for that country to assert its nuclear-age ambitions. These had been somewhat thwarted by a mistrustful USA under its postwar *McMahon Act*, which put a stop to the sharing of nuclear secrets, a state of affairs not fully reversed until 1962. It was a time of increasing paranoia as the Cold War set in. The Soviet Union, with considerable input from nuclear spies such as Klaus Fuchs, Alan Nunn May and the notorious Cambridge gang of Philby, Burgess, MacLean and Blunt, was able to test its own atomic bomb in 1949, dropping the Cold War temperature still further and sending a chill through Britain, which was still a few years away for testing its own device. Much nuclear weaponry information from the wartime Manhattan Project, which developed the atomic bombs dropped on Hiroshima and Nagasaki, was in Britain's possession already, and the country had set up an atomic weapons and energy project at Harwell, near Oxford. Indeed, Britain was at the forefront of the fundamental physics research that had made atomic weaponry possible.

But what it didn't have was space. When the UK prime minister at the time, Clement Atlee, wrote to Australian Prime Minister Robert Menzies on 16 September 1950, seeking permission to use Western Australia's Monte Bello islands for atomic testing, Menzies was eager to oblige.

It wasn't all sycophantism—there is evidence that Australia under Menzies had aspirations to join the nuclear club in its own right, and this was seen to be the way in; Menzies may not have been expected to know at that point just how tight the British would be with their information (but Menzies didn't ask too many questions either). Most of what Menzies agreed to was not publicised at the time, and, as the 1985 Royal Commission into the British nuclear tests makes clear, there were active attempts to limit or deny media access to information. While there were some protests from the media about the silence that prevailed over the test program, on the whole not much got out and the Australian public was largely oblivious at the time.

It was not too difficult to secure the test sites—in fact, it was achieved almost with a stroke of Menzies's pen. In the case of the Monte Bello islands bomb tests, he did so without informing or consulting Cabinet. Cabinet was, however, consulted about a permanent test site at Maralinga, and gave formal assent in 1954. Maralinga was active from 1956 to 1963, though it never hosted more than two series of mushroom cloud atomic bomb tests. It was used much more extensively for the top secret and significantly more dangerous minor trials.

The minor trials

At Maralinga, a series of innocent-sounding minor trials—as distinct from the mushroom-cloud atomic bomb blasts—let loose more than 20 kilograms of one of the deadliest materials known: a form of plutonium known as plutonium-239. Its radioactive half-life, during which it may cause serious illness in humans if ingested, is 24,000 years. This means that it takes longer than *Homo sapiens* has been in existence (100,000 years) for all traces of radioactivity to disappear. Vixen B involved non-nuclear explosions and deliberate destruction intended to test how bombs and related paraphernalia would behave if, for example, an aeroplane laden with nuclear warheads crashed on take-off. All the Vixen B tests were undertaken from firing pads at the far west of the Maralinga range at a site called Taranaki, which was the focus of later concern about plutonium contamination.

At the conclusion of Vixen B, a substantial area around Maralinga was saturated in plutonium. Plutonium is picked up readily in dust and can swirl around the landscape, making it easily inhaled by anyone in the vicinity. It is an insoluble particle that, if inhaled, lodges in the lungs where it can stay throughout a person's lifetime, it also irradiates its surroundings, potentially causing lung cancer. Given the dusty lifestyle of the original inhabitants of the Maralinga lands, this was a major, unacceptable risk. The other risk was of visitors to the site picking up souvenirs to place on the mantelpiece, from where the objects would emit their radiation. To this day, no one knows if such mantelpiece ornaments are still out there—there was a period of several years during the 1970s when the test range was not patrolled and anyone could have picked up a lump of plutonium-soaked rock.

While the British atomic bomb test program was reported by media in the 1950s, what was covered was tightly controlled by the UK and Australian governments, and the media did not undertake investigative journalism to more fully examine the tests. In addition, the minor trials were not covered by the media at all—not even superficially. Active measures were put in place by the test authorities to ensure, in particular, that Vixen B did not appear in the media. The Australian people did not find out about Vixen B until some important investigative journalism appeared years later.

Brian Toohey's Maralinga stories

Investigative journalist Brian Toohey was the first to break open the Maralinga story for a national audience, through a series of articles in the *Australian Financial Review*. The series began on 5 October 1978 with a story based upon a leaked Defence Department Cabinet submission that had been prepared by the Defence Department under its then minister Jim Killen. Headlined 'Killen warns on plutonium pile', with a strapline (subheading) of 'Terrorist threat to British atomic waste', the page-one story revealed the ticking time bomb of Maralinga. It was a factual account of the contents of the submission, with added commentary on the consequences arising from those contents.

The 5 October story was widely picked up by the broader media and caused considerable consternation to the federal Coalition government of Malcolm Fraser. However, an even greater impact was felt after Toohey's follow-up story on 11 October 1978. This article, titled 'Maralinga: The "do nothing" solution', brought down the wrath of Minister for Defence Killen on Toohey's head. The story put pressure on the Australian government to declare what it would do about the plutonium, since the British at that stage were refusing to remove it. The British stance had been backed by a supportive statement from Australian Acting Minister for Foreign Affairs Ian Sinclair, who played down any risks. Toohey was not deterred, particularly as the leaked Cabinet submission had made strong statements about the terrorist threat that the material at Maralinga posed. The 11 October story quoted a media release issued by Killen on the evening of 5 October, after publication of the first *Australian Financial Review* story, in which he also denied there was an immediate threat.

Upon publication of this story, Killen responded even more forcefully. He took the unusual step of castigating Toohey and the *Australian Financial Review* in federal parliament. The attack was detailed and sustained. Killen claimed that the submission did not make assertions about an immediate terrorist threat, although one could conceivably exist if no action were taken, and that publicising this threat 'was an act of irresponsibility'. Toohey was not put off by the attacks and continued to publish more stories in this series on 12 and 13 October, opening new angles for public scrutiny.

In May 1984, when Toohey worked for the now-defunct *National Times* and a few months before the Royal Commission into the British nuclear tests began taking evidence, he also published a landmark feature on the legacy of Vixen B. The feature, titled 'Plutonium on the wind: The terrible legacy of Maralinga', was a detailed summing up of the Vixen B issue, with full weight given to the relevant science in a way that had not been done before in the media. One of the points of difference between the contemporary media coverage and the later coverage was the ease with which later journalists dealt with the scientific and technological aspects of the story.

Toohey's coverage of the Maralinga issue was pivotal in it entering the public domain. While the Royal Commission later sparked considerable media coverage, Toohey's stories, and those that followed by other reporters, were not only informed by the science of the tests, but they also showed a much clearer understanding of the politics of the British tests than any stories of the tests themselves published at the time. They were not dictated or guided by politicians or other authorities, and their sources included both leaked information and independent corroboration from scientists and test participants. A clear change had taken place in how the events at Maralinga were approached by journalists and media organisations.

The breakthrough investigative reporting undertaken by Toohey set a new standard for how the tests would be reported in the future, with a distinct Fourth Estate approach to keeping democratic government accountable.

Dirty Deeds: Ian Anderson and Maralinga

Ian Anderson's 1993 *New Scientist* story, 'Britain's dirty deeds at Maralinga', was the first journalistic story to show the full extent of contamination at Maralinga. Even the McClelland Royal Commission—a thorough, and thoroughly hostile, investigation fronted by the former ALP politician 'Diamond Jim' McClelland in particularly colourful mode—didn't find what was left for Anderson to uncover. Anderson showed a particularly damaging untruth that had ramifications back in Britain and ultimately helped to force the British to pay for a clean-up at the site. Observers and participants claim that Anderson's story created a particular moral atmosphere in 1993, opening up for public debate disturbing new information that raised fundamental questions about the very nature of the Australia–UK relationship.

'Britain's dirty deeds at Maralinga' subsequently received two major science journalism awards. Anderson was by then a doyen of Australian science journalism, having made his name reporting for *New Scientist* from the USA, before returning to his home town of Melbourne in 1989, where set up the Australian edition of the publication.

Specialist journalists are (or should be) particularly good at cultivating excellent sources and Anderson had the best possible source for this story: the fallout expert and long-time secretary to the committee set up by the Australian government to oversee safety issues at Maralinga, John Moroney, an Australian. Moroney, once a loyal servant of the British test program, later became bitter and disillusioned when he discovered how much he and the rest of the country had been duped. His painstaking work, in the three years or so before Anderson's exposé, provided the scientific basis for showing that the British had covered up the extent of plutonium contamination. He was a key source for Anderson, but was desperately ill as the story was being prepared and died within days of publication. He is not mentioned by name in the story, but there is no question that it was Moroney's research that made Anderson's story possible.

Moroney's analysis of about 2500 pages of declassified nuclear contamination data from trials in the USA that were almost identical to Vixen B, known as the Roller Coaster trials, finally revealed the truth—that the British, who must have known what was happening, apparently thought (or hoped) that the Australians wouldn't notice. In essence, Moroney found that the British assertions about plutonium contamination at Maralinga were wrong by a factor of ten. There was ten times more radiation at the site than had been claimed. This made the area very much more dangerous than Australia had been led to believe, and made it impossible for the traditional owners to return without a proper clean-up. The British knew that the figures given to the Australian government were wrong, but they did not provide correct figures and attempted to sign away any responsibilities after a third ineffectual attempt at a clean-up in 1967. It was only with the declassification of US data and Moroney's commitment to understanding what those documents contained that the truth came out. It might have gone no further than Moroney's desk at the Australian Radiation Laboratory if Anderson hadn't become involved and taken on the story as a detailed and painstaking piece of investigative reporting.

When the *New Scientist* story came out, Anderson appeared on many shows, including as the lead story on ABC TV's *7.30 Report*—and it galvanised the Australian government. That it had a significant impact is certain, though the extent of it is difficult to measure. Anderson, a modest man, confirmed later that year that 'the article played a … general role—it added to the moral pressure that parliamentarians and others were bringing to bear on the British government to acknowledge its responsibilities and pay up'. The article was faxed to then Minister for Energy Simon Crean by his staff. The minister was already in Europe with Attorney-General Gareth Evans, preparing for a meeting with their counterparts in the UK to discuss the continuing political fallout from Maralinga. An obituary for Anderson (who died prematurely in 2000) in the *Guardian* by Philip Jones claimed that 'his evidence, and the media attention engendered by the material in such a prestigious science journal, played a crucial role in the successful conclusion of the talks'.

The outcome was payment by the British government of a total of £20 million (about $45 million) to be used to clean up the site—about half the actual cost. Before publication of the article, a number of prominent UK parliamentarians had been asserting that Britain had no obligations in this matter whatever. However, a deal was struck on 19 June by senior ministers from both governments and a clean-up was eventually carried out.

Conclusion

This case study demonstrates a fundamental difference in the behaviour of media towards the British nuclear test program between the two eras. The Maralinga Vixen B minor trials were of clear public importance and interest, but they were not subject to contemporary public scrutiny. However, the tests were covered extensively in Australian media from 1978 onwards, indicating their undisputed news value. Vixen B was extremely dangerous and had implications not only for human health but also for for Australia's treaty obligations and trade in radioactive materials. The fact that these tests did not attract any media scrutiny at all while they were under way reveals stark differences in the way the media operated in the two eras. At the time of the tests, the media activity around Maralinga was characterised by several features: first, media practitioners and proprietors were largely compliant to official wishes and mostly depended upon official sources for information about Maralinga. Second, despite a large program of Maralinga test activities after the end of the major trials in 1957, the media did not investigate or react to the activity at the site that could easily have alerted them to a continuation of testing. The Australian and British authorities, while doing all they could to deter journalistic investigation, in fact prepared for media interest that never came. The media did not go looking.

The Maralinga test site had been inspected by invited media contingents several times in the 1950s and its purpose was, in broad terms, known to the contemporary media. Officially staged media events at the site and in other locations discussing the Maralinga nuclear tests had been held. A significant portion of media material appearing in mainstream news outlets was made up simply of word-for-word official statements. The later era was completely different, with journalists actively seeking hidden information, cultivating informants and applying public pressure on politicians. The output of the later era shows greater depth, sophistication and knowledge of the science, technology and politics of nuclear weaponry.

Journalists were more familiar with the role of scientific issues in national affairs, were more prepared to challenge official information and more skilled at digging for hidden information.

This case study shows the evolution of the Australian media from a tentative and complaisant sector to an independent force capable of investigating complex scientific and technological stories with military and security implications, thus revealing an increased capacity for fulfilling a true Fourth Estate role.

KEY REFERENCES

Anderson, I. (1993). 'Britain's Dirty Deeds at Maralinga'. *New Scientist.* 12 June.

Toohey, B. (1978a). 'Killen Warns on Plutonium Pile'. *Australian Financial Review.* 5 October, 1.

Toohey, B. (1978b). 'Maralinga: The 'do nothing' solution'. *Australian Financial Review.* 11 October, 1, 10, 37.

TOOLS 4:

WRITING FEATURES

LIZ TYNAN

Introduction

Feature writing is the most varied of all journalistic styles. Many journalists enjoy this form of writing because of the scope afforded to them in choosing a topic and applying a broader vocabulary and more varied structure. Many kinds of features are possible, up to and including pieces that could be classed as literary. While journalists usually have more freedom of expression in feature writing than they do in news writing, this is not an invitation for undisciplined or self-indulgent writing. Part of the allure of features for the reader is being taken along for an exciting ride by a confident and skilled writer, who is aware that a good structure and engaging voice will instil confidence in the audience. The reader might not know where you are going, but hopefully they will trust you to get them there safely.

Feature writing complements the news

Features give depth, width, colour, gloss, sass, savvy, mind, heart and pathos to the media. They can give readers access to a level of understanding about a topic that cannot be achieved in the news format. Some use investigative journalism techniques in which the journalist finds, uncovers and elucidates hitherto obscured or disregarded information of great political, historical, scientific or social importance. Others explore the minutiae of individual experience to provide glimpses of private lives, traumas and triumphs. They may amuse or sadden, inspire or anger. They complement and extend the news, and are an indispensable part of public information as well as a great source of enjoyment for readers. As Ricketson (2004: 4) says, 'A first-rate feature can add almost as much to a newspaper as a breaking news story.'

Features cover a range of categories, although be aware that these have a tendency to overlap:

- news features, which flesh out a topic currently in the news
- investigative features, which uncover secrets and lies
- profiles, which reveal the lives of individuals
- human interest stories, which may be heartrending, gossipy or humorous
- special interest features, such as historical pieces, travelogues or how-to guides.

Pick up a broadsheet newspaper such as the *Weekend Australian* and see if you can identify all of these categories (and more). Hint: look into the 'Inquirer' section for news and investigative features and the colour magazine for profiles. Note how news features are almost always connected in some way to what appears in the first part of the paper, while other kinds of features may not be.

Structuring features

Once journalism students move on from the news story to learning how to write features, they sometimes become alarmed and confused that the strict forms of print news seem to be dispensed with, and that anything goes. That is not the case, as features have their own set of disciplines that do differ from the disciplines of news. Versatility is a useful characteristic among journalists, so it is wise to cultivate the ability to flip between the different styles, as you may find yourself doing both news and features in your professional life.

News stories are almost always shorter than features, although supplying a blunt statement of relative word counts is tricky—there is simply too much variation. Mainstream hard news stories rarely exceed 700 words, and most are much shorter. Features cover a broad range, usually (in Australia) from around 800 words up to no more than 3000 words. The standout exception is the famous literary magazine the *New Yorker*, which has been known to run features of up to 35,000 words.

Another distinguishing characteristic is structure. Feature articles are not written in the inverted pyramid form. The inverted pyramid (see Chapter 14) is intended to provide an efficient and streamlined way of providing information. Features have more space and, while still demonstrating disciplined writing, can be more discursive. Features tell a more detailed and comprehensive story, and they often do so using narrative devices that are entertaining and interesting for the reader. For example, a feature may begin with a pungent anecdote or a striking direct quote. It may play around with timeframes, perhaps beginning in the present, and then moving to the past, then back again. They balance out colour or evocative description with factual information—but be aware that they are always factual. In fact, the most entertaining and enjoyable journalistic features are grounded strongly in well-researched fact. This should give you the hint that while features may be creative in many ways, they are not flights of fancy or works of fiction. They are tied to reality and express facts about the world. Nevertheless, the story you tell may well take some twists and turns, like all good creative stories do. Stories can contain sudden surprises, revelations and wow moments. They can lead to a conclusion that you didn't allude to or reveal at the start. They can contain vivid descriptions of the people and places you are writing about. This is often best done using a strong structure that begins with a colourful anecdote, leads to statements about the factual basis of the topic, is bolstered and supported by a range of quotes from your sources, perhaps includes another compelling anecdote, then is wrapped up in a satisfying and circle-completing manner at the end. A structure such as this provides a rhythm to your piece, and is a helpful starting point. Experienced writers take pleasure in subverting the formula, but will do so in a knowing way.

Anecdotes

Anecdote: A vignette or brief word picture that describes an incident, which is often used to illustrate the main theme of a journalistic feature.

Anecdotes are vignettes, brief word pictures that describe an incident relating to your main theme. In feature writing they must be short and pithy, or they may become shaggy dog stories that try the reader's patience. Here's a brief guide to constructing anecdotes:

- Compose a simple story based on your interview or interviews and/or research.
- Use concrete imagery that will enable readers to create pictures in their heads.
- Flesh out the detail and character descriptions.
- Stay in one time and place.
- Use short quotes and facts if possible.

The following in an example of an anecdote used at the start of a feature by Kate Legge in the *Weekend Australian Magazine*:

> Margaret Wood's Uncle Len—a bookie well known for the 10-bob note he'd twist into a bow tie—failed to deliver a single winning tip when she went with a girlfriend to Melbourne's spring carnival in 1962. 'I'd never been to the races before. Mum said "Go and see Len and get your tips from him", which we did. They all lost. The whole lot of them', she recalls. But luck visited her when she least expected its golden touch with a tap on the shoulder from a racing official, who suggested she enter the inaugural Fashions on the Field. (Legge 2010)

In anecdotes, things happen to people, or people make things happen. They can be encapsulated in a few words or they may extend to a few paragraphs. And, as Legge's example shows, they give readers the capacity to imagine the scene. We can see Uncle Len's bow tie and we can also see the racing official tapping a young woman on the shoulder at a racetrack. By helping us see things, anecdotes provide a mental landscape for the story that is to follow. When you read features in the media, watch for the many anecdotes writers use to help you understand the story. Here are a few examples of the kinds of action that can be conveyed using an anecdote:

- It is raining, and Mikhail Baryshnikov is standing in a courtyard in Riga.
- Early this year, villagers noticed that hundreds of dead fish started floating in the muddy river near the Bakun dam site.
- When the verdict was read she started sobbing.
- In Andy Warhol's new loft studio, 'The Factory', Viva leaned against the whitewashed plaster wall, her cotton-candy hair bright blonde under the spotlights.

Creating compelling anecdotes does take some practice and sensitivity. Listen intently during your interviews, and follow up when you hear a good descriptive story developing.

Creating a theme

A good writer guides the reader through the story. One important way to do this is to ensure that you have a single, coherent theme that unifies the whole piece and that can make the reader feel confident they understand the landscape you will be traversing. Going off on tangents confuses the reader. Even as you surprise and delight your reader with new insights and compelling imagery, you must stick to a single context. A way to do this is to provide an overarching statement near the beginning that makes the theme explicit. A recapitulation of the theme in supporting statements further on will enable the reader to keep the context in mind. These statements should tie together the article and provide it with a fruitfully narrowed focus.

Statement of theme: Summary sentence to remind the reader of a feature article of its main idea.

Each of the following sentences could work as a **statement of theme** in a feature story:

- The war in Chechnya was one of the world's most brutal conflicts.
- Venture to the epicentre of our resources boom—the Pilbara—to see Australia's split personality economy at its most intense.
- Several measures of social capital are on the wane.
- The San Bernardino Valley lies only an hour east of Los Angeles by the San Bernardino Freeway but is in certain ways an alien place.

A statement to set the theme doesn't have to be the first thing you write—use a good anecdote if you have one—but you will need to make a context statement somewhere in your story. Not placing a statement of theme might disorient your readers.

Quotes

Quote: A statement attributed to someone; a direct quote is a statement in quotation marks, while an indirect quote has no quotation marks.

It may not exactly have eternal life, but a media quote is not as ephemeral as most human utterances, so it should be carefully chosen. A **quote** is a statement attributed to someone. A direct quote is a verbatim statement in quotation marks. An indirect quote summarises what someone has said and has no quotation marks, but it still includes an attribution. We obtain quotes from the people we interview—the primary sources—or from secondary sources, such as published material (see Tools 1).

Quotes give stories the voices of the participants and the commentators. They lend authority and colour and interest, and are essential in most journalistic writing—perhaps especially so in features. Record them carefully and reproduce them accurately. While you are doing your interviews, highlight in your notebook those quotes that strike you as the most vivid and insightful.

Here are some tips for using quotes in features:

- Choose quotes carefully, being mindful of their need to advance the story and add life and colour.
- Keep them short and to the point: avoid large slabs of verbatim transcript.
- Reserve especially pungent quotes to open or close your story.
- Edit quotes for grammar if necessary, but never distort the meaning or intent of the original statement.

Facts and figures

Your writing will benefit from a variety of facts and figures, which are a sign of research and will give your work solidity and authority. Wafty, unresearched writing is ultimately unsatisfying for the reader. Consider the following statements:

- The National Broadband Network (NBN) is Australia's largest infrastructure project. (fact)
- The fibre optic network is projected to cost $43 billion. (fact)
- The NBN has grown to Godzilla-like proportions. (simile)

- The project has been initiated without a full cost-benefit or risk analysis, and large sections of the public are unconvinced that it will be the panacea for the nation's broadband problems. (comment)

Notice that the comment, while slanted in a particular direction, must also be factual. Everything in a feature story has to be factual, even if the writer uses facts to structure a particular argument.

Facts alone, though, are rarely engaging. Some people call them factoids to disparage them, and certainly if they are used in a dull way they will, in fact, be dull. But they can be used to great effect by a skilled writer.

A feature about the effect of climate change on coral reefs, for example, will contain factual information on how corals are affected by higher temperatures and particularly the crucial symbiotic relationship between coral and algae that is damaged by warmer seas. It may also include information on recent large-scale coral bleaching events, a description of how the acidity of seawater affects animals that build calcium carbonate skeletons, and scientific projections on likely future scenarios. This is important baseline information you need to provide a foundation for the overall theme and for the anecdotes and colourful quotes that you provide. To persuade your reader that your feature is trustworthy, you must use accurate factual material.

Here are some tips on the use of facts:

- Don't overdo facts and figures but never omit the important ones.
- Avoid placing too many facts into one paragraph—spread them through the article.
- Obtain facts from authoritative sources.
- Always check that the facts are accurate.

Smooth joins

It's important to make seamless transitions between your anecdotes, your theme-setting prose, your quotes and your facts. The example below, from a *Vanity Fair* feature about the famous trial of a man accused of defrauding the estate of his mother, celebrated society philanthropist Brooke Astor, shows an effective combination of various elements. Notice how you can picture the scene being set and also learn new things, while you are developing an understanding of the territory this feature is going to cover.

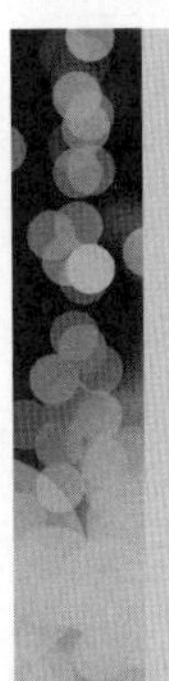

The New Astor Court

By Meryl Gordon

Room 1536 at Manhattan's 100 Centre Street courthouse, with its utilitarian brown linoleum floor and fluorescent lighting, hardly seems like the setting for an emotionally riveting society drama. Yet as the case of *The People of the State of New York v. Anthony Marshall and Francis Morrissey Jr.*—more popularly known as the Brooke Astor trial—entered its third month, the room bristled with electricity. Even the veteran court stenographer admitted, 'Every day, I feel like I'm in a Jackie Collins novel.'

Source: Gordon (2009).

Show, don't tell

Show-don't-tell principle: The advice given to all media writers to use interesting material to illustrate a point rather than bluntly state something you want the reader to know.

The **show-don't-tell** principle means that you use interesting material to illustrate a point rather than just bluntly state something you want the reader to know. For instance, in a profile, instead of just writing the bland fact 'Johanna Bloggs is great with children', describe a scene where Johanna is interacting with children. Then readers can draw their own conclusion about how the profiled person relates to children. You show action in scenes rather than give summaries of the outcomes of actions.

Elaborating the structure

Not every sentence in your feature story will fit neatly into the feature writing elements we have been looking at. One of the joys of feature writing is that there is more room to deviate from prescriptive forms such as news writing. But you must understand the notions of structure before you start mucking about with them. Undisciplined writing might be fun for the writer, but it is not much fun for the reader. You have a duty to your readers to perform a service for them, and part of that is the unspoken, unwritten agreement that you will take them on a journey that they can really enjoy without feeling confused or alienated. So, keeping in mind your need to consider your reader, you can consider elaborating the basic structure in various ways, for example:

- when the basic elements are in place, you can build on them with passages of description and exposition
- beware of extended passages in telling mode, as there is a danger the feature story will then resemble an essay, an instruction pamphlet or an excerpt from an encyclopaedia
- always return to the basic elements, using description and exposition to occasionally fill in the gaps and provide background information.

The language of feature writing

Features are great vehicles for fine writing. You should aim for grace, economy, correctness and style, as in all your media writing. You can add compelling narrative and literary merit too—if you want to and if your editor agrees.

Tips to achieve forceful prose include the following (also see Chapters 4 and 14):

- write in the active voice where possible; use passive voice sparingly
- use concrete rather than abstract words and images
- edit every sentence for brevity and conciseness
- minimise adjectives and adverbs where possible
- remove redundancies and tautologies
- avoid exclamation marks
- avoid rhetorical questions

As a general principle, simplify your writing as much as possible. Overblown, flowery and ornate language is not journalistic. Aim for clear, straightforward, tight language. This form of language is more likely to grab and hold the reader, and keep them enthralled to the end.

First person

The feature writer has more scope than the news reporter to engage personally with the story, and some choose to do this by using first person, placing themselves into the narrative. The trend to greater use of the first person in journalism is unmistakeable and it would be wrong to counsel dogmatically against its use. Nevertheless, those new to journalism should proceed cautiously and ensure that the presence of the 'I' is justified by the theme and content of the article. Few articles are primarily about the reporter, so even if the 'I' is used, it will be there to show a relationship between the journalist and the main participants in the story, while still endeavouring to keep the focus on the participants. Friedlander and Lee (2004: 195) agree that the first person pronoun may be justified when the writer has personally experienced extraordinary events. Do not use the personal pronoun gratuitously—there must be a point to it. It must pass the 'Who cares?' test; that is, if there is no reason for the readers to care about the personal experiences or opinions of the reporter, there is no place for the personal pronoun.

Keep the ego in check

While we are free to push the limits of journalistic writing further in feature writing than we are in news, we are not free to be self-indulgent—a characteristic that irks editors (not to mention readers), and is to be avoided. Good editors like feature writers to primarily be writers: people who have talent for the craft of writing and a respect for its conventions and disciplines. Being paid to write can be a difficult gig to get and to keep. Acceptance of the need to keep the ego within bounds is helpful for a long-lasting career.

Colourful landscapes

The best features have an X factor that, to the extent it can be analysed, is most likely a magical combination of logical and clever structure, fine language use, a great topic, thorough research, illustrative quotes and anecdotes, and a visual or mental landscape that draws the reader in.

Sometimes a mechanism for achieving this is colour or atmosphere. To paraphrase Matthew Ricketson (2004), where hard news is about information, colour is about emotion. Colourful writing is not all of feature writing, and its scope may be limited, because colour alone does not give the full story. But where the use of colour works, stories are given an unforgettable quality that lives on after the reader has put down the newspaper or magazine. It is deceptively difficult to do well, because it depends upon the journalist's ability to observe and describe. To a certain extent, too, it depends upon the writer's sensitivity and depth of knowledge.

It really helps to be culturally literate, to understand and use a wide range of references that add depth and nuance to your work. To illustrate this, here are the opening passages from a Clive James piece, 'Postcard from Japan 1: An Exchange of Views' (1984):

> By courtesy of a British Airways Boeing 707 I was crossing in a few hours the same distance that cost Marco Polo years of his life, but the speed of modern travel has its penalties. Among these had been the inflight movie, which I dimly remember was about bears playing baseball.
>
> From the air, Siberia looks like cold nothing. The Sea of Japan looks like wet nothing. But Japan itself, at your first glimpse of it, looks like something. Even geographically it's a busy place.
>
> Immediately you are impressed by the wealth of detail—an impression that will never leave you for as long as you are there. Only a tenth of the land is useful for anything. The remaining nine-tenths, when you look down on it, is a kind of corduroy velvet: country so precipitously convoluted that the rivers flowing through it look like the silver trails of inebriated slugs. The useful tenth is inhabited, cultivated and industrialised with an intensity that boggles the Occidental mind. I have never seen anything like it in my life.
>
> Seen from high up, the basic agricultural pattern of Western countries is of accumulated squares. America looks like a patchwork quilt; France like another quilt but with smaller patches; Britain like yet another quilt with smaller patches still. The basic agricultural pattern of Japan is of proliferating brain cells. Everywhere a rice paddy can possibly be put a rice paddy has been put, even if it is only the size of a table napkin.
>
> Merging with this nervous tissue, like bionic grafts, are the areas of urban habitation and industry. One hundred and ten million live and work down there, most of them in conurbations which to the stratospheric eye look like infinitely elaborate printed circuits. You can tell straight away, before you even touch the ground, that in Japan there is nowhere anybody can hide. They're all in it together.

This amusing and insightful piece on Japan demonstrates a range of skill not limited to knowing how to write well. James also demonstrates historical and geographical knowledge, and an understanding of geopolitics, agricultural practices, electronic circuitry, arcane but apposite terminology (such as Occidental), and concepts in science, specifically, neurology.

In other words, there is no point just observing if you don't have the knowledge to give flesh to your observations. You can look but you won't be able to see. And you won't be able to write. The James piece is simple in its words and structure for the most part, but that simplicity hints at a wide, sophisticated base of knowledge upon which he is drawing. Being able to see the connection between the agricultural pattern of Japan from the air and the notion of brain cells is not a given. A prepared mind has to make that connection.

James has deftly provided the reader with a visual image of the country that he is about to explore. He has created an atmosphere of nervousness, multitude and elaborateness. After setting the scene, he moves to an amusing anecdote about his difficulties getting past Japanese officials at the airport, an anecdote made all the more effective by the atmosphere that has already been invoked. Anyone reading this feature will form an emotional connection as well as an intellectual one.

Conclusion

The Clive James feature demonstrates the essence of good feature writing: connecting readers to the subject matter. This is the whole point and ultimately the key to successful feature writing: you need to bring the topic to life for the reader, crafting your words so that the reader can see the events and the people you are evoking. There are few more enjoyable things to read than a well-written feature. The nice thing is that there are few journalistic tasks more enjoyable as well.

TIPS ON WHAT TO DO AND WHAT TO AVOID

Make sure you always:

- be mindful of the need for accuracy, as much as you must be for a news story
- find a workable blend of anecdotes, theme statements, quotes and facts to make a satisfying and well-rounded story
- choose quotes with care
- add colour by deep observation refined through cultural literacy.

Make sure you never:

- use a feature as an opportunity for an ego trip or a dazzling display of experimental grammar
- overdo the pronoun 'I'
- allow anecdotes to run on too long
- neglect the strict architecture of structure, even if you are subverting that structure.

To really shine, you should:

- keep in mind that features are an important part of the conversation of humanity, and they should be written with due consideration to their role.

KEY REFERENCES

Conley, D. & Lamble, S. (2006). *The Daily Miracle.* Melbourne: Oxford University Press.

Friedlander, E. J. & Lee, J. (2004). *Feature Writing for Newspapers and Magazines: The Pursuit of Excellence.* Boston: Allyn & Bacon.

Gordon, M. (2009). 'The New Astor Court'. *Vanity Fair,* September.

Johnson, C. (2005). *21st Century Feature Writing.* Melbourne: Pearson Education.

Ricketson, M. (2004). *Writing Feature Stories: How to Research and Write Newspaper and Magazine Articles.* Sydney: Allen & Unwin.

PART 5

FRAMEWORKS AND SOCIAL CONTEXTS

The history of media, in terms of its development and research, is marked by a series of moral panics: moments of anxiety when media industries and media texts alike are accused of challenging societal norms and values and therefore contributing to the breakdown of society as a whole.

Media industries do not act unfettered. Aside from the watchdog role journalism plays, media operate in frameworks of legislation, regulation and obligation. Chapter 16 looks at ethics in communication. The implications of legal issues in the media are profound and Chapter 17, Media Law, provides the need-to-know essentials.

This section also reflects on the many novel and evolving aspects of the brave new media world. In Chapter 18, The New Media Environment: Digital and Social Media, we extend our analysis of media by considering the contemporary social contexts in which media functions, in particular the technological revolution engendered by the rise of digital media. In Chapter 19, Convergence, we examine developing media intersections. We go on to examine the evolving relationship between media, society and culture that can be characterised as part of postmodernity. This is an analysis of where media have come from, where they are now and where they might go in the future.

Case Study 5, New Media and Ethical Practice: Journalism and Blogging on the World Wide Web, uses an ethical frame to understanding twenty-first century journalism practice in the digital age at a time when the production of news is increasingly taking place within and outside of professional news organisations.

Tools 5, New Media and Journalism Practice, provides an overview of the new media tools essential to contemporary journalism. As we move into the second decade of the twenty-first century all professional journalists are expected to have the skills to produce news stories across multiple platforms (at the very least, print and online). These new formats have put new demands on journalists and changed the way journalists go about their craft.

CHAPTER 16

ETHICS IN COMMUNICATION

NICOLA GOC AND LIZ TYNAN

Introduction

Few areas in society are more subject to charges of ethical compromise than the communication professions, particularly media and public relations. These are major components of the public sphere, and encroach on people's lives in many ways. They deal in information, and that information can be manipulated for many purposes. Media and public relations practitioners have attempted to diffuse ethics-based criticism by producing codes of ethics that seek to monitor the behaviour of those working in these fields. Most practitioners also recognise that working sustainably and ensuring that the media and public relations play positive roles in modern society require a high standard of conduct. The record shows that only a relatively small proportion of media and public relations professionals actively seek to be unethical, but the intense scrutiny and visibility inherent in communication, and the power of what they do, make these professions especially vulnerable to complaint in this area. This chapter examines the ethical issues at stake, and outlines the ways the professions attempt to deal with these issues.

This chapter looks at:

- ethics in journalism
- the core ethical issues facing journalists today
- codes of ethics
- ethics in public relations
- the public relations ethics backlash.

Journalism ethics

Daily we see examples of journalists behaving badly. We know journalists don't always present balanced reports, that sensationalism, distortion and exaggeration can be used to create headline-grabbing news and that some journalists fabricate stories, for example, the infamous American journalists Jayson Blair and Stephen Glass, who defrauded their colleagues and readers at the *New York Times* and *New Republic*, respectively. But at the same time we are daily informed about despotic governments, political crises, contaminated waterways, bushfire threats, floods and tsunamis, traffic accidents, unsafe buildings, killers on the run, terrorist threats and impending wars—all through the work of news journalists.

In 1994, when more than a million people were massacred in Rwanda—despite a United Nations military mission being aware, in advance, of the killing plan—an inquiry into the slaughter concluded that the United Nations mission 'might have prevented genocide by leaking to the *New York Times* rather than reporting to their superiors' (Reeves 1998: 21). Journalism matters. Democratic societies simply cannot function without the practice of ethical journalism through a free press.

Moral philosophy: an overview

Ethics: A system of moral principles, by which a person can judge right and wrong in any field, for example, media ethics.

Deontology: Also known as rights-based ethics, it assumes that each individual has certain rights, no matter the circumstances, and that no innocent person should be harmed or killed for any reason.

Consequentialism: A branch of ethical philosophy in which notions of morality are based not on a set of rules but on observing the outcomes, the consequences, of every separate action. Consequentialists weigh up the consequences and decide where the majority of the benefit lies.

Virtue ethics: The emphasis on the virtues, or moral character, in contrast to the duties or rules (deontology) or the consequences of actions (consequentialism).

Utilitarianism: The ethical doctrine that the greatest happiness for the greatest number should be the criterion of a virtuous action.

The three major schools of thought in modern **ethics** are deontology, consequentialism and virtue ethics. **Deontology**, or rights-based ethics, tends to rely upon prescriptive arguments and rules, and is often, though not always, associated with various religions. In deontology, the underlying assumption is that each individual has certain rights, no matter the circumstances, and that no innocent person should be harmed or killed for any reason. Rights-based ethics features in many social questions, including euthanasia and abortion. In general, the deontologist would say that euthanasia or abortion should not be permitted, because an innocent person would be killed. However, a terminally ill person who is a deontologist might well claim a right to die as well, so you can see that it is not a clear-cut matter.

The second school, **consequentialism**, bases notions of morality not on a set of rules but on observing the outcomes or consequences of every separate action. Consequentialists weigh up the consequences of, for example, euthanasia and abortion, and decide where the majority of the benefit lies. They might well take the line that euthanasia is ethically acceptable, because it would lead, in the country's health system, to the unclogging of the system from one where people are needlessly being kept alive to a world in which fewer people suffer pain.

Virtue ethics may be identified as the approach that emphasises the virtues, or moral character, in contrast to the duties or rules (deontology) or the consequences of actions (consequentialism). Suppose it is obvious that someone in need should be helped. A **utilitarian** will point to the fact that the consequences of doing so will maximise well-being, a deontologist to the fact that, in doing so, the agent will be acting in accordance with a moral rule (such as 'Do unto others as you would be done by') and a virtue ethicist to the fact that helping the person would be charitable or benevolent.

These underlying principles inform much discussion around public sphere ethics, although they have much wider implications as well.

Moral philosophy and journalism

The usefulness of moral philosophy in the practice of journalism can be illustrated through the contentious issue of reporting grief. When tragic events happen, they attract media attention. While many tabloid journalists long ago gave up any ethical considerations when interviewing grief-stricken people, responsible journalists need to weigh up whether reporting on personal grief will actually be of benefit to the community at large, and to consider whether their reporting may exacerbate the suffering of the grieving person. This issue provides us with the dilemma of rights-based theories versus consequentialism.

Journalists need to weigh up the public's right to know in making a decision as to whether to publish or broadcast a story about personal grief. They have to decide if the story is in the wider interests of the community. If they make the judgment that the public does have a right to know, the journalist then may feel obliged to file a report, even when the person concerned does not want their grief reported. Consider, for example, the case of the married man who is the victim of a serial killer who targets married men who frequent gay bars. The wife of the victim tells the media that for the sake of her four teenage children she does not want it known that her husband was frequenting gay bars. However, if the media comply with her wishes while the killer is still at large, they may be putting other potential victims at risk. If they do not report to the public that the latest victim was killed by a man who picked him up in a gay bar, it could be argued that members of the media are denying the public—and particularly married patrons of gay bars—the right to be aware of the risk and take measures to protect themselves. If all the public hears about the case is that a man has been killed, but it is not told all the circumstances, are not the media taking a decision to put other people at risk in order to protect the sensibilities of one family? But what about the right to privacy of the wife and children of the family involved? Don't they have a right to their private lives being kept private and their grief remaining a private family matter?

Australian media professionals can be guided by their particular **code of ethics**. Journalists who are members of the Media Entertainment and Arts Alliance (MEAA) are required to respect private grief and personal privacy. Clause 11 of the MEAA/AJA Code of Ethics states that journalists have a right to resist the compulsion to intrude. In such a case, individual journalists have to make a moral judgment—weighing up questions such as the greater good versus the right to privacy—and they generally have to make their decision within a very short time frame.

Code of ethics: A set of rules prescribing the ethical practices that all members of a profession should follow.

Deadlines deny journalists the luxury of time to consider such issues at length, which is why responsible journalists are constantly thinking about their journalism practice from within an ethical framework. Ethics in journalism is complex and challenging, and the best practitioners wrestle regularly with ethical issues.

Media ethics in contemporary society

In a world of nonstop news, the World Wide Web, news blogs and podcasting, journalists today are facing unprecedented pressures and demands. News content has changed significantly in the past decade, with stories that were once regarded as soft news, such as celebrity and

Frontline

> In the year *Frontline* went to air, Australian current affairs were plagued with controversy…media practices which had caused public concern included…the graphic re-enactment of a shark attack on the nightly news, footage of journalists interviewing gunmen holding hostages, and numerous clips of journalists aggressively hassling people about their alleged wrongdoing. (Lumby 1999: 52–3)

ABC's spoof current affairs show, *Frontline*, questioned many aspects of populist current affairs journalism, particularly **chequebook journalism**, and encouraged debate about the role of television current affairs and journalistic ethics. More recently, *The Chaser's War on Everything* has taken over this role, particularly through its 'What have we learned from current affairs this week?' segment.

Chequebook journalism: Journalism that involves the payment of money to a source for the right to publish or broadcast information.

human-interest stories, now taking the place of hard news stories. While some commentators, such as cultural critic and journalist Jon Katz (1992), see the shift to infotainment news as part of an exciting new era, for others the changes are a threat to journalism itself. Academic and former *New York Times* chief political journalist Richard Reeves argues that it is possible to bypass older values and standards of journalism in a world of 'dazzling new technologies, profit driven owners, celebrated editors, reporters and broadcasters' (Reeves 1998), and that the press must go back to doing what it was hired to do long ago: to stand as an outsider and to 'keep an eye on politics and government for readers and viewers busy in the pursuit of happiness' (Reeves 1998: 16).

Journalist and academic Ian Hargreaves argues that in this new era of journalism 'the ethic of truthfulness and accuracy' must remain at the 'heart of the morality of journalism', and that without these qualities, 'journalism cannot inspire trust and without trust, there is no worthwhile journalism' (Hargreaves 2003: 11). Ethical journalism remains central to the future of news journalism. Without credibility, journalism has lost its effectiveness and its ability to animate democracy.

Ethical journalism

Although there are no easy answers, and ethical journalism is fraught with contradictions, ethical decision making and objectivity are worthwhile goals, even when journalists know that they are going to fall short of fully achieving them.

Kovach and Rosentiel

American journalists Bill Kovach and Tom Rosentiel were so concerned about the future of journalism that in the late twentieth century they founded the Concerned Journalists Group, which aims to promote ethical journalism. Kovach and Rosentiel acknowledge

that the concept of truth is no longer uncontested: 'We understand truth as a goal—at best elusive—and still embrace it' (Hargreaves 2003: 221). The journalists created a nine-principle manifesto setting out the values they believe the news media must adopt if they wish to be trusted and wish to fulfil the democratic mission of a free press. This rather old-fashioned mission statement offers optimism to journalists and journalism students who believe that the craft of journalism remains central to the existence of a democratic state:

- Journalism's first obligation is to the truth.
- Its first loyalty is to citizens.
- Its essence is a discipline of verification.
- Its practitioners must maintain independence from those they cover.
- It must serve as an independent monitor of power.
- It must provide a forum for public criticism and compromise.
- It must strive to make the significant interesting and relevant.
- It must keep the news comprehensive and proportional.
- Its practitioners must be allowed to exercise their personal conscience.

Journalism codes of ethics

In 1923, the American Society of Newspaper Editors adopted the first journalism code of ethics, followed by the American Society of Professional Journalists three years later. However, it was not until 1944 that the Australian Journalists Association introduced its own code of ethics. This code was revised in 1984, and reviewed in 1993 and 1996. The 1996 ethics review committee saw the MEAA/AJA Code of Ethics as a 'statement by members to the public of the ethical considerations which will guide them in their activities on behalf of keeping the public informed' (MEAA 1996). The committee's aim was to influence the actions of practitioners, making them conscious of their responsibilities and of the various interests at play in a particular set of circumstances. The existence of a code allows journalists to be aware of the standards expected of them by their peers and by the public, and to make ethical decisions with prior knowledge of the code of practice.

The MEAA/AJA Code of Ethics

The opening statement of the MEAA/AJA Code of Ethics (MEAA 1996) defines the core principles of the code:

> Respect for truth and the public's right to information are fundamental principles of journalism. Journalists describe society to itself. They convey information, ideas and opinions, a privileged role. They search, disclose, record, question, entertain, suggest and remember. They inform citizens and animate democracy. They give a practical form to freedom of expression. Many journalists work in private enterprise, but all have

these public responsibilities. They scrutinise power, but also exercise it, and should be accountable. Accountability engenders trust. Without trust, journalists do not fulfil their public responsibilities. MEAA members engaged in journalism commit themselves to:

- honesty
- fairness
- independence
- respect for the rights of others.

The code contains twelve clauses, which cover the core ethical issues facing journalists today and which are discussed briefly in this chapter. The Guidance clause, which has attracted debate, provides journalists with the choice, when faced with 'substantial advancement of the public interest or risk of substantial harm to people', to override the code.

Guidance clause

'Basic values often need interpretation and sometimes come into conflict. Ethical journalism requires conscientious decision-making in context. Only substantial advancement of the public interest or risk of substantial harm to people allows any standard to be overridden' (MEAA 1996).

Effectiveness of codes of ethics

Reeves acknowledges that 'the deepest fault line in the geography of press standards is self-censorship: reporters and correspondents generally give editors and owners what they want, because what they want is what they print or show' (Reeves 1998: 68). But perhaps the greatest weakness of the MEAA/AJA Code of Ethics is not that it is regulated by journalists, but that in Australia in the twenty-first century, individual workplace contracts mean that many journalists are not members of the MEAA, and cannot be sanctioned for breaches of the code. Furthermore, many of the key decision makers in media organisations—the editors, producers and owners who wield the power, and who should be accountable for unethical behaviour—are also not MEAA members, and are not subject to the code and its enforcement system. Quite simply, the MEAA/AJA Code alone cannot deliver media accountability in Australia.

Other watchdogs: industry codes of ethics and regulatory bodies

Other regulatory bodies and watchdogs exist in Australia to oversee the behaviour of journalists. All print journalists, editors and newspaper proprietors can be brought before the Australian Press Council, a non-statutory authority set up to answer complaints from the public about the print media. The APC was formed in 1976 as a voluntary organisation made up of representatives from major publishers, newspaper associations, journalists and public representatives. It sees its role as promoting freedom of the press and upholding journalistic standards. As a non-statutory authority, the APC cannot enforce sanctions; however, it can make findings, and newspaper members are required to publish retractions or corrections.

The broadcast media have different regulators and, arguably, the journalists, editors, producers and owners in this field are subject to more stringent codes of conduct. The Australian Communications and Media Authority (ACMA), which replaced the Australian Broadcasting Authority (ABA) in 2005, enforces the *Broadcasting Services Act 1992* (BSA), which covers commercial and community broadcasting in Australia. Since ACMA has the power to grant and withdraw broadcasting licences in many sectors of Australian broadcasting (excluding the ABC and SBS), it wields considerable (at least theoretical) power in this sphere. The ABC and SBS have their own codes, under their own legislation, that are not enforceable by ACMA, although they must be notified to ACMA. Under section 123 of the BSA, industry groups have developed codes of practice in consultation with ACMA. These codes are not restricted to ethical issues, but cover a whole range of matters. ACMA monitors the codes, and deals with unresolved complaints made under them. The current Commercial Television Industry Code of Practice, for example, was registered with ACMA, and came into effect on 1 July 2004. It covers a wide range of commercial television activities, including program classification, advertising time, accuracy, fairness and privacy in news and current affairs, disclosure of commercial arrangements and the handling of complaints. Similarly, commercial radio and community radio and television are subject to their own codes, each registered with ACMA.

One example of the predecessor to ACMA, the ABA, acting to enforce broadcast codes of conduct was the 1999 inquiry into the infamous cash for comment scandal involving high-profile Australian commercial radio broadcasters Alan Jones and John Laws. Although the radio station and the announcers were found to have breached the Act, the penalties were criticised by many commentators as being far too lenient.

Censorship, sedition and freedom of expression

The United Kingdom embraced the Declaration of Human Rights when it joined the European Union, and the USA has a Bill of Rights that protects freedom of speech. Australia is one of the few common law jurisdictions without explicit constitutional provisions to protect the rights of citizens. When Australia again holds a public discourse on the issue of a republic, the question of whether we need a Bill of Rights to protect freedom of speech and freedom of the press, as well as other freedoms, will need to be discussed.

US academic Dale Jacquette (2007: 136) argues that to whatever extent we limit freedom of the media, we also limit the optimisation of truth available to the members of a free society to that same extent. However, he agrees that in certain instances censorship may be imposed for the sake of satisfying a morally greater obligation, that is, for the greater good:

> The question then is always how, under such circumstances, the regulation and limitation of free inquiry by a free press is morally valuable. A free press and the free flow of information it helps to sustain is one of the most important ways in which a

> free society safeguards its freedoms. It is not the only way, however, and there are circumstances under which the publication of certain kinds of information is more of a threat than a benefit to the maintenance of a society's freedom. (Jacquette 2007: 136)

In late 2005, the Australian government introduced new sedition laws as part of a package of anti-terror legislation, despite widespread criticism that the laws were unnecessary and would stifle free speech. Then chair of the Australian Press Council, Professor Ken McKinnon, argued that the sedition laws were such 'catch-all laws that they are an insult to a modern country' (Pullin 2005). McKinnon told the media that Australia's sedition laws dated from the First World War, 'but that no one had been convicted of the offence since 1949, and similar laws had been ditched in countries such as Canada and New Zealand'. Law Professor George Williams, of the University of New South Wales, argued that the laws would make people think twice before speaking out, particularly in a more security-conscious world. He said, 'It's a risk you are taking and that means there is a real chilling effect on what people are prepared to say' (Pullin 2005).

Ethics in public relations

Ethics is a major issue in public relations practice, as it is in media practice, and a source of much angst from within and much condemnation from outside. People entering the profession will find several levels for thinking about public relations ethics, including two we canvass in this section. There is the level of the everyday practitioner faced with how to best portray a piece of information he or she is required to promote. Then there is the level of great societal trends, in which the individual tends to get swallowed up and ceases to have much immediate individual importance. It is in the bigger picture where campaigns of spin have been used to change world events (see, for example, Case Study 2 on the first Gulf War). However, it is important to note that the individual practitioner can observe how public relations has come to dominate the presentation of information in the public sphere—and wonder about whether this is a potentially dangerous development—while nurturing ethical behaviour in their own public relations work. There are well-documented cases where public relations has been spectacularly unethical, but the individual practitioner, even knowing that, can choose to behave ethically at all times and not be adversely affected.

As discussed above, all Australian journalists, at least notionally, are governed in their behaviour by a code of ethics that stresses honesty, fairness, independence and respect for the rights of others. It is an essential part of the ethos of the profession that its adherents may operate unfettered by the kinds of constraints that work against free speech, such as commercial or political expediency.

So how does this accord with the way in which public relations practitioners operate? On the surface it may appear that the two professions are hopelessly at odds, even though they must work in tandem. While that may well be the case in some areas, for the most part they actually do work rather well together, perhaps because their aims are not as far apart as they may seem. They both deal in the organisation and exchange of information. The problem for individual public relations people may be, to a certain extent anyway, one of perception. The media has a long-standing ethos of disinterested independence, an ethos that is not enjoyed by the public relations industry. This tends to make public relations people even more vulnerable to ethical criticism than journalists.

There may even be excessive emphasis on ethics in PR, and indeed, other professions may not bear up so well if they were subject to the same kind of ethical scrutiny. Often, this scrutiny has come from media practitioners, who may have something of a vested interest in disparaging one of their major sources of information—as slamming PR can be a cheap and easy way to polish up one's own ethical image—just as long as they remain journalists and don't move over to the dark side.

PR people are employed across many sectors, including all levels of government, business and industry, community organisations, educational institutions such as universities and schools, scientific and medical research organisations, charities, celebrities and international organisations such as UNESCO and WHO. This is a huge range of activities, so it is hard to generalise about all of them. One thing you can say is that the PR people in all these types of organisations will be seeking to place their employers or clients in the best possible light to the various publics they seek to inform. They will also be assisting them to overcome any existing or potential image problems they may encounter, by releasing positive information or material designed to create a certain impression.

This automatically seems to put practitioners at risk of ethical compromise. If we can agree that the underlying fact of public relations is to help win public acceptance for a product, service, plan or idea, does that not imply being selective with the truth at the very least? It can be looked at slightly differently. If PR people understand the way journalists operate, as they certainly should, then their task when they carry out media liaison may simply involve selecting those pieces of information that assist the journalist to get to the point of a story, leaving out extraneous and time-consuming irrelevancies. This would also be the case when PR professionals are interacting with publics other than the media, such as government, shareholders or direct to members of the public.

The best and most useful forms of PR do exactly this—the practitioners, mindful of media (or other audience) needs, evaluate the available information and present it in a form acceptable to the recipients. They make information less complicated, and therefore more readily understood, or they frame positions and issues for clarity. The success of this approach is apparent in the way media journalists accept this information and use it readily, often coming back for more. So long as the information fits with what the journalist is hoping to achieve, then the journalist will have no qualms about making use of it, and ethics will not enter into it. On countless occasions, the information prepared by a PR person is simply absorbed into the reporter's copy, often without attribution. It is the lot of the PR person not to receive bylines. This practice of just slotting material into what should be researched journalism is part of the ethical problem shared by media and PR people.

In dealing with the problems posed by PR practice, professional groups in Australia and elsewhere have developed codes of ethics. The most important one in Australia has been devised by the Public Relations Institute of Australia (PRIA), which is reproduced towards the end of this chapter. Point three of the code specifically forbids members to 'knowingly disseminate false or misleading information', and to 'take care to avoid doing so inadvertently'.

So the notion of promulgating falsehood, the single biggest ethical charge levelled against PR practitioners, is specifically forbidden by the profession's most important organisation. This requirement can be found in the equivalent organisations in other countries as well. But, as with the print media, these ways of behaving are essentially voluntary—there is no enforceable sanction within the profession against people who choose not to behave this way.

The only remedies outside public relations are laws such as the *Trade Practices Act 1975* (Cth), which do limit the ability of any organisation to convey misleading information, but which tend to deal with extreme and persistent cases of deceptive or misleading conduct. The Act does not cover the small distortions or omissions or little white lies that can be employed to give a nice spin to something.

Jim Macnamara, an Australian public relations theorist, takes the view that PR is often the victim of sheer prejudice, and that the more realistic view about the profession is that it is an essential part of a pluralistic society. As he puts it (Macnamara 2001):

> The growth of PR is clear evidence of the market telling us something. PR is not going away and needs to be recognised. Most journalists think that the entire public relations industry exists for no other function than trying to manipulate or stonewall the media, leading to negative and often paranoid attitudes towards PR. Accordingly, the growth of public relations is viewed with fear—and some loathing—by many journalists.

Macnamara maintains that this is largely driven by ignorance and a kind of knee-jerk derogatory response that is unjustified. In fact, he claims that most public relations activities are not related to the media, quoting a breakdown of PR activities, based on recent US research, as follows: 60 per cent of PR budgets were for functions other than media liaison and publicity, based on 10 per cent for internal communication, 10 per cent for special events, 8 per cent for investor relations, 7 per cent for community relations, 6 per cent for fundraising, and 9 per cent for public affairs and government relations, with other funds spent on advice, research and issues advertising (Macnamara 2001).

Macnamara sees the rise of these functions as commendable, because it shows that corporations and other large organisations are actually taking communication seriously; it is a very positive move away from the bad old days of opaque decision making and distant management not interacting with employees or the outside world. In effect, he says, PR has actively improved corporate and organisational culture substantially, including its ethics. He also notes that the media themselves has played a dominant role in encouraging the rise of public relations:

> Economics have forced the shrinkage of reporting staff in most media. Many small town and suburban newspapers and many trade journals are produced by one or two people. From days when 'roundsmen' proactively covered all key areas of civic and business activity … today many companies and organisations have no likelihood of the media contacting them. They have to take their news to the media, or directly target audiences, or they will not get their message across. (Macnamara 2001)

The image of PR people as ethically compromised still persists, however. A 2000 survey carried in the USA caused an uproar in the industry. The *New York Times* of 8 May 2000 carried a story headlined 'In Public Relations, 25% Admit to Lying'. This story emerged from a survey carried out by a trade newspaper, *PR Week*, of 1700 PR executives. The survey showed that 25 per cent admitted to lying on the job, 39 per cent had exaggerated the truth, 44 per cent had felt 'ethically challenged at work' and 62 per cent had felt 'compromised by lack of information or lying clients'.

Adam Leyland, then editor of *PR Week*, commented that he would like to survey business people at large to find out how many of them lied, and how many media people had lied to get or enhance a story. The speculation in the industry at this point was: Why should PR people constantly have their truthfulness disputed or discussed when business people, journalists and politicians routinely tell lies as well, and it is often impossible to know when anyone is really telling the truth?

The PR ethics backlash

Perceived unethical behaviour inevitably causes a public backlash, and that is certainly the case with the PR industry. Not surprisingly, the backlash originated in the same place that spawned public relations: the USA. A voice of dissent against the influence of PR is a group called PR Watch, which can be found at <www.prwatch.org>. On this site one can find, depending upon their inclination, bracing honesty or unbelievable polemic, all to do with the consequences of PR in modern society.

One of the gurus of this anti-PR movement is John Stauber, who, with his colleague Sheldon Rampton, published a famous anti-PR tome, *Toxic Sludge is Good for You: Lies, Damned Lies and the Public Relations Industry* (1995). If the authors are to be believed, the public face of many companies is frequently far removed from a shadowy and immoral reality.

An article called 'War on Truth: The Secret Battle for the American Mind' by Derrick Jensen (1999), which is based upon an interview with John Stauber, quotes Australian academic Alex Carey. Carey said: 'The twentieth century has been characterised by three developments of great political importance: the growth of democracy, the growth of corporate power and the growth of corporate propaganda as a means of protecting corporate power against democracy.' Carey's book, *Taking the Risk out of Democracy: Propaganda in the US and Australia* (1995), was published posthumously—Carey had died in 1988 and his essays were later collected. Like the influential philosopher Noam Chomsky (who wrote the foreword to this book), Carey takes the view that there is something specific and unique about Western democratic society that leads to abuses of power that are different from those found in non-democratic societies, but are just as damaging. He says that in a technologically advanced democracy, 'the maintenance of the existing power and privileges are vulnerable to popular opinion' in a way that is not true in authoritarian societies. Therefore, elite propaganda must assume a 'more covert and sophisticated role'.

This means, says Carey and others, not just putting forward positive assertions but also subtly undermining all potential sources of dissent, indeed, vilifying those who do not hold to corporate values, many of which are equated with democratic values. This amounts to the active discouragement of a diversity of views and the concomitant rise and celebration of mediocrity and conformity. Large communities that are in a state of mediocrity and conformity are unlikely to look too deeply at how they are being manipulated. Carey saw this as nothing less than social engineering designed to make people feel free, while they are in fact enslaved by the need to buy products produced by the corporations.

One of the most prominent figures in the way PR developed its practices towards this very goal was the so-called father of PR, Edward Bernays. Bernays (1947) said: 'It is impossible to overestimate the importance of engineering consent. The engineering of consent is the very essence of the democratic process. It affects almost every aspect of our daily lives.' Bernays believed that, with a little help from the theories of his uncle Sigmund Freud, average people could have their views engineered to the benefit of elite groups, whether they were politicians or corporations. Maybe the best summing up of the thinking of these pioneering PR people comes from a quote from a contemporary of Bernays, Harold Lasswell (1927), who wrote: 'More can be won by illusion than by coercion.' It is in the context of these views and behaviours that a lot of the criticism of PR has arisen.

In his brief introduction to *Toxic Sludge is Good for You*, Mark Dowie uses as a focus Edward Bernays's infamous rally in New York—allegedly in support of the right of women to smoke cigarettes, but really a piece of consent engineering paid for by a cigarette company—before developing an overview of the critique of PR. It is a critique largely based upon both ethical considerations and the usurping of the watchdog role of the news media. Dowie writes:

> Academicians who study media now estimate that about 40 per cent of all 'news' flows virtually unedited from the public relations offices, prompting a prominent PR exec to boast that 'the best PR ends up looking like news' ... It is critical that consumers of media in democratic societies understand the origin of information and the process by which it is mediated, particularly when they are being deceived. Thus it is essential that they understand public relations. (Dowie 1995: 4)

The many critiques of PR ethics have considerable strength, and all prospective practitioners need to be aware of the nature of the criticism—and do whatever they can in their own practice to ensure that they are not adding to the causes of dissent. Some of these issues are not for PR people alone to solve, however. The decline of traditional Fourth Estate media is a broader societal issue that has no simple cause or solution, although it is looking increasingly likely that the watchdog role has moved online. And online is where the loudest voices warning about PR are often to be found.

Public Relations Institute of Australian (PRIA) Code of Ethics

1 Members shall deal fairly and honestly with their employers, clients and prospective clients, with their fellow workers, including superiors and subordinates, with public officials, the communications media, the general public and with fellow members of PRIA.

2 Members shall avoid conduct or practices likely to bring discredit upon themselves, the Institute, their employers or clients.

3 Members shall not knowingly disseminate false or misleading information, and shall take care to avoid doing so inadvertently.

4 Members shall safeguard the confidences of both present and former employers and clients, including confidential information about employers' or clients' business affairs, technical methods or processes, except upon the order of a court of competent jurisdiction.

5 No member shall represent conflicting interests nor, without the consent of the parties concerned, represent competing interests.

6 Members shall refrain from proposing or agreeing that their consultancy fees or other remuneration be contingent entirely on the achievement of specified results.
7 Members shall inform their employers or clients if circumstances arise in which their judgment or the disinterested character of their services may be questioned by reason of personal relationships or business or financial interests.
8 Members practising as consultants shall seek payment only for services specifically commissioned.
9 Members shall be prepared to identify the source of funding of any public communication they initiate or for which they act as a conduit.
10 Members shall, in advertising and marketing their skills and services and in soliciting professional assignments, avoid false, misleading or exaggerated claims and shall refrain from comment or action that may injure the professional reputation, practice or services of a fellow member.
11 Members shall inform the Board of the Institute and/or the relevant State/Territory Council(s) of the Institute of evidence purporting to show that a member has been guilty of, or could be charged with, conduct constituting a breach of this Code.
12 No member shall intentionally injure the professional reputation or practice of another member.
13 Members shall help to improve the general body of knowledge of the profession by exchanging information and experience with fellow members.
14 Members shall act in accord with the aims of the Institute, its regulations and policies.
15 Members shall not misrepresent their status through misuse of title, grading, or the designation FPRIA, MPRIA or APRIA.
16 Adopted by the Board of the Institute on 5 November 2001, this Code of Ethics supersedes all previous versions.

Conclusion

No human society in history has ever fully worked out how it should organise and behave for the benefit of all. The base side of human nature constantly militates against the noble side. The very power of information automatically confers much potential for dishonourable behaviour that must be balanced by structures that attempt to ameliorate this power. Because media and public relations professionals deal with information, and sometimes powerful and influential information, they must be more mindful than most of the consequences of their actions. Most practitioners do acknowledge the need for an ethical framework and strive to work within it. Spectacular examples of those who do not tend to dominate discussions on this issue, but what tends to get overlooked is the daily quiet adherence of millions of practitioners who know they are part of an endeavour that can affect how the world is constructed, so they do their best to keep it real.

KEY REFERENCES

Bernays, E. L. (1947). 'The Engineering of Consent'. *Annals of the American Academy of Political and Social Science.* Thousand Oaks: Sage.

Hirst, M. & Patching, R. (2005). *Journalism Ethics: Arguments and Cases.* Melbourne: Oxford University Press.

Keeble, R. (2001). *Ethics for Journalists.* London: Routledge.

Macnamara, J. R. (2001). *Impact of PR on the Media.* Washington: CARMA International.

Tanner, S., Phillips, G., Smyth, C. & Tapsall, S. (2005). *Journalism Ethics at Work.* Sydney: Pearson.

WEBSITES

Ethics in Journalism: <www.spj.org/ethics.asp>.

FAIR: Fairness and Accuracy in Reporting: <www.fair.org/>.

MEAA/AJA Code of Ethics: <www.alliance.org.au/>.

PR Watch: <www.prwatch.org>.

Public Relations Institute of Australia: <www.pria.com.au>

CHAPTER 17

MEDIA PRACTICE, INDUSTRY CHANGE AND THE LAW

TIM DWYER

Introduction

The terms 'media' and 'law' can be combined in many different contexts. For some media and journalism students, the first thought that comes to mind will be *Underbelly*, *Wire in the Blood*, *The Sopranos* or some other mediatised formats of criminality and general grievous bodily harm. But media practitioners learning the ropes will need to develop an understanding of a range of key concepts, frameworks and general legal literacies that are relevant to their roles as content creators. On one level, this is simply a matter of self-protection, but on another it is about acquiring the confidence to create well-informed, quality content for a media citizenry.

To begin to get a sense of the legal implications of our media practice, we can consider these different scenarios. Do you ever write for a university newspaper or a sports club newsletter? Have you helped produce content for community television or radio? And to these more traditional activities we can now add various new media practices:

- What messages do you post on blogs or send in multirecipient emails?
- What content do you include on websites—including on your Facebook profile—or take from other people's profiles?
- Do you have a Twitter account and tweet about events or people?
- Have you uploaded video to a video-sharing site such as YouTube?
- Do you share images or video between mobile devices?
- Do you use recorded images or sound without people's express consent?

If you have created, used or distributed content in any of these ways, you would have been bound by the same legal principles as journalists and other media workers who write or produce content for metropolitan dailies, radio or television, or 24/7 online. Everyone in the publishing industry has the same rights and obligations as other citizens. All are subject to the same laws. But the distinctive nature of media and journalistic work brings it into contact with specific areas of law every day. The two most important of these are the laws of defamation and contempt of court, while issues of confidentiality, privacy and copyright can also affect media practitioners in their everyday work.

It is not necessary to have a lawyer's knowledge, but media practitioners do need to recognise risky words and phrases, know when to seek legal advice in relation to controversial content, estimate whether a publication is likely to land them in court, and make informed judgments about whether to proceed with a publication. These can be complex topics, for which this chapter aims to provide an overview. Students can refer to Beattie and Beal (2007) and Forder and Svantesson (2008) for more detailed information.

In this chapter we look at:

- the structure of the Australian legal system
- defamation law
- contempt of court
- confidentiality
- privacy
- copyright
- law in changing mediaspheres.

The Australian legal system

Courts

Jurisdiction: Refers to either the power granted to a legal body, such as a court or tribunal, to administer justice within a defined area of responsibility, or a geographically delimited area within which certain laws apply (for example, a state, territory or nation).

Knowledge of the court hierarchy and the **jurisdiction** of particular courts will assist journalists in assessing the general significance of a case.

The highest court in the Australian legal system is the High Court of Australia. Its role is to interpret the Constitution and to hear appeals from other courts: federal, state or territory. As the highest court, its decisions are binding on all other Australian courts. Freedom of expression cases, which are heard in the High Court, are of great interest to media practitioners.

Next in the court hierarchy is the Federal Court, which has original and appellate jurisdiction. The states and territories also have their own courts, which interpret and apply the law. In ascending tiers, these are:

- *Magistrates' Courts*, which deal with the most common criminal offences, such as traffic infringements and minor assaults, and smaller civil claims such as debt recovery
- *Intermediate courts*, such as District or County Courts, which hear the majority of serious criminal offences (often with a jury), and more serious civil claims up to certain monetary limits
- *Supreme Courts*, which are the highest courts in Australian states and territories, and deal with the most serious criminal and civil claims; these courts may sit with either a single judge, or a bench of three judges as an appeal or full court to hear appeals from decisions made by judges in courts or tribunals lower in the hierarchy. Supreme Courts usually have specific categories or lists of matters they can hear. Defamation cases (on the Defamation List), for example, are heard at this level.

Sources of law

There are two principal sources of law: statute law and common law. The former refers to laws enacted by state or federal parliaments, while the latter refers to judge-made law as decided in specific cases over time and through the interpretation of statutes; together, these are known as the 'doctrine of precedent'. The mechanism of precedent, then, is a feature of common law systems.

Common law systems derive from the English legal system, and are followed mostly in those countries with a previous colonial connection to Britain, such as Australia, Canada, New Zealand and the USA. The application of the common law system diverges in the USA from other former colonies as a result of its system being shaped by a powerfully independent Congress and Supreme Court. However, in all common law system countries the outcome of cases can be uncertain, depending on the interpretation of the legislation and the relevance of judgments in previous cases. Parliaments may change legislation at any time, and judges must work within the current Acts and rules of statutory interpretation.

The common law system may be contrasted with **civil law systems**.

Common law system: The basic structure of law in Australia, based on a combination of the decisions that judges make according to statute, and case law, meaning precedents set by earlier judgments in higher courts.

Civil law system: The legal systems based primarily on the interpretation of statutory codes, such as those existing in much of Europe (as opposed to systems based on the doctrine of precedent, such as the UK common law system).

Civil and criminal cases

Media practitioners might be parties to criminal or civil actions, depending on the nature of the published material. **Criminal actions** are brought by the state. A driver who breaks road speed limits knows there is a risk of encountering the criminal justice system. Likewise, a publisher who interferes with the business of the courts might face criminal charges. Compare this with **civil actions**. These occur when legal proceedings are commenced by private individuals or entities to obtain compensation or redress from those who they claim have caused them harm. If a publisher is responsible for material that impugns the reputation of a person, then they may well be sued for the hurt and pain caused.

One major difference is that in criminal cases, the accused is presumed innocent until a court finds otherwise. In civil cases, there is usually no notion of guilt or innocence in the criminal sense. The **plaintiff** attempts to obtain some kind of **remedy** for the perceived wrongdoing, and a court might award **damages**. This distinction is essential knowledge for media practitioners, as we shall see later in this chapter.

Criminal action: A court case brought by the state against somebody who has committed a crime.

Civil action: A court case relating to disputes between two parties.

Plaintiff: A person bringing a civil action to court.

Remedy: Compensation to a plaintiff in a civil action.

Damages: An amount of money awarded by a court as a remedy in a civil action.

A further difference may be illustrated by way of an example. In 2005, a high-profile community leader, Mr X, faced rape charges. The Crown lost the case on the evidence before the court. Mr X was therefore found by the court to be innocent of the rape charges. The following year, a woman claiming to be the victim in that same rape case, sued Mr X in a civil action for damages—and won. Guilt in a criminal case must be proven beyond reasonable doubt, but in a civil action the evidence is sifted through and a case is won or lost on the balance of probabilities.

Freedom of expression: For media workers, the fundamental legal right to discover important information and convey it to the public.

All parties to a legal action have rights and obligations. The fundamental right of great interest to media professionals—writers, playwrights, novelists, musicians, performers, producers, publishers and other media workers—is that of **freedom of expression**. Without this freedom, the law can impinge on the efforts of media to report important information and ideas to the public. First in the newsroom, and then in the courts, we see the tensions between the right to freedom of expression and other rights and freedoms. Such rights include the following:

- the right to a good reputation (defamation laws)
- the right to a fair trial (contempt laws)
- the right to safeguard secrets (confidential information laws)
- the right to privacy (laws protecting personal information and communications)
- the right to protect intellectual and creative property (intellectual property laws, including copyright).

In the newsroom, a team of editorial staff—including the journalist, the editor, possibly a legal adviser, and sometimes the executive manager or proprietor—may all have advice regarding the constraints of the law.

Predicting the exact extent of freedoms for media practitioners is not always clear cut, and this is why the media take a special interest in cases that may have implications for future media practice. When a case is before a court, one party will be arguing for the freedom to publish, the other for restrictions on publication, for redress or for compensation, because the publication may have harmed the plaintiff in some way. The role of the court is to tease out all the available evidence, interpreting the circumstances according to the relevant legislation and previous case law.

A brief history of free speech

In the USA, freedom of the press is called the 'first freedom': free speech and freedom of the press were written into the US Constitution from its inception. In Australia there is no absolute right to free speech. However, Australia is a signatory to the UN's 1948 Universal Declaration of Human Rights, the International Covenant on Civil and Political Rights, and the International Covenant on Economic, Social and Cultural Rights, which protect limited rights. The High Court of Australia has ruled on several occasions since 1971 that there is an implied constitutional freedom of expression in political and government matters (see Beattie & Beal 2007: Chapter 5). Australian law, then, has a precedent for freedom of expression, even though it has no constitutional **bill of rights**. In Australia, only the Australian Capital Territory (*Human Rights Act 2004*) and the state of Victoria (*Human Rights and Responsibilities Act 2006*) have enacted their own charters of human rights.

Bill of rights: Legislation, through parliament or a clause in the Constitution, that guarantees citizens a legal right to certain freedoms.

To understand the evolution of freedom of speech, it is helpful to trace events back more than 500 years. Even before the development of the printing press in the fifteenth century, powerful people feared the spoken word. Death, imprisonment and mutilation were punishments for the spreading of gossip. How much more then would the written word create fear among the nobility, when they realised the damage a free press could do to their reputations? In the eighteenth century, John Milton made his speech in parliament in defence of free speech and a free press: 'A Speech for the Liberty of Unlicensed Publishing', later published as the *Areopagitica* (see Butler & Rodrick 2007: 4). The law of treason may have declined along with the absolute powers of monarchy, but the lineage of laws of sedition and seditious libel flows right through to present-day Australia. Amendments to Commonwealth sedition laws were enacted through Schedule 7 of the *Anti-Terrorism Act (No 2) 2005* (Cth). This development should be illustration enough that the idea of freedom of speech is a matter that ultimately depends on specific, historically contingent expressions of power within a particular jurisdiction.

But free speech has been philosophically justified in relation to arguments linking it to individual autonomy and liberties, famously invoked by John Stuart Mill's essay 'On Liberty' (1859), in addition to arguments underpinned by the fundamental debates about the value of truth and democracy. It should be clear, then, that debates about the media and the role of media practitioners in the public sphere are closely connected with these wider, historically rich, debates in liberal democracies.

As Beattie and Beal note:

> From their earliest inception these rights had a public character, protecting public assembly and distribution of information, and a private character, protecting individual communications from state scrutiny and keeping the state out of private spaces. The spatial nature of these rights influences the ways in which broadcasting and communications are regulated today. (2007: 89)

As democracies have evolved, so too has a recognition of human rights, among them the right to hold and express a view, particularly a view about those people in government who represent the citizens. Arguing for the democratic merits of a written constitution that enshrines freedom of expression and of the media, John Keane makes the point that: 'A great variety of legal means can help to promote freedom of expression and access to information among transacting citizens' (Keane 1991: 128). Publication through the media is the key vehicle by which citizens exercise this right to express their views in the public sphere.

Tolerance and vilification

Democratic governments, to a greater or lesser extent, tolerate a range of views, including those many might disagree with. Famously, the French philosopher Voltaire described freedom of speech in these terms: 'I disapprove of what you say, but I will defend to the death your right to say it.' The argument is that in the tolerance of all views, even false ones, the truth will emerge; in bits and pieces perhaps, dispersed, and variously revealed, but eventually it will shine through, and this is the incontrovertible quality of freedom of expression.

Taking a long view of the development of free speech, it can be argued that there has been a general shift in focus away from individual political figures and towards the regulation of 'dangerous speech' (Beattie & Beal 2007: 89). Such speech includes vilification or hate speech. Anti-vilification laws are in conflict with the concept of free speech and are justified on the basis of an overriding public interest. These laws use an anti-discrimination model and are regulated at state and federal level through anti-discrimination agencies such as the Human

Rights and Equal Opportunity Commission, which relies on the *Racial Hatred Act 1995* (Cth) to operate a complaints-based scheme. If unsuccessful, conciliation is supported by other remedies, including the application of monetary penalties (Beattie & Beal 2007: 99).

Arguably, to suppress one view, which we might believe to be false and damaging, is to risk suppressing worthy views closer to the truth. Furthermore, any suppression of views raises the question: Who shall have the right to exercise this control? Governments and other powerful institutions, such as courts, that suppress freedom of speech are frequently in conflict with the media. Journalists, and often courts as well, hold very strongly to the principle of freedom of expression, though the relationship is perennially unsettled. Consider these events that were widely reported by the media:

- A Danish newspaper, the *Jyllands-Posten*, published cartoons of the prophet Mohammed carrying a suicide bomb in his turban. Many lives were lost in the violent civil protests following their publication.
- The British historian David Irving was jailed in Austria for denying aspects of the mid-twentieth-century holocaust in Europe.
- The Australian historian Keith Windschuttle disputed historical accounts of mass killings of Indigenous Australians in colonial times.

These ideas are unpalatable to many, because they are false, offensive, unsubstantiated or highly contentious; however, advocates for free speech say it is better to discuss such views publicly than to suppress them, for public discussion takes all citizens closer to the truth by fostering the emergence of strong reasoning and vital debate, which energise democracy.

It is important that media practitioners become familiar with the jurisdictions in which they work. Even within particular countries, differences might apply between the states, which have their own legislatures. Democracies themselves vary significantly in the legal guarantees for publishers. Yet even though legal systems vary from one jurisdiction to another, the principles discussed warrant ongoing discussion.

Armed with the foregoing points, we can now consider specific laws relevant to journalists in their daily work.

Defamation

The meaning between the lines

Imagine this. You are a cadet journalist with a story about a famous elite athlete who has been seen behaving badly at an after-competition party. Your source is near where you live so you go and interview them and a couple of other people in the same area, who were also at the party. They all tell the same story: the celebrity athlete had consumed a great deal of alcohol, and then driven her car into another athlete's car on leaving the party. She has been under a probationary warning from her sport's governing body and was facing charges over a violent domestic incident with a previous boyfriend. According to witnesses, when police arrived at the party to investigate, she became abusive. Onlookers were horrified by the Jekyll-and-Hyde character change in the telegenic sports star. You take some quotes, and the revellers tell you other stories about what the celebrity sportswoman gets up to when she is not training for the next personal best. The quotes state that she is crazy, abusive and irresponsible in party mode. You try unsuccessfully to contact her closer friends or family to get their side of the story. It is close to deadline, and this is looking like a powerful article with international interest for the front page. Should you proceed with the information you have? The subeditor is uncomfortable about the story. What solid evidence do you have that the athlete has a split personality, is an unsuitable role model and needs to attend anger-management therapy? A colleague suggests that you take a visit to the athlete's Facebook profile. There, in jiving, scantily clad detail is your elite athlete in full party mode. There are various perhaps raunchy, not debauched party images updated on her profile, with a variety of partygoers, so you feel confident of the truth of the events as they have been reported to you. You download all the images from Facebook to your laptop. The subeditor discusses your article with the chief editor, who, under the pressure of time, goes ahead with the story without sending it first to the lawyers to check its safety. The next day, when the paper is out, lawyers for the young sports celebrity call the editor and threaten to sue.

Here, a person's reputation is at stake. Both the images and the words are open to interpretation. The damage is done, not only by the literal words but also by the meanings arising from them. **Defamation** is about perceptions. If the sports star sues, the publisher will need to prove the truth of your story in court. The reported events are relatively minor criminal offences that concern her dubious lifestyle and party behaviour. To prove them, people will have to appear in court as witnesses under oath. The images may convey real events, but they prove little about the overall suitability of the person to be a national sports icon. Not only is her team membership on the line, but all those celebrity product endorsements could be at risk, too. Regarding the Facebook images, media practitioners should also be aware that legal relationships and the general content liability of platform providers, members and third parties are usually matters determined by websites' specific terms and conditions and ethical codes of practice.

Defamation: The reduction of the reputation of another person in the minds of people, by exposing that person to ridicule, or by causing them to be shunned and avoided.

Anyone can be defamed by what we call 'imputations': the meanings between the lines; for example:

- suggestions of incompetence, which might offend a professional practitioner
- suggestions of duplicity, which might offend someone who values the trust of the community, such as a youth worker or a real estate agent
- negative references to physical traits such as obesity, which might offend a sportsperson
- suggestions of financial mismanagement, which might offend an accountant
- stories of slovenly hygiene habits in the kitchen, which might offend a restaurateur
- shocking party revelry, which might offend the kind of person who values their reputation as a role model for younger elite athletes.

Here are other examples of potentially risky scenarios:

- In a suburban newspaper, a photograph of a youth acclaimed for his community service appears next to an article about a homeless drug addict, prompting discussion with the lawyers.
- A well-known media commentator tweets a random, seemingly jokey comment about the sexuality of a sports star that may damage that person's reputation.

- In a coastal town, a letter to the online editor, from the president of a residents' association, implies that a developer is anti-conservationist. The developer threatens legal action for defamation.

Although these publications seem to be reasonable not innocent enough, each could lead to a successful claim through the courts for damage to reputation.

The media have the potential to defame people every day. It is not only indirect imputations that you need to be aware of: direct statements, even if partially true, can trigger a defamation suit because the named person is prepared to contest the claim. Unintentionally defaming an individual is expressly not a defence for media workers. Care and attention to detail is always necessary when a person's reputation is at stake. Nonetheless, it is only when someone has the will, the money and the knowledge to sue that the publisher is held to account. Often there is a chilling effect on media work: the actual or perceived threat of possible legal action leads to self-censorship and tends to limit, or completely prevent, the publication of important public interest material. As media law academic Andrew Kenyon has argued: 'Media speech is chilled directly when lawyers recommend editing the content of publications, and is chilled structurally when journalists internalise the law's restrictive principles' (Kenyon 2006).

An action for defamation is usually a civil action, defined in an Act of parliament; however, it has a long and complex common law history (Rolph et al. 2010: 204). From January 2006 uniform defamation laws took effect around Australia. Each state and territory introduced a defamation Act, in very similar terms, enabling a nationally consistent approach to defamatory publications. The key changes from previous laws relate to introducing standardised defences around Australia. Truth (or justification) is now a complete defence in New South Wales, Queensland and Tasmania (truth has always been a complete defence in Victoria, South Australia and Western Australia), apologies (or offers of amends) and innocent dissemination have been made statutory defences and the category of qualified privilege for fair reports has been expanded. Potential monetary damages were capped at $250,000 (although this is indexed to the cost of living, and courts may override in certain situations and compensate for specific economic loss), and corporations can no longer sue for defamation, with the exception of non-profit organisations with fewer than ten employees (Beattie & Beal 2007).

Good intentions

In media workplaces, where the threat of defamation is constant, journalists often check only the articles they think might be defamatory, sometimes overlooking the very ones that turn out to be offensive. Just as ignorance is no excuse in criminal law, so the intentions of the writer are usually irrelevant in a civil defamation action, and it will be insufficient to argue as a defence that you did not intend to defame someone.

The rules of defamation also apply irrespective of the means of distribution: you may be publishing in the traditional media to a multinational, national or local audience, microblogging on Twitter, making a comment on Facebook, emailing a small number of recipients or even just sending a fax. In addition, anyone involved in the publication may be liable: publishers, editors, journalists and their sources. Newspaper printers, distributors, newsagents and retailers and internet service providers can be sued, but they have available to them a defence known as 'innocent dissemination'.

A question of identity

Another pitfall for publishers can occur with mistaken identity. The plaintiff need not be the person the journalist intended to identify in the story, but for an action to proceed, it is sufficient that the readers could presume the plaintiff was the person referred to in the article. Mistaken identity can occur with substitute names, group references, typing errors or omission of a name.

An article about an unnamed shonky pool builder, in a particular suburb where there were three pool builders, could defame all three in that suburb, because readers could assume any one of them was the subject of the article. Conversely, an article containing a general statement about the untrustworthiness of television journalists would be safe, because no particular person would be identifiable in such a large field. Substitute names and absence of names are risky if the field is small enough for identification. Video footage or images that accompany reports can also imply unintended identity, as can textual inference: an apparently de-identified story may contain material that certain audiences will recognise as referencing a particular individual.

The action

In commencing a defamation case the plaintiff must first show that:

- the material was **published** (communicated to at least one other person)
- it contained defamatory content, so there was a loss of reputation
- readers could identify the plaintiff as the one referred to in the article.

So to have any chance of succeeding in an action the plaintiff must meet these three conditions.

Publication: In a defamation action, a communication must reach at least one other person; hence, a fax, a postcard, an email, a comment on Facebook or a tweet may be a publication.

To show loss of reputation, the plaintiff lists imputations. These are the messages that might result from the actual words—the meaning(s) or sting readers might infer from the published material. Media practitioners become adept at predicting imputations by adopting the walk-in-my-shoes approach. 'How would I feel if someone wrote this about me?' they might ask. 'How might another interpret my words?' 'Could I defend in court the truth of these words and their intended or unintended meanings?' The priority of the media should be on publishing important public interest material and, on legal advice, finding the right defences to fit the facts of the story.

The defence

If the plaintiff is successful in meeting the three elements of defamation, the case proceeds. In the next stage, the burden of proof falls on the publisher, whose task it is to defend the words that have caused offence. It is, then, possible to defame someone legally, if the publisher has a valid defence. In other words, the defendant needs to produce evidence to prove their case.

The defences are defined in the uniform defamation Acts, and the main ones are truth (or justification), privilege, and opinion or comment. There are also other minor defences: triviality, consent, innocent dissemination and offer of amends. Which applies will depend on the circumstances.

Let us look more closely at each of the main defences, because practitioners must know and understand them in order to make informed judgments about whether to publish.

Truth

Truth is the first defence in a defamation action. In Australia, it is nearly impossible to defend words and imputations that are untrue. In the USA, though, where the First Amendment gives greater legal protection to freedom of expression, it is possible.

Here is a story of two men in the USA, each with the same family name. A reporter writes a news piece about the criminal behaviour of one. The other is the mayor of the town and a well-known citizen. The editor, not knowing of the criminal but knowing of the mayor, presumes the reporter has made a mistake with the first name, and changes it so that the article names the mayor as having been engaged in criminal behaviour. The mayor sues for defamation. The court agrees his reputation has fallen as a result of the publication. The newspaper cannot prove the truth of the story, because it is plainly false, so there appears to be no defence. The court awards damages to the mayor. But the newspaper appeals the decision on the basis of freedom of expression, which is enshrined in the US Constitution. The court of appeal overturns the earlier decision, finding that, despite the imputations being false (that the mayor was a crook), the First Amendment right to freedom of expression should prevail, providing there was no malice in the defamation.

While Australian journalists have no such protection for untrue publications, the scenario above shows how the defence of truth can be affected by the constitutional guarantee of freedom of expression. This guarantee does not negate the need for truth and accuracy, either in the USA or in other Western democracies; rather, it illustrates legal historical differences. In Australia, as in all free speech countries, truth is crucial. No media outlet ought to be publishing unsubstantiated material, whether or not there is a constitutional freedom of expression.

The defence of truth, sometimes called 'justification', is not always as straightforward as it might seem. Imagine that two people meet in a dark city lane. One is a police sergeant, the other a shady underworld identity. The crook hands a brown paper bag to the sergeant. A crime journalist sees the exchange and writes in an article that the policeman accepted a parcel from the other person in a city laneway. The words are true, but the many meanings that spring from them might be untrue. The literal words imply a bribe.

If the publisher can show in court that the imputations are true, then those imputations set or confirm the level of the reputation of the plaintiff; hence, defamation would be impossible. A plaintiff usually lists several imputations, and if the defendant fails to prove just one of them, the defence of truth will fail. In one of the most famous contemporary libel cases—and the longest-running in Britain—the fast-food chain McDonald's sued campaigners Helen Steel and David Morris, a gardener and a postman, over the distribution of a leaflet: *What's Wrong with McDonald's?* The court found the pair had defamed McDonald's. Having proved the truth of some of the imputations, but unable to prove the others, the defendants were ordered to pay damages of £60,000.

So in order to mount a successful defence of truth, defendants need to prove that all of alleged defamatory imputations in the matter complained of were substantially true. This can be a very difficult task: defendants may be able to establish the truth of an imputation, but to prove the facts upon which the imputation is based can be much more difficult.

Privilege

Defamation law recognises that on certain privileged occasions the public interest in people speaking out will outweigh an individual's right to protect their reputation.

There is an **absolute privilege** to publish otherwise defamatory material in reports of open sessions in parliaments and the courts. Accordingly, the publication of defamatory material from such proceedings will be completely immune from the laws of defamation, even if it is in the most scurrilous terms.

A second form of privilege arises in circumstances of **qualified privilege**. This allows the defence to be available provided certain specific conditions are met. The following types of statements would be protected:

Absolute privilege: Complete immunity from the laws of defamation based on the principle of open justice, which allows the courts and the parliaments to function in a fearlessly independent manner.

Qualified privilege: Material that otherwise might be regarded as defamatory, but which is protected from prosecution.

1 Fair and accurate reports of absolute privileged statements. In these situations journalists need to select and summarise complex information from public proceedings in order to create stories in newspaper style, but they must do so with great care to retain the essential meaning. While the words they take must be verbatim and the selection fair, the actual meanings of the words need not be true or provable. For example, an untrue and unprovable statement made in a parliament or a court by a participant in the proceedings (such as a politician, a witness, an accused person, a lawyer or any other party), and later published by the media, will not place the journalist in jeopardy, so long as the journalist's report is accurate.
2 Defamatory communications based on a moral, social or legal duty, where the recipient has a reciprocal duty to receive them. The media are not generally considered as satisfying this requirement.
3 Reports of public meetings, where the gatherings relate to matters of public interest.
4 Official notices published in accordance with an official request, for example, when the police publish an identikit construct of a suspected criminal, the media may report this without being sued for defamation provided it is a bare facts report of the police notice.
5 Where the media provide a space for a person to respond to a public attack; however, no further counter-attack is permissible.
6 Discussion of political and government matters, referred to as the 'political qualified privilege', and treated as a defence in its own right. This defence has a special significance in Australian jurisprudence, as it has its origins in a series of free speech cases in the early 1990s, including the Lange case (in which a former prime minister of New Zealand sued the ABC for defamation over imputations in a *Four Corners* program). In that case, the High Court held that the Constitution created an 'implied guarantee' of a freedom to communicate on political and government matters. This defence is sometimes called the 'Lange defence'.

Lange case

The High Court held that the Constitution created an implied guarantee of a freedom to communicate on political and government matters: *Lange v Australian Broadcasting Corporation* (1997) 189 CLR 520; online at <www.austlii.edu.au>.

Opinion and comment

The publication of opinion and comment are protected from a defamation action provided certain conditions exist. Essentially, this defence enables the free expression of opinions and comments and can apply to commentary, analysis, reviews, satire and cartoons. The defence protects an honestly held opinion, however extreme or unreasonable it seems. The **honest opinion** defence (similar to the common law defence of fair comment) applies to material presented as opinion, not fact. For example, a statement such as 'The steak was tough and overcooked' is presented as fact. The fair comment defence would therefore be unlikely to hold. But if the journalist had written, 'In my opinion, on that occasion it seemed to me that the steak was tough and overcooked', the fair comment defence may apply, if the statement were the genuinely held opinion of the reviewer journalist, properly researched, and without malice. Beattie and Beal note that:

Honest opinion: A defence in defamation; the right to publish opinion and comment so long as it is reasonably and honestly researched, and without malice.

> To rely on the defence the imputations that arise from the published comment (or opinion) must be a matter of public interest, must be honestly held and the facts upon which it is based must be either set out or well-known. (2007: 48)

The honest opinion defence is particularly useful for restaurant reviewers, music and theatre critics, and editorial writers, but it can apply to anyone publicly expressing a view. By definition, opinion and comment need not be provable, just fairly based.

Defamation on the internet

In the events leading to the landmark Dow Jones case (*Dow Jones & Company Inc v Gutnick* (2002) 210 CLR 575), defamatory material published in the USA was downloaded in Victoria, where the reputation and identity of the plaintiff, businessman Joseph Gutnick, was well known. In this landmark case the defendant, Dow Jones, operated an online news subscription service 'Barons'. The content was uploaded to servers in New Jersey in the US. Certain material was claimed to be defamatory by the plaintiff, Joseph Gutnick, a Melbourne investment/share trading businessman, who downloaded the material in Victoria. Basically, the imputations were that Gutnick had connections to a convicted money launderer and fraudster.

The plaintiff commenced proceedings in the Supreme Court of Victoria. The defendant, meanwhile, sought to have the action struck out on the grounds that Australian law should, like that applied in the USA, recognise that in the case of the internet, publication occurred when the subscription magazine content was uploaded in New Jersey. They also argued, unsuccessfully, that the case should be heard in the USA under US law where defamation laws tend to be more favourable to defendants (publishers) than in Victoria. The plaintiff's legal team successfully argued that Victoria was the most appropriate place to bring the action, since Gutnick lived in Victoria, and that was where he was most likely to suffer the greatest harm to his reputation.

The High Court established that the action could proceed in Victoria, despite the fact that the material was written, produced and published on a US website. In a unanimous judgment in Mr Gutnick's favour, the High Court held that the general rule was that defamation occurs at the place where the material is made available in a comprehensive form. In the case of the internet, this occurs when material is downloaded and read via a browser, and it is the place where the content is downloaded that any damage to reputation may occur. The action was therefore validly commenced in Victoria, and the High Court found that Mr Gutnick had indeed been defamed, awarded him significant damages, and ordered Dow Jones to pay his legal costs.

Dow Jones case

The High Court held that the general rule was that defamation occurs at the place where the material is made available in a comprehensive form: *Dow Jones & Company Inc v Gutnick* (2002) 210 CLR 575; online at <www.austlii.edu.au>.

The wider significance of the case is that it illustrates how the internet problematises jurisdiction. In other words, since defamation laws have evolved in specific geographic jurisdictions, the internet—which crosses all boundaries—now complicates the situation. It cannot be assumed that statements can be made safely online just because they relate to individuals in another country, or because someone has already said it on a website.

The first consideration is the identity of the publisher and disseminator of the material. The internet service provider (ISP) cannot be expected to check all content in the same way that traditional media can check content prior to broadcast or print publication. Hence the ISP, and in some cases also a website, might have the defence of innocent dissemination (just as a newsagent may have such a defence in relation to a traditional newspaper story).

The second consideration is the place of publication and location of the audience. The location of the ISP, the location of the sender (or uploader) of the material and the location of the audience all might be anywhere in the world.

The Dow Jones case means that any person in the world who places content on the web that could be viewed in Australia does so not only subject to the local laws of the jurisdiction where they happen to be, but also subject to the potentially different laws of Australia. And, in reverse, material uploaded in Australia may fall foul of laws in other places where content is downloaded. This will be particularly significant where the foreign laws are more advantageous to a plaintiff identified in the publication than under Australian law. These questions now have to be considered in relation to the place where the plaintiff's reputation is most at stake.

Legislation in the USA and the UK has attempted to define the separation between internet provider and publisher, thus creating a demarcation to protect the ISP from liability. However, the widespread uptake of the internet now means that there could be significant (financial) global implications for this relatively new medium. Although the case specifically concerns defamation laws, Dow Jones has wider implications for internet law and governance in general because it has established the importance of a distinction between origination of content (uploading) and the point of consumption (downloading). In effect, the case means that a person or media organisation making material available online could potentially be sued in just about any jurisdiction where a media platform can be accessed and proceedings can be commenced. However, in practice, there are many other complex jurisdictional issues that may bear on this process (sometimes called 'conflict of laws' principles), including how the specific laws and their enforcement operate internationally (see Goldsmith & Wu 2008; Forder & Svantesson 2008).

Contempt of court

Four principles

Contempt of court: Any action with the potential to damage a fair trial.

The second key area of legal concern for the purposes of this chapter is **contempt of court**. Contempt laws aim to preserve the justice system so that it works fairly for all citizens. Four principles underpin Australian contempt laws:

- open justice
- the right to a fair trial
- the presumption of innocence
- public confidence in the legal system.

Beyond these is the idea that justice must not only be done, but also must be seen to be done. Hence any publication with the potential to damage a fair trial could lead to a contempt charge. With this in mind, media practitioners in general, and journalists in particular, need to tread carefully when presenting content about matters relating to the courts.

Contempt of court is usually a criminal offence, punishable by a fine or jail.

Sub judice

The two main ways in which media may be in contempt of court are by publishing material that could influence a trial and by disobeying a court order. (We discuss the second of these, disobedience contempt, in the later section, 'Confidential sources and confidential documents'.)

The right to a fair trial, uninterrupted by the media, is highly valued in Western democracies. Equally, as former High Court Justice Michael McHugh has argued, 'The publication of fair and accurate reports of court proceedings is vital to the proper working of an open and democratic society and to the maintenance of public confidence in the administration of justice' ('*Fairfax v Police Tribunal of NSW*' (1986) 5 *NSWLR* 465). The cost to society of trial by media can be high: delays and even acquittals can result, denying citizens justice as a consequence. Defence lawyers can also use prejudicial publications to their own advantage, arguing that their client could not receive a fair trial after media coverage.

Publications relating to a trial—when that trial is pending or under way—are called *sub judice* publications. We can divide the *sub judice* period into three parts: the pending period, the trial and the appeal process.

In criminal proceedings, the pending period lies between the time when a summons or warrant for arrest is issued, or when a person is arrested or charged, until the commencement of the trial. Proceedings are not pending just because police inquiries are under way. In civil proceedings, 'pending' refers to the period from the issuing of a writ, statement of claim or summons until the commencement of the trial.

Sub judice: the period, while a trial is pending or under way, when heavy restrictions are placed on the release of information about the trial.

During the pending period, journalists can report the charges and can identify the accused or respondents/defendants, so long as the charges do not involve children as victims or accused. Information that presumes guilt or innocence, that refers to any past convictions or that otherwise might be relevant to the case, is prohibited.

The second stage of the sub judice period is the trial itself, when journalists can report anything stated in an open court. In cases before a jury, more care needs to be taken in reporting the proceedings than in cases before a judge alone, as jurors are considered to be more susceptible to outside influence than a judge.

Children's courts are closed, not reportable, and identities of all participants are protected. Breaches of the law relating to children's courts are extremely serious.

The third stage of the sub judice period is the appeal process, which extends until the appeal process has been exhausted. Journalists can report anything already stated in open court, but can make no further comment that could affect the appeals.

Contempt of court and the media practitioner

We can now see how the law relating to sub judice publications might impinge on freedom of expression. Imagine you have witnessed a robbery. The police charge someone within hours. You know the person committed the act because you saw the event, but you cannot publish this fact in the sub judice period. It is the courts alone that decide the facts, not the media. Now imagine the accused is your brother or sister. You would expect a fair trial through proper court processes, not trial by media, wouldn't you?

All citizens are entitled to the rule of law and to the **presumption of innocence** until a proper court process finds otherwise. The media have great power to influence the fairness of this process.

Presumption of innocence: The right of an accused person to innocence in law until a court convicts that person.

Notorious cases often result in breaches of contempt laws. If the media and public are hungry for information about a sensational case, courts can be powerless to prevent abuses of the justice process. In December 2006, police in Britain charged a man with the murder of five prostitutes in what became known as the Suffolk strangler case. Although public discussion must cease after a suspect is charged, the *Sun* newspaper published prejudicial material, including a photograph of the accused mock-strangling his former wife, and quotes from two prostitutes alleging he had cruised for sex dressed in drag. Police and the attorney-general reprimanded the media for threatening the man's right to a fair trial.

Publications in other jurisdictions are harder to contain. A court has power only over its own state, territory or nation, and this explains why details of trials during the sub judice period might be published in another country. The trial of the murdered British backpacker Peter Falconio and his relationship with his girlfriend Joanne Lees, for example, were grist to the mill for the UK's tabloid media while proceedings were sub judice in the Northern Territory.

The magazine *Who Weekly* experienced the heavy cost of sub judice contempt in 1994 in relation to the so-called backpacker murders in New South Wales. *Who Weekly* published an image of the accused, Ivan Milat, during the sub judice period before his conviction. In the Milat case, the issue of identity was crucial to the trial, and in any event the publication of a photograph of an accused person is prohibited. The front cover of the magazine carried the words: 'Backpacker serial killings. The accused. The private life of road worker Ivan Milat, the man charged with slaying 7 hitchhikers, as told by his brother Wally.' The magazine was fined $100,000 and the editor $10,000. The Court of Appeal found that the publisher had a right to seek profit from providing information as entertainment, but had no right to do so at the expense of the administration of justice.

The media are prohibited from reporting material from a closed court, or from proceedings that are subject to suppression orders. Generally, this is in the interests of the administration of justice, for instance, to protect witnesses, to facilitate police informers coming forward to give evidence and to safeguard the rights of the accused to a fair trial. In early 2008, the Nine Network was ordered by the Supreme Court in Victoria not to broadcast specific episodes of the television drama series *Underbelly* on the basis that the material (referencing Melbourne's gangland murder subculture) would interfere with criminal proceedings in that state (*R v [A]* [2008] VSC 73). Controversially, the judge's suppression orders also prohibited the series being viewed over the internet, a measure which, together with the fact that bootleg DVD copies were easily available, was very publicly seen as unenforceable and was widely discussed in the media. It has been suggested that the Court of Appeal's judgment in *General Television Corporation Pty Ltd v Director of Public Prosecutions* ([2008] 19 VR 68) has now 'added to the list of categories where a court may derogate from open justice' (Rotstein 2010: 110). The disjuncture between the longstanding rationale behind contempt laws and the ways in which audiences are now able to consume their favourite media products was apparent for all to see.

Defences

A journalist charged with contempt of court has few defences, and truth is not among them.

To understand why, return for a moment to the robbery you have witnessed. Let's say you published the truth, that the accused committed the offence. But the case is sub judice, and your report has the potential to influence the jury, who must be free to decide their verdict on the basis of what goes before the court, not what they read or have the potential to read, see or hear in the media.

The main defence for contempt of court is that of a fair and accurate report under qualified privilege. You may report exactly what was said in the court and the bare facts of the case, and if your report is a true and accurate account of those proceedings, you will have a defence.

Another defence, that of public interest, might also apply but is less reliable. Australian broadcaster Derryn Hinch put the public interest argument when charged with contempt of court after referring to the prior convictions of a former priest, Michael Glennon, who was facing sex offences in 1985. Hinch argued the public had a right to know of the accused's history, but the court found there was risk of serious prejudice to the trial because the statements might stay in the jurors' minds.

Advice for journalists

The *ABC All Media Law Handbook* has the following advice for journalists reporting on court cases:

- It is a contempt to state a person is guilty or innocent before they have been convicted or acquitted.
- If reporting on a civil action, do not say a person is liable or negligent before a judgment is given.

- Do not publish an admission of guilt outside the court process.
- Do not publish the criminal record of the accused.
- Do not publish confessions.
- Do not publish evidence relating to the case.
- Do not publish any independent investigation of the case.
- Do not publish any statement in court when the jury is out of the court.
- Do not publish a photograph of an accused person.
- Do not publish a statement of a witness (or potential witness).
- Do not pressure anyone not to participate in a case.
- Do not publish that a trial is a retrial until the retrial is concluded.

Source: ABC (2006).

Confidential sources and documents

As mentioned in the previous section, as well as contempt by publication there is another area of contempt that is particularly relevant to media: **disobedience contempt**. We discuss this here in relation to confidential sources and documents: first, because it is unrelated to sub judice contempt, and second, because it is distinctive in the whole area of confidentiality.

Disobedience contempt: The refusal by journalists to reveal their sources when asked by a court to do so.

Historically, only a fairly narrow number of circumstances have qualified as confidential information. They have included trade secrets, program ideas, domestic confidences, and tribal, cultural, religious and government secrets. It is the latter category, government secrets, that tends to trigger disobedience contempt. This occurs when journalists refuse to reveal their sources when asked by a court to do so; in other words, the law of contempt is on occasion relied upon by the state to protect legal proceedings from certain kinds of journalistic practices (Beattie & Beal 2007: 59).

Confidential sources

Confidential sources can provide important information that might otherwise not be available to the public. But when sources leak such information, they often do so at risk to themselves; hence, the journalist might promise anonymity to the source in return for the information. The MEAA Code of Ethics (1996) states that journalists must respect all confidences, thus ensuring that they keep the trust of those upon whom they depend for information. But if a trial, in which the identity of a source is vital to the case, is under way the judge might decide to call the journalist as a witness to reveal the name of the source.

Confidential sources: People who provide—while keeping their identities secret—important information that might otherwise not be available to the public.

Since the 1980s, at least twelve journalists have faced contempt of court charges in Australia for refusing to reveal their sources. Two *Herald Sun* journalists, Michael Harvey and Gerard McManus, pleaded guilty to contempt of court at a pre-trial hearing in 2006 for refusing to reveal the identity of a source who had provided them with leaked documents that revealed that the government had refused a bid for an increase in war pensions of more than $500 million). They were convicted and each fined $7000. The leaking of confidential documents is an offence, and a senior public servant was charged, but the decision was later overturned by the Supreme Court. In the contempt case that followed in February 2007, the County Court Chief Judge Michael Rozenes said the two journalists had put their professional ethics ahead of the justice system, and asked how any court could tolerate such a circumstance (MEAA 2007).

Shield laws: Legal protection for journalists who refuse to reveal their confidential sources to a court.

The conflict between journalists' protection of their sources and the requirements of the courts remains unresolved. **Shield laws** are legal mechanisms to safeguard journalists against prosecution, and are available in some jurisdictions to protect journalists in relation to disclosure of their sources. In the USA, the overwhelming majority of states have shield laws and they are expected soon to be available at the federal level, having been debated in Congress for over six years—although the WikiLeaks controversy has now complicated the passing of laws to protect conventional journalistic sources (*LA Times* 2010). In the UK, there is limited protection for journalists under the *Contempt of Court Act 1981*. This means that in the UK no court

> can require a person to disclose, nor is a person guilty of contempt of court for refusing to disclose, the source of information contained in a publication for which they are responsible unless it is established to the satisfaction of the court that disclosure is necessary in the interests of justice, or national security, or for the prevention of disorder or crime. (Butler and Rodrick 2007: 329 [7.395])

In New Zealand, the *Evidence Act 2006* contains a specific privilege protecting journalists' sources. In Australia, after a long period of delayed promises, the *Evidence Amendment (Journalists' Privilege) Act 2010* was passed in 2011, and as amended, will apply to bloggers and citizen journalists using 'any medium', as well as to traditional journalists.

The new laws strengthen provisions relating to information provided to journalists and requires Courts to consider whether:

- information was passed contrary to the law in determining whether evidence should be admitted, or whether a source should be revealed; and
- there will be potential harm to the source and/or the journalist if evidence is given.

The laws are modeled on the New Zealand law that provides a rebuttable presumption in favour of journalists not disclosing information in court proceedings that would identify their source. The Act provides that if a journalist has promised an informant not to disclose his or her identity, neither the journalist nor his or her employer is compellable to answer any question or produce any document that would disclose the identity of the informant.

Many observers stress the important connection between effective shield laws and laws protecting the disclosure of confidential information in the public interest. For example, the Australian Press Council argues: 'the Council has always advocated that the introduction of effective public interest disclosure legislation, that includes provisions for disclosure to the media, also requires the introduction of effective shield laws to allow journalists to protect their sources.' (APC, 2010:13).

A rarely used mechanism is provided for under s. 202 of the *Broadcasting Services Act 1992* (Cth), when the Australian Communications and Media Authority undertakes investigations that may involve calling journalists to give evidence. In these circumstances it is a reasonable excuse for a journalist to refuse to answer a question or produce a document that has been used for the purposes of making a program, when to do so may disclose the identity of a confidential source.

The MEAA Code of Ethics (1996) warns against promising anonymity and advises journalists to find the information elsewhere. But extremely sensitive information, such as that which reveals fraud or malpractice, is usually not easily available elsewhere, hence the need for members of the media to obtain and maintain the trust of their sources.

The journalist's relationship with confidential sources is a grey area where law and ethics can easily be in conflict. Recognising this ethical complexity, in 2008 the ABC's managing director requested that the director of editorial policies review the organisation's policy and procedures (ABC 2008). The review was triggered by the so-called Brissenden affair, involving an 'off-the-record' interview between Michael Brissenden of the ABC's *7.30 Report*, the then Federal Treasurer Peter Costello and two other journalists. The event became controversial when it was suggested that the journalists had breached a confidence with the treasurer.

These cases show the conflict between freedom of expression, the processes of justice and wider public interests. To yield to a court order to reveal a confidence is at the very least to lose face among professional colleagues and, more significantly, to betray a trust. To withhold the information is to deny justice to one or the other party in a case. The courts tend to respect this conflict and are reluctant to convict, but that has not stopped them from punishing journalists such as Harvey and McManus when the administration of justice and ethical media practice were clearly relying on different decision-making frameworks.

Confidential documents

The law protects people's secrets, but, as we have discussed above, it has not in the past protected journalists' secret sources. There are, however, crucial differences between protecting a confidential arrangement a journalist might have with a source, and protecting the disclosure of confidential documents. And in a contemporary blurring of this distinction, we need look no further than the highly publicised activities of the WikiLeaks organisation in releasing a video onto YouTube, 'Collateral Murder', which shows a US Army Apache helicopter slaughtering innocent Iraqi civilians, including children, in Baghdad. WikiLeaks, in the few short years it has operated, has facilitated the disclosure of hundreds of thousands of confidential government and corporate documents into the public domain (Khatchadourian 2010).

It is possible that journalists will face legal action if they publish material that has the status of confidentiality. A document does not need to have 'confidential' written on it in order to be confidential—many commercial communications, for example, are in confidence. Journalists develop a sense for confidential material, that is, they can often identify it even if it is not marked as such. The material must have a quality of confidence; it must have been imparted in a way that carries an obligation of confidentiality. Accidental disclosure of such material is still a breach. To publish is to risk being sued by the party whose confidence has been broken, or to risk being charged with contempt of court if the publication is in breach of a suppression order.

Leaks are the lifeblood of investigative journalism. The person revealing sensitive information usually believes the public has a right to know. But if the leaked material is confidential (and by its nature, it usually is), then any publication carries risk. In the next section we consider the media and privacy: the public's right to know and related ideas of the public interest are often invoked to justify actions by media when individuals' privacy is breached.

The right to privacy

In Australia there is no specific statutory privacy tort or wrong defined in legislation. However, the Australian Law Reform Commission (ALRC), at the culmination of an extensive investigation, has recommended that such a tort be implemented (ALRC 2008).

Privacy in Australia has arisen as a patchwork of laws and regulations, and several broad categories of privacy tend to get collapsed together to offer protection. These categories relate to personal information (or data held by corporations and government), communications (telecommunications interception, the use of listening devices and other types of surveillance devices) and laws relating to invasions of private space (autonomy against intrusion into private lives).

The ALRC surveyed the Australian public in relation to their privacy concerns: the results may surprise. Almost three-quarters of all respondents (73 per cent) cited telemarketing as a major concern, followed by:

- the handling of personal information by the private sector (19 per cent)
- the handling of personal information by government (9 per cent)
- the protection of privacy on the internet (7 per cent)
- national identity cards and smart cards (7 per cent)
- problems accessing and correcting personal information (7 per cent)
- surveillance in public places (4 per cent)
- workplace surveillance (2 per cent).

Amid concerns about the impacts of more restrictive privacy laws on the Fourth Estate role of the media, the ALRC suggests that the courts should be required to consider whether the public interest in maintaining the claimant's privacy outweighs other matters of public interest, including the interest in informing the public about matters of public concern and facilitating freedom of expression. The ALRC's recommended statutory cause of action for serious invasion of privacy includes the following types of scenarios:

> After the break-up of their relationship, Mr A sends copies of a DVD of himself and his former girlfriend (B) engaged in sexual activity to Ms B's parents, friends, neighbours and employer;
>
> Mr C sets up a tiny hidden camera in the women's toilet at his workplace, capturing images of his colleagues that he downloads to his own computer and transmits to a website hosted overseas, which features similar images; and

> Ms D works in a hospital and obtains access to the medical records of a famous sportsman, who is being treated for drug addiction. D makes a copy of the file and sells it to a newspaper, which publishes the information in a front page story. (ALRC 2008)

The main federal legislation, the *Privacy Act 1988* (Cth), sets out different principles for how private organisations and government agencies should manage personal information or data. On top of that, each state and territory has its own privacy laws or guidelines and some also have separate laws on health privacy. The federal *Privacy Amendment (Private Sector) Act 2000* contains an exemption for journalists in the course of their work as they gather information for news or documentaries for the purposes of making that material available for the public. Arguably, as privacy rights increase, the right to publish decreases. Journalists need also to be aware of prohibitions on electronic surveillance. The Victorian *Surveillance Devices Act 1999*, for example, prohibits the taking of photos and videos in private places and proscribes the use of material from hidden cameras or audio recording devices.

Privacy laws affect media practitioners at two critical points in the production process: the gathering of information and the publication of information. The MEAA and industry co-regulatory sector codes (administered by ACMA) have provisions that deal with best practice behaviours in relation to protecting individuals' privacy. In addition, the Australian Press Council's Statement of Principles and Print Media Privacy Standards offer a practical guidance framework for media practitioners in the preparation of publications to observe the 'privacy and sensibilities of individuals'. These guidance materials also expressly acknowledge that the right to privacy 'should not prevent publication of matters of public record or obvious or significant public interest' (Australian Press Council 2007).

Privacy is an area of law that can, in certain situations, cross over with questions of defamation and confidentiality, blurring neat demarcations between rights, responsible media performance and legal redress. We live in times of shifting relations between the public and private spheres. Media and communications are actively implicated in this process of redefining social and cultural understandings of the behaviours we refer to as 'privacy'. Think of the way we now communicate in public spaces. When we travel on public transport, we use mobile communication devices to have, on occasions, fairly intimate conversations with those we care about, or other conversations that could be defined as private. Or, to take another example from the mediated public sphere, think of reality television formats. Contestants (and it usually is a some kind of contest) are a weird mix of celebrity and ordinary, and audiences can engage with a hybridity of personal, private and yet highly public human interactions. Social networking sites such as Facebook and Bebo, and other kinds of 'mass self communication' as Castells (2007) describes it, also have these hybrid private and public elements. In fact, the software usually allows people to have a binary private/public switch on their personal profiles, which is capable of recognising social distinctions between family and friends who are in a closer network, and all the others whom they permit to become part of the wider network of generic friends. The Federal Trade Commission and congressional privacy committee members in the USA have investigated the way third-party applications gather and transmit personally identifiable information about Facebook site users and those users' friends. It is possible that 'do not track' regulations will be introduced to protect privacy and prevent data collection by advertisers and other third parties in social networking sites (Canning 2010).

In all the above examples, we can see that the line between the public and private spheres is somewhat fuzzy. But it should be becoming clearer that 'privacy is essentially normative and, as such, the idea of the private changes over time, with part of that change being driven by technological change affecting communications' (Morrison et al. 2007: 199). The ALRC in its 2008 report notes:

> It does appear that young people are more comfortable than their parents, and certainly their grand-parents, in sharing personal information, photos and other material on social networking websites. The question is whether this represents the beginnings of an enduring cultural shift, or simply the eternal recklessness of youth, played out in a new medium and utilising new technology. Put another way, will today's teenagers be horrified in a decade's time when prospective employers—and prospective partners and in-laws—can easily 'google up' intimate and potentially embarrassing images and information?

Through Article 8 of the European Convention on Human Rights, a right to privacy is now enshrined in UK law; in the USA, the right to privacy is a strong legal right with a long history (based on a *Harvard Law Review* article entitled 'The Right to Privacy' in 1890 by Warren and Brandeis), giving litigants an alternative to defamation laws, which are much weaker (see Case Study 3 for more on this issue).

The case of the wedding of actors Michael Douglas and Catherine Zeta-Jones in 2000 illustrates how a loosening of one law can be neutralised by a tightening of another. A media discussion over privacy, confidentiality and defamation was sparked when the magazines *Hello!* and *OK!* published photographs taken at the wedding. *OK!* paid for exclusive rights to publish the Douglas–Zeta-Jones wedding photos, while *Hello!* published paparazzi shots. Zeta-Jones called the paparazzi snaps 'sleazy' and 'offensive', and took issue with shots showing her new husband spooning cake into her mouth. Meanwhile, *OK!* sued *Hello!* for breach of confidentiality. Six years later, the Britain and Wales Court of Appeal (Civil Division) ruled in favour of *OK!*, treating the photographs as akin to trade secrets for the purposes of the law of confidences.

The House of Lords had earlier, in *Campbell v Mirror Group Newspapers Ltd* [2004] 2 AC 457, confirmed the legitimacy of the new privacy right in the UK, with a ruling that a newspaper had breached supermodel Naomi Campbell's right to privacy when it published a correct statement that she had visited Narcotics Anonymous. Under the European Convention of Human Rights, an individual's Article 8 rights are engaged if one has a 'reasonable expectation' of privacy in the information concerned.

Typically, in debates about media and privacy laws, there is a view expressed that the role of paparazzi and 'stories about the private lives of celebrities amount to big business, and poor practice would leave media organisations exposed to liability for damages' (ALRC 2008). In this context, many media commentators and practitioners see a general international shift from the right to publish towards the right to privacy.

Privacy case study: CCTV

How often do you hear a news report say 'Police are reviewing CCTV footage' to assist in solving a crime? The increasing use of CCTV cameras in public spaces is one of the more visible changes to privacy in recent years. Broadly speaking, their usefulness in reducing incidents of criminal activities has tended to outweigh civil libertarian arguments in relation to growing surveillance trends in society and a general reduction in personal privacy. On the one hand, it is difficult to argue with statistics showing that criminals suspected of very serious crimes (such as murder and rape) have been apprehended after the police have examined CCTV footage. On the other hand, the police have got it wrong at times, and apprehended the wrong people after relying on CCTV footage.

A television current affairs item, examining the use of CCTV cameras in inner London, illustrated the excessive surveillance now prevalent in cities, when the reporter was captured on camera more than a dozen times as he commuted by bicycle from where he lived to where he worked (*Foreign Correspondent* 2007).

Another concern is the increasing tendency for surveillance systems to be linked together in cities and for them to run by computerised systems with little human intervention. As security experts are quick to point out, such systems are only as good as the component elements from which they are constituted. Should one system get it wrong, there is a cumulative error in all the systems.

The case of Joey De Mesa is an example of the use of CCTV surveillance going out of control. A 23-year-old fruit shop worker noticed himself on CCTV footage on the news in an item concerning a serial rapist, so he handed himself in to Mount Druitt police, hoping to clear up any uncertainty. He had records to prove that he had been at work on the day in question. Unfortunately for Mr De Mesa, he was left in a cell for several days and refused bail. There were eleven charges against him, including three counts of aggravated sexual assault, three counts of aggravated robbery, indecent assault, and stalking and intimidation linked to assaults on five women in Sydney's northwest between April and June. All the charges were eventually dropped on the basis of forensic tests when his case went to the Supreme Court.

Source: *Sydney Morning Herald* (2008).

Freedom of Information

Freedom of Information (FoI) laws are now a characteristic of open government in democratic societies. FoI laws in Australia are mostly based on a US precedent, which has been mirrored in all states and territories except the Northern Territory.

Freedom of Information: Laws that grant some rights of access to government documents of public interest.

The legislation exists to create an enforceable right to access documents held by governments, their departments and agencies. There are various exempt agencies (for example, the security organisations ASIO and ASIS), as well as specific categories of exempt documents, including:

- essential interests or functions of government, such as national security
- relations between state and territory governments
- Cabinet documents
- Executive Council documents
- documents that would jeopardise the deliberative processes of government (internal working documents) against the public interest
- law enforcement documents
- documents that would prejudice a fair trial, breach a confidence or constitute contempt of court.

Even though FoI remains an important channel for access to government information by the media, most users of FoI are non-journalists seeking personal information.

Access is by way of filling in an application form, paying the required fee and waiting the prescribed thirty days to be notified of the outcome of the request. If access is refused (and the grounds for such refusal will be stated), applicants have a further thirty days within which to lodge a request for an internal review. There is a further appeal process through the Administrative Appeals Tribunal.

The FoI process is sometimes criticised on the basis of the number of exemptions and the high costs involved, which has tended to thwart its original objectives. A controversial feature of Australia's FoI scheme has been the mechanism of a 'minister's certificate', or 'conclusive certificate', which allows a minister to make a declaration that a disclosure of particular documents would be contrary to the public interest. These ministerial decisions are beyond the ambit of a full merits review, unlike many administrative decisions made by bureaucracies. There have been recent measures to reform FoI laws by state and federal governments in terms of lowering fees and charges, and increasing general accessibility and workability. At their heart, these reforms are being driven by attempts to reignite the original intentions of these laws, which were to make government more open and accountable to its citizens and to allow the use of freedom of information by journalists to ensure that matters of public concern are brought to the public's attention through the media (Australian Press Council 2010).

Copyright

You have had an idea for a news feature story. You meet a writer friend at a city cafe and discuss it. Your friend goes away and turns your idea into an online article. She then meets a third friend to discuss the article, leaving a copy for comment. The third friend has connections with the *New York Times*, and with the best intentions sends the article (based on your idea) for publication.

In this scenario, there may have been a breach of **copyright**. The article has been published without permission. Who owns the copyright? Not you, but the person who turned your brilliant idea into a material form: your writer friend. She is the one who might sue the third friend and the *New York Times* online.

Copyright: The exclusive right, granted by law for a period of time, to control the publishing and copying of a particular publication or artistic work. It does not protect ideas, only the material form of those ideas.

Intellectual property: A broad term used to refer to intangible property created by the mind.

Who owns an idea?

The *Copyright Act 1968* (Cth) protects all creative and **intellectual property**. It does not protect ideas, only the material form of those ideas.

Copyright is automatic. It needs no registration, and while the universal copyright symbol is a warning against misuse, it is not essential. The owner of a work of writing, art, photography, music, poetry, performance, or a logo, house plan, design or cartoon, is the only person entitled to publish the work for any purpose. Another may use it only with permission.

The copyright owner in a work has the exclusive rights to:

- reproduce the work (for example, convert it to a digital format)
- publish the work (for example, in a newspaper, magazine or book)
- communicate the work to the public (for example, post it on the internet or make it available to download on mobile phones).

Most creative and intellectual works are copyright. Publication of a line of a song or a paragraph of prose needs permission from the owner. Building a website using video, images, sounds, links to other websites, text quotes or news items published elsewhere will all require permission from the copyright owner (Forder & Svantesson 2008). The idea of culture as property is the main metaphor that underpins all intellectual property laws: copyright, moral rights, patents, designs, trademarks and passing off in common law.

The advent of digitalisation and convergence processes has radically reconfigured these laws and their wider cultural implications for creativity and innovation. User-generated and DIY media creation in general have altered the balance and expectations of deriving income from intellectual property. The inability of traditional legal concepts to adapt to these processes has led to alternatives to conventional intellectual property laws, for example, in **creative commons licensing** and **open source licensing** (Beattie & Beal 2007).

In response to obligations under Article 11 of the World Intellectual Property Organization (WIPO) Copyright Treaty 1996 to introduce **technological prevention measures** (or TPMs), Australia introduced its own digital copyright laws with the *Copyright Amendment (Digital Agenda) Act 2000* (Cth). This Act updated copyright laws for digital media and communications by introducing a 'broad-based technology-neutral' right of communication to the public, which subsumes and extends the previous broadcast and cable rights.

Creative commons licensing: A form of licensing that encompasses the spectrum of possibilities between full copyright (all rights reserved) and the public domain (no rights reserved). Creative commons licences help owners keep their copyright while inviting certain uses of the owner's work—a some rights reserved copyright.

Open source licensing: A copyright licence to modify computer software code, generally entailing a requirement to make available to others any modifications that are made.

Technological prevention measure: A device, product, technology or component (including a computer program) that in the normal course of its operation controls access to or use of the copyright-protected work, for example, software coding that prevents a CD from being used in a car.

A consolidated version of the *Copyright Act 1968* (Cth)—including the amendments under both the *Copyright Amendment (Digital Agenda) Act* and the *Copyright Amendment Act 2006* (Cth)—can be found at <www.austlii.edu.au/au/legis/cth/consol_act/ca1968133>.

Broadly, the purpose of these laws was to introduce tougher restrictions on consumers' use of digital products such as recorded music and film, including the criminalisation of illegal use. So-called digital rights management and specific TPMs have attempted to limit widespread infringement. There has, for example, been a number of high-profile cases in the USA and Australia in relation to peer-to-peer (P2P) music and film file sharing. Overall, however, the effects of these cases on creation, distribution and consumption trends in media consumption have been very limited. Despite a great deal of commentary to the effect that these changes signal the end of intellectual property, corporations continue to invest a great deal of money, time and energy in fighting these battles.

How can this apparent impasse be resolved? In Lessig's view, the 'copyright warriors' continue to frame the debate 'at the extremes—as a grand either/or; either property or anarchy, either total control or artist won't be paid'. In his view, and it is a persuasive argument, 'the mistake here is the error of the excluded middle'. What is actually needed, he suggests, is 'neither "all rights reserved" nor "no rights reserved" but "some rights reserved"—and thus a way to respect copyrights but enable creators to free content as they see fit' (Lessig 2005: 277).

Copyright: key points to note

Copyright lasts for the lifetime of the creator, and for fifty to seventy years thereafter (also, twenty years for a patent, ten years for a trademark or five years for a design).

Copyright can be transferred to another owner by sale or assignment (for example, to a publisher in return for royalties or a lump sum), by inheritance or by licensing for a fixed period.

Copyright permissions usually incur a fee, in the case of books, for use of more than 100 words. For journalists, it is usually sufficient to request permission by telephone, while book publishers obtain written permission, specifying the nature and extent of the use.

Breach of copyright must involve a substantial part of the work. Consider the opening sentence from Charles Dickens's *A Tale of Two Cities*: 'It was the best of times, it was the worst of times', or the famous lines from Leo Tolstoy's *Anna Karenina*: 'All happy families resemble one another but each unhappy family is unhappy in its own way', or these words from Samuel Taylor Coleridge's poem *Kubla Khan*: 'In Xanadu did Kubla Khan a stately pleasure dome decree'. In each case, the lines are only a tiny part of the whole work, but they are crucial part nevertheless, and hence they illustrate what the courts could debate as being a substantial part.

While the *Copyright Act* distinguishes between commercial and educational use, it does not make any judgment about the quality of the work or the talent of the creator: a bad poem has as much significance in copyright as one written by a Nobel Prize-winning literary genius.

The *Copyright Act* allows some limited copying of protected materials in certain situations; for example, artistic works displayed in public spaces may allow copying by photography or filming.

The *Copyright Act* provides a limited number of exceptions to copyright infringement under fair dealing sections covering the following generic situations:

- research or study
- criticism or review

- reporting the news
- legal advice or judicial proceedings
- parody and satire.

Despite the fact that copyright laws operate in national jurisdictions, they have become increasingly globalised through international treaties and international trade agreements. These have the affect of setting minimum standards for rights and providing avenues for enforcement, including trade sanctions in the case of World Trade Organization (WTO) treaties. Several of the Digital Agenda amendments, for example, were subsequently repealed and replaced by laws to implement Australia's free trade agreement with the USA (AUSFTA), including the *Copyright Amendment Act 2006* (Cth).

The Australian Copyright Council website contains full details in relation to copyright laws in Australia; see <www.copyright.org.au/information>. For information about intellectual property more broadly, visit IP Australia's website at <www.ipaustralia.gov.au>.

Moral rights

Another category of rights exists for creators of certain copyright-protected works, called moral rights. Moral rights impose separate rights and obligations that are associated with copyright in a work, and accompany copyright if the work is eligible for copyright. As Beattie and Beal explain: 'Moral rights differ from copyright in that they are personal non-economic rights. They cannot be sold or licensed and even if copyright is sold moral rights remain with the creator' (2007: 122).

Moral rights require the creator to be attributed whenever their work is reproduced, communicated to the public, exhibited or published. They prevent people from falsely attributing a work, treating a work in a derogatory way, or modifying it in a way that is prejudicial to the reputation of the creator. Consent is required for each particular event that may breach the moral rights of a creator.

Law in changing mediaspheres

The ways in which media are produced, distributed and consumed by audiences continue to change relatively rapidly. Communications media are constantly undergoing significant transformations in this era of deregulation, concentrating ownership and the internet. Therefore, it is important to recognise that the fundamental debates involving communication and society both change and stay the same.

An important implication of this evolutionary process is that the traditional media of television, radio and newspapers are changing alongside the popular new media forms. Accordingly, many of the laws that have been developed in the context of existing media may also be relevant to new media, such as the internet and social media applications.

Enduring concerns will include the wider set of law, policy and regulation that grapples with the following issues, as listed by Dwyer (2007, 2010):

- the media and democracy
- media concentration and ownership

- public service media and market liberalism
- universal service and net neutrality
- the representation of race, ethnicity and other diversities
- news and the coverage of elections
- the availability of a full range of programming genres
- protection of the child audience
- the provision of services for less able audiences.

Clearly, traditional concerns do not just disappear because of new media delivery and audience consumption modes. We can safely predict that new modes will change social and cultural uses as a result of innovation by, for example:

- developments in the way people are using media while in transit, based on their specific locations, accessing content that originates almost anywhere in the world
- the ease of falsifying identity, or the altering of content itself, through software that enables such modification
- other forms of as yet unseen creative media use.

As social and cultural uses of media evolve, these will find expression in the law. The law, after all, is a formal system for the governance of culture.

Conclusion

Media practitioners are subject to the same laws as are all other citizens. Everyone who publishes on any media platform needs to be mindful of the potential to defame or breach contempt laws, to breach a confidence, to illegally invade privacy or to breach copyright. Safe publishing does not require a lawyer's knowledge, but rather an awareness of the boundaries of particular laws. Breaches of media law are constantly occurring, but equipped with a working knowledge of concepts, frameworks and general legal literacies relevant to their roles as content creators as discussed in this chapter, media practitioners will be able to confidently and effectively work in the evolving media and communications industries.

KEY REFERENCES

Beattie, S. & Beal, E. (2007). *Connect and Converge. Australian Media and Communications Law*. Melbourne: Oxford University Press.

Kenyon, A. T. (2006), *Defamation: Comparative Law and Practice*. London: UCL Press.

Morrison, D., Kieran, M., Svennevig, M. & Ventress, S. (2007). *Media and Values. Intimate Transgressions in a Changing Moral and Cultural Landscape*. Bristol and Chicago: Intellect.

Rotstein, F. (2010). 'Chewing the Fat of a Soft Underbelly'. *Media and Arts Law Review*, 15(1).

CHAPTER 18

THE NEW MEDIA ENVIRONMENT: DIGITAL AND SOCIAL MEDIA

JASON BAINBRIDGE, CAROLYN BEASLEY AND LIZ TYNAN

Introduction

During the rolling news coverage of the Queensland floods in 2010–11, Channel Nine news presenter Wendy Kingston commented on the liberal use Nine had made of consumer-generated content, particularly footage taken on mobile phones, accessed via Facebook, and tweets. She noted that 'the landscape to communicate and report news has now changed' (Kingston 2011). Her comment points to one of the most wondrous things about being alive in the twenty-first century: the sheer pace of change. It is exhilarating, even though sometimes we feel it might be out of control. Indeed, the pace of change is so rapid that this chapter is becoming obsolete even as we write it.

Paul Saffo of the Institute for the Future (Kluth 2006) described what's going on right now as a 'Cambrian explosion' of technology-driven creativity, echoing the huge biological proliferation on Earth hundreds of millions of years ago.

One area that is continually changing, updating and rebooting itself is that of media. The new mechanisms that these changes are producing are referred to collectively as 'new media', and more specifically, as digital and social media.

Some would argue that these new media have democratised and invigorated the media; others that they have sent them into a downward spiral. Whatever you think, change is inevitable, particularly as technology burgeons. Just as the invention of the transistor in the late 1940s was the start of the (then unimaginable) computer revolution, so we are now inventing technologies that will take us to who knows where. As information is one of the most important commodities in the world, the rise of information-based technology has transformed the way we receive and process information. Boundaries of all kinds are being blurred and if we thought we could see the future a generation ago, we certainly cannot see it now.

Throughout this book we have made reference to a variety of ways in which digital and social media have had an impact on traditional media industries and ideas, from the possibility of an online Fifth Estate to the effects of DVD technologies on television. While we all think we know what is meant by the new media environment, in this chapter we define what it means to be one of these new media forms and why it is important. We also address some of the features and impacts of digital and social media that we haven't looked at before. Finally, we provide some suggestions for future directions and, in the context of journalism more specifically, examine how the shift in most traditional newsrooms to part online operation has profoundly changed news.

In this chapter we examine:

- the new media environment
- specific examples of new media
- online journalism and the switched-on newsroom
- computer-assisted reporting
- the consequences of the rise of new media for old media.

What is the new media environment?

The new media environment comprises information and entertainment transmitted digitally. This definition is almost the same as our definition of media that opened this book. The difference is in the addition of the word 'digital'. We use digital as the point of demarcation because, strictly speaking, all media are new media. As John Hartley (2002a: 164) notes, 'The first new media technology we know about was writing, invented about 3100 BC in Egypt and Sumeria, and separately in China around the same time'. All media are new for the era that spawned them; media are constantly developing with advances in technology.

New media: The mechanisms for digitally transmitting information and entertainment.

The term **new media** is most often used as a catch-all term to differentiate between old media, such as newspapers, magazines, radio and television, and new media, which are based on digitalisation, such as mobile phones, DVDs, gaming systems and the internet. Mobile phones and social networking sites such as Twitter and Facebook are also referred to as social media because they encourage audiences to be socially engaged, establishing the type of audience networks discussed in Chapter 10. These audience networks so profoundly challenge the old broadcasting models and the way that we communicate that it would be wrong to consider them just a fad; sixty million updates occur daily on Facebook alone.

Understanding the new media environment is not just a matter of listing all the new gadgets and widgets that are being introduced. According to media theorist Terry Flew (2002), we have to understand all of these things in terms of 'how they are actually altering our society'. This is because digital media and social media are doing something very important: they are 'promoting a culture based upon interactivity and virtuality' (Flew 2002: 207). This is the essence of the new media environment. According to Flew, simply characterising them as new things beginning with C (such as computers, communications networks, content and convergence) is not sufficient (Flew 2002: 10), especially since new media are often based upon old forms of media, and the lines of demarcation are not clear. A lot of internet content is made up of text or visuals that existed in other, older media forms long before they went online. Much of new media has involved taking, say, a newspaper and turning it into an online version of itself. But the online newspaper is not just another version of itself; it is updatable, it is interactive, it can be corrected and it is available to many more people than before. It is a digital media form. Increasingly, too, this new form of the newspaper includes moving pictures and audio associated with the stories. This took some time to be widely available, largely because it depended upon its users having access to broadband. Now that broadband is commonplace, an increasing amount of internet content includes moving images and sound.

How has digital technology changed news production?

There are several ways in which established newspapers have altered the structure and form of their stories for online broadcast. First, they tend to place less importance on the 'when' of a story, with the lead omitting any reference to the time or day that the event took place. Rather, this information tends to appear in the second paragraph or later, which could be seen as a way of making the story seem more current, as if it has happened only moments ago. This sense of currency means the story can be used across a number of updates and over a period of time.

Second, specific details about the 'who, what and where' of the lead—such as names and places—that used to be held back to the second paragraph are now used in the headline as a way of ensuring that the story is picked up during a Google metasearch. Headlines are written with search engines in mind (Lohr 2006). Some publications also now include dot point summaries after the second paragraph as a way of keeping the reader's attention after the lead.

What do we mean by digital technology?

Digital technology is distinct from **analogue technology**. Analogue (which means 'analogous to the original' or 'continuous') signals are transmitted as continuous waves, whereas digital information is transmitted as binary code that has to be converted by the receiving equipment. This code consists of bits (binary digits) of information, arranged in ones and zeros that represent two states: on and off. This arrangement of ones and zeros determines how that material will subsequently be decoded and put back together. Whereas analogue transmissions can be subject to interference (interruptions from competing signals) and degrade with excessive copying, digital information is received well or not at all (either on or off), and can be infinitely replicated without degradation. This has the positive result of enabling interactivity (see below), but its negative result is that it makes near-exact copying (piracy) very easy.

Digital technology: The transmission of electronic information using binary code to store and transmit data; replaces analogue technology.

Analogue technology: The transmission and storage of electronic information via continuous waves, especially in recordings and radio signals, and along telephone wires.

Digital technology is compressible. Therefore:

- its ability to compress information is dense: vast amounts of information can be digitalised and stored in a small space, such as, on a single CD, USB stick or network server
- it is manipulable: it can be reshaped constantly, from creation through to delivery and usage, which allows for interactivity and the audiences' ability to shape content
- it is impartial: it is indifferent to ideas of representation, ownership, creation or usage, and is accessible to most forms of hardware
- it is networkable: content can be distributed to numerous audiences at once.

Understanding digitalisation is important to understanding why new media are important. Because new media are digitised, they have radically changed the mediasphere. Digitalisation allows for:

- content to be distributed across multiple delivery platforms (see Chapter 17)
- content to be distributed at a much faster rate
- content to be made interactive
- consumers to be provided with the tools of media production, blurring the lines between media production and consumption.

The internet

A product of the Cold War and the USA's desire to keep pace with the Soviet Union (following its launch of the Sputnik satellite in 1957), the internet began life in 1969 as APRANET, a decentralised computer network designed by the American Department of Defense's Advanced Projects Research Agency (DAPRA), later to become APRA. APRANET provided a nuclear war contingency that would enable information to continue to exist and to be exchanged outside a central location if all central defence locations were destroyed.

The first email and mailing list

The first email program was developed in 1975. The first mailing list, the MsgGroup, followed shortly afterwards. On 12 April 1975, Kevin McKenzie emailed the group with the suggestion that symbols (emoticons) be used in emails to indicate emotion; for example, the emoticon :) would indicate a smile. It was the beginning of a new language for emails, one based very much on the principles of semiotics, signs and signifiers, that we have discussed in previous chapters, and similar to the texting conventions that have been taken up by mobile phone users. Each media form, it seems, develops its own vocabularies, often in their infancy.

The internet (or net) developed throughout the decades, thanks to the ongoing interest of military scientific research, that often relied on civilian scientists communicating between university campuses, and state funding. In the 1970s, a number of state-funded computer networks started appearing. They became compatible because of a 1985 decision by the National Science Foundation network (NFSNET) to make the Transmission Control Protocol/ Internet Protocol (TCP/IP) mandatory. Between 1981 and 1989, with this infrastructure in place and the ongoing collaboration of universities and private research bodies, the number of computers linked to the net rose from 300 to just over 90,000. Subsequent developments of USENET, which enabled students at Duke University to network computers over a telephone line, and the NFSNET, which linked five university computing centres, meant that when APRANET was decommissioned in 1995, TCP/IP became the infrastructure of the internet as we know it today, enabling global communication.

In 1989, the internet moved one step closer to the modern idea of the **World Wide Web**, the digital system that potentially links every computer in the world with every other computer, thanks to the development of a protocol based on **hypertext**, the embedding of links to one text inside another. This replicates the dialogic relationship (see Chapter 1) between texts that we call the mediasphere, and helps to develop those audience networks that have come to displace traditional broadcasting networks (as discussed in Chapter 10). Users no longer need to be culturally competent to recognise the intertexts, when a simple finger click will take one user straight to another.

World Wide Web: The digital system that potentially links every computer in the world with every other computer; first named as such in 1991.

Hypertext: The embedding of links to one internet text from another.

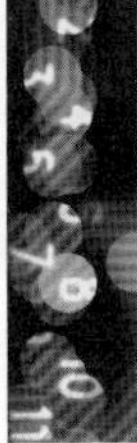

NEUROMANCER

William Gibson's novel *Neuromancer* (1984) gave us the term **cyberspace** to describe the way in which computer users can inhabit a new kind of mental space, within and between computers. Gibson refers to this space as a 'consensual hallucination'.

The final step was the development of a **web browser**, a mechanism by which every computer user can navigate the World Wide Web. This began with the development of Marc Andreessen's Mosaic browser in 1992.

The central feature of the World Wide Web in the 1990s was the lack of control by any one company of the whole, but the issue soon arose of whether it could it remain a public resource. During the 1990s, Microsoft emerged as the major supplier of software for all the world's computers, and made various attempts to take control of people's access to the Web. Since 2000, vast new companies, such as Google, Yahoo and Amazon, have begun to rival Microsoft's power. These companies, in turn, have been accused of attempting to take control of the world's electronic knowledge through their control of internet **portals**, the entry points to the Web from which users gain access to news websites, **search engines**, email pages and databases. Thus far, it has been difficult for even the most litigious of organisations—or even the most ambitious of lawmakers—to maintain any degree of control over what appears online.

Cyberspace: The virtual space entered by a computer user who is constantly online.

Web browser: The mechanism by which every computer user can navigate the Net.

Portals: Entry points to the World Wide Web, from which a user gains access to news websites, search engines, email pages and databases.

Search engine: A system for searching and analysing the content of all non-hidden websites, analysing the relationship between websites and ranking sites on the basis of links from other highly relevant sites; the most famous search engine is Google.

GOOGLE

The enormous growth of the World Wide Web posed a major problem: How could any individual user find the internet address of any other user who had some desired piece of information? This problem was solved by the invention of the **search engine**, of which the foremost example is Google.

Google works by searching and analysing the content of all non-hidden websites, analysing the relationship between websites and ranking sites on the basis of links from other highly relevant sites. Google has become the premier internet search engine and one of the largest online advertisers. Google is so well known that the name has become a verb (to google) for searching the net, and a metaphor for research more generally ('I'll just google it'). The name comes from a misspelling of 'googol', referring to the number 10 to the power of 100. Since 2000, Google has also sold advertisements associated with search keywords. More recent innovations have included Google News, Google Maps, Google Product Search (a price comparison site) and Google Scholar (indexing scholarly journals and articles)—its aim is to make the internet world a Google world.

The world goes online, followed by journalism

Worldwide use of the internet is growing so quickly that any listing of statistics is almost immediately out of date. That said, the largest region for internet use in sheer numbers is Asia, and it is estimated that by 2020 Chinese will be the most common internet language (which is reflected in the television science fiction series *Firefly*, in which the world's language is an amalgamation of English and Chinese). Europe and North America come in second and third in numbers of internet users, with a fast-growing internet population in Africa not far behind. **Broadband** access is also quickly outstripping **dial-up** access, particularly in the developed world. Broadband access is a significant advancement on dial-up access because it makes many new forms of online interactivity possible, such as uploading videos or taking part in **metaverses**. It brings more potential for connecting to a wider world, or, more accurately, to a larger range of small, specialised worlds, what some theorists have referred to as public sphericules (see Chapter 1).

Broadband: Currently, the most advanced form of internet access, offering high-speed access and wide bandwidth; transmitted via telephone, cable and wireless services, which has almost entirely replaced dial-up.

Dial-up: The earliest form of access to the internet, via slow signals sent through a telephone wire.

Metaverse: A fictional, virtual world.

The sheer numbers of people with online access has also been noticed by the existing media industries that want to go on existing. In September 2006, four major News Limited daily papers—the *Daily Telegraph* in Sydney, the *Herald Sun* in Melbourne, the *Courier-Mail* in Brisbane and the *Adelaide Advertiser*—announced that they were becoming twenty-four hour operations, with their newsrooms operating continuously to ensure regular online updates on stories (Australian Press Council 2006). This brought News Limited into line with the two major Fairfax outlets, the *Sydney Morning Herald* and the *Age*, which had gone to a nonstop newsroom about eighteen months earlier.

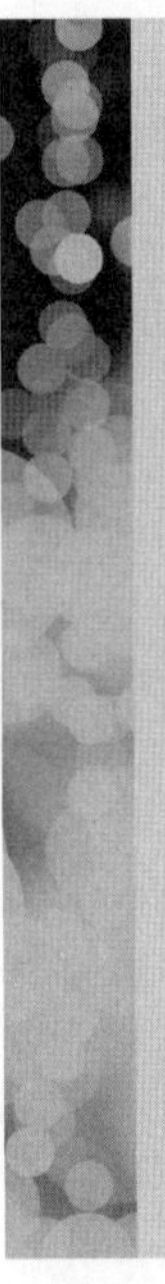

Blogs

As you saw in Chapter 3, 'blog' is the contraction of the word 'weblog', an online journal comprised of postings of personal observations, answers from respondents, and links to other websites.

While blogging is frequently held out as a completely new phenomenon, this is not the case. People have always kept journals and expressed opinions. Blogs are simply a new, far-reaching and very public way of doing it. They are also increasingly associated with the passage from old to new media being undertaken by many newspapers. Australia's most visited online newspaper site is that of the *Sydney Morning Herald*, which also hosts blogs. The country's only national mainstream daily, the *Australian*, has a burgeoning blogging enterprise, as do many other Australian newspapers that have decided to set up their own blogs.

The important thing to remember is that blogging and most other new media forms are new media developments of pre-existing media forms, industrial byproducts of the digitalisation of media.

The twenty-four hour news cycle

The twenty-four hour news cycle has become a daily reality for many journalists, particularly those in metropolitan newspapers or on mainstream electronic media. News on the Web is updated regularly, and constantly changes. It is increasingly accompanied by digital photographs, audio grabs or video footage, sometimes from citizen journalists and sometimes from journalists who are now expected to write a print story and produce electronic material for the website as well. Reporters trained in convergent journalism are growing in number, and are prized for their ability to move between print and electronic reporting formats with ease.

Similarly, television networks have been quick to ally themselves with online sites. In Australia, Channel Seven has formed a connection with Yahoo! to create Yahoo!7, Channel Nine has followed US network NBC's lead in connecting with Microsoft to form ninemsn. The ABC has an enormous online presence, which features iView, accessible archived episodes of some of their series, podcasts, vodcasts and transcripts from its television and radio programs. Increasingly, these sites are not only advertisements and portals to other television sites, but also produce their own exclusive content that provides clues and gossip about ongoing series, as well as behind-the-scenes information and catch-up episodes of certain programs. These alliances seem to be in anticipation of **Internet Protocol Television (IPTV)**, essentially, television content on demand, of which YouTube is the best known example.

Internet Protocol Television (IPTV): Television content on demand through the internet; YouTube is currently the best-known example.

YouTube

YouTube, founded by several former employees of ebusiness PayPal, is a video-sharing website where users can upload, distribute, create, share, comment on and view videos; most users are individuals but media corporations are increasingly posting their own content, too.

YouTube has evolved beyond its original aims to become a central part of the public sphere, an archive of pop culture moments and a shorthand way of becoming a celebrity. By 2006, when it was acquired by Google for $US1.65 billion, close to 100 million video clips were, according to a 16 July 2006 survey and the Nielsen/Net ratings, being viewed daily, 20 million viewers logged on per month and an additional 65,000 videos were being uploaded every 24 hours. By 2010, 24 hours of video were being uploaded per minute, the average person spent 15 minutes a day on YouTube and views per day had exceeded 2 billion, nearly double the prime-time audience of all three major US television broadcast networks combined. Importantly, 70 per cent of those viewers and users came from outside the USA (Website Monitoring).

The significance of YouTube was confirmed by *Time* magazine's cover featuring a silver foil monitor that proclaimed 'You' as the 2006 Person of the Year; the cover was specifically referring to user-created media on sites such as YouTube. The most important ability YouTube has is to throw an event, issue or person into the public eye within hours. See, for example, how YouTube was used as a platform for US citizens to quiz the Democrat nominees in the lead-up to the 2008 presidential election, and in 2010 streamed a live interview with President Obama. This ability to create and disseminate the hot topic of the day, or even multiple topics, marks YouTube as being a natural source of news. It functions as a free and democratic view into what is galvanising the public at any time. As well as using YouTube as an eye and ear on what the buzz topics are in their world, journalists can add to the narratives surrounding this buzz and bring these issues into the purview of mainstream culture, often creating YouTube celebrities along the way.

YouTube celebrities

As noted in Chapter 11, YouTube is becoming an increasingly important part of celebrity culture. YouTube celebrities who have attracted publicity through their videos include Smosh, lonelygirl14 (the New Zealand actress Jessica Rose) and the 'Star Wars kid' (a fourteen-year-old boy recorded acting out Darth Maul moves). The 'kid' has been viewed over 900 million times, and, while not originating on YouTube, currently resides there as the basis of a number of **mashups**. Some YouTube celebrities have used YouTube (some would say successfully, some not) as a way to become offline celebrities, among them Brooke Brodack (Brookers), Lisa Donovan (LisaNova), Chris Crocker (who tearfully defended Britney Spears after her 2007 MTV Music Awards performance) and, most famously, Justin Bieber.

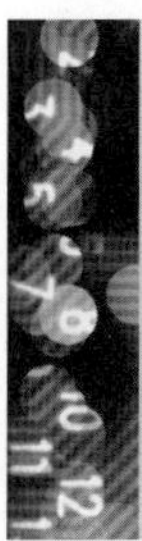

YouTube also assists celebrities in promoting themselves. The YouTube posting of OK Go's treadmill video for 'Here it Goes Again', Susan Boyle's first extraordinary performance on *Britain's Got Talent*, which exposed her to a global audience that may have never otherwise seen her on the program, and Sick Puppies, who garnered international attention when their music accompanied the YouTube video of the Free Hugs Campaign. All of these examples can still be sourced from YouTube.

The power of internet news

Internet news breaking and associated independent analysis has become a game changer in what was a fairly tame, safe media environment. The rise in the early 2000s of the Australian news and comment site, crikey.com.au, for example, caused a major stir in the Australian media. Such sites provide not only a free-flowing exchange of news but also of opinion.

Mashup: A website or application that combines content from more than one source into an integrated experience.

In 2002, crikey.com.au ran with the first news of the former Australian Democrat turned Labor member Cheryl Kernot's alleged affair with former Attorney-General Gareth Evans. An entire edition of the *Media Report* on ABC Radio National at that time was devoted to examining the Kernot matter, and a significant part of that dealt with the new style of journalism practised by Stephen Mayne, the creator of crikey.com.au, and others who have gone down this path. Another spectacular earlier example is Matt Drudge's *The Drudge Report*, which revealed the Monica Lewinsky story in the US in 1998, which in turn led to impeachment proceedings against President Bill Clinton over his alleged affair with the White House intern. Some have argued that this is a new form of journalism in action. Others see it as something less than real journalism. What do you think?

Stephen Mayne and crikey.com.au

Stephen Mayne, who sold crikey.com.au in 2005 for $1 million, told the ABC Radio National's *Media Report* that he published only about 20 per cent of the stories that he heard, but he stuck his neck out further than traditional media would have in the past. Mayne said that online journalism is significantly different from traditional journalism, in that incorrect information can be pulled immediately and corrected.

In the same program, Cheryl Kernot made the point that a feature of internet-based news breaking through blogs or other forms of Web news is that questionable material remains in circulation in an unbalanced form (in the form of unchallenged allegations) before balancing fact and comment is supplied. She says that journalism has fundamentally changed to allow this sort of thing to happen. Whereas once in the past, she said, journalists would not go public with any story without an attempt to research all sides, now it was possible to let an allegation run for a period of time before seeking that balance (O'Regan 2002).

In 2006, the Australian Press Council conducted a survey into how the new media had changed Australian media consumption habits in the ten years since Australian newspapers took to the internet. It found that 'through the twin benefits of having content on tap and established reputations, the traditional newspaper publishers dominate the online news field' (Australian Press Council 2006). It's clear some trends are emerging. A 2005 analysis of the online habits of *Sydney Morning Herald* readers showed that they have a distinct preference for stories containing either violence or celebrities (or possibly both). While stories on the big issues that year—the Asian tsunami, the London bombings, Hurricane Katrina, the death of Pope John Paul II and the hanging in Singapore of the convicted Australian drug mule Nguyen Tuong Van—were read widely, the most read story concerned a triple murder in the Indonesian province of Central Sulawesi, in which three schoolgirls were beheaded. According to the Australian Press Council report (2006: 2), the online report on this story was read 192,202 times. This is remarkable for a story that did not receive widespread regular press coverage.

Alternative models of newsgathering in the new media environment

As part of the larger shift towards audience networks, digitisation has enabled alternative community media to evolve, along with opportunities for audiences to pay to help journalists investigate and write about stories that mainstream media overlook. Under this model, if a news outlet buys the story, donations made to help get the story off the ground are reimbursed. For more information, see <www.spot.us/pages/about>. Other sites that follow this or a similar model include the following:

The Centre for Investigative Reporting: <www.centerforinvestigativereporting.org/about>.
The Centre for Public Integrity: <www.publicintegrity.org/about/>
ProPublica: <www.propublica.org/about/>

But are not-for-profit and indie journalism outlets as good for us as we think they are? See <www.slate.com/id/2231009/pagenum/all/#p2> for a discussion on the downside of nonprofit journalism.

Social networking site: A social structure composed of individuals and or organisations that become nodes connected to each other through multiple interdependencies such as friendships, common interests, sexual relationships, prestige and any other number of emotions and concerns.

Social networking sites

The internet also assists in community building through the creation of social media, **social networking sites**, such as Facebook, Twitter, MySpace, Friends Reunited, and Flickr. These are media designed specifically for social interaction, thanks to accessible and easily changeable layouts and designs. Here, individuals become 'nodes' in a network connected by friendships, common interests, sexual relationships, prestige and any other number of emotions and concerns.

All of these social networking sites are essentially evolutions of internet **chatrooms**, where users can communicate with each other via a series of short messages. Today, communication is enhanced by visuals, music or anything else the user chooses to put up on a page. They are miniature archives of how this person chooses to represent themselves in the public sphere. The economic value of such sites was first realised in 2005 when News Corporation acquired MySpace for $US576 million and British television company ITV acquired Friends Reunited (see Nightingale 2007a).

Chatroom: A site on a computer network where online conversations are held in real time by a number of users.

K RUDD AND MySpace

When he was Opposition Leader, Kevin Rudd used MySpace as a platform from which to develop his 'Kevin 07' campaign in the lead-up to the 2007 Australian federal election. The election of 24 November 2007 marked a turning point in how Australian political parties used the internet, taking the lead from politicians in the USA. Analysts agree that the social networking sites and the cool Kevin07 site—as described by pioneering Australian online media analyst Stephen Quinn (2007)—may have had a substantial role in delivering the youth vote to the ALP at that time.

Social media and journalism

Social media, or online sites and tools that encourage social networking (Lariscy et al. 2009) and the dissemination of information through social interaction, have also had an impact on the way news is collected and presented to the public.

As Lariscy and colleagues make clear (2009), journalists may regularly visit blogs, chatrooms, Facebook and MySpace for story ideas and information updates. Some even use these forums to check facts and check the veracity of rumours. Interestingly, the larger a publication, the more likely its journalists are to consult social media sites as a source of verification and information. Social media are also widely used by businesses as a type of media release, enabling companies and organisations to attempt to influence the issues that are reported on and given attention in the media, making them a prime news source for journalists (Lariscy et al. 2009).

But social media are not just for journalists wanting a story; they can also be used to get a story to the widest possible audience. Social media have the ability to disseminate a range and rate of information in sometimes startling ways. Bursts of gunfire from a US helicopter in Bagdad in 2007 killed a dozen people in the streets, including two Reuters journalists. Reuters spent three years attempting to find out the circumstances of the deaths, using Freedom of Information Acts and government pressure. On 6 April 2010, the WikiLeaks site released a video of the shooting. Within thirty-six hours, 2.5 million people had seen it (Greenwald 2010). This was the start of the whole WikiLeaks phenomenon we have mentioned throughout this book, and an important reminder of how such sites are altering ways in which we think about what journalism can be. All aspiring journalists should already be blogging and using Twitter.

Carolyn Beasley

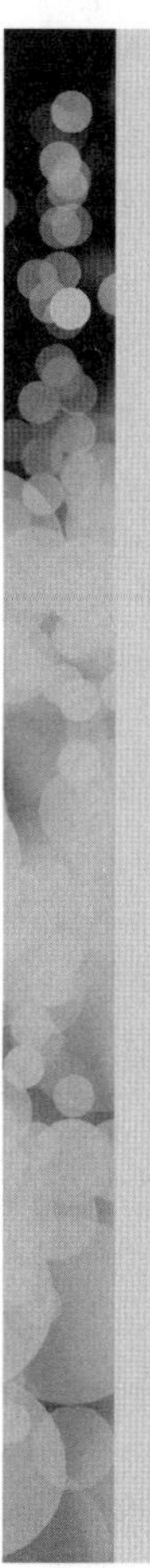

Social media in disaster management

On midnight of Wednesday, 2 February 2011, the biggest cyclone ever to hit Queensland, Severe Tropical Cyclone Yasi, crossed the coast. The destructive winds had started many hours before and would continue well into the next day. It was a terrifying time for people all along the north coast of the state. Satellite images showed a gigantic cyclonic system moving with awful inexorability towards several large population centres, including Townsville. On the morning of 2 February, the cyclone was upgraded to Category 5, the highest measure of cyclonic power.

For the first time, the Townsville City Council took the decision to include the social networking sites Facebook and Twitter in its disaster management communication plan. Regular updates in a calm and informative tone gave residents directly in the cyclone's path practical advice on what to do and a sense that they were not alone—far better than the more distant traditional news bulletins could do.

The council's Cyclone Yasi Facebook page recorded 6,063,152 page views, peaking in the days before the cyclone, and about 13,000 friends. Of these, 77 per cent were female and 12,643 were from Australia. Council staff did not moderate comments but found instead that the site became 'self-moderating'. However, they did use the platform to correct any misinformation. Twitter was not as popular as Facebook, but still proved useful. There were 329 tweets and around 900 followers.

As someone who lived through the fear of the approach of Yasi, I hung off every word posted on the council Facebook site and was grateful for the advent of new media in disaster management.

Liz Tynan

Twitter

Twitter is most often used as a tool to track the minute-by-minute activities of friends and celebrities. It lets you send tweets to a designated website. As of 2010 there were more than 106 million accounts on Twitter and the number of users is increasing by 300,000 every day (Website Monitoring). This ability to communicate short messages immediately and to an open audience means it has also become an unintentional tool of citizen journalism.

This shift from pure social networking to social alerts was made clear when people sending tweets were the first to tell the world about the terrorist attacks in Mumbai and the Hudson River plane crash in New York. Recognising Twitter's power as a device for immediate updates or serialisations, major news organisations now allow their journalists to report on summits and events via Twitter.

Of all the social media tools, Twitter is the most comfortable for print journalists to use as it allows them to communicate in the medium of the written word. With this in mind, we could argue that it is the print journalist who can best use Twitter as a reporting device (Ahmad 2010). This natural adoption is reflected in the irony that the *Guardian*'s journalists have gathered three times the number of followers on Twitter than the number of newspapers sold daily (Ahmad 2010).

Why is Twitter so useful for journalists?

Twitter's instantaneousness is one of its key allures. It provides instant updates on news and events straight to the mobile phones, email inboxes and websites of subscribers and readers. A journalist's message can reach its audience within seconds of being sent, and can be updated without limit. A second important aspect is that Twitter enables a journalist to build a highly personal and/or highly public, and certainly intensely interactive, relationship with their reader (Ahmad 2010). Once having received a tweet, the audience can tweet back directly to the journalist and the journalist can choose whether to have that response streamed to the newspaper's site or on the journalist's own blog.

This immediacy is also a boon for the print industry as it enables online editions to compete with radio and television news when it comes to presenting immediate and breaking news (Ahmad 2010).

Journalists can also use Twitter as a way of calling for information, sources and verifications. In a sense, it can be seen as a collaborative research tool. The *Guardian*'s legal correspondent, Afua Hirsh, is renowned for using Twitter in this way and will present ideas, theories and questions in an effort to get feedback and direction when building stories (Ahmad 2010). This represents the purest form of the dialogic relationship between media texts and texts and audiences that we first raised back in Chapter 1.

Twitter's use as a tool of citizen journalism became obvious with the 2008 Mumbai terrorist attacks, the communication of immediate and hitherto inaccessible on-the-street information during the 2009 Iranian election and the emergency landing of a passenger jet in New York's Hudson River in 2009. During the terrorist attacks in Mumbai, CNN reported that approximately eighty SMS messages per five seconds were being sent to Twitter (Ahmad 2010). The upside is that readers are exposed to what may be uncensored and unmediated eyewitness accounts of events as they unfold in real time. The downside is that without the skills of journalistic practice, citizen journalists may not be able to contextualise, analyse or distance themselves from what they are seeing occur around them. It is in the hands of the citizen journalist, then, that Twitter becomes a way of communicating what it's like to be immersed in the immediacy of an event. As Ahmad (2010) notes, it is this gap that demonstrates the need for the trained journalist. While anyone can relay what they are seeing, the journalist is uniquely positioned to offer informed commentary, analysis, synthesis and collation.

Twitter also serves the interest of the newspaper and its organisation by drawing people to the online site of the publication during times of crisis or emergency. Due to the immediacy of the tweets from the street level reporter or citizen journalist and the ability of these to be streamed to a central site, Twitter is the fastest way to collate, spread and share information about a disaster or any other event (Lenatti 2009).

Newspapers use Twitter as a marketing device by sending tweets to followers announcing the titles and links to articles that appeared in the printed and online editions of the paper that day. In these instances, Twitter is functioning as a supplement rather than challenge or substitute for the more traditional forms of journalism (Ahmad 2010).

There are, of course, some deeper theoretical issues that need to be explored when we think about how journalists might use Twitter. There's a high level of interest in citizen journalism reporting on elections and events in developing nations on the grounds that Twitter and other social media can offer an unmediated and uncensored eye into closed societies.

Critiquing this, we might want to think about whether these reports are indeed coming from the average uninvested observer on the street or whether only a certain type of citizen is able to participate in these types of electronic exchanges. To use Twitter and other social media, a person must have access to a mobile phone and internet connection, the technological skill to connect these two, and the financial means to be able to afford a network account. The type of citizen who can afford these is more likely to be middle class, of good means and have a degree of political and international awareness. Are these individuals likely to be the 'value-neutral progressive technology embraced by cosmopolitan youth ushering in democratic modernity to authoritarian' nations? (Ahmad 2010) We should also consider the degree to which the use of Twitter, and indeed, any new technology, functions as a device of corporate information capitalism and a lure for consumerism (Ahmad 2010).

MMPORGs

MMPORG: Massively multiplayer online role-playing games; a genre of gaming in which large numbers of players interact with each other in a virtual world.

Another form of social networking occurs in the massively multiplayer online role-playing games **(MMPORGs)**—such as *World of Warcraft*, described in more detail below—which also enable players to talk and interact in real time in completely fictional virtual environments. The *Second Life* site takes this even further. It has over nine million users, who design the way they look, choose their friends, set up businesses, buy and sell things, have sex and build houses, though not necessarily in that order. Increasingly, a number of real-world businesses have been setting up sites in *Second Life*; Australia's ABC, for example, now has a radio station based there.

Second Life's residents own all the intellectual property rights in the things they create, which has created a burgeoning second life economy inside the *Second Life* world itself, using the game's virtual currency, Linden dollars, and also on eBay for US dollars, using the Linden exchange rate. The *Economist* (2006: 99) estimated that for an average month, ten million *Second Life* objects are created, and 230,000 are bought and sold.

***Second Life*: Check out the *Second Life* website for yourself at <http://secondlife.com>.**

Virtual community: An online community where communication is achieved through technology rather than face-to-face interaction.

Virtual identity: A fictional identity invented by an online member of a virtual community.

Ultimately, all of this is happening in a virtual space, because the internet itself is virtual rather than tangible. The communities that gather there are therefore **virtual communities**, that is, their communication is achieved through technology rather than face-to-face interaction.

Perhaps more significantly—as the internet has all of the capabilities afforded by digitalisation, including manipulability—the identities of the individuals that make up these virtual communities are similarly manipulable. They are **virtual identities**. Unlike the relative fixity of identities offline, through gender, sexuality, age and race, though it is conceded that these can all be challenged in various and sometimes surgical ways, a virtual identity enables a computer user to completely transcend materiality. An overweight man of fifty can become a petite young girl with pigtails. An overworked accountant can become a muscular barbarian. Virtual identities enable us to live out a number of lives, where how we look and what we do is only limited by our imaginations.

The negative result is that virtual identities allow for the greater possibility of internet stalking, including people posing in chatrooms under different ages and genders. This includes paedophiles posing as children to talk online to other children. At the very least, the relative facelessness of virtual identities can result in practices that would not be undertaken in the real world, practices that the relative lack of online accountability seems to permit.

The extreme example of a virtual identity is the **avatar**, a digital character that is created online by the user. These can range from the female dwarves of *World of Warcraft* to the eCommerce tycoons of *Second Life*.

Avatar: An online construct that allows a member of a virtual community to transcend age, gender, race or geography, and make a fluid new identity.

In 1992, Neal Stephenson's novel *Snow Crash* was one of a number of novels that helped to popularise the idea of an avatar living in a virtual world.

eBay

eBay primarily exists as a trading centre for online shoppers. Launched in 1995, eBay started as a place to trade collectables and hard-to-find items. Today, eBay is a global marketplace where businesses and individuals can buy and sell practically anything.

eBay also serves as a kind of cultural barometer by which we can measure the changing tastes of consumers and the importance they attach to cultural artefacts. eBay can function as a type of research tool: as an archive of consumer tastes, as a way of exploring how desire for cultural products is generated (usually based around nostalgia) and as a way of circulating culture, continually reinvigorating cultural products by giving them currency.

eCommerce

Opportunities for online businesses (**eCommerce**) are based around two principles: disintermediation and reintermediation.

Traditionally, business transactions occur through a series of intermediaries. Products flow from manufacturers to wholesalers, then to distributors, then to retailers and on to consumers.

The internet facilitates **disintermediation**, the removal of wholesalers, distributors and retailers (the middle men) from the intermediary processes, so manufacturers can deliver products directly to consumers. An example of this is a manufacturer's website that offers products for sale directly to a consumer. This removal of intermediaries, and their attendant fees and costs, enables manufacturers to keep a greater cut of the profit, while enabling the consumer to receive the product at a significantly reduced price.

But, as we have seen from the eBay example, the internet also allows for the possibility of **reintermediation**, the reintroduction of an intermediary—an electronic intermediary. This is a new business (or businesses) designed

eCommerce: Business conducted online; internet-based, interactive, networked connections between producers, consumers and service providers.

Disintermediation: The removal of wholesalers, distributors and retailers (the middle men) from the intermediary processes, so manufacturers can deliver products directly to consumers.

Reintermediation: The reintroduction of a business intermediary; an electronic intermediary, a new business (or businesses) designed to link manufacturers to consumers.

to link manufacturers to consumers. eBay is a classic example of reintermediation, especially where artists or customisers are selling their items through the website. Amazon.com is another.

Reintermediation can also add value to products by offering extra material, in the form of extra content or promotional material, customised to the individual consumer.

How do websites make money?

As we have previously seen in our discussion of audiences (in Chapter 10), specifically in the context of television (see Chapter 7), broadcast media obtain their revenue from the sale of audiences to advertisers. Online media face a more complicated situation. Advertising revenue is not simply based on how often an advertisement is seen, or the number of times users click through to the advertiser's home page, or even the volume of sales or sales prospects, but also on the length of time users spend on one site. This is because internet users generate commercially useful information every time they visit a website, and this information can be valuable regardless of whether they look at the advertising displayed. Therefore, online advertisers are really interested in sites that prompt a great deal of internet traffic, just as broadcast advertisers are interested in programs that attract large audiences or a certain type of audience. However, this can also negatively impact on journalism; there are reported instances of editors rejecting stories because they don't appeal to online readers and therefore won't generate enough hits. For more information see: <www.siliconvalleywatcher.com/mt/archives/2010/05/mediawatch_mond_7.php>.

Pay per view for news

Both News Limited and the Fairfax stable of papers have outlined plans to charge for their online news sites. They're looking at a mixed model where general news content will remain free but more specific targeted information will be subject to a paywall or payment per viewing. Whether the paywall or pay per view approach is adopted, it amounts to the same thing: a reader has to pay to read an article.

This change has been fuelled by declining advertising revenues from their print editions. The shortfall has not been filled by online advertising revenue, which alone is not enough to finance newsrooms, despite Fairfax and News Limited's websites recording about 10 million users a month.

There is still great debate over whether pay per view or paywalls are the way forward for online news. Some suggestions that have been offered include the following:

- Paywalls work best with specific or niche articles and information, such as those offered by trade publications, insider news such as the politics beat, parliamentary updates, topic collections or celebrity stories. This is not a new conclusion as there are enewsletters that do well by subscription. The trick will be to persuade the general newspaper reader that there is a niche for them.

- The best way forward for the average newspaper is a mix of paid and free content. Perhaps an article could be read for free for a month, but then it becomes payable. This is a model used by some publications, but it's easily circumvented due to URL archiving services such as the Way Back Machine (<www.archive.org>). Alternatively, some articles could be offered for free, but follow-up pieces would have to be paid for.
- Papers should position themselves as authorities on a particular area, and then people would pay more in the belief that the content is unique. For example, the *Washington Post* alone gives you the real insider news on Washington and politics. The concept here is to sell the idea of Washington, not local stories about Washington.

Wikis

New media optimists point to a remarkable phenomenon that epitomises the democratic and unregulated nature of the internet: that of **wikis**. The first software to be called a wiki, WikiWikiWeb, was said to be named by a fellow called Ward Cunningham, who remembered a Honolulu International Airport counter employee telling him to take the so-called Wiki Wiki shuttle bus line between the airport's terminals. According to Cunningham (2006), 'I chose wiki-wiki as an alliterative substitute for "quick" and thereby avoided naming this stuff "quick-web" '. Wiki Wiki is a doubling up of 'wiki', a Hawaiian word for fast. The word is sometimes interpreted to be an acronym for 'What I know is', which describes its knowledge contribution, storage and exchange functions.

Wiki: A server program that allows users to collaborate in forming the content of a website. Users edit the content of other users.

Wikipedia: An online encyclopedia that is continually edited and added to by its users.

Wikis enable people using the internet to go into an online document and edit it or add new information. The best known example of this is **Wikipedia**, an online encyclopedia famously compiled by an army of online contributors, who regularly dispute and bicker over information. For all its potential for agendas and false information, it still does remarkably well to remain up to date and useful. This proves to many people's satisfaction that the self-regulatory nature of the internet does not allow egregious errors to stand for too long; someone will come along soon and fix it if the information is wrong.

There have been some well-publicised wiki-based disasters in the media. Among them, in 2005 the *Los Angeles Times* attempted to establish a wiki as part of its Iraq war editorial column, an inherently tricky topic for editing and additions. After an unedifying virtual battle over two days among highly polarised contributors, some of whom plastered the site with pornographic images, the paper withdrew the wiki and chalked it up to experience. As the ABC *Media Report*'s host Richard Aedy commented (2005) in relation to the *Los Angeles Times* debacle:

> I think the fundamental issue … is that wikis work best when people are trying to establish facts or truth, or something that can be objectively realised, whereas the editorial page is inherently opinion.

Some disturbing trends

A disturbing and sinister new aspect of the internet was all too apparent in the aftermath of the invasion of Iraq in 2003: its use to webcast the execution of hostages in Iraq, Saudi Arabia and Afghanistan. Both the immediacy and the nature of the content make this phenomenon unique: public executions that can be viewed by anyone with internet access. Many television news programs then showed at least the lead-ups to the beheadings, stopping short of the act itself. Even allowing for this restraint on the broadcast airwaves, surely this is a retrograde step, taking us back to the barbarity of public executions. Perhaps this is inevitable as the full range of possibilities of the internet—positive and negative—are mapped out. Similarly, acts of violence and animal abuse have been recorded on mobile phones and put up on YouTube. Extreme instances of bullying in schools were put up in Britain and Australia, prompting much debate in the media.

The gaming industry

Ironically, given the attention that we have lavished on print, radio, film, television and public relations, it is the gaming industry that, at the time of writing, is the single largest media industry in the world, making $55 billion to $60 billion internationally, $1 billion of which comes from Australia. Game budgets are equivalent to those for feature films (the latest *Grand Theft Auto* cost $60 million to develop) and their sales far outstrip them (*Halo 3* sold more than $170 million worth of copies in the first twenty-four hours of its release). Currently, there are an estimated 142 million regular games players worldwide, making games much more than child's play.

The gaming industry is also culturally significant in that computer games remain the first mass media form not to have been invented in the West. They are of Japanese and Korean origin, the product of companies such as Nintendo, Sega and Sony.

Even the name of the industry has evolved as the industry has evolved. It has progressively shed the adjectives 'video' games or 'computer' games as the industry has continued to move beyond outdated analogue technologies. Utilising a variety of software and consoles, and played across a variety of media, from televisions to computer screens, in a variety of environments, domestically and in arcades, the gaming industry is perhaps the best equipped of all media industries to forge links with the latest technological developments and take advantage of the opportunities offered by convergence. Some writers, such as Lalor (2007), refer to game systems such as PlayStation and Xbox as providing an 'intravenous connection' to old media such as the television. Rather than being seen as extensions of traditional media, they are now propping up older media as distribution systems for their graphics and ideas. Their function as a convergent industry is considered in more detail in Chapter 19.

The earliest video game is 1972's *Pong*, and from there the graphics continued to develop through games such as *Space Invaders* and *Centipede*. It became a domestic media form with the Atari 26000 game system in 1977, and reached critical mass with *Pac-Man* in 1980. From there the industry continued to produce a range of iconic characters capable of moving between media forms, such as television series, comic books, cartoons and films, from the barrel-throwing monkey Donkey Kong, through to the Italian plumbers Mario and Luigi and

Mario's evil counterpart Wario, to the blue hedgehog Sonic, the English archaeologist and adventurer Lara Croft, in the tiny, tiny shorts and the grim and gleaming Master Chief of *Halo* fame. Rather than simply adapting other properties into games, the gaming industry itself has become a content provider.

Current estimates place the overall figure of digital immigrants at 800 million (based on registered members of online computer games). In Australia, Jeffrey Brand's study, *Interactive Australia 2007*, found that 79 per cent of Australia households have some form of computer game device. Furthermore, the average age of the Australian gamer is twenty-eight (up from twenty-four, two years before); in Europe and the USA it is thirty (Brand 2007). Gaming is certainly no longer just an adolescent pursuit.

A content industry

Properties such as *Resident Evil*, *Silent Hill*, *Doom* and *Super Mario Brothers* have all been adapted into films, with varying degrees of success. *Resident Evil* and *Halo* have also featured in toy lines, comic books and novels (see Chapter 19 for more on this).

WORLD OF WARCRAFT

Over eight million people are registered inhabitants of the fantastical world of Azeroth. It is Blizzard Entertainment's fourth *Warcraft* game, and took over five years to develop. *WoW*, as it is popularly abbreviated, involves controlling an avatar within the continuing Tolkienesque game world, interacting with other players (and non-player characters), exploring the landscape and fighting monsters. Players belong to one of two factions, the Alliance or the Horde, and the game continues to expand with the opening of new territories and eras, such as the dark home world of the Orcs, Draenor, in the *Burning Crusade* expansion.

Aside from the communal aspects of adventuring in Azeroth, *WoW* also supports a vibrant online community, offering prizes, forums and the opportunity to submit and display fan artwork and comic-strip storytelling. But the game has also received its fair share of criticism—over 40 per cent of *WoW* players are said to be addicted to the game to the point that they are neglecting other parts of their lives in favour of adventuring in Azeroth.

A few types of games

Just to give an indication that gaming is a lot more complex and multifaceted than most critics realise, here is an overview:

- First-player shooter games, including *Doom*, *Quake* and *Half-Life 2*, offer worlds where the game world is rendered from the point of view of the player character.

Currently, the most famous of these is the *Halo* series, which focuses on the combat between the human super-soldier Master Chief and a collection of alien races known as the Covenant. The *Halo* trilogy of games has been spun off into books, comics and action figures.

- Role-playing games, the *Final Fantasy* series, for example, is modelled on the dice-and-pencil role-playing game *Dungeons & Dragons* and its ilk, where adventurers face a number of perils while building up experience points.
- Platform games, for example, *Super Mario Brothers* and the *Mega Man* series, are the earliest form of gaming, characterised by game play that involves moving between platforms. They are largely the province of handheld consoles now.
- Simulation games, as the name implies, are simulations of such situations as flight and tank warfare. A subgenre is God games, in which players completely control, build and develop a world, whether that world involves a suburban family or an entire civilisation. The most famous of these is *The Sims*, which is essentially the world as a digital dollhouse created by Will Wright after his home burnt down and all his family possessions were lost. Others include *Spore,* from Sims creator Wright, which starts with a single-cell organism that evolves into other forms, and *Okami*, which uses the notion of a Celestial Brush so gamers can paint their own realities.
- Massively multiplayer online games, as described above.

The importance of gaming

While academics have been slow to analyse gaming, seeing it as a largely adolescent and trivial pursuit, some theorists, such as Terry Flew (2002), note that gaming does raise interesting questions about media and culture. Among these, Flew includes 'debates about the cultural appropriateness of digital content, gender identities, the experience of childhood, and intellectual property regimes' (Flew 2002: 108).

Gaming and the appropriateness of digital content

Gaming can often be seen as contributing to an overly imperialist pro-American hegemony, through its use of stereotyping villains. *America's Army*, for example, was a product of US Army investment in computer games to create a recruitment tool for the military.

Gaming technology also permits sites of resistance. *Under Siege*, for example, is similarly a military-type game, but from the perspective of the Syrian designers. It was produced as a direct response to games such as *America's Army* by designers upset by the portrayal of Arabs as the enemy in other military games.

Gaming and gender and gender roles

Traditionally, gaming is viewed as a male pursuit, but the Entertainment Ratings Software Board found that almost 40 per cent of gamers were women (ESA 2009). Perhaps this should not be so surprising. Female characters appear in *Tomb Raider* (Lara Croft) and *Metroid*, and as early as *Ms Pac-Man*, the gaming industry was providing strong female characters (Ms Pac-Man being one of the first popular cultural characters to take the 'Ms' title and thus be claimed as a feminist icon). Opportunity gaming and digital avatars allow for subverting gender, thus appealing to female players.

Is there a difference between male and female players? Studies have found that, on average, female gamers prefer problem-solving games, while male gamers prefer first-person shooters.

Gaming and social contact

Gaming provides a high degree of social contact, often more than other media forms. Multiplayer games challenge the idea of gaming being a solitary pursuit, and this social dimension also extends to the offline contexts in which people play games—not just in the domestic space of the home but in internet cafes and at local area network parties (LAN). In South Korea, for example, hundreds of thousands of people gather to watch teams of gamers competing on large screens, and in late 2007 Australian theatre chain Hoyts exhibited game playing along with cinema releases.

Gaming also requires a high level of interactivity from players on many levels. Understanding the game controls and objectives often requires a high degree of flexibility and literacy; some game guides run to over 50,000 words. They are, in a sense, unfinished texts that interpellate the player into the space left in the game, making the gamer the final part of the game text.

This space permits the games consumer to become a **prosumer**—the convergence of a producer and consumer—by actually adding to the content of the game.

The final level of interactivity is that derived through open source models of game design, which allow for development and engineering. This is sometimes also referred to as **modding**. Modding comes in two forms. One is partial mods, which add a minimal amount of new content to the underlying structure of a game, Id Software, for example, the producers of first person shooter *Doom*, released the source code allowing for partial mods of the game. The other is total conversions, which create an entirely new game, such as *Counter-strike*, a total conversion of *Half Life*.

Prosumer: Where the consumer becomes a producer in their own right, actually contributing to the content of the media form in some way. An example would be a computer user whose activities, such as influencing the rules of the computer games, amounts to production.

Modding: A contraction of 'game modification'; the addition of new content to games.

Modding also raises questions about intellectual property rights. Can modders legally make money onselling their mods? What does the law say about producers of mashups using copyrighted texts to produce something new on YouTube? Who ultimately owns the land that people are building on in *Second Life*? For the moment, these questions remain unanswered, though it has already been suggested that this is fertile ground for future litigation by industries wanting to protect their intellectual property.

The digital environment of new media encourages production and use, rather than mere consumption. As Henry Jenkins notes, the new generation of prosumers is one that is disinclined to pay for content they can access for free; equally, they are armed with, and prepared to use, the tools that enable them to repurpose copyrighted material (Jenkins 2006a). We return to some of these ideas in Chapter 19.

Gaming as journalism?

The line between journalism and game development may also be being blurred in the future. One US newspaper is already exploring the use of a games engine to present news, potentially offering a completely immersive news environment in which audiences can engage with events directly rather than just watch them.

Computer-assisted reporting (CAR)

Computer-assisted reporting (CAR): Internet research by journalists, involving deep analysis of databases using spreadsheets and database managers.

Electronic interconnectivity has many benefits, which the media have been quick to exploit. One major benefit has been the rise of a new way of sourcing information by using vast reserves of online data that otherwise would remain just strings of zeros and ones stored somewhere that no one would look. **Computer-assisted reporting (CAR)** operates on three main levels: basic, intermediate and deep (or investigative). Just about every reporter in Australia will use basic CAR in some form, even if it is just sending emails or looking at a website. That is a given in the job these days. It is at the investigative end that it is most interesting, and requires the most specialised training. One US CAR guru, Brant Houston (2004), lists some examples of CAR-derived stories:

- Swedish reporter Stefan Lisinski exposed questionable practices involving bankrupt companies by using a massive Swedish database of information on the companies and directors.
- Dutch journalist Marjan Agerbeek probed government data with spreadsheet software and was able to document poor financial planning by the country's thirteen universities.
- A Brazilian journalist dug into Brazilian government statistical reports to show that in Sao Paulo the first cause of death among children between 10 and 14 years old was homicide, and that often the killer was a parent.

It is probably true to say that without the techniques of CAR, these stories and many others would not have been exposed. CAR is not just internet searching; it also involves deep analysis using spreadsheets and database managers. Journalists commonly use Microsoft Excel or Lotus 1-2-3 and the database managers Microsoft Access or Paradox. New software that is designed to probe datasets is emerging all the time. Most journalists do not start out as computer experts, but many have become so because this form of journalism is turning up some great stories.

The world's leading centre for CAR practice and research is the National Institute for Computer-Assisted Reporting (NICAR) in the USA. NICAR is run by a group called Investigative Reporters and Editors, Inc., which is based on the Missouri School of Journalism, a nonprofit US organisation dedicated to improving the quality of investigative reporting in that country. Founded in 1989, NICAR has trained thousands of journalists in the practical skills of finding and analysing electronic information.

According to an article by Melisma Cox (2000), CAR predates widespread use of the internet by a generation. She says that University of North Carolina's Professor Philip Meyer was one of the innovators of computer-assisted reporting, with his coverage of the Detroit riots in 1967:

> He conducted a survey among African-Americans during the Detroit riots and along with John Robinson and Nathan Kaplan at the University of Michigan employed an IBM 360 mainframe to analyze survey data. The analysis revealed that, contrary to the assumed hypothesis, people who had attended college were equally likely to participate in riots as were high school dropouts. The story won him a Pulitzer Prize and signaled the beginning of a new era in computer-assisted reporting.

Back in 1967, computers were ridiculously cumbersome things, nothing like the compact and far more powerful desktop or laptop machines we know today. It took some years for computers to find their way into the routine of journalism. The rate of CAR has increased markedly since the internet provided freer access to all kinds of databases. Using CAR is a sign that journalism continues its rightful place as a watchdog and a keeper of records.

Old media versus new media

As we have mentioned throughout this book, this new media environment has greatly undermined the old order of media operation. The old media moguls have had to adapt—sometimes painfully. They have been very successful for over 150 years, the argument goes, and now they are feeling the impact of forces outside their control. Media moguls associated with mainstream media are either getting in or getting out:

- The Packer family, since the death of its patriarch Kerry Packer in December 2005, has been divesting itself of old media such as the Nine Television network, apparently heeding advice that old free-to-air television stations are on their way to becoming dinosaurs. Even James Packer's investment in television station Ten seems more about exploiting its online potential.
- That other well-known (former) Australian mogul, Rupert Murdoch, is making up ground initially lost, and has become a convert to the idea of the digital native, a consumer more at home in an online environment than with a newspaper or television show. Murdoch owned up, on behalf of all old media barons, to being 'remarkably, unaccountably complacent' (Kluth 2006). He said that young readers 'don't want to rely on a god-like figure from above to tell them what is important. And to carry the religion analogy a bit further, they certainly don't want news presented as gospel.'

The dynamics of the media industry have been altered beyond recognition. When the world's biggest media company is now said to be Google (Kluth 2007), which does not produce anything that even resembles media content, we can safely say that the media industry has become a very different beast.

The shift, then, seems to be away from the traditional divide between content and distribution, and towards interactivity and convergence. This is a measurable change between new media and traditional media due to the level of interactivity afforded consumers, eroding the old distinctions between producers and audiences as new media allow consumers to participate directly in the evolution of the narrative, to choose between a variety of events and control their sequence.

Increasingly, new media designers are creating a space in which gamers make their own stories. New media are left incomplete on purpose, leaving gaps in which users can create (as in *Civilization IV*, where gamers create cities, countries and civilisations, their actions deciding the path of the game and the fate of their world) as well as modify and develop. This is an even more evolved form of interpellation, where producer and user enter into a co-creative partnership.

This, together with digitalisation, is another defining characteristic of new media—that it remains unfinished. It requires the user to become part of the text in order to complete it.

Conclusion

Paul Saffo (Kluth 2006), from the Institute For the Future, said that 'revolutions tend to suck for ordinary people'. There are pitfalls for many people in the switch from old to new media, not least because we don't know where we are headed. What does it all mean for broad human social interaction? Are we are headed into narrower and narrower virtual enclaves, interacting with disembodied avatars and receiving information that only confirms our own narrow views of the world instead of expanding our knowledge and our horizons? The days of broadcast appear have already ended, replaced by increasingly smaller narrowcasts. The public sphere is breaking into smaller and smaller public sphericules (see Figure 19.1).

Saffo wrote: 'Each of us can create our own personal-media walled garden that surrounds us with comforting, confirming information and utterly shuts out anything that conflicts with our world view.' This is social dynamite, which could lead, he says, to 'the erosion of intellectual commons holding society together … We risk huddling into tribes defined by shared prejudices' (Kluth 2006).

The injury being inflicted on our languages is of enormous importance to the continuity of ideas, and the preservation and cultivation of intellectual activity. It is hard to convey profundity—or at least profundity as we now know it—using SMS-speak. To be optimistic, new techno-based languages could emerge that will help us convey ideas that were not possible in previous eras. The evolution of languages is not necessarily to be feared, although we must all do what we can to ensure that as languages change we don't lose our capacity for the thought associated with them. George Orwell's novel Nineteen Eighty-Four was not only a brilliant evocation of a political dystopia but also a warning about what could happen if we don't value our languages and the complex meanings they represent. His 'Newspeak' was a language devoid of humanity and complexity in meaning. We should all be aware of the risk of allowing the language we use to interact in the new media to go down the same path.

A more optimistic view is that opening up a marketplace of ideas, something the internet does so well, can only be good and positive, and that allowing for previously impossible connections between geographically diverse areas must aid mutual understanding. Some of these ideas are explored in more detail in Chapters 19 and 20.

No one can say with any certainty what the future of media will actually be. All that is certain is that the pace of change will continue, so for the person starting out in the communication industries, the big issue is how to ride the wave and adapt to make the most of this new media environment.

KEY REFERENCES

Aedy, R. (2005). 'Wikis, Journalism and Watching the PR Industry', *Media Report*, ABC Radio National, 29 September.

Cox, M. (2000). 'The Development of Computer Assisted Reporting'. 17–18 March. <http://com.miami.edu/car/cox00.htm>. Accessed 11 June 2007.

Flew, T. (2002). *New Media: An Introduction.* Melbourne: Oxford University Press.

Houston, B. (2004). *Computer-Assisted Reporting: A Practical Guide* (3rd edn). New York: St Martin's Press.

Kluth, A. (2006). 'Among the Audience'. *Economist.* 20 April.

WEBSITES

TWITTER

<http://reportr.net/2008/12/04/bbc-considers-how-twitter-and-the-mumbai-attacks-affected-its-journalism/>

<http://blogs.telegraph.co.uk/kate_day/blog/2009/04/01/is_the_g20_summit_a_turning_point_for_twitter>

<http://tunedin.blogs.time.com/2009/06/15/iranians-protest-election-tweeps-protest-cnn/

<www.time.com/time/world/article/0,8599,1905125,00.html>

PAY-PER-VIEW NEWS

<www.cjr.org/feature/open_for_business.php?page=all>

CHAPTER 19

CONVERGENCE

JASON BAINBRIDGE

Introduction

In the previous chapters we have considered a number of media industries, including print, radio, film and television, as discrete entities. As you read through the chapters you may have noticed that they are often quite interdependent, that is, many of the industries overlap, and almost seem to come together at certain points. This is becoming even more prevalent in the new media environment we outlined in the previous chapter. Convergence is one of the ways we can describe this coming together of media industries.

In this chapter we look at:

- what convergence is
- forms of convergence
- the impacts of convergence.

What is convergence?

Convergence: The coming together of what were once separate media texts and industries.

Convergence is the coming together of what were once separate media texts and industries. As Jenkins (2006a: 282) notes, convergence is both 'an ongoing process' and a 'series of interactions between media systems, not a fixed relationship'. Convergence is a historical process that is now accelerating, thanks to the new media environment and the possibilities afforded by digital and social media (see the previous chapter).

We can understand media industries operating quite similarly to the media texts that they produce, as they often rely upon each other to produce meaning. We can therefore think of media industries, such as media texts, working together (becoming convergent) in a number of ways:

- As we saw in Chapters 9 and 10, media industries can work hegemonically to produce certain ways of looking at the world (discourses) and thus reinforce a certain ideology. We could think here of Fox News (television) and News Limited (print) working together hegemonically to produce a certain discourse of US foreign policy, for example, that intervention in Iraq was the correct foreign policy, that the USA is justified in intervening in other areas of the world, reinforcing the ideology that US foreign policy is correct and should be exported to other countries.

- Media industries can also work pluralistically, offering different discourses. For an easy example of this, think about the differences between radio and television coverage of a cricket match. In radio coverage listeners are guided by the voice of the commentator, but much is left to the imagination of the individual listener. On television, exceptional catches or points scored can be fetishised by being replayed over and over again from different angles. Radio, then, foregrounds the sounds of the game and the skills of the entire team, while television foregrounds—often through the use of sophisticated technology—the individual players and the environment in which the game is played.
- Media industries can also work intertextually; for example, a number of television series have been turned into films, radio series have become television series and comic books have become films. As we have previously seen, an increasing number of new media texts are often the product of media companies raiding their own back catalogues of media product to develop media texts that may work in other formats. *Tron, Star Trek* and *Green Lantern* are examples of this.
- As we saw in Chapter 11, we can think of some media industries, such as the music and celebrity industries (both as industries in their own right and through their attendant industries of publicists, PR, agents and spin doctors), as already being convergent media industries.
- Convergence has an impact on the ways in which media industries participate in the mediasphere.

Carriage: Those industries responsible for distributing media content.

Content providers: Media industries that actually produce content, which is then distributed by the carriers.

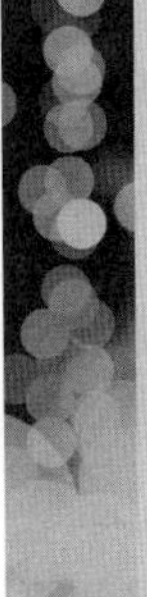

Blurring the distinction

Convergence fundamentally affects not only the structure of media industries but also the ways in which they participate in the mediasphere, because it blurs the distinctions between production and distribution, between content and **carriage**.

Through convergence, a number of industries that were previously involved only in carriage, such as the Australian telecommunications company Telstra, have now moved into the production of content. Similarly, **content providers**, such as film studios, have moved into carriage by, for example, buying cinema chains that show their films. Increasingly, any industry that wants to be part of the global connectivity that is the internet must invest in network carriage systems.

Reasons for convergence

Convergence seems to be primarily motivated by two concerns: economics and power.

- Convergence is often economically motivated, to maximise profits by managing media industries to work together on a common project. The *Idol, X Factor* and *America/Britain/ Australia's Got Talent* programs, for example, are the products of convergence between (at least) three media industries: television, where the series is aired, telecommunications,

where voting is conducted, and music, where the end product will be distributed. Programs such as these provide economic benefits for the television, telecommunications and music industries by increasing exposure across the three platforms, thereby maximising the profits that could have been made if it had been broadcast across only one platform.
- Convergence can also be ideologically motivated, to hegemonically promote a certain discourse (see Chapter 1): the media moguls who own multiple media industries can preserve their power base by reinforcing their views on a certain issue consistently across multiple platforms.

There is a tension at the heart of convergence between those who have traditionally controlled the tools of production and those who are increasingly being provided those tools to participate and engage more directly with media industries. We will explore this tension in more detail below.

Types of convergence

Convergence describes a series of changes that take four forms:

- cultural convergence
- industrial convergence
- technological convergence
- narrative convergence.

Before we look at each of these in detail, it's worth briefly examining the relationships between convergence, different media industries and the audience.

The above forms of convergence are not exclusive Industrial convergence, for example, usually depends upon technological convergence to produce narrative convergence, which can then lead to a wider cultural convergence, depending on the extent of ownership. They frequently overlap to such a degree that we could almost call them a convergence of convergences.

Convergence also involves a number of other media industries that, for reasons of space, we cannot explore in greater detail in this book, such as the merchandising and telecommunications industries. We'll refer to them briefly in this chapter to illustrate certain points around how convergence works.

The relationship between convergence and the audience takes three main forms:

- cultural convergence can produce mass audiences by broadcasting media products across the globe.
- technological convergence can also produce niche audiences by narrowcasting to a few thousand people.
- to function well, convergence often depends upon another increasingly important type of audience, the fan audience.

Fans are people who follow a particular media form, genre or personality with great enthusiasm, for the pleasure of doing so rather than a desire to earn an income. Developing a fan base or fan following for certain media texts is becoming increasingly desirable as audiences fragment, and even more desirable for convergent industries, as fans will often lead investment in media texts and pursue media texts across multiple delivery platforms.

Fans are therefore economically important to media industries, for their loyalty to various media properties and for their investment in said properties. More importantly, it is fans who increasingly generate the move towards convergence, either through their investment in media properties or by more actively pressing for convergent opportunities themselves.

We can think of this as **fan culture**, which is increasingly converging with mainstream or industrial media culture, to the point that the two are becoming more and more indistinguishable.

Fan culture: Term derived from *fanatic*; those people who follow a particular media form, genre or personality with great enthusiasm, for the pleasure of doing so rather than a desire to earn an income.

While fans have been the subject of ridicule and derision in the past, for such behaviour as wearing anoraks and singing Klingon death chants at funerals, it is worth acknowledging the increasing importance of fan audiences in contemporary media culture.

Convergence can, then be thought of as a double-edged sword, at once reinforcing the economic power of those controlling media industries and giving economic power back to the consumers, especially the fans. This is the tension at the heart of convergence.

Tron

A number of these ideas are demonstrated in Disney's Tron franchise. *Tron*, released in 1982, took the audience inside the Grid, a virtual reality and forerunner of the internet literally made up of humanoid programs in blue light suits and, in the central struggle between the Master Control Program (MCP) and the individual user Flynn (Jeff Bridges) and 'program' Tron (Bruce Boxleitner), offered a metaphor for the struggle between private ownership and private access that was to become an important issue for cyberspace in the subsequent decades. A critical and commercial failure on release, *Tron* nevertheless developed a strong fan following over the succeeding decades as an innovator in special effects (it features some of the earliest digital animation and was thereby excluded from Oscar contention that year for cheating) and cyberpunk sensibility (as embodied by the anti-establishment Flynn), so much so that Disney revived the franchise with a successful 3D sequel in 2011, *Tron Legacy*. Extradiegetically, the existence of the *Tron* franchise is a confirmation of fan power, while diegetically it speaks to the ongoing problematic tension between fans and producers—between freedom and control.

Figure 19.1 Cultural convergence

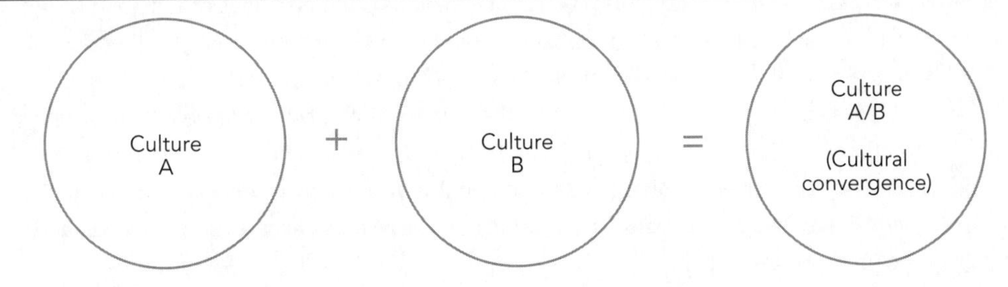

Cultural convergence

Cultural convergence: The intersection of cultures: locally, nationally and globally.

Cultural convergence refers to the ways in which different cultures are coming together through media. This is not a homogenisation of culture, as is sometimes suggested—that is, the argument that US culture is becoming the sole media cultural form in the world—but rather the tendency of cultural convergence to mix cultures rather than dilute them and, more importantly, the way one culture can inform another.

Cultural convergence is increasingly being enabled by technology because technological advances have produced a world where global technology is erasing issues of geographical distance. As we saw in the previous chapter, the compression of time and space is one of the facilities offered by social media, which we can see manifested in social networking websites such as Facebook and Voice over Internet Protocol (VoIP), which converts voices into digital signals that can travel over the internet via a broadband connection.

During the 1800s, technologies such as the telegraph, the railway and the steamship did much to bring the world together and compress time and space. In that era, **globalisation** was pursued aggressively through imperialism and colonialism, as evidenced by the British empire, which sought to unify the world according to one common global set of standards—its own.

Globalisation: The tendency toward increasing standardisation of life, markets and economies around the world.

We can think of cultural convergence as being a positive or a negative aspect of the modern multimediated world.

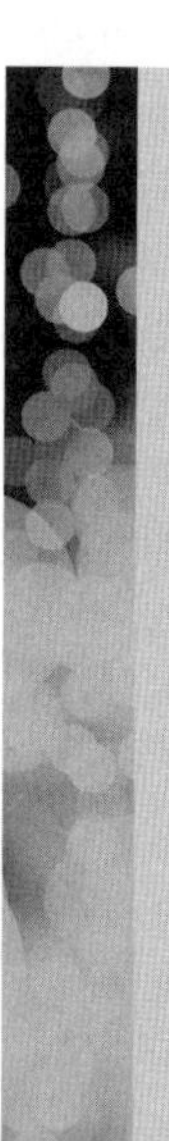

Why cultural convergence and not globalisation?

Since cultural convergence shares a great deal in common with globalisation, why not just use that term? Globalisation refers to the increasing standardisation of life, markets and economies around the world. It can be used negatively to refer to a process of homogenisation, where everything is becoming the same, or it can be used positively to refer to the ways some cultures can influence others. Essentially, it refers to a change in perspective, from thinking about individual nation-states to thinking globally in terms of global poverty, global markets and global issues, such as environmental degradation.

Cultural convergence refers to the coming together of cultures, not just world cultures, such as, say, Indian, American, Japanese and Russian, but also subcultures, such as goth, queer and punk, and cultures based around questions of taste and class, such as high culture, low culture, pub culture or working-class culture. It is therefore a more general and inclusive term than globalisation, and is more closely allied to media.

Examples of cultural convergence, then, would not only include *Ugly Betty* (Latino culture) and *Iron Chef* (Japanese culture), but also *Queer as Folk* and *Queer Eye for the Straight Guy* (queer culture), *Roseanne* and *The Royle Family* (working-class culture), and *Frasier* and *My Name is Earl*, which can be viewed as deconstructions of high and low culture, respectively.

The cultural imperialism hypothesis

The cultural imperialism hypothesis of globalisation and cultural convergence maintains that the current move towards global thinking reinforces a form of media imperialism, in which the dominance of a few multinational media conglomerates causes not only a narrowing of opinion but also an increasing homogenisation of media product and opinion.

The cultural imperialism hypothesis states that there is a unidirectional flow of media and culture, by which everything in the world is becoming the same (homogeneous). It is also referred to as 'Americanisation', as the USA is the world's largest producer of popular culture, or, more specifically, 'Disneyisation', 'McDonaldisation' or 'Coca-Colonisation' (with reference to popular global brands). This negative view of US brands is hardly surprising when you consider that fifty-seven of the world's 100 most valuable brands are owned by US companies <www.interbrand.com>; for more on this view, see Dorfman and Mattleart (1991).

Anime and manga: Styles of Japanese animation and comic books, covering a wide variety of genres, and often appealing equally to adults and children; *manga* often provides the basis for *anime* productions.

Anime and *manga*

Anime and ***manga*** are, respectively, animation and comic books from Japan, directed at adults rather than children. Increasingly, both forms have become a global form of media, not only original *anime* and *manga*, such as the films of Studio Ghibli and television series such as *Pokemon, Naruto* and *Yu-Gi-Oh*, which are doing well in the global market, but also the *anime/manga* look (and occasionally the sensibility), which is becoming the standard for Western animation. Look at animated series such as Nickelodeon's *Avatar* or *Super Robot Monkey Team Hyperforce Go*. Other forms of Western media are being revised and remodelled with an *anime/manga* look, such as Nancy Drew and Alex Rider. Here, then, is cultural convergence in action, where the coming together of Japanese and Western cultures creates new media properties.

In the same way, global reality television franchises—emerging from such countries as Germany and New Zealand—influence and shape global media cultures. For an example of a truly convergent text, look again at Nickelodeon's cartoon *Avatar*. It features a largely Chinese-derived storyline (both the avatar Aang's journey and relationship with the Fire Nation parallels that of the Dalai Lama) and is produced in the USA with a Japanese *anime* style and sensibility.

Hybridity, domestication and indigenisation

Other theories about globalisation prefer to concentrate on the differentiation and diversification that can occur through cultural convergence. These are collectively referred to as forms of **glocalisation**, whereby global texts are transformed to become relevant to local cultures. They are hybridity, domestication of texts and indigenisation.

Glocalisation: The transformation of global texts so that they become relevant to local cultures.

Hybridity: The mixture of media cultures to create a multi-origined media.

Diaspora: The scattering of a population from one geographical area throughout the world.

Domestication of texts: The adaptation by individuals and local media cultures of global texts.

Indigenisation: The appropriation and reframing of globalised texts to make them relevant to local cultures.

- **Hybridity** is the mixing of cultures to create something new, a multi-origined approach to media (see Chapter 20). Hybridity is often the result of the creation of a **diaspora**, the scattering of populations, voluntary or otherwise, throughout the world from a single geographic area. The reasons for travel can be diverse, ranging from the slave trade (the movement of African-American communities from the 1600s to the 1900s) through to famine, the desire for better education and travel, but the end result is the creation of dispersed and hybrid communities, such as African, Greek, Irish, Jewish and Italian communities, that bring elements of their own cultures to other cultures.
- **Domestication of texts** is the way in which global texts are adapted for use by local individuals and communities. Just as animals, such as dogs and horses, and plants were domesticated for use by ancient communities, so too are media texts. Television franchises, for example, such as *Dancing with the Stars* or *Idol*, are domesticated for local audiences with some adjustments in format, a local host and local celebrities. Domestication can also negatively impact on a text, as when local areas impose censorship on scenes that offend particular cultural, religious or racial sensitivities.
- **Indigenisation** is similar to domestication in its reference to the ways in which global texts are adapted for use by local individuals and communities. But indigenisation more often refers to the process by which this occurs: how global texts are appropriated and remodelled, reframed or reinscribed, to be made relevant to local cultures. An interesting by-product of this appropriation and reinscription is that the end product can then be re-exported to other markets. Some Japanese *anime* in the 1970s and 1980s, for example, were appropriated and reinscribed in the USA as *Robotech*, then re-exported to English-speaking countries around the world. The classic US sitcom *All in the Family* is a US adaptation of the British sitcom *Till Death Do Us Part*, with both being exported to Australia.

Multiculturalism: The conferring of equal rights on the many distinct cultural groups that make up a society.

Interculturalism: The interaction, sharing and exchange between cultures, wherein each culture benefits from exposure to the other.

What is common across these three forms of glocalisation is a shared focus on the positive aspects of cultural convergence: the new and very different media texts that can be produced through this sharing of cultures.

What about multiculturalism?

Multiculturalism is an ideology that advances the idea that society should consist of a number of distinct cultural groups that are afforded equal status. It is ideologically opposed to the notion of monoculturalism.

Whereas multiculturalism is based around the idea of cultures being distinct and separate, cultural convergence is founded on an ideology of **interculturalism**, allowing for mutually beneficial cultural exchanges, whereby cultures can be influenced and educated by and about other cultures. It the differs quite substantially from multiculturalism, and is the preferred term for our purposes.

What about national cultures?

One of the common arguments against cultural convergence and globalisation is that we need to protect national cultures. This stance underpins Australian local content laws, and certainly is an attractive idea for ensuring that communities continue to see their own stories and hear their own voices in the media that they consume.

What, really, is a national culture? Media theorist Tom O'Regan (1993: 59) refers to the 'double face' of popular culture, be it European, British or Australian. This is the blend of local and imported product that produces 'an amalgam of different cultures ... and multiple identities' (O'Regan 1993: 96). Here, O'Regan is pointing out that national cultures are already a product of cultural convergence, and while any attempt to protect local content should be applauded, we should not lose sight of the fact that national cultures are already convergent ones.

O'Regan is more particularly referring to the Australian media culture here, but in his description of the 'Australian and US trade in drama programs' as 'part of a wider system of exchange and similarity' (O'Regan 1993: 88), we can find parallels with British and European program exchanges, particularly franchises in reality television such as *Big Brother* and game shows such as *Dancing with the Stars*, suggesting his notion of a 'double culture' can be more broadly applied.

Cultural convergence and media

How, then, can we account for the popularity of media texts across global cultures, particularly those with very different norms and values? There are two schools of thought, one that views cultural convergence positively, the other negatively.

A number of media commentators have argued that the ubiquity of US television is producing a global, hegemonic monoculture generated by a collective desire among most countries to emulate the Western lifestyle. This is leading to increased homogenisation and Americanisation of local content and hence, a loss of national cultures.

In contrast, media theorist Scott Robert Olson (2004, following Bhabha 1994, among others) argues that 'although readers around the world are increasingly gaining access to the same materials to read, they do not have access to the same ways of reading' (Olson 2004: 114). Rather, Olson suggests that producers of US media texts, in particular, are good at making and exporting texts that easily blend into a variety of cultures. Olson calls this **narrative transparency**, which he defines as:

> any textual apparatus that allows audiences to project indigenous values, beliefs, rites, and rituals into imported media or the use of those devices. This transparency effect means that American cultural exports [such as television] manifest narrative structures that easily blend into other cultures. (Olson 2004: 114)

Narrative transparency: A textual process by which audiences can project their own values, beliefs, rites and rituals into imported media and make use of these devices.

The end result is that US media texts 'seem familiar regardless of their origin [and] seem a part of one's own culture, even though they have been crafted elsewhere' (Olson 2004: 120).

Narrative transparency therefore allows for cultural convergence by allowing other cultures' artefacts to be folded back into, and made a part of, the receiving culture's culture.

Industrial convergence

Industrial convergence: The intersection of a variety of media industries through cross-media ownership and cross-promotion.

Cross-ownership is the consolidation of the control of a variety of media companies and industries (and therefore power) in the hands of a few major companies.

Industrial convergence refers to the convergence of different media industries. It involves two aspects: cross-ownership and cross-promotion.

Figure 19.2 Industrial convergence

$$\text{Industrial convergence} = \frac{\text{Crosspromotion (seen)}}{\text{Crossownership (unseen)}}$$

Cross-ownership is the consolidation of the control of a variety of media companies and industries (and therefore power) in the hands of a few major companies through their acquisition of a number of smaller media companies.

Historical examples include:

- William Randolph Hearst at the end of the nineteenth century
- Rupert Murdoch during the last forty years
- the Time-Warner conglomerate since the early 1970s
- the state, in countries where it is the government that controls television, radio and newspapers.

Some facts on media ownership

Four Western news agencies supply 90 per cent of the world's press, radio and television.

Roy Greenslade (2003), a journalist at the *Guardian*, reviewed the editorial stance of the 175 Murdoch-owned newspapers worldwide, and found that all supported the invasion of Iraq. Rupert Murdoch himself admitted as much to an ABC journalist in October 2004. 'With our newspapers,' said Murdoch, 'we have indeed supported Bush's foreign policy. And we remain committed that way.'

Consolidation of ownership (and therefore power and control) remains an issue in most countries. The European Union has introduced regulations regarding cross-ownership; the US opposes monopolies through antitrust laws; and Australia and Britain have competition laws designed to prevent this consolidation of power. Given the above statistics, we'll let you decide how well you think these laws are working.

Cross-ownership is also a behind-the-scenes aspect of industrial convergence because members of the public are rarely made aware of the connections between industries—who owns what. As we have demonstrated throughout this book though, ownership of particular industries can have a profound impact on media content.

Cross-promotion is the promotion by celebrities, programs and industries of other celebrities, programs and industries that have the same owner.

Cross-promotion: The promotion by celebrities, programs and industries of other celebrities, programs and industries that have the same owner.

Examples include:

- the Australian media product *Better Homes and Gardens*, which exists as a television series and a magazine, and asks its readers and viewers to follow up stories in both formats
- *Dancing with the Stars*, which features contestants who are often celebrities from the host television network's other programs
- the US police franchise *Law & Order*, which regularly features crossovers between the various series in the franchises. Here the crossovers function as a form of cross-promotion, as they draw attention to these other series through the use of continuing narratives.

A move away from production?

Clearly, cross-ownership and cross-promotion overlap.

Industrial convergence is an important process not only because it raises concerns about ideology and hegemony, but also because it has the potential for shifting the focus of media industries away from production and towards the distribution and exploitation of archive material. In Chapter 18, we saw how a distributor of media, Google, rather than any content provider, has become the world's biggest media company.

Frequently, companies will be bought and sold on the value of their back catalogue of media properties, which are then developed into different media forms. The *Superman* comic, for example, from DC Comics, existed as a television series *Smallville* on the WB network and a film franchise through Warner Brothers, all companies that are part of the larger Time-Warner conglomerate.

In part, this shift is a recognition of the importance of recognisable brand names and franchises for building audiences—audiences respond well to names they know and brands that have brought them pleasure in the past. Hence we have a film version of *The A-Team* and an updated version of the television series *Hawaii Five-O*.

But as media industries are also responsible for the production of culture, any change in this structure, such as a move away from production towards distribution and exploitation, could have a major impact on us as a creative society.

Technological convergence

Figure 19.3 Technological convergence

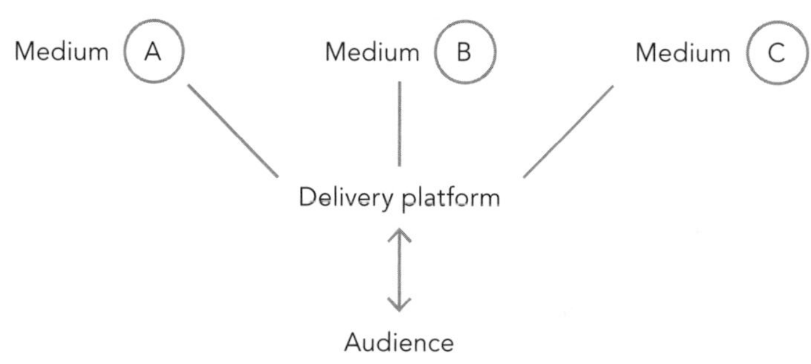

Technological convergence: Media intersection enabled by technological development.

Technological convergence is the intersection of media enabled by technological developments. When we think about technological convergence, we often think of the gaming industry, the internet or the telecommunications industry:

- The gaming industry is currently the most economically profitable media industry, with a regular turnover much greater than that of the film industry.
- The internet has completely revolutionised the way we communicate, do business and access the media, because it allows for ever-increasing interactivity.
- The growth in the telecommunications industry is a direct result of convergent applications, to the point that mobile phones are now a media platform in their own right, capable of accessing the internet and radio, taking photos, playing music and viewing television.

Delivery platforms: The ability of media to act as platforms for the delivery of media texts.

The only problem in writing about technological convergence is that inevitably, by the time this book is published it will be hopelessly out of date. That said, in principle, technological convergence actually promises a variety of delivery systems or **delivery platforms** that are responsible for the dissemination of media texts and the ways in which those platforms and systems are increasingly converging into one site. Whereas media texts were once delivered across a variety of systems and platforms—print, television, cinema—increasingly one platform or system is being used to deliver a variety of different media texts. Think, for example, of the iPad or Xbox.

For more on the technology at the heart of technological convergence, see Chapter 18.

THE iPAD

Most people know what an iPad is, but what does it actually do? It's been heralded as a device that can capture a new set of users who want more portability than their laptop can offer, but a greater range of interactivity and information supply than their mobile phone can perform. As does the iPhone, what it can do relies on the innovation

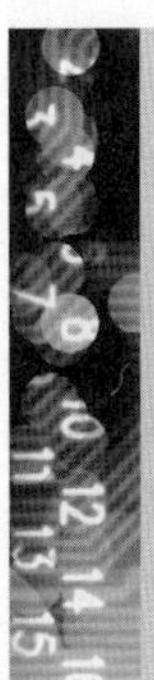

and range of the applications (apps) other people create for it. From the newspapers' perspective, it enables them to charge for online content and offer interactivities such as navigation maps, games and magazine-style interfaces. Indeed, it is predicted that around 45 per cent of iPad owners will use the device to view news, so news organisations hope that the enriched engagement experience offered by the growing range of iPad applications will make audiences happy to pay for content. For more detail see <http://technology.timesonline.co.uk/tol/news/tech_and_web/personal_tech/article7138592.ece>. But some people may view it as a big iPhone that can't make calls.

MICROSOFT'S XBOX 360

Gaming systems are now seen as one of the most effective delivery platforms because they are very popular, domestic, as are television and radio, which means that they can become part of the living space, and allow for interactivity, especially through devices such as the Nintendo Wii and Microsoft's Kinect, which encourage more physical activity as part of the gaming experience.

Microsoft's development of the XBox 360 game console is a good example of convergent technology. The XBox 360 is designed to play games, but can also display photos, play music, screen films and connect to the internet. According to the promotional literature around its launch in 2005, it was marketed as a 'multitalented, multitasking, multimedia machine'. It is, therefore, a perfect example of an all-purpose delivery platform.

Underscoring this development is, in Microsoft terms, a move towards the digital entertainment lifestyle (DEL). Here, through digital technology, all media will merge into a single integrated, portable, customisable media gestalt; one writer even calls it an 'electronic ecosystem'.

Although this development reinforces Microsoft's economic power, it also returns some power to the fans, because the projected XBox Live permits fans to sell their customised versions of Microsoft games online.

As Bill Gates, founder and then CEO of Microsoft, noted on its initial release in 2005: 'You can't just sell it [the XBox 360] as a convergence device. You gotta get it in there because certain members of the family think it's a must-have item.'

THE INTERNET

Unsurprisingly, the internet is at the forefront of convergent applications, not only because it has the capability to carry all forms of media from newspapers and radio to film and music, or that it can bring them together, but rather because it:

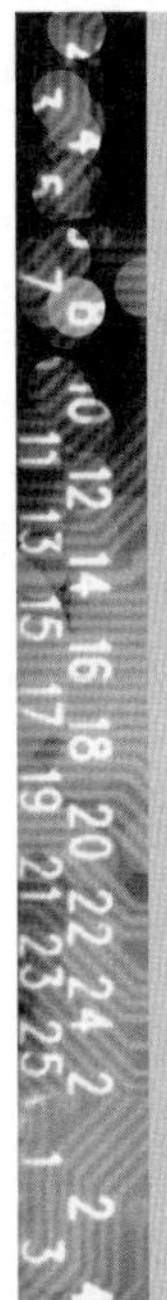

- empowers people to produce, converging producers and consumers into the notion of the prosumer (see Chapter 10)
- enables people to receive information from all over the world, thus assisting cultural convergence
- permits the free flow of information, from reviews of films to neo-Nazi rhetoric, to porn, and through downloading and shareware, circumvent other media industries.

The internet can also be seen as a confirmation of fan power, because it builds on ideas that fan communities have been involved with for years: interactivity, community and production. It also provides fans with multiple ways of maintaining a stake in media properties, via sites such as YouTube and illegal downloading sites, or by burning illegal copies.

The internet really transfers the tools of production into the hands of the fans, which means that fan interest can have a real impact on the shelf life and future development of media, frequently leading to petitions for DVD releases.

Just look at Ain't It Cool News (<www.aintitcool.com>) if you want a confirmation of how the internet has empowered the fan.

THE MOBILE PHONE

The mobile phone has become the pre-eminent delivery platform. In the past decade, the telecommunications industry, of which mobile phones are a part, along with data services, online services, search engines and rapid information transfers, particularly electronic commerce, has become the world's fastest growth industry and the mobile phone the world's fastest developing delivery platform.

Currently, the mobile phone can connect to all of the telecommunications services mentioned above, take photos, download media content and play music. There is even content generated exclusively for the mobile: mobisodes, which deliver five-minute episodes of popular television dramas such as *Doctor Who*.

Narrative convergence

Narrative convergence: Narrative that does not originate from a single textual site, but flows across, between and through a number of different delivery platforms.

Narrative convergence is narrative that does not originate from a single textual site, but instead flows across, between and through a number of different delivery platforms. This is possibly the most contentious of the forms of convergence presented here: the notion that a narrative can, in itself, function as a form of convergence. Other theorists refer to the concepts of transmedia narratives or synergy (see below), rather than considering narrative as a form of convergence in its own right. But given the fact that communication is central to media, and that narrative and the permutations of narrative, from interpellation through to news narratives, celebrity metanarratives and the metanarratives, or grand narratives, that underpin modernity, and which we consider in the final chapter, have been part of our focus—it makes sense to think about the importance of narrative in the context of convergence.

Figure 19.4 Narrative convergence

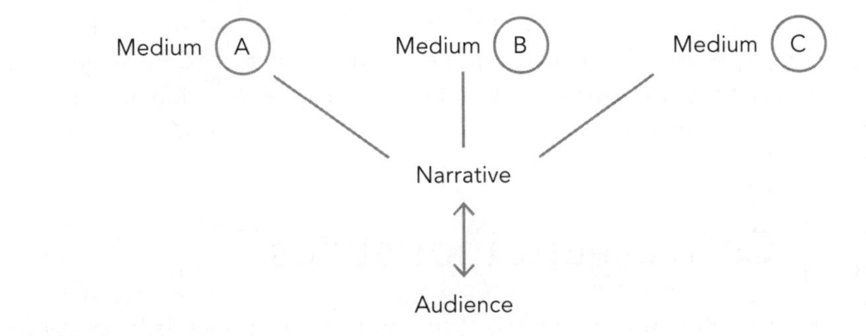

A recognition of narrative convergence is a recognition of the power of narrative and the emergence of a new narrative form that will have an impact on media production and distribution well into the future.

Narrative convergence really exists distinct from technological convergence. Rather than bringing platforms together to create one portal, it acknowledges that there are different audience pleasures and engagements to be derived from consuming different media forms. It takes advantage of these differences by producing narratives that can work across a variety of different media platforms and systems. It is the narrative that provides the convergence rather than the underlying technology. It is the narrative that connects the different delivery systems and platforms.

Narrative convergence is built around the idea of **transmedia storytelling**. Henry Jenkins (2006a: Chapter 3) coined this expression to describe stories that are told across a number of different delivery platforms, each platform highlighting different aspects and characters in the story. Jenkins looked at the concept in connection to *The Matrix*, which incorporated three films, games, graphic novels and an *anime* DVD, *The Animatrix*.

Transmedia storytelling: Stories that are told across a number of different delivery platforms, each platform carrying a slightly different aspect of the story.

Synergy: The combined marketing of products, owned by the same corporation, such that the total effect is greater than the sum of the parts.

Virginia Nightingale (2007a) notes that this process makes stories similar to brands such as Disney and celebrities such as Britney Spears, in that they depend on an accumulation of intertexts to develop a complete narrative (just as celebrities did back in Chapter 11).

Narrative convergence can, therefore be thought of as a development of **synergy**. Synergy is 'the combined marketing of products which are owned by the same corporation such that the total effect is greater than the sum of the different parts' (Branston & Stafford 2006: 373). Synergy confers prominence through repetition: *Star Wars* books, toys, comics, games, cards, DVDs and soundtracks all work together to promote the *Star Wars* films and subsequent television series. As we saw in Chapter 10, intertexts work together to make a text significant. Repetition of a text across multiple intertexts will increase the prominence and perceived significance of that individual text. This is the basis for promotion—and the basis for synergy.

The total effect produced can be more complex than just synergistic. Narrative convergence occurs where the extratextual elements of media's cultural circulation actually contribute to, and develop or enrich, its narrative—where merchandising actually advances the story.

Why is transmedia storytelling a form of convergence? Because it brings all of these delivery platforms together around one media text, thereby encouraging audiences to adopt

Fanzine: An amateur magazine produced for fans of a pastime or celebrity; the concept originated among science fiction fans in the 1930s, spread gradually among other interest groups during the 1960s, and was adopted by a wide range of groups during the last twenty years.

Merchandising: The marketing of a wide range of consumer goods bearing images from a specific media product.

multiple delivery options over the text's run. It also alters the dynamics of the producer–consumer relationship.

For now, it is enough to make a distinction between synergy, that is, purely about economics and promoting a certain media text, and narrative convergence, also economic, but also in some way developing the media text's narrative.

Convergent industries

We can now start to think of several media industries as being convergent industries in the context of narrative convergence.

The comic industry

We can think of the comic industry as a convergent industry because it supplements other industries' narratives by adapting their stories into comic format, a process already popular before the rise of the video industry, and fulfils fans' desires for new, ongoing narratives featuring beloved characters such as *Star Wars, Star Trek, The A-Team* and, most recently, the *Buffy the Vampire Slayer Season 8* comic book series. It also develops other industries' creations into narrative forms such as *The Transformers, The Micronauts* and *GI Joe*. Finally, it is increasingly a content provider of stories and concepts for current Hollywood and television entertainment, reflected in the change from Marvel Comics to Marvel Characters and the development of Marvel Studios, DC's role as part of Warner Bros and Dark Horse Comics' establishment of Dark Horse Entertainment to develop film properties based on their comic characters.

The comic industry is one of the first media industries where we can see fans in a dialogic relationship with media texts through conventions and **fanzines**. Because of the longevity of this industry, it is also one of the first media forms in which fans (consumers) such as Roy Thomas and Jim Shooter themselves became producers (writers and editors).

The merchandising industry

Merchandising is the marketing of a wide range of consumer goods bearing images from a specific media product. The merchandising industry is usually credited as beginning with Walt Disney animations of the 1930s, including Mickey Mouse and *Snow White and the Seven Dwarfs* (1937). It was fully realised with *Star Wars* (1977), and became a common global practice with the introduction of McDonald's Happy Meals in 1979, which started with a tie-in to *Star Trek: The Motion Picture*. The practice actually goes back to the beginning of the twentieth century, with the efforts of early entrepreneurs such as L. Frank

Baum and Edgar Rice Burroughs, creators of the *Wizard of Oz* and *Tarzan* respectively, to merchandise their creations.

Merchandising is important to narrative convergence because it can enrich narratives by providing greater background detail about places and characters, as well as enabling consumers to create their own narratives through play.

More significantly, the merchandising industry really gives fans pure economic power. The enormous sales of its merchandise, particularly DVDs, was one of the reasons the animated television series *Family Guy* was returned to the airwaves by Fox following its cancellation.

Whereas fans of *Cagney and Lacey* and the original *Star Trek* could only write letters to the networks pleading for the television series to be spared from cancellation, now fans have real economic power to influence the decisions of media industries. This can keep a series such as *Buffy the Vampire Slayer* on air; while ratings were never stellar, attendant merchandise sales kept the series profitable. It also explains how the science fiction western *Firefly* became the film *Serenity* (DVD sales, again, made it a potentially profitable venture) and how the shelf life was improved for equally short-lived series such as *Life As We Know It, Wonderfalls* and *Space: Above and Beyond*, which all continue to sell well as DVD boxed sets, even though they were axed after just one broadcast season apiece.

Why is narrative convergence important?

Narrative convergence encourages consumers, particularly fans, to be producers—the prosumer. This is the final evolution of the active audience we first discussed in Chapter 10: the final crossing of the divide between producers and consumers. Increasingly, these properties continue to be important over generations: *Superman* has been with us since the 1930s, *Star Wars* since the 1970s, *Star Trek* since the late 1960s and *Doctor Who* since the early 1960s, and fans, the former consumers of the product, are moving into positions where they can take control of and responsibility for the content.

Until recently, fans of particular media texts were limited to illegal activities or playing in the margins of media texts. Scholars such as Jenkins (2006a) have explored the ways in which fan communities became participatory communities through conventions, **fan fiction**, unauthorised fiction based on the media products, and **slash fiction**, fiction that serves as unauthorised extensions of the media products, generally sexual and often homosexual in nature.

Fan fiction: Fiction, written by fans of a particular media text, that features characters from that text.

Slash fiction: Unauthorised fiction, written by fans of a particular media text, that features characters from that text in narratives that are sexual, often homosexual, in nature.

With technological and narrative convergence, fans suddenly have the opportunity to engage directly with the media product. It's no longer just fan fiction, they can actually bring the property back, as in the comic book revivals of 1980s properties *GI Joe* and *The Thundercats*, or write official tie-ins to extend the life of the property, as with *Buffy the Vampire Slayer* and *Star Trek*. In effect, they become the authorised producers of the text. This has several consequences:

- The status of commercial or popular culture is affected, as it becomes 'a potential source of status rather than the thing the elite define themselves against' (Seabrook 2001).

Think, for example, of the economic value of the nostalgia industry, of eBay as the cultural barometer of what is valuable and therefore highly praised by society, or the phenomenon of geek chic, where it is almost trendy to be geeky about popular culture.

- It changes the way media texts are produced. Media designers are encouraged to think in terms of world-building, of creating a universe, or detailed secondary world, that can be exploited for franchise potential or marketing spinoffs. They are encouraged to create media properties that have the potential for narrative convergence built into them.
- Narrative convergence is economically important, as it increases the shelf life, and therefore the profitability, of a property by increasing its cultural circulation. This makes us rethink how capitalism, the ideology underlying commercial culture, works. Capitalism becomes not only a process of making money but also a process of generating new ways of making money. Capitalism becomes a productive discourse.

Our modern myths?

It can be argued that convergence is part of mythmaking in that it enables media texts to become our modern myths. Increasing the shelf life of a media product recasts the product as a modern myth because jumping media is quite similar to the ways in which the ancient myths of Greece and Rome were told across different media, such as pottery, painting, poetry, plays and song. This is even parodied in a scene from Disney's *Hercules* film. This serial repetition and development across different delivery platforms creates a sense of being mythic and, judging from the sheer volume of sites devoted to these often obscure media texts, a great number of these media properties have indeed become cultural touchstones and modern myths for a vast array of people, especially those born in the 1970s and 1980s.

What are the impacts of convergence on media?

Convergence has had three significant impacts:

- *On control:* convergence is a double-edged sword. Because of changes in the means of production, fans have greater power over media than ever before, from having the opportunity to become authorised producers to participating in and archiving what is important to them on YouTube. Yet these platforms are still the properties of media corporations, so fans as authorised producers are still involved in the perpetuation and maintenance of these corporations' power bases. Only through illegal or illicit activities is some form of fan resistance maintained, which is usually disempowered or undermined by the fact that it is inauthentic.
- *On journalism:* just as the means of production empowers fans, so it also empowers citizens to become journalists. The phenomenon of the citizen journalist, who operates through blogs and web pages or by being witness to breaking news and taking photos with

mobile phones, is also a result of convergence. Consumers of news are having a great deal more influence over news production than they would have had in the past. Furthermore, it is technology that is altering the delivery of news stories and the recording of new events. For more on this, see Bromley (2004), who refers to the ways in which journalism is being affected by the convergence of technologies and ownership, which alters attitudes towards the previously distinct forms of journalism in press and broadcasting. Branston and Stafford (2006: 200) also refer to some of these.

- *On image:* as celebrities function across a number of different media platforms, the ability to speak publicly and present well becomes increasingly necessary, regardless of whether they are rock stars, politicians or authors. Maintaining a consistent image can become a full-time job, and create its own subindustries, such as public relations agents, stylists, personal assistants and image consultants, teams of people dedicated to constructing and maintaining the most familiar representations of these public figures in the mediasphere.

Conclusion

Convergence, the various intersections developed between aspects of the media, has always been a part of media's development, and will continue to be so in the new media environment for the foreseeable future, continually changing in response to new technological developments and innovative ideas.

Convergence, involves questions of economics and power, which can broadly be divided into four forms: cultural, industrial, technological and narrative. Most importantly, convergence will become the site where issues of power and control will continue to be contested between those who originate media content and those who engage with it.

FURTHER REFERENCES

Jenkins, H. (2006a). *Convergence Culture: Where Old and New Media Collide.* New York: New York University Press.

Nightingale, V. & Dwyer, T. (2007). *New Media Worlds: Challenges for Convergence.* Oxford: Oxford University Press.

CHAPTER 20

POSTMODERNITY

JASON BAINBRIDGE

Introduction

Nobody likes postmodernity, alright? Postmodernity is one of those words that provokes great debate among academics ... and stifled yawns among almost everyone else. It's often regarded as outdated, a bad word and really quite rubbish. And that's just the view of the people who do like it. So why are we making it the last chapter of our book? Because it's important.

In the past we did not recognise the rights of women to vote. We did not recognise Indigenous ownership in Australia or the wrong that was done to the Stolen Generations. We did not fight for equal rights for homosexuals or refugees. We did not debate environmental issues. So what are the things we don't see today? What are the problems that will make people ask in the future: How could they not see that? How could they not act on that?

That is why postmodernity can help us. It is about optimism, about idealism, about thinking of the alternative point of view, about thinking outside the box. Postmodernity is about the potential and the possibility of media and journalism to make real, lasting, positive change. That is why it is so important and that is why it is our final chapter.

The problem is that postmodernity is also a big complex idea that has been made even more complex by being extended to explain just about everything. 'Postmodernity', 'postmodern' and 'postmodernism' are used fairly interchangeably in academia and in the wider community. Indeed, 'postmodernity' has been used so widely, in so many contexts, that the word itself is at risk of having no meaning: everything seems capable of being classed as postmodern—from art and film through to thought and writing.

In textual analysis terms we could almost call postmodernity an empty signifier, because the term has been stretched and adapted so much that it no longer produces a clear signified.

Even so, postmodernity remains a useful tool, particularly for people engaging with the media, as it is a way of:

- understanding the changing relationship between media and society
- analysing the textual and industrial structure of media forms
- taking account of different points of view when making decisions or producing your own media texts.

These are all important considerations for anyone working with media. We should all be aware of the history of media and the history of ideas. Similarly, we should all be respectful of difference and diversity.

This is our last full chapter. It relies on all that you have read in the previous chapters; it also takes us back to theoretical approaches discussed in Chapters 2, 9 and 10.

This chapter is, therefore, part rehabilitation and part definition of the importance of postmodernity, for now and for the future. It aims to:

- provide a workable definition of postmodernity applicable in the context of media theory and media practice
- explain why postmodernity is an important concept for media practitioners
- provide examples of postmodern media texts.

In so doing, we acknowledge that other theorists and other practitioners will have their own definitions, and that debates over the correct use or utility of the term postmodernity will be ongoing. But this is the formation of postmodernity that works for us, and the one we would encourage producers and consumers to hang onto in the years ahead.

What is postmodernity?

Let's start by taking the word itself and breaking it down bit by bit:

Postmodernity

or

Post Modern Ity

The word has three parts:

- post
- modern
- ity

Post modernity

The first thing to notice is the prefix 'post'.

The common misconception is that *post* means *after*, as in 'post mortem' or acting 'post haste' People assume that postmodernity comes after modernity (we look at modernity in more detail below).

But in this instance post means *it isn't something any more.* It's a break with something, an alternative perspective on something. So in this case it isn't modern: it's a break with the modern, an alternative perspective on the modern. It's a break with tradition. It's thinking outside the box, or standing in someone else's shoes. 'Post' here means something new, something different.

This means that postmodernity does not come after modernity. Rather, it coexists with modernity, as a corollary to modernity, running parallel to modernity. Think of two streams running side by side and you'll have a sense of the relationship between them. The view from one stream is slightly different from the view from other stream, but they are both running in the same direction, and they originate from the same source (see below.)

In fact, postmodernity is an inadequate word—*countermodernity* or *paramodernity* would be more accurate terms. But though postmodernity is a problematic term, we use it here because academics and the general populace use it so much that it still serves as a convenient way of describing a challenge or, more precisely, an alternative to modernity.

Post *modern* ity

The second part of the word is 'modern'.

Modern here means *a particular way of representing or thinking about the world*, such as a discourse or a myth or an ideology (see Chapter 10). As we see below, modernity involves a number of discourses, myths and ideologies that work together to produce a way of looking at the world and/or organising the world that is so convincing that we often refer to it as *conventional* thinking.

Post + modern = a break with thinking about the world or looking at the world in a certain way. Postmodernity is, therefore, a new perspective on the modern, a challenge to the modern or an alternative view of the modern. In so doing, it recognises that there are limits to what modernity can provide.

Postmodern *ity*

Notice the suffix 'ity'.

In some ways this is the most contentious bit of our definition, because we're using 'ity' rather than 'ism', which means that we are talking about post + modern + ity rather than post + modern + ism.

Though many writers conflate the two—they use postmodernity and postmodernism interchangeably—they are quite different terms: *modernity* is a form of social organisation, but *modernism* is an artistic movement (see Felski 1995: 13).

The distinguishing factor, then, is that one is a social force (modernity) and the other is an aesthetic force (modernism). Postmodernity, is a new way of thinking about the world in terms of the social rather than the aesthetic forces. It represents a break with, and a new alternative to and new perspective on, what has come before.

Postmodernity certainly involves ideas of postmodernism—but postmodernism, the aesthetic, is only a symptom of postmodernity the social movement. John Frow (1997), for example, refers to postmodernism as a genre of theoretical writing rather than a way of thinking about the world.

What about other isms?

You might ask, what about communism or fascism? Aren't these examples of isms that are ways of thinking rather than aesthetic movements? Of course they are and many

more besides. The point we are trying to make here is to draw a distinction between postmodernism and postomodernity. More broadly, these other -isms like commmunism and facism are ideologies whereas postmodernity is a much larger way of thinking that can subsume ideologies like communism and facism. The difference is therefore one of scale, as will be demonstrated below.

To describe postmodernity as postmodernism would be like describing the flu as a cough.

The relationship between postmodernity and postmodernism

A number of academic and popular texts do use these terms interchangeably, and a great deal more favour postmodernism over postmodernity, so it is important that we set out the relationship between postmodernism and postmodernity in some more detail:

- Postmodernity represents a break with conventional (modern) thinking.
- Postmodernity is therefore a change in the way that we think.
- Postmodernism is a change in the way we see.
- Postmodernism is also a change in the way that we produce.
- Postmodernism is often produced by a change in the way that we think (postmodernity).
- Postmodernity, the change in the way that we think, can therefore express itself through changes in the way that we see and the way that we produce (postmodernism).
- In turn, postmodernism can then be expressed through art, the change in the way that we see and economics the change in the way that we produce.

Postmodern forms

Examples of postmodern art include the work of Andy Warhol, the architecture of the Bonaventure Hotel and the media form of comic books.

Examples of postmodern economics include the work of Robert Venturi, and the layout and development of theme parks such as Disneyland.

These are all postmodern forms because they are all marked by a return to the popular, the low culture and the vernacular. As such, represent a break with the modern, because they place an emphasis on the local and particular as opposed to the universality of modernism.

Many texts run through examples of postmodern aesthetics in detail. See the Key references list at the end of the chapter for more on postmodernism.

The assumptions of postmodernity

Having defined what we mean by postmodernity, let's now have a look at the theoretical assumptions that lie behind postmodernity. These are all derived from the pioneering work of French cultural theorist Jean-Francois Lyotard (1984):

- As noted above, postmodernity is a corollary to modernity, not something that follows it or represents its conclusion. Postmodernity therefore represents a break with conventional thinking.
- Postmodernity is concerned with alternative knowledge structures and theories, rather than authorised or legitimate theories and institutions. Ultimately, this translates into a new economy, which we will return to below.
- Postmodernity believes that modernity can be a limited way of thinking about and organising the world. It encourages us to question, to think outside the box and seek out alternative viewpoints.
- Postmodernity favours oscillation between, or consideration of, a number of points of view, even points of view that are in competition.
- To ensure that all viewpoints get a fair hearing, postmodernity will often favour the minority view.
- Postmodernity believes in a multiplicity of meanings rather than one unitary meaning. (You should already be noticing the utility of postmodernity for media studies, because it is in keeping with two concepts we have already considered: the polysemy of individual media texts and the pluralism of groups of texts or discourses.) Postmodernity celebrates this diversity and the possibility of this diversity.
- Postmodernity encourages consideration of premodern as well as modern knowledge structures.

One history of Western thought

As postmodernity does encourage the consideration of premodern and modern ways of thinking about the world, it is important to consider some previous streams of Western thought. One way of describing such a history is to divide it into three ways of seeing, representing and organising the world:

- premodern
- modern
- postmodern.

All three of these ways of thinking about the world are still with us today. But we can point to periods in time when premodernity and modernity (at least) were ascendant—and in this way understand where postmodernity is coming from, and what it is responding to.

Premodernity

Premodernity: The mainstream of Western thought until the nineteenth century; its underlying beliefs based on religion, nature and a sense of divine justice.

Premodernity is the form of Western social organisation that held sway until the sixteenth century, involving:

- belief
- nature
- divine justice.

Premodernity is therefore defined by some form of religion: the belief that everything comes from a god or multiple gods. Hence, it is marked by mythology or paganism, or the beginnings of organised religion. At the very centre of premodern society we find churches and storytellers. These are the origins of our modern media: organisations and individuals who mediate events to larger audiences through a series of representations.

Premodernity is still important for the following reasons:

- Religious discourse remains important in the public sphere, for example, in the current religion-based debates around teen sex and contraception, intelligent design, stem cell research and the language used to justify the War on Terror.
- In premodern times we first see large numbers of people (congregations) being brought together (in church) and/or mobilised around a common ideology (religion), which set the template for today's media and politics.
- It gave us an oral and visual tradition that is the basis for most mass media forms. John Hartley (1992a, 1999, 2002b), for example, has argued that television performs some of the functions of the family and church in modern societies, in that it teaches us citizenship and how to place ourselves in relation to the rest of the world.
- It still informs a number of texts, for example, the belief in divine justice that underpins the superhero genre, a large number of police procedurals and violent government-sanctioned heroes, such as James Bond, *24*'s Jack Bauer and Arnold Schwarzenegger in pretty much all of his films. These heroes embody the premodern ideal of divine justice in that they dispense their own brand of justice (beating up people or shooting them in the kneecaps) without resorting to the law.

Remember our analogy of modernity and postmodernity as streams running side by side? Premodernity is the lake from which our streams of modernity and postmodernity flow. That means premodern ideas continue to run through the waters … but the world has moved away from the ascendancy of premodernity.

To help you identify premodern ideas, here is a checklist:

- Premodernity is a form of social organisation based on belief rather than researched evidence. As you will see throughout this chapter, all of these '-ities' are forms of social organisation based around a way of thinking about the world.
- Premodernity is expressed through discourses of religion and nature, which often overlap. Therefore the symbol of premodernity (the signifier) is the pastoral scene.
- Premodernity can be gendered as either male or female. Most of these '-ities' tend to be gendered in certain ways. The Judaeo–Christian–Islam God, for example, is usually gendered male ('Our Holy Father'), whereas alternative religions privilege the Goddess.

Relics of this thinking can be found in the conspiracy theory at the heart of Dan Brown's bestseller, *The Da Vinci Code*, and the debates over the recognition versus the exclusion of femininity from religious thinking, including the traditional resistance in the churches to female clergy.

Modernity

Modernity: The mainstream of Western thought, from the nineteenth century until the late twentieth century, that is based on ideas of progress, rationality and equality.

Modernity is a form of social organisation based around notions of:

- progress
- rationality (evidence-based thought, and freedom and justice through the law)
- equality of human beings.

According to Childs (2000: 15), modernity was produced by 'a societal shift ... a way of living and of experiencing life which has arisen with the changes wrought by industrialization, urbanisation and secularisation'. This can be called modern living or the condition of modern life.

Modernity, as Felski (1995: 12) describes it, is not a:

> homogeneous Zeitgeist which was born at a particular moment in history, but rather ... comprises a collection of interlocking institutional, cultural and philosophical strands which emerge and develop at different times and which are often only defined as 'modern' retrospectively.

As Sarup (1996: 50, citing Bauman) says, 'Modernity is associated with order, certainty, harmony, humanity, pure art, absolute truth.' Therefore, modernity marks a:

> general philosophical distinction between traditional societies, which are structured around the omnipresence of divine authority, and a modern secularised universe predicated upon an individuated and self-conscious subjectivity. (Felski 1995: 13)

It might be easier if you think of modernity as an attitude rather than a specific time or place.

The beginnings of modernity

There are multiple and contested accounts describing the beginnings of modernity. Here are three of the most prominent.

Possible historical origins

Modernity has been linked to the Renaissance, to the seventeenth-century scientific discoveries of Galileo, Newton and Descartes, to the eighteenth-century Age of Enlightenment (Habermas 1989) and to the period of European expansion (colonialism) (see Bhabha 1990).

The three-phase approach

- 1500–1800, the ascent of modern life
- the 1800s, the period of revolution
- the 1900s, global modernisation, incorporating early modernist theorists such as Emile Durkheim, Max Weber and Ferdinand Tonnies at the turn of the century, and later, the Frankfurt School, including Theodor Adorno, Max Horkheimer and Walter Benjamin (see Berman 1983).

The multi-origined approach

Modernity begins:

- in politics with the French Revolution (eighteenth century)
- in philosophy with the Enlightenment (eighteenth century)
- in science with the experimental method (early seventeenth century)
- in industry, with the Industrial Revolution in Britain (late eighteenth and early nineteenth centuries) (Hartley 1999: 39).

The main elements

While a variety of theories have been advanced regarding the origin of modernity, generally all theorists agree that modernity involves the following elements:

- progress
- rationality
- equality.

These three elements are generally associated with the process of **enlightenment**, the process that marked the societal change from the Middle Ages to the Renaissance, from traditional to more democratic societies and from premodernity to modernity.

Enlightenment: The period, from about 1500 to about 1800, when feudal, religion-based societies gave way to secularised, more democratic societies.

The feudal hierarchies of the Middle Ages gave way to the 'modern secularised universe' made up of 'democratic' societies. They were democratic because they were founded on these Enlightenment values that were 'used as a guide to organising society' (McKee 2003: 6).

While there was a transition from premodernity to modernity, not all elements of premodernity vanished overnight. Elements of premodern thinking remain a part of our societies to this very day. Enlightenment values include that:

- all citizens are of equal worth and importance (equality)
- everyone should be treated fairly (justice/equality)
- everyone should have control over their own lives (freedom)
- everyone has a right to a basic level of material welfare (equality/justice/comfort) (McKee 2003: 6).

The Enlightenment recognised that everyone could somehow make a contribution to society. It was the first recognition of the individual contribution to the greater good, and so marked the beginnings of democracy. That's why we can say modernity is a form of social organisation based around equality, rationality (leading to freedom and justice) and progress, because it is a desire to look forward to a perfectible future. In this sense modernity is always modern—always of the now—because it is always looking to the future.

Two mechanisms evolved to simultaneously enshrine and promote these Enlightenment values in modern societies:

Public sphere: The public spaces of work, leisure, politics, religion, academia and the mass media, where issues and ideas are encountered, articulated, negotiated and discussed as part of the ongoing process of reaching consensus or compromise in democratic societies.

Rule of law: Consistent, fair rules of society that apply equally to all citizens.

- The **public sphere** (Habermas 1989): 'Where information, ideas and debate can circulate in society, and where political opinion can be formed' (Dahlgren 1995: ix). In such a society, citizens gain an input into political debates, thereby enshrining and promoting equality and, ideally, rationality. See Chapter 1 for more detail.
- The **rule of law**: a society in which law is a mechanism to ensure equality, fairness, justice, freedom and the right to comfort, as opposed to arbitrary rules imposed by rulers on citizens. The rule of law became fundamental in transforming arbitrary authority into rational authority subject to the scrutiny of a citizenry, because it was law that organised this public body. The rule of law enshrines rationality and equality, while at the same time enabling progress based on clear rights and duties.

Together, the public sphere and the rule of law transformed feudal hierarchies into democratic modern societies based around Enlightenment values. Again a checklist, this time of modernity would include:

- Modernity is a form of social organisation based around the idea of the democratic society.
- Modernity is expressed through discourses of knowledge such as law, science, medicine and philosophy.
- The symbol of modernity (the signifier) is the city.
- Modernity is often gendered as male.

Modernity is a stream running off the lake of premodernity. It is a manufactured stream, incorporating the work of people from all levels of society, redefining ways of organising the world.

Why is modernity important?

Modernity is still the dominant way of organising, seeing and thinking about the world:

- Almost by definition, modernity is always modern. It is an ongoing project because, as Habermas writes (1981: 9), it consists of 'efforts to develop objective science, universal morality and law … for the rational organization of everyday life', that is, because it is based around progress, modernity is always in the process of becoming.
- Modernity intends to replace premodernity. It sidelines premodern religion and natural authority in favour of reason and knowledge, and absolutes in place of abstractions, absolute in the sense they are empirically testable and verifiable. Modernity stresses the increasing importance of the secular realm, based on evidence, as opposed to the spiritual realm, based on faith.

- Modernity gave birth to popular culture and mass media. While premodern societies, with their forums, agoras and organised religions, their gathering together of people in one space, set up the metaphorical model or possibility for mass media to exist, it was modern society that ultimately gave birth to mass media and our contemporary understanding of popular culture. This was because modernity gave birth to a corresponding rise in capitalism and entertainment. Technological development permitted advancements in production, circulation and consumption that allowed for the development of popular culture and the mass media as we know them today (Harvey 1989: 23).
- Modernity produced the modern idea of the institution, including the media institution. These include capitalism (commodity production and circulation), industrialism (the transformation of nature and use of inanimate sources of power), surveillance (the capacity of the state to monitor the activities of its citizens) and military power (legitimately monopolised by the state instead of by individual warlords).
- Modernity itself is frequently the subject of media texts. Ideas of modernity are constantly being debated, contested and supported in media texts. Examples include:
  - the television series *Law & Order* (a celebration of the modern legal system, with police and lawyers working together), *ER* (a celebration of the modern hospital system), *CSI* (a celebration of forensic science) and *Star Trek* a celebration of the perfectible modern future: in the Star Trek franchise, equality, rationality and progress are the benchmarks of the United Federation of Planets' future
  - the nightly news, which often hegemonically reinforces these notions of equality, rationality and progress, making these the benchmarks by which we judge other societies
  - entire genres, such as science fiction and the western, are often based on modernity's central ideology of progress and the perfectible future.
- Similarly, a great number of texts look at crises in modernity (which we return to in greater detail below). These include *Desperate Housewives*, which picks apart suburban life, and literary texts that have latterly been adapted for the screen such as Elizabeth Gaskell's *North and South* and Kenneth Grahame's *The Wind in the Willows*, which feature the premodern/modern relationship between the city/urban setting and the country/rural/pastoral setting.

As modernity is an ongoing project because it is always in the process of becoming, it means that modernity is always incomplete. That means that there's a gap in modernity. And that's where postmodernity comes in.

Postmodernity

Postmodernity is a form of thinking based around notions of difference and respect.

It is not a form of social organisation. It is a way of thinking that informs social organisation, not a complete form of social organisation in itself.

The crucial difference between modernity and postmodernity is that, while postmodernity still accepts the importance of the basic Enlightenment ideals—equality, freedom, justice and comfort—it

Postmodernity: A type of Western thought that, while sharing the basic ideals of modernity, accepts that a wide variety of groups within a society have different perspectives on society and ways of being in that society, and that these differences should be respected and alternative viewpoints considered.

also, according to McKee (2005: 17), 'accepts that different groups think and communicate differently about issues and we should respect that'.

Thus, postmodernity is against fixity, objectivity and, taken to the ultimate extent, reality, terms that we return to below, while encouraging oscillation, fragmentation, difference and respect for alternative perspectives, including the trivial, the commercial and the spectacular.

Postmodernity should be exciting, because it's about alternative ideas and letting them be heard. It is really a way of considering a wide variety of perspectives and encouraging debate—and isn't that what we want in our media and in the public sphere more generally?

Where did postmodernity come from?

The term 'postmodernity/ism' (note the slippage) first emerged in the 1870s, when it was used by British artist John Watkins Chapman as a term to describe the move away from accepted genres in art, literary criticism and architecture (Litowitz 1997: 41). Later, sociology and anthropology took up the term to discuss the ways cultural variety and economic indeterminacy are reflected in advanced industrial societies (Litowitz 1997: 42–5).

We can actually link postmodernity to a certain historical period, the Second World War, which was the ultimate crisis in modernity (at least before 11 September 2001).

As we can see, postmodernity is a stream that has been running parallel with modernity for at least fifty years. Postmodernity is a period that John Hartley describes as being 'coterminous' with modernity itself (Hartley 1999: 39). Indeed, Lyotard himself (1987: 8–9) viewed postmodernity as the necessary corollary to modernity, not 'a new age [but rather] the rewriting of some features modernity had tried or pretended to gain'.

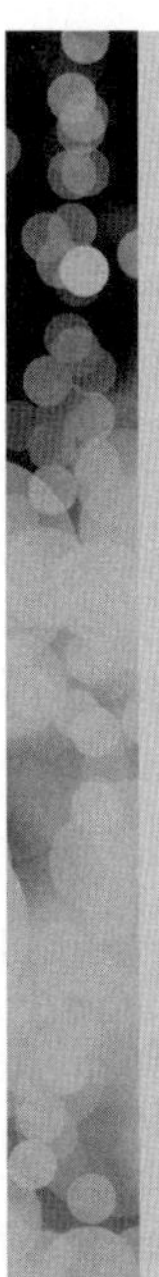

Second World War

In the late 1930s, just before the beginning of the Second World War, then Chancellor of Germany Adolf Hitler, justified the Holocaust in terms of modernity: he justified the extermination of millions of Jewish people as being rational and necessary for the future progress of Germany. To that end he had facilities purpose-built for genocide.

The most infamous of these was Auschwitz, the name loosely used to identify a compound that comprised three main Nazi concentration camps and forty-five to fifty subcamps. The name was derived from the Germanised form of the nearby Polish town, situated about 60 kilometers southwest of Krakow. Beginning in 1940, Nazi Germany built several concentration camps and an extermination camp in the area, which at the time had been annexed by Nazi Germany. The camps were a major element in the perpetration of the Holocaust.

The total number of casualties at Auschwitz is still under debate, but most modern estimates are between one million and 1.5 million.

It was the images of these camps that became the signifiers of the crisis in modernity.

How could anyone believe in modernity—progress, equality and rationality—in the face of these atrocities? How could anyone believe in modernity, when modernity had been used to justify this genocide? And how could anyone believe in modernity's notion

of a universal unity (a 'we'), when our fellow humans were capable of committing such acts for what they saw as a greater good?

After the Second World War

With the end of the Second World War came the end of the economic conditions, based on prosperity in the USA, that had persisted up until this time. Japan and Western Europe had to rebuild their own economies without relying on the USA for production facilities and technologies. This marked a turn away from a unified economy. In place of the old economies came new, information-based technologies, the beginning of a new economy that was to increasingly blur the divide between producers and consumers.

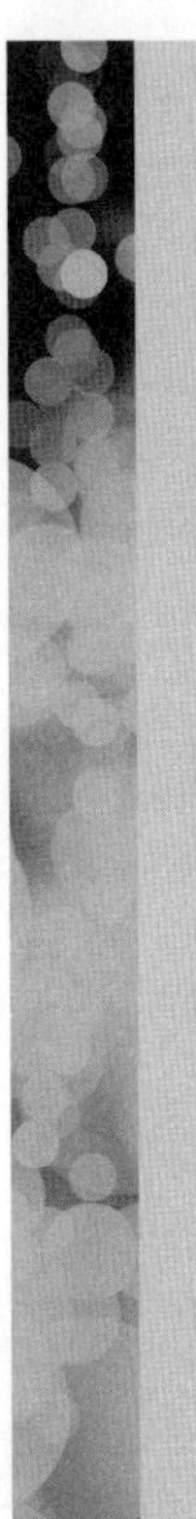

First signs of postmodernity

With a degree of hindsight, we can see that postmodernity has been part of modernity from the very beginning:

- In literature, novels such as *Tristram Shandy* (Laurence Sterne), dating from 1772, ignore all accepted rules of structure and plot.
- In journalism, as Hartley (1999: 40) suggests, we can now understand the press as containing postmodern elements from its inception, because it was 'dedicated to the irrational and emotional as well as to reason and truth; to feminized, privatized, non-metropolitan knowledges as well as to public affairs; to questions of identity as well as power'.
- In science, the founders of modern science, Francis Bacon and Isaac Newton, were essentially premodern heretics. Science, therefore, began as a mix of alchemy, magic and rational thought.
- In television, pioneers of the medium, such as Graham Kennedy in Australia, frequently engaged in what we would now refer to as postmodern strategies, breaking the wall between performer and audience to talk directly to viewers, adopting a variety of points of view over the course of a show, referring to other programs and advertisers (intertextuality), making fun of television and his own sponsors, and drawing attention to camera operators (and thereby breaking down the form).

Postmodernity, therefore, can be conceived as Heller's (1999: 4) 'self-reflective consciousness of modernity itself … a kind of modernity that knows itself in a Socratic way'; McGuigan's (1999: 122) 'reflexive modernity' or 'the other' to modernity that Derrida (1982) speaks of. To use Heller's (1999: 9) terms, modernity is simply subjected to a constant process of erosion by postmodernity.

Hartley (1999: 40) refers to postmodernity as the 'necessary twin to modernity, in conditions that were always there but only recently resolved into analytical coherence'. So postmodernity is something that's always been there. It only took the atrocities of the Second World War to make us realise how important it could be.

When did postmodernity become a theoretical position?

Postmodernity's broad use as a philosophical response, a way of thinking or reflecting on the world, didn't really arrive until 1979 with the publication of Lyotard's *The Postmodern Condition: A Report on Knowledge* (trans. 1984).

Here, Lyotard defined postmodernity as 'an incredulity to metanarratives' (1984: xxiv). As Lyotard's definition forms the foundations of our understanding of postmodernity, let's look at what Lyotard means here in a bit more detail.

What are metanarratives?

Metanarratives are the underpinnings of modernity. They are where discourses such as reason or unity turn for legitimation. Think of metanarratives as really big narratives that structure discourses into stories in the same way that regular narratives structure texts into stories. Metanarratives include 'We need science for progress' and 'We need law for unity'.

As we saw in Chapter 11, metanarratives help to structure the many narratives that appear around celebrities' public lives (the texts they appear in) and their private lives into one cohesive, or reasonably cohesive, whole. The metanarrative thus becomes a way of making sense of a celebrity. In a similar way, the metanarratives that Lyotard refers to help to structure and make sense of modern discourses, such as law and science.

Lyotard's (1984: xxiv) incredulity to metanarratives, therefore, encourages people to become sceptical about the established, to recognise the limits of modern thinking and to create something new: a new perspective, an alternative point of view or a challenge to the pre-existing modern discourses.

What is legitimacy?

Legitimacy: The process that each discourse employs as it seeks to authorise it's truth, rightness and superiority.

Lyotard's (1984) main concern is with the altering status of science and technology, which he uses as a springboard for discussing the problem of **legitimacy**.

Lyotard (1984: xxvi) claims discourses seek to legitimate themselves by 'making an explicit appeal to some grand narrative [or metanarrative; he uses the two terms interchangeably], such as the dialectics of the Spirit, the hermeneutics of meaning, the emancipation of the rational or working subject, or the creation of wealth', be they classical (resorting to enlightened notions of truth) or modernist (communicative).

Lyotard saw discourses legitimating themselves with reference to what were essentially a larger set of myths built around wealth creation or emancipation. For more on discourses and myths, see Chapter 10. These mythic metanarratives continue to be used today.

The two key metanarratives Lyotard discussed were unity ('the speculative narrative') and reason ('the emancipatory narrative').

- The metanarrative of unity is still frequently used. It refers to something done for the greater good, in the national interest or otherwise refers to the national spirit. This is precisely the myth used in relation to the US's War against Terror, the introduction of the US *Patriot Act* or the arguments for relaxing cross-ownership laws in Australia.
- The metanarrative of reason is grounded in the political visions of Immanuel Kant ('Reason will emancipate us from tyranny') and Karl Marx ('Science enables the proletariat to emancipate themselves') (Lyotard 1984: 37). It is the metanarrative that law appeals to in order to legitimate itself. It is also the myth used to justify cloning, animal experimentation and rape in marriage. It also legitimates most governmental and occasionally media responses to social (contentious) issues.

Lyotard claims that metanarratives have 'lost [their] credibility' (1984: 37) because they have not fulfilled their aims of unity and liberation (1987: 179–80). In the wake of the Second World War, you can see why the credibility of metanarratives were challenged. Hitler justified the Nazi regime as being modern and progressive, based on ideas of reason and unity twisted to his own ends.

The breakdown of metanarratives represents the shift from modernity to postmodernity. Lyotard (1984: xxvi) uses the term 'modern' to 'designate any science [science defined to include disciplines from physics to philosophy] that legitimates itself with reference to a meta[narrative] of this kind'. In contrast, 'postmodern' refers to '[discourses] that are legitimated by smaller, localised narratives' (Litowitz 1997: 111).

We can see the shift towards postmodern discourses in some of the previous chapters, where we examined such processes as the shift from the public sphere to public sphericules, from mass audiences to niche audiences and from journalism to citizen journalism. In each case, the larger metanarrative fragments to be replaced by 'smaller, localized narratives' (Litowitz 1997: 111).

What are alternative knowledge structures?

What Lyotard is encouraging people to do here is to think of alternatives. He is arguing for people to consider multiple, parallel, competing, dissenting and often minority viewpoints when coming to a decision, rather than just following the majority, authorised or commonsense view. Lyotard wants people to question and so *Postmodern Condition* (1984: 512) ends with an argument for dissent and multiplicity, a 'splintering', but not in a nihilistic sense. Lyotard's desire is to return to the people the power to think for themselves. Lyotard (1984: 37) not only encourages us to resist metanarratives but also presents the idea of **alternative knowledge structures**:

Alternative knowledge structures: Knowledges derived from the consideration of multiple, parallel, competing, dissenting and often minority viewpoints.

> In contemporary society and culture—postindustrial society, postmodern culture—the question of legitimation of knowledge is formulated in different terms. The [metanarrative] has lost its credibility, regardless of what mode of unification it uses, regardless of whether it is a speculative narrative or a narrative of emancipation.

Modernity is also based on an idea of democratisation, the recognition that everyone has the capacity to contribute to society and therefore has the capacity to think for themselves. Lyotard (1984: 512) offers a different way of achieving this aim: 'What saves [the people] from [the force of metanarratives] is their knowledge that legitimation can only spring from their own linguistic practice and communicational interaction.'

Here, then, we see a powerful recognition of selfhood and individualism. Lyotard wants people to think for themselves, to take account of a variety of points of view and perspectives, rather than simply listening and doing what they are told.

Once again, these are ideas we can currently see being played out in the mediasphere, in the move from the passive to the active audience and from the consumer to the producer. This is the basis for interpellation, polysemy and pluralism (see Chapters 9 and 10).

Other definitions of postmodern

Some theorists in this area have, though not very convincingly, attempted to link these shifts in thinking to the aesthetics (the style and structure) of particular texts, especially television series such as *Miami Vice*, with its fragmentation of soundtrack, *Twin Peaks* and *Moonlighting*, with their blurring of genres, and *Ally McBeal*, with its splintering of narrative, broken by music, song and fantasy sequences.

While all of these series can be viewed as postmodern, they are postmodern in terms of their thinking, in terms of the way they view the world, rather than merely the way they present that world aesthetically or the structural and stylistic considerations they employ. That is, they reflect postmodernity rather than postmodernism.

What is the aim of postmodernity?

What is central to all these forms of postmodernity is an interest in fragmentation, contingency, textuality, uncertainty and the indeterminacy of ideas, in breaking them down and remaking them as it does so. This approach overlaps with the tenets of poststructuralism, as discussed below.

Glee: postmodern television you can dance to

For an example of truly postmodern television, look at the television series *Glee*. Using a form that is intrinsically postmodern, the musical, which is postmodern because it disrupts the narrative with song and is based around spectacle and emotion, *Glee* is truly postmodern because it celebrates diversity in that it gives equal time to all of the very different viewpoints of its characters, and presents these viewpoints without judgment, even the increasingly bizarre antics of coach and Glee club nemesis Sue Sylvester (Jane Lynch).

What is poststructuralism?

These aims of uncertainty and the indeterminacy of ideas are something that postmodernity has in common with the theorists often labelled as poststructuralists, frequently leading these theorists also to be labelled as postmodernists.

As the name implies, poststructuralism is essentially an intellectual outgrowth of structuralism. While it still clings to the basic structuralist methodology of breaking

down structures, and the basic structuralist idea of signs being made up of signifiers and signifieds, poststructuralism rejects definitions that claim to be absolute or universal. It focuses less on the author and more on the reader as the producer of meaning. The author's intended meaning is, therefore, of secondary importance to the meaning that the reader perceives. Thus, texts can have multiple meanings rather than one preferred reading. You can see a number of these poststructuralist ideas informing the ideas of textual analysis we have derived from Hartley (1999) and McKee (2003).

In contrast to structuralism, poststructuralism has never been a defined movement (with its own manifesto). Rather, it has been a label that has been selectively applied to those who criticised some aspects of structuralism, including prominent structuralists such as Claude Lévi-Strauss, Jacques Lacan, Roland Barthes and Michel Foucault, along with theorists such as Jacques Derrida, Gilles Deleuze and Julia Kristeva.

In contrast to postmodernity, poststructuralism does not refer to a particular form of study. It just exists as a label for a form of structuralist critique. Therefore, it may be better to think of poststructuralism as a necessary development of structuralism that certainly informs the ideas of media, culture and textual analysis that we use today, and points towards some of the central concerns of postmodern thinking.

The aim of postmodernity, then, is to accentuate insight into the polysemic or splintered character of the social, and place legitimation back into the hands of the people, based on the assumption that you can move outside the boundaries and binaries that modernity imposes. Therefore, postmodernity:

- encourages you not only to think for yourself but also to think about others' perspectives
- encourages you to challenge conventional thinking
- repudiates certainties and boundaries to reveal the way power is manifested through institutions, language (according to Lyotard) and discourses (according to Foucault)
- aims to give voice to marginalised groups, and delights in the subsequent play of paradoxes, the oscillation between different points of view (according to Lyotard).

Are you still having trouble working out the difference between modernity and postmodernity? If so, try the *Scooby Doo* test.

Try the *Scooby Doo* test

The two incarnations of the *Scooby Doo* franchise are a good illustration of modern and postmodern thinking in action.

The classic *Scooby Doo,* the 1960s Saturday morning cartoon series with limited animation and lots of recycled scenes of Scooby and the gang running around, has the following characteristics:

- It uses logic, reason or rational thought (such as Velma).
- Actions are justified as being for progress, profit or the greater good (such as Old Man Whatever used to say when he dressed up as a ghost, a monster or another troublemaker).

- An action appears completely sensible and makes perfect sense until you think about it from another perspective (as in a 'And I would have got away with it too, if it wasn't for you pesky kids' ending).

This is an example of *modernity*.

The more recent *Scooby Doo*, the 2000s live-action films with a computer-generated Scooby and starring Sarah Michelle Gellar from *Buffy the Vampire Slayer*, has these characteristics:

- It is illogical, emotional, unreasonable or irrational (such as Shaggy and Scooby confronted by a monster … or a Scooby snack).
- An action is justified by a bizarre or out-there motivation, or a completely unexpected cultural or subcultural context (such as real ghosts or real monsters).
- It makes no sense until you think about it from another point of view (the It's breaking the walls between realities' endings).

This is an example of postmodernity.

So here is a checklist of points to remember about postmodernity:

- Unlike premodernity and modernity, postmodernity is not a form of social organisation. Rather, it is a tool that encourages us to consider different ideas, different points of view, and different cultures and subcultures. It works with modernity, and sometimes, necessarily, against it.
- Postmodernity is based on the idea of difference and diversity. It celebrates difference by making us think about different ways of seeing, organising and thinking about the world.
- Postmodernity is expressed through ideas of hybridity, intertextuality and bricolage, which we define in more detail below.
- If postmodernity has one symbol, it is, as some students have suggested, the question mark (?). Also, postmodern texts tend to favour female gendering.

The X-Files

Long-running series *The X-Files* reverses the gendering we usually associate with postmodernity. The modern thinker, FBI agent and forensic scientist Dana Scully, is female, while the postmodern thinker, intuitive and emotional FBI agent Fox Mulder, is male.

Postmodernity in practice

So postmodernity is breaking down what is already out there and encouraging us to form a new perspective, either by putting the pieces back together in a different way or just finding another viewing position (from another text or another cultural perspective).

There are three terms we can use to describe what postmodernity is doing in practice, one of which you will already be familiar with from previous chapters. While some authors use these terms interchangeably, we prefer to think of them as different postmodern positions:

Bricolage: (From the French for 'striking together'); the intersection of a variety of styles to create something new.

Intertextuality: The idea that texts do not exist in isolation, but rather are interdependent. Texts frequently make meaning through their relationship with other texts. These other texts (or secondary texts) are called intertexts.

Hybridity: The mixture of media cultures to create a multi-origined media.

- **Bricolage** describes how different styles are juxtaposed, or clash, to create something new; for example:
  - In the realm of fashion, Doc Martens boots, a short black skirt, a black sweater and heavy dark eye make-up are brought together to create an Emo style.
  - In the realm of Hollywood musicals, Fred Astaire performs a dance routine that includes the items in the room around him (dancing with a hatstand, dancing up the wall).

  With bricolage, you can still pick out the various components, such as the boots, the skirt and the make-up, that form the style, and therefore understand how they all work together.
- **Intertextuality** (see Chapter 9) is the way texts refer to, and help us make sense of, each other. Intertextuality is clearly postmodern in that it encourages us to look at one text in relation to another text. Therefore, it encourages us to think about the relationship between different ideas and look at ideas from different perspectives. Whereas you can still pick out the individual components involved in bricolage relatively easily, intertextuality can be a lot harder to detect. It requires audiences to have that level of cultural competency where we can either recognise the presence of a reference to an intertext or recognise when an intertext might help us make meaning in this instance.
- **Hybridity** relates to the mixing and sampling of different elements to create something new. Hybridity does not depend on juxtaposition because, unlike bricolage, the audience is rarely aware of the pieces that make up the whole until, or unless, they are pointed out. An example is the cyborg T-100 in *The Terminator*. We are unaware that this is a cyborg (part machine and part man) until it is injured and we can see the metal armature beneath its human skin. It is a hybrid—a mixture of different elements to create something new—but we are not aware of those different elements until they are revealed to us.

  As hybridity relies on different elements it also refers to something that is multi-origined, which has origins in robotics and humanity and brings them together, as in *The Terminator* cyborg. If we expand these concepts a little further, we can think about elements as being cultural, not just physical, so media texts could be simultaneously Japanese and American, as demonstrated by some *anime*, businesses can be simultaneously commercial but environmentally focused, brought together in the concept of sustainable development, and teaching can be simultaneously educational and entertaining, brought together in the genre of edutainment, to which *Sesame Street* would belong.

Each of these terms can be used to discuss what postmodernity is doing in practice. For example, postmodernity challenges modernity by making us think in a wide variety of ways and take in different perspectives (intertextually). It encourages us to develop new styles and approaches in conjunction with what is already there through bricolage. It ultimately compels us to create something new through sampling or mixing different elements, by hybridity.

Postmodern industries

We can think of a number of media industries as being postmodern:

- *The fashion industry:* Fashion is continually reinventing itself, developing trends and blending styles. Think of the bricolage involved in bringing together boots, dresses, hats and jewellery.
- *The music industry*: Jazz and rap offer new ways of thinking about the world from the perspective of different cultures and subcultures, while sampling in dance and techno is surely an example of bricolage. Similarly, a film such as *Moulin Rouge* makes the postmodernity of music explicit: the lead characters blend different lyrics and songs from different times and styles to express their emotions.
- *The comic industry*: Structurally, comics are very postmodern as they splinter narrative into pictures and words. They therefore create an experience that oscillates between the viewpoint of the writer and that of the artist. Industrially, too, the text itself oscillates between periodicals—newspaper strips and comic books—and trade paperback books and graphic novels. Textually, comics are postmodern, presenting a superhero figure who oscillates between two or more identities and contrasting ideas of law and justice.

Postmodern perspectives

Postmodern perspectives exist in the wider society, and media frequently take up these perspectives as the basis for their own texts. Here are a few examples:

- history—arguments about invasion versus settlement
- journalism—the rise of literary journalism and blogging
- medicine—herbal treatments and alternative medicine
- law—the new perspectives that have arisen from the Mabo decision, *Roe v Wade* and *Brown v Board of Education*
- religion—not only *The Da Vinci Code* but also *Hitchhiker's Guide to the Galaxy* and *Dune*
- sustainability—a bricolage of perspectives offered by premodern environmentalism and modern ecological science
- social movements—which manifest themselves as subcultures such as punk, from the Sex Pistols to Bart Simpson, and the gothic, from Edgar Allen Poe through to Lemony Snickett.

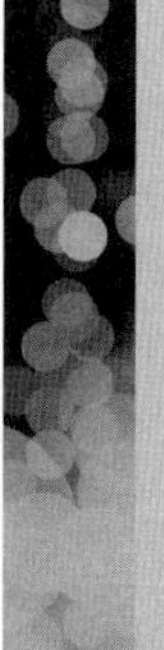

Is postmodernity conservative?

While postmodernity encourages us to adopt a variety of different viewpoints and take into account a number of alternative perspectives, here's a challenge that's worth considering: is postmodernity conservative?

In encouraging us to consider alternative viewpoints and perspectives, postmodernity also constructs one viewpoint as the mainstream or normal one. It therefore privileges this perspective, even as it encourages us to look beyond it.

The problem is that to move outside the boundaries, one has to be made aware of the boundaries that exist, even though this does serve to enshrine the white, male, heterosexual, Western perspective that is at the heart of modernity. Some could argue that, while postmodernity is trying to be very democratic, it still, ultimately, reinforces the dominance of the modern viewpoint.

Postmodern ideas

Postmodernity's questioning of some of the tenets of modernity have also resulted in a number of postmodern ideas that have been foregrounded in today's media, particularly in relation to news and popular media forms. Four of the most famous, and most controversial, are:

- Identity is mutable.
- There is no reality.
- Emotion is just as important as rationality.
- Postmodernity has produced a new economy.

We now look at each of these and how they work in the context of the mediasphere.

Identity is mutable

Postmodernity fundamentally believes in a world without fixity, where everything is changeable. This carries over to identity as well—whether it's our physical, spiritual or cultural identity. For postmodernists there is no one truth, only multiple truths. This means that age, gender, nationality and sexual preference are all merely ways of being that can be challenged, deconstructed and changed through hybridity, intertextuality or bricolage.

As we have seen in Chapters 18 and 19, new media clearly allow us to manipulate, reform and reconstruct every aspect of ourselves. They provide us with a virtual postmodern space in which we can become anything. Examples include:

- the cyborg and plastic surgery (the mutable body)
- the avatar (the mutable identity)
- the tourist compared with the refugee, the immigrant with the emigrant, and the terrorist with the patriot (the mutable cultural identity)
- celebrities in general—people who change their identities, sometimes in a very short time.

More recently, this has evolved into the idea of posthumanism: that humanity itself is limited and we need to move beyond humanity to truly develop. This is reflected by a growing interest in the posthuman in popular culture, for example, the perfect man in the *Twilight* series is not presented as human but rather a choice between a vampire (Edward Cullen) or a werewolf (Jacob Black). James Cameron's *Avatar* similarly presents the journey of its protagonist Jake Sully (Samuel Worthington) from a (literally) crippled human to a free and environmentally aware posthuman Na'vi—a truly posthuman character in that it is a 3D motion-captured animation. Thus the posthuman represents the latest evolution of postmodernity's interest in mutable identities.

Those who consider postmodernity an abstract theory might well consider the possibilities of the new media environment in which millions of ideas are accessible and millions of ways of being are possible. New media may, necessarily, be the product of modern technology, but it provides us with a very postmodern vantage point on our culture and our society.

Philip K. Dick

Postmodern ideas of reality, authenticity, hyperreality and simulacra are well illustrated in the novels and short stories of Phillip K. Dick, many of which have been loosely adapted into Hollywood films, with varying degrees of success. See, for example, *Blade Runner,* based on Dick's novel *Do Androids Dream of Electric Sheep?*, *Total Recall* or *A Scanner Darkly*. Dick's collective works, most of which are in print, add up to an omnibus of postmodern ideas and speculations.

There is no reality

As postmodernity believes in a virtually infinite range of perspectives and viewpoints that make up the world, it has questioned whether there can ultimately be any reality, and consequently any form of objectivity or truth. This is problematic, especially for scientists and journalists, but it doesn't have to be.

The idea of there being no reality most famously manifests itself in Baudrillard's notion of hyperreality: nothing is real and all we perceive are the representations of reality (the simulacra) (Baudrillard 1994).

Note the connection with the ideas about media that we have been discussing in Part 5 of this book—media texts are representations, and many different representations make up the mediasphere, which is a part of the larger public sphere. We can examine the ways in which these representations present themselves and the significance of certain texts, but we would not say that one is a better representation of reality than another. They are all representations, but some merely seem more real, that is, they are more authentic representations of reality.

Think of this in response to the media coverage of the Gulf Wars, the original one in 1991, where these ideas were first raised, the post-2001 War on Terror and the post-2003 war in Iraq. Are we being shown the reality of war? How are statistics used to insulate the viewer from the suffering? How do embedded journalists function as propaganda for the forces they are supposed to be reporting on? (See Case Study 2 for a discussion of these issues.)

Constant questioning is a vital part of the scientist's and journalist's role, so anything that encourages that can't be all bad, can it? Alan Sokal was one who didn't agree.

A word of dissent: Alan Sokal's assault on postmodernity

Not everyone is happy with the rise to prominence in academic circles of postmodernity and postmodernism. These theories and ways of thinking are either ignored or scorned by people from the so-called hard sciences, disciplines such as physics, chemistry and mathematics that are concerned with empirical data that represent the physical world. If scientists are even aware of the existence of postmodernism, and many are only vaguely so, talking about it is likely to provoke dismissive chuckles or looks of irritated bemusement. But when postmodernity does intrude into the scientific domain, some scientists hit back. Given that this is a chapter that encourages you to think about diversity, it seems only fitting to present the alternative point of view: that postmodernity has intellectual flaws that decrease its usefulness, at least in relation to science.

The most famous critic is Alan Sokal, a physicist with New York University. In 1996, his article 'Transgressing the Boundaries: Towards a Transformative Hermeneutics of Quantum Gravity' appeared in the cultural studies journal *Social Text*. Regular consumers of postmodern theory will recognise the style of the article title instantly: it exactly matches the forms of words often used in this field, as indeed does the language of the whole piece. Immediately upon publication of his article, Sokal revealed it to be a hoax, and an international scandal erupted, which was covered in the mainstream media, including the front page of the *New York Times*. 'Transgressing the Boundaries' was abject nonsense, but it so pushed all the right postmodernist buttons that it was accepted by the editors of *Social Text*.

Sokal had become increasingly angry at the incursions into science by social theorists, whom he believed did not understand anything about physics and mathematics (in particular), but were simply posing and name-dropping (or equation-dropping). He was accused of being a right-wing reactionary, obsessed beyond reason with science, intellectually inflexible and explicitly anti-French. Much of the theory he included in his parody came from European thinkers, and particularly the French.

In a book, cowritten later with physicist Jean Bricmont, titled *Intellectual Impostures* (2003), Sokal rejected the criticisms, saying that he was forced to act to show up the inaccuracy of some of the things being said about science, though he did not reject humanities theories in toto. As a left-leaning individual, he also rejected the idea that he was pushing a right-wing agenda. He said that his aim was, 'quite simply, to denounce intellectual posturing and dishonesty' (2003: 14). His bogus paper cited many authorities, from great quantum theorists such as Niels Bohr to the current superstars of postmodernism. A huge range of genuine quotes was assembled to back a nonsensical argument that asserts an extreme form of relativism: no less than the idea that all physical reality is 'at bottom a social and linguistic construct', that the pi of Euclid or Newton's gravity are simply products of the cultural origins of their theorists. To a physical scientist, this is demonstrably untrue, and yet to a postmodernist editor of a cultural studies journal it appeared completely reasonable.

Liberally employing the jargon of postmodernism, Sokal dumped on the usual suspects in postmodernity of white males and objective reality, and asserted a melange of trendy ideas that included a feminist interpretation of physical phenomena. To quote from one of his supporters, Gary Kamiya, 'Sokal will no doubt be smeared as a reactionary for having the effrontery to place a whoopee cushion under the Supreme Throne of Post-Modernist Progressive Rectitude' (Kamiya 1996), and he certainly was.

His critique of postmodernism should be taken seriously as a genuine attempt to show some of the absurdities that have accumulated around parts of this theoretical landscape. *Intellectual Impostures* makes great reading, written as it is in clear, eloquent and often humorous prose. This, it has to be said, contrasts with the prose of the many postmodern theorists quoted in the book, who end up looking self-important, puffed up and rather ridiculous, just like the emperor in the famous fable about new clothes.

Liz Tynan

Emotion is just as important as rationality

Postmodernists call for a reappraisal of emotion in the face of modernity's insistence on rationality. Emotion can still be a powerful rhetorical tool: emotional arguments, for example, can be as persuasive, if not more so, than rational ones. Therefore, the privileging of emotion and public displays of emotion is encouraged by postmodernity. Think of the following:

- *Current affairs interviews:* How do emotional outbursts compare to rational arguments?
- *Talk shows:* How do public displays of emotion function? As therapy? As shared trauma? How do they make you feel as an audience member?
- *Narrative television, such as Grey's Anatomy or Damages:* How important is emotion to these characters? Why must they hide their emotions to be better doctors or lawyers? Does this make them stronger or lesser people?
- *Media events that centre on tragedy:* What is the media's role in foregrounding emotion, in bringing us together at Princess Diana's funeral or in the wake of the 2001 attack on the Twin Towers in New York? Is the mediasphere a place for shared mourning? Is this therapeutic? And how does the media deal with trauma?

Postmodernity has produced a new economy

Finally, and perhaps most importantly, postmodernity has created a new economy through its splintering of unity, reappraisal of divisions between, for example, producer and consumer and increased focus on the importance of alternative knowledge structures and alternative sources of information. As noted earlier, this new economy emerged out of the aftermath of the Second World War, when countries had to rebuild without US support (and therefore US control). What this produced was a new economy, based on the commercialisation and capitalisation of information. This is enshrined in new media, especially the connectivity, and interactivity of new media. But also carries across to all media, because all media, in some way, are involved in the communication of information and entertainment.

Conclusion

Postmodernity has been represented as a very complex idea, endlessly applicable to a vast number of scenarios and situations. It has often been ridiculed and questioned, both for its relevance and for what it can offer discourses such as science and journalism. This chapter has set out to reveal the ways in which postmodernity can be a useful tool. Indeed, we would argue that postmodernity is increasingly important in an age of fundamentalism, embedded journalists and cross-media ownership. Anything that makes us question and critically reflect upon what is being represented to us can only be a good thing, for the following reasons:

- It introduces new ideas into the public sphere.
- It permits the recognition of a wide variety of cultures and subcultures.
- It allows for the possibility of mutable identities.
- It encourages an interactive and participatory audience.
- It allows for greater pluralism in the public sphere.
- It encourages us to question the modes of media manipulation: what is real, what is authentic, what is objective and what is credible.

Postmodernity is a social context for thinking about media, but more importantly it is a tool through which we, as media producers and consumers, can understand what the relationship between media and society has been and what it can be in the future.

KEY REFERENCES

Butler, C. (2003). *Postmodernism: A Very Short Introduction.* Oxford: Oxford University Press.

Hartley, J. (1996). *Popular Reality: Journalism, Modernity, Popular Culture.* London: Arnold.

Lyotard, J. F. (1999). *Toward the Postmodern.* Amherst: Humanity Books.

Malpas, S. (2005). *The Postmodern.* Abingdon: Routledge.

Sokal, A. & Bricmont, J. (2003). *Intellectual Impostures.* London: Profile Books. This book contains the original Sokal, A. Transgressing the Boundaries: Towards a Transformation, Hermeneutics of Quantum Gravity. In *Social Text* article, as well as a great deal of argument around the issue of postmodern incursions into the physical sciences.

CASE STUDY 5:

JOURNALISM AND BLOGGING ON THE WORLD WIDE WEB

NICOLA GOC

Introduction

In many ways the internet is the new agora, the new global coffee house, a place where public opinion is shaped and formed, and citizens, responding to posts, provide checks and balances on truth-telling and accuracy. Journalism is mutating in the digital age as new news delivery systems evolve on the web and traditional news organisations lose their exclusive power of publication. Media barons and their editors and journalists are no longer exclusively setting news agendas. Bloggers, user-generated content (**UGC**) and new hybrid online news sites are challenging this power structure. In the new online environment, the linear news paradigm has been destroyed as news audiences are no longer passively receiving news, and citizens can be both consumers and producers of news.

UGC: An acronym for user-generated content on the Web.

Journalism is a particular communication practice that has implications for the success of democratic societies, so the issue of journalism practice in the digital world has implications for all of us as citizens.

In this age of citizen journalists on the web—of bloggers and J-bloggers, of YouTube, wikis and Twitter and digital media news delivery systems yet to be thought of—the question of who is a journalist and what is journalism in the twenty-first century is the focus of much discussion. Are bloggers journalists? Where does journalism as a public service fit within the new media construct? What is the role of the traditional journalist within the open, inclusive news discourse of the global agora? How has this devolution of journalism to the World Wide Web affected truth-telling and accuracy? Where do the highly structured routines and practices of the traditional twentieth-century news journalist fit within the world of new media and the 24/7 news cycle?

Journalism practice on the internet through an ethical frame

Journalism ethics is a cornerstone of how professional journalism should be defined. This case study examines journalism practice in the digital environment through an ethical frame as a way of understanding contemporary practice. At a time when the production of news is increasingly taking place within and outside of professional news organisations, an analysis of ethical practice provides a way to understand journalism in the digital world, a space where anyone can be a journalist because, as Mark Deuze argues, journalism is an 'editorial act, one that can be equally found among the millions of amateur bloggers as among the tens of thousands of professional journalists' (2009: 86).

There is a sense 'that technology is responsible, partially or wholly, for a devaluation of journalistic standards—amateur bloggers who do not adhere to practices of fact-checking, deadlines that become shorter or even continuous because the internet is 'always on', sloppier writing, and more inaccuracies' (Tsui 2009: 53). In his analysis of interviews with Finnish journalists in 2003, Ari Heinonen found that the journalists at the start of the twenty-first century believed journalism would survive in the digital world 'by adhering to its traditional ethical values' (Heinonen 2006: 137). But as journalism practice evolves on the web, new previously unthought of ethical issues have arisen, such as when to link, and the archiving and updating of content. One journalist said that the biggest problem was that the 'quality of online journalism outside of … traditional media is so varied. And it can be unreliable because it does not rely on the old traditions' (Heinonen 2006: 137).

Another journalist in Heimonen's study was concerned that the technology was corrupting good journalism practice, 'because of the [screen] resolutions and things like that, the net favours short presentations … Especially when you are reading from the screen, there are special requirements for the text and that will begin to affect the text. You have to spice up the text to make it juicier and that leads easily to bending the truth' (Heinonen 2006: 139). Yet another acknowledged the challenges of anonymity on the web: 'It is entirely compatible with the spirit of the net, completely suitable that you can remain anonymous in discussions and chats … But as far as journalistic contents are concerned, that of course doesn't apply—that's a totally different matter' (Heinonen 2006: 140).

The outing of Grog's Gamut

The online challenges to journalism practice have created tensions around the issue of who is a journalist and what is journalism on the web. The internet affords every individual user enormous freedom to communicate news, opinion, knowledge and ideas, and allows every user 'near total responsibility for how that freedom is exercised' (Singer & Ashman 2009: 3). It is the way this freedom is exercised that is creating tensions between professional journalists and mainstream media (MSM) on the one hand, and citizen journalists and bloggers on the other. When journalist James Massola from the *Australian* newspaper outed blogger Grog's Gamut as Canberra-based public servant Greg Jericho, there was much discussion about journalism and the web, and the rights and wrongs of Massola's actions.

James Massola argues that Grog's Gamut had become an influential public figure, whose identity was a matter of public interest after he published a post on 30 July 2010 in which he wrote that Australian news editors should 'bring home' their journalists from the 2010 election campaign trail, 'because they are not doing anything of any worth except having a round-the-country twitter and booze tour' (Jericho 2010).

Grog's Gamut's critique of the lack of policy questions from the press during the 2010 Australian federal election started a media debate across old and new media platforms about the quality of the election coverage. Jericho argued that he was not acting in his role as a public servant when posting his blogs, and that for him the failure of journalists in the 2010 election campaign was personal. As he had a daughter with Down Syndrome, he argued that he wanted

MSM: An acronym for mainstream media; that is, established mainstream television and radio stations and large established newspapers.

answers as to whether Opposition leader Tony Abbott's policy on disabled schoolchildren would make his daughter eligible for the $20,000 assistance payment when she started school.

Jericho's criticism of journalists covering the 2010 election hit a raw nerve with some journalists and media commentators. The 30 July post catapulted the Grog's Gamut blog into the public arena, attracting more than a thousand new followers on Twitter in the following days, and hundreds of supportive comments on his blog, reflecting the public's concern at the state of political journalism and the role of blogging in the political sphere.

ABC chair speaks out

Grog's Gamut: A blog maintained by Australian public servant Greg Jericho. Jericho maintained his anonymity until Australian journalist James Massola outed him during the 2010 federal election.

Grog's Gamut's influence reached its zenith when one of the most influential media executives in Australia, ABC managing director Mark Scott, picked up on Grog's Gamut's criticism, and sent a directive to his ABC newsrooms across the country to change their coverage:

> Halfway through the campaign, the ABC Executive met on a Monday morning and discussed the weekend blog by the Canberra public servant, writing under the tag Grog's Gamut. It was a lacerating critique of the journalists following the candidates, their obsession with transient matters, the political scandal of the day. He met a chorus of praise and support, triggering a barrage of criticism of campaign coverage. (Scott 2010)

Scott says he brought Grog's Gamut's criticism to the meeting because 'dynamic political news was crowding out proper reporting of policy initiatives in some news bulletins … We adjusted our strategy as we listened to critics, our audiences and critiqued our own coverage' (Massola 2010a).

Massola argued that the Grog's Gamut blogger had a responsibility to step out from behind his anonymous blog and defend his writing in the same way that journalists are expected to be accountable for their stories—because they have the power to influence public opinion—and therefore exposed Jericho's identity.

In his response to Massola, Jericho wrote in his 27 September blog (Jericho 2010a): 'So because the head of the ABC took notice of something I wrote anonymously about journalism, I need to be named. I guess the lesson here is if you want to blog anonymously, don't do it effectively.'

While accountability is one of the foundations of ethical journalism, Jericho argued that he was not a journalist and therefore there was no ethical imperative for him to disclose his identity. His posts, though, clearly were influential, and swayed one of Australia's most powerful media executives to change the way journalists covered the campaign.

Anonymity and blogging

This case highlights the issues around anonymity and blogging, particularly political blogging, the blurring of the lines between blogging and journalism, and the issue of accountability. It also reflects the tensions within journalism as practitioners face the challenges of tight deadlines in a 24/7 news cycle, diminishing resources, the pressure to be multiskilled in the world of convergence, a public appetite for infotainment rather than hard news journalism and the concerns within mainstream journalism at the development of a mass communication system that allows anyone to potentially act in the role of a journalist.

The vast majority of Twitter and online comments about Massola's story outing Grog's Gamut saw his actions as 'professional arrogance'. The responses extended worldwide with New York University lecturer and media commentator Jay Rosen responding: 'Let's see @jamesmassola answer the blogger he outed and explain how @GrogsGamut violated policy for public servants in Oz.'

One Australian reader, 'Glen of Southport', commented:

> I will continue to believe that investigative journalism is dead and that the majority of the media are left wing sympathisers with no desire to report anything that might cause the general public to think. The reporting of election policies was abysmal … My message to the media is do your job investigate and report and people like Greg Jericho won't be forced to do your job! ('Glen of Southport', posted at 11:26am, 27 September 2010; Massola 2010b)

Reader Liz Aitken was concerned that the *Australian* was implying that 'only journalists are "allowed" to blog. If that is the case, then partisan political discourse is dead, and democracy is threatened' (Liz Aitken of Melbourne, posted at 11:20am, 27 September 2010; Massola 2010a).

Massola acknowledged in his update later on the same day, that his outing of political blogger Greg Jericho had unleashed a firestorm of protest on Twitter. One tweeter responded: 'What I think […] is that @jamesmassola should have to answer to every blogger and political journalist in Oz: why did he do it?' (@Kimbo_Ramplin).

The *Australian Financial Review*'s political editor, Laura Tingle, tweeted: '@GrogsGamut I think you are supposed to start trembling and crawl terrified into a hole at this point. I hope you don't.' However, ABC political writer Annabel Crabb argued: 'I don't think anonymity should be a right. Disclosure of identity would be a rebuttable presumption in my ideal world' (Massola 2010b).

Codes of ethics

While adherence to a code of ethics is a foundational requirement of credible journalism, and professional integrity is the cornerstone of a journalist's credibility, codes of ethics and principles of practice have been slow in evolving on the Web. Traditional news organisations, desperate to attract and maintain audiences in the online environment, have been reluctant to place restrictions on UGC and have for more than a decade allowed freedom of comment from anonymous citizens, without setting guidelines that protect both citizens and journalists.

The McCanns

This open slather approach was abruptly modified in March 2008 when Kate and Gerry McCann, the parents of missing toddler Madeleine McCann, sued the Express group in the UK. Overnight UGC relating to the McCanns and their missing daughter was removed from online editions of all UK news media. For almost a year the unfounded speculation that the McCanns had been involved in their daughter's disappearance continued to have legs in the UK news media. This unprecedented media frenzy was fuelled to a great degree by journalists reacting to the intemperate and irresponsible UGC that mainstream news organisations allowed to be posted with little or no moderation.

Journalists created news stories based on rumour, speculation and unsubstantiated allegations as they reacted to the rabid mob mentality of many online reader responses (Goc 2009). This case also opens up questions of accountability in terms of historical records. The removal of UGC content from online sites denies future journalists, historians and citizens access to influential material. Governments in the UK and Australia have yet to make it mandatory for newspapers to supply national libraries with the entire contents of their online sites.

Consequences of the absent gatekeepers

By allowing readers to respond anonymously, and therefore without accountability, media organisations provide not only a platform from which members of the public can vent their ill-informed prejudices, but also one from which many reputable online journalists feel their integrity is compromised, for example, by being compelled to participate in online discussions with the likes of BIGDICK119 and Rooty, whose level of discourse was reduced to what journalists call 'bile' (Turner 2007, cited in Goc 2009).

As prolific blogger Nick Douglas argues: 'During the New Media Revolution, old-school journalism has learned one thing about bloggers: They're incoherent. Rough drafts and an insidery feel render blog posts nearly unreadable' (Douglas 2006).

Not only are they often unreadable, but too many blogs also reflect a laissez-faire attitude to notions of accountability and accuracy, and there has been considerable resistance from bloggers to any requirement that they should adopt existing journalism codes of practice.

The International Principles of Professional Ethics in Journalism

While there is no universal code of conduct for journalists, journalism and journalistic practice adheres to the fundamental notion of a free press, and an adherence to accuracy, independence, accountability and fairness. In 1978, after consultative meetings with journalists and news media around the globe representing 400,000 working journalists, UNESCO helped establish an International Principles of Professional Ethics in Journalism.

These principles were prepared to represent an international common ground, to act as a source of inspiration for national and regional codes of ethics and to be promoted autonomously by each professional organisation. The principles are:

- people's right to true information
- the journalist's dedication to objective reality
- the journalist's social responsibility
- the journalist's professional integrity
- public access and participation

- respect for privacy and human dignity
- respect for public interest
- respect for universal values and diversity of cultures.

Margo Kingston—webdiary

For over a decade, journalist and J-blogger Margo Kingston has negotiated the challenges of ethical practice while promoting a more inclusive journalistic discourse on the World Wide Web. Her case provides a useful starting point for understanding the complexities of the evolving journalism in the online environment.

Kingston was one of the first journalists to confront the challenges of ethical practice in the online environment. In creating 'Margo Kingston's Webdiary' in 2001, while working as a journalist for the *Sydney Morning Herald*, she was one of the first Australian journalists to seek to have an online conversation with her audience. In her first post Kingston told readers: 'The idea of this space is to write something each day and for you to give me your feedback' (Kingston 2001).

When she established Webdiary, she acknowledged up front that there was a different expectation of ethical practice between her readers and herself. In the preamble to her expectations of her contributors, Kingston made clear the difference between her role as a journalist and her contributors' role as respondents: 'As a journalist I have ethical obligations to readers; as a contributor you do not.' She went on:

> I want you to trust Webdiary. Trust is the ideal at the core of all professional ethics codes, which are guidelines for conduct which aim to achieve that ideal. I'm a journalist bound by a code of ethics drafted to apply to traditional journalism. I've adapted the code to meet the responsibilities of running Webdiary, and set out guidelines for your contributions. These guidelines are always open for discussion and debate on Webdiary and can be clarified and added to as issues arise. (Kingston 2003)

In July 2003, Kingston first published 'Webdiary's Ethics', after writing a chapter on the topic for *Remote Control: New Media Ethics* (Kingston 2003). Kingston encouraged contributors to follow guidelines that covered the core issues of truth, honesty, accuracy, accountability, fairness and respect, which are embedded in all journalists' codes of ethics.

Her contributor's policy included a policy on anonymity (accountability), disclosure of affiliations (conflict of interest), plagiarism (honesty and accuracy), truthfulness (accuracy) and respect (fairness).

In August 2005, after her relationship with the *Sydney Morning Herald* ended, Kingston moved to a new portal—WebDiary: Independent, Ethical, Accountable and Transparent—where she changed the format away from blogging and her single editorial or authorial voice, and handed the site over to an editorial team who moderated reader's comments on the site:

> What was once 'an open conversation' between Margo and her readers has become an open conversation between the readers, based on articles written by readers (and from time to time by Margo). It isn't really a blog, since there is no single editorial or authorial voice, and it's rare for two entries in a month to come from the same Webdiarist. The mission remains as set out by Margo in the Webdiary Charter. (Webdiary 2010)

The change from blog to WebDiary Pty Ltd, along with the appointment of a board, enabled the site managers to have more editorial control over the discourse and to exclude offensive and abusive comments (Kingston 2005):

> Another thing that distinguishes Webdiary from a blog is the ongoing attempt to keep conversations and debates on the site relatively civil, at the same time as censoring as little as possible. This ongoing balancing act is maintained by a team of volunteer editors who check each submitted comment before publication. The rules they work by are set out in the following statements:
>
> - Webdiary Ethics
> - Editorial Policy, and
> - Comment Moderation

Today 'Webdiary Ethics' contains Margo Kingston's original 2003 obligations, which proclaim her allegiance to the MEAA/AJA code of ethics: 'I will strive to comply with the Media Alliance codes of ethics, which will be in a prominent position on this site at all times' (Kingston 2005).

In 2006 the following was included to the Editorial Policy of Webdiary:

> Webdiary will not publish comments or host discussion on the following matters:
>
> 1) Denial of the existence of the holocaust
> 2) Allegations that a Western power or powers were behind the attacks on the United States on September 11, 2001
> 3) 'False flag' theories.

Why these three? It isn't just because of the content, but is also because experience of these debates tells us that in fact no debate is possible: the two (or more) sides endlessly repeat the same arguments to which the other side isn't listening. There are plenty of sites around devoted to these subjects where the interminable repetition is welcome: go debate them there. When you're there, remember that the complete lack of any evidence just shows how well the conspiracy is working. Obviously, it can be difficult to draw the line, particularly when debating 9/11, and that can lead to some inconsistencies between editors, but that's life (Webdiary 2006).

Kingston committed to Webdiary being a 'space to which all readers, whatever their views or style, feel safe to contribute' and she has a commitment not to 'publish any material which incites hatred' (Webdiary 2008). Significantly, in 2008 Kingston took on the role of ombudsman to investigate reader's complaints. In August 2008, the following addendum was added to the site at Kingston's request (Webdiary 2008):

> There will be no response to
>
> 1) repeated allegations that have already been investigated and ruled upon or
> 2) complaints from former Webdiarists who have been banned from Webdiary for harassing the editors. (Webdiary 'Webdiary Ethics' 2008)

By 2010, the Webdiary's 'Ethics' had been further modified 'to reflect its independence and the change in the means of Webdiarists' contributions from emails to comments' (Webdiary 2010).

The evolution of this site's code of ethics and Kingston's experience reflects the complexities and challenges the online environment creates for ethical journalistic practice in the new media environment. Where audiences have enormous freedom to participate in media discourse, journalists are compelled to come out from behind their bylines to respond and to defend their journalism.

Conclusion

Technology has acted as an amplifier and accelerator of change in journalism (Deuze 2009: 82) and journalism is increasingly being practised outside of traditional delivery systems (old media) where the fragmentation of news production is further facilitated by outsourcing, subcontracting and offshoring (see the World Press Association of Newspapers Report 2006).

The World Wide Web has thrown open the barriers to the publication of news. In the digital age, the public expects journalists to 'step out from behind articles, defend and discuss them' (Singer & Ashman 2009: 16). Bloggers, user-generated content and new hybrid online news sites are challenging the old news structures. The digital age has transformed, and is continuing to transform, journalism. The rejection of a top-to-bottom approach to news by citizen journalists and citizen journalism websites, and the embracing of a peer-to-peer approach to the communication of news, have opened up new possibilities for journalism in the twenty-first century.

The tension between journalists, their audience, bloggers and citizen journalists in the online environment suggests that journalism is evolving into a more inclusive and therefore stronger fourth (or fifth) power. However, for journalism as a practice to evolve in any meaningful way in this new environment, it must continue to be seen as ethical and develop a new code of practice that embraces the ethical minefield of the new, inclusive journalism environment of the World Wide Web.

The digital revolution provides a platform for the establishment of a new, vibrant, inclusive, democratic exchange of news and information—a new conversation with the promise of reinvigorating journalism in the twenty-first century.

KEY REFERENCES

Deuze, M. (2009). 'Technology and the Individual Journalist: Agency Beyond Imitation and Change'. In Zelizer, B. (ed.) *The Changing Faces of Journalism: Tabloidization, Technology And Truthiness.* London: Routledge Taylor and Francis, 82–98.

Friend, C. & Singer, J. B. (2007). *Online Journalism Ethics: Traditions and Transitions.* New York: M. E. Sharpe.

Goc, N. (2009). '"Bad Mummy"—Kate McCann and the Media'. In Burns, C. (ed.) *Mis/Representing Evil: Evil in an Interdisciplinary Key.* Interdisciplinary Press Fisher Imprints, 169–93.

Scott, M. (2010). 'Quality Journalism and a 21st century ABC'. *The Drum,* 3 September. <www.abc.net.au/news/stories/2010/09/03/3001302.htm>. Accessed 12 November 2010.

WEBSITES

Grog's Gamut: <http://grogsgamut.blogspot.com/>.

EthicNet: Journalism ethics: <http://ethicnet.uta.fi/international/international_principles_of_professional_ethics_in_journalism>.

Webdiary.com: <http://webdiary.com.au/>.

TOOLS 5:

NEW MEDIA AND JOURNALISM PRACTICE

NICOLA GOC

Introduction

Vlog: Short for video blogging. It is a form of blogging in which the medium is video.

Audioblog: A blog that includes audio clips in MP3, AAC or other audio format with brief text descriptions of their content. If the audioblog is made available in a syndication format such as RSS, it is a podcast.

Wiki: A server program that allows users to collaborate in forming the content of a web site. Users edit the content of other users.

IM: Short for instant messaging. Exchanging text messages in real time between two or more people logged into a particular instant messaging (**IM**) service.

Social bookmarking: A system for Web users to store, manage, organise and search for bookmarks of resources online.

As we move into the second decade of the twenty-first century, all professional journalists are expected to have the skills to produce news stories across multiple platforms, at the very least in print and online. Digital media such as blogs, **vlogs**, **audioblogs**, **wikis** and **IM**, and social networks such as Facebook, Twitter and Tagworld, along with podcasts and **social bookmarking** services such as MyWeb, Digg and Furl, have put new demands on journalists and changed the way journalists go about their craft. Professional and citizen journalists alike have been quick to utilise new media tools, particularly blogs, mobile phones and social networking sites to create news.

The internet and mobile technologies are 'at the center of the story of how people's relationship to news is changing. In today's new multi-platform media environment, news is becoming portable, personalized, and participatory' (Purcell et al. 2010). Thirty-three per cent of mobile phone owners now access news on their cell phones, 28 per cent of internet users have customised their home page to include news from sources and on topics that particularly interest them, and 37 per cent of internet users have contributed to the creation of news, commented about it or disseminated it via postings on social media sites such as Facebook or Twitter (Purcell et al. 2010).

The online world has seen journalism become a 24/7 global activity. Journalists are no longer restricted to traditional office hours to contact sources, obtain information, and file and update stories; instead they are expected to post and update stories around the clock.

Multiskilled journalists

Multiskilled: In journalistic terms a journalist who is adept in producing news across multiple media platforms.

Today journalists need to become **multiskilled** in the digital environment, because the future of news consumption, according to several recent studies, is across multiple media platforms. According to a 2010 study by PewInternet and the Project for Excellence in Journalism (Purcell et al. 2010), the overwhelming majority of Americans (92 per cent) use multiple platforms to get their daily news. This study also showed that 75 per cent of people surveyed, from a sample of 2259 adults, who access news online get it forwarded through either email or posts on social networking sites, and half of them forward the news through social networking. The report showed that almost 60 per cent of Americans are getting their news from offline and online news sources and, significantly, that less than 10 per cent of people obtain their news from a single media platform. Nearly half (46 per cent) claimed that on a typical day they obtained news from four to six media platforms. Television is still the biggest source of news, with the internet coming in second.

Facebook

Many journalists, particularly freelance journalists, now use Facebook as a way of profiling their work, and also as a way of cultivating and communicating with sources and their audience. Creating an online identity and cultivating it well on different platforms, using as many social platforms as possible, is increasingly important for journalists.

Facebook managers have recognised these shifts in consumption behaviour, and are now making partnerships with, and providing resources for, news organisations and publishers to more effectively use the platform: 'Most noticeably, you can now see what your Facebook friends have "liked" or "recommended" on sites like CNN or *Washington Post. Washington Post*, for example, has prominently integrated Facebook's social plug-ins into its site for a social news experience' (Purcell et al. 2010). Social networking sites have become important platforms for the delivery of personalised news in the twenty-first century.

Twitter

Tweeting is the latest social networking tool to be taken up by journalists. It is believed that news about the 2008 Mumbai terrorist attacks broke first on Twitter. Journalist Neha Viswanathan said, 'Even before I actually heard of [the attack] on the news, I saw stuff about this on Twitter. People were sending in messages about what they were hearing. There were at least five or six blogs from people who were trapped or who were very close to what happened' (Busari 2009: 1).

The advantage of Twitter is that journalists can quickly provide ongoing succinct updates in real time. While each single tweet is restricted to 140 characters, it is important to note that the individual **tweet** doesn't sit in isolation in a user's Twitter feed—it is surrounded by the context of other tweets, creating a far more comprehensive discourse. News organisations are beginning to think of their Twitter feeds as a separate product, not just a place to push their journalism but to do journalism that is adapted to the Twitter format.

Tweet: The term originally referred to a posting on Twitter, but is now both a noun and a verb.

Twitter is attracting huge audiences. In 2009, for example, David Gregory of the US television show *Meet the Press* had more than 520,000 followers, Rachel Maddow of MSNBC had more than 500,000 followers and the *New York Times*'s David Pogue had more than 300,000 followers (Farhi 2009: 27–8). Farhi says, 'Some well-known news media names now have Twitter followers that are almost as large as the circulation of their newspapers or viewerships of their TV shows' (Farhi 2009: 27).

Court and parliamentary reporters now use Twitter to post breaking news and update stories, though the use of mobile phones and computers inside courts was something unheard of until very recently. In 2010, the Lord Chief Justice for England and Wales allowed journalists to report some court proceedings using Twitter. Until this time, the use of mobile phones in British (and Australian) courts was forbidden. The Lord Chief Justice said the use of an unobtrusive, hand-held, virtually silent piece of modern equipment for the purposes of simultaneous reporting of proceedings to the outside world as they unfold in court is unlikely to interfere with the proper administration of justice. He argued that the most obvious purpose of permitting the use of live, text-based communications would be to enable the media to produce fair and accurate reports of the proceedings. With this ruling, at least in England and Wales, journalists can now use their mobile phones and computers to text and email. This ruling on the use of Twitter in court proceedings was prompted after journalists used Twitter at the bail hearing of WikiLeaks founder Julian Assange to provide updates.

This decision is likely to lead to courts throughout the Commonwealth to allow the use of new media in courtrooms and the creation of a set of guidelines for journalists on the use of social media and internet-enabled laptops in courts of law.

Australian journalism academic Julie Posetti found herself grappling with the legal ramifications of Twitter in late 2010 when she tweeted updates from the Journalist Education Association Conference in Sydney. During a session at which former *Australian* journalist Asa Wahlquist was talking about her experiences of writing for the *Australian*, Posetti paraphrased several of Wahlquist's remarks. Her tweets included: 'Wahlquist: 'Chris Mitchell goes down the Eco-Fascist line' on #climate-change' and 'Wahlquist: 'In the lead-up to the election the Ed in Chief was increasingly telling me what to write.' It was prescriptive' (Hooton 2011: 13). When the editor in chief of the *Australian* saw the tweets, he contacted Wahlquist, who claimed she had been quoted inaccurately and taken out of context. According to Hooton, an audiotape 'appeared to confirm the accuracy of Posetti's reported tweets' (2011: 12). Nevertheless, Mitchell said he would sue Posetti for defamation. Posetti maintained that her tweets were a fair report of a matter of public interest: 'I was tweeting summaries of matters of public interest being discussed in a public forum' (Hooton 2011: 12).

Guardian journalist David Banks argues that in terms of court reporting using Twitter, it is important that journalists have legal guidelines to make sure they retain their defences against libel and contempt. The challenge for journalists is the brevity of tweets. 'Court reporters have defences against charges of contempt of court and an action for libel so long as their reports are fair and accurate. Can they fairly sum up what might be complex legal points in 140 characters?' (Banks 2010). Banks says the use of links, or **Tweetlonger**, might address this, but 'there is a danger of cherrypicking the juiciest moments when tweeting court and possibly producing a report which is not a fair account of proceedings' (Banks 2010).

Tweetlonger: Also known as Twitlonger it is a simple service that allows the posting of messages of more than 140 characters on Twitter. Long Reply is a similar service.

Twitter is also used for gathering information from sources. According to Farhi, Twitter is a 'living, breathing tip sheet for facts, new sources and story ideas' (Farhi 2009: 28). He says it can provide 'instantaneous access to hard-to-reach newsmakers, given that there's no PR person standing between a reporter and a tweet to a government official or corporate executive. It can also be a blunt instrument for crowdsourcing' (Farhi 2009: 28). According to Dan Gillmor, veteran news media blogger and Arizona State University journalism professor, 'Journalists should view Twitter as a "collective intelligence system" that provides early warnings about trends, people and news' (cited in Farhi 2009: 29).

However, Twitter is not without its problems. The 140-character limit means links to websites and articles must be short, and viewers might not know what they are clicking on before they click.

Despite the popularity of Twitter among media organisations and journalists, it may not be the most popular social medium with the public. According to Adam Ostrow, of the online media and review site Mashable, Facebook dominates the social media landscape as the most popular way to share information online. Email comes in second, followed by Twitter and, in last place, MySpace (Ostrow 2010, cited in Harper 2010).

Blogs, social media and RSS

According to a 2009 report, almost 30 per cent of journalists surveyed reported regularly reading five or more blogs to research stories, and nearly 75 per cent followed at least one blog regularly (Johnson 2008a). More than 75 per cent of journalists say they use social media to research stories, and nearly 38 per cent of journalists say they visit a social media site at least once a week as part of their reporting. Almost 19 per cent of journalists receive five or more **RSS** feeds of news services, blogs, podcasts or videocasts every week, and about 44 per cent receive at least one regular RSS feed.

RSS: An acronym most commonly expanded as 'Really Simple Syndication', RSS feeds enable frequently updated content, such as news headlines, news feeds, news stories, excerpts from discussion forums and corporate information, to be delivered to a computer or mobile device as soon as it is published.

New media and the ABC

Managing director of the ABC, Mark Scott, says the 2010 federal election changed the way political journalists go about their craft. He argues that the single most salient aspect of the media coverage of the election was 'the voices of the public being heard more than ever before. The first example is through blogs and the Twitter traffic' (Scott 2010). He adds that the election offered 'a remarkable opportunity to use old tools and new tools to bring the story to the Australian people' (Scott 2010). He acknowledges the 24/7 news cycle and the pressures on journalists today, but believes that the campaign offered 'a depth and richness' through online coverage that was never before available, certainly not at the ABC.

Scott is excited about the possibilities of the internet for news journalism: 'The space is there online to tell the story properly' (Scott 2010). He says the ABC was able to offer more policy and political insights through the ABC website, *The Drum*, than it had ever been able to offer before:

> One of the joys of online is that you have space. Space to run details on every candidate in every seat on Antony Green's election pages. Pendulums and calculators and demographic analysis. Detailed policy briefings. Press conferences available in full. Debates. Archival material. All there for anyone who is interested, anyone who wants it. (Scott 2010)

Scott acknowledges that traditional news organisations need to take heed of what their audiences are saying. He also acknowledges Grog's Gamut's contribution: 'Twitter and the mass of amateur blogs contain many smart people who for some bizarre reason enjoy writing about policy … the media should not scorn these people, they should feed off them for ideas and research (properly acknowledged of course).' He believes the future of news journalism is a closer interaction with audiences. However, he also recognises that this new interaction can be challenging for journalists:

> The blogosphere is no place for the faint-hearted. You know that by reading comments on stories—and they are the ones that got through the moderation process. There is no filter on Twitter. And I expect there will now always be savagery in the criticism of much mainstream media performance, just as most weeks there is robust criticism of the professionals who run out onto sporting fields or those who get elected to office. (Scott 2010)

Ethics in the digital environment

There are many ethical issues surrounding the social media shift and some of these are discussed in Case Study 3. There are significant challenges for journalists in the new interactive online environment, where they are expected to interact with an audience that does not have the same obligations to adhere to a code of practice.

In this new world of digital interaction, the ethical and professional practice of journalism, with its declared emphasis on objectivity and facts, is even more vital, such is the alleged poor quality and unreliable nature of much of the amateur blogosphere (Carlson 2007, cited in O'Sullivan & Heinonen 2008).

Australian political journalist and commentator, Annabel Crabb has spoken candidly about the challenges—and opportunities—for journalists in the new media environment.

Annabel Crabb's new media experience

Annabel Crabb provides an insight into the practice of journalism in the new media environment. Crabb left the *Sydney Morning Herald* in 2010 to become ABC's online political editor. She started working as a journalist before the presence of the internet in newsrooms and is now working at the cutting edge of digital technology. She recalls the introduction of the internet into the newsroom:

> I can remember when my newspaper first got the internet. It was 1998 and I was a cadet, and in the police rounds room, where I worked the 4:00pm til midnight

> shift, there in a corner was the brand spanking new desktop computer which had the internet on it. Just the one terminal, for the whole newspaper, and there it sat, like a freshly-ditched meteorite in a Kalahari camp. Not many of us touched this weird apparatus. Every now and again, senior journos would walk past it and wrinkle their noses. 'I'd like to see it ever give me a story,' and so on.
>
> That was 12 years ago. We get so preoccupied with the threats of the internet that we forget how bizarrely object-dependent we used to be before its invention. When getting hold of a government report meant cycling across town to collect it. Often to pay for it, if you can imagine that. When working on a Sunday meant a total information blackout, with no access to public service information, and when foreign newspapers were inaccessible, apart from the two-week-old *Guardian* which might turn up from time to time on the news floor. (Crabb 2010)

Crabb left newspapers because she says she was witness to the 'internecine warfare' that still rages in newspapers 'around the control of the websites'. She says that at Fairfax it felt as though 'an absurd structural roadblock was obstructing a great company's adaptation to the new media environment', while at the ABC 'a group of enthusiastic executives' were embracing the new terrain with vigour. Today Crabb writes online for The Drum, which had 4.5 million page views in the third quarter of 2010 and The Drum/Unleashed, which had nine million views in the third quarter of 2010.

For Crabb, the mother of two small children, the change to her journalism practice has been significant. She now works from home most of the time and no longer has a 7pm deadline: 'I can write anytime, often late at night,' she says. 'I file directly to my editor … and it can be posted in minutes. I don't even have a desk at the ABC; I just have an iPad with its little keyboard, and I set up wherever I happen to be working' (Crabb 2010).

In the online environment Crabb says she also has much more flexibility in terms of word length:

> My word length is anywhere between three words and 3000. I file when I feel like there's something to say. If it's short, I'll say it on Twitter; my main account, in my own name, has about 24,000 followers and I use it mainly for news, sharing links to stories, comments on news events as they happen, or pointers to especially delicious recipes.

She has a second Twitter account @CrabbTwitsard, which she set up for live tweeting during Question Time at federal parliament. Crabb says she can 'churn out tweets every 20 seconds about how things are going down in the House of Representatives'. She uses this second Twitter, which she admits is for 'hard-core nerds', to gain inspiration for her column: 'I use it as a sort of notebook. I send out the thoughts that first spring to mind, and later I might develop a column of it. The feedback I get during Question Time often gives me ideas I wouldn't have had by myself.' This new interaction with her audience through comments is one of the hallmarks of digital journalism.

Crabb is indeed a model of the new journalist of the digital age. She works across several platforms in old and new media, and regularly provides comment on ABC national and local radio. She is a regular guest on the ABC TV's *Insiders* program and also provides analysis and comment on the ABC 24-hour news channel, ABC News 24.

She is the first to admit she not a tech head, even confessing to once baking an Apple Powerbook in the oven. 'My relationship with information technology hardware is one of intense mutual suspicion,' she admits.

What significant difference has Crabb found working in the online environment? The first things she noticed were the immediacy of reader response and the vigour. In the past, readers incensed or inspired by something a journalist had written or produced did not have the ability to respond instantly. A letter to the editor was the only recourse for a reader. Today, those gatekeepers are absent and readers can respond directly to the journalist and, as Crabb has found, they often do in intemperate language:

> You get the kitchen table response. Straight away. Right in the kisser. 'Make a comment!' suggests the tag at the end of the story. And ABC *Online* readers do. Oh yes, my word, they do. As do the denizens of the Twittersphere. One of the funniest moments I've had was on my first day back at work after the abrupt end to my maternity leave occasioned by the calling of the 2010 election. I raced into Ultimo on Saturday morning, doing my own hair and make-up with the skill and dexterity that only a print journalist can manage, and when I was finished with my live television cross, I found a fusillade of commentary awaiting me on Twitter. 'You will never be taken seriously,' wrote one correspondent in a direct message, 'until you do something about your ridiculous hair.' The correspondent's name, by the way, was @hairy_ballsack. I wanted to reply, but struggled for appropriate words. 'Dear Mr, er, Ball-sack. Thank you for your tweet of 10 minutes ago…' In the end, I maintained what I like to think was a dignified silence. (Crabb 2010)

While Crabb has found being 'publicly shellacked by people who have clearly only half-read your piece, or have never read anything you have written' is one of the challenges of twenty-first century interactive journalism, she admits that what is worse is the readers who have read her article, and 'really quite seriously think you are a loser, and whose argument is so compelling that by the end of it you feel quite obliged to agree'.

Both of these experiences are, as she says, part of the new media landscape. 'It's what happens when the damn system is democratised':

> News journalism as we have known it in the past—a sort of daily feeding-time in which news is distributed to a passive audience at a designated hour and in the order selected by the zookeeper—is over, or well on its way to being so. Audiences are splintered, but demanding. They want new news, and if something complicated has happened, they want instant analysis. Commonly, they want an opportunity to express their own views—not only on the event itself, but on how it has been reported. (Crabb 2010)

News, Crabb says, is no longer about newspapers, journalists or radio bulletins 'delivering a chunk of news, and that being the end of it. It's more likely to be the beginning of something; something you can't much control after pressing "Send". This loss of control is such a hallmark of the new media' (Crabb 2010).

Studies on journalists and social media

Crabb's engagement with the Web reflects the findings of a study of US journalists' views on social media conducted in 2008 by Brodeur and Marketwire. It found that while all journalists surveyed said they actively read and created content online, it was political reporters who created the most online content and social media, particularly blogs. This study also found that over half of reporters surveyed said they spent more than an hour per day with online news sources and blogs, and nearly half (47 per cent) of all technology reporters and over one-third (38 per cent) of political reporters said they blogged as part of their reporting (Johnson 2008b).

When it came to making judgments about the positive and negative influences on their work practices, over half of all reporters from all rounds said social media and blogs were having a positive influence on the editorial direction of reporting and the diversity of reporting, but more than two-thirds of political reporters (77 per cent) and half of lifestyle reporters (53 per cent) said social media had a negative impact on the tone of coverage in their area (Johnson 2008b).

Another study by TEKgroup International and Bulldog Reporter in 2010, that questioned more than 2000 journalists on how they use new media, found that while almost one-third of journalists don't cover blogs, more than one-quarter said they read five or more blogs to research stories and nearly 70 per cent follow at least one blog regularly (TekGroup 2009). The survey was conducted on 11–23 September 2008 and reflects the practices of 2386 respondents, of which approximately 48 per cent were editors or editorial staff and 34 per cent were reporters or writers.

The survey found that more than one-quarter of journalists surveyed said they visit a social media or networking site at least once a week, while more than 44 per cent visit at least once a month. Other findings reflect the ways in which journalists use new media as a way of sourcing information for stories and communicating with sources and the public (TekGroup 2009).

Conclusion

The most significant changes to journalism practice in the past half century have undoubtedly been the introduction of computers into newsrooms and the advent of the World Wide Web. While journalists have always had to adapt to new technologies, today's journalist is faced more than ever with new ways of delivering news and information. To be successful in the digital world, today's journalist has to embrace new technologies across multiple platforms. This is indeed an exciting and challenging time to be working in the news media.

KEY REFERENCES

Busari, S. (2009). 'Tweeting the Terror: How Social Media Reacted to Mumbai.' *CNN*. 27 November. <http://articles.cnn.com/2008-11-27/world/mumbai.twitter_1_twitter-tweet-terror-attacks?_s=PM:WORLD>. Accessed 21 October 2009.

Crabb, A. (2010). 'The End of Journalism as We Know it (and Other Good News)'. ABC. 27 October. <www.abc.net.au/news/stories/2010/10/27/3050027.htm>. Accessed 2 November 2010.

Farhi, P. (2009). 'The Twitter Explosion'. *American Journalism Review*, 31(3), 27–31.

Leach, J. (2009). 'Creating Ethical Bridges from Journalism to Digital News.' *Nieman Reports*. 21 October.

Purcell, K., Rainie, L., Mitchell, A., Resentiel, T. & Olmstead, K. (2010). 'Understanding the Participatory News Consumer'. *Pew Internet.* 1 March. <www.pewInternet.org/Reports/2010/Online-News.aspx?r=1>. Accessed 2 January 2011.

Scott, M. (2010). 'Quality Journalism and a 21st century ABC'. *The Drum*, 3 September. <www.abc.net.au/news/stories/2010/09/03/3001302.htm>. Accessed 12 November 2010.

WEBSITES

Mashable: <http://mashable.com/>

Pew Internet: <www.pewinternet.org/>

The Drum: <www.abc.net.au/thedrum/>

The Drum Annabel Crabb: <www.abc.net.au/thedrum/people/annabelcrabb/>

The Drum Unleashed: <www.abc.net.au/unleashed>

CONCLUSION: THE VIEW FROM HERE: CLOUDING, MEDIATION AND THE END OF PRIVACY

Media is always in the state of becoming.

Upgrading, innovating, reconfiguring to meet societal changes, developing along with the latest technological advancements. Media 2.0, the most recent iteration of media, has this built into its very design because it involves the audience more than ever before, as producers rather than simply consumers, and in so doing gives us all the potential to be journalists, catching images, posting stories, writing blogs.

In a similar way, a book such as this can't really conclude, not in the sense of coming to a final word on the subject of media and journalism. We are dealing with dynamic professions that are on the frontline of global societal change. Anything can happen in the future—and probably will.

What we have done is offer you new approaches to understanding what is out there. We have provided you with theoretical tools to understand how to make the best of the Media 2.0 environment, whether you want to be a producer, a consumer or a prosumer. We have provided you with an active, practical and transferable skill set referred to as journalism that can be used across a number of media platforms and contexts. We have offered a range of contemporary and historical case studies and contexts that show these tools and skills in action. We have offered new models for media industries by comparing television to a zoo and interrogating what it means for film to be an art form, and offered new insights into the many forms convergence can take, the hierarchy of celebrity and the utility of postmodernity. For those of you who want more, you can find more new approaches to assessments, tutorial content and media in our online supplement to all of the chapters, tools and case studies on the website accompanying this book. Like media, this too will always be in a state of becoming, with regular updates and new additions over the coming months.

What we can also offer you is the view from here, a view looking back over where media and journalism have come from and a view looking forward, with some helpful ways for you to navigate through whatever the future holds. One of our goals with this book is to arm you with the theoretical knowledge and practical tools for a career in media. We want you to go forward with confidence and a determination to make sense of the media world you will inhabit, whether as a journalist, screenwriter, director, games designer, actor, blogger or some other public figure.

At the conclusion of Ridley Scott's seminal science fiction film, *Blade Runner* (1982), Rick Deckard (Harrison Ford) has a final confrontation with his nemesis, the replicant (android) Roy Batty (Rutger Hauer) high atop a dilapidated building. Instead of fighting him, Batty, his life drawing to an end, calmly sits down and delivers a monologue that has since become famous for film scholars and screenwriters:

> I've seen things you people wouldn't believe. Attack ships on fire off the shoulder of Orion. I watched C-beams glitter in the dark near the Tannhauser gate. All those moments will be lost in time, like tears, in rain …

We do not know what C-beams are, or the nature of the attack ships off Orion, or where the Tannhauser gate is located. We don't have to, to understand the loss that Batty (and Deckard) are feeling, or the awesome sense of history and progress that has brought them to this point.

The history of media and journalism are similarly marked by such moments, some of which we have shared with you in this book, memories of productions and papers and events that may seem as far removed from you now as C-beams and attack ships. Many more are archived on YouTube or fansites or referred to (often incorrectly) on Wikipedia. Each, in its own way, is important to being able to understand where these disciplines come from … and where they are going.

This book is littered with contemporary examples of media change—from Wikileaks to tweets from Iran, from the transcendant YouTube celebrity of Justin Bieber to the postmodern challenges of *Glee*—each of these examples reminds us of the enormous technological changes and pressures driving media and journalism ever forward. Our book has taken you from the beginnings of print media, when single sheets of news were handed out on street corners, to a world of global media and technological revolution, which has taken human communication to levels that were unimaginable just a few decades ago. Every day the possibilities for what media can do and the definition of what it means to be a journalist continually blur and change.

Here, through an examination of what it is to be a journalist or a media practitioner—and what that means for the world, both past and present—we have brought together an overview of media and journalism in all of their forms, with the aim of providing a better understanding of the role and impact media and journalism have had and continue to have on society. We have sought to explore the relationships between journalism and the broader media, and by doing so, have tried to expose the often complex and dynamic interconnections between the two. We have, for example, seen how news journalism influences novels and screenplays, think of the many films that feature journalists as their lead characters and draw upon the news media for their plots, from *Superman* and *Smallville* to the representations of real-life characters such as Truman Capote (*Capote, Infamous*) and Edward G. Murrow (*Good Night, and Good Luck*). We have also examined how the world of entertainment is represented through news journalism in front-page or leading news stories about actors and celebrities (think of Lady Gaga, Charlie Sheen or Angelina Jolie).

In this book we have also tried to draw together theory and practice in a way that aims to inform all of you, whether you have an ambition to practise journalism in its various forms or to work in the media, from the budding Walkley Award-winning journalist, to the latest public relations guru, to the documentary filmmaker or movie producer, to those who wish to analyse and interpret what it is that journalists and those working in the media do, and how this has an impact on society in the twenty-first century, to the future media analysts, media advisers to government or big business, or public policy developers, researchers and teachers.

We have seen how the Fourth Estate has evolved from debates in the forums and agoras of the ancient world, through to the creation of *corantos*, then newspapers, and much later, radio and television, to the advent in the late twentieth century of the World Wide Web and the attendant unlimited possibilities for communication, production and distribution, perhaps best represented by WikiLeaks. Now we communicate with each other and receive news and information and are entertained—and entertain ourselves—interactively while we are in the office or at the beach through laptop computers, iPods and mobile phones. We play games, watch movies and television shows, and listen to music on these devices while we go about our daily lives. We access the latest news online, whenever we want, wherever we are, through our computers or on our phones through news-text messages, video-streamed news bulletins and the latest apps. We are J-bloggers and citizen journalists, commentators, bloggers, spruikers, prosumers and entertainers, providing the global world with news and information and entertainment live on blogs, YouTube and Facebook. Instant global communication is at the fingertips of those of us with access to the technology. Social media connect us to people we may not have wanted to see again after high school, helps rescue workers find suvivors in the wake of natural disasters and rallies activists in pursuit of democracy in the Middle East. Suddenly, for the first time in history, we all have the ability to be media practitioners.

It is a great time to be studying media and journalism, but what does it mean in practice?

In this exciting, transforming, technological revolution, the role of journalists and journalism is changing. WikiLeaks has shown us that the Fourth Estate is transforming into a Fifth Estate, providing news and information in formats that often have little semblance to the old static forms of journalism. Back on 1–2 May 2008, the MEAA and the Walkley Foundation hosted a summit on the future of journalism at the ABC's Eugene Goossens Hall in Ultimo, New South Wales. Among the topics canvassed were the decline in readerships of newspapers, particularly in the USA and Europe, and the even greater decline in advertising revenue. This latter decline has led to serious concerns that without classified advertising newspapers might not be able to afford to pay journalists' salaries.

The reason for both these declines was identified as being the migration of readers and advertisers to the internet. Mike van Niekerk, from Fairfax, has argued that the only way old media companies can survive into the future is through diversification, that is, working across different media platforms; newspapers alone would no longer be enough to sustain them.

The major problem highlighted here, as noted by ABC *Media Watch*'s Jonathan Holmes ('Wired for the Future', 5 May 2008) is that 'there's no obvious substitute for the newspaper business model when it comes to funding quality journalism', that is, there is simply no comparable way through online delivery to afford the hundreds of journalists currently employed at newspapers. One of the major questions for the future of journalism is a purely economic one: how to get money from readers for news websites. As *Guardian* media columnist and commentator Roy Greenslade notes:

> In the future there will be advertising, it won't be enough to fund huge staffs as there are now, but we'll have a core of professional journalists. We can fund them and then, in company—in participation with journalists, bloggers, user-generated content, however you want to describe that, amateur journalists … will form a different kind of approach to journalism. (interview with *Media Watch*, 5 May 2008)

The flow-on effects of this economic change are two-fold. First, news corporations will increasingly rely on amateur journalists, from citizen journalists to J-bloggers. This was seen first-hand during the run of natural disasters at the beginning of 2011, from the flooding in Queensland to the earthquake and tsunami in Japan, where images captured on mobile phones, tweets and blogs provided the most confronting, illuminating and often informative representations of what was occurring.

Second, there are already indications that the most popular news stories online are soft rather than hard news, moving the mediasphere ever closer to the dissemination of entertainment and identity-based stories, that is, celebrity culture rather than information. The antics of Charlie Sheen, the royal wedding between Prince William and Kate Middleton and the ever-changing fashions and actions of Lady Gaga have all received the most attention on online sites. In the face of these changes it becomes imperative that journalists understand and become aware of the broader mediasphere and their changing place within it. For while the future of journalism may remain unknown, what is still certain is that wherever individuals acknowledge the importance of free speech, and are committed to respecting the truth and the public's right to information, journalism will survive.

Here are three recent elements that demonstrate how the mediasphere is changing and will be impacting on media and journalism in the future.

The first is clouding. If you have used webmail services such as Yahoo! Mail, Gmail or Hotmail, or you have stored your photos and videos online, if you have used Facebook and other social networking sites, or if you have used applications such as Google Documents or Adobe Photoshop Express, then you have participated in cloud computing. Cloud computing is a system through which your personal information is transmitted, processed and stored by a third party. Today, computer users rely heavily on clouding. Some examples are Amazon's Simple Storage Service, Elastic Computing Cloud to store unlimited photos on the online photo service, SmugSmug and others, using Google Apps for word processing, virtual worlds such as Second Life that enable users to build 3D environments combining Web pages and Web applications (Cavoukian: 2009: 6). According to Correy (2008): 'All our stuff which we imagine is held in that black box under our desk will in fact be in China somewhere, or America, or Europe'. Cloud computing means that when you are using internet browsers you are 'taking information off your laptop, off your desktop computer, out of your office, out of your home or apartment and putting it into giant data centres owned by Google and others' (Correy 2008).

Significantly, most internet users are unaware of cloud computing and do not realise that they have little involvement in or control over their stored personal data. No longer do you have autonomy over the data on your personal computer. Clouding has significant implications in terms of privacy, ownership and copyright, so how will we as individuals control our personal data in the future? Indead, who will have control of our data? Many large organisations, including universities, are already using cloud storage. With the personal computer, a users' privacy and security was largely assured by restricting physical access to the stand-alone computing devices and storage media. Now users' personal information is stored away from their control, often without their knowledge. Carr argues that personal data that is being supplied through cloud computing can be

> extremely sensitive information in that when you aggregate it, you have it in one central place, you get a very clear view of a person's behaviour, a person's interests, even a person's motivations, and the danger is that corporations or even governments, can begin to tap into these central stores of information and use them in ways that should make us uncomfortable, whether it's monitoring what we do, or manipulating us for commercial ends. (Carr 2008)

Cloud storing has implications not only for privacy, but also for the practice of journalism. WikiLeaks currently relies on whistleblowers to pass on documents, but in the future whistleblowers, or journalists themselves, may be able to access large amounts of citizens' personal data. Information is a commodity and in the future unscrupulous media organisations may buy an individual's personal data without their knowledge or permission. In repressive regimes the potential risk to dissidents is obvious. The issues around clouding and privacy and sourcing information have yet to be adequately addressed. According to Cavoukian (2009: 26) 'The brave new world of clouding computing offers many benefits provided that privacy and security risks are recognised and effectively minimised' (2009: 26).

The second example of the changing mediasphere is an increase in a term we already considered earlier in this volume, but which is increasingly significant in all aspects of our lives, mediation. There has long been debate (modern, postmodern and the like) over the relationship of media and journalism to reality, and it is a debate that we have rehearsed in these very pages. But it seems that the world is becoming more and more mediated. As the mediasphere continues to consume much of our public sphere and our waking time, and now that we all have access to the tools of production, our lives are themselves tending to turn into media products. We can score our days with our iPods. We can build our own documentaries on web pages with webcams. We can publish and distribute our own opinion pieces online. Screenwriters and game designers are now encouraged to think of narratives in terms of worlds rather than stories and with many of us colonising these new worlds, the mediasphere is increasingly becoming the new frontier. Facebook statuses and tweets increasingly make us the stars of our own lives and, when the rest of the world starts to notice (cue: Justin Bieber), we can actually move up that hierarchy of celebrity.

In late 2010–11 two films, both contenders for Best Picture at the 2011 Academy Awards, highlighted the increasing importance of mediation as part of communication practice. The first, *The King's Speech* (2010, dir. Tom Hooper), explores the challenges that the stammering newly crowned King of England, George VI (Colin Firth), faces when forced to use the then relatively new medium of radio in 1939 to make an important speech to his subjects following Britain's declaration of war with Germany. Thanks to the services of an unorthodox Australian speech therapist, Lionel Logue (Geoffrey Rush), the king successfully makes the speech, and many more during the course of the conflict. But the film often laments the need for mediation, with King George V (Michael Gambon) noting that:

> In the past all a King had to do was look respectable in uniform and not fall off his horse. Now we must invade people's homes and ingratiate ourselves with them. This family is reduced to those lowest, basest of all creatures, we've become actors!

More particularly, the dangers of mediation are highlighted when the Royal Family is watching a newsreel of Adolf Hitler speaking at a rally in Germany. King George VI admits he can't understand what Hitler is saying but 'he seems to be saying it rather well'. Of course, it was Hitler's consummate skill in using media that assisted him in his rise to power.

The second film, *The Social Network* (2010, dir. David Fincher), referred to earlier, explores the founding of Facebook (commencing in 2003) and the subsequent lawsuits served on Mark Zuckerberg (Jesse Eisenberg) by his co-founders. Even more than *The King's Speech*, the film uses a real historical event to provide an examination of how mediation has increasingly become our only form of communication, with Zuckerberg continually depicted as being unable to communicate, with his girlfriend, his friends and his colleagues, without his computer. At the end of the film, he is alone and forced to settle because he will be unsympathetic to a jury, trying to reconnect with the girlfriend who dumped him at the beginning of the film by sending her a friend request on Facebook and refreshing the page over and over again.

Both films feature lonely and isolated protagonists who, despite their ages being over 70 years apart, are both increasingly reliant on media to communicate. In so doing they highlight the problems with that reliance, as the mediasphere continues to grow. When King George VI complains that:

> If I'm King, where's my power? Can I form a government? Can I levy a tax, declare a war? No! And yet I am the seat of all authority. Why? Because the nation believes that when I speak, I speak for them. But I can't speak

he may be referring to his stammer. But in part he is also referring to a need to understand how to speak through media, how to use media to communicate. He is speaking to the inexorable rise of mediation that will ultimately lead to the development of social-networking sites.

It seems a given that such mediation is always in the service of communication. Indeed, we define media in this book as being the mechanisms of communication. But could there be a time when rather than simply enabling us to communicate, media will actually communicate for themselves? On Thursday, 10 February 2011, *Time*, in an article written by Lev Grossman, provocatively entitled '2045: The Year Man Becomes Immortal', reported on the technological singularity theory. While it may sound more like the futures envisioned in *The Matrix*, *Battlestar Galactica* or *Terminator* franchises, the technological singularity theory postulates a time when, based on the accelerating pace of change and the exponential growth in the power of computers, technology will surpass humanity, thereby creating superhuman intelligence. While opinions differ on when or even if this will occur such an idea carries profound implications for media for, as we have seen throughout this book and in the filmic examples above, the evolution of media is inextricably linked to the evolution of technology. If the technological singularity, or even something approximating it, were to occur, Media 2.0 provides us only a hint of what is to come. The lines between media, technology and humanity would blur to the point that they would become indistinguishable. The reality is that mediation is already an indelible part of the human experience; rightly or wrongly we can no longer function as individuals or as a society without media. As Sean Parker (Justin Timberlake) puts it in *The Social Network*: 'We lived on farms, then we lived in cities, and now we're going to live on the internet!' This will only become more pronounced in the future.

The third example of the changing mediasphere is something that touches on both clouding and increasing mediation—the erosion of privacy. With so much of our lives being lived online or on a screen there has been a commensurate loss of the private sphere; indeed, wearable media has made such a space virtually (pun intended) non-existent. By way of example, 23 exabytes of information is recorded and uploaded to the web weekly and Google street view is in the process of photographing the entire planet. Even Facebook's new privacy settings make profile information and photos public by default. But while privacy advocates have long raised concerns about this perceived loss of privacy, online advocates trumpet this as an evolution in connectivity, borne out by Google's assistance in finding survivors in the wake of natural disasters and the aforementioned use of social networking to organise mass democratic change movements in, say, the Middle East. In March 2011, the ABC television series *Hungry Beast* conducted a privacy survey. Among its findings were that eighty-two per cent of respondents (over 10.7 million Australian adults) are members of at least one social networking site; one in three children under 18 are also members of social networking sites. Seventy-seven per cent of respondents said they had adjusted the privacy settings on their social networking sites. That said, over fifty per cent said they had posted comments on what they were doing at any given moment along with their marital or relationship status. Such findings suggest that the very concept of privacy may be changing. In an era when the possibilities of celebrity and fame are more attractive than ever and every life is considered worthy of online dissemination, privacy itself appears to be in danger of becoming outdated, a value of the past. Celebrity has taught audiences that self-transformation is possible. In a similar way the audiences of the future may transform themselves, that is, change their names, create new identities, to escape the online sins of their past.

A major support structure for navigating current and future changes throughout the mediasphere remains an ability to grasp the most basic element of media and journalism: language. It is useful to be aware of a distinction between the creative evolution of the language and the destructive erosion of the language; no matter what violence is being done to our dominant means of communication, there will still be a place for efficient and careful communication in the information-based professions. A fluke of evolution has given humans the capacity for language. Whatever whistles and clicks and grunts other creatures use to communicate with each other, miraculous as these are in themselves, only humans form words, sentences and paragraphs, and from these, media such as books, journal articles, newspaper columns, and, with more dubious benefits, political slogans, fast food menus and Blu-Ray instruction manuals.

As far back as the 1940s, George Orwell was warning us about the risks of allowing language to degrade to the point where abstract concepts, including ideas of political dissent, become difficult or even impossible to express. While the process of systematic and deliberate corruption of the language that created what Orwell called Newspeak in his novel *Nineteen Eighty-Four* is not exactly what we have to fear now, we do need to ensure that denizens of the public sphere are not, by either neglect or agency, faced with difficulty in manoeuvring a language that has lost its capacity for fine nuance and has therefore turned to slush. There is an argument that some forms of new media have slush-creating potential, a destructive erosion rather than a creative evolution, but we do not need to accept this process as inevitable.

It is an old-fashioned notion these days, but many professional writers remain interested in standards. Standards matter. As that great exponent of clear English writing, Clive James, once wrote, 'If you lose the language, you lose everything'. This statement has a rhetorical flourish, but there is a lot of truth in it. We would even suggest that it goes to the heart of who we are as people. Our capacity for language is one of the defining characteristics of humanness; it is one of the reasons we should not just see ourselves simply as naked apes, essentially the same as our simian relatives. We are different; we have language. We have the capacity, not always realised, for ethics and morals. We can make choices about how to behave, rather than blindly follow a set of base instincts. We can speculate, verbally, about the past and the future, and consider the concept of death. We can see this reflected in our greatest pieces of media, in the films that move us, the television series that make us think, the music that defines a moment of our lives, the newspaper article that reveals a new facet of the world.

It is this capacity for language that has also given us belief systems, another human characteristic, probably an inevitable consequence of the abstract thinking essential for language. Language is the primary way by which we project from our internal, subjective world into the wider external world. That bridge between the inner and outer worlds is tenuous, and can create any number of potential barriers and pitfalls. Imprecise language use is one of them.

Abusing semantics by, for example, detaching meaning from words is downright dangerous, and in these dangerous times we need more than ever to be clear about what we mean.

A professional communicator can go a long way with a fine appreciation for language and a facility for its use. Language is a precision instrument that you can wield to your advantage. Think about your words. In many of the communication professions these are the main things you are being paid for. Whatever may come in the future, this fact is unlikely to change.

Be aware that whatever work you do in the mediasphere matters. Any form of media, from the comic strip to the film, the newspaper column to the advertisement, has the capacity to carry meaning and therefore make change. When the news media were rallying behind US President George W. Bush in the opening days of the war on Iraq, it was left to popular media, to films as disparate as *Batman Begins* and *War of the Worlds*, television series such as *Boston Legal* and *Battlestar Galactica*, and comics such as *The Ultimates* to step into the breach and comment on the erosion of civil liberties, the justness of war and the power of fear. More recently television series such as *V* have commented on the Obama regime and *Glee* has spoken out against homophobia and bullying in schools. Sometimes you may just want to make the bloodiest, scariest zombie film with a few mates and a bottle of tomato sauce—and that's OK too. But always remember the capacity for media to make critical comment and to enact change. After all, even the granddaddies of zombie movies, *Romero's Night, Dawn* and *Day of the Dead*, offered insightful and satirical commentaries on racism and consumerism.

Thanks to Media 2.0 we are all part of this same mediasphere, part of a conversation that has been running since we first learnt to communicate with one another on a plain or in a cave somewhere in Africa. So go on. Put the book down and go out there. Make your own moments. Add to the conversation. We wish you well.

GLOSSARY

10BA Cycle of Films:
A group of Australian films produced in the 1980s, assisted by the 10BA tax scheme, introduced in 1981, that provided generous tax relief for film investors. The films spanned a number of genres (horror, exploitation and action) and were particularly commercial, stylistically imitative of Hollywood and more focused on the US film market than providing any quintessential depictions of Australianness.

A movie:
In a double bill at a movie theatre, the feature attraction, made with higher budgets and well-known stars.

ABC:
The Australian Broadcasting Corporation (the Australian Broadcasting Commission from 1932 until 1983); Australia's public broadcaster, which is funded by the federal government rather than advertising.

Absolute privilege:
Complete immunity from the laws of defamation based on the principle of open justice that allows the courts and the parliaments to function in a fearlessly independent manner.

Actuality:
Location sound, which may sometimes be an interview with talent, and in some newsrooms is used interchangeably with *grab*.

Address:
The way the text hails us, calls us over or otherwise demands our attention.

Addressee:
The audience implied by being addressed.

Addresser:
The position that is actively attracting us to the text.

Agenda setting:
The way the media determine what will be communicated as news to influence what audiences think about and discuss.

Agora:
An open space in a town where people gather, especially a marketplace in ancient Greece.

Alternative knowledge structures:
Knowledges derived from the consideration of multiple, parallel, competing, dissenting and often minority viewpoints.

Analogue technology:
The transmission and storage of electronic information via continuous waves, especially in recordings and radio signals and along telephone wires.

Analysis:
Examination in detail of the elements of something in order to determine how the whole functions.

Anchorage:
The tying down of an image text (through a caption) or a written text (through a headline) to a certain meaning.

Anecdote:

A vignette or brief word picture that describes an incident, which is often used to illustrate the main theme of a journalistic feature.

Anime and manga:

Styles of Japanese animation and comic books, covering a wide variety of genres, and often appealing equally to adults and children; *manga* often provides the basis for *anime* productions.

Antenna:

The device used to send or receive electromagnetic signals, a crucial part of radio and television? broadcasting.

Audience identification:

Encouraging audiences to adopt the viewpoint and share in the emotions (especially hopes and fears) of a character in the text.

Audience networks:

Where audience members themselves access media texts through links with other audience members, replacing the broadcast one-to-many media networks.

Audioblog:

A blog that includes audio clips in MP3, AAC or other audio format with brief text descriptions of their content. If the audioblog is made available in a syndication format such as RSS, it is a podcast.

Auteur theory:

From the French *auteur*, meaning author; at its most basic, it is the theory that a film has an author, just as a book does, and the author of a film is its director. In its more complex variations, it is a theoretical tool that concedes while it is impossible for there to be a unitary author of a film, given the number of people who contribute to its making, it is still possible to analyse individuals' ability to leave some form of distinctive style or signature on what is essentially an industrial product.

Authenticity:

The way in which media try to represent ideas or situations as near as possible to how they occur in reality—the principal aim of journalism.

Avatar:

An online construct that allows a member of a virtual community to transcend age, gender, race or geography, and make a fluid new identity.

B movie:

In a double bill at a movie theatre, the supporting or second feature, made with lower budgets and lesser-known stars.

Backgrounder:

Material provided in addition to a media release, consisting of more detailed information than the release and providing journalists with a range of new angles.

Bankability:

The ability of a celebrity to make a guaranteed profit for his or her employer; a bankable Hollywood star can make a film succeed on the strength of his or her name alone.

Berliner:

A compact newspaper measuring 470 mm × 315 mm, which has become a popular newspaper format in recent years.

Bill of rights:

Legislation, through parliament or a clause in the Constitution, that guarantees citizens a legal right to certain freedoms.

Bingeing:

The watching of a succession of television episodes in one sitting.

Blockbuster film:

A very costly film that the studio hopes will make a profit as a result of the enormous amounts of money spent on publicity and wide distribution.

Blog:

An online journal comprising links and postings; both a noun and a verb with various inflections, such as 'blogger' and 'blogging'. Its origin is 'weblog', a regular online journal.

Brand:

A name, person, sign, character, colour, font, slogan, catch-phrase or any combination of these that operates as the signifier of a particular product, service or business. A legally protected brand is called a trademark. A brand is a perfect example of metonymy and an aspiration for many celebrities.

Bricolage:

(From the French for *striking together*); the intersection of a variety of styles to create something new.

Broadband:

Currently the most advanced form of internet access, offering high-speed access and wide bandwidth, transmitted via telephone, cable and wireless services, which has almost entirely replaced dial-up.

Broadcast:

The transmission of knowledge (ideas and information) in the widest possible circles. It can operate as a verb: to broadcast; a noun: a television broadcast; and as an adjective: a broadcast program.

Broadsheet:

Historically, a cheap single page of entertaining news, usually crime or sensationalised accounts of disasters and a precursor to the newspaper. By the 1860s, cheap newspapers had largely taken their place. Today, broadsheet refers to a large format newspaper (in Australia, generally 841 mm × 594 mm). In some countries, including Australia, broadsheet newspapers are commonly perceived to contain more quality or in-depth journalistic reporting than their tabloid counterparts.

Broadside:

A precursor to the newspaper, cheap single pages of entertaining news, usually crime or sensationalised accounts of disasters. By the 1860s, cheap newspapers had largely taken their place.

Canon:

The set of texts regarded as forming the essence of a particular body of work.

Carriage:

Those industries responsible for distributing media content.

Celeactor:

A fictional character who has both a private and public life, and exists independently of his or her creator; for example, Dame Edna Everage.

Celebrity:

The familiar stranger (Gitlin): a celebrity is simultaneously a text and an industry.

Celebrity culture:

A culture based on the individual and individual identity; for example, news that consists mainly of gossip, scandal or snippets from celebrities' PR handouts, or where social issues are constantly reframed as personal issues.

Celebrity image:

The image of the celebrity as it appears in the media, a construction designed to connote the ideas and values of the celebrity.

Celetoid:

A celebrity created to fill a gap in an industry, or for some specified purpose (such as reality show winners).

Chatroom:
A site on a computer network where online conversations are held in real time by a number of users.

Chequebook journalism:
Journalism that involves the payment of money to a source for the right to publish or broadcast information.

Churnalism:
A term coined by British journalist Nick Davies to describe the way media rely on media releases, public relations and wire copy for most content.

Cinematography:
The industrial process of shooting, manipulating and developing film.

Citizen journalist:
A member of the public who acts in the role of a journalist gathering news and new information (including images), which are communicated to an audience.

Civil action:
A court case relating to disputes between two parties.

Civil law system:
The legal systems based primarily on the interpretation of statutory codes, such as those existing in much of Europe (as opposed to systems based on the doctrine of precedent, such as the UK common law system).

Closed questions:
Questions whose answers are limited to yes, no, or similar precise information.

Closed texts:
Texts that focus on a specific meaning and permit little space for the reader to generate a variety of interpretations.

Cloud, clouding, cloud computing
A system through which personal information is transmitted, processed and stored and over which the individual has little knowledge, involvement, or control.

Code of ethics:
A set of rules prescribing the ethical practices that all members of a profession should follow.

Codes:
Usually parts of the signs that make up texts; including such elements as colour, dress, lighting, angles, words used and format on the page.

Commodification of news:
The view that news is a commodity that can be valued, and bought and sold like any other good in the market place, reflecting the globalisation and deregulation of news.

Commodity:
An economic good; in relation to celebrities, it refers to someone who is subject to ready exchange or exploitation within a market.

Common law system:
The basic structure of law in Australia, based on a combination of the decisions that judges make according to statute; and case law, meaning precedents set by earlier judgments in higher courts.

Commutation:
The replacement of one element of a text with another to see how this affects how meaning is made.

Computer-assisted reporting (CAR):
Internet research by journalists, involving deep analysis of databases using spreadsheets and database managers.

Confidential sources:

People who provide—while keeping their identities secret—important information that might otherwise not be available to the public.

Conflict:

A state of opposition or hostilities. In the context of judgements about what makes news, this might be a significant violent conflict like a war or a non-violent conflict such as a disagreement.

Connotations:

The possible signifieds that attach to a signifier.

Consequentialism:

A branch of ethical philosophy in which notions of morality are based not on a set of rules but on observing the outcomes, the consequences, of every separate action. Consequentialists weigh up the consequences and decide where the majority of the benefit lies.

Consumerist model:

Under the consumerist model the manufacture of news is profit driven; news is seen primarily as a business enterprise, with news as a commodity.

Contact book:

An electronic or hard copy listing of journalistic sources of information, often with notations to update the information. Journalists refer to their contact book regularly when seeking comment for stories.

Contempt of court:

Any action with the potential to damage a fair trial.

Content:

The subject of the text, and how that subject is presented to us.

Content analysis:

Analysis that focuses on the frequency of the presence or absence of words or categories within texts.

Content providers:

Media industries that actually produce content, which is then distributed by the carriers.

Content words:

Nouns, verbs, adjectives and adverbs; the words that supply substance in the English vocabulary.

Context:

The location of the text; the point in time and space where an audience will locate it.

Convergence:

The coming together of what were once separate media texts and industries.

Conversationalisation of news:

The way the language of news is structured to mirror ordinary conversation; blurring the boundary between the public and private and reflecting the fact that while most news is public in nature, much of it, especially broadcast and online news is consumed in private domains like lounge rooms.

Copyright:

The exclusive right, granted by law for a period of time, to control the publishing and copying of a particular publication or artistic work. It does not protect ideas, but only the material form of those ideas.

Coranto:

The earliest predecessor of the newspaper, a *coranto* was a small news pamphlet that was only produced when a newsworthy event occurred. From the Spanish *coranto* (runner); that is, fast-delivered news.

Creative commons licensing:

A form of licensing that encompasses the spectrum of possibilities between full copyright (all rights reserved) and the public domain (no rights reserved). Creative commons licences help owners keep their copyright while inviting certain uses of the owner's work—a some rights reserved copyright.

Criminal action:
A court case brought by the state against somebody who has committed a crime.

Cross-media ownership:
The ownership of one major source of news and information (such as a television station) in the same territory as another other major source (such as a daily newspaper or radio station).

Cross-promotion:
The promotion by celebrities, programs and industries of other celebrities, programs and industries that have the same owner.

Cultural competency:
Knowledge and ideas that are gained from experience; cultural knowledge is insider knowledge that is known only by people within a particular culture or by people who have learned about the culture through interaction with that culture.

Cultural convergence:
The intersection of cultures: locally, nationally and globally.

Cultural currency:
The knowledge we acquire from consuming media.

Cultural product:
A product that contains meanings, values and ideas; that is, a product that functions as a form of communication.

Culture jamming:
Resistance to cultural hegemony by means of guerrilla communication strategies such as graffiti, satire or some other reappropriation of the original medium's iconography to comment upon itself. It differs from other forms of artistic expression or vandalism in that its intent is to subvert mainstream culture for independent communication or otherwise disrupt mainstream communication.

Currency of news:
The impact of recent and breaking news arising from controversial and emotionally charged events.

Current affairs:
The news media's delivery of political and social events or issues of the present time, usually on television or radio.

Cut and paste:
The transfer of information, by a journalist, from a PR release to a news item, without the application of journalistic editing skills or judgment.

Cyberspace:
The notional realm in which electronic information exists or is exchanged; the imagined world of virtual reality.

Damages:
An amount of money awarded by a court as a remedy in a civil action.

Defamation:
The reduction of the reputation of another person in the minds of ordinary people, by exposing that person to ridicule, or by causing them to be shunned and avoided.

Delay:
The way in which consumption of television is indefinitely postponed through advertising, narrative or scheduling.

Delivery platforms:
The ability of media to act as platforms for the delivery of media texts.

Demographic analysis:
Statistical analysis of audiences, based upon selected population characteristics such as age, gender, race, sexuality, income, disability, mobility, education, employment status and location; showing distributions of values within a demographic variable and changes in trends over time.

Denotation:
The most likely connotation of a signifier, often determined as a matter of common sense or by looking at the relationship of the text to other texts or the context in which the text is found.

Deontology:
Also known as rights-based ethics, it assumes that each individual has certain rights, no matter the circumstances, and that no innocent person should be harmed or killed for any reason.

Détournment:
The reuse of a well-known text to create a new text that often carries a message contrary to the original.

Dialogic:
Descriptive of texts that are structured as dialogue.

Dial-up:
The earliest form of access to the internet, via slow signals sent through a telephone wire.

Diaspora:
The scattering of a population from one geographical area throughout the world.

Digital divide:
The gap between those who can access media technology (thanks to wealth, culture and geographical location) and those who cannot.

Digital technology:
The transmission of electronic information using binary code to store and transmit data, replacing analogue technology.

Discourse:
A way of representing the world.

Discourse analysis:
Analyses how texts support or subvert overall views of the world, such as patriarchy or media power.

Disintermediation:
The removal of wholesalers, distributors and retailers (the middle men) from the intermediary processes, so manufacturers can deliver products directly to consumers.

Disobedience contempt:
The refusal by journalists to reveal their sources when asked by a court to do so.

Disposable celebrity:
A celebrity manufactured on a production line in order to be replaced in the near future by the next disposable celebrity.

Docugames:
Interactive reality games where players are involved in role-play scenarios that are based on real events. They blend reality with interactive entertainment by allowing the player to control and alter historical figures and events. Throughout the game there are links to articles and interviews from or about the real event.

Documentary film:
A fact-based film that depicts actual events and people.

Domestication of texts:
The adaptation by individuals and local media cultures of global texts.

eCommerce:

Business conducted online; internet-based, interactive, networked connections between producers, consumers and service providers.

Embargo:

A notice forbidding release of information about an event before a certain time or date.

Empowered reading:

A reading of media informed by an understanding of how media work, how audiences can be manipulated and the choices being offered to audiences in the larger mediasphere.

Enlightenment:

The period, from about 1500 to about 1800, when feudal, religion-based societies gave way to secularised, democratic societies.

Epistemology:

The use of logic, psychology, philosophy and linguistics to study knowledge and how it is processed by humans.

Ethics:

A system of moral principles, by which a person can judge right and wrong in any field; for example, media ethics.

Euphemism:

A mild or vague word or phrase that is used instead of a blunt, harsh word.

Evidence:

Signs or proofs of the existence or truth of some proposition; information that helps somebody to reach a particular conclusion, through empirical materials (physical items) and observable phenomena (such as heat or cold).

Exclusivity:

The exclusion of an audience member, as if he or she has been excluded from a certain community.

Exnomination:

The process by which dominant ideas become so obvious they don't draw attention to themselves; instead they just seem like common sense.

Expressive medium:

The notion that film works best by expressing the feelings of the artist, through metaphor, allegory and performance.

eZine:

A magazine that is published in an electronic form.

Facebook:

An online social networking site.

Fan culture:

Term derived from *fanatic*; those people who follow a particular media form, genre or personality with great enthusiasm, for the pleasure of doing so rather than a desire to earn an income.

Fan fiction:

Fiction, written by fans of a particular media text, that features characters from that text.

Fanzine:

An amateur magazine produced for fans of a pastime or celebrity; the concept originated among science fiction fans in the 1930s, spread gradually among other interest groups during the 1960s, and was adopted by a wide range of groups during the last twenty years.

Fifth Estate:

The new media technologies, such as the internet, as modes of news delivery; originally applied to radio and television.

Film genres:
Film categories, such as westerns, mysteries and melodramas, produced in order to keep costs low while building presold audiences.

Film movement:
Groups of films loosely directed towards similar formal or social ends.

Flack:
A term often used to describe PR practitioners; thought to have been formed by melding flak—for flak catcher, someone paid to catch the flak directed at their employer—with hack (a mediocre writer).

Flow:
In television, the way one moment of drama or information leads to the next.

Form:
The shape of the text and the way it appears before us.

Formalist medium:
The notion that film works best by presenting the best possible examples of film styles and techniques (the form).

The Fourth Estate:
Journalists as a group.

Forum:
In ancient Rome, a public square or marketplace where business was conducted and the law courts were situated.

Framing:
A process of selecting and rejecting information in the construction of a news story by placing emphasis on a particular aspect or angle.

Freedom of expression:
For media workers, the fundamental legal right to discover important information and convey it to the public.

Function words:
Conjunctions, prepositions and articles; words that help to show the relationships between content words, thus giving meaning to the substance of the content words.

Gatekeeper:
Media professional, such as a subeditor, who decides which news stories or other types of information will be selected or rejected for public consumption.

Gazette:
One of the earliest forms of a newspaper, including official government information. Named after a *gazetta*, a small coin in the Republic of Venice that was the price of their early news sheets, the name was later applied to many types of newspaper.

Genre:
Categories of texts according to shared narrative and iconographic features and codes, as well as categories of commercial products provided by producers and marketers and expected by audiences of texts.

German expressionism:
A form of filmmaking, developed in Germany, particularly Berlin, during the 1920s, that featured highly stylised sets and symbolic acting to reveal the internal emotional struggles of its protagonists (and society).

Globalisation:
The tendency toward increasing standardisation of life, markets and economies around the world.

Glocalisation:

The transformation of global texts so that they become relevant to local cultures.

Grab:

An excerpt of a journalist's interview with the talent (or source).

Grammar:

The rules of the relationship that words have to one another in a sentence.

Grog's Gamut:

A blog maintained by Australian public servant Greg Jericho. Jericho maintained his anonymity until Australian journalist James Massola outed him during the 2010 federal election.

Hard news:

News stories that aim to inform the community about events and happenings and to provide citizens with the information they require to be able to participate as fully informed citizens in the democratic process.

Hegemony:

The ability of elite groups to acquire and/or remain in power by convincing subordinate groups that it is in their best interests to accept the dominance of this elite.

Home theatre:

Electronic facilities in the home, such as large screens and five-speaker sound systems, that emulate facilities once found only in cinemas and theatres.

Honest opinion:

A defence in defamation; the right to publish opinion and comment so long as it is reasonably and honestly researched, and without malice.

House style:

The particular set of grammatical rules, conventions and organisation preferences chosen by individual publishers and media organisations; usually prescribed in a style guide.

Human interest news:

News stories that revolve around stories of ordinary people, or issues judged to be socially interesting or important.

Hybridity:

The mixture of media cultures to create a multi-origined media.

Hype:

Extravagant and overstated publicity; a contraction of the word hyperbole, which means an exaggerated statement not meant to be taken literally.

Hypertext:

The embedding of links to one internet text from another.

Iconography:

From icon; the most recognisable aspects of a text's form and content, which represent that text; for example, white hats (the good guys) and black hats (the bad guys) in Western movies.

Ideology:

An all-encompassing set of ideas for thinking about the world.

IM (instant messaging):

Exchanging text messages in real time between two or more people logged into a particular instant messaging (IM) service.

Impact:

The size of the consequences of a news story: the greater or wider the consequences of a news story, the greater will be its impact.

Inclusivity:
The inclusion of an audience member, as if he or she belongs to a certain community.

Indigenisation:
The appropriation and reframing of globalised texts to make them relevant to local cultures.

Industrial convergence:
The intersection of a variety of media industries through cross-ownership and cross-promotion.

Infotainment:
Originally, a term that referred just to television programming that dealt with serious issues or current affairs in an entertaining way; today the term applies across all media, and refers to the way in which soft news style, in both form and content, is delivered in news and current affairs stories.

Intellectual property:
A broad term used to refer to intangible property created by the mind.

Interculturalism:
The interaction, sharing and exchange between cultures, wherein each culture benefits from exposure to the other.

Internet Protocol Television (IPTV):
Television content on demand through the internet; YouTube is currently the best-known example.

Interpellation:
Actively seeking out an audience; encouraging the audience to contribute to the text in some way.

Intertextuality:
The idea that texts do not exist in isolation, but rather are interdependent. Texts frequently make meaning through their relationship with other texts. These other texts (or secondary texts) are called intertexts.

Intro or announcer read:
The introductory part of an electronic media story, usually read live by the newsreader, and scripted by the reporter.

Inverted pyramid:
The style of writing news that places the most important information at the beginning of the story, followed by less important information, and so on to the end of the story; this enables the story to be cut from the bottom in order to fit the available space.

J-bloggers:
Internet bloggers who act in the role of journalists disseminating newsworthy information, and who subscribe to the journalistic ideals of an obligation to the truth and the public's right to know; term coined by Nicola Goc.

Journal:
From the French *journal*: a daily record of events; therefore, a daily newspaper or magazine.

Journalism:
The gathering and disseminating of new information to a wide audience about current events, trends, issues and people.

Journalist:
A person who practises journalism; someone who gathers and disseminates new information about current events, trends, issues and people to a wide audience; from the French *journal*, which comes from the Latin *diurnal* (daily).

Jurisdiction:
Refers to either the power granted to a legal body, such as a court or tribunal, to administer justice within a defined area of responsibility; or a geographically delimited area within which certain laws are seen to apply (for example, a state, territory or nation).

Legitimacy:
The process that each discourse employs as it seeks to authorise its truth, rightness and superiority.

Literary merit:
Intrinsic value or worth of a literary work based on the quality of writing, inventiveness of story or ability to capture a certain period of time or emotion; often used to demarcate literature from other formulaic or genre fiction and from the wider body of popular culture.

Mainstream:
The most familiar, popular or otherwise generally available of any art form, especially films.

Manufacturing consent:
The way in which Western mass media act to subdue popular dissent and to assist in the realisation of political and corporate objectives while giving the illusion of freedom; coined in 1922 by the American writer Walter Lippmann and popularised later by Noam Chomsky and Edward Herman.

Maralinga:
The nuclear weapons test site established in the South Australian desert where the United Kingdom tested seven major atomic bombs and conducted hundreds of smaller nuclear experiments between 1956 and 1963.

Mashup:
A website or application that combines content from more than one source into an integrated experience.

Mass media:
Media designed to attract the greatest number of audience members.

Media:
Content and distribution mechanisms through which information and/or entertainment is transmitted.

Media alert:
Also known as a diary note; a document used by PR practitioners to alert journalists and editors to a forthcoming event, often a media conference or a speech by a prominent person. It is a form of invitation tailored to the needs of the media, and is generally distributed by email or facsimile between one week and one day before the event.

Media baron:
The term, which replaces press baron, refers to the early English newspaper proprietors, such as Lords Beaverbrook, Rothermere and Northcliffe, and contemporary media owners such as Rupert Murdoch.

Media conference:
A public relations event in which a major news announcement is made to assembled journalists. The announcement is usually followed by questioning of the news source by journalists.

Media effects model:
The injection (like a hypodermic syringe) of ideas by media into an essentially passive and vulnerable mass audience. Sometimes also referred to as the direct effects or hypodermic syringe model.

Media event:
A news story that becomes an historically important communication event, interrupting the flow of all other news.

Media kit:
A folder that contains a range of material relevant to a media event such as a media conference. As well as a media release, they may include background information, photographs and pens.

Media monitoring organisation:
A company that may be contracted to track media activity and provide print media clippings and audio and video recordings of media coverage. These companies generally also offer analysis of news trends. Media monitoring organisations are used extensively by PR professionals to measure the impact of various publicity activities.

Media practitioner:
Any person involved in the production of media.

Media release:
A document, written by a PR practitioner in journalistic style, that provides a story intended for use by the media.

Mediasphere:
The subtle and obvious connections between media texts, whether fictional (popular media) or factual (journalism), that form a larger whole.

Media text:
Anything produced and/or distributed by a media industry from which we can make meaning.

Mediation:
The function of media; the communication of messages, whether information, entertainment or a mixture of both, by media.

Merchandising:
The marketing of a wide range of consumer goods bearing images from a specific media product.

Metanarrative:
A supernarrative built up from all the narratives in all of the intertexts that represent the celebrity.

Metaphor:
An implicit or explicit comparison between signs, where the qualities of one are transferred to another.

Metaverse:
A fictional, virtual world.

Methodology:
A systematic way of producing knowledge, involving both the production and analysis of data; a way of testing, accepting, developing or rejecting a theory.

Metonymy:
The standing in of a part or element of a text for the whole.

MobLog:
Weblogs where participants appear to behave like regular mobs, but unlike their flesh-and-blood counterparts, their ideas can have an instantaneous impact on a worldwide platform.

Mockumentary:
A melding of the words 'mock' and 'documentary'; a film or television program presented as a documentary recording real life but which is in fact fictional—a commonly used medium for parody and satire.

Modding:
A contraction of game modification: the addition of new content to games.

Modernity:
The mainstream of Western thought, from the nineteenth century until the late twentieth century, that is based on ideas of progress, rationality and equality.

Mise en scène:
Literally 'placing on stage' it refers to all the physical elements of a shot; that is, everything that is placed before the camera—props, sets, actors, costumes, make-up and lighting—and how these are arranged to tell the story (for example, revealing narrative information, emotion or even a character's mental state).

MMPORG:
Massively multiplayer online role-playing games; a genre of gaming where large numbers of players interact with each other in a virtual world.

MSM:
An acronym for mainstream media; that is, established mainstream television and radio stations and large established newspapers.

Muckraker:

A term coined by President Theodore Roosevelt, referring to investigative journalists who challenged his government. The term came from John Bunyan's *The Pilgrim's Progress* (1678), where it was used to describe men who look nowhere but down.

Multiculturalism:

The conferring of equal rights on the many distinct cultural groups that make up a society.

Multiskilled:

In journalistic terms a journalist who is adept in producing news across multiple media platforms.

Myth:

An ideology that has become so accepted, so commonplace, that it is no longer recognised as an ideology.

Narrative convergence:

Narrative that does not originate from a single textual site, but flows across, between and through a number of different delivery platforms.

Narrative transparency:

Textual process by which audiences can project their own values, beliefs, rites and rituals into imported media and make use of these devices.

Narrative tropes:

Words, phrases or expressions that recur in particular narratives; for example, the *femme fatale* (sexually attractive but dangerous woman) in crime movies of the 1940s.

Narrowcasting:

The distribution of media content to increasingly segmented audiences, to the point where the advertising or media message can be tailored to fit the special needs or consumer profile of members of the targeted audience.

Natsound:

Natural sound, recorded on location.

Network-centric warfare (NCW):

A new military doctrine or theory of war, pioneered by the American Department of Defense, that seeks to translate an information advantage into a competitive war fighting advantage through the robust networking of well-informed, geographically dispersed forces allowing new forms of organisational behaviour.

New media:

The mechanisms for digitally transmitting information and entertainment.

News agenda:

The influence of news providers on the way both members of the public and people in power absorb and react to public events.

News culture:

The predominating attitudes and behaviours that characterise the operations of newsrooms and media organisations.

News discourse:

The way in which news professionals express ideas in written and spoken language, including their evaluation of such elements as newsworthiness.

News story:

Information packaged in order to afford maximum readability; either in the pattern of beginning–middle–end, or in the inverted pyramid pattern of most important–slightly less important–least important.

News values:

Criteria that the media apply to determine if and what information will be produced as news; including impact, proximity, prominence, human interest, novelty, conflict and currency.

Novelty news:
News that reveals rare, unusual or bizarre information.

Object:
The thing being acted upon in a sentence; the subject of the sentence acts on its object.

Object of study:
What you are studying; the focus of your research.

Objectivity:
The application of observation and experimentation to reality in order to avoid bias or prejudice; the principle that requires journalists to be fair, nonpartisan, disinterested and factual.

Op-ed:
Contraction of opinion editorial.

Open questions:
Questions whose answers can elicit a wide range of responses; usually these questions begin with the words Who?, What?, When?, Where?, How? and Why?

Open source licensing:
A copyright licence to modify computer software code, generally entailing a requirement to make available to others any modifications that are made.

Open texts:
Texts that have many possible meanings.

Outro or back announce:
The announcement made by the live announcer or newsreader after the packaged part of an electronic media script has finished.

Pacing:
The speed at which a reporter, newsreader or presenter speaks.

Paradigm:
The greatest spread of possible connotations that any signifier can have.

Penny press:
Cheap nineteenth-century newspapers that cost a penny and were marketed to the newly literate working class, leading to a dramatic increase in newspaper circulation.

Performative documentary:
A style of documentary film that is constructed around a performance by the filmmaker.

Periodical:
A magazine or journal published at regular intervals, such as weekly, monthly or quarterly.

Plaintiff:
A person bringing a civil action to court.

Pluralism:
Diversity in society, and therefore in the media; pluralist media offer us a wide range of choices.

Podcast: (iPOD broadCAST):
An audio broadcast that has been converted to an MP3 file or other audio file format for playback in a digital player. Although today many podcasts are played on a computer, the original idea was to listen on a portable device; hence, the 'pod' name from 'iPod'. Although podcasts are mostly verbal, they may contain music, images and video.

Polysemy:
The openness of texts to many different interpretations; a splintering of interpretations.

Popular media:
Media watched or listened to by the majority of the population; for example, tabloid newspapers, soft news, commercial television and radio, computer games and comic books.

Portals:

Entry points to the World Wide Web, from which a user gains access to news websites, search engines, email pages and databases.

Postmodern:

A way of thinking about the world that considers that there is no single representation of any aspect of the world: rather, there are multiple ways of making sense of the world.

Postmodernity:

A type of Western thought that, while sharing the basic ideals of modernity, accepts that a wide variety of groups within a society have different perspectives on society and ways of being in that society, and that these differences should be respected and alternative viewpoints considered.

PR consultancy:

A company set up specifically to carry out contract public relations (PR) work, in contrast to a PR person who is on the staff of a company or organisation.

Premodernity:

The mainstream of Western thought until the nineteenth century, its underlying beliefs based on religion, nature and a sense of divine justice.

Presumption of innocence:

The right of an accused person to innocence in law until a court convicts that person.

Primary text:

The original information that forms the basis of the rest of textual analysis.

Proactive PR:

Often called agenda setting; the creation of a story, usually a positive story, where none existed; examples include calling a media conference to announce the establishment of a new award, or sending out a media release about the findings of a specially commissioned study.

Prominence:

The likely impact of a news item, according to whether the person in the news is already well known.

Propaganda:

The deliberate, systematic attempt to shape perceptions, manipulate cognitions and direct behaviour to achieve a response that furthers the desired intent of the propagandist.

Propaganda model:

Noam Chomsky's argument that the mass media is a tool used by its owners and by governments to deliver a capitalist ideology, rather than to scrutinise governments and other powerful groups in society.

Prosumer:

A computer user whose activities, such as influencing the rules of computer games, produce a convergence between a producer and consumer.

Proximity:

The distance of the news event from the audience: the closer the proximity of news to the environment of the person absorbing a news story, the greater the impact of the news item.

Publication:

In a defamation action, a communication must reach at least one other person; hence, a fax, a postcard, an email, a comment on Facebook or a Tweet may be a publication.

Public relations (PR):

The controlled release or exchange of information in various ways and through various outlets, most visibly through the news media.

Public Relations Institute of Australia (PRIA):

The peak professional body for PR practitioners in Australia.

Public sphere:

The public spaces of work, leisure, politics, religion, academia and the mass media, where issues and ideas are encountered, articulated, negotiated and discussed as part of the ongoing process of reaching consensus or compromise in democratic societies.

Public sphericules:

Multiple smaller public spheres—based on particular cultures and subcultures relating to age, sexuality, gender or race—that interconnect with each other.

Publics:

In PR, a buzzword that refers to the different audience sectors, such as employees, investors, media, community sectors and government, that often require separate communication skills, with emphasis on dialogue rather than one-way communication.

Qualified privilege:

Material which otherwise might be regarded as defamatory, but which is protected from prosecution.

Quasar:

A shooting star: a celebrity whose popularity remains only for the duration of a major event. The term is scientifically inaccurate, as a quasar is not a shooting star (transitory), but a quasi-astronomical object: a mysterious far-off object that might be a star, or perhaps a mini-galaxy in violent turmoil.

Quote:

A statement attributed to someone; a direct quote is a statement in quotation marks, while an indirect quote has no quotation marks.

Radio:

The wireless transmission through space of electromagnetic waves, and the device designed to collect these signals and turn them into sound that you can listen to.

Ratings:

Nightly and weekly surveys are conducted to determine how many viewers are watching particular programs on particular channels. These results are used to attract advertisers and determine programming schedules. The practice of ratings surveys is often referred to as the ratings war between commercial television or radio stations.

Rational media:

Media that promote political and social debate, including broadsheet newspapers, political pamphlets, hard news reports, political websites and public broadcasters.

Reading a text:

The first act in interpreting the text; the point at which we start to make meaning.

Realism:

The way in which media try to represent ideas or situations in ways that members of the audience believe are real.

Realist filmmaking:

A style of filmmaking, seeking to show great fidelity to real life, often through unscripted dialogue and the use of handheld camera and long takes, necessarily limiting the intrusion of the filmmaker; best seen in the British documentary movement and the neo-realist movement in Italy.

Receiver:

The text's destination.

Reception studies:

Studies of the ways in which audiences consume (receive) media.

Reintermediation:

The reintroduction of a business intermediary: an electronic intermediary, a new business (or businesses) designed to link manufacturers to consumers.

Remedy:
Compensation to a plaintiff in a civil action.

Representation:
The selection of elements that media communicate to audiences; those aspects of the world that media re-present to audiences.

Round:
A form of reporting where the journalist specialises in a particular subject area and covers that area in depth. Examples include court or police rounds. This same role is known as a beat in the US.

RSS:
An acronym most commonly expanded as Really Simple Syndication, RSS feeds allow frequently updated content—such as news headlines, news feeds, news stories, excerpts from discussion forums and corporate information—to be delivered to a computer or mobile device as soon as it is published.

Rule of law:
Consistent, fair rules of society that apply equally to all citizens.

Russian montage:
A form of filmmaking, developed in the USSR in the 1920s, based on Sergei Eisenstein's notion of using separate, contrasting images to construct combined new images for the viewer.

Script:
The written part of a radio or television story.

Search engine:
A system of searching and analysing the content of all non-hidden websites, analysing the relationship between websites and ranking sites on the basis of links from other highly relevant sites; the most famous search engine is Google.

Secondary texts:
Analytical or descriptive studies that interact, inform or otherwise elucidate the original information you are studying.

Segue:
Pronounced *seg*-way; the transition between elements of a broadcast story or show, including the throw that the news reader uses to introduce a pre-recorded package.

Semiotics:
Sometimes also referred to as semiology or semiotic studies, it's the study of the role of signification in communication, including, but not limited to, how meaning is made (both how it is produced and how it is understood by an audience member).

Sender:
The text's point of origin.

Seventh art:
As an art new to the twentieth century, cinema was added to the traditional arts, such as painting, sculpture, architecture, poetry, theatre and philosophy.

Shield laws:
Legal protection for journalists who refuse to reveal their confidential sources to a court.

Shorthand:
A system of rapid handwriting made possible by using abbreviations of words.

Shot–reverse shot:
The standard method of showing two actors interacting in films and on television: first the image of one speaker, then the image of the other speaker.

Show business:
The business of entertainment, especially in the USA, that seeks to strike a balance between the show (entertainment spectacle) and the business (making a profit).

Show-don't-tell principle:
The advice given to all media writers to use interesting material to illustrate a point rather than bluntly state something you want the reader to know.

Sign:
A unit of meaning; a structural element of a text that produces meaning(s).

Significance:
The impact of a particular media text's representation of the world. It refers to both social and political significance, and is derived from the number of times a media text is referenced in other texts; the more it is referenced, the more significant a media text will become, and the more impact that text's representation of the world will have.

Signification:
The *signifier* is the physical part of the sign. The *signified* is the mental part of the sign, the abstract concept represented by the sign. *Signification* is the relationship between the signifier and the signified.

Signposting:
Words and sentence structures that show listeners, readers or viewers the context of a story and/or the way in which they should react to it; for example, broadcast news journalists structure their lead stories in such a way as to provide context for the story first before revealing the new thing that has happened.

Slash fiction:
Unauthorised fiction, written by fans of a particular media text, that features characters from that text in narratives that are sexual, often homosexual, in nature.

Social bookmarking:
A system for users of the Web to store, manage, organise and search for bookmarks of resources online.

Social networking site:
A social structure composed of individuals and/or organisations that become nodes connected to each other through multiple interdependencies such as friendships, common interests, sexual relationships, prestige and any other number of emotions and concerns.

Socialisation:
The process by which individuals are embedded into a culture, consequently learning, absorbing and practising particular characteristics of that culture.

Soft news:
News (sometimes called infotainment) that does not have a high priority in the news values scale, and encompasses such fields as entertainment, sport, lifestyle, human interest, celebrity and the arts.

Source:
In journalistic terms, someone who communicates information to a journalist.

Spin:
The process whereby an organisation or individual ensures that information placed into the public sphere, usually through a PR channel, puts them in the best possible light. This word has a negative connotation, as it implies information manipulation.

Spin doctors:
People who are paid to bend information to the needs of their bosses or clients, often beyond what a PR person might normally do.

Splurge journalism:
The up-to-the-minute, immediate saturation coverage of major events.

Spoiler:
A source of information that reveals important details about narrative before the wider audience has had access to it.

Star:
A celebrity who commands prominence, longevity and power in his or her particular field.

Statement of theme:
Summary sentence to remind the reader of a feature article of its main idea.

Stereotype:
An oversimplified, standardised image or idea held by one person or social group about another.

Structuring absences:
Elements in the text that have meaning despite (or because of) the fact they have been left out.

Studio system:
The set of practices that dominated the American movie industry from the 1920s to 1950s, chiefly based around vertical integration and the conception, scripting and production of films with a factory-style efficiency.

Style:
The overall use of a language, whether written (journalism, broadcasting, television or literature), aural (film and television sound) or oral (radio and television presentation); in journalism, it combines grammatical rules, journalistic conventions and the individual preferences of writers, editors and managers.

Subeditor (sub):
A member of a media organisation who edits and corrects material submitted by other people, such as reporters and columnists.

Subject:
The topic of a sentence; what or who is performing an action in a sentence.

Subjective viewing position:
The taking on of the viewpoint of a character in a text by an audience member; the addressee position actually created as a space within the text itself.

Subjectivity:
The addressing of reality through individual experience, perception and interpretation; the expression of an individual's point of view.

Sub judice:
The period, while a trial is pending or under way, when heavy restrictions are placed on the release of information about the trial.

S–V–O (subject–verb–object) sentence:
A standard sentence structure in English containing a *subject* (what is acting), the *verb* (the action being taken) and *object* (what is being acted upon).

Synergy:
The combined marketing of products, owned by the same corporation, such that the total effect is greater than the sum of the parts.

Syntagm:
The selection that an audience member makes from the paradigms of possible connotations.

Tabloid:
In a literal sense, a type of newspaper that is smaller and easier to read than a broadsheet paper. Generally, it refers to news that focuses on the sensational, and is recognised by an informal

vernacular delivery, featuring such subjects as crime, sex, scandal and sport. Today, hard news stories, even in serious news organisations, are often delivered in a tabloid style.

Tabloidisation:

News that is made as easy to read and absorb as possible, often featuring photographs accompanied by sensational news delivered in an informal style.

Talent:

In electronic media, the person interviewed for a story.

Talkback radio:

Radio programming that includes telephone conversations with members of the audience.

Technological convergence:

Media intersection enabled by technological development.

Technological prevention measure:

A device, product, technology or component (including a computer program) that in the normal course of its operation controls access or use of the copyright-protected work; for example, software coding that prevents a CD from being used in a car.

Technological Singularity

The point at which technology surpasses humanity to create superhuman intelligence; appropriated from astrophysics by science-fiction novelist Vernor Vinge in the 1980s and applied to L.J. Good's idea of an intelligence explosion (1965).

Text:

Anything we can make meaning from.

Textual analysis:

An educated guess at some of the most likely interpretations that might be made of the text.

Theory:

The body of rules, ideas, principles and techniques that applies to a particular subject, as distinct from actual practice.

Throw:

A brief line introducing the person who is about to speak, often an electronic media reporter whose voiceover is about to be played.

Timings:

The times allowed in the script for various sound elements: an overall timing for the whole package, and a timing for the pre-recorded part of the package.

Transmedia storytelling:

Stories that are told across a number of different delivery platforms, each platform carrying a slightly different aspect of the story.

Tweet:

The term originally referred to a posting on Twitter, but is now both a noun and a verb.

Tweetlonger:

Also known as Twitlonger a simple service that allows the posting of messages on Twitter of more than 140 characters. Long Reply is a similar service.

Twitter:

An instant messaging service launched in 2006 that allows users to send brief text messages up to 140 characters to a list of friends and approved followers.

UGC:

An acronym for user-generated content on the Web.

Utilitarianism:

The ethical doctrine that the greatest happiness for the greatest number should be the criterion of a virtuous action.

Van Diemen's Land:

Tasmania, the island state of Australia, was known by Europeans as Van Diemen's Land until 1853 when the name was changed to Tasmania (after Dutch explorer Abel Jansoon Tasman). The name change came in the same year that transportation of convicts ceased.

Verb:

The word in a sentence that conveys action.

Vertical integration:

The ownership by one company of all levels of production in any industry; in the film industry, it was the combined production, distribution and exhibition of films in the USA before the 1950s.

Virtual community:

An online community where communication is achieved through technology rather than face-to-face interaction.

Virtual identity:

A fictional identity invented by an online member of a virtual community.

Virtual space (also Cyberspace):

An alternative space to generally accepted reality, experienced by people interacting with other people and their environment via computers and not through face-to-face contact.

Virtue ethics:

The emphasis on the virtues, or moral character, in contrast to the duties or rules (deontology) or the consequences of actions (consequentialism).

Vlogs:

Short for video blogging. It is a form of blogging in which the medium is video.

Voiceover, voicer or VO:

The recorded voice of the reporter explaining an aspect of the story.

Water-cooler show:

A film, televison or radio program that generates great interest wherever members of the public gather in discussion, especially around the office water cooler.

Web browser:

The mechanism by which every computer user can navigate the World Wide Web.

WikiLeaks:

A non-profit online media organisation that publishes otherwise unavailable documents from anonymous sources.

Wiki:

A server program that allows users to collaborate in forming the content of a web site. Users edit the content of other users.

Wikipedia:

An online encyclopedia that is continually edited and added to by its users.

World Wide Web:

The digital system that potentially links every computer in the world with every other computer; first named as such in 1991.

YouTube:

A user-created online video bank.

REFERENCES

ABC—see Australian Broadcasting Corporation.

Aedy, R. (2005). 'Wikis, Journalism and Watching the PR Industry'. *Media Report*. ABC Radio National, 29 September. <www.abc.net.au/rn/mediareport/stories/2005/1471019.htm>. Accessed 13 June 2007.

Ahmad, A. N. (2010). 'Is Twitter a Useful Tool for Journalists?'. *Journal of Media Practice*, 11(2), 145–55.

Allan, S. (ed.) (2005). *Journalism: Critical Issues*. Maidenhead: Open University Press.

Allen, C. (1992). *Channels of Discourse, Reassembled: Television and Contemporary Criticism* (2nd edn). Chapel Hill: University of North Carolina Press.

Allen, R. C. & Hill, A. (2004). *The Television Studies Reader*. London: Routledge.

ALRC—see Australian Law Reform Commission.

Althusser, L. (1971). *Lenin and Philosophy*. New York and London: Monthly Review Press.

Anderson, I. (1993). 'Britain's Dirty Deeds at Maralinga'. *New Scientist*, 12 June.

Archard, D. (1998). 'Privacy, the Public Interest and a Prurient Public'. In M. Kieran (ed.), *Media Ethics*. London: Routledge, 82–96.

Arnett, P. (1994). *Live from the Battlefield: From Vietnam to Baghdad, 35 Years in the World's War Zones*. New York: Simon and Schuster.

Aspinall, A. (1945). 'The Social Status of Journalists at the Beginning of the 19th Century'. *Review of English Studies*, xxi, 216–32.

Australian Broadcasting Corporation (1994). 'Code of Practice'. <www.abc.net.au/corp/pubs/codeprac04.htm>. Accessed 21 March 2011.

——(2002). 'The Art of the Interview'. *Cultures of Journalism*. Radio National, November. <www.abc.net.au/rn/learning/lifelong/stories/s1174641.htm3>. Accessed December 2007.

——(2006). *ABC All Media Law Handbook*. Sydney: ABC Books.

——(2008). *Sources and Conflicts: Review of the Adequacy of ABC Editorial Policies Relating to Source Protection and to the Reporting By Journalists of Events in which They Are Participants*. ABC Corporate. <www.abc.net.au/corp/pubs/documents/200806_confidentialsources_finalreport_july2008.pdf>.

ABC1 (2008) 'Wired for the Future'. *Media Watch*, Jonathan Holmes. 5 May.

ABC Radio National (2003). 'Propaganda Wars'. *Media Report*, interview with John Pilger, 30 January. <www.abc.net.au/rn/talks/8.30/mediarpt/stories/s771659.htm>. Accessed 10 November 2010.

ABC Television (2007). *Foreign Correspondent*, 1 November.

Australian Law Reform Commission (2005). *Uniform Evidence Law: Report*. <www.alrc.gov.au/sites/default/files/pdfs/publications/ALRC102.pdf>. Accessed 15 March 2011.

——(2008). *For Your Information: Australian Privacy Law and Practice, Report No. 108*. September. <www.austlii.edu.au/au/other/alrc/publications/reports/108/>.

Australian Press Council (2006). *State of the News Print Media in Australia 2006*. Sydney: Australian Press Council.

——(2007). *State of the News Print Media in Australia 2007*. <www.presscouncil.org.au>. Accessed 13 June 2007.

——(2008). *State of the News Print Media in Australia 2008*. <www.presscouncil.org.au>. Accessed 13 June 2007.

——(2009). 'Statement of Principles', February. <www.presscouncil.org.au/pcsite/complaints/sop.html>. Accessed 2 December 2010.

——(2010). *Annual Report*, 34. Sydney: Australian Press Council.

Banks, D. (2010). 'Tweeting in Court: Why Journalists Must Be Given Guidelines'. *Guardian*, 15 December. <www.guardian.co.uk/law/2010/dec/15/tweeting-court-reporters-julian-assange>. Accessed 29 December 2010.

Baratay, E. & Hardouin-Fugier, E. (2004). *Zoo: A History of Zoological Gardens in the West*. O. Welsh (trans.). London: Reaktion.

Barthes, R. (1957/1993). *Mythologies* A. Lavers (ed. and trans). London: Vintage.

Bates, D. (2006). *'Mini-Me' History: Public Relations from the Dawn of Civilisation*. Sydney: Institute for Public Relations. <www.instituteforpr.org>.

Baudrillard, J. (1994). *Simulacra and Simulation*. Michigan: University of Michigan Press.

Bazin, A. (1997). *Bazin at Work: Major Essays and Reviews from the Forties and Fifties*. A. Piette & B. Cardullo (trans.), B. Cardullo (ed.). New York: Routledge.

BBC—see British Broadcasting Corporation.

Beattie, S. & Beal, E. (2007). *Connect and Converge. Australian Media and Communications Law*. Melbourne: Oxford University Press.

Beecher, E. (2010). 'Tabloid Media Laughing All the Way to the Pub on Campbell'. *Crikey*, 24 May. <www.crikey.com.au/2010/05/24/beecher-tabloid-media-laughing-all-the-way-to-the-pub-on-campbell/>. Accessed 3 June 2010.

Bell, A. (1999). *The Language of News Media*. Oxford: Blackwell.

Benjamin, D. (1995). 'Censorship in the Gulf'. <http://web1.duc.auburn.edu/~benjadp/gulf/gulf.html>. Accessed 14 October 2010.

Bennett, W. L., Lawrence, R. G. & Livingston, S. (2007). *When the Press Fails: Political Power and the News Media from Iraq to Katrina*. Chicago: University of Chicago Press.

Berman, M. (1983). *All That is Solid Melts into Air: The Experience of Modernity*. London: Verso.

Bernays, E. L. (1947). 'The Engineering of Consent'. *Annals of the American Academy of Political and Social Science*. San Francisco: Sage.

——(1965). *Biography of an Idea: Memoirs of Public Relations Counsel*. New York: Simon and Schuster.

——(1972). *Propaganda*. Port Washington: Kennikat Press.

Beystehner, K. (1998). 'Psychoanalysis: Freud's Revolutionary Approach to Human Personality'. <www.personalityresearch.org/papers/beystehner.html>. Accessed 20 March 2011.

Bhabha, H. (1990). *Nation and Narration*. London and New York: Routledge.

——(1994). *The Location of Culture*. London: Routledge.

Bishop, J. & Woods, O. (1983). *The Story of the* Times. London: Michael Joseph.

Bonner, F. (2003). *Ordinary Television: Analysing Popular TV*. London: Sage.

Boorstin, D. (1961). *The Image: A Guide to Pseudo-events in America*. New York: Atheneum.

Bordwell, D. & Thompson, K. (2008). *Film Art: An Introduction* (8th edn). Boston: McGraw-Hill.

Bourne, H. R. F. (1887). 'The State of our Trade'. *Fortnightly Review*, February, 196–210.

Boyce, G., Curran, J. & Wingate, P. (eds) (1978). *Newspaper History: From the Seventeenth Century to the Present Day*. London: Constable.

Brand, J. (2007). *Interactive Australia 2007: Facts About the Australian Computer and Video Game Industry 2007*. National research prepared by Bond University for the Interactive Entertainment Association of Australia. <http://epublications.bond.edu.au/hss_pubs/95>.

Brandeis, L. D. & Warren, S. D. (1890). 'The Right to Privacy'. *Harvard Law Review*, iv(5), 193–220.

Branston, G. & Stafford, R. (2006). *The Media Student's Book*. London: Routledge.

BBC (2001). *Faces* Dir. by James Erskine and David Stewart. (4 parts).

British Broadcasting Corporation (2001). *The Human Face*, part 2.

Broadcasting Services Act 1992, Section 123.

Bromley, M. (ed.) (2004). *Online Journalism*. New York: Sage.

——(2005). 'Subterfuge as Public Service: Investigative Journalism as Idealised Journalism'. In S. Allen (ed.), *Journalism: Critical Issues*. Maidenhead, England: Open University Press.

Bruzzi, S. (2000). *The New Documentary: A Critical Introduction*. London: Routledge.

Bryant, D. (2006). 'The Uncanny Valley: Why are Monster-movie Zombies So Horrifying and Talking Animals So Fascinating?'. <www.arclight.net/~pdb/nonfiction/uncanny-valley.html>.

Burns, G. & Thompson, R. (1989). *Television Studies: Textual Analysis*. New York: Praeger.

Busari, S. (2009). 'Tweeting the Terror: How Social Media Reacted to Mumbai'. CNN, 28 November. <cnn.com/asia>. Accessed 18 March 2010.

Butler, C. (2003). *Postmodernism: A Very Short Introduction*. Oxford: Oxford University Press.

——(2004). *Australian Media Law*. Sydney: Lawbook Company.

Butler, D. & Rodrick, S. (2007). *Australian Media Law* (3rd edn). Sydney: Lawbook Company.

Byatt, A. S. (2003). 'Harry Potter and the Childish Adult'. *New York Times*, 11 July. <www.countercurrents.org/arts-byatt110703.htm>.

Calabresi, M. (2010). 'Winning the Info War. Julian Assange's Arrest Fortifies his Insurgency'. *Time*, 20 December, 12.

Canning, S. (2010). 'Click of Approval for Online Privacy Tool has $2bn Ad Industry in Spin'. The *Australian*, 6 December.

Carey, A. (1995). *Taking the Risk out of Democracy: Propaganda in the US and Australia*. Sydney: University of New South Wales Press.

Carlyle, T. (1841). *On Heroes and Hero Worship*. London.

Castells, M. (2007). 'Communication, Power and Counter-Power in the Network Society'. *International Journal of Communication*, 1, 238–66.

Cavoukian, A. (2009). *Privacy in the Clouds: A White Paper on Privacy and Digital Identity: Implications for the Internet*. Ontario: Information and Privacy Commissioner of Ontario.

Chalke, D. (2005). 'Personality Speaking'. *Sydney Morning Herald*, 19 March. <www.smh.com.au/articles/2005/03/17/1110913718713.html>.

Chappell, W. (1999). *A Short History of the Printed Word*. Vancouver: Hartley & Marks.

Childs, P. (2000). *Modernism*. London and New York: Routledge.

Christensen, C. (2010). 'WikiLeaks: Three Digital Myths'. *Le Monde Diplomatique*, 9 August. Cited in <http://chrchristensen.wordpress.com/>. Accessed 18 January 2011.

Commonwealth Consolidated Acts. <www.austlii.edu.au/au/legis/cth/consol_act/bsa1992214/s123.html>. Accessed 21 March 2011.

Conley, D. (2002). *The Daily Miracle* (2nd edn). Melbourne: Oxford University Press.

——& Lamble, S. (2006). *The Daily Miracle: An Introduction to Journalism* (3rd edn). Melbourne: Oxford University Press.

Cook, D. A. (1996). *A History of Narrative Film* (3rd edn). New York: Norton.

Correy, S. (2007). 'Iraq: New Team, New Strategy, New Tensions'. *Background Briefing*. ABC Radio National, 15 April. <www.abc.net.au/rn/backgroundbriefing/>.

——(2008) 'Cloud Computing, Background Briefing'. *ABC Radio National*, Transcript 14 September. http://www.abc.net.au/rn/backgroundbriefing/stories/2008/2359128.htm. Accessed 26 September 2008.

Cowen, Z. (1969). 'The Private Man'. *Boyer Lectures 1969*. Sydney: ABC Books.

Cox, M. (2000). 'The Development of Computer Assisted Reporting'. 17–18 March. <http://com.miami.edu/car/cox00.htm>. Accessed 11 June 2007.

Crabb, A. (2010). 'The End of Journalism as We Know It (and Other Good News)'. *ABC*, 27 October. <www.abc.net.au/news/stories/2010/10/27/3050027.htm>. Accessed 2 November 2010.

Craig, D. (2006). *The Ethics of the Story*. Lanham: Rowman & Littlefield.

Crook, A. (2010). 'The Minister, The Gay Sauna, and a Reporter with Scores to Settle'. *Crikey*, 21 May. <www.crikey.com.au/2010/05/21/the-minister-the-gay-sauna-and-a-reporter-with-scores-to-settle/>. Accessed 3 June 2010.

Cryle, D. (1997). *Disreputable Profession: Journalists and Journalism in Colonial Australia*. Brisbane: Central Queensland University Press.

Cunningham, M. (2005). *The Art of Documentary*. Berkeley, CA: New Riders.

Cunningham, W. (2006). 'Wiki'. <http://en.wikipedia.org/wiki/Wiki>. Accessed 6 June 2007.

Curthoys, A. & Schultz, J. (eds) (1999). *Journalism: Print, Politics and Popular Culture*. St Lucia: University of Queensland Press.

Dahlgren, P. (1995). *Television and the Public Sphere: Citizenship, Democracy and the Media*. London: Sage.

——(2002). 'In Search of the Talkative Public: Media, Deliberative Democracy and Civic Culture'. *Javnost/The Public*, 9(3), 5–26.

Davis, W. (2000). 'Just an Online Minute … The Ginger-Mary Ann Question: Blogs vs Mainstream Media?'. *MediaPost*, 20 March <http://blogs.mediapost.com/online_minute/>. Accessed 19 March 2007.

Dayan, D. & Katz, E. (1994). *Media Events: The Live Broadcasting of History*. Cambridge MA: Harvard University Press.

Defamation Act 2005 (NSW). No 77, Explanatory note, NSW Government Printing Service.

Deloitte (2011). 'Television's 'Super Media' Status Strengthens'. 18 January. <www.deloitte.com/view/en_GX/global/industries/technology-media-telecommunications/tmt-predictions-2011/media-2011/b6ea8f036907d210VgnVCM2000001b56f00aRCRD.htm>. Accessed 26 January 2011.

Derrida, J. (1982). 'Difference'. In A. Bass (trans.). *Margins of Philosophy*. Chicago: University of Chicago Press.

de Saussure, F. (1986). *Course in General Linguistics*. C. Bally, A. Sechehaye and A. Riedlinger (eds), R. Harris (trans.). La Salle: Open Court.

Deuze, M. (2009). 'Technology and the Individual Journalist: Agency Beyond Imitation and Change'. In B. Zelizer (ed.), *The Changing Faces of Journalism: Tabloidization, Technology And Truthiness*. London: Routledge Taylor and Francis, 82–98.

Dorfman, A. & Mattelart, A. (1991). *How to Read Donald Duck: Imperialist Ideology in the Disney Comic*. D. Kunzle (trans.). New York: International General.

Douglas, N. (2006). 'Disturbing Blog on Respected News Sites of the Day'. 31 August. <htttp://valleywag.gawker.com/197996/disturbing-blog-on-respected-news-site-of-the-day-screens>. Accessed 30 March 2009.

Dowie, M. (1995). 'Torches of Liberty'. In J. Stauber. & S. Rampton (eds), *Toxic Sludge is Good for You: Lies, Damned Lies and the Public Relations Industry*. Monroe: Common Courage Press.

Dwyer, T. (2007). 'The Policy Agenda'. In V. Nightingale & T. Dwyer (eds), *New Media Worlds: Challenges for Convergence*. Melbourne: Oxford University Press.

Dwyer, T. (2010). *Media Convergence*. UK: McGraw Hill/Open University Press.

Dyer, R. (1998). *Stars* (2nd edn). London: BFI.

Economist (2006). 'Living a Second Life'. 30 September, 97–9.

Elliott, M. (2010). 'Briefing: The Moment'. *Time*, 20 December, 7.

Ellis, J. (1999). 'Television as Working-through'. In J. Grisprud (ed.), *Television and Common Knowledge.* London: Routledge, 55–70.

——(2000). *Seeing Things: Television in the Age of Uncertainty.* London: Tauris.

Entertainment Software Association (2009). *Industry Facts.* Washington, DC: Entertainment Software Association. <www.theesa.com/facts/>.

Entman, R. (1993). 'Framing: Towards Clarification of a Fracture Paradigm'. *Journal of Communication,* 43(4), 51–8.

ESA—see Entertainment Software Association.

Ester, H. (2007). 'The Media'. In C. Hamilton & S. Maddison (eds), *Silencing Dissent.* Sydney: Allen & Unwin.

Ewart, J. (2005). 'What's New in Newspapers? Reconnecting with Readers'. Conference paper, Journalism Education Conference, Griffith University, 29 November–2 December.

Fairclough, N. (1995). *Media Discourse.* London: Hodder Headline.

Farhi, P. (2009). 'The Twitter Explosion'. *American Journalism Review,* 31(3), 27–31.

Felski, R. (1995). *The Gender of Modernity.* Cambridge, MA: Harvard University Press.

Ferguson, J. A. (1965). *Bibliography of Australia, Vol One 1851–1900.* H-P Sydney: Angus and Robertson.

Ferguson, J. A., Foster, A. G. & Green, H. M. (1936). *The Howes and their Press.* Sydney: Sunnybrook Press.

Fiske, J. & Hartley, J. (1978). *Reading Television* (2nd edn). London: Methuen.

Flew, T. (2002). *New Media: An Introduction* (3rd edn). South Melbourne: Oxford University Press.

Flew, T. & Sternberg, J. (1999). 'Media Wars: Media Studies and Journalism Education'. *Media International Australia, 90,* February, 9–14.

Flew, T., Sternberg, J. & Adams, D. (2007). 'Revisiting the 'Media Wars' debate'. *Australian Journal of Communication, 34*(1), 1–28.

Forder, J. & Svantesson, D. (2008). *Internet and E-Commerce Law.* Melbourne: Oxford University Press.

Foucault, M. (1972). *The Archaeology of Knowledge.* A. M. Sheridan Smith (trans.). New York: Pantheon.

——(1977). *Discipline and Punish: The Birth of the Prison.* A. Shenden (trans.). London: Vintage.

Fowler, C. (2002). *The European Cinema Reader.* London and New York: Routledge.

Fowler, H. W. (2002). *A Dictionary of Modern English Usage.* Oxford: Oxford University Press.

Freeman, N. B. (1995). *National Review,* 11 December. Cited in *Forbes Media Critic,* 1(3), 98.

Friedlander, E. J. & Lee, J. (2004). *Feature Writing for Newspapers and Magazines: The Pursuit of Excellence.* Boston: Allyn & Bacon.

Friend, C. & Singer, J. B. (2007). *Online Journalism Ethics: Traditions and Transitions.* New York: M.E. Sharpe.

Frith, S. (2004). *Popular Music: Critical Concepts in Media and Cultural Studies.* London: Routledge.

Frow, J. (1997). *Time and Commodity Culture: Essays in Cultural Theory and Postmodernity.* Oxford: Clarendon Press.

Galtung, J. & Ruge, M. H. (1965). 'The Structure of Foreign News. The Presentation of the Congo, Cuba and Cyprus Crises in Four Norwegian Newspapers'. *Journal of Peace Research,* 2, 64–9.

——(1981). 'Structuring and Selecting News'. In S. Cohen & J. Young (eds), *The Manufacturing of News: Social Problems, Deviance and the Mass Media* (rev. edn). London: Constable.

Giblin, W. R. (1939). *The Early History of Tasmania, vol. 2: 1804–28.* Melbourne.

Gitlin, T. (1980). *The Whole World is Watching.* Berkeley: University of California Press.

——(2001). *Media Unlimited: How the Torrent of Images and Sounds Overwhelms Our Lives.* New York: Metropolitan Books.

Goc, N. (2009). 'Bad Mummy—Kate McCann and the Media'. In C. Burns (ed.), *Mis/Representing Evil: Evil in an Interdisciplinary Key.* Interdisciplinary Press Fisher Imprints, 169–93.

Goldsmith, J. & Wu, T. (2008). *Who Controls the Internet? Illusions of a Borderless World* (2nd edn). New York: Oxford University Press.

Goodrick, J. (1978). *Tales of Old Van Diemen's Land.* Adelaide: Rigby.

Goodwin, A. (1992). *Dancing in the Distraction Factory: Music Television and Popular Culture.* Minneapolis: University of Minnesota Press.

Gordon, M. (2009). 'The New Astor Court'. *Vanity Fair*, September.

Grabe, M., Zhou, S., Lang, A. & Bolls, P. (2000). 'Packaging Television News: Effects of Tabloid on Information Processing and Evaluative Responses'. *Journal of Broadcasting and Electronic Media*, 44(4), 581–98.

Gramsci, A. (1971). *Extracts from Prison Notebooks.* London: Lawrence & Wishart.

Greenslade, R. (2003). 'Their Master's Voice'. *Media Guardian*, 17 February. <www.ojr.org/ojr/stories/050524glaser/>.

Greenwald, G. (2010). 'Iraq Slaughter Not an Aberration'. Salon.com. <www.salon.com/news/opinion/glenn_greenwald/2010/04/06/iraq>.

Gripsrud, J. (1997). 'Television, Broadcasting, Flow: Key Metaphors in TV Theory'. In C. Geraghty & D. Lusted (eds), *The Television Studies Book.* London, 17–32.

Grisprud, J. (1999). 'Scholars, Journalism, Television: Notes on Some Conditions for Mediation and Intervention'. In J. Grisprud (ed.), *Television and Common Knowledge.* London: Routledge, 34–54.

Habermas, J. (1981). *The Theory of Communicative Action.* London: Beacon Press.

——(1989). *The Structural Transformation of the Public Sphere: An Inquiry into a Category of Bourgeois Society.* Cambridge: MIT Press.

——(1992). *Habermas and the Public Sphere.* Cambridge: MIT Press.

——(1997). 'Institutions of the Public Sphere'. In O. Boyd-Barrett & C. Newbold (eds), *Approaches to Media.* London: Arnold.

Hargreaves, I. (2003). *Journalism: Truth or Dare?.* Oxford: Oxford University Press.

Harper, R. (2010). 'Why talk about social media?'. 22 November. <http://justruthings.com/2010/11/22/why-talk-about-social-media/>. Accessed 3 December 2010.

Harrell, E. (2010). 'WikiLeaks Founder Julian Assange'. *Time*, 26 July. <www.time.com/time/world/article/0,8599,2006496,00.html>. Accessed 15 January 2011.

Hartley, J. (1992a). *The Politics of Pictures: The Creation of the Public in the Age of Popular Media.* London: Routledge.

——(1992b). *Teleology: Studies in Television.* London and New York: Routledge.

——(1996). *Popular Reality: Journalism, Modernity and Popular Culture.* London: Arnold.

——(1999). *Uses of Television.* London and New York: Routledge.

——(2002a). *Communication, Cultural and Media Studies: The Key Concepts* (3rd edn). London: Routledge.

——(2002b). 'Textual Analysis'. In T. Miller (ed.), *Television Studies.* London: British Film Institute.

Harvey, D. (1989). *The Condition of Postmodernity: An Enquiry into the Origins of Cultural Change.* Cambridge and Oxford: Blackwell.

Hecht, M. (2007). 'Watch the Hillary Ad'. *Sacramento Bee*, 20 March. <www.sacbee.com/770/story/140959.html>. Accessed 27 March 2007.

Heinonen, A. (2006). 'Journalism Online: Ethics as Usual?'. In K. Richard (ed.), *Communications Ethics Today.* London: Troubador Publishing, 134–42.

Heller, A. (1999). *A Theory of Modernity.* Malden, MA: Blackwell.

Helmore, E. (2007). 'YouTube: The Hustings of the 21st Century'. *Observer*, 25 March.

Herman, E. S. & Chomsky, N. (1994). *Manufacturing Consent: The Political Economy of the Mass Media.* London: Vintage.

Heyer, P. (2003). 'America Under Attack 1: A Reassessment of Orson Welles' 1938 *War of the Worlds* Broadcast'. *Canadian Journal of Communication*, 28, 149–65.

Hickey, N. (1998). 'Money Lust: How Pressure for Profit is Perverting Journalism'. *Columbia Journalism Review*, July/August, 28–36.

Hirst, M. & Harrison, J. (2007). *Communication and New Media: From Broadcast to Narrowcast.* South Melbourne: Oxford University Press.

Hirst, M. & Patching, R. (2005). *Journalism Ethics: Arguments and Cases.* South Melbourne: Oxford University Press.

Holland, P. (2000). *The Television Handbook* (2nd edn). London: Routledge.

Hooton, A. (2011). 'A Little Birdie Told Me …'. *Good Weekend*, 22 January, 11–15.

Houston, B. (2004). *Computer-Assisted Reporting: A Practical Guide* (3rd edn). New York: St Martin's Press.

Huffington, A. (2007). 'Who Created 'Hi Hillary 1984?': Mystery Solved!'. 21 March. <www.huffingtonpost.com/arianna-huffington/who-created-hillary-1984_b_43978.html>. Accessed 27 March 2007.

Jacquette, D. (2007). *Journalistic Ethics: Moral Responsibility in the Media.* Upper Saddle River, NJ: Pearson.

James, C. (1984). *Flying Visits.* London: Picador.

Jarlov, M. (n.d.). 'What Fourth Estate?'. Medialens.org. <www.medialens.org>. Accessed 8 July 2007.

Jefferson, T. (1787). 'Letter to Edward Carrington 16 January 1787'. *Papers*, 11, 48–9, Amendment I (Speech and Press), Document 8 <http://press-pubs.uchicago.edu/founders/>.

Jenkins, H. (2006a). *Convergence Culture: Where Old and New Media Collide.* New York and London: New York University Press.

——(2006b). *Fans, Bloggers and Gamers: Exploring Participatory Culture.* New York: New York University Press.

Jensen, D. (1999). 'War on Truth: The Secret Battle for the American Mind'. Interview with J. Stauber, 28 March. <www.ratical.org/ratville/PRcorrupt.html>.

Jericho, G. (2010). 'Election 2010: Day 14 (or waste and mismanagement – the media)'. http://grogsgamut.blogspot.com/2010/07/election-2010-day-14-or-waste-and.html. Accessed 12 August 2010.

Johnson, C. (2005). *21st Century Feature Writing.* Upper Saddle River, NJ: Pearson Education.

Johnson, J. (2008a). 'Blogs Influence Journalists, Nearly all Facets of News Coverage'. *Brodeur*, 9 January. <www.marketingcharts.com/print/blogs-influence-journalists-nearly-all-facets-of-news-coverage-2982/>. Accessed 21 January 2011.

——(2008b). *Brodeurhttp.* <//www.brodeurmediasurvey.com/>. Accessed 3 January 2011.

Johnson, S. (2005). *Everything Bad Is Good For You: How Popular Culture Is Making Us Smarter.* London: Allen Lane.

Johnston, J. & Zawawi, C. (2000). *Public Relations Theory and Practice.* Sydney: Allen & Unwin.

Jolly, R. (2008). 'Going Digital—Digital Terrestrial Radio for Australia'. Social Policy Section, Department of Parliamentary Services, Parliament of Australia, 19 December. <http://202.14.81.34/Library/pubs/rp/2008-09/09rp18.pdf>. Accessed 20 March 2011.

Kaleem, K. (2010). 'isamaa.tv/2010-12-11 Could Become as Important a Journalistic Tool as the Freedom of Information Act'. 11 December. <'isamaa.tv/2010-12-11-could-become-as-important-a-journalistic-tool-as-the- freedom-of-information-act-Time>. Accessed 24 January 2011.

Kamiya, G. (1996). 'Transgressing the Transgressors: Toward a Transformative Hermeneutics of Total Bullshit'. *Salon*, 17 May. <www.salon.com/media/media960517.html>. Accessed 26 June 2007.

Kaplan, B. (2003). *Editing Made Easy.* Melbourne: Penguin.

Katz, J. (1992). 'Rock Rap and Music Bring the News'. *Rolling Stone,* 5 March.

Keane, J. (1991). *The Media and Democracy.* Cambridge: Polity.

Keeble, R. (2001). *Ethics for Journalists.* London: Routledge.

Kent, J. (1990). *Out of the Bakelite Box: The Heyday of Australian Radio.* Sydney: ABC Books.

Kenyon, A. T. (2006). *Defamation: Comparative Law and Practice.* London: UCL Press.

Khatchadourian, R. (2010). 'No Secrets: Julian Assange's Mission for Total Transparency'. *The New Yorker,* 7 June. <www.newyorker.com/reporting/2010/06/07/100607fa_fact_khatchadourian>.

Kingston, M. (2001). 'Webdiary Charter'. 26 April 2001. <www.smh.com.au/articles/2002/04/29/1019441338099.html>. Accessed 3 June 2008.

——(2003). 'Diary of a Webdiarist: Ethics Goes Online'. In C. Lumby & E. Probyn (eds), *Remote Control: New Media, New Ethics.* Melbourne: Cambridge University Press.

——(2005). 'Webdiary Ethics'. 24 October. <http://webdiary.com.au/cms/?q=node/1/printWebdiary>. Accessed 12 June 2008.

Kirkman, D. (1999). 'What is News?'. Australian Press Council Public Forum, Launceston, Tas. <www.presscouncil.org.au/pcsite/apcnews/feb00/laun/html>.

Kirkpatrick, R. (2000). 'Covering Every Dogfight: A Century and a Half of Local News in the Provincial Press'. *Australian Journalism Monograph,* 5–6 May–November.

Kluth, A. (2006). 'Among the Audience'. *Economist,* 20 April.

Kress, G. (1997). 'Visual and Verbal Modes of Representation in Electronically Mediated Commu-nication: The Potentials of New Forms of Text'. In I. Snyder (ed.), *From Page to Screen: Taking Literacy into the Electronic Era.* Sydney: Allen & Unwin, 53–79.

Kuczynski, A. (2000). 'In Public Relations, 25% Admit to Lying'. *New York Times,* 8 May <http://query.nytimes.com/gst/fullpage.html?res=9C00E5D91238F93BA35756C0A9669C8B63&sec=&spon=>. Accessed 12 December 2007.

Kurtz, H. & Vargas, J. A. (2007). 'A Brave New World of Political Skulduggery?'. *Washington Post,* 23 March.

Lalor, P. (2007). 'Game On'. *Australian,* 'Business', 15 September.

Lariscy, R., Avery, E. J., Sweetser, K. & Howes, P. (2009). 'An Examination of the Role of Online Social Media in Journalists' Source Mix'. *Public Relations Review,* 35, 314–16.

Lasswell, H. (1927). *Propaganda Technique in World War I.* New York: Alfred A. Knopf. <http://nielsenhayden.com/makinglight/archives/2006_06.html>.

Launceston Examiner (1842). 'Editorial'. 1(1), 12 March.

Leach, J. (2009). 'Creating Ethical Bridges from Journalism to Digital News'. *Nieman Reports: Nieman Foundation for Journalism at Harvard,* Fall 2009. <www.nieman.harvard.edu/reports/article/101899/Creating-Ethical-Bridges-From-Journalism-to--Digital-News.aspx>. Accessed 12 January 2011.

Lee, D. (2010). 'Trying to Exclude WikiLeaks from Shield Law Stinks'. First Amendment Centre, 25 August. <www.firstamendmentcenter.org/commentary.aspx?id=23303>. Accessed 18 January 2011.

Legge, K. (2010). 'Vintage Model'. *Weekend Australian Magazine,* 30–31 October, 30.

Lenatti, C. (2009). 'All A-Twitter: Social Networking as a Tool for Newspaper Journalists?'. *Seybold Report,* 5 February.

Lessig, L. (2005). *Free Culture. The Nature and Future of Creativity.* London: Penguin.

Levy, B. & Bonilla, D. M. (1999). *The Power of the Press.* New York: H. W. Wilson.

Lindoo, E. C. (1998). 'The Future of Newspapers: A Study of the World Wide Web and its Relationship to the Electronic Publishing of Newspapers'. May. <www.wan-press.org/article.php3?id_article=2821>.

Litowitz, D. E. (1997). *Postmodern Philosophy and Law.* Lawrence: University Press of Kansas.

Lohr, S. (2006). 'This Boring Headline Is Written For Google?'. *New York Times*, 9 April. <http://query.nytimes.com/gst/fullpage.html?res=980DE4D61130F93AA35757C0A9609C8B63&pagewanted=1>. Accessed 9 April 2006.

Los Angeles Times (2010). 'WikiLeaks and a Journalism 'Shield Law''. Editorial, 5 August. <http://articles.latimes.com/2010/aug/05/opinion/la-ed-shield-20100805>.

Lotman, Y. (1990). *The Universe of the Mind: A Semiotic Theory of Culture.* Bloomington: Indiana University Press.

Lumby, C. (1999). *Gotcha: Life in a Tabloid World.* St Leonards, NSW: Allen & Unwin.

——(2004). 'The Democratisation of Celebrity'. *Griffith Review*, 5, September.

Lyotard, J. F. (1984). *The Postmodern Condition: A Report on Knowledge.* G. Bennington & B. Massumi (trans.). Minneapolis: University of Minnesota Press.

——(1987). 'Rewriting Modernity'. *Substance*, 16(3), 3–9.

——(1999). *Toward the Postmodern.* Amherst: Humanity Books.

MacArthur, R. (1992). *Second Front: Censorship and Propaganda in the First Gulf War.* New York: Hill and Wang.

Macnamara, J. R. (2001). *Impact of PR on the Media.* Washington, DC: CARMA International.

Malpas, S. (2005). *The Postmodern.* Abingdon: Routledge.

Massola, J. (2010a). 'Controversial Political Blogger Unmasked as a Federal Public Servant'. *Australian*, 27 September. <www.theaustralian.com.au/business/media/controversial-political-blogger-unmasked-as-a-federal-public-servant/story-e6frg996-1225929679443>. Accessed 8 December 2010.

——(2010b). 'Twittersphere Hit by Storm over Whether Political Blogger had a Right to Anonymity', 27 September. <www.theaustralian.com.au/business/media/twittersphere-hit-by-storm-over-whether-political-blogger-had-a-right-to-anonymity/story-e6frg996-1225929874704>. Accessed 8 December 2010.

Mayhew, H. (1861). 'Of the Street-Sellers of Stationery, Literature, and the Fine Arts. Of the Recent Experience of a Running Patterer'. *London Labour and the London Poor*, 1, chap. 11. London: Griffin, Bohn.

McGuigan, J. (1999). *Modernity and Postmodern Culture.* Buckingham, Philadelphia: Open University Press.

McKee, A. (2001). *Australian Television: A Genealogy of Great Moments.* South Melbourne: Oxford University Press.

——(2003). *Textual Analysis: A Beginner's Guide.* London: Sage.

——(2005). *The Public Sphere: An Introduction.* Melbourne: Cambridge University Press.

McLuhan, M. (1967). *Understanding Media: The Extensions of Man.* London: Sphere.

——(1967). 'Radio: The Tribal Drum'. In *Understanding Media: The extensions of Man.* London: Sphere Books.

——& Fiore, Q. (1967). *The Medium is the Massage.* New York: Bantam.

MEAA—see Media, Entertainment & Arts Alliance.

Media, Entertainment & Arts Alliance (1996). 'Ethics Review Committee Final Report November 1996'. <www.gwb.com.au/99a/ethics.html>.

——(2006). *The Media Muzzled: Australia's 2006 Press Freedom Report.* Sydney: Media Entertainment and Arts Alliance.

——(2007). *Official Spin: Censorship and Control of the Australian Press 2007: The Media, Entertainment & Arts Alliance Report into the State of Press Freedom in Australia.* <www.alliance.org.au/>.

——(n.d.). 'Journalist Code of Ethics'. <www.alliance.orgu.au>. Accessed 21 March 2011.

Melville, H. (1835). *A History of Van Diemen's Land.* G. Mackaness (ed.). Sydney: Sydney Review Publications.

Mill, J. S. (1859). *On Liberty.* <www.constitution.org/jsm/liberty.htm>.

Miller, M. (1952). *Pressmen and Governors.* Sydney: Sydney University Press.

Miller, T. (1998). 'Hollywood and the World'. In J. Hill. & P. C. Gibson (eds), *The Oxford Guide to Film Studies.* Oxford: Oxford University Press.

Morison, S. (1980). 'The Origins of the Newspaper'. In D. McKitterick (ed.), *Selected Essays on the History of Letter-Forms in Manuscript and Print.* Cambridge: Cambridge University Press.

Morris, D. J. (2004). *Storm on the Horizon: Khafji—The Battle That Changed the Course of the Gulf War.* New York: Random House.

Morrison, D., Kieran, M., Svennevig, M. & Ventress, S. (2007). *Media and Values. Intimate Transgressions in a Changing Moral and Cultural Landscape.* Bristol, UK and Chicago, USA: Intellect.

Murrow, E. (1958). 'Address to Radio-Television News Directors Association and Foundation Convention'. Chicago, 15 October. Association of Electronic Journalists <www.cultsock.ndirect.co.uk>.

Naughton, J. (2010). 'The War on Free Speech'. *War in Context.* December 7. <http://warincontext.org/2010/12/07/the-war-on-free-speech/>. Accessed 2 January 2011.

Neale, S. (2000). *Genre and Hollywood.* London: Routledge.

Nightingale, V. (2007a). 'Lost in Space: Television's Missing Publics'. In R. Busch (ed.), *Media and Public Spheres.* London: Palgrave, 185–97.

——(2007b). 'New Media Worlds? Challenges for Convergence'. In V. Nightingale & T. Dwyer (eds), *New Media Worlds: Challenges for Convergence.* South Melbourne: Oxford University Press, 19–37.

——& Dwyer, T. (2007). *New Media Worlds: Challenges for Convergence.* Oxford: Oxford University Press.

North, L. (2009). *The Gendered Newsroom.* USA: Hampton Press Inc.

Olson, S. R. (2004). 'Hollywood Planet: Global Media and the Competitive Advantage of Narrative Transparency'. In R. C. Allen & A. Hill (eds), *The Television Studies Reader.* London and New York: Routledge, 111–30.

O'Regan, M. (2002). 'Cheryl Kernot and the Politics of the Personal'. *The Media Report,* ABC Radio National, 4 July. <www.abc.net.au/rn/talks/8.30/mediarpt/stories/s596309.htm>. Accessed 10 June 2007.

O'Regan, T. (1993). *Australian Television Culture.* St Leonards, NSW: Allen & Unwin.

Orwell, G. (1938). *Homage to Catalonia.* London: Victor Gollancz.

——(1946). 'Politics and the English Language'. *Horizon,* April. <www.orwell.ru/library/essays/politics/english/e_polit>. Accessed 16 July 2007.

Ostrow, A. (2010). 'Sharing on Facebook Now More Popular than Sharing by E-mail'. *Mashable,* 20 July 2009. Cited in R. Harper, 'Why Talk about Social Media?', 22 November. <http://justruthings.com/2010/11/22/why-talk-about-social-media/>. Accessed 3 December 2010.

O'Sullivan J. & Heinonen, A. (2008). 'Old Values New Media: Journalism Role Perceptions in a Changing World'. *Journalism Practice,* 2, October, 357–71.

O'Sullivan, T., Hartley, J., Saunders, D., Montgomery, M. & Fiske, J. (1994). *Key Concepts in Communication and Cultural Studies* (2nd edn). London: Routledge.

Padmanabhan, M. (2005). 'Publicising the Private: The Right to Privacy against Media Intrusion'. In R. Nalini (ed.), *Practising Journalism: Values, Constraints, Implications.* London: Sage, 76–7.

Palmer, S. (2006). 'BlogMobs: The Attack of the Fifth Estate: Comment'. MediaPost Publications, 29 June <http://publications.mediapost.com/index.cfm?>. Accessed 12 March 2007.

Patterson, C. (n.d.). 'Inventing the Newspaper: John Lienhard Presents Guest Catherine Patterson'. *Engines of Our Ingenuity.* Ep. 1983. Audio <www.uh.edu/engines/epi1983.htm>. Accessed 21 August 2006.

Parvaz, D. (2007). ''Hillary 1984' Shows Internet is a Clever Slambook'. *Seattle Post-Intelligencer,* 24 March. <http://seattlepi.nwsource.com/saturdayspin/308769_parvaz24.html>. Accessed 25 March 2007.

Pearson, M. & Brand, J. (2001). *Sources of News and Current Affairs.* Sydney: Australian Broadcasting Authority.

Penberthy, D. (2010). 'Why David Campbell has a Lesser Right to Privacy'. *The Punch*, 21 May. <www.thepunch.com.au/articles/why-david-campbell-has-a-lesser-right-to-privacy/.May>. Accessed 12 November 2010.

Peters, J. (2010). 'WikiLeaks Would not Qualify to Claim Federal Reporter's Privilege in any Form'. <http://works.bepress.com/jonathan_peters/1>. Accessed 15 January 2011.

Pew Centre for Research (2007). 'Public Blames Media for Too Much Celebrity Coverage Cable and Network TV Worst Offenders'. 2 August. <http://people-press.org/report/346/public-blames-media-for-too-much-celebrity-coverage>. Accessed 2 January 2011.

Phillips, G. & Lindgren, M. (2006). *Australian Broadcast Journalism* (2nd edn). Melbourne: Oxford University Press.

Pike, A. & Cooper, R. (1998). *Australian Film 1900–1977.* Melbourne: Oxford University Press.

Pitt, G. H. (1946). *The Press in South Australia, 1836–1850.* Adelaide: Wakefield Press.

Pretyman, E. R.(1966). 'Bent, Andrew (1790–1851)'. *Australian Dictionary of Biography, Volume 1.* Melbourne: Melbourne University Press.

Pullin, R. (2005). 'New Australian Sedition Law Sparks Censorship Fear'. Reuters, 3 December <www.newsdesk.org/archives/003549.html>. Accessed 26 January 2006.

Purcell, K., Rainie, L., Mitchell, A., Resentiel, T. & Olmstead. K. (2010). 'Understanding the Participatory News Consumer'. *Pew Internet.* 1 March. <www.pewinternet.org/Reports/2010/Online-News.aspx?r=1>. Accessed 2 January 2011.

Quinn, S. (2007). 'Online Federal Election Battle Hots Up'. *Sydney Morning Herald*, 15 November. <www.smh.com.au/news/web/online-federal-election-battle-hots-up/2007/11/13/1194766680943.html?page=2>. Accessed 6 December 2007.

Reeves, R. (1998). *What the People Know: Freedom and the Press.* Cambridge, MA: Harvard University Press.

Rein, I., Kotler, P., Hamlin, M. & Stoller, M (2006). *High Visibility* (3rd edn). New York: McGraw-Hill.

Revkin, A. C. (2001). 'US Losing Status as World Leader in Climate Change'. *New York Times*, 11 June. <www.nytimes.com/2001/06/11/us/us-losing-status-as-a-world-leader-in-climate-science.html>. Accessed 12 March 2004.

Ricketson, M. (2004). *Writing Feature Stories: How To Research and Write Newspaper and Magazine Articles.* Crows Nest: Allen & Unwin.

Robins, B. (2010). 'A History of Support for Gay Issues'. *Sydney Morning Herald*, 22 May 2010. <www.smh.com.au/nsw/a-history-of-support-for-gay-issues-20100521-w1r5.html.>. Accessed 23 May 2010.

Robson, L. (1983). *A History of Tasmania.* Melbourne: Oxford University Press.

Rojek, C. (2001). *Celebrity.* London: Reaktion.

Rolph, D., Vitens, M. & Bannister, J. (2010). *Media Law: Cases, Materials and Commentary.* Melbourne: Oxford University Press.

Rosen, J. (2005). 'Each Nation Its Own Press'. In *Barons to Bloggers: Confronting Media Power.* Melbourne: Miegunyah Press.

Rotstein, F. (2010). 'Chewing the Fat of a Soft Underbelly'. *Media and Arts Law Review*, 15(1).

Sanders, K. (2003). *Ethics and Journalism.* London: Sage.

Sardar, Z. & Van Loon, B. (2000). *Introducing Media Studies.* Crows Nest: Allen & Unwin.

Sarup, M. (1996). *Identity, Culture, and the Postmodern World.* Athens: University of Georgia Press.

SBS—see Special Broadcasting Service.

Schatz, T. (1981). *Hollywood Genres: Formulas, Filmmaking and the Studio System.* Boston: McGraw-Hill.

Schechter, D. (2010). 'UN Wants Probe of WikiLeaks Torture Revelations: Iraq War Crimes and Media Response', OEN OpEdNews.com, 24 October. <www.opednews.com/articles/UN-Wants-Probe-of-Wikileak-by-Danny-Schechter-101024-327.html>. Accessed 23 January 2011.

Schirato, T. & Yell, S. (2000). *Communication and Cultural Literacy: An Introduction.* St Leonards, NSW: Allen & Unwin.

Scott, M. (2010). 'Quality Journalism and a 21st century ABC'. *The Drum*, 3 September. <www.abc.net.au/news/stories/2010/09/03/3001302.htm>. Accessed November 12, 2010.

Seabrook, J. (2001). *NoBrow: The Culture of Marketing and the Marketing of Culture.* New York: Vintage Books.

Sellers, F. (2006). 'Embracing Change'. *American Journalism Review*, October–November <www.ajr.org/Article.asp?id=4223>. Accessed 8 October 2007.

Shepard, A. C. (1997). 'Celebrity Journalists'. *American Journalism Review*, 19 September.

Silfry, M. (2007). 'Who is ParkRidge47?'. Techpresident.com. <www.techpresident.com/node/130>.

Singer, J. B. & Ashman, I. (2009). 'Comment is Free, but Facts are Sacred: User-Generated Content and Ethical Constructs at the *Guardian*'. *Journal of Mass Media Ethics*, 24(1), 3–21.

Smith, A. (1979). *The Newspaper: An International History.* London: Thames & Hudson.

Society for Professional Journalists (n.d.). 'Code of Ethics'. <www.spj.org/ethicscode.asp>. Accessed 21 March 2011.

Sokal, A. & Bricmont, J. (2003). *Intellectual Impostures.* London: Profile Books.

Sorensen, R. (2007). 'Time You Turned on the Tube'. *The Australian*, 17 March.

Special Broadcasting Service (2010). 'Codes of Practice'. <media.sbs.com.au/home/upload_media/site_20_rand_2138311027_sbscodesofpractice2010.pdf>. Accessed 21 March 2011.

SPJ—see Society for Professional Journalists.

Stauber, J. & Rampton, S. (1995). *Toxic Sludge is Good for You: Lies, Damned Lies and the Public Relations Industry.* Monroe: Common Courage Press.

Stockwell, S. (2004). 'Reconsidering the Fourth Estate: The Functions of Infotainment'. Conference paper, Australian Political Studies Association, 29 September–1 October.

Strunk, W. & White, E. B. (2000). *The Elements of Style* (4th edn). Boston: Allyn & Bacon.

Sydney Morning Herald (2008). <http://news.smh.com.au/national/alleged-sex-attacker-refused-bail-20080828-44pq.html>.

Tanner, S., Phillips, G., Smyth, C. & Tapsall, S. (eds) (2005). *Journalism Ethics at Work.* Frenchs Forest: Pearson Longman.

Tapsall, S. & Varley, C. (2001). *Journalism Theory in Practice.* Melbourne: Oxford University Press.

TekGroup (2009). 'Bulldog Reporter/TekGroup Study Shows Increased Usage of Online and Social Media Resources'. <http://newsroom.tekgroup.com/releases/mediarelationspracticessurvey.htm.>. Accessed 2 January 2011.

Thwaites, T., Davis, L. & Mules, W. (2002). *Introducing Cultural and Media Studies: A Semiotic Approach.* Basingstoke: Palgrave.

Tiffin, R. (1989). *News and Power.* Sydney: Allen & Unwin.

Toohey, B. (1978a). 'Killen Warns on Plutonium Pile'. *Australian Financial Review*, 5 October.

——(1978b). 'Maralinga: The 'Do Nothing Solution''. *Australian Financial Review*, 11 October.

Truffaut, F. (1977). 'A Kind Word for Critics'. *Harper's Magazine*, October, 95–100.

Truss, L. (2003). *Eats, Shoots and Leaves.* London: Profile Books.

Tsui, L. (2009). 'Rethinking Journalism Through Technology'. In B. Zelizer (ed.), *The Changing Faces of Journalism: Tabloidization, Technology and Truthiness.* London: Routledge Taylor and Francis, 53–55.

Turner, G. (2004). *Understanding Celebrity.* London: Sage.

——(2006). *Film as Social Practice.* London: Routledge.

——& Cunningham, S. (eds) (2000). *The Australian TV Book.* St Leonards, NSW: Allen & Unwin.

——& Cunningham, S. (eds) (2002). *The Media and Communications in Australia.* Crows Nest, NSW: Allen & Unwin.

——, Bonner, F. & Marshall, P. D. (2000). *Fame Games: The Production of Celebrity in Australia.* Cambridge, New York: Cambridge University Press.

Turner, J. (2009). 'Face it: We Need the McCanns to be Guilty'. *Times,* 15 September. Cited in N. Goc, 'Bad Mummy'—Kate McCann and the Media'. In C. Burns (ed.), *Mis/Representing Evil: Evil in an Interdisciplinary Key.* Interdisciplinary Press Fisher Imprints, 2009, 169–93.

Tye, L. (2002). *The Father of Spin: Edward L. Bernays and the Birth of Public Relations.* New York: Owl Books.

Tymson, C., Lazar, P. & Lazar, R. (2000). *The New Australian and New Zealand Public Relations Manual.* Chatswood: Tymson Communications.

Tynan, E. (2011). 'Atoms and Empty Space: Media and the Most Dangerous Scientific Experiments in Australia'. Unpublished PhD thesis. Australian National University.

Wasko, J. (2001). *Understanding Disney: The Manufacture of Fantasy.* New York: Polity Press.

Watson, D. (2003). *Death Sentence.* Milsons Point, NSW: Random House.

Webdiary (2006). 'Editorial Policy', October. <http://webdiary.com.au/cms/?q=node/4&page=1&order=2&from=0&comments_per_page=5>. Accessed 12 June 2008.

——(2008). 'Webdiary Ethics', August. <http://webdiary.com.au/cms/?q=node/257>. Accessed 28 June 2009.

——(2010). 'Webdiary Ethics', June. <http://webdiary.com.au/cms/?q=node/1>. Accessed 23 June 2010.

Welles, O. (1938). 'Opening Narration to *War of the Worlds*'. Mercury Theatre on the Air. New York, 30 October.

West, J. (1842). 'Editorial'. *Launceston Examiner,* Launceston, 3.

West, J. (1852). *A History of Tasmania.* Launceston: Henry Dowling.

WikiLeaks (2011a). <http://213.251.145.96/>

——(2011b). 'About. What is WikiLeaks?'. *WikiLeaks Archives 2006–2010.* <http://213.251.145.96/About.html>. Accessed 16 January 2011.

Williams, B. (2009). 'Good Contacts, Extraordinary Stories'. *Police Journal,* February 2009.

Williams, F. (1957). *Dangerous Estate: The Anatomy of Newspapers.* London: Longmans Green.

Williams, R. (2000). 'Advertising: the Magic System'. *Advertising and Society Review,* 1(1).

——(2004). *Science Show,* 24 October. ABC Radio National.

Windschuttle, K. (2000). 'The Poverty of Cultural Studies'. *Journalism Studies, 1*(1), 145–59.

Woodberry, Joan (1972). *Andrew Bent.* Hobart: Fullers Bookshop.

World Association of Newspapers (WAN) (2000). 'World Press Trends: Newspaper Growth Continues: World Newspaper Congress and World Editors Forum'. <www.wan-press.org/ce/previous/2000/leaders2000/index.html>. Accessed 26 July 2006.

World Association of Newspapers (2004). 'Newspapers: A Brief History'. <www.wan-press.org/article2821.html>.

Zelizer, B. (2004). *Taking Journalism Seriously: News and the Academy.* Thousand Oaks, CA: Sage.

Zelizer, B. (2005). 'The Culture of Journalism,' in Curran and Gurevitch (eds), *Mass Media and Society* (4th edn). London: Arnold.

Zelizer, B. (2009). *The Changing Faces of Journalism: Tabloidization, Technology and Truthiness.* London: Routledge Taylor and Francis.

WEBSITES

Australian Broadcasting Corporation: <www.abc.net.au>

Australian Communications and Media Authority: <www.acma.gov.au>

Australian Media History Database: <www.amhd.org.au/associations.html>

Australian Press Council: <www.presscouncil.org.au>

Colonial Times: <http://trove.nla.gov.au/>

Cyberjournalist.net: <www.cyberjournalist.net>

Drum: <www.abc.net.au/thedrum/>

EthicNet: <www.uta.fi/ethicnet/>

Ethics Connection: <www.scu.edu/SCU/Centers/Ethics/>

Ethics in Public Broadcasting: <www.current.org/ethics/>

FAIR: Fairness and Accuracy in Reporting: <www.fair.org/>

Grog's Gamut: <http://grogsgamut.blogspot.com/>

Gutenberg Press: <www.mainz.de/gutenberg/english/erfindun.htm>

Hobart Town Gazette: <http://trove.nla.gov.au/>

Huffington Post: <www.huffingtonpost.com/>

Journalism Education Association of Australia: <www.jeaa.org.au>

Mashable: <http://mashable.com/>

Media, Entertainment and Arts Alliance: <www.alliance.org.au>

Pew Internet: <www.pewinternet.org/>

PR Watch: <www.prwatch.org>

Public Relations Institute of Australia: <www.pria.com.au>

Society of Professional Journalists: <www.spj.org/ethicscode.asp>

Tao of Journalism: <www.taoofjournalism.org>

Webdiary.com: <http://webdiary.com.au/>

WikiLeaks: <http://wikileaks.ch>

INDEX